KURT WEILL

KURT WEILL

A LIFE IN PICTURES AND DOCUMENTS

DAVID FARNETH WITH ELMAR JUCHEM AND DAVE STEIN

DESIGNED BY BERNARD SCHLEIFER

THE OVERLOOK PRESS

WOODSTOCK • NEW YORK

for Lys Symonette

This book is published in conjunction with
Musical Stages: Kurt Weill and His Century, an exhibition
created and sponsored by the Kurt Weill Foundation for Music and
The New York Public Library at Lincoln Center,
in association with the Akademie der Künste, Berlin.

First published in the United States in 2000 by
The Overlook Press, Peter Mayer Publishers, Inc.
Lewis Hollow Road
Woodstock, New York 12498
Web: http://www.overlookpress.com

Library of Congress Cataloging-in-Publication Data

Farneth, David.
Kurt Weill: a life in pictures and documents
p.   cm.
Includes index.
1. Weill, Kurt, 1900-1950 Chronology. 2. Weill, Kurt, 1900-1950
Pictorial works. I. Title
ML410.W395F37   1999   782.1'092—dc21   [B]   983357

Type formatting by Bernard Schleifer Company
Manufactured in the United States of America
First Edition
1 3 5 7 9 8 6 4 2
ISBN 0-87951-721-2

Contents

ACKNOWLEDGMENTS

THIS PROJECT WAS A TRUE COLLABORATION DEPENDENT ON THE DEDICATED AND EXPERT participation of co-compilers Elmar Juchem and Dave Stein, both colleagues at the Kurt Weill Foundation for Music. Even before the time-intensive work of making the book began, both spent weeks sifting through hundreds of files of correspondence, programs, press clippings, and music to compile a master wish list of documents and photographs to include. Elmar brought his sharp, critical eye to the project as well as invaluable native German language skills. He assisted in the selection of documents, provided translations, compiled the appendix, time lines, and production histories, and generously shared information from his unpublished dissertation about the collaboration between Weill and Maxwell Anderson. He also translated the book for a German edition. Dave Stein brought six years of experience at the Weill-Lenya Research Center to the project. He assisted in the acquisition and selection of documents and photographs, provided and edited translations, drafted captions, compiled the manuscript and indexes, and organized and prepared hundreds of digital and printed photographs gathered from sources around the world. Moreover I am especially grateful for his excellent copy editing at every step along the way. Both brought to the project a discriminating knowledge of Weill's life and works and the sources that document them, as well as a commitment to teamwork, an irrational love for long working days, and a generous spirit of collegiality.

This book is a publication of the Kurt Weill Foundation for Music, which is dedicated to preserving and promoting Weill's legacy. The Foundation contributed the salaries and expenses related to compiling and editing the intellectual content. The Foundation's Board of Trustees also established the Weill-Lenya Research Center in 1983 and has supported it with the funding, personnel, and facilities required to acquire, catalog, preserve, and provide access to the collection. The Research Center also benefited from a grant in 1994 from the National Endowment for the Humanities, Division of Preservation and Access to support the cataloging of the core collection.

The groundwork for this book was laid in 1983, when the Weill-Lenya Research Center took on the task of assembling sources and documenting Weill's career. That effort has been helped along the way by numerous employees of the Kurt Weill Foundation, a wide range of libraries and archives, the various publishers of Weill's music, and a host of Weill devotees around the world. Foundation president Kim H. Kowalke contributed the preface to this book and encouraged the project since its inception. Lys Symonette, musical executive of the Foundation, worked over the years to make many of the translations and responded energetically to requests for new ones. Valued colleagues Edward Harsh and Carolyn Weber lent unqualified support and took a remarkably flexible approach to sharing office resources and personnel during an extremely busy period of preparing the Weill centenary. Special thanks go to Brian Butcher, whose accomplished office management and cheerful disposition insulated us from the major catastrophes and minor irritations involved in running an organization in a congested and frenetic urban area.

Kendall Crilly, music librarian of the Yale University Music Library, and public services librarian Suzanne Eggleston responded with enthusiasm to our request for a massive amount of reproductions from the Weill-Lenya Papers and devoted generous time and resources to the project. Suzanne, in particular, organized the electronic scanning of approximately 200 pages of music scores, photographs, and documents for inclusion in this book. We thank Suzanne and her staff for their extraordinary assistance. A number of other non-profit archives, libraries, and institutions graciously provided photos for this book. They are the Margaret Herrick Library, Academy of Motion Picture Arts and Sciences; Hochschule der Künste Berlin (Wolfgang Rathert and Markus Hilbich); Leo Baeck Institute (Sandra Gebbeken and Diane Spielmann); Bertolt-Brecht-Archiv, Stiftung Archiv der Akademie der Künste (Erdmut Wizisla); University of California at Los Angeles Music Library (Stephen Davison and Timothy Edwards); Rare Books and Manuscript Library, Columbia University (Bernard Crystal); Stadtarchiv Dessau (Antje Geiger); Deutsche Stiftung Kinemathek (Wolfgang Jacobsen); Staatsoper Dresden; University of Georgia Libraries; Harvard Theatre Collection, The Houghton Library; Indiana University School of Music; Jewish National and University Library; Levy Sheet Music Collection, John Hopkins University; Institut für Theater-, Film- und Fernsehwissenschaft, Universität zu Köln (Anja Hellhammer, Hedwig Müller, Jürgen Trimborn); Leipzig Stadtgeschichtliches Museum; Music Division, Library of Congress; Stadtarchiv Lüdenscheid (Dieter Saal); Stadtarchiv Mannheim; University of New Hampshire; New York Public Library for the Performing Arts; Museum of the City of New York (Marty Jacobs and Anne Easterling); Stadt Norderney (Herr Bätje); Southern Literature Collection, University of North Carolina; Sibley Music Library, Eastman School of Music, University of Rochester (Mary Wallace Davidson and David Coppen); Rodgers and Hammerstein Organization (Theodore Chapin); Staatsbibliothek Preußischer Kulturbesitz; Galston-Busoni Archive, University of Tennessee (Nick Wyman); Harry Ransom Humanities Research Center, University of Texas; University of Utah Libraries; Wiesloch Standesamt; Beinecke Library, Yale University. For permission to published photos from commercial archives, we thank Bildarchiv Preussischer Kulturbesitz, Corbis-Bettmann, Culver Pictures, Margo Feiden Galleries, The Raymond Mander & Joe Mitchenson Theatre Collection, Photofest, Roger-Viollet, and Ullstein Bilderdienst. Special thanks go to the collectors, scholars, and photographers Irma Commanday, James Fuld, Pascal Huynh, Tamara Levitz, Patrick O'Connor, H. Schulze-Brinkop, and Jürgen Schebera.

The publishers of Weill's music responded to numerous requests for materials and information about Weill's publishing history. They are: Ronald Freed of European-American Music Corporation, Marion von Hartlieb of Universal Edition, Peter Hanser-Strecker of Schott Musik International, and Don Biederman of Warner-Chappell. Amy Guskin, Corey Field, Suzanne Hagadorn, and Caroline Kane of European-American Music Corporation have been particularly helpful. Judy Bell at The Richmond Organization was always on the lookout for interesting items that were needed by the Weill-Lenya Research Center, and the staff at Universal Edition in Vienna was especially responsive to numerous requests for reproductions and information about Weill's publishing history.

Special thanks go to designer Bernard Schleifer for his impressive knowledge of bookmaking, unflappable demeanor, and refreshing humor. Bernie worked in a supportive, collaborative spirit and manipulated the myriad images and text elements into a cohesive design. Christoper Hailey translated most of the letters between Weill and Universal Edition in the 1980s. Stephen Kampmeier and Richard Miller helped with some last-minute translation editing and copy editing, respectively. At The Overlook Press, gratitude goes to President Peter Mayer, whose passion for this period of history brought about the release of this book by a commercial publisher, to Publishing Director Tracy Carns for overseeing every step of the way, and to Hermann Lademann for working out the legal details.

Personal gratitude goes to my partner David Gilbert for his sage professional advice and for his patience while this book further exacerbated the constraints of a long-distance relationship.

D. F.

FOREWORD

LIEBESLIED FOR WEILL
Luciano Berio

IT HAS OFTEN ENOUGH BEEN SAID THAT THE MUSIC MARKET AND THE culture industry tend to perpetuate themselves through stylistic imitation and conformity. Although I can't pretend to an insider's view of that industry, I like to think that a musical work might also acquire its *raison d'être*, market considerations apart, from the fact that its meaning and identity don't just conform to a certain style but consistently take account of "otherness." This is a central feature of all Kurt Weill's works, in particular those he created in collaboration with Brecht and which contributed to a genuine revolution in musical theater.

I think that the modernity of Kurt Weill, with his constant search for the "other" and the "elsewhere," is due not only to his conception of epic theater (theorized by Brecht but prefigured musically by Weill himself) but also to the way in which he defines and puts to use his specific musical ingredients. Song is only one of these, but one of the most significant. Weill had made his way into the world of European and American song with a prestigious passport, stamped with the widely differing neoclassicisms of Busoni, Schoenberg (which was Hanns Eisler's downfall), Hindemith, and Stravinsky, and also with surrealism, *Gebrauchsmusik*, and the aesthetic-ideological acrobatics of *neue Sachlichkeit*. I think that Weill followed a path diametrically opposed to that of Gershwin, who, inspired by the short time spans of songs and jazz, looked for his "other" and "elsewhere" in the longer time spans of rhapsodic structures. With centrifugal agility, Leonard Bernstein was to carry this pursuit of the "other" forward in many directions at once.

Though Weill fled Nazi Germany, once he arrived in the United States he never gave the impression of the German or Viennese musician who felt obliged to educate America musically. In fact, he immediately made himself at home, happily and of his own free will. But that doesn't mean that Weill gives the impression of being just a songwriter. He is always an "other," and his songs are never just "the real thing." They never become commercial goods, as they always transmit more or less explicit signals of knowing other dimensions—and not just musical ones.

Songs can be instruments of revolution. And Weill's songs are indeed revolutionary, because they are aimed above all at the listener rather than the consumer wanting to purchase escape. Weill's songs are not always narratives and are often dialogues—dialogues of solitude, even when the protagonists talk to each other. It is the music itself which implies, as music, a virtual dialogue and tends to transform the listener into a narrator. The listener recognizes the *Gestus* and the ready-made ingredients that are an integral part of the songs as if they were relics from a lost world, or as if they were dear, longtime friends who reappear laden with memories that are not always happy. Yet these ingredients assimilate with the "other" and are at the same time distanced from it, so that they in turn acquire alienating functions. A face-to-face confrontation of the two "others" hardly ever happens.

In the famous "Liebeslied" from *Die Dreigroschenoper*, for example, after a parody of operatic recitative, the expected thirty-two bars of a Boston waltz set off down a very illegitimate harmonic path, all the more seductive in its impact. So our old friends find themselves subtly infiltrated by alien characteristics and functions (above all, harmonic ones) which distance them from us and subvert their original sense, rather like Caspar Neher's projected captions on Brecht's stage, which break into the action and prevent straightforward emotional identification.

In Weill's music—and not only his songs—there are no elementary and irreconcilable conflicts. Instead there emerges a sort of unstable complementarity, a dialectical coexistence: what I might metaphorically call a Beckett-like dialogue between musical characteristics and functions that are genetically distant. Within Weill's creative development, this dialogue signals the search for an essence or, as Theodor Adorno might have it, for intermittency of dramaturgy and structure. But in effect it also signals a stylistic renunciation and, as such, an exemplary act of musical morality.

The first time I encountered Weill's music and theater was in Milan in 1956, when Giorgio Strehler, with Bruno Maderna as musical director, mounted an unforgettable production of *Die Dreigroschenoper* at the Piccolo Teatro. (It was on this occasion that I met Brecht.) Perhaps in my case the personal memories linked to Weill's music are excessively diverse, and this is not the place to evoke them. The sense of involvement that I have always felt with his songs might provoke uselessly conflict-ridden feelings. I just want to record that, in the 1950s, I arranged several of Weill's songs for Cathy Berberian (who was my Lotte Lenya).

We need to stay in dialogue with the musical theater of Weill, just as we do with the musical theater of other times, from Monteverdi to Verdi, Wagner, or Berg. With its fragmentation of narrative structures, its hybridization of genre, its difficult and often enigmatic sense of voice, its diversified and pared-down means that are conditioned and often ineffably contradicted by the music, the musical theater of Weill is, even now, one of the most significant events of the twentieth century.

Florence, April 1999

PREFACE

THE SUBTITLE OF THIS VOLUME, *A Life in Pictures and Documents*, seems resolutely unpolemical. A neutral designation for a documentary biography, it appears to be blissfully detached from the critical controversies that have shadowed the reception of Kurt Weill and his works throughout the century that is now coming to a close, coincident with the composer's own centenary of birth. The title makes no overt attempt to situate Weill geographically "in a divided world" or somewhere along the path "from Berlin to Broadway." He is not identified as an extension of his most famous librettist (a "Brecht composer") or his most famous work (a "threepenny songwriter"). There is no promise that the book might reveal the "real Weill" or join the debate over whether this "might-have-been" can actually be considered, from a modernist perspective, a "genuine" composer. Only in the singularity of the innocent-appearing *A Life* could one perhaps intuit a revisionist agenda, implicitly challenging the two-Weill theory—the double-identity construct, coined during Weill's lifetime, that has shaped virtually all previous critical discourse about the composer. We might infer, therefore, a unitary answer to the fundamental question recently articulated so succinctly by the German musicologist Hermann Danuser: "Are they one and the same artistic person, or should we think of Weill in terms of two distinct personalities?"

"Where does the stable essence of an 'I' reside?" asks Milan Kundera in *Testaments Betrayed*, his remarkable collection of essays on modernism. "Over what period of time can we consider a man identical to himself?" Such Weill-relevant questions arise as Kundera interrogates the modern novel, seeking in particular to understand the differences between Dostoyevsky and Tolstoy. Kundera maintains that the stable identities of Dostoyevsky's characters lie in their personal ideology, whereas "in Tolstoy, man is the more himself, the more an individual, when he has the strength, the imagination, the intelligence, to transform himself." In *War and Peace* Bezukhov and Bolkonsky surprise—"They make themselves different"—and thereby offer another conception of man: "He is an itinerary; a winding road; a journey whose successive phases not only vary but often represent a total negation of the preceding phases." Kundera quickly refines this metaphor, however: "I've said *road*, a word that could mislead, because the image of a road evokes a destination. Now, what is the destination of these roads that end only randomly, broken off by the happenstance of death?"

In the musical realm Kundera focuses not on Weill, but on Stravinsky, "whose conscious, purposeful eclecticism" he finds "gigantic and unmatched." Stravinsky's life, Kundera notes, "divides into three parts of roughly equal length: Russia, 27 years; France and French-speaking Switzerland, 29 years; America, 32 years." Despite the corresponding radical shifts in Stravinsky's musical language and style, Kundera argues not for three "distinct personalities" but for a single artistic persona who changes as he attempts to master the past, an agenda central to the modernist project. "Without a doubt, his artistic evolution would have taken a different path if he had been able to stay where he was born. In fact, the start of his journey through the history of music coincides roughly with the moment when his native country ceases to exist for him: having understood that no country could replace it, he finds his only homeland in music." But elsewhere in his book, in a nuanced unpacking of irony entitled "Paths in the Fog," Kundera might well have chosen Weill (rather than Janáček) to stand as the musical counterpart to Kafka: "One might say that the various phases of an itinerary do have an ironic relation to one another. In the kingdom of irony, equality rules; this means that no phase of the itinerary is morally superior to another. . . . And just as one cannot pass judgment on the various phases of one's life from a moral viewpoint, similarly one cannot judge them as to authenticity."

Such axioms seem to have guided the editors in assembling the present book. The six chapters covering Weill's mature years divide equally between his European and American careers, with each covering roughly a five-year period. The nature and presentation of documents remains consistent throughout, and, other than the selection process itself, the only obvious imposition of emphasis or interpretation is chronologically mandated, as dates serve even as chapter headings. In an attempt to contextualize both broadly and deeply what can be apprehended from an assortment of pictures and documents, detailed chronologies of Weill's life and works intersect and interact with year-by-year chronicles of developments in other arenas. (In this sense the book will serve admirably in lieu of a catalog for the centenary exhibition, evocatively and ambiguously called "Musical Stages: Kurt Weill and His Century.") The layout is, in Kundera's terms, wonderfully alive to the possibility of irony, "which is by definition discreet": "None of the assertions . . . can be taken by itself, each of them stands in a complex and contradictory juxtaposition with other assertions, other situations, other gestures, other ideas, other events."

The reader is invited to search for common denominators across contradictory and complementary *stages*—in each of the several senses of that word. Just as Kundera inquires, "What is the common essence that lets us see Bezukhov the atheist and Bezukhov the believer as the selfsame person?" we are challenged to reconcile the multiplicities of Weill's life, oeuvre, and style. At once "serious and popular," "European and American," "Jewish and German," "commercial and universal," Weill has been called the most problematic composer of his century. Challenging traditional aesthetic boundaries and expectations, his legacy is as diverse as his individual works are hybrid. In a lifelong effort to articulate values of humane justice, freedom, and dignity, Weill manages somehow to be both the quintessential "Brecht composer" and the consummate "Whitman composer." Though he frequently chose to write in a popular vein for a broad audience, his works on both sides of the Atlantic reserved the freedom to resist, to defy expectations and challenge conventions, to break with tradition and ultimately to find fulfillment in that liberation.

Amid such cross-currents of duality and ambiguity, then, is it possible to determine what makes Weill really Weill? What makes him identical to himself over the course of a life, which neatly spans the first half of the twentieth century and reflects its turbulence? Is it, as Harold Clurman suggests, that he was always "all theater, all mask"—so much the adaptable artist that "he could write music in any country as if he were a native"? Or was he, as Virgil Thomson eulogized, an indefatigable musico-dramatic experimenter, whose every work was "a new solution of dramatic problems." Or rather, as Adorno disparagingly described him, a type of *Musikregisseur*, "hardly commensurate with the concept of 'composer' at all."

Weill actually responded to this question himself. In an "Opera News on the Air" feature broadcast from the Metropolitan Opera in 1949, after a discussion of what makes Puccini Puccini, Boris Goldovsky inquired, "Tell me, Mr. Weill, as a composer yourself, are you conscious of what brings out the most characteristic in you; what brings out the Weill in Weill, so to speak?" Weill replied, "In retrospect, looking back on many of my own compositions, I find that I seem to react very strongly to the suffering of underprivileged people, of the oppressed, the persecuted. When my music involves human suffering, it is, for better or worse, pure Weill." Tolstoy is indeed not far removed.

Shortly after that interview, as Weill approached his fiftieth birthday, he wrote to his parents with some astonishment that "people are beginning to talk generally about the 'historical significance' of my works." That debate has only intensified in the subsequent half century. *Kurt Weill: A Life in Pictures and Documents* will surely serve as a reliable marker and memorable milestone within that ongoing process.

KIM H. KOWALKE
President, Kurt Weill Foundation for Music
New York, 28 July 1999

INTRODUCTION

MUCH HAS CHANGED IN THE FIFTY YEARS SINCE COMPOSER KURT WEILL'S death. Even principal landmarks in his two favorite cities are barely recognizable. The Berlin Reichstag is topped with a futuristic sphere overlooking a city still scarred from thirty years of division and neglect. New York is homogenized, and Times Square disneyfied. Still, if Kurt Weill could see us celebrating his one hundredth birthday in 2000, he would no doubt be more interested in observing the human condition than surveying the altered landscape. "What keeps mankind alive?"

Balancing on the cusp of a new century, we are well positioned to look back at the past one hundred years as an era indelibly marked by the rapid development of technology and its growing presence as a dynamic, driving force in society. This book reflects that force; it relies on advancements in the creation of visual images for its content and on innovations affecting the transmission of music for its subject matter. The history of recent times no longer hinges on a written account of events. Instead, the twentieth-century has been captured in pictures, which continue to be manipulated, transmitted, and replayed by ever-evolving technologies, allowing the viewer to evaluate individual images and montage as carefully as a written text. The early twentieth century also saw the emergence of audio recording and radio, which worked in tandem to ignite the explosion of popular music as a valued form of entertainment and to provide easy and affordable access to all kinds of music. Music became a powerful transmitter of global culture. Weill recognized and utilized the power of popular music. He was also one of the first composers to write expressly for radio, and he incorporated film and audio recordings into his early operas.

Today, fifty years after his death, Weill's music remains fresh to modern ears, and his compositional techniques continue to inspire young composers. The humanistic themes in his stage works remain universal, and their political commentaries continue to resonate when applied to modern-day situations. But there is something in Weill the man that appeals to us as well. We are seeing ourselves more and more as citizens of the world, and, in the process, gaining an understanding and appreciation of the artistic expressions of different cultures. In this context Weill might be viewed as a type of new world citizen: a person with the intellectual savvy and emotional sensitivity to maneuver in diverse cultures, able to make his voice heard in a foreign environment.

Kurt Weill's name means different things to different people. "Mack the Knife," Broadway musicals of the 1940s, Nazi persecution, social consciousness, a quiet man who died before his time. His life spanned precisely the first half of the century: he was born in 1900 in Dessau, Germany, and died in New York in 1950. Most book-length studies of Weill divide his life by longitude and latitude and define his music in terms of the culture in which it was written: German, French, or American. This book takes a slightly different approach, with chronological chapter divisions reflecting identifiable stages of his career. While these stages are sometimes informed by political and social events in Germany and by Weill's two emigrations—to France in March 1933 and to the United States in September 1935—the chapter divisions reflect the time needed by Weill to adjust to the environments in which he found himself.

Kurt Weill: A Life in Pictures and Documents presents a visual overview of Weill's prolific career and places his works within the context of social changes and political events happening around him. By featuring images chosen to illustrate his works, writings, compositional process (with and without collaborators), and theories about his art, the book is perhaps more akin to a biography of works than an account of a life, in that greater prominence is given to the development and reception of Weill's compositions than to personal relationships or the nuances of social and political context. It is organized chronologically to show more clearly the various projects occupying Weill's attention at any one time. Small departures from strict chronology are taken to avoid confusion or to make a connection. For instance, documents pertaining to the genesis of a major stage work are generally grouped together rather than spread over the entire period of composition. This group precedes the principal section devoted to that work, which is placed chronologically by the date of the first performance and includes a list of the work's production history during Weill's lifetime, followed by reviews and photographs related to the premiere. Readers should keep in mind that works were not always performed in the order in which they were composed.

There is virtually no prose commentary in the main body of the book. Instead, each chapter opens with a chronology of Weill's life and work. Brief contextual information pertaining to music and theater, literature and film, science and society, and politics is provided in yearly time lines. Captions identify the illustrations, again without subjective commentary from the compilers. An appendix gives English translations for most of the foreign-language documents and the original language for documents that have been translated into English. "A Brief Life," which follows this introduction, summarizes each chapter to provide a mini-biography.

A complete documentary account of Weill's life and works, even without including the music itself, would probably consume more than fifty volumes of this size. To keep this book to a manageable length (and therefore accessible to a general audience), choices were made. The selection process for texts favored items previously unpublished. As a result, this book is most effectively used in conjunction with Weill's published correspondence and writings. Approximately equal space is given to each of his major stage works, regardless of familiarity or success. Whenever possible, a sampling of positive and negative reviews was assembled. The selection of correspondence is weighted heavily toward letters written by Weill rather than to him. This approach, admittedly, gives a somewhat one-sided view of the collaboration process that was fundamental to Weill's work as a theater composer, but it serves the goal of investigating more fully Weill's attitudes about similar topics throughout his lifetime. The selection also favors business-related letters over personal ones. As for photographs, again the compilers favored those that are the least known, except when a familiar image was required to fill a gap in the chronology. Photographs of stage productions were chosen to illustrate musical sections or turning points in the plot rather than to provide a clear view of the individual performers. Only a few non-Weill-related photographs are included; the reader might wish to consult books devoted to the Weimar Republic and American musical theater of the 1930s and 1940s for additional perspective. No individual topic or work is treated comprehensively; the selection offered here is a mere sampling of the range and diversity of the sources that are available for study in libraries and archives.

What do these photos and documents reveal, individually and collectively, about Weill's personality and attitudes toward his work? They show an unflagging devotion to literature and a lifelong search for high-level collaborators who could provide the kind of words he needed for inspiration. We see a composer open to a wide range of possibilities, often reluctant to take a definitive viewpoint on a subject. This trait (or tactic?) surely allowed him to negotiate the compromises required in his artistic collaborations. Weill's letters reveal his many self-images: the mentor (when writing to Maurice Abravanel), the philosopher (when writing to his parents), the protector (when writing to Lotte Lenya), the innovator, the businessman, the showman, the catalyst. Throughout his life we see an irrepressible ambition, a passion for work, a desire to have his successes publicly acknowledged, a need for financial security.

Some of Weill's compositional techniques are illustrated, such as his use of mixed compositional styles for dramatic effect and his practice of self-borrowing, an attempt to give new life to his previously composed music rather than letting it fall into obscurity. Multiplicity is a unifying characteristic in his music, just as an attraction to hybrid genres (musical play, song-style opera, musical tragedy, American opera, film operetta) marks his entire oeuvre. Weill also seemed uninterested in the notion of linear development; at the time of his death he was contemplating an opera for Lawrence Tibbett while drafting simple folk-like songs for a show based on *Huckleberry Finn* (both with Maxwell Anderson). His continual search for new dramatic musical forms is espoused not only in his public writings, but it informs almost every step of his career. It is a recurring theme in his correspondence with collaborators, publishers, and colleagues and, most obviously, in the works themselves, each of which is built upon a distinctive "sound world." Rather than allowing his experiments to wander into the realm of the arcane, or the "new," he directed them toward making his music more accessible, simpler, more immediate, so that the complexity of the messages contained in the words was readily communicated to a wide array of listeners.

While these are some possible inferences that might be drawn from these pictures and documents, the book is really intended to allow each reader to make connections and draw her or his own conclusions. For the Weill specialist, the documents published here begin to shed light on some of the vexing issues in the current scholarly discourse, such as whether he "sold out" to Broadway or continued on a path already established in Europe, or if he conformed to the modernist concept of the "composer." They also show the process by which Weill adapted to American culture, and they illuminate his preferred methods of collaboration. Also evident is Weill's constant search for new solutions to the problems of musical theater and indications of his lasting contributions to the development of the Broadway musical.

Interesting as these topics are to Weill specialists, other readers will be more interested in how these photos and documents further our understanding of the German state-subsidized opera system, cultural life in the Weimar Republic, the timing and method of the encroachment of Nazi ideology on artistic expression, or the artistic climate in Paris before World War II. They also illustrate the effect of forced immigration on both the refugee and the new country and provide examples for the uses of music in furthering political and social agendas during the 1930s and 1940s and in supporting the American war effort. Weill's experiences in composing for stage and film, supplemented by his commentary, will illuminate the wider worlds of Broadway and Hollywood between 1935 and 1950. Some might also find evidence of Weill anticipating the more recent trend to seek broader, less defined musical theater genres.

Of course no amount of study of the past can show us how Weill's contributions will be viewed in the future. Will his now unfamiliar works rise to the popularity of his violin concerto, the music from *Die Dreigroschenoper*, and "September Song"? Will Germany ever see him as more than "Brecht's composer"? Will Weill's place in the development of the Broadway musical and an indigenous American opera be routinely acknowledged? In time, if Weill's complete body of work can been heard and seen in faithful performances as easily as paging through this book, posterity might indeed find the closing statement of David Kilroy's 1992 dissertation applicable to his entire career: "The sound of his art may have changed over the course of his lifetime, but its essential purpose remained constant. Weill sent many messages to the American public in the postwar years. Broadway audiences who heard them could . . . walk out into the night air in an awakened state."

DAVID FARNETH

A BRIEF LIFE

1900-1918. THE WEIL/DE VEIL/WEYL/WEILL FAMILY, ONE OF THE OLD-EST Jewish families in Germany, can trace its lineage back to the four-teenth century through a long line of rabbis. As the son of a cantor, Weill's early musical education centered on the synagogue. He first studied piano with the organist and mounted amateur performances of concerts and dra-matic works at the Jewish community center. At age fifteen he began study-ing piano and theory with Albert Bing, the first kapellmeister of the highly respected Dessau opera, known then as "the Bayreuth of the North." Soon he was accompanying singers from the opera and studying conducting, score reading, and orchestration. Letters to his brother Hanns from this period show his early interest in literature and the development of his musical observations. Weill shared the community's wish for the end of the war and concern with the fate of his classmates serving in the army. Buoyed by hear-ing Richard Strauss conduct *Salome*, he eagerly anticipated a new life in Berlin, freed from family life in Dessau.

From **1918-1924** Weill pursued his formal education and settled on a career in music composition. In April 1918, he began studies at the Hochschule für Musik, where he took lessons in composition, counterpoint, and conducting while attending lectures by Ernst Cassirer and Max Dessoir at the Friedrich-Wilhelms-Universität. He witnessed the November Revolution of 1918 and the formal establishment of the Weimar Republic early the next year. At the Hochschule he explored various musical styles, from the classicism of Mendelssohn to the modernism of Schreker, Reger, and Strauss. After con-sidering the idea of studying with Schoenberg in Vienna and then rejecting it, probably for lack of money, he took a job as an opera coach (in Dessau) and conductor (in Lüdenscheid) to sharpen his practical skills. Returning to Berlin in late 1919, the music critic Oskar Bie arranged for Weill to meet Ferruccio Busoni, who accepted him in his new master class in composition at the Preußische Akademie der Künste. For the next several years, Weill led a double life: he was a loyal student and disciple, a mainstay in the almost mystical, Eastern atmosphere of Busoni's salon, while at the same time he eked out a near-poverty existence during Germany's period of hyperinflation by giving theory lessons and directing synagogue choirs. Philipp Jarnach, who had offered to teach him counterpoint and composition for free, arranged for his first commissions and important performances. 1924 was a

pivotal year. Weill traveled to Italy and returned to Berlin with a signed publishing contract with Universal Edition virtually in his pocket. He wrote a masterful violin concerto in three months, began a collaboration with play-wright Georg Kaiser that would soon lead to his first major success as an opera composer, got to know his future wife Lotte Lenya, and experienced Busoni's final illness and death. He was becoming known as one of the lead-ing composers of his generation; letters from this period show confidence in his compositional talent and an acknowledgment that "my future develop-ment depends entirely on myself now."

Weill's rise to fame during **1925–1928** paralleled the rise in prosperity of the Weimar Republic. He chose the path of a theater composer and began his life long search for new music theater forms and significant, well-crafted librettos. In 1925 he completed the one-act opera *Der Protagonist*, the cantata *Der neue Orpheus* (which he saw as a turning point towards a new, simpler style) and most of the score for *Royal Palace*, an opera-ballet with a libretto by Iwan Goll. Weill and Lenya formalized their living arrangement with a civil marriage ceremony on 28 January 1926. The success in March 1926 of *Der Protagonist* eased the way for productions of new works and brought offers for commissions of operas. He introduced film and audio recordings onto the stage and incorporated popular dance forms into the music, working towards a new style where unity was achieved with a carefully constructed presentation of multiple idioms. *Mahagonny Songspiel* (1927) represented the first product of the collaborative trio of Weill, Brecht, and the designer Caspar Neher. (Weill maintained a friendly but complicated relationship with Neher until 1933, and resumed it by mail after World War II.) The *Songspiel* shows Weill bringing his harmonies into sharper focus and introducing the "song style," with numbers including the now-famous "Alabama Song." Weill and Brecht interrupted work on a full-length opera version of *Mahagonny* to write *Die Dreigroschenoper*, which became an instant success and secured fame and financial stability for both author and composer, not to mention multi-faceted rewards to publishers, performers, and the producer. At age twenty-eight, with a new apartment, a new Fiat, a new level of financial independence, and Lenya happy with acting engage-ments at Berlin's major theaters, Weill was poised to take advantage of his *Dreigroschen* success. Proud of having proven his ability to reach a popular audience, he was eager to keep his hand in the concert world and composed *Das Berliner Requiem* for the Frankfurt Radio in a new, austere, lyrical style.

Confident of his place in the development of German music theater, Weill's compositions from **1929-1934** are marked by continued experimentation. In summer 1929, after a tangle with Hindemith over their collaboration on *Der Lindberghflug*, Brecht, Elisabeth Hauptman, Weill, and Neher collaborated again, on *Happy End*. Weill wrote one of his best scores, but Helene Weigel, Brecht's wife, sabotaged the production, probably to infuriate Brecht's two "other women" who were also involved in the production: Hauptmann and Carola Neher. By the time *Aufstieg und Fall der Stadt Mahagonny* premiered in Leipzig in March 1930, artistic differences left Brecht and Weill barely speaking to each other. Although Nazi demonstrations marred the opening and were repeated during the Frankfurt production six months later, he was buoyed by the German and international success of the school opera *Der Jasager*. His personal life, however, was marred by increasing estrangement from Lenya. Weill and Caspar Neher began collaboration on *Die Burgschaft*, a three-act opera in which Weill sharpened his command of large-scale musical structures while treating popular idioms with a new sophistication and understatement, but the introduction of a totalitarian regime into the plot brought Weill still more venom from the Nazis. By the time *Der Silbersee* premiered in February 1933, Hitler's plan to take over Germany was nearly complete. Weill was warned to leave Germany, and he made preparations for what he hoped would be a temporary stay in Paris, where he had had a major success with the musical elite four months earlier with performances of *Mahagonny Songspiel* and *Der Jasager*. He left Germany during the night of 21 March 1933. An unexpected commission from Edward James to write *Die sieben Todsünden* that spring brought some much-needed income. While critics in Paris and London were penning mixed-to-negative reviews of the "ballet with singing," cadres of Hitler Youth were burning Weill's music in Germany's public squares. When it became clear that he was more than a temporary visitor in Paris, an anti-Semitic faction began to work against him. In late October he signed a publishing contract with Heugel for his new compositions, but Universal Edition terminated his German contract. He was now officially divorced from Lenya, and, as per their agreement, she sold his cherished house in the Kleinmachnow section of Berlin. He moved from Paris to an apartment in the quiet, medieval town of Louveciennes, where he could compose at a safe distance from his detractors. By now he knew that he would not be returning to Germany in the near future, nor could not continue to write the kind of music that made him successful in Germany's subsidized theaters. To succeed in France, he would have to be as un-German as possible.

1934-1940 was a frustrating period of transition during which Weill's personal future seemed uncertain and his career remained in flux. By the end of summer 1934 he was working on three major stage works at once, in three different genres: an operetta (*Der Kuhhandel*), a massive spectacle (*Der Weg der Verheißung*) that combined elements of opera, oratorio, spoken drama, and pageantry, and *Marie galante*, a play with music (text

by Jacques Deval) intended for a commercial run in Paris. The ill-fated collaboration with Deval broke down early on and the show ran only three weeks at the end of 1934. Early in 1935 Weill began to refashion *Der Kuhhandel* as *A Kingdom for a Cow* for a commercial run in London. Its disappointingly short run in July 1935 left Weill disheartened and made the need for a success with *Der Weg der Verheißung/The Eternal Road* even greater. But his time in London was not a total loss; he and Lenya were reunited there and began a period of reconciliation. They sailed together to America on the SS *Majestic* and arrived in New York Harbor on 10 September 1935 with Weill eager to prepare *The Eternal Road* for a January 1936 opening. Collaboration disputes, production delays, and lack of proper financing caused producer Meyer Weisgal to postpone the opening indefinitely, leaving Weill again in a new country looking for a means of support, having lost his publishing contract with Heugel. Harold Clurman introduced him to Cheryl Crawford, the producer for the Group Theatre, an acting company dedicated to producing plays that addressed essential social and moral issues of the time. Crawford arranged a collaboration between Weill and Pulitzer Prize-winning playwright Paul Green for an anti-war play called *Johnny Johnson*. Weill's score, reflecting the lean economy of *Die Dreigroschenoper*, proved a bit ambitious for many of the non-singing actors, but the show brought him much-needed exposure. In the meantime, Weisgal had found enough money to open *The Eternal Road* in January 1937 and it brought laudatory reviews, even though Weill and the librettist Franz Werfel were largely overshadowed by the celebrity of director Max Reinhardt. Shortly after the opening Weill and Lenya quietly remarried in a New York suburb. For the next two years he split his time between New York and Hollywood, relying on income from film work while he tried out new collaborations. In May he accepted an offer to write the score for a new Fritz Lang film, *You and Me*, starring Sylvia Sidney and George Raft, a project in which he explored the dramatic possibilities of musical underscoring. Summer 1938 brought the opportunity Weill had been waiting for: a full-blown musical with Maxwell Anderson. *Knickerbocker Holiday* attracted more notice for its anti-New Deal politics than it did for Weill's score, but Broadway producers recognized Weill's potential and Broadway composers acknowledged a new competitor. In a February 1940 newspaper interview, Weill committed himself publicly to the development of Broadway's musical theater, but the projects he had tried during the previous years indicated that he would continue taking advantage of all opportunities.

Weill had his two biggest Broadway successes during the years **1940-1945**: *Lady in the Dark*, a show about psychoanalysis, and *One Touch of Venus*, a comic wartime entertainment. With the success came the extra work that accompanies increased publicity, making recordings, marketing hit songs, and quarrels with producers. With money earned from the sale of the film rights for *Lady in the Dark*, Weill and Lenya bought a farmhouse in rural New City, New York, one hour from Manhattan and a short walk from Maxwell Anderson's home. Here for the first time since leaving Germany he felt settled in an environment conducive to concentrated work. After America's entry into WWII, Weill assisted in the war effort by registering for the draft, contributing music to fundraisers, radio programs and a propaganda film, scouting for enemy aircraft, and producing morale-boosting shows for factory workers. True to his Jewish roots, he contributed music for Ben Hecht's pageant *We Will Never Die*, which called attention to the Holocaust before the U.S. government and organized Jewish groups were willing to do so. Brecht, who was now living in the U.S, contacted Weill about collaborating on musical versions of two plays, but Weill lost patience with his unreasonable financial demands and lack of understanding of the American theater system. Using contacts in government, he was able to expedite his U.S. citizenship. He renewed his collaboration with Ira Gershwin, first for a movie musical *Where Do We Go from Here?* and then for an operetta-style stage musical *The Firebrand of Florence*. The film featured some clever musical numbers and an extended musical sequence, but, by the time it opened in April 1945, audiences were not very interested in its wartime theme. *The Firebrand of Florence* became Weill's biggest Broadway flop, sending him to Hollywood to rest and regroup while working on the film version of *One Touch of Venus*.

The end of WWII gave Weill the freedom to plan large-scale works that addressed serious subjects, and his induction into The Playwrights' Company cemented his reputation as a dramatist-composer. During the last five years of his life, **1945-1950**, he composed three works for Broadway, each with different collaborators, on themes that challenged America's post-war optimism. *Street Scene* fulfilled his longtime dream to compose a successful American opera, a remarkable achievement in 1946 when there were few venues for this type of work and such projects were not valued by the cultural elite. In 1947, when Americans were free to travel to Europe again, Weill visited his parents in Palestine to deliver the news of his brother Hanns's death. He avoided Germany, but surveyed the effects of the war on Paris and London. For *Love Life*, repeating a technique he had used in *Die Dreigroschenoper*, he and Alan Jay Lerner used vaudeville numbers to comment on the effect of industrialism on traditional families, and in *Lost in the Stars* exposed apartheid in South Africa (and U.S. segregation) without commenting upon it directly. Weill was the only Broadway composer of his period who orchestrated his own music, thus giving him subtle control over the dramatic underpinnings of each work. When he died in 1950 from a heart attack brought on by congenital hypertension, Weill thought that the full scores for all of his major German works had been forever destroyed by the Nazis. He was still hoping for an effective American adaptation of *Die Dreigroschenoper* and seeking ways to introduce idiomatic performances of his Broadway works in Europe. His obituaries reflected a life and career still fractured by pre- and post-war attitudes.   D.F.

1900 – 1918

I would love to have a nice little room in Berlin, in Leipzig, in Munich and a closet filled with scores and books and music paper, and work until I drop— to write down uninterruptedly all the things that make my head practically burst, and to hear only music and be only music.

Kurt Weill

1900

March 2 — Born Curt Julian Weill to Albert Weill (b. 2 January 1867; d. 30 December 1950) and Emma Ackermann Weill (b. 15 December 1872; d. 22 June 1955), Leipziger Straße 59, Dessau, Germany. The third of four children: Nathan (b. 8 January 1898; d. 17 July 1957), Hanns Jakob (b. 14 January 1899; d. 1 March 1947), Ruth (b. 6 October 1901; d. 1975?) The family traces its roots to Juda (c. 1360) and his son Jakob Weil (c. 1390), a rabbi in Nuremberg, Augsburg, Bamberg, and Erfurt.

1904 — Attends Fröbel-Kindergarten on Fürstenstraße. The Weill family moves from their residence at Franzstraße 45 (where they moved in 1902) to Muldstraße 20.

1906 — Starts elementary school.

1907

Spring — Weill family moves to quarters in first floor of the Jewish community center, which adjoins the new synagogue on Steinstraße.

1909 — Attends Herzogliche Friedrichs-Oberrealschule (secondary school). His music teacher is August Theile and his German teacher is Dr. Max Preitz.

1912–13 — Studies piano with synagogue organist Franz Brückner and, later, with Margarethe Evelyn-Schapiro.

1913 — *Mi Addir: Jüdischer Trauungsgesang.*

Es blühen zwei flammende Rosen. Song fragment.

1914 — *Ich weiss wofür* (Guido von Güllhausen).

Reiterlied (Hermann Löns).

August — Outbreak of the First World War.

Autumn — Joins the nationalist youth group Dessauer Feldkorps.

1915 — *Gebet* (Emanuel Geibel), Dessau. Four-part chorale composed for sister Ruth's confirmation.

January — Earliest known public performance by Weill: *Für uns*, January 1915, Dessauer Feldkorps.

December — Performs a Chopin prelude and the third nocturne from Liszt's *Liebesträume* in a recital at his school in Dessau.

1915–17 — Studies piano and theory with Albert Bing, a former student of Hans Pfitzner. Bing's wife Edith is the sister of the Expressionist playwright Carl Sternheim. The Bings later become second parents to Weill.

1916 — *Sehnsucht* (Joseph von Eichendorff).

Ofrahs Lieder (Spring 1916–September 1916, Jehuda Halevi), cycle of five songs. The date of the first performance is unknown. (Weill later considered this to be his starting point as a composer.)

Zriny, opera after the play by Theodor Körner (lost).

Im Volkston (Arno Holz).

Gives piano lessons to Duke Friedrich's niece and nephews.

1917 — *Volkslied* (Anna Ritter).

Das schöne Kind (author unknown).

Employed as a volunteer accompanist and coach at the Dessau Court Theater. Undertakes intensive studies in conducting, orchestration, and score-reading with Albert Bing. Shows an avid interest in literature and philosophy and is reading Hermann Bang, Otto Julius Bierbaum, Richard Dehmel, Goethe, Sven Hedin, Hendrik Ibsen, Else Lasker-Schüler, Alois Riehl, Rainer Maria Rilke, Romain Rolland, Shakespeare, and Friedrich Theodor Vischer.

March — Appears in concert with Emilie Feuge in Cöthen. Weill is writing fugues for music teacher Mr. Köhler, who finds them "too modern, too chromatic," but free of mistakes and full of musical ideas.

April — Begins taking piano lessons every other day, practicing in the morning and composing in the afternoon. The piano lessons include etudes by Moscheles, Bach chorales in four clefs, and score-reading from *Tristan*. He is reading novels by Albert Brachvogel, Hermann Bang, and Emile Zola and looks forward to the end of the war with anticipation. During this month he is particularly taken with performances of Humperdinck's *Hänsel und Gretel* and Bruckner's Symphony no. 4.

May — Weill's brother Nathan is called to the front lines. Weill studies *Fidelio* and reads novels by Björnstjerne Björnson.

July — Visits relatives in Bad Kreuznach, Mannheim, Wiesloch, and Heidelberg with sister Ruth.

August — Conducts a student orchestra, directs a male chorus, and performs with the Cöthener Jungwehr Musik. Begins taking trumpet lessons in the hopes of being placed in a military band if drafted.

October — Studies *Rigoletto* with Bing.

November — Attends *Die Schneider von Schönau* by Jan Brandts-Buys and *Hamlet* starring Alexander Moissi.

December — Piano studies include a Brahms sonata and Chopin etudes.

Intermezzo, piano solo.

Visits Hanns at the end of the month in Halberstadt.

1918

February 6 — *Maikaterlied* and *Abendlied* (April 1917–January 1918, Otto Julius Bierbaum) Saal des Evang, Vereinshauses, Dessau; Clara Oßent and Gertrud Prinzler.

March — *Andante aus der As-dur Sonate von C. M. von Weber*, orchestration exercise.

Performs in a concert in Cöthen; attends *Rappelkopf* by Ferdinand Raimund and Tolstoy's *Macht der Finsternis* starring Moissi and Max Pallenberg. Weill has become thoroughly acquainted with the standard operatic repertoire, especially Wagner.

Finishes studies at Herzogliche Friedrichs-Oberrealschule in Dessau and travels to Berlin to make arrangements for his further education.

---

1. The palace of the Duke of Anhalt, located in the center of Dessau.

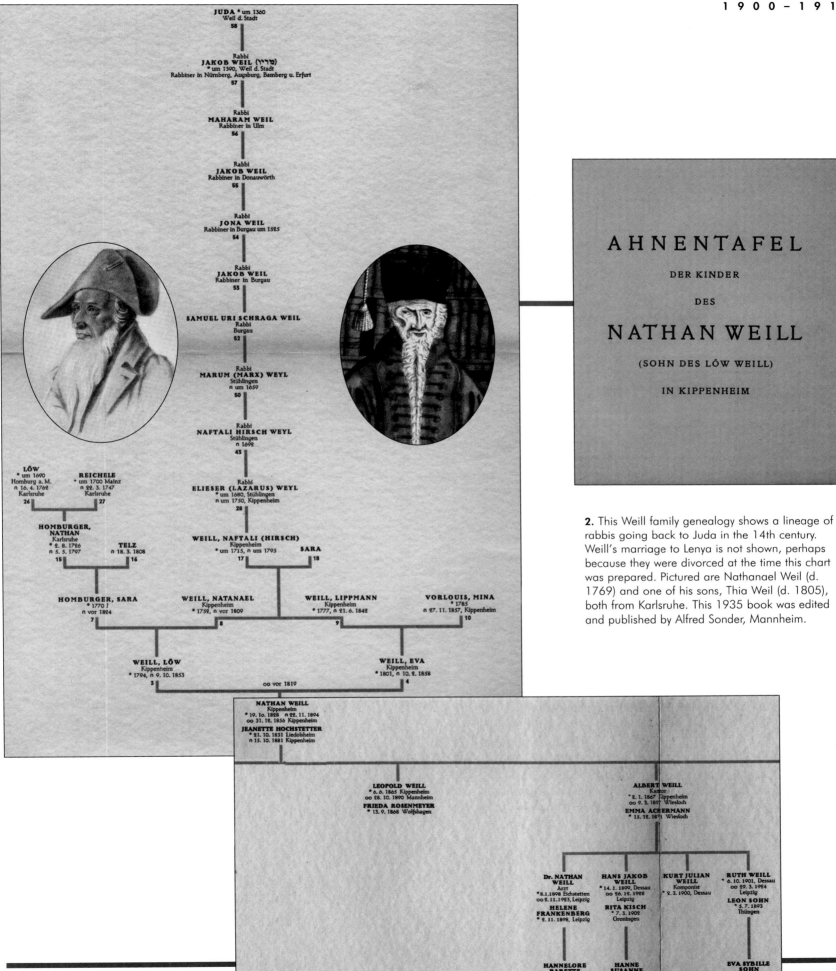

2. This Weill family genealogy shows a lineage of rabbis going back to Juda in the 14th century. Weill's marriage to Lenya is not shown, perhaps because they were divorced at the time this chart was prepared. Pictured are Nathanael Weil (d. 1769) and one of his sons, Thia Weil (d. 1805), both from Karlsruhe. This 1935 book was edited and published by Alfred Sonder, Mannheim.

WEIL - DE VEIL

A Genealogy, 1360-1956

Important figures among the descendants of Juda Weil:
Generations of rabbis, teachers, priests, ministers,
writers and a composer

A guide to German, Dutch and English sources,
with special emphasis on their interrelationship

BY ERNEST B. WEILL

Scarsdale, New York, 1957

The reason the Weil family could be traced for six hundred years into the past is explained by the fact that many of its members were scholars who had handed down in writing and print, from generation to generation, in books and on gravestones, the information about their origins, origins which may have gone back to Spain.

The changes and differences in the spelling of the family name are of no importance. They were, in many cases, simply the result of the whim or ignorance of some town or village registrar. As one of the oldest traceable Jewish families in Germany, the Weils and Weills formed a part of the Jewish population which had already lived in that country for many centuries when Adolf Hitler, an Austrian immigrant, persecuted and destroyed them as foreigners.

We find the earliest records of the family in what is now Southern Germany, first in that part which was then called "Schwaben," later in Baden and the Black Forest, Alsace, Lorraine, Prague, Austria, Poland, and Switzerland. In the seventeenth century Weils were recorded in Stühlingen in the Oberland of Baden. From there, early in the eighteenth century, members of the family moved to Kippenheim in Baden, others to Karlsruhe, the capital of Baden. Of course, not all persons by the name of Weil, whatever the spelling, are descendants of the fifteenth century Rabbi Jacob Weil. The name Weil and Weiler, which in German means hamlet, was used in those days by several villages east and west of the upper Rhine River. Quite a number of persons, not related to one another, on leaving these towns, would have chosen the name Weil or Weiler as a family name to be added to the first name which had been sufficient identification in their old home towns.

The first known Weil of this tree was named simply *Juda* [also *Jehuda*]. He was a Jew born in 1360 who lived in the hamlet Weil der Stadt, not far from Stuttgart. His son *Jacob Weil*, born about 1390, named himself after this little town. A former pupil of the Rabbi Jacob Moeln (1365-1427) of Mainz, Jacob

was ordained in Nuremberg in 1427. He was first a rabbi there and later in Augsburg, Bamberg and Erfurt [after 1444]. Though the exact date of his death is not known, it was concluded that he died before 1456. Jacob Weil's wife counted among her ancestors the illustrious Talmudists Rabbi Meir (Maharam) of Rothenburg (1215-1293). Jacob Weil's book *Ohel Jisrael* (The Tent of Israel) was first printed in Venice in 1523. It has two parts: *She Elot u Teschubot* (Questions and Answers — Responsa) and the important appendix entitled *Shehitot u Bedikot* (Jewish rules for the slaughtering and inspection of animals). These rules have been regarded as authoritative by later rabbis. They were reprinted as well as translated from the Hebrew in many European countries from the sixteenth to the nineteenth century. The book has run through seventy-one editions and the rules stipulated by Jacob Weil in this work have been the subject of various commentaries and additions. The Hebrew Union College Library in Cincinnati, for example, has 49 different editions.

Jacob Weil's son became the Rabbi *Maharam Weil* in Ulm and Maharam's son, again named *Jacob (Jequil) Weil*, was a rabbi in Donauwörth and later in Landau. This trio of grandfather-father-son forms the common trunk of this Weil-de Veil genealogical tree. . .

Rabbi Jacob (Jequil) Weil had a son, *Jona*, who became rabbi in Burgau (about 1525). Jona's son, Rabbi *Jacob*, also lived in Burgau, and his son, Rabbi *Samuel Uri Schraga Weil*, stayed in Burgau. Samuel's son, *Marum (Marx) Weyl*, was a rabbi in Stühlingen until 1659, and Marum's son, Rabbi *Naftali Hirsch Weyl*, died in Stühlingen about 1692. Two of Naftali's sons became rabbis: *Elieser (Lazarus) Weyl* (born 1680 in Stühlingen and died about 1750 in Kippenheim) and Naftali's younger son, Nathanael Weil (1687-1769), who was elected to the high office of "Oberlandrabbiner" in Karlsruhe, the capital of Baden. As he had been highly respected among Christians as well as Jews, the margrave of Baden-Baden ordered a commando of cavalry and infantry to escort his funeral procession from Rastatt to Karlsruhe.

Nathanael Weil is the author of several works known to scholars to this day: *Korban Nethan'el* (published in Karlsruhe in 1755), *Netif Chaim* (published in Fürth in 1779) and *Thorath Nathanael* (published in Fürth in 1795). *Korban Nathanael*, meaning "The Offering of Nathanael" is a Talmudic work, a supercommentary on Asher ben Jechiel's compendium on the Talmud. In the past, educated people, Jewish scholars in particular, considered a person's ancestry and background (called their "Jichus") as very important. In the introduction to his work Nathanael Weil passed on to future generations proof of his descent from Rabbi Jacob Weil of the fifteenth century. It was based on reliable documents and annotations in books which linked him with Jacob and were handed down by the seven generations of rabbis whom he quotes. A mention of his descent also appears on his gravestone. Probably due to a lack of money to pay a printer, three of Nathanael Weil's works were still in manuscript form when he died in 1769. These were printed posthumously by one of his sons, *Simon Hirsch Weil*, a scholar and writer in his own right. Nathanael's book *Netif Chaim* (The Pathway of Life) offers annotations and supplements to the code of the Law, *The Prepared Table*. They are critical studies to the ritual code *Orach Chaim*. This publication was followed by two more books, under the collective title *Thorath Nathanael*. The first is a collection of comments on the law which Rabbi Nathanael had given to his contemporaries during his lifetime; the second deals with the Pentateuch, the five books of Moses.

One of Nathanael's sons, *Thia Weil*, (1721-1805), succeeded him in the high office of chief rabbi in Karlsruhe. Thia's son, Rabbi *Abraham Weil*, born in 1754 in Prague, was a rabbi in Mühringen in the Black Forest. Later, until his death in 1831, he was "Provinzialrabbiner" in Sulzburg, Baden. *Jacob*

Weill, one of Abraham's sons, was a scholar and author of *Thorath Shabbat*, published in Karlsruhe in 1839. This book is a collection of laws and rules for the sanctification of the Sabbath, its customs and ceremonies. The text is in Hebrew, with facing pages in German. The German, however, is also printed in Hebrew characters. Jacob Weill, just as his grandfather Nathanael had done, refers in the introduction of his book to his ancestors, calling himself the "grandson of Thia of the tenth generation after the *gaon* Jacob Weil." Jacob Weill died in Karlsruhe in 1851. His brother, *Hirsch Weil*, lived in Sulzburg from 1780-1856 and had a son, again named *Nathanael Weil* (1818-1892) who was entrusted with the office of "Stiftsrabbiner" in Karlsruhe, where he had the reputation of a teacher of high learning.

The line branching off from the Rabbi Elieser (Lazarus) Weyl (d. Kippenheim 1750), the ninth rabbi generation, leads four generations later to *Carl Weill*, born in Kippenheim 1818 who died in Karlsruhe in 1894. He was the author and publisher of a Hebrew language grammar, dictionary and textbook, published in Karlsruhe in 1879.

Another branch down from Rabbi Elieser (Lazarus) Weyl leads six generations later to the composer *Kurt Weill*. Probably best known internationally for his *Dreigroschenoper* (Threepenny Opera), Kurt Weill was born in 1900 in Dessau, Germany, the youngest son of cantor Albert Weill. . . .

Another highly gifted and promising musician of the same generation [was] *Rudi Weill*, born 1891 in Karlsruhe, a grandson of Carl Weill. At the age of twenty-three he became conductor at the opera house in Breslau, but only a few years later he met his death as an officer in the First World War. More musical talent is found in the fifteenth and sixteenth generation of the Dutch family branch, composer and conductor *Sijmen de Weille* and his son *Bernardus Adrianus Sijmen de Weille*.

3. Weill's parents, Emma Ackermann and Albert Weill, around the time of their wedding on 8 March 1897 in Wiesloch, and their marriage certificate.

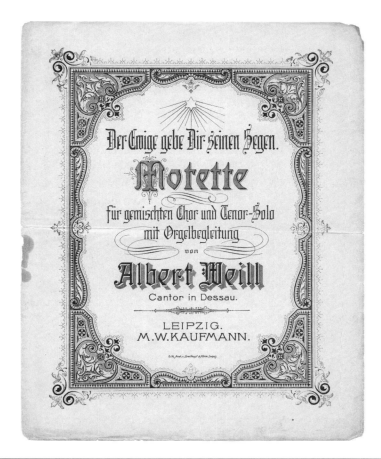

4. Weill's father published a few compositions, including this undated motet and a collection of "Synagogen-Gesänge" for cantor and men's chorus (1893).

5. Map of central Dessau, 1900, showing the location of:
1. Weill's birthplace and home until 1902 at Leipziger Straße 59. (The building was demolished in 1967.)
2. Weill family residence from 1902–1903: Franzstraße 45.
3. Weill family residence from 1904–1907: Muldstraße 20.
4. The new Dessau synagogue, opened 18 February 1908. The Weill family moved into the adjoining Jewish community center (Gemeindehaus) during the spring of 1907. (The synagogue was burned in November 1938 and further destroyed by Allied bombs in 1945.)
5. The school Weill attended from 1909–1918 (Herzogliche Friedrichs-Oberrealschule). (The building was destroyed by Allied bombs in 1945.)
6. The palace of the Duke of Anhalt (Herzogliches Palais). (It was demolished in 1927.)
7. The ducal theater (Herzogliches Hoftheater, renamed Friedrich-Theater in November 1918 and destroyed by fire in 1922).

7. The new Dessau synagogue officially opened in February 1908. Cantor Weill and his family lived on the ground floor of the building at the right.

6. Weill's birthplace at Leipziger Straße 59, where his family lived until 1902.

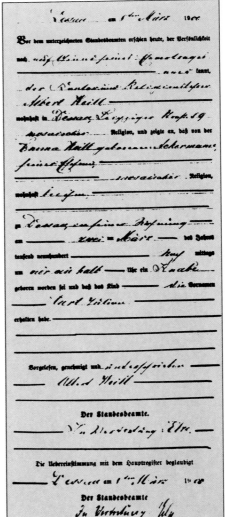

8. "Curt Julian" Weill's birth certificate dated 2 March 1900.

9. Emma Weill and son Kurt.

MUSIC + THEATER	LITERATURE + FILM	SCIENCE + SOCIETY	POLITICS
1900-1904 Puccini *Tosca* Mahler *Symphony No. 4* Cabaret *Überbrettl* founded in Berlin Debussy *Pelléas et Mélisande* Caruso makes first recording Humperdinck *Dornröschen* D'Albert *Tiefland* Janáček *Jenufa* Wedekind *Die Büchse der Pandora*	**1900-1904** Dreiser *Sister Carrie* Mann *Buddenbrooks* Stefan Zweig *Silberne Seiten* Doyle *The Hound of the Baskervilles* *The Great Train Robbery* (film by Edwin Porter) London *The Call of the Wild* Hudson *Green Mansions* Chekhov *Vishnevyi sad* (*The Cherry Orchard*)	**1900-1904** German Civil Law Code (BGB) comes in force New German orthography adopted Wright Brothers successfully fly a powered airplane Henry Ford, with capital of $100,000, founds Ford Motor Company New York policeman arrests a woman for smoking in public Max Weber *Die protestantische Ethik und der Geist des Kapitalismus*	**1900-1904** Boxer Rebellion in China against Europeans Bernhard von Bülow is named German Chancellor Queen Victoria dies, succeeded by her son Edward VII William McKinley assassinated, succeeded by Theodore Roosevelt Triple Alliance between Germany, Austria, and Italy renewed Alaskan frontier is settled
1905-1908 Strauss *Salome* Lehár *Die lustige Witwe* Cohan *Forty-Five Minutes from Broadway* Busoni *Entwurf einer neuen Aesthetik der Tonkunst* The first *Ziegfeld Follies* staged in New York Schoenberg's *String Quartet op. 10*	**1905-1908** Rilke *Das Stundenbuch* First regular cinema established, in Pittsburgh, Pa. O. Henry *The Four Million* Sinclair *The Jungle* Conrad *The Secret Agent* Forster *A Room with a View* Anatole France *L'île des pingouins*	**1905-1908** Sigmund Freud *Drei Abhandlungen zur Sexualtheorie* Clemens von Pirquet introduces the term "allergy" to medicine Night shift work for women forbidden internationally San Francisco earthquake kills 700 people Ivan Pavlov studies conditioned reflexes Louis Lumière develops color photography Fritz Haber synthesizes ammonia Sven Hedin explores Persia and Tibet	**1905-1908** Demonstration in St. Petersburg brutally crushed by the czar Sailors' mutiny on the battleship *Potemkin* France and Spain control Morocco U.S. troops occupy Cuba William II of Germany and Nicholas II of Russia meet Oklahoma becomes 46th state of the U.S. Union of South Africa established Leopold II transfers the Congo to Belgium
1909-1912 Strauss *Elektra* Molnár *Liliom* Herbert *Naughty Marietta* The tango arrives in Europe Strauss *Der Rosenkavalier* Schoenberg *Harmonielehre* Schreker *Der ferne Klang* Schoenberg *Pierrot Lunaire*	**1909-1912** Wassermann *Caspar Hauser* D. W. Griffith features Mary Pickford, the first film star May *Winnetou* (German novel for boys) Dreiser *Jennie Gerhardt* *Afgrunden* (film starring Asta Nielsen) Hauptmann *Atlantis* Maugham *The Land of Promise* *Les amours de la reine Elisabeth* (film by Henri Desfontaines)	**1909-1912** Women admitted to German universities T.H. Morgan begins research in genetics Halley's comet observed The English wife-poisoner H.H. Crippen executed Marie Curie wins Nobel Prize in Chemistry Roald Amundsen reaches South Pole Polish chemist Kasimir Funk coins the term "vitamin" S.S. *Titanic* sinks on her maiden voyage	**1909-1912** Bethmann-Hollweg becomes German chancellor Japan annexes Korea King Edward VII dies, succeeded by George V Kaiser Wilhelm asserts Germany's "Place in the Sun" Winston Churchill appointed First Lord of the Admiralty Lenin takes over editorship of *Pravda* Woodrow Wilson wins presidential election
1913-1916 Stravinsky *Le Sacre du Printemps* Shaw *Pygmalion* Vaughan Williams *A London Symphony* Graener *Don Juans letztes Abenteuer* American Society of Composers, Authors, and Publishers (ASCAP) founded Reger *Mozart Variations* Schillings *Mona Lisa* Schubert-Berté *Das Dreimäderlhaus*	**1913-1916** Mann *Der Tod in Venedig* The first Charlie Chaplin movies appear Joyce *Dubliners* Dreiser *The Titan* Van Wyck Brooks *America's Coming of Age* *Birth of a Nation* (film by D.W. Griffith) Brod *Tycho Brahes Weg zu Gott* *The Pawn Shop* (film by Chaplin)	**1913-1916** Panama Canal opened Jack Dempsey starts fighting under the name "Kid Blackey" Albert Einstein postulates his general theory of relativity The largest railroad station in Europe completed in Leipzig Margaret Sanger jailed for writing book on birth control Food rationed in Germany	**1913-1916** Balkan War Mahatma Gandhi arrested Austria-Hungary declares war on Serbia Germany declares war on Russia and France, World War I starts German submarine sinks *Lusitania* German dirigibles attack London Czar Nicholas II takes over command of Russian army Battle of Verdun Italy declares war on Germany

10. Kurt between his brothers, Nathan (left) and Hanns. Photo by Hartmann.

11. The four Weill children: Hanns, Nathan, Kurt (seated, in front), and Ruth. Photo by Clasen.

12. Kurt, Nathan, and Hanns flanking their grandfather Daniel Ackermann, a teacher. Photo by Meder.

13. Weill (at far left) in a play at the Jewish community center. His sister Ruth is standing third from the left.

Emma Weill Remembers . . .

On my dear departed mother's birthday I used to travel home with one of our children, although the journey was a long one. It was always the first of March—the day of joy, called *Purim* by the Jews. That particular year it was little Kurt's turn. He was a charming traveling companion and so full of fun. On the night of *Purim*, when it got to be late in the evening, the children of the small town stormed into our apartment wearing masks and doing all kinds of monkey business—as used to be the custom then—and little Kurt got terribly scared. He was only five years old and cried and cried and cried. I got angry at him and scolded him for doing this, when my mother tore Kurt away from me, screaming at me quite loudly: "Don't you touch this child. He is somebody special."

Our apartment was next to the huge synagogue—a present to the Jewish community from the Baroness von Cohn-Oppenheim—in a big building used for all social activities. It was there that dear Kurt was able to spend his diligent and happy young years. All of the interesting people who gathered around our family participated in Kurt's development as well. I must include here that Kurt was an *extremely* conscientious student, and that he also wrote the most magnificent and interesting essays. All three boys were very well liked in school; after we had gotten them a tuxedo, they regularly alternated in conducting the student concerts. Kurt's fellow students always called him *Musikerappel* [musician apple].

Kurt had his first piano lessons with our dear father. Then they were taken over by a young French woman who studied music in Leipzig until he eventually got [Albert] Bing as a teacher. How happy the boy was when we could afford to buy a magnificent grand piano!

As his parents, we had to decide whether or not Kurt should study music. To be on the safe side, his dear father wanted him to study medicine as well. But Nathan and Hanns came and begged their father to let him study music. Hanns said, "Nathan will become a great doctor, and I will become a successful businessman. We will see Kurt through this."

Ruth Weill Remembers . . .

We all brought our friends home after school and on weekends. Our apartment was on the main floor of the Jewish community center and the social rooms were on the second and third floors. One of the rooms had a small stage where plays were produced, sometimes classics, sometimes modern plays, or even plays made up for special occasions. We all acted in the plays, and Kurt always chose or played whatever music was needed. Sometimes he would conduct a small orchestra.

School lasted from eight until one, when we went home for midday dinner. Kurt had a great gift for mimicking, and he was always imitating his teachers. Kurt took higher mathematics instead of Latin. He did his homework right after dinner and then twice a week went over to the Bings' house for music lessons. Every afternoon promptly at 5:30 was the *Bummel*, or afternoon stroll, for the teenagers. Kurt never missed it, no matter how deeply absorbed he was in something else. He would jump up, wash his face and hands, slick his hair, and take off with Hanns, who was the real lady-killer in the family. They would walk back and forth in front of the theater, boys walking with boys, girls with girls, everyone flirting and giggling. Kurt used to discuss with me all the great problems of the world and big questions about God, the universe and stars, and why people existed.

Our parents were deeply involved in their feelings toward each other, and we children understood. Oftentimes we would come home to find the apartment empty, because our parents were out walking together. Our parents had a great deal of pride, especially Mother, and that quality always impressed Kurt. Even during the war when food was scarce, they never discussed our needs with anybody. Kurt and I would sometimes hike to small nearby villages in search of butter and eggs, but usually without success. People were living on turnips and barley soup then.

When Nathan was in the army at the French front and Hanns was already in business, I remember Kurt being very anti-military. In his last year of school they tried to take Kurt into the army. The night before his physical exam he took a hundred aspirin tablets. I sat up all night to keep him company in the music room. At the exam his heart was pounding and he was rejected. Several months before he had started to learn the trumpet so that he could play in a band if he was drafted. When soldiers marched past our house, Kurt would run around closing all the windows so that he couldn't hear the military music.

Dr. Willy Krüger Remembers. . .

Our school was the Herzogliche Friedrichs-Oberrealschule, located in the Dessau Friedericianum. I attended classes with Kurt Weill from 1909 to 1917. He was a very talented boy, but he never pushed himself. He was satisfied with his class rank, which was usually between fourth and sixth in the class. Most of the boys played sports after school, but not Kurt. He would practice for hours at the piano or at the organ in the synagogue. Kurt was already a musical expert at school, and the music teacher, August Theile, quickly recognized his talent. I remember a school concert in 1916 when the choir sang some war choruses which Kurt had composed. His brother Nathan conducted.

In the tenth grade we all had to participate in public speaking (*Rede-Akt*), where we would address the class for about thirty minutes on a selected topic. Kurt chose to speak about the composer Felix Mendelssohn-Bartholdy, and Theile arranged for him to speak for a whole hour before the entire student body. Everyone was impressed with Kurt's lecture and his performance of Mendelssohn's music at the piano. It was at this time, about 1916, that Kurt sent his first compositions to a music publisher in Leipzig. The publisher (I don't recall his name), responded that the music was very interesting but suggested that, because of his young age, it would be better to wait a few years before publication.

Kurt was also very knowledgeable on the subject of literature and knew most of the books in his father's library. One literature teacher was an avid collector of rare books, and we used to encourage Kurt to divert the teacher's attention when we had an exam scheduled. When class began, Kurt would rise and innocently ask a question about rare editions. The teacher would launch into a long discussion with Kurt, and we didn't have to worry about the exam!

Sometimes Kurt would invite us to the synagogue, and I remember spending many hours listening to him practice the organ. One visit in particular impressed me very much. We obtained permission to attend a Jewish festival, the *Laubhütten-Fest* (Succoth). Another vivid impression I have is that of the entire Weill family together in one of Dessau's large parks. It was a very peaceful scene: the cantor—he always wore his hat—his wife, and the four children walking and talking together.

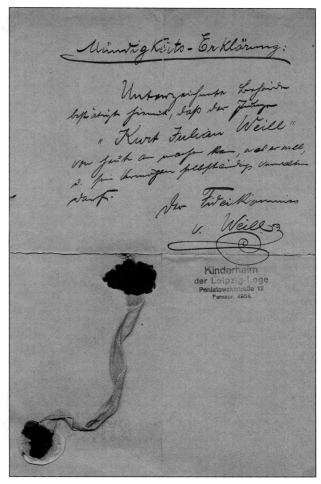

14. Weill's "Mündigkeits-Erklärung" (coming-of-age certificate), signed by his father, 1913.

15. Weill's first surviving composition, *Mi addir*, a Jewish wedding song, 1913, shows that he was fairly new to writing musical notation.

16. Top, the Herzogliche Friedrichs-Oberrealschule in Dessau (Weill's high school, also called Friedericianum Gymnasium), built in 1882. Bottom, class picture in 1915; Weill is seated at the far right, first row.

17. Program of concert given by the Dessauer Feldkorps, January 1915. "Kundschafter [roughly "scout," a rank within the Feldkorps] Weill" is named as the pianist for the sixth item, *Für uns.*

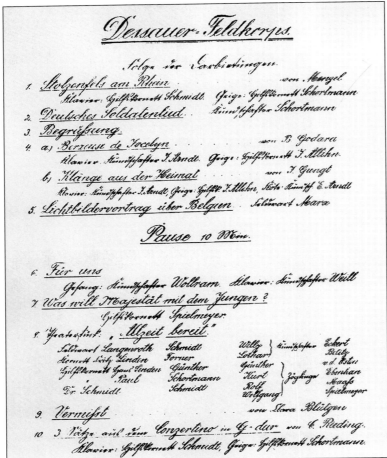

Dr. Werner Spielmeyer Remembers. . .

Yes, it is true that Weill composed war choruses. As you know, World War I inspired a great nationalist wave in Germany. As boys of fourteen, we were strongly influenced by the surge and wanted to do anything we could to be involved. All of our studies in school were focused on nationalist themes. Everything German was emphasized: language, literature, art, and even nationalistic music. We were being prepared to serve the Emperor and the army.

We all joined the Dessauer Feldkorps, the German equivalent of the Boy Scouts. We were issued uniforms and assigned rankings such as *Hilfskornett* (flag carrier), *Feldwart* (field lookout), and *Kundschafter* (scout). Kurt Weill was a *Kundschafter*. In addition to weekend exercises, we organized public evenings where we presented special sketches, songs, and recitations. In January 1915, we held one of these programs at the Zentrale, a Dessau restaurant. Kurt Weill played the piano and sang one of the war songs, *Für uns.* This certainly must be one of the earliest programs to include the musician Weill.

In 1915 or 1916, the boys from our school had to join the army, and soon we received word that some of our schoolmates had been killed in action. At the school commemoration services, Kurt Weill usually spoke on behalf of the students. He always found the right words.

Weill (in Dessau) to Nathan and Hanns Weill, 22 March 1917:
During the first part of the week I was very busy with rehearsals, giving lessons, etc.; on top of that we had nothing but bad weather so I wasn't exactly in a good mood. Tuesday there was a tremendously ridiculous gala to raise war bonds. Thursday at seven o'clock I went to Cöthen with Mrs. [Emilie] Feuge. Bing really wanted to come along because I had played the "Liebestod" very well for him. He even seriously considered walking home the same night. In Cöthen I ate magnificently at the Thormeyers again. Green peas with boiled potatoes and two eggs sunnyside up (fried in butter) and marvelous chocolate pudding. In the afternoon I practiced by myself in the concert hall, then met the Hofgaardens in the cafe and at nine everything got started. The concert was well attended, and I received quite a bit of applause at my entrance (I was the first).

Without self-praise, I did play very well, especially the memorized pieces, the "Liebestod," and the accompaniment to the Jensen *Lieder*, after which the audience applauded more for me than for Mrs. Feuge. I had tremendous applause, especially for *Tristan*. After the Grieg they brought me a huge bouquet of flowers, from Mr. Thormeyer; nice, wasn't it? After that I had to come out three times. The rest of the concert also received lots of applause, mainly, of course, for Mrs. Feuge, who got more flowers than any Dessau flower shop could muster. Afterwards we gathered together as one small, cozy group: Thormeyers, Bankewitzes [Käthe Bankewitz was the soprano soloist], Mrs. Feuge and I. There was coffee and cake and afterwards wonderful champagne; we went home at midnight, where there was another supper waiting. I went to bed at 1:30, got up at a quarter to five (the first night during which I did not sleep for one minute!); I had to catch the train at a quarter to six, since it was impossible to play hooky again. You can imagine that I'm dead tired today. Of course I'm very curious about the review. It will run in the *Staatsanzeiger* again. Besides all of this, I've also received forty Marks. The knight's castle will soon be ready!

Weill (in Dessau) to Hanns Weill, 30 March 1917: Here in school—much like last fall during the inspection of the 98ers—there is quite a bit of anxiety [about the draft] because last night the [names of the] dischargees from the 99th appeared in the newspaper. . . . You'll have to find out over there whether it would be more advisable for you to get your army physical in Halberstadt or here, and then decide accordingly. But Father will write you more about that. In any case, I do hope that you won't let them intimidate you, and that you'll use your famous big mouth effectively, and that you'll make up a good story for those almighty doctors. Under no circumstances must you become a soldier! Any questions?—At ease!

I've written a very good fugue for four voices. Of course again it was too modern, too chromatic, for Mr. Köhler, but he could not discover any mistakes and admitted "there's a lot of musical stuff in there." I especially wanted to write in a very simple manner, but I couldn't do it. Might this be a good sign? Now I'm working on a larger fugue on the theme of "Thank ye the Lord, because He is kind, His goodness is everlasting." Also, during the vacation I want to write a canon for two female voices with simple piano accompaniment, something I've promised Mrs. Feuge, but I haven't found a suitable text yet.

Weill (in Dessau) to Hanns Weill, 17 April 1917: I did get one piano lesson [from Albert Bing] and a very interesting one at that. After the etudes (I've started on the first one by Moscheles), we got to talk about the orchestra. I'm supposed to start score reading seriously now. He showed me a few passages of the *Tristan* score and that slowed us down so much that we had to postpone the rest of the lesson until Monday. . . . *Hänsel and Gretel* was simply wonderful. Although [Engelbert] Humperdinck is working faithfully according to the Wagnerian model in his development of themes as well as in the orchestration—Bing tells me that he actually belongs to Bayreuth's most enthusiastic supporters and collaborators, is Cosima's best friend, and supposedly has even written most of Siegfried Wagner's concoctions [*Machwerke*]—yet he is entering entirely new paths in the choice of themes and overall structure. . . . By highest order of His Highness [Duke Friedrich II of Anhalt], the witch had to be made over into a Good Fairy so the children would not be scared! That produced an utterly ridiculous effect. The same with the Finale, into which Humperdinck had woven the "Dessauer Marsch" in order to suck up to the Duke [*sich beim Herzog anzuscheißen*]. That ruins the effect of the magnificent final chorus. . . .

Yesterday afternoon I had another lesson. In order to learn how to read the different clefs Bing gave me four-voice chorales by Bach. . . . In every lesson I have to play some of these for him "but only if my Jewish heart won't be offended by these 'ecclesiastical chorales.'" By this method I'm getting pretty well into the score-reading process.

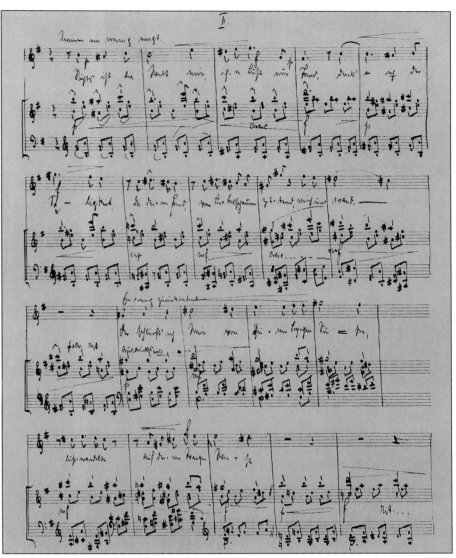

18. The second song from *Ofrahs Lieder*, "Nichts ist die Welt mir," 1916.

| 1 | 9 | 1 | 7 |

Music + Theater:	**Literature + Film:**	**Science + Society:**	**Politics:**
Hans Pfitzner *Palestrina*	Lion Feuchtwanger *Jud Süss*	Sigmund Freud *Vorlesungen zur*	WWI
Ferruccio Busoni *Turandot*	Sinclair Lewis *The Job: An American*	*Einführung in die Psychoanalyse*	U.S. and Cuba declare war on
First recordings of the Original	*Novel*	Trans-Siberian Railroad completed	Germany
Dixieland Jazz Band	UFA becomes foremost German film	U.S. Senate rejects President Wilson's	October revolution in Russia
	company	suffrage bill	The Allies execute dancer Mata Hari
			as a spy

19. Weill with Peter Bing, the son of his music teacher Albert Bing, ca. 1916.

22. Weill at the piano in the family's new music room, about which Weill reported to his brother in March 1917: "Our 'salon' turned out to be gorgeous: very impressive blue wallpaper, and the grand piano situated smack in the middle of the room from the corner where the desk stands."

25. The music room in the ducal palace, where Weill gave lessons to the duke's niece and nephews.

20. Albert Bing, Weill's music teacher and "second father," was first kapellmeister at the Dessau opera.

23. Weill stands to the immediate right of the banner in this photo of members of the Dessauer Feldkorps.

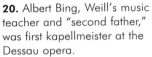

24. *Ich weiss wofür*, a four-part setting from 1914 of Guido von Güllhausen's patriotic poem.

26. Weill with two unidentified boys near a pond in the Harz mountains. The Weills apparently participated in the Freikörperkultur naturist movement in Germany.

21. Weill played a Chopin prelude and a nocturne from Liszt's *Liebesträume* at his school in a charity concert organized by the "Society for German Culture Abroad," 18 December 1915.

Weill (in Dessau) to Hanns Weill, [20 April 1917]: Every morning I'm still going to school until 11:30. I haven't missed a day yet because physics and mathematics require a lot of attention. In the afternoon I work by myself, and in the evening I'm mostly in the theater. Friday evening there was a very beautiful concert. Once again, Mikorey wasn't up to the Bach concert. However, he handled the Romantic Symphony by Bruckner very well. By reading the full score and working through the piano score that Bing had given to me, I've gotten to know that work well enough to consider it one of the most beautiful of symphonies. . . .

   I think that a decent *Tristan* performance will always be a special event for me. No other opera score contains so much. One can hardly sink so deeply into any other kind of music when listening, or be pulled into it when learning or performing it. Last night I saw *Die verlorene Tochter* by Ludwig Fulda. In order to get mother to see a play for once, I used a trick: I bought a seat in the orchestra at the box office and told her that Ruth had gotten it in school for just one Mark. Then Ruth and I took standing room. The play is a very nice, rather freewheeling comedy, which made us laugh a lot.

Weill (in Dessau) to Hanns Weill, 1 May 1917: I'm anxious to find out whether Bing will be able to stand this choral conducting [in Berlin] for any length of time, since, as he told me, it's very strenuous to stand up in front of a herd of people and let them to scream into your face; also, he's never conducted a chorus before. Sunday he gave me the last lesson for the time being. I've got to work on the 1st [C major] Weber sonata, beautiful but difficult. I also have to study the woodwinds thoroughly on the basis of several books, read the various clefs, and work very diligently on the Moscheles etudes; therefore I really have quite a lot to do. The canon will be finished soon. I had a lot of pleasure and joy working it out because the accompaniment—much to my surprise—turned out to be quite contrapuntal and orchestral. I think I'm gradually getting closer and closer to understanding orchestral writing.

Weill (in Dessau) to Hanns Weill, mid-May 1917: Mäkke [Preitz] has been nagging me all day to give my lecture, and I've hardly started to work on it. You probably know already that I'm supposed to talk about Mendelssohn-Bartholdy? For that purpose I've bought a very fine book from the series "From the World of Nature and Mind: The Golden Age of German Musical Romanticism" by Edgar Istel. I'll prepare myself especially for the subjects of: "Mendelssohn-Wagner" and "Mendelssohn the Jew" (of course, musically he is no more Jewish than Mozart). . . . Besides the usual piano technique and clef-reading exercises we are now doing the following: we take both the full score and the piano vocal score from any opera. First Bing plays from the vocal score and I conduct from the full score, and afterwards vice versa. For homework he has given me the first scene from *Fidelio*: to play from the full score and then to conduct—specifically with every cue for stage and orchestra and all nuances. You can imagine how much fun I'm having, but also how much work this is. . . .

   Have your hopes for peace been improving? Yesterday we suddenly had to spend four hours writing a French essay. *La guerre sous-marine allemande* [the German submarine war]. What a pile of shit!

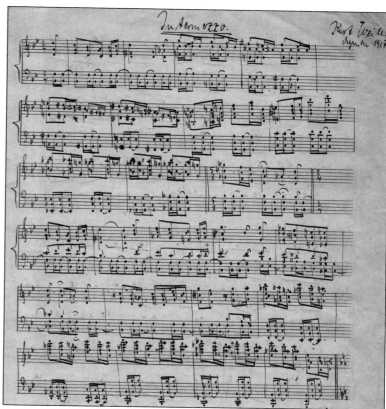

27. The *Intermezzo* for piano solo (1917) is Weill's only work for that instrument.

Weill (in Dessau) to Hanns Weill, 16 May 1917: Monday I finished my lecture, which I'm going to send to you. For musical examples I'm going to play the Scherzo from *Ein Sommernachtstraum* and something from an oratorio. Besides this, I have to read and comment on a historic novella by Gottfried Keller. Then I have to reorganize the student orchestra and the men's chorus. Perhaps I'll be successful with the latter. I believe there'll be quite a few who may want to participate. . . .

   I have started a little string quartet with Köhler, of course still very basic.

Weill (in Dessau) to Hanns Weill, [16] June 1917: What do you say about *Palestrina* [by Pfitzner]? I've read a long, very interesting review in the *Frankfurter Zeitung* from the 15th and 16th [of June 1917] which Bing had picked up at [Carl] Bömly's. It really seems to be a gigantic work; just imagine twenty-four large male solo parts! And most important of all, it also seems to be pointing in an entirely new direction: away from exaggerated, modern chromaticism and back to the Wagner of *Die Meistersinger*! Mind you, Paul Bekker characterizes it as the last, highly spiritual work of musical romanticism, as the final conclusion of a great musical epoch. I wonder if he is right? In any case, the humble [Hans] Pfitzner has finally succeeded in winning the esteem he deserves on Germany's musical scene, although the work probably won't get more than a few performances with minimal popular acclaim.

Weill (in Dessau) to Hanns Weill, 26 June 1917: The poems by Franz Werfel (is he Jewish?) are really good. Although Bing advised me against it, I'll still try and compose them. This might become my first "philosophical composition" à la *Palestrina*.

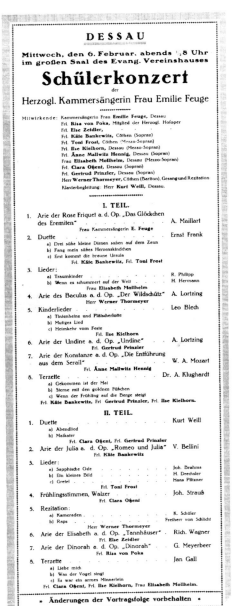

28. *Maikaterlied*, a duet for two sopranos and piano accompaniment, was performed in Dessau by Clara Oßent and Gertrud Prinzler, both voice students of Emilie Feuge.

29. Program from a 6 February 1918 concert in which Weill accompanied his two duets, *Maikaterlied* and *Abendlied*.

30. The quotation from *Hänsel und Gretel* from Weill's 20 August 1917 letter to his brother Hanns.

Weill (in Dessau) to Hanns Weill, 20 August 1917: I would love to have a nice little room in Berlin, in Leipzig, in München and a closet filled with scores and books and vocal scores and music paper, and work until I drop. And just for once to be without the concerns of a head of the household, without all the school stuff and without worries about being drafted, to write down uninterruptedly all the things that make my head practically burst, to hear only music and be only music. Oh well, the kind of things one dreams about and which Herr Hindenburg has no intention of being a part of. But you must not think that I always hang my head low like this, and that I have a black outlook on everything. No, first of all I still believe that the war is going to end this year, I still believe that [quotation from *Hänsel and Gretel*] "when the need is the greatest, God will hold out his hand."

31. Advertisment for a concert in Ostercöthen on 2 February 1918 in which Weill accompanied soprano Emilie Feuge, assisted by some of her voice students; he also played solo pieces by Mozart, Raff, and Weber. Due to a paper shortage, the announcement also served as the program.

Weill (in Dessau) to Hanns Weill, [January 1918]: I am really scared that this *Abitur* [graduation exam] is going to happen right in the middle of my concerts. You know that I am participating in two of Mrs. Feuge's farewell concerts in Cöthen, in which I also will play some solos, and—if Mikorey doesn't louse it up—two ladies are supposed to sing the *Maikaterlied* here in Dessau. I have to put a lot of work into the latter because I have to coach the canon myself. But this is much more fun than the *Abitur*. . . . The Brahms sonata is making progress. I am almost on top of the first movement, which is the most difficult one.

Weill (in Dessau) to Hanns Weill, [19 March 1918]: I'm finally getting around to giving you a more detailed report about my stay in Berlin. . . . Well, Monday morning I ran around for hours trying to get a ticket for *Salome* on Tuesday, but no luck. So I went to the box office again on Tuesday morning and actually did get a seat on the fourth tier, first row. You can imagine my happiness! And so this became the greatest treat I've ever experienced. *Salome* is the greatest musical work of genius you can possibly imagine. Practically without leitmotifs, but rather in true Straussian manner concerned only with sound effects, and this in such a masterly fashion that I didn't miss even the most subtle moments of the action, although I didn't have the vaguest idea about it beforehand and the text could not always be understood. And thus the accumulated impressions grew into a veritable intoxication, and at the end I couldn't do anything but yell "Strauss"—and again and again "Strauss," until he finally—with a very modest gesture—turned the evening's success over to [Barbara] Kemp, who did indeed present a Salome that couldn't possibly be surpassed. You can well imagine that the giant orchestra (twenty first violins!) under Strauss himself played magnificently.

1918 – 1924

I need poetry to set my imagination in motion, and my imagination is not a bird, but an airplane.

1918

April
Moves to a pension on the Winterfeldplatz in western Berlin. Attends classes at the Hochschule für Musik, Berlin, and studies philosophy at the Friedrich-Wilhelms-Universität, where his teachers include Ernst Cassirer and Max Dessoir. With the consent of Albert Bing and his parents, Weill decides at the end of three months to concentrate on musical studies instead of medicine.

May
Begins studies with Friedrich Koch and Engelbert Humperdinck. Weill describes himself as ahead of his fellow students in the areas of piano, score-reading, organ, conducting, and theory but behind in improvisation and counterpoint. Accepts the position of choir director of the Religionsgemeinde Friedenau, begins accompanying at Stern's Conservatory, and immerses himself in Berlin's cultural life.

June
Piano studies include Bach suites and score-reading of Beethoven symphonies.

July
Spends term break in Dessau.

August
Prepares the synagogue chorus in Friedenau for Yom Kippur services.

September
Begins full-time studies at the Hochschule für Musik, Berlin. His teachers include Paul Juon and Humperdinck (composition), Koch (counterpoint), and Rudolf Krasselt (conducting). Weill's reading includes *Auch Einer* by Friedrich Theodor Vischer and *Novellen um Claudia* by Arnold Zweig. Also begins informal violin lessons.

String Quartet in B minor (1917–18).

October
Visits family in Dessau. In Berlin, hears Richard Strauss conduct *Ein Heldenleben* and attends a performance of *Der Rosenkavalier*.

November
Signing of the armistice ends the First World War. Abdication of the Kaiser in Germany. The Republic is proclaimed by Philip Scheidemann. A national assembly convenes in Weimar in February 1919 and ratifies a new constitution for the "Weimar Republic."

December
Spends Christmas vacation with his family in Dessau. The Novembergruppe is established in Berlin.

1919

January
Continues studies at the Hochschule für Musik, where he remains until July.

March
Orchestra Suite in E major (1918–March 1919).

April 12
Bauhaus opens in Weimar.

March–July
Die Weise von Liebe und Tod des Cornets Christoph Rilke, symphonic poem on a text by Rilke, Berlin. Manuscript lost.

July
Schilflieder (Nikolaus Lenau). (May have been composed earlier.) Lost.

Despite winning a Felix Mendelssohn-Bartholdy scholarship for composition, Weill agrees with his parents that he should leave the Hochschule and gain more practical experience as a vocal coach and conductor, with the intention of continuing composition lessons with Hermann Wetzler in Cologne or Pfitzner in Munich.

August
Visits the Convalescence Home Ebert, Benneckenstein im Harz with his father. Returns to Dessau to accept with reluctance a post as repetiteur at the Dessau Hofoper under Hans Knappertsbusch.

Die stille Stadt (Richard Dehmel).

September
Accompanies Elisabeth Feuge, who sings his songs and works by others in highly successful recitals in Dessau, Cöthen, and Zerbst.

December
Upon a recommendation from Humperdinck, begins a six-month tenure as second kapellmeister at the newly formed municipal theater in Lüdenscheid.

1920

January
Takes over the duties of the chief conductor at Lüdenscheid, where he is responsible for a mixed repertoire of operettas and popular opera.

April
Conducts *Die Fledermaus*, *Cavalleria Rusticana*, *Zigeunerbaron*, and the premiere of an operetta, all within two days in Lüdenscheid.

May 15
Travels to Leipzig, where his father has accepted the directorship of the B'nai B'rith children's home. His parents live in the suburb of Kleinsteinberg.

June 22
Accompanies Elisabeth Feuge in a recital sponsored by the Berend-Lehmann-Verein, Halberstadt, where his brother Hanns is responsible for musical activities.

Summer
Negotiates for, but does not accept, a position at the summer theater in Norderney working under Arthur Kistenmacher, director of the Lüdenscheid theater.

Sonate für Violoncello und Klavier (ca. spring 1919–summer 1920). Possible premiere in Hannover; Martin Missner, cello, Albert Bing, piano, February 1921.

Ninon von Lenclos (1919–summer 1920, one-act opera after the play by Ernst Hardt). Manuscript lost, probably unfinished.

Visits parents in Leipzig.

August–September
Sulamith. "Chorfantasie" for soprano, chorus, and orchestra. Incomplete draft survives.

September
Moves back to Berlin, first to Beerenstraße 48 in Zehlendorf, then to Flensburger Straße 11 in Lichterfelde.

Weberlied I and *Weberlied II* (Gerhart Hauptmann).

December
Accepted to study in Ferruccio Busoni's master class at the Prussian Academy of Arts in Berlin after Oskar Bie's recommendation in November.

1921

April–June
Sinfonie in einem Satz (no. 1). A four-hand piano version is performed in Busoni's master class.

Langsamer Fox and *Algi-Song*, the first for piano solo, the second a parodic cabaret number. Possibly performed by Weill himself in the *Bierkeller* where he played piano.

Works as the choral conductor at a synagogue on Münchener Straße.

June	Considers writing a dissertation (*Doktorarbeit*) on synagogue music, supervised by Max Friedlaender, and taking his exams in the fall.
July	Officially begins composition studies with Ferruccio Busoni (some evidence points to an earlier date). Other students in the class are Luc Balmer, Erwin Bodky, Svetislav Stancic, and Vladimir Vogel. He later supplements composition studies with counterpoint lessons from Philipp Jarnach, who teaches him for several years without a fee. Jarnach also arranges many of Weill's early performances.
October	*Die Bekehrte* (Goethe), an assignment for Busoni's master class. Busoni makes his own setting as well.
November	*Rilkelieder*, for piano and voice (Rainer Maria Rilke). Partly missing. Begins composing *Divertimento*, op. 5.

1 9 2 2

	Psalm VIII. Composition date uncertain. Incomplete.
Spring	Joins music division of the Novembergruppe. *Divertimento für Flöte und Orchester*, op. 52, by Ferruccio Busoni, arrangement for flute and piano. (November 1921–22.)
Winter	Begins composing String Quartet, op. 8.
November 18	*Zaubernacht* (Summer 1922, ballet-pantomime with scenario by Vladimir Boritsch). Theater am Kurfürstendamm, Berlin; George Weller, conductor; Franz-Ludwig Hörth, director.
December 7	*Divertimento für kleines Orchester mit Männerchor* (last movement only). Sing-Akademie; Berlin Philharmonic Orchestra; Heinz Unger, conductor. Entire work: 10 April 1923, Berlin Philharmonic Hall; Berlin Philharmonic Orchestra; Heinz Unger, conductor. The full score is lost.

1 9 2 3

From 1923 until 1926	Weill supplements his income by giving private theory and composition lessons. His initial students include Claudio Arrau, Nikolaos Skalkottas, and Maurice Abravanel.
March 12	*Fantasia, Passacaglia und Hymnus für Orchester*, op. 6 (February–May 1922). Berlin Philharmonic Orchestra; Alexander Selo, conductor. The full score is lost.
June 14	*Quodlibet*, op. 9 ("Orchestersuite aus der Pantomime *Zaubernacht*"). Friedrich-Theater, Dessau; Albert Bing, conductor.

June 24	*String Quartet no. 1*, op. 8 (1922–23). Frankfurt Kammermusikwoche; Hindemith-Amar Quartet. The quartet becomes part of the repertory of the Roth Quartet, which performs it twice in Paris in 1924 and tours it throughout Spain.
September	*Recordare*, op. 11 (Text: Lamentations V), Berlin. In 1925 Weill asks Universal Edition to suggest a performance of *Recordare* at the Donaueschingen music festival, but it is not performed there. Begins composing *Stundenbuch* (Rilke), op. 13.
December	Completes his third and last year in the master class; Busoni recommends Weill to Universal Edition (Vienna), with particular praise for his String Quartet, op. 8.

1 9 2 4

January	Meets Expressionist playwright Georg Kaiser.
January 24	*Frauentanz, sieben Gedichte des Mittelalters*, op. 10 (June–July 1923). Saal der Singakademie, Berlin; Nora Pisling-Boas, soprano; Fritz Stiedry, conductor.
February	Begins work on *Pantomime*, scenario by Georg Kaiser. Unfinished. Partly lost.
February–March	Visits Nelly Frank, Villa Bergfried, Davos, Switzerland. Makes extensive tour of Italy and meets with Universal Edition in Vienna.
April 22	Signs first publishing contract with Universal Edition, Vienna.
May	Moves to a new apartment in Berlin at Winterfeldstraße 21.
Summer	Meets Lotte Lenja at Georg Kaiser's home in Grünheide, a suburb east of Berlin. (She changes the spelling of her name to Lenya in 1937.)
July 27	Death of Busoni.
August	Kaiser and Weill stop work on a ballet pantomime they have begun and start on a one-act opera based on an earlier play of Kaiser's, *Der Protagonist*.
November	Takes a job as the chief Berlin music correspondent for the weekly journal *Der deutsche Rundfunk*. The first issue containing his writing appears on 30 November.

---

1 9 1 8

MUSIC + THEATER:	LITERATURE + FILM:	SCIENCE + SOCIETY:	POLITICS:
Igor Stravinsky *Histoire du Soldat* Franz Schreker *Die Gezeichneten* New York Philharmonic Society bans compositions by living German composers	Heinrich Mann *Der Untertan* ("The Loyal Subject") Aldous Huxley *The Defeat of Youth* *Die Augen der Mumie Ma* (German film by Lubitsch)	Max Planck, Nobel Prize in Physics Harlow Shapley discovers true dimensions of the Milky Way World-wide influenza epidemic strikes; by 1920 nearly 22 million are dead	Wilson proclaims Fourteen Points for world peace Wilhelm II abdicates, Philipp Scheidemann proclaims German Republic Armistice signed between Allies and Germany

33. The Hochschule für Musik in Berlin, where Weill studied music for sixteen months, April 1918–July 1919.

34. Engelbert Humperdinck in front of his house in Berlin, 1919.

Weill (in Berlin) to Hanns Weill, 2 May 1918: I am sitting here in the beautiful reading room of the Hochschule to thank you for your various news reports. . . . I am so accustomed to this place that now this Jewish characteristic of mine, this mania for criticizing, is already beginning to arise in me. So today, after the second lesson, I found my piano studies with old Heymann to be of really poor quality. . . . I have met some rather nice fellow students who are ahead of me in improvisation, counterpoint, etc., but in other things like piano, score reading, organ, conducting, and theory they can't touch me. For the most part they come here from teachers like Paul Ertl and Leopold Schmidt.

Weill (in Berlin) to Hanns Weill, 9 May 1918: I've already had two lessons with old Humperdinck. For the first one he had me come to his home, so on a brilliant May morning I went to the idyllic Wannsee where he owns a magnificent villa situated on large grounds. The maid already knew my name and led me through the vestibule where a bright-colored, oaken grand piano caught my eye, and on to the music room. The master, who was still quite ill but had gotten out of bed only on my account, had a hard time breathing. The manuscript score of

35. A weekly class schedule from May 1918, when Weill was studying at the Hochschule für Musik and attending lectures at the Friedrich-Wilhelms-Universität (which became Humboldt-Universität in 1945).

Monday	12:00-2:00	Organ practice
	6:00-8:00	German Literature Röthe
Tuesday	5:30-6:30	Organ practice
Wednesday	9:00	Music History
	10:00	Meeting Range
	6:00-8:00	Dr. Reich-Antikes Drama
Thursday	11:45	Piano lesson
	1:00	(History) Hochschule
	4:45	Partitur
Friday	4:00-5:00	Cassirer Greek Philosophy
	6:00	Organ practice
Saturday	1:00	History of Literature
	4:00-6:00	Dessoir

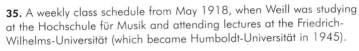

his new opera [*Gaudeamus*] was lying on the piano. He asked me about this and that, gave me some homework, and then dismissed me. But yesterday he came to the Hochschule, gave me new homework, and told me that at the next lesson I should show him the sketch of my string quartet. I immediately dug it up and now I'm working on it. . . . Although the esteemed professors speak rather disparagingly of him, I hope that—if I work hard—I will learn at least as much from him as from Professor Koch, whose opera [*Die Hügelmühle*] is causing the Deutsche Opernhaus quite a few problems. In any case, altogether it actually does mean something to have studied with Humperdinck.

I've already heard two magnificent lectures at the university. In [Max] Dessoir's "Philosophy and Art" every single word is a revelation for me, and I follow [Ernst] Cassirer's discussions about the philosophy of the Greeks with great pleasure and interest. We are not yet reading [Gustav] Roethe (History of Literature from 1830 on) or Reich (Antique Drama). It's a wonderful thing to be able to follow the completely unique range of ideas of these illustrious intellects. It opens one up to entirely new worlds of thought, to new concepts and new stimulations. And yet, this student life is a curious thing. It's never completely satisfying because you never know exactly what you are striving for, and you don't work regularly enough. Thank God, it's not quite the same with the study of music, although with music too, one has to depend almost entirely on oneself, and so far I haven't found real inner satisfaction there either. But after studying for only two weeks that's hardly possible.

Weill (in Berlin) to Hanns Weill, early June 1918: I'm using a free hour at the Hochschule to answer your letter, which I enjoyed tremendously. If you drag my title "stud. mus. et phil." through the mud once more with your snooty remarks, you can expect a "call to arms" from me, you apprentice you! You mustn't be overly impressed by my "first performance in the Imperial Capital." It's a students' concert consisting of fourteen different pieces with three accompanists, and the only extraordinary thing is the fact that: 1) it's the semester's final concert of the Stern Conservatory, 2) because I'm the youngest, and because it's the first time that someone who is not from Stern's—and a student at the Hochschule at that—appears as accompanist there, and 3) the fact that they already have three other accompanists is an honor for me, because I can assume that [Nikolas] Rothmühl did not ask me because of some emergency, or because of an absolute need, but rather because I'm good at it.

Only an ignorant layman like you could ask whether the string quartet is already finished. I was glad when I could show Humperdinck the finished score of the first movement yesterday, after I had sweated like a madman for the last few days. It's a somewhat sustained but very passionate movement with the following themes: [see illustration]. The second movement, on which I'm working now, is fast, and I want to title it "Nachtstück," *pp*, very fast with a lot of pizzicato and chromatic envelopment of the main melody and the following themes: [see illustration]. On Humperdinck's advice, I'm going to choose an Intermezzo for the third movement and for the finale the usual presto.

37. A page from Weill's letter to his brother Hanns, early June 1918.

36. The 1917–18 Hochschule für Musik yearbook shows the faculty in the Department of Composition and Theory and lists Weill as a composition student under Humperdinck.

Königliche
akademische Hochschule
für Musik in Berlin
zu Charlottenburg

Jahresbericht

für den Zeitraum vom 1. Oktober 1917
bis zum 30. September 1918.

A. Direktorium.

Herr Geheimer Regierungsrat, Professor Dr. Hermann Kretzschmar, kom. Direktor und Vorsteher der Abteilung für Orchesterinstrumente.
- Professor Heinrich Barth, Vorsteher der Abteilung für Klavier und Orgel.
- Professor Dr. Engelbert Humperdinck, Vorsteher der Abteilung für Komposition und Theorie. Vertreter: Prof. Friedrich E. Koch, siehe unter B 1.
- Professor Felix Schmidt, Vorsteher der Abteilung für Gesang.

B. Lehrer.

1. Abteilung für Komposition und Theorie.
Herr Prof. Dr. Engelbert Humperdinck, Komposition.
- Prof. Leopold C. Wolf, Theorie, Komposition und Partiturspiel.
- Prof. Paul Juon, Theorie und Komposition (seit 3. 6. 1915 im Heeresdienst).
- Leo Schrattenholz, Theorie und Komposition.
- Prof. Robert Kahn, Theorie, Komposition und Zusammenspiel.
- Prof. Friedrich E. Koch, Theorie und Komposition; zugleich mit der vertretungsweisen Wahrnehmung der Geschäfte des Vorstehers der Kompositions- und Theorie-Abteilung beauftragt.
Fräulein Elisabeth Kuyper, Theorie und Komposition.
Herr Rudolf Tobias, Theorie.
- Prof. Dr. Karl Krebs, Zweiter Ständiger Sekretär der Kgl. Akademie der Künste, Geschichte der Musik und des musikalischen Stils.
- Prof. Dr. Max Seiffert, Ältere Musik

Herr Prof. Theodor Grawert, 1. Armee-Musikinspizient, Militärmusik.
- Oskar Hackenberger, 2. Armee-Musikinspizient, Militärmusik.

2. Abteilung für Gesang.
Herr Prof. Felix Schmidt.
- Prof. Max Stange.
Fräulein Helene Jordan,
- Meta Lippold,
Herr Prof. Johannes Messchaert, } Gesang.
- Paul Knüpfer, Königl. Kammersänger,
Fräulein Ida Hiedler, Königl. Kammersängerin,
Herr Rudolf Krasselt, Leitung der dramatischen Übungen und Aufführungen (siehe 1. Abteilung).
Frau Marie Gagliardi, Italienische Sprache.
Herr Prof. Dr. med. Jacob Katzenstein, Anatomie, Physiologie der Stimme und Hygiene des Gesanges.
- Großherzoglich Mecklenburgischer Oberregisseur Heinz Sattler, Deklamation, dramatischer Unterricht, Mimik und Bewegungslehre.
- Prof. Hugo Rüdel, Königl. Hof- und Domchor-Direktor. Leitung d. Gesangchöre.
- Romuald Wikarski, Korrepetitor (seit 28. 11. 14 im Heeresdienst).
Fräulein Charlotte Pfeffer, Rhythmische Gymnastik, Gehörsbildung u. Improvisation.

210	Herr Wagner	Max	Berlin
211	*Frl. Warschauer	Margot	Berlin
212	Frl. Weigel	Ilse	Werdau (Chemnitz)
213	Herr Weill	Kurt	Dessau
214	Herr Weissgerber	Joseph	Volo (Griechenland)
215	*Frl. Wenig	Dora	Hohen-Schönhausen
216	Fr. Weymann geb. Werner	Klara	Schafau
217	Frl. Wilcke	Anneliese	Charlottenburg
218	Herr Wilensky	Richard	Bielefeld
219	*Herr v. Wilpert	Otto	Ruhenthal (Kurland)
220	Frl. Wodtke	Charlotte	Berlin
221	*Frl. Wolffenstein	Andrea	Charlottenburg
222	Frl. Zbylicki	Elisabeth	Danzig
223	Frl. Zimmermann	Margarete	Berlin.

38. The earlier of two extant fair copies of the String Quartet in B Minor, 1918. The first performance has yet to be documented; however, Martin Missner, the cellist in a quartet based in Hagen, wrote to Weill on 2 June 1920 that he was copying the parts again so that the quartet could begin rehearsing after the summer break.

39. Envelope addressed to "Hanns Weill, Kaufmannslehrling" from "Kurt Weill, Kapellmeisterlehrling," 30 August 1918.

40. The November Revolution, 9 November 1918: A truckload of revolutionary soldiers at the Brandenburg Gate; soldiers and workers at the barracks of the Second Uhlan Guard Regiment on Invalidenstraße.

Weill (in Dessau) to Hanns Weill, 9 August 1918: It's as difficult for me to get anything done here as it was easy for me to work in Berlin. You see how dependent I am on inspiration from my teacher, from my fellow students, and from the opera and concerts in Berlin. Will I ever be able to create true art if I don't continue to be exposed to these influences? Sure, we all know that I'll never become another Schubert or Beethoven, and the others, I believe, have also suffered from the same "disease."

Weill (in Berlin) to Hanns Weill, 8 November 1918: Although it can hardly be taken for granted that this letter will actually get to you, I don't want to leave it unwritten. Well, through the unbelievable stupidity of these "*melechs*" [royalists] we've finally come to a point when every single minute we must deal with the outbreak of an uprising. I don't know whether you're still getting newspapers and whether you're informed about everything. Berlin is completely cut off from the outside, and since I don't have any news from home, I'd appreciate it if you could try and telephone me Sunday afternoon or Monday morning. After the tumultuous jubilation over the imminent armistice, on the very same evening an enormous tension and nervousness arose—caused by the events in the Northern cities and by the precautionary measures of the police—which now is widening by the minute, especially after the ultimatum to the Kaiser. So far order has been kept by brute force, so that one has to be afraid that—should it keep on growing—it will develop into one of the most gigantic evolutions in history. But the main thing is: the end of the world war. . . . The Suite [in E major] is slowly progressing and is conceived as more of a study than an opus.

Weill (in Berlin) to Hanns Weill, 12 November 1918: I've had indescribable experiences during the last few days, indescribable mostly because they're still too fresh in my mind. Saturday's great revolution broke forth with such an elemental force and fantastic speed that out there in the country you probably won't be able to understand it all. Even the night before I was walking around and seeing how brilliantly everything had been prepared. Admittedly, only precautionary measures against a revolution were noticeable. Saturday I stayed close to the Reichstag all day, saw the surprise attack on the military barracks, the formation of the A. and S. [Arbeiter und Soldaten: workers' and soldiers'] councils, the speeches by [Karl] Liebknecht, [Johannes] Hoffmann, [Georg] Ledebour and others, and finally in the evening the heavy fighting at the Marstall. I was also present at the pitched battle at the Reichstag. Aided by subterranean bunkers, the officers are defending themselves with such gallantry that so far they're undefeated and will be shooting proficiently during the night. The university is closed and I'd like to make myself available to the A. and S. councils. But the Hochschule is still open. I could fill volumes. But I'm too tired.

Weill (in Berlin) to Hanns Weill, 15 November 1918: Sometimes I still can't believe that all arms have been put to rest, that everything has turned out quite differently, that I no longer have to fear this ominous thing called the "draft" lurking in the future, and there is no longer the possibility that I will have to become a *royal Generalmusikdirektor*. The revolution, here too, is now steered toward calmer waters and several excellent, completely trustworthy men have taken the reins. All would be fine if only one did not have to be afraid of one thing: that instead of having a dictatorship of the aristocracy, we might now get a dictatorship of the proletariat. Admittedly, only the Spartacists have set their goals in that direction; but here in Berlin, the parties in the middle have allowed themselves to become so totally bereft of any kind of influence that it will be very difficult to repair the damage. If they don't insist energetically on a convocation of the national assembly (which will not turn out in favor of the independents) and on the middle's participation in government, we can expect Russian conditions and *pogroms*, which, as an effective means of attracting the masses, will be recommended warmly in pamphlets carrying the endorsement of both the independents and the ultra-conservatives. And Mr. [Hugo] Haase is not going to change that, despite his two orthodox sons in Königsberg. Under pressure, the Jews will be used as an effective means of distraction by each party. Of course, we can be working against all of this, especially by voting for the middle or, at the most, for a socialist majority. The kind of politics exercised by the German citizens of Jewish faith, who merely want to stand by in a state of indifference, is impossible. By the way, a Jewish bulwark has been founded here (secretly!) by Zionists recruited from former soldiers. For all that, the mob is only waiting for a cue to pillage and mutiny, aiming preferably at the Jews. But enough of it! . . .

I've had one tremendous concert impression: [Emil von] Sauer. He overshadows all the piano virtuosi I've heard so far; he reminds one tremendously of Liszt and plays simply ideally. Tomorrow [Maximilian] Harden, Monday *Missa solemnis* under [Siegfried] Ochs, Tuesday [Bronislav] Hubermann-Strauß, Wednesday the *Deutsches Requiem* by Brahms in the Opernhaus Unter den Linden [Staatsoper] under Mr. [Hugo] Rüdel. I saw Shylock played by [Paul] Wegener; an outstanding acting job, but enormously spiteful, purposely distorted and unnatural. The performance itself was of course masterful.

Weill (in Berlin) to Hanns Weill, 3 December 1918: Humperdinck was really enthusiastic again about the second movement of the Suite [in E major] and actually embraced me. . . . I've also been voted into the student council of the Hochschule. I accepted only in order to fight against *Risches* [anti-Semitism].

Weill (in Berlin) to Hanns Weill, 7 December 1918: In general I notice that a "modern" clique has sprung up around me at the Hochschule, strangely so, because the teachers themselves are definitely not modern: Humperdinck—well, maybe in his bold carelessness toward contrapuntal voice-leading. Koch is a stiff contrapuntalist and as a composer an ultramodern, much-ado-about-nothing type; and Kahn—he's a truly naive Mendelssohnian, for whom every augmented triad is like a box on the ear. But in the midst of this, a small circle of students has formed a group in which you have to feel ashamed if you don't know all the music of Richard Strauss and Reger, and also Korngold, Debussy, Schreker, Bittner, Marx, etc. That is, of course, very exciting.

41. Cover label and the opening measures from Weill's first extant orchestral work, the Suite in E Major.

1 9 1 9

MUSIC + THEATER:	LITERATURE + FILM:	SCIENCE + SOCIETY:	POLITICS:
Richard Strauss *Die Frau ohne Schatten*	Hermann Hesse *Demian*	J. M. Keynes *The Economic Consequences of the Peace*	Spartacist revolt in Berlin
Henry Cowell completes his book *New Musical Resources*	André Gide *La Symphonie pastorale*	Ernst Cassirer *Erkenntnisproblem in der Philosophie und Wissenschaft der neueren Zeit*	Habsburg dynasty exiled from Austria
Max Reinhardt opens the Großes Schauspielhaus, Berlin	H.L. Mencken *The American Language*	Austria abolishes death penalty	German peace treaty signed at Versailles

Weill (in Berlin) to Hanns Weill, 18 February 1919: Today I heard that one of the candidates for the job of Director of the Hochschule is supposed to be one of the most modern of all the moderns: [Ferruccio] *Busoni.* Of course, the old Teutonic, behind-the-times, idiotic flock of asses, the Hochschule teachers and students, are fighting this tooth and nail. But this man would be a healthy choice for this old place, although I don't know whether he's a suitable teacher for composition. Anyway, I think it quite out of the question that he'll be accepted. They're already spreading the rumor that he is a Jew, and when a student says that about you, then God help you.

Weill (in Berlin) to Hanns Weill, 21 February 1919: For the time being, I'm leaning more toward a finely constructed comic opera; for all that, I now seem to be drifting into modern currents again because of my close association with my fellow student [Walter] Kämpfer, with whom I study only the most modern music (Schreker, Reger, Schoenberg, etc.). However, regarding my own music, I see that I am not at all well balanced yet. With the Suite I've definitely gone a step backwards. I really began to realize this when I noticed at the first rehearsal of my string quartet how modern, how "Regerish" it is. This retrogression can only be explained by the fact that I'm still clinging convulsively to this form even though I've practically mastered it. But I'm not yet the thoroughly modern person that Mahler exemplified so well. I still carry the smell of the provinces; I'm not sufficiently saturated with the cultures of the present. For that very reason I'm planning a larger modern orchestral work, which I'll model closely on a modern literary subject, now that I've completed my conception of the Suite (which should really be called a "symphony" instead). I still hold dear my original idea of a prelude to Grillparzer's *Des Meeres und der Liebe Wellen*—which one could easily shape into a modern form—however this isn't what Kämpfer wants from me: the most modern formulation of the most modern poetry, such as *Die Weise von Liebe und Tod* [Rilke] as simple symphonic poetry with Strauss's *Don Juan* as the august model. . . . I'm extremely happy with my new teacher [Paul Juon]. Since I'm also his only student in composition, he works with me most intensively (one-and-a-half hours), is a thoroughly modern musician, and I can accumulate more positive knowledge than would ever have been possible with Humperdinck, especially as to orchestral tone, color of orchestration, etc. (all of which up to now I didn't have the slightest notion of). . . . Of course, the string quartet is idiotically difficult, but the students are showing quite a bit of interest. [Willy] Heß's judgment: "Devilishly modern, devilishly difficult, and devilishly beautiful." I go to concerts almost every night; in Nikisch's last one, I not only got to know *Tod und Verklärung* thoroughly, but also learned to love it for all of eternity.

Weill (in Berlin) to Hanns Weill, 27 March 1919: The conception of the symphonic poem [*Die Weise von Liebe und Tod*] is progressing only slowly. I want to divide the piece into three parts within one movement. The first part will describe the Knight's gloomy mood, which is only interrupted here and there by a ray of light: the boy's courageous thirst for adventure; the second part will be lyric in character and describe the night of love and later on, in the transition, the sudden awakening of the castle, the racing-around, the fire; and the third part will be the battle and death. Of course I don't want to proceed just programmatically. Although my music should be stimulated by the varying moods of the poetry, it should nevertheless be intelligible, even without any sort of program. The whole thing is a difficult, but rewarding task. It's too bad that I have so many other things to do. Krasselt is placing higher and higher demands on the budding correpetiteur. He wants to outfit me now with all of the things Bing wanted to keep in store for me in Dessau. Now he also insists that I must get further ahead with my piano technique, and I have to resign myself to practicing piano diligently this summer to bring my technique up to par. Since I'm busy almost every evening, the days slip by long before I've finished my work. And when I think that this coming winter my composing will probably have to stop altogether . . .

On Tuesday there was a big event: *Elektra* under Strauss with [Marie] Gutheil-Schoder from Vienna. It definitely is the climax of Strauss's stage works, not just a music drama, not even merely music, but music—not to say clamor—only as a means to an end, as a heightening of the dramatic effect, but—as seen from this point of view—the masterful work of a genius.

Weill (in Berlin) to Hanns Weill, 29 April 1919: Now I've landed again in Berlin's bustle but can't get to work until I'm in the clear about my living quarters. After a long search I found yesterday an old lady who lives near aunt Eva who wants to let me have a room for—would you believe it—30 Marks; it's rather primitive and simple and dangerously close to the train tracks, but I can get used to that. A piano was supposed to cost 40 Marks, but I just received an offer through Uncle Markus for one for 20 Marks; I'll look at it tomorrow.

I have already talked to Krasselt. He has nothing against a volunteer job if they give me enough to do. But—after I told him my age for the first time—he said I could also stay on for one more winter in Berlin; we're definitely going to get a semester in conducting and I also could concertize. If Bing doesn't find anything for me, that would be something to think about. Of course, I'd love to be on my way, the sooner the better.

Weill (in Berlin) to Hanns Weill, 9 May 1919: After two almost sleepless nights, I now hardly hear the trains anymore and hope soon to be so toughened up that I can sleep with the window open. The piano is very good and the room so isolated that I can work undisturbed. However, I still will have to go often to the university. I'm going to hear [Ernst] Cassirer's "Philosophy from the Time of the Renaissance up to Kant," [Alois] Riehl's "Logic," [Max] Herrmann's "History of Theater in Germany," [Max] Friedländer's "The German Lied," and then some other public lectures. I really enjoy the philosophical ones. And *Zarathustra* is coming up too! That's going to be extra special. There's nothing to report about concerts. I don't dare go to hear Weingartner because I'm afraid that it would blur the deep impression that Nikisch's Beethoven interpretation left with me. I saw a magnificent performance of the *Faschingsfee*, a quite significant operetta—even musically—by the *Czárdásfürstin* manufacturer [Emmerich Kálmán]. I believe that this man does not write only for money, but spontaneously and from an inner impulse, because he produces such sweeping, if slightly worn out, music—so much so that I became doubtful whether I could do this kind of thing, too. There's much more to it than merely writing an acceptable waltz.

Last night I experienced the ultimate bliss: *Figaro* under Strauss. Although I had really studied this work quite thoroughly, I hardly recognized it. For the first time in my life I really understood what Mozart is all about, the meaning of Mozart. It was a great joy to discover that I'm now mature enough to understand this.

42. Leipzig, ca. 1918. Photo: E. Hoenisch.

Weill (in Berlin) to Hanns Weill, 15 May 1919: You needn't be concerned about Dessau; I'm not about to write to those girls, since I might give the game away. And they don't understand us anyway, they haven't got the brains for it. However, I must confess, that to me these types of girls are quite preferable as far as females in general are concerned. The other kind, with whom I can converse more or less intelligently, I consider to be more like comrades, like-minded people. What I require of a woman, what every one of us, we artists perhaps the most, needs from a woman—not only in the sensual but also in psychological and spiritual aspects, that which Goethe with his "eternal feminine" [das ewig Weibliche] raised up to its highest potential—this very thing one rarely finds in intelligent girls. The Dessauers have got a monopoly on the other kind. And where will we find the one who offers a happy medium between the two?

Weill (in Berlin) to Ruth Weill, [ca. 20 June] 1919: There are several young girls living in my neighborhood who sing all kinds of folk songs in harmony every evening—right now they are starting again. I love this kind of fresh, unspoiled girlish voice. . . . By chance, is there among your acquaintances someone marriageable for me (conditions: very pretty, very stupid, unmusical, 1 million Marks dowry)?

Weill (in Berlin) to Hanns Weill, 27 June 1919: It keeps going around and around in my head: Should I stay here? And always the answer: To Vienna! And then every time the same disappointment when I realize that such a plan right now would be impossible for me. The constant increase in the cost of living there, which is actually causing people to starve, defies all description. Will this get better within two months' time? If I had a job and were not a burden on father's purse, I could console myself and wait until next fall, especially since by then I'd be much better prepared for the tremendous impressions of Vienna and studies with Schoenberg. . . . Thanks to Providence, I'm looking for new things and understand what it means to be "new." Strauss is fading away. Think of everything in Strauss that is false, trivial, whitewashed, and far-fetched and replace it with the ultimate in modernism—in Mahler's sense—with deepest penetration into a great personality: then you have Arnold Schoenberg, as I'm getting to know him now from his *Gurrelieder*. . . . I must get to Vienna—sooner or later. Schoenberg brings something so new to me that I'm entirely speechless.

To think about working productively is, of course, impossible. Not even a little Lied is taking shape. Today I had a very beautiful idea for the beginning of a cello sonata and I wrote it down right away. But right now I feel already like tearing it up. I had come to the definite conclusion of giving up this scribbling altogether and throwing myself totally into the conducting business. Well, we Jews are simply not creative, and when we are, we are destructive rather than constructive. And if the young movement in music views the Mahler-Schoenberg guidelines as being constructive and heralding the future (as I, alas, do too!) then it must consist of Jews or Gentiles with Jewish accents. No Jew could ever write a work like the Moonlight Sonata. Following this train of thought is enough to force the pen out of one's hand. I want to accomplish this much—and only through Schoenberg could I do it—that I write only when I have to, when it comes most honestly from the depths of my heart. Otherwise it will merely turn out to be music of the intellect, and I hate that. The *Weise* comes to me from the heart. I really live in this music, but even this is an embarrassment; I do need poetry to set my imagination in motion, and my imagination is

not a bird, but an airplane. The only small consolation is the fact that the young composers around me are no better, often even worse. However, they do not aspire to such heights as I do. They set their goals lower and reach them sooner.

Weill (in Berlin) to Hanns Weill, 14 July 1919: By the way, did I write you that I received an extremely nice postcard from Schoenberg, from Vienna, in which he advises me in the most genteel manner about his willingness to be obliging in every respect. The message is composed in such modern style that we here, and also our parents, are enthusiastic about it.

Weill (in Dessau) to Hanns Weill, 5 September 1919: I owe you a report on the last few days. I had noticed already in the first rehearsal that my most exaggerated ideas about Elisabeth's abilities had been justified; she has a thrilling, brilliant voice, knows how to use it, is as musical as no other, and adds her own touch to every work. Only a musician could notice that her voice is still not quite even in the highest register, which is understandable considering her youth and the short time she has been studying. Of course she was very nervous at the Cöthen concert and therefore had a tendency to rush, but nobody noticed that. The applause was as strong as it could be from a Cöthen audience; of course, she was somewhat disappointed because she had expected storms of applause like she was used to at concerts in Munich. But to make up for that, we concocted a concert for Dessau like they've never seen before. The program, which I'll be sending you along with the reviews, was put together very effectively and consisted of—aside from three arias—only modern songs. The auditorium of the Hoftheater was overcrowded with the cream of society, especially with the nobility, since the entire Court had gathered together. The whole thing breathed an aura of festive expectation and it inspired us to make better music than in the best rehearsal. She sang my songs

43. Elisabeth Feuge

fantastically well, but because of their modernity they were misunderstood by most of the audience. If the applause for me was extraordinarily strong it was due to my accompaniment—executed quite perfectly—and to the opulent shower of flowers, with which both of us were overwhelmed (to mother's greatest and my lesser joy). Elisabeth then was asked to Prince Aribert's [regent of the duchy of Anhalt, who had formally abdicated when the Weimar Republic was declared] and she and I have been invited to make music at the hereditary Princess's next week. After the 9th of November that's quite something for Dessau! Also, since the entire theater was present at the concert, I've introduced myself well into my new position. The first baritone has already approached me and asked me to coach him every day for one hour with pay! Of course there was no lack of envy either.

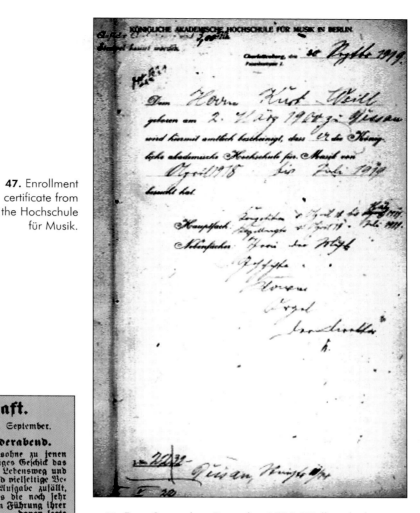

47. Enrollment certificate from the Hochschule für Musik.

> Aus dem Wettbewerb um die **Felix Mendelssohn-Bartholdy-Stiftung** für 1919 ist folgendes zu erwähnen:
> Die Hälfte des Staatsstipendiums für ausübende Tonkünstler in Höhe von 750 M erhielt der Pianist **Richard Wilenski**, Schüler der akademischen Hochschule für Musik in Berlin, und die Hälfte des Staatsstipendiums für Komponisten der Komponist **Max Tauber** von derselben Anstalt.
> Außerdem erhielten Unterstützungen: der Waldhornist **Hermann Blume** und der Komponist **Kurt Weill** von derselben Hochschule je 300 M.

44. This announcement of Weill's award from the Mendelssohn-Bartholdy-Stiftung for 1919–1920 appeared in the Hochschule für Musik yearbook.

45. *Die stille Stadt*, composed on a text by Richard Dehmel, was probably premiered by Elisabeth Feuge in Dessau on 4 September 1919. Weill accompanied the recital.

Kunst und Wissenschaft.

Dessau, 5. September.

Elisabeth-Feuge-Arien- und Liederabend.

Fräulein Elisabeth Feuge gehört zweifelsohne zu jenen glücklichen musikalischen Naturen, denen ein gütiges Geschick das Beste und Schönste von vornherein mit auf den Lebensweg und auf die Künstlerlaufbahn gegeben: eine reiche und vielseitige Begabung, angesichts derer die Schule nur die Aufgabe zufällt, mühelos zu leiten und zu entfalten. Und was die noch sehr junge angehende Künstlerin unter der gediegenen Führung ihrer Mutter bereits gelernt — und das ist sehr viel —, davon legte sie in ihrem gestrigen Konzert nach allen Richtungen hin vollberedtes Zeugnis ab. Die Atemführung, der Ansatz des Tones und sein gesponnenes Entwickeln, die lockere Leichtigkeit der Koloratur, die Klarheit und Deutlichkeit der Textbehandlung, das gab sich so frei, so ungezwungen, so vollkommen natürlich, daß man daran eine fast ungetrübte Freude haben konnte. Was noch abzustellen wäre, ist eine bei einigen Vokalen nicht ganz einwandfreie Lippenstellung, die hier und da eine kleine Klanghemmung im Gefolge hatte. Mit den eben erwähnten, mehr der reinen Gesangstechnik angehörenden Vorzügen verband sich ein starkes Vortragstalent. Man merkte es der jungen Sängerin auf Schritt und Tritt an, daß all ihre Liedergaben nicht nur den Lippen, sondern vielmehr noch einem gesunden und tiefen Empfinden entquollen. Ernstes und Heiteres, beides in den mannigfachsten Abstufungen, gelangte voll zu seinem Recht und führig zu eindringlichen Wirkungen. Ob die junge werdende Künstlerin Meyerbeer, Rossini oder Thomas sang, ob sie in ihrem reichen und sein gewählten Liederprogramm sich für Liszt, Wolf, Reger, Rüzner oder Herrmann einsetzte, überall traf sie mit staunenswerter Sicherheit die Stilart dieser Meister und schuf aus natürlichem Einfühlen und Einempfinden manch feines Kabinettstück. Sicher vermag Fräulein Feuge in der Schule ihrer Frau Mutter noch manches zu lernen, dann aber möge sie noch anderen Meisterinnen der Gesangs- und Vortragskunst sich zugesellen, um somit dem freien und letzten Endes ureigenen Künstlerschaffen entgegenzureifen. Am Flügel hatte Fräulein Feuge in Herrn Kurt Weill einen in jedweder Hinsicht ganz ausgezeichneten Begleiter, der vorzüglich in der Technik und musikalisch poesievoll mitgestaltend in allem voll auf der Höhe stand. Viel Interesse erweckten auch zwei Liedkompositionen dieses jungen vielverfprechenden Musikers, die — namentlich das erste — ausgesprochen expressionistisch angelegt, ein starkes, auf sich selbst gestelltes Talent verrieten. Daß die den Konzertsaal bis auf den letzten Platz füllende Zuhörerschaft die beiden Vortragenden mit Beifall reichlich überschüttete, sei zum Schluß nur noch nebenher erwähnt.   E. H.

46. Ernst Hamann's review of Elisabeth Feuge's recital in Dessau appeared in the *Anhalter Anzeiger*.

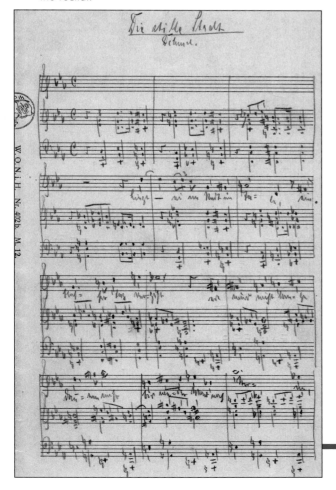

48. From September–December 1919, Weill worked as a Repetiteur under Hans Knappertsbusch at Dessau's Friedrich-Theater. Knappertsbusch is pictured here ca. 1923, after assuming Bruno Walter's position in Munich.

49. Lüdenscheid, 1920.

50. Hotel zur Post in Lüdenscheid, ca. 1920. The theater occupied the first floor.

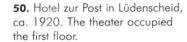

Weill (in Dessau) to Hanns Weill, 19 December 1919: The *Weise* is finished (except for the dynamic markings). Bing, to whom I showed the score, was enthusiastic about it, thinks the work is ready for performance, and wants to get in touch with Nikisch and Strauss. I don't quite believe this. The agency for the "Bühnengenossenschaft" [state agency for artist's employment in theaters], to which I turned in order to get a job, has already sent me a contract starting right now as second *Kapellmeister* in Lüdenscheid in Westphalia. I signed it right away and am now waiting for the countersignature of the management. Therefore, my days in Dessau are probably numbered.

Weill (in Lüdenscheid) to Ruth Weill, 28 January 1920: If indeed theater life will allow me more time and leisure for my own writing, I intend to complete the one-act piece by Ernst Hardt [*Ninon von Lenclos*]. In this work I would want to give—and would want to achieve—only one thing: beauty. . . . Now if, together with a poet, I were to create a new work of art, I would come up with totally new ideas for it. . . . All that words cannot express—and there is a lot of that—must be said through music, pantomime, dance (in a modern sense), color, light—but mostly through music, because it best expresses what cannot be said in mere words. Perhaps this could be a life's work, and I wouldn't find many who would understand me. . . . Right now there is no chance for composing anything at all. No one could possibly imagine how this makes me suffer. I only hope that this summer I can manage my time better. . . . Again, the next few days will be heavily loaded with work. Three new and difficult things, one of which gives me great pleasure because it is the first opera I am conducting and one of the most difficult ones at that: *Die schöne Galathea*. Once again, I have to do this with only one rehearsal, of course. That's hard on my nerves. The other night I spent a very stimulating evening with friends from Benneckenstein in Gelsenkirchen, where I met a tremendously talented, very modern painter and a very interesting young composer and talked and made music until 2:30 with marvelous red wine in between. That was a most pleasant change.

Weill (in Lüdenscheid) to Engelbert Humperdinck, 16 March 1920: You may be wondering why you have not heard from me in such a long time, but my new field of activity brings so much work that only today at a late hour of the night have I found the time to thank you most cordially for your nice letter. In the short time I have been here I have advanced tremendously in my development as a conductor. What I want to achieve is the following: To stay far enough above day-to-day affairs that I can find enough time in any conducting position to attend to my own work. The main thing is to achieve a certain routine, and I'll have

---

1 9 2 0

MUSIC + THEATER:	LITERATURE + FILM:	SCIENCE + SOCIETY:	POLITICS:
Igor Stravinsky *Pulcinella*	Jaroslav Hašek *Osudy dobrého vojáka Švejka za světové války* (*Good Soldier Schweik*)	C. G. Jung *Psychologische Typen*	Wolfgang Kapp stages short-lived monarchist *coup d'état* in Berlin
Paul Whiteman tours Europe with his band	Karl Kraus *Die letzten Tage der Menschheit*	First radio station opened in Pittsburgh, Pa.	Treaty of Rapallo signed
Jazz records become available in Germany	*Das Kabinett des Dr Caligari* (film by Robert Wiene)	The sport of water skiing pioneered on Lake Annecy, France	Danzig declared a free city
Georg Kaiser *Gas*			

plenty of opportunity to acquire it here. I have to coach everything myself and have to conduct almost every night. Besides all of the classical and modern operetta repertoire, I have also produced several operas (*Freischütz, Waffenschmied*). That has given me special pleasure, but also a great deal of work. This week I have *Zigeunerbaron*, after that probably *Martha*. I am assured from all sides that the musical quality of the theater has experienced a fresh impetus since I got here.

The Academy is going to give out the second prize of the Michael Beer Foundation (for a work for full orchestra and a chamber music work). One of the conditions is that one must be at least twenty-two; I am only twenty years old. Despite this, would it be possible for me to participate, perhaps through your recommendation? My symphonic poem has been deposited with Professor Nikisch for some weeks. Could you perhaps say a few good words on my behalf? A performance of this work would make me the happiest of people. . . .

I have a good offer as principal conductor for the summer at the Spa Theater at Norderney. I do not know as yet what I will be doing during the winter. I am hoping to be in Berlin in May for several days and to be visiting you then.

51. Weill (front row, left) with singers in costume from the Lüdenscheid opera house.

Weill (in Lüdenscheid) to Hanns Weill, 1 April 1920: For Easter I have the following obligations: Sunday afternoon *Fledermaus*, in the evening *Cavalleria*; Monday *Zigeunerbaron*, in the evening *O schöne Zeit, O selige Zeit* (premiere). So you can imagine how much I have to do this week. Just to reduce that huge *Cavalleria* score to my minimal orchestra and to coach them in it, not to mention this small chorus, the difficult stage conditions, etc. No wonder that I'm about at the end of my rope. After Easter I won't be doing anything anymore. Tonight is the dress rehearsal for *Cavalleria*; before this we had only two rehearsals with half of the orchestra. This is going to be some fun. Just the same, it's a joy to dig oneself into that passionate music, though mind you, the difficulties with the orchestra are unbelievable.

52. Programs from performances conducted by Weill in Lüdenscheid.

Weill (in Berlin) to Albert Weill, 29 November 1920: Busoni had written to [Oskar] Bie that I should come to see him. You have no idea how difficult it is to get to Busoni. The doorman has orders to send everyone away. Despite this, I spent a most interesting afternoon with Busoni. His conversation is tremendously stimulating, and he insists so strongly on complete freedom and openness that it is difficult for people like us to handle him. . . . He is amazed by my youth and has kept my compositions, he but does not want to make a decision yet because so many big shots have applied [for the master class].

53. Program from a concert in Halberstadt arranged by Weill's brother Hanns, featuring Elisabeth Feuge. The program included works by Reger, Trunk, Schreker, Pfitzner, Marx, and Schoenberg, along with Weill's *Abendlied* and *Die stille Stadt*.

54. Ferruccio Busoni is surrounded by his "disciples" from the master class: Kurt Weill, Walther Geiser, Luc Balmer, and Wladimir Vogel.

55. Only the first movement of Weill's Cello Sonata (1919–1920) survives in his autograph. (A copyist's manuscript of the entire work was preserved by Peter Bing, the son of Weill's teacher Albert Bing.)

Weill (in Berlin) to Ferruccio Busoni, 20 January 1921: Permit me to unburden my heart in this manner to thank you once more for your kind willingness to be of assistance. This afternoon I could only hastily stammer my thanks in my surprise that the one person whom I venerate most ardently above all others could so energetically take an interest in me. Already before this day I've been so grateful for everything you have said, for the friendly personal association with which you have honored me, for the undreamed-of prospects your music opened up to me, so that now I hardly know how to pay back this debt of gratitude. Therefore I hope that you'll understand when I join my thanks today with a request: allow me to assist you further, as far as you might need me and as far as I may be able to; let it be a matter of course, that with everything I have, I will be at your and your work's disposal. I would be most happy if I could always be thought of as your sincerely devoted *famulus* [scholarly servant].

1 9 2 1

MUSIC + THEATER:

First new music festival in Donaueschingen

Paul Hindemith *Mörder, Hoffnung der Frauen* and *Das Nusch-Nuschi*

Luigi Pirandello *Sei personaggi in cerca d'autore*

LITERATURE + FILM:

Kurt Tucholsky *Träumereien an preußischen Kaminen*

John Dos Passos *Three Soldiers*

The Kid (film by Charlie Chaplin)

SCIENCE + SOCIETY:

Albert Einstein wins Nobel Prize for discovering the photoelectric effect

T. H. Morgan postulates chromosome theory of heredity

German reparation debt amounts to $33.2 billion

POLITICS:

Walter Rathenau appointed German Minister for Reconstruction

Hitler's Storm Troopers (SA) begin to terrorize political opponents

German finance minister Matthias Erzberger assassinated

Weill (in Berlin) to Hanns Weill, 12 April 1921: A thousand thanks for sending me that cash present—it arrived just when I was about to hit somebody up for a loan. Well, I'm now the officially appointed choral director of the synagogue in the Münchener Straße, receiving 400 Marks, but for the time being I've accepted for one month only. I have to start by getting a chorus together and rehearsing them in time for Pesach, which will be a lot of aggravation because the time is so short. . . . The only diversions are the visits with Busoni, who is leaving for Italy today (for a short time only).

Ferruccio Busoni (in Berlin) to Raffaello Busoni, 15 July 1921: So far there are four [pupils in the master class]: a headstrong Russian, who always likes to be in the right and accomplishes little [Wladimir Vogel]; a somewhat perfumed Croatian who is already "professor" in Zagreb [Svetislav Stancic]; a very fine little Jew (who will certainly make his way and is already something of a factotum around the house) [Weill]; and finally a small podgy youth who looks like an inflated tire, wears enormous glasses perched on his nose and is undoubtedly talented [Erwin Bodky]. The two latter are a source of pleasure. But *where* does one begin to teach? At the moment this is quite a problem. They have great ability and are yet incapable of the simplest things, their forms are complex and yet not diversified, and they exercise the general right of today's youth to proclaim every crooked line as individuality and freedom. Where does one start? I can bring them to reason only gradually and patiently. Were I to "drive my point home," I would become ridiculous in their eyes and fail to convince them. Am I not one of the "leaders of modern trends"? Are they not fulfilling—this is what they feel—my boldest dreams? Oh, what misunderstanding!

Weill (in Berlin) to Ferruccio Busoni, 13 February 1922: I received your letter only today due to this disastrous rail strike. I am very happy that you thought of me, and I thank you most sincerely. I found the *Athenaeum* in your apartment and have read Mr. Dent's essay with great interest. It is truly amazing what great understanding of your work and its influence he shows. How he describes the atmosphere of your home, how he speaks about the favorable effect of Romanism on German art, how he speaks about the cordial relationship between yourself and us—all of these are phrases which correspond to our own thoughts and perceptions experienced during this past half-year. To be sure, your influence reached far deeper than to mere compositional matters: for me it culminates in the realization that before we are able to create a true work of art we first have to guide our own humanity [*Menschentum*] through all complexities, scaling them down to the simplest and most concise formula.

56. Weill gives a lecture-demonstration about Beethoven in Halberstadt.

57. Weill made a four-hand piano arrangement of his Symphony no. 1 for a performance in Busoni's class. Pictured here is the first page of the *seconda* part.

1 9 2 2

MUSIC + THEATER:
International Society for Contemporary Music formed in Salzburg
Louis Armstrong joins King Oliver's band in Chicago
Bertolt Brecht *Baal*

LITERATURE + FILM:
James Joyce *Ulysses*
Herman Hesse *Siddhartha*
Nosferatu (film by F. W. Murnau)

SCIENCE + SOCIETY:
Wittgenstein *Tractatus logico-philosophicus*
American cocktail becomes popular in Europe
Unrest in German cities due to increasing food prices

POLITICS:
Walter Rathenau assassinated by German nationalist fanatics
Mussolini's march on Rome
France threatens to occupy the Ruhr area

There isn't much to report from here. The strike—in its ramifications probably the worst Berlin has ever experienced—had the one good effect of paralyzing, at least for one week, the Americanism which has gripped Berlin for several years now. Some images remain: A gentleman in top hat and fur coat carrying water on the Kurfürstendamm, a lady at night looking for an escort through the pitch-dark Tiergarten, and finally the Charlottenburger Chaussee resembling the Red Sea through which the Israelites move toward the West on dry feet. . . .

As for me, I've been occupying myself a lot with Mozart again and what I meant above with the inner mental balance relates to him and all those who follow in his footsteps. Among the latter I have also studied Bizet more closely; *L'arlésienne* suite has transported me into true rapture because of its warmth of expression and the mastery with which it has been created. With great enthusiasm and much urgency I'm working on a passacaglia for orchestra, which I hope will be finished in time for your return.

Weill (in Berlin) to Ruth Weill, September-October 1922: After the great joys of composing it, the Pantomime [*Zaubernacht*] now will be entering the troublesome and grinding phase of rehearsals, and I'm afraid that in the next few weeks I'll have more aggravation on account of that than the whole thing is worth. But this, too, represents some kind of education. Besides, there are the other performance possibilities, but they are hanging by a thread, which means I have to remain as calm as possible and wait for that thread to tear. The best possibility seems to be a performance in Dessau, where it's likely that Bing will be getting the position of first *Kapellmeister*. He wrote me the dearest, most cordial letter.

Personally I'm experiencing a lot; few, very few pleasant things, but some very dramatic scenes. And I'm beginning to realize that no poet ever invented anything that a real person couldn't experience just as well. The worst of all is that every day I have to give these boring lessons. Naturally, with all of this, working conditions are not the best, especially since for three to four weeks I'll still have plenty to do with the orchestrations.

59. First page of an incomplete pencil short score of the *Fantasia, Passacaglia, und Hymnus* for orchestra (1922). The full score and parts are missing. The Berlin Philharmonic Orchestra gave the premiere on 12 March 1923 with Alexander Selo conducting.

58. Vocal score of the "Lied der Fee" from the pantomime *Zaubernacht*, 1922. The full score is missing. The work includes a few set pieces which foreshadow Weill's future song style. Four years later, Weill commented on the piece: "I wrote the pantomime *Zaubernacht* for a Russian troupe at the Theater am Kurfürstendamm. I have learned two things from the concentrated intensity of Russian theater art: that the stage has its own musical form, which develops organically out of the flow of the plot, and that important events can truly be expressed only through the simplest, least conspicuous means. An orchestra of nine, a singer, two dancers, and a few children—that was the entire apparatus of this dream dance." (*Bekenntnis zur Oper* [reproduced on page 49])

60. Newspaper advertisement for *Zaubernacht* at the Theater am Kurfürstendamm.

Kindertheater „Märchentruhe"
im Theater am Kurfürstendamm
Sonnab. d 18 Novbr., nachm. 3 Uhr:
Zaubernacht
Pantomime von W. Boritsch.
Musik: Kurt Weill. Regie: F. L. Hörth.
Ballett: Mary Zimmermann.

Aus den Konzertsälen.

In der Singakademie traten die staatsakademischen Schüler aus der Kompositions-Meisterklasse des Prof. Dr. Ferruccio Busoni — jetzt weiß man wohl Bescheid — der Reihe nach auf das Podium und dirigierten dem Philharmonischen Orchester und dem tit. Publikum ihre Schöpfungen vor. Wie schön es doch jetzt diese jungen Herrschaften haben. Man lebt entschieden großzügig in der Nachkriegszeit. Man findet für die Papiersetzen ideale Zwecke und der Meister behütet nicht ängstlich seine Sprößlinge. Erstaunlich ist, wie sich die musikalische Jugend des formal-technischen Apparates zu bedienen weiß. Gar keine Blödheit mehr. Wie überall, so auch in der Kunst. Das Schwabenalter rücke man auf 15 Jahre vor! Walther Geiser und Robert Blum sind zwar, wie aus den Lebensläufen der Schüler auf der letzten Programmseite ersichtlich, erst seit 1922 bei Busoni, aber ihm schon wesensverwandt im flotten Ton, in der witzigen Episode. Wo Geiser tiefer furchen will, geschieht es nur nebenbei und ohne Ueberzeugung. Blum entwickelt im Intermezzo eine ruhige Fläche, die wohl etwas leer, aber doch da ist. Uebertreibungen kommen nicht vor und kompositionstechnisch ist alles schön geraten. Eine andere Nummer ist Kurt Weill — nebenbei bemerkt der einzige Deutsche unter diesen Zöglingen auf Staatskosten —; er ist Metaphysiker, eigenwillig, schreibt eine eher abstrakte Musik. Er könnte bedeutend werden, wenn er die sinnliche Plastik hinzugewänne; andernfalls verdorrt er leicht zu einem kahlen Stumpf. Luc Balmer ist der vollkommenste Repräsentant des Meisterschülers. Thema, Gegenthema, Rezitativo, Reprise, Finale enthält sein symphonischer Satz. Wie wohl wird's mir! Tüchtiges Können, solide Arbeit, aber auch größere Architektonik im Sinne und teilweise auch in der Sprache der klassisch-brahmsschen Kunst machen ihn zu einem Zentrum dieses Schülerkreises. Er ist auch gewandter im Dirigieren als die Vorgenannten, die ihre lustigen Stücke teilweise mit unfreiwilliger Komik ausstatteten. Der Außenseiter, das enfant terrible, ist Wladimir Vogel. Er bekommt das Schlußwort zu einem „Symphonischen Vorgang", bleibt aber klugerweise im Hintergrund und überläßt die Lüftung dieses „Vorgangs" dem Dr. H. Unger. Dieser hatte sich mit liebevollster, eindringlichster Kenntnis in die schwierige Partitur versenkt und gab mit einer ganz ausgezeichneten Dirigierleistung eine Probe von dem, was ein Kapellmeister vollführen soll. Nur diese Aufgabe „jedes Werk durchleuchten" gibt es für den Dirigenten: Der Routinier besingert es dagegen wie von weitem, ist er ja doch in allen Sätteln sicher. Vogel gab neurussische Exzesse — instrumental mit Strawinsky, melodisch mit Skrjabin liebäugelnd — und bewies, daß bei Busoni auch dies gestattet ist. Dies war die selbstbewußteste Komposition des Abends, was durchaus anerkennend gesagt sei. Sie benötigte kein Schülerkonzert mehr. Die grauen Häupter entsetzten sich, die Jugend war begeistert und trampelte vor Entzücken. Eine orchestral glänzende Leistung, inhaltlich aber ein schrullenhaftes Chaos, weil ihm eine faszinierende Ausdruckskraft vorläufig nicht vorhanden ist. Alles zusammen ein imponierender Abend, ein Abend, der vor 30 oder 50 Jahren als Zukunftsmärchen gegolten hätte. Man rief am Schluß nach dem Meister, aber er blieb unsichtbar, wie Wotan vor seinem Sprößling Siegmund. **R. S.**

Berlin, den 1. Dezember 1922.

Ew. Hochwohlgeboren

gestatten sich die Staatlich akademischen Schüler aus der Kompositionsklasse des Herrn Prof. Dr. Ferruccio Busoni zu der am 7. Dezember abends 7½ Uhr in der Singakademie stattfindenden Aufführung eigener Kompositionen ergebenst einzuladen. Es würde ihnen zur hohen Ehre gereichen, Sie an diesem Abend erwarten zu dürfen.

Mit ausgezeichneter Hochachtung

Walther Geiser, Kurt Weill, Luc Balmer, Robert Blum, Wladimir Vogel.

---

61. The Berlin Philharmonic performed the last movement of Weill's *Divertimento* for orchestra and male chorus in a concert of music by students of Busoni. A review appeared in the 15 December 1922 edition of the *Berliner Börsen-Courier*.

Konzertdirektion Hermann Wolff und Jules Sachs   Preis 40,— Mk.
Berlin W.9   Linkstrasse 42

Sing-Akademie

Donnerstag, den 7. Dezember 1922, abends 7½ Uhr

KONZERT

mit

Kompositionen der Staatsakademischen
∴ Schüler aus der Meisterklasse ∴

Prof. Dr. Ferruccio Busoni

Ausführende:

Das Berliner Philharmonische Orchester
Der Chor der Kaiser Wilhelm Gedächtnis-Kirche

Dirigenten:

Dr. H. Unger und die Komponisten

PROGRAMM

1. Walther Geiser:
Ouvertüre zu einem Lustspiel

2. Kurt Weill:
Letzter Satz aus dem „Divertimento"

3. Robert Blum:
Drei kurze Stücke für Orchester
Ouverture, Intermezzo. Rondo

4. Luc Balmer:
Letzter Teil einer Symphonie (c-moll, d-moll)
Thema, Gegenthema, Recitativo, Reprise, Finale

5. Wladimir Vogel:
Symphonischer Vorgang (in einem Satz)

KONZERTFLÜGEL: BECHSTEIN

Während der Vorträge bleiben die Saaltüren geschlossen

Weill (in Leipzig) to Ferruccio Busoni, 31 March 1923: You probably have heard that my *Divertimento* (in the 5 movement version) will be performed at the Singakademie under [Heinz] Unger's direction. At the moment, the revisions of the String Quartet are demanding a lot of my time. But I heard from Donaueschingen that the programs are as good as completed and that greatest haste is in order; therefore, for the time being, I decided to send off the Quartet in the first version.

---

1 9 2 3

MUSIC + THEATER:
Arthur Honegger *Pacific 231*
Ernst Křenek *Der Sprung über den Schatten*
Elmer Rice *The Adding Machine*

LITERATURE + FILM:
Franz Werfel *Verdi*
Romain Rolland *Mahatma Gandhi*
Robin Hood (film by Douglas Fairbanks)

SCIENCE + SOCIETY:
Sigmund Freud *Das Ich und das Es*
Regular radio broadcasting starts in Germany
Gregorian calendar introduced in the USSR

POLITICS:
Hitler's "Beer Hall Putsch" in Munich fails
Hyper inflation in Germany
July: US$1 = 170,000 RM
October: US$1 = 12 billion RM
November: US$1 = 4.2 trillion RM
French army occupies Darmstadt, Karlsruhe, Mannheim

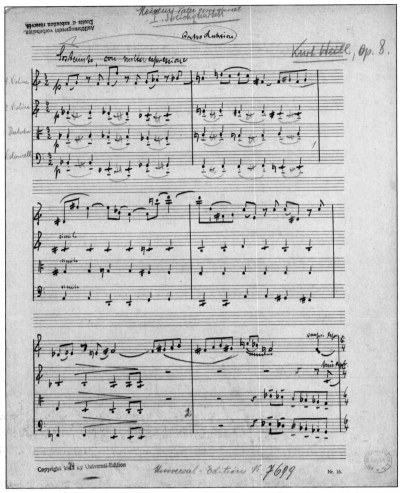

62. First page of the String Quartet no. 1, op. 8, "dedicated to my father."

Weill (in Frankfurt) to Ferruccio Busoni, 21 June 1923: There was an experiment [here] that made one sit up and take notice: Stravinsky's *L'histoire du soldat*. This is some kind of "folk play with singing and dancing," something in between pantomime, melodrama, and farce; as far as this form allows, the music has been masterfully shaped and the search for the smell of the street is tolerable because it fits the subject matter.

I'm going to hear my quartet for the first time only today because the Hindemith people are terribly overburdened. Strangely enough, the last movement—which for me as well as for you is the most mature one—seems to meet with the least approval from those four gentlemen. I'm afraid that Hindemith has already danced his way a bit too deeply into the land of the foxtrot.

Ferruccio Busoni (in Berlin) to Emil Hertzka, Universal Edition, July 1923: I have given my pupil Kurt Weill a letter addressed to you, which you ought to receive in a short time. It concerned Weill's string quartet, a work of splendid qualities with power and invention. I hardly know a piece by a 23-year-old of the present day that is so attractive and worthwhile. It is thoroughly "modern," without any unattractive features. I emphasized in the letter that you should promptly grab this talent. Incidentally (and yet it is so important), Weill is a man who thinks and is well-read, a man of the most upstanding character.

Weill (in Berlin) to Ferruccio Busoni, October 1923[?]: There is only one excuse for my long silence, and that is the desire to shield you from lamentations [referring to his choral work *Recordare*]. Hereabouts it looked almost as if there wasn't any hope at all; the transition from millions to billions was so violent, that even those who ordinarily are indifferent to money matters were stunned. But even now we have grown accustomed to our lot, and people have begun grasping at new straws. From abroad it may look even worse than it actually is. After all, having lasted through all of those various crises, this country can hardly be written off, and the patience of the people is truly admirable.

As far as one can judge from here, Berlin has not changed much since you left. The concert season has opened with the same devil-may-care attitude as ever. Bruno Walter, who now seems to be completing his development into an American Heldentenor, conducts Mozart overly precise, affected, and sugary. I don't like this type of jabbering [*mauschelnde*] conductor, whose intellect knows of nothing better than to create a mirror in which he may admire his own beautiful backside. Sometimes I'm tempted to doubt whether Mahler was entirely free of this flaw; or does one not dare to draw an inference about the interpreter from the compositions? Schnabel seems to me to have grown more manly, more definite in his playing; he succeeds in everything he attempts as he has intended, but the deficiency lies in the intention itself and that is a matter of basic concept, of temperament. Claudio Arrau is trying his best to play in your spirit; he succeeds less in your own *Carmen* than in Liszt's *Don Juan Fantasy*.

And then there's the new Generalissimo of the opera [Erich Kleiber]! I've told you about the excellent *Fidelio* performance. I liked *Aida* less, because this stylizing, this overdoing every phrase does not agree with Verdi, and if someone happens to be a German conductor, he cannot simulate the presence of Italian theater blood simply by exercising arbitrary tempo fluctuations. And yet, Kleiber is a fine musician and also the right man for the job, because he will rejuvenate the repertory from the bottom up. For the time being he is letting all the Bayreuth demi-gods and full-gods parade around.

One glance into the audiences of the concert halls makes one realize that Berlin will not give up its music. To be sure, a flock still gathers at the Philharmonic concerts; they try to look "cute" when it's Mozart, "heroic" when it's Beethoven, and "severe" when it's Bach, beating the quarter notes with the left leg and tinkling the eighths with the right hand. But what all their faces do have in common is a touching look of blissfulness, that despite of all that's been happening they're still able to sit in an illuminated concert hall and are allowed to listen to music. And so, a mere layman's judgment is bound to be more naive, more sincere, and of greater value to the artist. And at the box office one hears of fantasy prices for tickets (up to a billion Marks on Monday evening).

There is little news to report about me. I've given up on the battle for a room and for the time being I'll be staying here in my friends' apartment. There's been no chance to do any work, although I would have been in good shape for it. But I have been reading quite a bit: Mozart quartets, of which I give the prize to the one in C major from the year 1785 [the "Dissonanz" Quartet, K. 465]. You remember the Adagio introduction with the famous cross relation in the beginning?—one of the most deeply stirring and at the same time boldest movements I know. Then a lot of Berlioz full scores: now it's dawned on me that it's not a matter of styles of orchestration, but rather that there exists only a certain way to compose for orchestra, just like a painter sketches differently for an etching than he would for a pencil drawing.

63. *Quodlibet*, op. 9, a suite from *Zaubernacht*, is dedicated to Weill's Dessau teacher and friend Albert Bing.

64. The premiere of *Quodlibet* in Dessau is reviewed by the *Volksblatt für Anhalt*, 15 June 1923.

65. ca. 1923.

I believe I am in strong opposition to the majority of the concertgoers when I declare this op. 9 a piece of high interest. One has to accept, however, the special features of all our moderns as given facts: the almost completely dissolved tonality; the intricate, apparently uneven harmony; the elevated dominance of dissonance; the multifariousness of rhythm and meter; the multicolored orchestral sounds and things similar. Kurt Weill already handles all these elements with surprising virtuosity, including a remarkable orchestral technique. . . . Kurt Weill, possessing strong musical talent, will not stop at the style of this orchestral suite, which aims for orchestral virtuosity. It represents a transitional stage for him, out of which the artist will escape—to speak in the voice of Walter Riemann—the superficial, artistic, and modern art of nerves, sounds, and moods, and reach a spiritualized form of music making that comes from the heart and soul. (*Anhalter Anzeiger*, 17 June 1923)

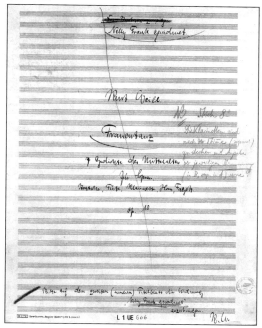

66. Ferruccio Busoni (seated) and Philipp Jarnach (standing behind Busoni) with the Amar-Quartett: Paul Hindemith, Maurits Frank, Licco Amar, and Walter Caspar. The quartet premiered the String Quartet no. 1, op. 8 on 24 June 1923 at the Frankfurt Kammermusikwoche.

67. *Frauentanz* for soprano and chamber ensemble is a set of seven medieval poems dedicated to Nelly Frank. In February 1924, Busoni arranged the chamber instrumentation of the third song, "Ach wär' mein Lieb' ein Brünnlein kalt," for piano. This was the last piece he lived to complete.

68. German radio began with a broadcast from Vox House at Potsdamer Straße 4 in Berlin, 29 October 1923. Pictured here is the radio program schedule for 23 December 1923–6 January 1924.

69. After currency reform ended Germany's hyperinflation in November 1923, the useless notes were pulped.

Ferruccio Busoni (in Paris) to Philipp Jarnach, 7 October 1923: I don't know Weill's *Frauentanz*. Considering his reserved vein and painstaking efforts, this youngster's productivity is surprising. He has any amount of "ideas"— as you say—but they are concealed or inferred, so that only "the likes of us" can discover and admire them. He—Weill—does not seem to be conscious of when he has arrived at the right place; instead, he passes over it as if over sand and rocks between which beautiful, individual flowers grow, which he neither tramples on nor plucks, and over which he does not linger. His wealth is great, his selectivity at present inactive. One envies and would like to help.—But he will come to the right thing of his own accord!—The eternal question: is he still developing, or has he already reached his peak?

Weill (in Berlin) to Emil Hertzka, 16 February 1924: In your letter last fall you had announced your intention "to accept my entire oeuvre into your catalogue" as of the beginning of 1924. I therefore consider it a welcome obligation to ask once more today for your final decision, as I am about to sign contracts with a German and a foreign publisher. Since I have now had several big successes, you won't be needing to raise a complete unknown out of obscurity. A major local stage publisher has just acquired two pieces of mine: the children's pantomime *Zaubernacht*, which will be performed this fall in New York (premiered in the Theater am Kurfürstendamm here in 1922), as well as a full-length stage work I am presently working on and for which Georg Kaiser is writing the libretto. My string quartet, op. 8, will be performed more often now by the Roth Quartet; a well-known foreign publisher has just made an offer for this piece, but if you are interested in it I would very much appreciate hearing your suggestions. Op. 9 is *Quodlibet, eine Unterhaltungsmusik* (four pieces for small orchestra based on the above-mentioned children's pantomime); it had a big success in Dessau, is accessible, easy to play and unpretentious (here, too, there are good reviews at your disposal). The *Frauentanz*, op. 10 (seven songs for soprano, viola, flute, clarinet, horn, bassoon), was performed by the I.N.M.G. by Frau Pisling and Stiedry; you will be particularly interested to know that *Ferruccio Busoni* has arranged one of these songs for voice and piano and will presumably do the same with the others. Op. 11 is an *a cappella* choral work with a Latin text (fifth chapter of Jeremiah's Lamentations), for four-part chorus and children's chorus. It is to be premiered, as I have heard, at this year's ADMV [Allgemeiner Deutscher Musik Verein] music festival. My next plans are: a violin concerto (already begun), a new string quartet, and a new (comic) opera.

1924

MUSIC + THEATER:
George Gershwin *Rhapsody in Blue*
Maxwell Anderson and Laurence Stallings *What Price Glory*
Krolloper becomes Berlin's third opera house

LITERATURE + FILM:
Thomas Mann *Der Zauberberg*
Klabund *Der Kreidekreis*
The Navigator (film by Buster Keaton)

SCIENCE + SOCIETY:
The Berlin S-Bahn (city train) is electrified
German airship crosses the Atlantic
First Winter Olympics held at Chamonix

POLITICS:
Giacomo Matteotti, leader of Italian socialists, murdered by fascists
Dawes plan comes into effect
The new Reichsmark introduced

Weill (in Davos, Switzerland) to Ferruccio Busoni, 25 February 1924:
Up here, idleness seems like a real pleasure for the first time. Going from Berlin to a mountain village in one day brings on so many surprises that I hardly have room for any thoughts besides amazement. We live idyllically here on a mountain slope 100 meters above the village of Davos; on one side we look into a steeply ascending forest, in which the sun plays the loveliest color games on the shimmering bluish snow; and toward the south the crest of a long chain of mountains cuts sharply into the sky. The sky is bluer than I have ever seen before; it seems to be a first foreshadowing of the south. Already in Helgoland I felt elated to sense a sort of solidarity with the earth, because daily events do depend on the weather, on happenings within nature; it brings on a certain symmetry of daily routine, but it never degenerates into monotony. I spend the mornings in the mountains, where the snow is two meters high and we walk without our coats in the radiant sunshine. At noon, while lying on open terraces facing south, the sun is so hot that one has to seek protection from it. This is where I made a wish for the first time—one that will probably be wished repeatedly during this journey: if only you could be here! This brilliant winter sun, this pure, thin air, and the view of the clouds, darkly hovering over the flat land below, puts one in an exalted mood.

You'll laugh when you hear that I'm being active in sports, but it's a good feeling to race on a small sled down a smooth ice track of four km and taking curves with merely a slight movement of the body. This isn't really dangerous because I'm doing it without being overly ambitious. . . . I had an encouraging telegram from Hertzka: "Have a lively interest to take on your works, request proposals concerning conditions." Although I am very skeptical when it comes to publishers, I will pass through Vienna on my return trip and try to reach an agreement with Hertzka in person.

If I think back on Berlin and all that lies behind me, my thoughts rest almost exclusively with you and I regret greatly not having received any reports about your state of health. I do so hope and wish that the decisive improvement which we were able to observe before my leaving has been keeping up and that you will soon be able to go south, to find there all of what you still miss so desperately.

Weill (in Bologna) to Ferruccio Busoni, 6 March 1924: I've been in this country for several days now, but whatever I've found Italy to be I've only found right here today. . . . I've taken the shorter and more beautiful route via the Bernina [mountains]. It is overwhelming when from the height of 2,400 meters you see green valleys lying below and then, in a circling descent, slowly you come closer to a deep-blue Italian lake. In Poschiavo the sun was shining warmly and in Tirano I already witnessed a regular Italian street scene with gypsies, scuffles, and such beautiful tenor voices that I could think of the Berlin State Opera only with melancholy. It is a bit early in the season for Lake Como and the much heralded Bellaggio did not quite live up to its promised effect. Milan, too, was somewhat disappointing. Compared to the magnificence of the cathedral and the archbishop's Palace, the city itself is a bit too average. But La Scala! What a magnificent theater! What a total fulfillment of the concept "theater"! How festive the picture of the wide, broad rows of orchestra seats and the five tiers of boxes! And what a performance!

Of everything I have ever seen, this comes closest to Mahler's ideal of "no concessions." They gave *Louise* by Charpentier. Toscanini conducted and this event alone was worth the entire journey. I didn't know that one could play

70. Between 1923 and 1926 Weill instructed private students in theory, orchestration, and composition. His early students included Claudio Arrau (above), Maurice Abravanel (right), and Nikolaos Skalkottas (not pictured).

71. The Internationale Gesellschaft für Neue Musik premiered *Frauentanz* on 25 January 1924 with soprano Nora Pisling-Boas and a chamber ensemble led by Fritz Stiedry.

72. Sledding with his cousin Nelly Frank in Davos, Switzerland.

73. Emil Hertzka, the director of Universal Edition. Photo by Fayer.

74. Excerpt from Weill's letter to Busoni, 15 March 1924.

75. First contract with Universal Edition, dated 22 April 1924.

"on" an orchestra by using such arbitrary rubati. The singing was marvelous and the chorus was flabbergasting in the musical and histrionic execution of its task. I don't know whether the opera gained a lot because of this performance—I found it to be beautiful in parts (as in the beginning of the fourth act). You can imagine the kind of verve with which they performed the great spectacular scene in the third act. I'll be thinking about this evening for a long time. . . . Now I'm sitting in a cafe while the orchestra is playing *Traviata* and they're all singing along; I feel happy and elated and wish for nothing more fervently than that you'll be well enough soon so that you can be here.

Weill (in Florence) to Ruth Weill, 8 March 1924: The trip to Florence was amusing. For six lire one gets a bag with salami, a piece of cold veal roast, a cucumber, oranges and a basket with a bottle of Chianti. Now all of the people on the train are sitting in there, stuffing themselves and guzzling wine. One family just entered, bringing with them a whole chicken, which they offered to everybody to eat. And they all are singing and chattering and screaming away—what a happy people! A city like Florence couldn't have been created if these people weren't so happy and completely integrated with the concept of beauty. In this city one can get a sense of how fathers have taught their sons which stones are considered valuable enough to build the cathedral, and one senses how these people have consciously been creating these treasures to last an eternity, and how everyone who had some talent became a servant in this cause. And each new generation begins there, where the previous one has left off, giving expression to its very own individuality but never forgetting the context of what has gone on before. . . . I'm living here so intensely, falling from one shudder of bliss into another, so that I can't sleep at night and often have to take hold of myself so as not to cry like a baby. Everything is alive: the churches are crowded with people who kneel there, there are as many priests as there are grains of sand by the sea, people are laughing and drinking Chianti, and Neapolitan singers are beating every colleague from the Berlin Opera out of the field—for two *Soldi*! Last night I was intoxicated by all this beauty and drunk from this wine.

Weill (in Rome) to Ferruccio Busoni, 15 March 1924: These present days in Rome will count among the most wonderful of my life. I am experiencing the much-praised Roman spring, and I can't stop taking in the sight of this truly divine city as it lies there shimmering in the sun. A view from the Pincio [one of Rome's seven hills] over the city toward the green hills, or the sight of marble ruins and the black cypress trees which form the background of Raffaello's Madonnas—it's become part of my sensibilities and I will always retain a longing for all of this.

And I am experiencing the Vatican's art treasures. Every day I visit three places: the Sistine Chapel, Raffaello's Stanze, and his ornamentations of the Villa Farnesina, and again and again I fall on my knees before this kind of perfection. I'm far too satiated by all this to find the right words, but I know full well that there must be some explanation for this deeply stirring aftereffect—that these people were incredibly able craftsmen, and that their sentiments were of the kind of purity that would in itself be justification for their presentation of godlike subjects in human terms. The relationship to the music of Bach and Mozart is plentiful, reaching into formal and melodic details, but to whom are such coherences as familiar as to you? . . . It's a warm spring day today [in Tivoli]. I was in the grottos near the waterfalls, which offer the most beautiful scenario for the *Freischütz*. And now I'm lying on the slope of an olive grove in the Sabine Mountains—a flock of sheep is grazing next to me and the shepherd with his Phyllis is singing

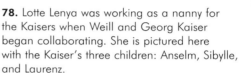

MUSIKBLÄTTER DES ANBRUCH

Monatsfchrift für moderne Mufik

Geleitet von Dr. Paul Stefan

Richard Strauß bedeutet für mich: an der Schwelle vom 19. zum 20. Jahrhundert ein Rückblick und eine Verheißung. Er ist Abschluß einer Epoche, der n Mittel nicht immer die gewähltesten waren, und deren Endziel der Naturalismus sein mußte. Und er ist Anfang einer neuen, weil alle „Schilderungen" unter seinen Händen sich in reines, unbeschwertes Musizieren wandeln. Er schafft sich eine Form, welche die Unmusikalität der beabsichtigten Tonmalerei vergessen macht. Er schafft sich eine Harmonik, die Dissonanzen bereits als Ausdrucksmittel benutzt; seine Linienführung gelangt zu jener weiten Ausdeutung der Tonalität, die einer gänzlichen Loslösung von tonaler Harmonik den Weg bereiten half. Er schafft sich ein Orchester, das alle — auch die platten — Einfälle in die günstigste Beleuchtung rückt, das auch über eine gewisse Leichtigkeit und Selbstverständlichkeit verfügt, obgleich es auf die Dickflüssigkeit Wagnerscher Partituren nicht ganz zu verzichten vermag.   Kurt Weill

76. Weill's first published article appeared in *Musikblätter des Anbruch: Monatsschrift für moderne Musik* 6, no. 5 (May 1924): 207.

77. Playwright Georg Kaiser, whose first collaboration with Weill began in 1924. Photo: Atelier Rieß, Berlin.

79. ca. 1924. Photo: Becker & Maaß.

78. Lotte Lenya was working as a nanny for the Kaisers when Weill and Georg Kaiser began collaborating. She is pictured here with the Kaiser's three children: Anselm, Sibylle, and Laurenz.

Neapolitan songs. I'm experiencing a light-heartedness, a fullness, an abandonment—and I'm singing along [see illustration 74]. That's better than the music I heard yesterday in a concert of the Corporazione delle nuove musiche (not the *Internationale*). It was the second of five evenings of exclusively French and Italian music (characteristic of what they perceive as new music over here). The best was a quartet by Milhaud and a few little jokes by Poulenc. Stravinsky's Suite for piano, violin, and clarinet sounds horrible. The best thing about the concert was that I met with and talked to Edward Dent there. He confirmed what Jarnach had hinted at on a postcard: that my *Frauentanz* has been accepted by Salzburg. This makes me terribly happy, especially since I never dared to have any hopes.

Weill (in Berlin) to the Weill family, 29 May 1924: My work has made such demands on me and outside obligations have been increasing as well. Two movements of the violin concerto are finished, but for three days now I've been stuck—so that my plan to have the whole thing finished before my visit with you can't be realized. But it's going to be great! Kaiser still hasn't delivered the ending of the libretto. But it doesn't bother me, because I've got such an endless amount of plans. [Eduard] Erdmann, up to now one of my enemies, seems to suddenly have been converted since he wants a large work for piano from me. In the *Anbruch* (May issue) my paragraph on Richard Strauss has appeared in very distinguished surroundings. Lotte Leonard, the most eminent German concert singer, will sing the *Frauentanz* in Salzburg. I've been in Dresden again and this time I spent an entire day with [Fritz] Busch—in every respect a most valuable acquaintance. Much—if not everything—in my future development depends entirely on myself now: I've got to work enormously hard in the next few years in order to take advantage of the favorable take-off I'm experiencing right now. Financially I don't have to be afraid anymore, I not only have better opportunities to earn something but little by little I'll be having some recurring income as well.

Weill (in Berlin) to Universal Edition, 3 June 1924: Along with *Frauentanz* I am sending you the two other compositions: the first string quartet, which belongs to the standard repertoire of the Roth Quartet—they have played it abroad; and the orchestra piece, *Quodlibet*, a piece of light entertainment music for which there are various projected performances in Germany (Dresden and Bochum, among others) as well as New York. It is based on the music for my children's pantomime *Zaubernacht*, which—as I have just been informed by the agent and author of the libretto, Dr. Vladimir Boritsch—will almost certainly be done by

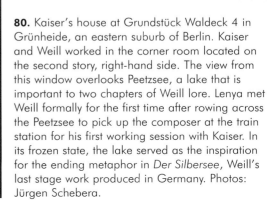

80. Kaiser's house at Grundstück Waldeck 4 in Grünheide, an eastern suburb of Berlin. Kaiser and Weill worked in the corner room located on the second story, right-hand side. The view from this window overlooks Peetzsee, a lake that is important to two chapters of Weill lore. Lenya met Weill formally for the first time after rowing across the Peetzsee to pick up the composer at the train station for his first working session with Kaiser. In its frozen state, the lake served as the inspiration for the ending metaphor in *Der Silbersee*, Weill's last stage work produced in Germany. Photos: Jürgen Schebera.

Fokine in New York. As soon as I know anything more definite about the performance I plan to prepare a new score of the work for a Mozart scoring (the score for the performance here has only 9 instruments). Are you interested in acquiring the work now and would you assist in arranging the New York performance? All of the parts, except the full score, are already in America. . . .

One other point: I am working on a concerto for violin and wind orchestra, which I hope to finish in two or three weeks. The piece was inspired by the idea—which has never been tried before—of contrasting a single concertizing violin with a body of winds. Now I have just come across Schott's competition, which sets forth very similar goals. I would therefore appreciate it if you would place a notice about this work, perhaps in *Anbruch* in the "manuscript" column.

81. Busoni died on 27 July 1924 in his Berlin apartment. Pallbearers carry his casket from Viktoria-Luise-Platz 11 three days later.

82. Weill finished his Violin Concerto, op. 12, in June 1924, but it was not premiered until one year later. Then it quickly became his most frequently performed concert work until *Kleine Dreigroschenmusik*.

Weill (in Berlin) to Leo and Ruth (Weill) Sohn, June? 1924: You mustn't be angry about my silence; Busoni is deadly ill and none of us knows where our heads are. It wouldn't be as awful to be suffering oneself as it is to see another human being suffer so terribly. When I'm not with him I have to bury myself in work in order to forget what he looks like. Unfortunately it was raining when I visited the Kaisers last week in Grünheide; they've become dear friends and will probably be the only ones who can replace a small part of what I'm going to lose in Busoni. I've finished a new, long piece, a violin concerto. So now I can finally get back to the Kaiser *Pantomime*. If I can scrape up the money, I'll be going to Salzburg in August.

Weill (in Berlin) to Universal Edition, 10 October 1924: I am enclosing the piano score of *Frauentanz*, ready for print, and hope that you will be able to give it to the engravers immediately. Do you consider the reference to Busoni on the title page appropriate? Or do you prefer the following formulation: "The piano arrangement of Nr. 3 was the last work of Ferruccio Busoni"?

As you may already know, *Frauentanz* will be performed in December by Walter Straram in Paris. Straram also wants to perform the violin concerto in Paris as soon as I can send the material, if possible as early as January. In addition the Roth Quartet will play my first string quartet in Paris.

Negotiations are still pending here regarding the premiere of the violin concerto. If these come to nothing I will send you the score and piano reduction immediately.

I still do not have a piano reduction of the *Stundenbuch*.

Would it be possible for you to arrange a performance (possibly in Vienna) of my *a cappella* choral work *Recordare* (four-part chorus with children's chorus). There are some difficult passages, but these would pose no problem if an efficient choral director were willing to take the trouble of rehearsing.

Finally, I would be very grateful if you would decide soon about acquiring *Quodlibet* since I have just received an inquiry specifically regarding orchestra works from another quarter. At the time you urgently requested that I send the score and mentioned a Vienna performance. Furtwängler has held out a prospect of a performance in the Gewandhaus after his American tour. And I would have various other possibilities for the piece if it were published. Please let me know your intentions in this regard.

Weill (in Berlin) to Lotte Lenya, 15 or 22 December 1924: The memory of your blowup today is not painful. You were very beautiful—and you were right. I was to blame. My attitude was still wrong. But now—finally, finally—I've understood exactly where you want me to be. And now I also know that it isn't so hard after all. A shift, not even a weakening, of my feelings—that's all. How passionately I love you—today more than ever—is entirely my own private affair. The expression of this feeling can't be obvious to others; it must be perceived only by you—just as your love still radiated to me even during today's blowup. For you were right in everything, except in saying you never really "liked" me; too often you've proven the opposite is true (and written that you are tougher on me than on others). This makes me glad, because often such an outburst is the strongest proof of your affection. But you must still believe one thing: these little arguments are not the end; they are the insignificant frictions of the beginning, which are caused solely by my inexperience. That's over now. Today I give you a present: me. You may take this present without qualms; it

83. In composing the Violin Concerto and the opera *Der Protagonist*, Weill abandoned the free-tone classicism of Busoni in favor of non-tonal expressionism. Shown here is a page from near the end of the third and final movement of the concerto.

DAS ZWEITE INTERNATIONALE KAMMER-
MUSIKFEST IN SALZBURG

VON

ADOLF WEISSMANN-BERLIN

52   DIE MUSIK   XVII/1 (Oktober 1924)

allem Dogmatischen abholden, problematischen Wesen ohne weiteres zu
erklären.

Von hier spannt sich von selbst ein Bogen zu Kurt Weill, dem Schüler Busonis,
dessen »Frauentanz«, ein in eigenartige instrumentale Hülle gekleideter Zyklus
von Gesängen auf mittelalterliche Texte, dank seiner stilvollen Übertragung
in die Sprache der Gegenwart hier womöglich noch eindrucksvoller war als
bei seiner Uraufführung in Berlin. Denn Lotte Leonard hob diese sieben Lieder
durch die Schönheit ihrer Stimme und den sinnvollen Vortrag ebensosehr
empor, wie der taktierende Jarnach die keineswegs gleichwertigen Spieler zur
Einheit zusammenzufügen wußte.

84. Adolf Weissmann's review of the Salzburg Chamber Music Festival, where
Frauentanz was performed in August 1924.

85. *Frauentanz*, Weill's first published score, appeared in November
1924. The vocal score was issued
in January 1925.

86. The music for *Recordare* was lost for
many years, until a copyist's score was
discovered in a Paris music shop by
British musicologist O.W. Neighbour in
1970.

will bring you only good things. Let me be your "pleasure boy" [*Lustknabe*],
more than a friend but less than a husband. I'm in the world for you—that is
self-evident, and you don't need to feel obligated. You'll now sense it. Give me
just a small sign that you will accept the present. Please.

Weill (in Berlin) to Universal Edition, 28 December 1924: Meanwhile another
unpleasant situation has arisen. My six orchestra songs, *Stundenbuch*, was the
only new composition to be recommended by the German section of the
International Society for Contemporary Music for the Prague Music Festival;
the score is in Winterthur, where the jury is to begin meeting on the 27th.
However, that same piece is supposed to be premiered on *22 January* by Unger
in the Philharmonie (Gesellschaft der Musikfreunde). So if the score is
returned in time I have to have the parts copied out immediately. I would very
much appreciate it if you would assume the costs of preparing the parts. I could
hardly afford it and you will presumably acquire the work after the premiere.
Please let me know what you think by return post. I have urgently requested
that Dr. Wellesz return the score to me immediately. I hope it works out.

Weill (in Berlin) to Emma Weill, 31 December 1924: Because you will be alone
this evening, you should at least have a little fun by getting this letter tomorrow
morning. Console yourself, because I, too, will stay home on New Year's Eve;
in the afternoon I have rehearsals (as of now: every day until the 22nd of
January!) and won't be able to squeeze in Grünheide. And I would not want to
be anywhere else. I hate to stagger into the beginning of a new year being deliri-
ous from a night of booze, but rather stay at home and do some thinking at such
a time. Your half-funny and half-caustic remarks about Chanukah give me a
chance for some important elucidations. Whichever way you look at it: religion
is a question of certain convictions. There are three roads which lead to those:
the first one is based on education and habit; you've done your best to show us
that particular road. However, the present generation wants to rationalize
everything, and our young, destructive spirits can no longer hang on to the idea
of behaving on the basis of a child's simple faith, i.e. behaving outside of what
we've gotten used to by now. Today, after having departed from a second road
(the one represented by "society"), I feel again much closer to the first one. It's
easier to practice religious matters as a member of a community. I've searched
for access to such a community; I did believe I had found friendship within this
stratum of society, but it all miscarried because of that very same society; and all
that remained was a deep contempt for these Jewish circles, which made any
further intimacy with them quite impossible. And the other Jews (both the
assimilated ones and the Zionists) are impossible anyway. So that leaves only the
third road: to find the way back to one's childhood faith very gradually in the
course of one's own human development. This takes a long time and leads
through many detours—but it is the crowning of every major achievement—
because the one great truth must be something very simple.

And I'm looking for friendship only among my equals, after I had found
it and lost it so quickly with Busoni. The Kaisers are trying to fill that void
in my life and this touching attempt by itself makes me love them.

What presents did I get? A beautiful tablecloth, six raw silk handkerchiefs,
six Hutschenreuth tea cups, books and cigarettes and from Lello [Rafaello
Busoni] and Hide [his wife] a large basket with fruit, tobacco, preserves,
Chianti, Schnaps, sweets, etc.

1925 – 1928

Slowly I'm beginning to advance toward "my real self."
My music is getting to be much freer, looser, and simpler.

Kurt Weill

1925

January 22 *Das Stundenbuch* (1923–25, Rainer Maria Rilke). Berlin Philharmonic Hall; Manfred Lewandowsky, baritone; Berlin Philharmonic Orchestra; Heinz Unger, conductor. Manuscript partly lost.

March Completes *Der Protagonist*, op. 15, his first mature opera.

May Moves with Lenya to an apartment owned by Georg Kaiser: Berlin-Charlottenburg, Luisenplatz 3, bei Hassfort. The poet-playwright Rudolph Leonhardt shares this address, as do Iwan and Claire Goll. Weill and Lenya live here for more than three years.

May 11 The Funkstunde Berlin broadcasts an "Evening of the November Group," which includes Brecht's recitation of his "Ballade vom Mazeppa" and "Die höflichen Chinesen." Weill reviews the broadcast in *Der deutsche Rundfunk*, 24 May 1925.

June 11 *Konzert für Violine und Blasorchester*, op. 12 (April–June 1924). Théâtre de l'Exposition des Arts Décoratifs, Paris; Marcel Darrieux, violin; Walter Straram, conductor. Although Joseph Szigeti was pleased that Weill dedicated the concerto to him, he apparently never performed it.

July–September Composes the cantata *Der neue Orpheus*, op. 15 [i.e. 16], set to Goll's text.

October Begins composing the one-act opera *Royal Palace*, op. 17, which he completes in January 1926.

October 29 Attends German premiere of his violin concerto in Dessau.

December 27 Presumably the first performance of Weill's music in America (*Zaubernacht* at the Garrick Theater, New York).

1926

January 28 Marries Lotte Lenya, née Karoline Wilhelmine Charlotte Blamauer, in a civil ceremony in the Charlottenburg section of Berlin.

March Begins composing the comic opera *Na und?* to a text by Felix Joachimson.

March 27 *Der Protagonist* (1924–25, Georg Kaiser). Dresden Staatsoper; Fritz Busch, conductor; Josef Gielen, director. The premiere of *Der Protagonist* marks Weill's first major success in the German theater. Other performances soon follow in Nuremberg and Erfurt.

June 18–July Travels to Zurich with Lenya for a performance of his violin concerto at the fourth festival of the Société Internationale de Musique Contemporaine, after which they vacation in Milan, Genoa, Verona, Alassio, and Cannes. Violinist Stefan Frenkel replaces an ailing Alma Moodie; Fritz Busch conducts.

September 1 *Herzog Theodor von Gothland* (1926, incidental music for a radio performance of the play by Christian Dietrich Grabbe). Berliner Rundfunk; Bruno Seidler-Winkler, conductor. Lost.

1927

March? Weill meets Brecht, and they begin collaboration on the opera *Aufstieg und Fall der Stadt Mahagonny*.

March 2 *Der neue Orpheus* (1925, Iwan Goll) and *Royal Palace* (1925–26, Iwan Goll). Berlin Staatsoper Unter den Linden; Delia Reinhardt, soprano; Rudolf Deman, violinist; Erich Kleiber, conductor.

March–August Composes the one-act opera *Der Zar lässt sich photographieren* op. 21, to a libretto by Georg Kaiser.

Mid-March Receives a commission from the Deutsches Kammermusikfest in Baden-Baden for a short opera. After searching for a suitable text, Weill decides to set some of Brecht's *Mahagonny-Gesänge*. He finishes the "songspiel" in May.

April *Na und?* (March 1926–March 1927, Felix Joachimson). Two-act comic opera, unperformed. Universal Edition rejects the composition; only sketches survive.

May 4 Travels to Nuremberg to attend rehearsals and a production of *Der Protagonist*.

July 17 *Mahagonny Songspiel* (Bertolt Brecht). Deutsches Kammermusikfest, Baden-Baden; Ernst Mehlich, conductor; Bertolt Brecht, director (with Walther Brügmann). The other works on the program are *Die Prinzessin auf der Erbse* by Ernst Toch, *Die Entführung der Europa* by Darius Milhaud, and *Hin und zurück* by Paul Hindemith. This performance marks Lenya's first appearance in a work by Weill.

August Visits Lenya in Prerow on the Baltic Sea.

October 29 *Gustav III* (October 1927, incidental music for the play by Strindberg). Theater an der Königgrätzer Straße, Berlin; Walter Goehr, conductor; Victor Barnowsky, director.

November 23 *Vom Tod im Wald*, op. 23 (September 1927, Bertolt Brecht). Berlin Philharmonic; Heinrich Hermanns, bass; Eugen Lang, conductor. This is the last of Weill's works to bear an opus number.

December 14 *Klops-Lied* (September 1925, Jean de Bourgois [pseudonym]). Private performance.

87. The intersection of Friedrichstraße and Unter den Linden, in the center of Berlin, 1926.

1928

January 2   Is one of eight nominees to the Prussian Academy of Arts but is not elected.

February 18   *Der Zar lässt sich photographieren* (1927, Georg Kaiser). Leipzig Neues Theater; Gustav Brecher, conductor; Walther Brügmann, director. The one-act opera had thirty-nine performances in ten different productions during its first season. The next season brought seventy-five performances in twenty-six different productions.

March 10   *Leben Eduards des Zweiten von England* (incidental music for the play by Bertolt Brecht and Lion Feuchtwanger). Fragment survives.

April 8   *Konjunktur* (March 1928, incidental music for the play by Leo Lania with song texts by Felix Gasbarra). Partly missing. Lessing Theater, Berlin; Erwin Piscator, director.

April 25   *Katalaunische Schlacht* (March 1928, incidental music for the play by Arnolt Bronnen). Manuscript missing. Staatliches Schauspielhaus, Berlin; Heinz Hilpert, director.

May   Travels with Lenya to the south of France to work with Brecht on *Die Dreigroschenoper*, stopping in Paris to discuss a production of *Der Zar lässt sich photographieren* with Mme. Bériza-Grévin. They stay at Hostellerie de la Plage, St. Cyr sur Mer. Brecht, Helene Weigel, and Elisabeth Hauptmann stay at a rented villa in Le Lavandou.

June 9   Travels to Frankfurt to supervise rehearsals for a *Zar-Protagonist* double bill.

August 31   *Die Dreigroschenoper* (May–September 1928, Bertolt Brecht). Theater am Schiffbauerdamm, Berlin; Theo Mackeben, conductor; Erich Engel, director. *Die Dreigroschenoper* becomes an instant hit, and theaters throughout Germany announce future productions. At Weill's insistence Universal Edition produces popular editions of the songs.

October   Moves to a new address: Berlin-Westend, Bayernallee 14.

October 14   Berlin premiere of *Der Protagonist* and *Der Zar lässt sich photographieren* in a double bill at the Städtische Oper Berlin, directed by Walther Brügmann and conducted by Robert F. Denzler.

October 15   *Berlin im Licht* (October 1928, text probably by either Brecht or Weill). Military band version: Wittenbergplatz; Hermann Scherchen, conductor. Song version: 16 October 1928; Krolloper; Paul Graetz, voice.

November–December   Composes *Das Berliner Requiem* to poems by Brecht.

November 20   *Petroleuminseln* (November 1928, songs and incidental music for the play by Lion Feuchtwanger). Berlin Staatstheater; Jürgen Fehling, director.

December 15   Music from *Quodlibet* is used to accompany a showing of Lotte Reiniger's film *Doktor Dolittle und seine Tiere* at the Alhambra Theater in Berlin. Paul Dessau arranged music by Weill and Hindemith for the event and composed his own music for one part of the film; he also conducted the Alhambra Movie Orchestra.

---

1 9 2 5

MUSIC + THEATER:	LITERATURE + FILM:	SCIENCE + SOCIETY:	POLITICS:
Alban Berg *Wozzeck*	Franz Kafka *Der Prozeß* (posth.)	The Charleston becomes the fashionable dance	Hindenburg elected president of Germany
Franz Lehár *Paganini*	*Potemkin* (film by Sergei Eisenstein)	One million radio sets in Germany	French troops pull out of the Ruhr area
Ferruccio Busoni *Doktor Faust* (posth.)	*The Gold Rush* (film by Charlie Chaplin)	Neue Sachlichkeit exhibition opens in Mannheim	Hitler reorganizes Nazi Party, publishes *Mein Kampf*

88. Weill as pictured in the program for the premiere of *Der Protagonist* (March 1926). Photo by Becker & Maaß.

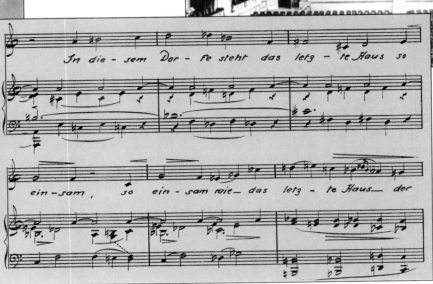

90. First page of a copyist's vocal score of one song from *Stundenbuch*, "In diesem Dorfe steht das letzte Haus." Weill's setting of Rainer Maria Rilke's poem was first performed on 22 January 1925 in the Berlin Philharmonic Hall (top right) with Heinz Unger conducting the Berlin Philharmonic Orchestra and Manfred Lewandowsky singing.

PULT UND TAKTSTOCK

FACHZEITSCHRIFT FÜR DIRIGENTEN

2. JAHRGANG — HEFT 6

Die großen Erfolge des

Pariser Musikfestes

Mai 1925

Alfredo Casella
Elegia eroica
(Dem unbekannten Soldaten)
U. E. Nr. 6983 Partitur Mk. 25·—

Vittorio Rieti
Concerto
für Blasquintett
und Streicher
U. E. Nr. 7613 Partitur . Mk. 15·—

"Ein lustiges, keckes, geistreiches Werk, dessen heimlichen, verführerischen Reiz man nicht analysieren kann. Eine außerordentliche Freiheit der Inspiration, Humor, fließen der melodischer Schwung und eine geradezu bezaubernde Technik zeigen einen geborenen Musiker, der neue und unfehlbare Effekte hervorzuzaubern weiß."
Excelsior.

Béla Bartók
Tanzsuite
U. E. Nr. 7545 Partitur Mk. 25·—
(Vergl. beiliegenden Prospekt)

Kurt Weill
Konzert
für Geige und Bläser
(in Vorbereitung)

"Weill ist einer der weulgen Deutschen, die hier Verständnis finden. Das Konzert zeigt ihn in seiner Reifezeit. Die Musik hat Nerven und Muskeln, ist rhythmisch sehr vital, ist stolz und von einer Spannkraft, die im Zaume schäumt. Es gefällt die Klarheit seines Stils."
Berliner Börsencourier.

Karol Szymanowski
Violinkonzert op. 35
U. E. Nr. 7260 Partitur Mk. 20 —
U. E. Nr. 6624 Kl.-Ausz. Mk. 6·—

"Die Ehre des Abends gebührt ihm. Ein Werk allerersten Ranges, so kühn und reich an Rhythmus, so voll orchestraler Feinheiten, wie die Schöpfungen der modernen Russen, voll melodischer Reize, sinnlich und abgeklärt zugleich."
L'oeuvre.

Universal-Edition A. G., Wien — New York

89. Weill and Lenya lived from 1925–1928 in Georg Kaiser's apartment at Luisenplatz 3, in the Charlottenburg section of Berlin. Iwan Goll lived in the same building for a time.

91. One of the earliest advertisements placed by Universal Edition for Weill's music called attention to the success of his violin concerto in Paris at a three-day festival of the local section of the International Society for Contemporary Music. Marcel Darrieux played and Walter Straram conducted. The announcement appeared in the June 1925 issue of Universal Edition's magazine for conductors, *Pult & Taktstock*.

Weill (in Berlin) to Albert and Emma Weill, 15 July 1925: The people at the radio station are talking more and more about hiring me as permanent musical editor. This gives them the advantage of not having to pay me for each line—and as for me, I will have quite a decent steady income. On the other hand, of course, I'm much more tied down and will have to go to the editor's office frequently, etc. But the mornings remain free for my work—that's the main thing. And sooner or later there'll be all kinds of money rolling in from the compositions (I can see Mother's face when she reads this sentence). The Paris performance did a lot for me.

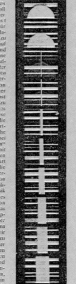

92. Weill began as a freelance writer for *Der deutsche Rundfunk* in late 1924. This cover is from the 30 November 1924 issue. His first front-page article, which appeared in the 28 June 1925 issue with the headline "Possibilities of Absolute Radio Art," is inspired by a flowering of experimental film. (The article is illustrated with excerpts of "absolute films" by Walter Ruttmann, who was to create the documentary *Berlin—Die Sinfonie der Großstadt* in 1927, and Viking Eggeling.) In his article Weill explores the relatively young medium of radio, pointing out two major effects: the social impact of the emergence of radio as a mass medium, and the steady technical progress that creates the possibility of incorporating natural and artificial sound effects into music, thereby creating an art form which is true to its medium and thus highly original.

93. In 1923, the director of the Mannheim Kunsthalle, G. F. Hartlaub, coined the term *Neue Sachlichkeit* [New Objectivity] as the title for an exhibition of paintings and prints. He distinguished between two directions: one that tended toward classicism, and another that showed "the true face of our time" by "the negation of art." After the exhibition opened on 14 June 1925, the term started to be applied to other arts as well. In music its use coincided with the call for socially relevant art, often referred to as "Gebrauchsmusik."

Weill (in Berlin) to Universal Edition, 18 August 1925: I found a review of the violin concerto in the *Revue musicale* by Prunière. Here are (in translation) the most important sentences: "K. W., only 25 years old, is one of the most talented musicians of the young German school . . . he possesses quite an extraordinary technique. . . . One must acknowledge the composer's polyphonic sense as well as his remarkable skill in weighing and balancing the orchestral sounds. In its way K. W.'s concerto is a completely effective work."

I just completed a new piece: *Der neue Orpheus*, concertino for soprano, violin and orchestra (text by Iwan Goll).

Or, ce concerto, écrit avec une rare ingéniosité, demeure dans l'atmosphère un peu grise des oeuvres de l'école allemande issue de Max Reger. Il se divise en deux mouvements, un Andante majestueux et massif et un Finale très vif en forme de tarantelle. Trois mouvements épisodiques viennent s'interposer entre l'Andante et l'Allegro. L'écriture est constamment tendue. La trame contrapontique est d'une finesse excessive. Musique dense et serrée. Pas d'air, pas de lumière. Je conçois fort bien que le public ne soit pas séduit par une oeuvre si peu faite pour plaire, mais on doit reconnaître la remarquable habileté de l'auteur dans l'art de doser et d'équilibrer les sonorités de l'orchestre et son sens de polyphonie. En son genre le Concerto de Kurt Weill est une oeuvre parfaitement réussie. — *La revue musicale* 10 (1925): 145.

94. Weill composed *Der neue Orpheus* during July-August 1925 to a text by Iwan Goll (pictured above). Delia Reinhardt sang the premiere in a triple bill at the Berlin Staatsoper Unter den Linden on 2 March 1927 with Erich Kleiber conducting and Rudolf Deman playing the violin solo.

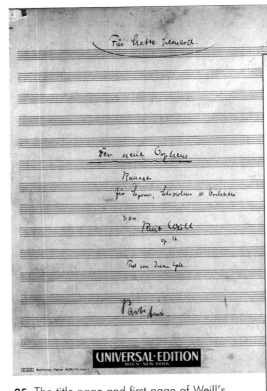

95. The title page and first page of Weill's autograph full score of *Der neue Orpheus.*

96. *Der neue Orpheus* makes reference to composers and music from the past, for instance to Gustav Mahler in Variation 6 and in the violin cadenza to Gluck's "Che farò senza Euridice" from *Orfeo ed Euridice*.

97. Weill dedicated *Der neue Orpheus* to Lotte Leonard, a Berlin-based soprano with an international reputation as a Bach and Handel singer. The performance he apparently had planned for her never materialized.

Weill (in Berlin) to Universal Edition, 22 August 1925: Important news! Busch called to ask me to come to Dresden yesterday. He wants to produce *Der Protagonist* as soon as possible (probably on 8 October!!). [Kurt] Taucher, the best tenor for the title role and on whose decision the acceptance depended, has already agreed in principle. On Tuesday Busch will show him the piano reduction; after that the final decision will be made. But Taucher is leaving for America at the end of October, after that I would have to wait until May for the premiere. But doing it now means that it would be the first event of the winter (also for Berlin). There's no danger that such great haste will hurt the performance since Busch himself will conduct.

Weill (in Berlin) to Universal Edition, 28 August 1925: Many thanks for your news. I am very happy that I was able to bring off the surprising acceptance in Dresden after all. General M[usic Director] Busch told me that the piano reduction will be prepared in Dresden and taken over by you. Please see to it that the dedication:

"Für Lenja"

appears on the title page (it is not on the manuscript, but I attach great importance to its being added!). I have changed the title; the work is now entitled: "Kulissen," one-act opera by Georg Kaiser, music by K.W. I will negotiate with Szenkar and Schulz-Dornburg regarding further acceptances. Things look especially favorable in Coburg, where my friend Albert Bing (who has written to me very enthusiastically about my opera) has become opera director.

In a few weeks I will receive the finished libretto for a new full-length stage work, a kind of operetta [*Na und?*], which I plan to compose in the course of this winter. . . . In view of the favorable outcome of the opera question you will not consider it immodest if I broach the financial question again. The fall looks very bad for me. I have no students and any other job would prevent my writing the new stage work. Since Director Hertzka has given me repeated firm assurances that with an acceptance in Dresden nothing would stand in the way of an increase and extension of my installments, I can, with a clear conscience, request that the monthly sum be set at 200 marks (immediately, if possible).

Weill (in Berlin) to Albert and Emma Weill, 17 September 1925: On Sunday, the Dresden stage director [Josef] Gielen will be coming to see me for a thorough pre-production meeting. Up to now I've not seen any scenic sketches or even a rehearsal, and you can imagine how curious I am. But you already have an idea how nerve-wracking it is for the composer during rehearsals of just an orchestral work. How much worse will it be with a stage work? The only thing that helps is a good deal of nerve and and an I-don't-give-a-damn attitude, both of which I have acquired in the course of time.

My string quartet is making a pilgrimage through nine cities in Spain. A strange feeling. But my best piece is now finished: *Der neue Orpheus*, cantata for soprano, solo violin and orchestra. Lotte Leonard is going to sing it.

Weill (in Berlin) to Universal Edition, 26 September 1925: I was in Dresden again yesterday and have finally come to the conclusion that it would be to my advantage after all to postpone the premiere of *Der Protagonist*. The work was already more than three-fourths rehearsed, and we could easily have met the 8 October deadline if Taucher hadn't suddenly lost his head out of nervousness over his America trip. Taucher, who really is the most ideal embodiment of the role and someone whom I would replace only with great reluctance, must leave for America on 12 November; in other words, the opera could only be done two, at most three times. Naturally that would be very detrimental for its success. Taucher himself, Busch, and the stage director Gielen are all firmly convinced that with Taucher in the title role, *Der Protagonist* could be a sensational success. They are constantly assuring me how much they are enjoying the work and how much they regret delaying it. Taucher has promised to have the role completely learned by the time he returns from America on *1 March*; the premiere would then take place on 20 March, whereupon the work will remain in repertory throughout April and, most important, it will be the only work by a young composer in the big opera festival that the Dresden State Opera is planning for May. Finally, I will tell you in confidence that in the very near future I will be getting a new libretto (half opera, half ballet) [*Royal Palace*] that I hope to finish by early 1926 and to place on the same evening in Dresden.

Weill (in Berlin) to Universal Edition, 15 October 1925: I find it absolutely incomprehensible that you delay so long in publishing my works. After Frenkel received first proofs of the violin concerto to correct several days ago, I continue to wait in vain for my own set of proofs to correct. At this rate it will of course be impossible to publish the violin concerto in time for the Dessau performance, a date you have known for months. You suffer the damage since I am very well known in Dessau and you could probably have sold a significant number of copies there. *Quodlibet*, too, which you've had for a year and which I proofread months ago, will appear too late to arrange a performance. I hope that it won't be the same story with *Der neue Orpheus*. It is extremely important to me that these pieces be published as soon as possible. I have prospects with Furtwängler, Klemperer, and Scherchen, but I can exploit them only if I receive the full score and piano reduction very, very soon. . . . Today I can inform you that I am working on a new opera, a ballet-like one-act opera, *Royal Palace*, text by Iwan Goll (a wonderful libretto). In addition I have begun a ballet *Maschinen*, by Terpis, that will be done here at the Staatsoper. I am also going to get a new libretto from Georg Kaiser and, finally, a young writer here is working on a full-length opera text for me according to my specifications. Since this is a good time to work, I hope to accomplish a great deal on these projects this winter.

Weill (in Dessau) to Lotte Lenya, [28 October 1925]: Hoesslin is actually quite incompetent. He can neither conduct nor rehearse; it's awful. People laugh and play wrong notes all the time (which he doesn't even notice), and there is not a trace of discipline. . . . I was stupid to give this somewhat rough, abstract, completely dissonant piece [Violin Concerto] to the Dessauers, who are the most ignorant and philistine of all. It will be unanimously rejected. You have to have willingly digested a portion of Schoenberg before you can understand this music.

Weill (in Berlin) to Universal Edition, 30 October 1925: Yesterday I attended the German premiere of the violin concerto in Dessau. The performance was not ideal, but Frenkel played beautifully. It was very successful, considering

Weill (in Berlin) to Emma and Albert Weill, [October 1925]: Sometimes I wish I could share in your lives more than I'm capable of doing. But I'm now going through that period in which an artist is constantly sitting on a powderkeg, where unused energies build up and explode, where an increased hypersensitivity creates a permanent condition of tension and excitement. Only by realizing this could you understand some things which perhaps seem incomprehensible to you. Right now, it's taken hold of me again. I am dug into this new opera [*Royal Palace*] and am leaving the house only to take care of the most necessary superficial things. I have to master an expression which is still new to me. And to my joy I can state—something I had already discovered in *Der neue Orpheus*—that slowly I'm beginning to advance toward "my real self," that my music is getting to be much freer, looser and—simpler. But that has to do with the fact that outwardly I've become more independent, more secure and less tense. Of course, living with Lenja has a great deal to do with this. It has helped me a lot. It's also the only way in which I can tolerate another person next to me: the coordination of two artistic interests connected by an inner bond which in its way furthers one and the other. How long will it last? I hope, a long time.

the reactionary audience which completely rejected the preceding dance suite by Bartók. What a shame that the piano reduction was not finished in time!

Weill (in Berlin) to Emma and Albert Weill, 7 November 1925: This goddamned stinking hole of Dessau has left me in such a state of depression that for days now I've been of no use to anyone. Never before have I experienced such a haughty, disapproving atmosphere as among these riff-raff. Since they responded with complete silence to the *Tanzweise* by Bartók—one of the most worthwhile, easily understandable contemporary works, which has received stormy applause in sixty cities—I couldn't possibly expect any success for my concerto. Besides, the set-up there is unfortunate. Hoesslin is very unpopular, and rightly so. I couldn't believe that such a degree of incompetence would be possible. The performance was bad except for the violinist, who was excellent. The reviews are completely negative, and as long as Mr. von Hoesslin holds the reins there, Dessau won't see me again.

Weill (in Berlin) to Emma and Albert Weill, 14 December 1925: I'm having a bad week right now. We have to get three issues [of *Der deutsche Rundfunk*] ready for the editor's office, one right after the other, so I've got to go into town every day. But I feel very good, especially when I'm sitting behind my desk. Last week I was supposed to participate in a musical tea party at [Gustav] Stresemann's; when the secretary called me, I told them to try [Philipp] Jarnach, the only composer who owns a dress suit. Instead, yesterday I went to a ball given by the *Börsen-Courier*, and today I'm going with Kaiser to the premiere of *Wozzeck*, an ultramodern opera (by Alban Berg). There was already a scandal during the dress rehearsal. In three months I'll be ready for one too.

Weill (in Berlin) to Albert Weill, 1 January 1926: I don't believe you could have the slightest notion of what it means to complete an opera of almost one hour's duration in just two and a half months. If I didn't have this heavenly quiet apartment and hadn't gotten rid of all social obligations, it wouldn't have been possible. I have rather high hopes for this new opera [*Royal Palace*] and I believe that it represents an important step forward in my development. During the Christmas holidays I spent one day with the Kaisers in Grünheide; but by the next evening I had to be back in the editor's office. The Kaisers are very good friends, and I had a long, very honest discussion with Georg.

98. ca. 1926.

99. Weill and Lenya married on 28 January 1926 in a civil ceremony in Charlottenburg. Lenya referred to this photo as their wedding picture. She recalled later: "We were quite poor at the time. Kurt was making money by giving music and theory lessons. He has our dinner here in a paper bag, which was some kind of herring and jelly. And I got some autumn leaves from the park in the back to decorate the table, and this was our wedding dinner."

Nr. 13.   1. April 1926.

Blätter der Staatsoper

Inhalt: Kurt Weill, Bekenntnis zur Oper — Adolf Aber, Goethe und Berlioz, Das Schicksal einer „Faust"-Musik

Kurt Weill
Bekenntnis zur Oper

Wir können nicht mit dem Snobbismus teilnahmslosen Verzichtes an die Oper herangehen. Wir können nicht Opern schreiben und zugleich über die Unzulänglichkeit dieser Gattung jammern. Wir können nicht in der Opernkomposition die Erfüllung einer rein äußerlichen Pflicht sehen, während wir unsere wahren Inhalte in anderen Formen erschöpfen. Wir müssen in den Gegebenheiten der Bühne unser Formideal erfüllt wissen, wir müssen überzeugt sein, daß das Bühnenwerk die wesentlichen Elemente unserer Musik wiederzugeben vermag, wir müssen uns jubelnd zur Oper bekennen. — Das Bewußtsein, daß der Gattung des Musikdramas nichts mehr hinzuzufügen oder zu entlocken war, machte uns zu Fanatikern der absoluten Musik. Wir wollten unser Jahrhundert gegen das vorige behaupten, das wir mit einem literarischen Einschlag, mit einer Materialisierung der Kunst belasteten. Musik sollte wieder der einzige Selbstzweck unseres Schaffens sein. Aus der Beschäftigung mit Bach und Vorklassikern und aus der Pflege der Kammermusik konnte eine Intensivierung des musikalischen Erlebens entstehen. Und doch konnte man

Rundfunkempfänger
Lautsprecher nach Prof. Dr. Koch
KOCH & STERZEL A.G. DRESDEN

100. Weill's essay "Bekenntnis zur Oper" appeared in conjunction with the premiere of *Der Protagonist* in Dresden, March 1926. *Blätter der Staatsoper Dresden,* Spielzeit 1925-26, no. 13 (April 1926): 97-99.

Seite 98.   Blätter der Staatsoper.   Nr. 13.

sich zu einer vollständigen Vernachlässigung der Opernbühne nicht entschließen. Die einen lockte die Möglichkeit breiterer Auswirkung, die andern die Gegensätzlichkeit zur eigenen Empfindung. Man schrieb Ballette, — d. h. man bereicherte die Wirkung der Konzertmusik um einen optischen Eindruck. Aber der Tanz gestaltete sich nach den Gesetzen der Musik, und es fehlte das Tempo der Bühne. Und durch die Verachtung dieses Bühnentempos glauben viele die Berechtigung ihres Nur-Musikertums zu beweisen.

Wesentlich ist die Erkenntnis, daß wir nicht mit einer musikalischen Umstellung an das Bühnenwerk herangehen dürfen, daß wir uns in der Oper mit der gleichen ungebundenen Phantasieentfaltung ausmusizieren müssen wie in der Kammermusik. Aber es kann sich nicht darum handeln, die Elemente der absoluten Musik in die Oper zu übernehmen; das wäre der Weg zur Kantate, zum Oratorium. Sondern umgekehrt: der dramatische Auftrieb, den die Oper verlangt, kann wesentlicher Bestandteil jeder musikalischen Produktion sein. Mozart lehrte mich das. Er ist in der Oper kein anderer als in der Sinfonie, im Streichquartett. Er besitzt immer das Tempo der Oper, darum kann er absoluter Musiker bleiben, auch wenn er den grausigen Höllenlärm über Don Giovanni hereinbrechen läßt. Wenn also unsere Musik die typisch opernhaften Elemente: die straffe Akzentuierung, die Prägnanz der Dynamik, die sprechende Bewegtheit der Melodie besitzt, so kann uns die Oper das kostbarste Gefäß sein, um Ströme inneren Gesanges aufzunehmen.

Erst als ich spürte, daß meine Musik die Gespanntheit szenischer Vorgänge enthält, wandte ich mich der Bühne zu. Ich schrieb für eine russische Truppe im Theater am Kurfürstendamm die Pantomime „Zaubernacht". An der geballten Konzentriertheit russischer Theaterkunst lernte ich zweierlei:

Alle Drucksachen
von den einfachsten bis zu den modernsten
Kaden & Comp.
Dresden, Wettinerpl. 10

Nr. 13.   Blätter der Staatsoper.   Seite 99.

daß die Bühne ihre eigene musikalische Form hat, deren Gesetzmäßigkeit organisch aus dem Ablauf der Handlung erwächst, und daß Bedeutsames szenisch nur mit den einfachsten, unauffälligsten Mitteln gesagt werden kann. Ein Orchester von neun Mann, eine Sängerin, zwei Tänzerinnen und eine Anzahl von Kindern — das war der Apparat dieses getanzten Traumes. Es hatte mir Freude gemacht, und ich war beglückt, als Georg Kaiser sich erbot, mir eine große, abendfüllende Balletthandlung zu schreiben. Wir gingen gemeinsam an die Arbeit. In zehn Wochen entstanden fast drei Viertel des Werkes. Die Partitur des Vorspiels und der beiden ersten Akte war vollendet. Da stockte es. Wir waren über den Stoff hinausgewachsen, die Schweigsamkeit dieser Figuren quälte uns, wir mußten die Fesseln dieser Pantomime sprengen: es mußte Oper werden. Georg Kaiser griff auf ein älteres Stück zurück, das früher schon in Gedanken an die Oper konzipiert worden war, den Einakter „Der Protagonist". Hier hatten wir das, was wir suchten: ein zwangloses unabsichtliches Ineinandergreifen von Oper und Pantomime. Das übersteigerte Schauspielertum des Protagonisten konnte nur in einer Opernfigur gestaltet, die großen Momente der Handlung nur durch Musik ausgedrückt werden: die Aussprache zwischen Bruder und Schwester, die heimlich hastige Liebesszene, der Übergang ins Tänzerische und der plötzliche Umschwung vom Heiteren ins Tragische. Die beiden Pantomimen gaben Gelegenheit zu lyrischer Entfaltung. Um dem ganzen Geschehen noch einen musikalischen Rahmen zu geben, erteilte ich den acht Musikanten gewissermaßen die Rolle des Chores in der antiken Tragödie: sie sollen das Drama eröffnen, sollen es in passiver Haltung begleiten, bis sie selbst eingreifen, und sollen am Schluß die Vorstellung erwecken, als seien wir nun Gäste des Herzogs und erlebten das einzigartige Spiel des Protagonisten.

Ein vornehmes Geschenk
für unsere Damen, das immer geschätzt wird und zu jeder Zeit anspricht, sei es im Winter für Theater und Ball, sei es im Sommer für die Reise, ist unstreitig ein schönes seidenes Kleid oder eine seidene Bluse
Seidenhaus Carl Schneider, Dresden, Altmarkt 8

1 9 2 6

MUSIC + THEATER:
Paul Hindemith *Cardillac*
George Antheil *Ballet mécanique*
Duke Ellington's first records appear

LITERATURE + FILM:
Franz Kafka *Das Schloß* (posth.)
Ernst Lubitsch leaves Berlin for Hollywood
Metropolis (film by Fritz Lang)

SCIENCE + SOCIETY:
J. M. Keynes *The End of Laissez-Faire*
Lufthansa Airline founded in Berlin
Gertrude Ederle (U.S.), first woman to swim the English Channel

POLITICS:
Germany admitted to League of Nations
Joseph Goebbels becomes *Gauleiter* of Nazi Party in Berlin
British troops pull out of Cologne

DER PROTAGONIST

Opera in one act; libretto by Georg Kaiser

1926 Dresden, Staatsoper (27 March)
Fritz Busch, conductor; Josef Gielen, director;
Adolf Mahnke, designer

Erfurt, Stadttheater (3 December)
1927 Nuremberg, Neues Stadttheater (5 May)
1928 *Altenburg, Landestheater (8 April)
Gera, Landestheater (22 April)
*Frankfurt, Städtische Bühnen (19 June)
*Berlin, Städtische Oper (14 October)
*Stuttgart, Landestheater (15 December)
1929 *Hannover, Städtische Bühnen (26 February)
Leipzig, Neues Theater (27 February)

1930-31 Essen, Städtische Bühnen

*performed with *Der Zar lässt sich photographieren*

101. Weill, conductor Fritz Busch, intendant Alfred Reucker, and director Josef Gielen before the premiere of *Der Protagonist*, March 1926.

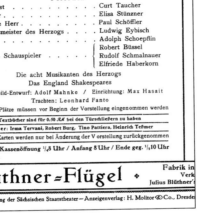

Weill (in Berlin) to Emma and Albert Weill, 1 April 1926: What do you say to this fabulous press? [Oskar] Bie's review, which I've just forwarded, is in his own opinion the best thing he's ever written about opera. Today's (Tuesday) *Dresdner Neueste Nachrichten* is fantastic, too. It really is exciting to become a world celebrity overnight. I find those few bad reviews very handy, too, because a unanimously favorable press would make the demands on me unbearably high.

Weill (in Berlin) to Emma and Albert Weill, 8 April 1926: Don't be angry about my silence. Last Saturday we drove out to the Kaisers'. It was quite wonderful out there, we sailed for hours, every afternoon there was a big bicycle tour, and in the evening marvelous Bordeaux. Kaiser is in a very good creative period, and we're already working on a sketch for a new opera subject [*Der Zar*]. I came home yesterday. Lenja will stay until the beginning of next week, because she is much in need of a rest.

Every day there are new reviews from newspapers in the provinces. The *Frankfurter Zeitung*, which is especially important, was excellent, also Breslau, Mannheim, Vienna, etc. I already have twenty rave reviews, ten of which are big feature stories. It was simply *the* big operatic success of the season. I don't know yet what the ramifications will be. . . . The people around me paid less attention, because my circle of acquaintances consists mostly of "colleagues" whose enthusiasm, understandably, does not express itself as noisily. Right now there are all sorts of intrigues against acceptance by a local opera house, and since my success has isolated me even more, a Berlin performance probably will not happen.

102. The Protagonist (Kurt Taucher) and his Sister (Elisa Stünzner) in the Dresden premiere of the opera.

103. Photo from the Dresden production of *Der Protagonist* showing Rudolf Schmalnauer, Robert Büssel, Kurt Taucher, and Elfriede Haberkorn. Photo by Ursula Richter.

Der Protagonist.

Dresdner Opernhaus.

Dieser erste Schauspieler und Direktor einer fahrenden Bühne in altenglischer Zeit wäre nicht ein so wertvoller Mensch, wenn er nicht trotz seiner leidenschaftlichen Begeisterung für seinen Beruf das Bedürfnis hätte, gegen die Lüge der Maske stets die Liebe zur Wahrheit bereit zu halten. Seine Schwester wird ihm dieser Wahrheitsspiegel. Ein Blick in ihr Auge und er ist den Teufel der Bühne los. Sie hat ihn nie getäuscht. Nur dies eine Mal hatte sie geschwiegen, von ihrer eigenen Herzensangelegenheit. Sie taumelt in Liebe. Sie taumelt in seinen Beruf hinein, in eine Probe der Pantomime. Der Schauspieler ist so bestürzt über die Entdeckung dieses Geheimnisses, daß er sie in der Erregung seiner Rolle wirklich niedersticht. Der Beruf tötet das Leben, das Leben zerstört den Beruf.

Georg Kaiser hat dieses Doppelspiel von Bühne und Leben zuerst als selbständigen Einakter herausgegeben, dann mit kleinen Aenderungen als Operntext gestellt. Er schöpft den Doppelsinn aus. Er denkt sich eine Aufführung vor einem Herzog, die geprobt wird, erst als buffoneske Pantomime, dann auf neuen Auftrag als tragische. Die tragische Szene geht ins Leben über. Er denkt sich zwei Orchester, eines für die Bühnenvorgänge, eines für das Stück selbst. Es soll alles in seine beiden Seiten zerlegt werden, Spiel und Ernst, komischer und tragischer Stil, Bühne und Leben. Man könnte sagen, es ist eine Kreuzung von Motiven Schnitzlers, von Ariadne und von Bajazzi, wenn es nicht ganz Georg Kaiser wäre in der Symbolik der Idee, der geistreichen Zuspitzung des Falls, der gezierten Kräuselung der Sprache. Es ist nicht so sehr musikalisch empfunden und ausgedrückt, als daß auf dem Untergrunde dieses Schicksals eine Musik ruht, die ein genialer Kopf heraushört und gestaltet.

Kurt Weill, Busonischüler, dessen Arbeiten sofort die Aufmerksamkeit auf seine starke Begabung gelenkt haben, findet diese Musik. Er sucht sie erst im Beginn des Stücks, noch unsicher schwankend, dann sieht er sie, packt sie an, steigert sie und vertieft sie so, daß sie die schwierige Katastrophe, in der die Figuren nur noch Tänzer von Ideen scheinen, vollkommen überwölbt.

Als Material an Instrumenten verwendet er sehr neu und sehr wirkungsvoll die beiden Orchester, unten das des Lebens, mit Streichern, Oboen, Baßklarinetten, Hörnern, Posaunen, Schlagzeug — oben das der Bühne als Oktett von zwei Flöten, zwei Klarinetten, zwei Trompeten, zwei Fagotten. Aber es ist nicht mehr die alte Teilung in Haupt- und Bühnenmusik. Es ist eine doppelte Seele. Die Bühnenmusiker (in Kostüm) steigen nach Ankündigung auf ein Podium im Orchesterraum herab und beteiligen sich an der allgemeinen Symphonie, da ja Bühne zuerst noch Leben ist. Zur Aufführung selbst steigen sie hinauf und begleiten die erste, die lustige Pantomime allein. Die zweite, die tragische Pantomime, spielen sie mit dem unteren Orchester zusammen: das Leben tritt wieder ein. Da das eine siegt, schweigen sie, um am Schluß noch einmal, von der Bühne aus, mit Fanfaren von einer höhnischen Feierlichkeit das Leben anzublasen. Niemals bisher in einer Oper ist die Vielheit von Orchestergruppen so seelisch, so symbolisch gefaßt worden. Es ist nicht hier Orchester, dort Kammermusik, es sind Ausdruckselemente verschiedener Welten, deren Kampf der Inhalt des Stückes ist. Es ist auch ein Drama des Orchesters.

Die Stimme behandelt Weill, der gar nicht naturalistisch, sondern stilisierend eingestellt ist, als ein vokales Instrument, nicht deklamatorisch, auch nicht instrumental, sondern eben als Stimme an sich. Er liebt darum eine neue Melodie mehr, als Rücksicht auf das Wort. Es ist ein wichtiger Weg ins modern Gesangliche hinein, Zukunft der Oper. Das Wort wird an entscheidenden Stellen ganz fallen gelassen. Bei Interjektionen feierlicher, tragischer, spottender Gefühle, die im Ton leben, bei lyrischen Steigerungen, die sich nur noch in der Koloratur aussingen, in dieser neuen Koloratur, die die Worte — Heimlichkeiten, Lüge, Liebe — diese andeutend spielenden Worte auf die singenden Lippen nimmt und in der absoluten Tonsprache des Duetts zergehen läßt, wie späten Schnee auf warmer Erde. Wie oft habe ich diese Perspektive der Oper empfohlen. Nun erlebe ich sie.

Der musikalische Stil von Weill ist etwa zwischen der psychologischen Intellektualität von Busoni und der fast gezeichneten Bläsergraphik von Strawinsky. Aber er ist durchaus eigen, selbständig, von Niemandem abhängig.

104. Oskar Bie's review of *Der Protagonist* appeared in the Berlin *Börsen-Courier*, 29 March 1926.

Er liebt den Bläserklang, der heut überall auf den Streicherton der Romantik reagiert. Jede Romantik, jede Ekstase ist vorüber, landschaftliche und seelische Schatten liegen leicht gebreitet, aber der Ausdruck der Empfindung ist irgendwie gebunden in der Sache der Musik, die ihre großen und starken Nuancen, ihre schweigenden Niederungen aus eigenem Wesen bildet. Es ist Klasse der antiromantischen trotz aller Charakteristik der Typen im Grunde absoluten und nur sich selbst verantwortlichen Musik, die heut über die Welt streicht. Ihre Sprache ist von letzter moderner Freiheit, ohne Grimasse und Bosheit. Sie reift sich im Laufe des Stücks immer mehr aus.

Der Aufbau ist grandios. Der erste Durchbruch erfolgt bei der Ahnung des Schauspielers vom kommenden Wahnsinn. Eine ungeheure Steigerung, auf die das große Sordinato der Liebesszene der Schwester gesetzt ist. Ein Duett, das in reiner Musik zerfließt. Die dummen, hochmütigen Akkorde des Hausmeisters, der die Buffopantomime befiehlt. Der tänzerische Uebergang. Das köstliche parodistische Oktett der oberen Bläser als Illustration der Bufffoneske. Die drolligen Vokalisationen der sprachlosen Spieler, Stimmenquartett zum Bläserakkord. Die erste Flut der schwesterlichen Beichte. Die tragische Pantomime, dunkle Farben, allmählich ein Kontinuo in Holzschlägelpauken, elementar sich verstärkend, h-ois, Riesenschaukel der Tragödie, ausbrechende Schreie der dissonanten Instrumente, reines D-dur der oberen Trompeten als Richter, übrig bleibendes G-moll der unteren Posaunen als Nachklang.

Wieder fuhr man nach Dresden, dem Vorort moderner Oper, gegen dessen Taten wir nur den einzigen „Wozzek", allerdings die Blüte der Gattung, gesetzt haben. Die Leistung ist erstaunlich. Busch dirigiert die gespaltene und vielumschlungene Partitur, als hätte er nie etwas anderes geprobt. Josef Gielen stellt eine sehr wirksame Bühne her, Saal eines Wirtshauses mit Gerüsten, vor die Mahnke die trefflich gemachten Balkonprospekte hängt, erst bunt und lustig, dann umgedreht schwarz und düster. Die beiden Pantomimen werden in der heiteren und tragischen Wendung zwischen zwei Paaren klar und scharf unterschieden gespielt. Curt Taucher ist ganz herrlich als wild bewegter abenteuerlich phantasievoller wahrhaft tragikomischer Held, von einer erfrischenden Kraft und Eindringlichkeit in Stimme, Figur, Bewegung, Gefühl. Die Schwester singt die Stünzner mit aller Liebe zum neuen Stil, unterstützt durch eine geübte Technik. Schöpflin ist der realistisch bedingte Wirt. Alles ist gut und sauber einstudiert, und es scheint keine Hemmung ungewohnter Aufgabe zurückzuhalten oder zu verwirren.

War es ein rein geistiger Genuß? War es verstandesmäßige Entdeckung neuer Opernwelten? Vielleicht war es etwas davon, aber nur im Bewußtsein des Kritikers, der die Fäden der Entwicklung dieses unüberwindlichen Genres in der Hand hält und prüft. Für den nicht philosophischen Theaterbesucher war es unmittelbare Wirkung, Bühnenerlebnis in neuer Form, Tatsache einer musikalischen Begabung, die nicht nur aus Wissen in die Zukunft blickt, sondern aus Können sie sich erobern wird, aus der zwingenden Kraft der Erfindung und Phantasie. Das ist der Schritt des Schülers über den Meister Busoni hinaus.

Bie.

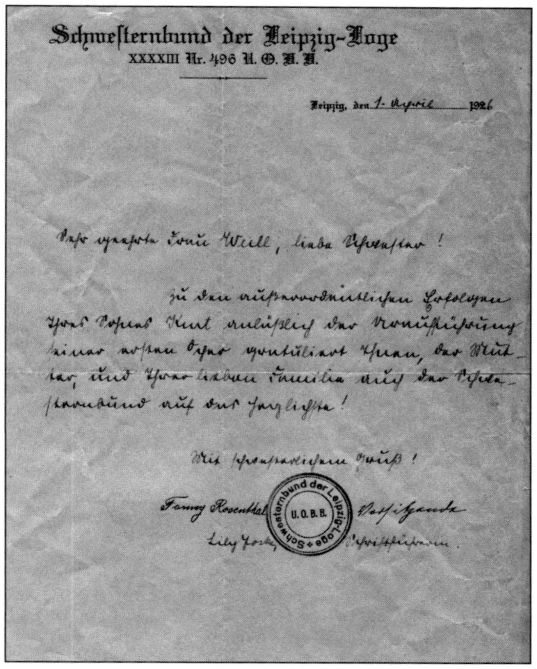

105. The Leipzig Women's Club sent congratulations to Emma Weill on the success of her son's opera.

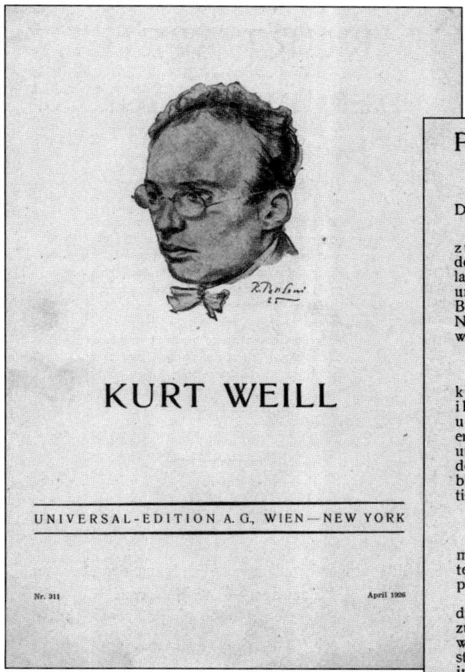

106. The cover of Universal Edition's publicity brochure for *Der Protagonist* featured Rafaello Busoni's drawing of Weill.

PRESSESTIMMEN ZUM „PROTAGONIST"

DRESDNER NEUESTE NACHRICHTEN

Ohne Umschweife: diese „Akt Oper" gibt den Glauben an ein zukünftiges musikalisches Theater wieder. Es wurde ein Weg gefunden, der mit einer kecken Wendung den Tummelplatz romantischer Gefühlsseligkeit verlassen hat, eine Zeit lang wohl durch die anarchischen Gegenden Schönbergs irrte, um plötzlich durch die erleuchtenden Erklärungen, die der geistvolle Wegweiser Busoni dem suchenden Schüler erteilte, in neuentdecktes Land zu führen. Noch steht der Fremdling erstaunt und verwirrt, doch der Weg zielt zur Höhe, wenn er weiter beschritten wird. . . . .

*

Der dramatische Impuls war unverkennbar, die Gegensätzlichkeit der beiden Pantomimen verlockten den Musiker. Und es gelang ihm tatsächlich, die dichterische Idee durch die musikalische unerhört zu steigern. Es gelang ihm sogar da, wo man es am wenigsten erwartet hätte: in der großen Auseinandersetzung zwischen dem Protagonisten und der Schwester, jener problematisch, philosophischen Zwiesprache, die den Sinn der ganzen Dichtung enthält. Es gelang ihm, weil seine Musik völlig unsinnlich bleibt, weil sie nirgends versucht auszudeuten, sondern mit der gleichen dramatischen Spannung geladen ist wie die Szene.

*

Den Umschwung der Stimmung zu charakterisieren, glückt Weill mit rein musikalischen Mitteln, die er mit echtem Theatersinn auswertet. Er teilt sein Orchester und gewinnt durch diese Teilung schon die Betonung der proteischen Idee der Dichtung.

. . . . Ein vortrefflicher Einfall, der bis dahin theoretische, jetzt aber wirklich dramatische Kraft erhält. Diese blasenden Musikanten geben nun allein die Musik zu einer im Kasperlestil travestierenden Pantomime, die durch ihre groteske Komik wirkt. Die Phantasie des Schauspielers ist mit sich allein, dem Leben abgewandt, steigert sich im Glücksgefühl des eigenen Wahnes. In der größten Tollheit dieser improvisierten Eifersuchtskomödie setzt ein Quartett ein, in dem die vier Stimmen der Agierenden nur Vokale singen, das in seiner Drastik zum Besten der Partitur gehört. Die Wahnwelt des Protagonisten erlangt stärkste Intensität. Dann ein plötzlicher Umschwung. Die Komödie wird zur Tragödie. Der imaginäre Herzog, eine Art Jourdain („Ariadne"), eine höhere, unsichtbare Gewalt, verlangt ein ernstes Spiel. Das Leben greift ein, das größere, versenkte Orchester spielt mit. Wirklichkeit und Wahn vermischen sich. Die Stimmung ist von unheimlicher Gewalt. Brennende Doppelsekunden stapfen wie das Schreiten der tragischen Muse selbst. Die Szene wird transparent. Die Musik sagt, was die Dichtung nicht allein sagen konnte. Die schmetternden D-dur-Fanfaren der phantastischen acht Musikanten verkünden schauerlich die Katastrophe des Wahnsinns. Der Vorhang hat sich über dem Spiel der Bühne geschlossen; das Spiel ist Wirklichkeit geworden. Zwischen echtem und gespieltem Wahnsinn gibt es keinen Unterschied mehr.

*

Die ausgesprochene Bühnenbegabung Weills wird auch in der Erscheinung des herzoglichen Hausmeisters deutlich. Dieser kommt zunächst als geschwätziger Hofschranze seines leichtlebigen Herrn, singt alberne Koloraturen und gefällt sich in sinnlosen Tiraden. Er kommt zum zweitenmal — und diese Umwandlung ist Weills eigene Idee —, kommt als düsterer Bote, der das tragische Schicksal heraufbeschwört. Das ist keine leere Symbolik, das ist von packender Dämonie, die mit theatralischen Mitteln wirksam gewonnen wird. Der jubelnde Glücksrausch des Protagonisten wird jäh in schauerliche Verzweiflung verkehrt. Die dramatische Konzeption von Musik und Dichtung dadurch zu unlösbarem Einklang verschmolzen.

Weill (in Berlin) to Universal Edition, 29 April 1926: A well-known German *Generalmusikdirektor* just wrote to me: "When will U.E. begin the customary publicity? I find the silence somewhat puzzling." It's nice to know that impartial musicians have begun to notice your silence regarding *Der Protagonist*. I must confess that this is deeply perturbing to me. Naturally the intendants say to themselves: "If the publisher is so quiet, there can't be much to the success." If the brochure isn't finished yet, you should have at least distributed an announcement. The success of *Der Protagonist* was not one bit less than that of *Wozzeck*, critical response was just as sensational, and in every place where modern operas are discussed, both works are mentioned in the same breath. Everyone who was there can confirm that there has never been such a successful first opera by a 25-year-old. But your conduct makes it look like an ordinary *succès d'estime*. You even continue your tactic of leaving all negotiations for future productions up to me. If you are interested in an acceptance by the Staatsoper here, then I must implore you to take the matter in hand immediately and energetically. Even if I continue to negotiate on my own, there are a few people who aren't well disposed toward me who will attempt to bring the negotiations to a standstill—something they have now achieved since I have heard nothing from either Kleiber or Hörth.

Berlin 9. Juni 1926

107. Letter from Weill to his friend and former pupil, conductor Maurice Abravanel, 9 June 1926. Weill writes: "In the ten weeks since the premiere of *Protagonist* I've been working feverishly, oblivious to my surroundings. . . . Within this span of time I have composed the entire first act of my new (third) opera (1 hour of music). . . . Kleiber has acquired the premiere of my second one-act opera, *Royal Palace*. The work is supposed to come out at the beginning of February under Kleiber and Hörth with sets by Chagall. . . . The work on my new opus, the musiquette *Na und?*, is occupying me more heavily than anything before it. Even when working with a very light and graceful subject matter, it is conspicuous how my dramatic aptitude achieves theatrical effectiveness."

108. Weill family photo from summer 1926 at Weill's parents' home in the Kleinsteinberg suburb of Leipzig. Seated: Leni Weill (wife of Kurt's brother Nathan) holding their daughter, Hannelore; Emma Weill; Lotte Lenya holding Eva Sohn (daughter of Kurt's sister Ruth). Back row: Ella (a maid), Albert Weill, Nathan Weill, Kurt Weill.

Weill (in Berlin) to Emma and Albert Weill, 27 May 1926: I'm developing more and more into a recluse, and if I didn't have Lenja—who always sends a new stream of freshness into my feeling for life—I would probably be a complete hypochondriac by now. This way I can afford to let my physical distance from people grow in the same proportion to which I'm distancing myself from them inside my mind. And out of the arrogance toward others grows humility toward one's own self (which one could also call godliness).

QUATRIÈME
FESTIVAL

DE LA

SOCIÉTÉ
INTERNATIONALE
DE
MUSIQUE
CONTEMPORAINE

PROGRAMME:

VENDREDI, le 18 juin:
Concert gala du Choeur mixte de Zurich
PSALMUS HUNGARICUS . . . . Zoltan Kodaly
ROI DAVID . . . . Arthur Honegger
Après le concert: Réception officielle à la Tonhalle

SAMEDI, le 19 juin:
A trois heures de l'après-midi: Inauguration de la plaque commémorative de Busoni
Premier concert
TRIO für Violine, Viola, Violoncello, Op. 8 . . . . Walter Geiser
QUINTETT für Flöte, Oboe, Klarinette, Horn und Fagott, Op. 26 . Arnold Schönberg
STRING-QUARTETT . . . . Frederick Jacobi
Après le concert: Nuit vénitienne avec illumination des bords du lac. Bal à la Tonhalle

DIMANCHE, le 20 juin:
Représentations du Théâtre suisse des Marionnettes
Les tréteaux de Maître Pedro (d'après Cervantes) . . . . . Manuel de Falla

LUNDI, le 21 juin:
Deuxième concert
LE MIROIR DE JÉSUS . . . . André Caplet
LITANEI, troisième musique spirituelle . . . . Felix Petyrek

MARDI, le 22 juin:
Troisième concert
PORTSMOUTH POINT, an Overture . . . . W. T. Walton
KONZERT FÜR ORCHESTER, Op. 38 . . . . Paul Hindemith
PARTITA per pianoforte ed orchestra . . . . Alfredo Casella
FÜNFTE SYMPHONIE für Violine, Trompete und großes Orchester . Ernst Levy
5 STÜCKE für Orchester, Op. 10 . . . . Anton Webern
FOULES . . . . P. O. Ferroud
DANSE DE LA SORCIÈRE (Fragment de ballet) . . . . Alexandre Tansman

MERCREDI, le 23 juin:
Quatrième concert
SONATE für Klavier, Nr. 4, c-moll, Op. 27 . . . . N. Mjaskowsky
SEPTUOR pour flûte, quatuor à cordes, voix de femme et piano . Arthur Hoerée
KONZERT für Violine und Blasorchester, Op. 12 . . . . . Kurt Weill
PASTORALE UND MARSCH, für Kammerorchester . . . . . Hans Krasa

109. Violinist Stefan Frenkel (left) was the chief exponent of Weill's Violin Concerto during the 1920s. He stepped in at the last minute to replace Alma Moodie in a performance at the 1926 Société Internationale de Musique Contemporaine festival in Zurich. In 1929 he arranged seven songs from *Die Dreigroschenoper* as showpieces for violin with piano accompaniment.

110. The Weill family. Front row: Emma Weill, Albert Weill. Back row: Kurt, Lenya, Rita Weill (wife of Hanns), Leni Weill (wife of Nathan), Nathan.

Weill (in Alassio, Italy) to Emma and Albert Weill, [after 26 June 1926]: Finally—after two days by the sea—I've recuperated sufficiently from the strain of Zurich to gather the patience to report to you in greater detail. Those days at the music festival were terribly strenuous after all. One imagines that being a celebrity is much easier than it actually is. Notwithstanding those exhausting rehearsals, the personal obligations, the almost 100 people who wanted to talk to me in detail, there were daily ceremonial receptions in the afternoon as well as at night, among them a fairytale-like garden party in the castle of the richest silk merchant, as well as a *déjeuner* with twenty-five courses given by Mrs. MacCormick in the fanciest of the hotels. . . . After that we arrived here via Milan and Genoa. It is unspeakably beautiful. The deep blue sky, the tropical vegetation, palm trees, cactuses, fig trees, the salty sea, and the hot sun—it makes one forget everything else.

Weill (in Berlin) to Lotte Lenya, [July 1926?]: Just one week ago we sat on the Piazza Signori in Verona and slowly discovered how beautiful it was there. As I think back now, I begin to feel a powerful yearning for you—so no more reminiscing! Anyway, I'll be seeing you the day after tomorrow. This very same thing has happened to me before: when I feel this longing for you, I think most of all of the sound of your voice, which I love like a very force of nature, like an element. For me all of you is contained within this sound; everything else is only a part of you; and when I envelop myself in your voice, then you are with me in every way. I know every nuance, every vibration of your voice, and I can hear exactly what you would say if you were with me right now—and how you would say it. But suddenly this sound is again entirely alien and new to me, and then it is the greatest joy to realize how affectionately this voice caresses me—it's almost like those first weeks, when I considered just thinking about you to be presumptuous. The wonderful thing is that I still have that same reverence toward you as I did in the very first hour, which makes it seem almost miraculous that you've come to me and all has turned out so beautifully. And now—just as it was on that first day—I'm no longer sad that somewhere else your voice resounds, and I'm not close by. . . . The evening at Mrs. von Nostitz's was funny. Two entire floors at the Lützowplatz, with furniture fit for a castle, very beautiful antiques, valets, and everything that goes with that. Amid all of it, this middle-aged lady, the wife of a diplomat, dabbling in aesthetics and literature, a board member of the PEN club, acquainted with every conceivable international literary or political celebrity. Her collection of luminaries lacked young musicians, and so I had to fill that void. Besides Arrau and myself, there were the former (imperial) intendant of the Wiesbaden opera and two young literati (one a hysterical Jew, the other a monocled Aryan), as well as Liszt's very last lady student, who played the piano in a fantastically antediluvian style. Later on they talked about "Goethe's breakthrough" or "Stravinsky's body temperature" and "the mysterious power of Catholicism." I played the worldly-wise raconteur, neither spilling my glass of lemonade nor burning anything with my cigarette; instead, approximately every half hour I dropped a well-pointed witticism. Whereupon Her Graciousness expressed her hope that I might come to see her again next fall. With a correct bow I bid my adieus. The valet got a one Mark tip. Amid a lively discussion about the totally unexpected results of the latest tennis matches (a real surprise for me, that's for sure!), we stepped out into the street. You see—I have become quite a man of the world. . . . The head of every note in *Der Protagonist* is a B-u-s-s-i [little kiss] for you.

Weill (in Berlin) to Emma and Albert Weill, 22 July 1926: My friend Jarnach has used my four-week absence to let loose a storm of intrigues against me. Since they can't get the better of me on artistic grounds, they now depict me as an unprincipled operator and use this line to try to influence the important professional circles. Every day I hear new gossip-mongering against me and all of it flows out of one single source. It would be senseless to do anything about it. One has to let them yap till they're tired of yapping.

Weill (in Berlin) to Universal Edition, 25 November 1926: Thank you very much for sending Hans Kafka's libretto draft, which I have studied in detail. The concept for the piece is excellent, and even if it seems more suitable at present for a play than an opera, I am nonetheless convinced that through a collaborative effort it could become a wonderful libretto, and I hope that I will have an opportunity in the near future to discuss in person with the author the possibility of such a collaboration. However, after *Na und?* it is my firm intention to interrupt my opera output for a while in order not to disturb the progress of my previous stage works with continual announcements of a new opera. (Just recently at the *Cardillac* premiere in Dresden I was able to observe that there is at present almost more interest for *Na und?* than for *Royal Palace*.) So if you have anyone who is interested in Kafka's libretto and who could begin working on it immediately, I would naturally step aside in the interest of the author. In any event I thank you for your suggestion.

To explain yesterday's telegram, Stanislawski is extraordinarily excited about the plot of the *Protagonist*, which the translator related to him (with a slight change to emphasize the revolutionary aspects). He wants to get to know the music as soon as possible and it is possible that he will still produce the work this winter. . . . The adaptation he has in mind is very clever; however, it is designed more broadly and would therefore require a few musical additions. But it would be worth the effort if it led to an acceptance, since Stanislawski would give performances of the work in an extended run.

1 9 2 7

MUSIC + THEATER:	LITERATURE + FILM:	SCIENCE + SOCIETY:	POLITICS:
Ernst Křenek *Jonny spielt auf*	Hermann Hesse *Der Steppenwolf*	I. P. Pavlov *Dvadtsatiletnii opyt* (*Conditioned Reflexes*)	Inter-Allied military control of Germany ends
Otto Klemperer becomes director of Berlin's Krolloper	Franz Kafka *Amerika* (unfinished novel, posth.)	Charles Lindbergh flies monoplane from New York to Paris	General strike in Vienna following acquittal of Nazis for political murder
Jerome Kern *Show Boat*	*The Jazz Singer* (film with Al Jolson)	Martin Heidegger *Sein und Zeit*	Trotsky expelled from Communist Party

Seite 908   *Die Funkstunde*   Nr. 35 vom 29. August 1926

Vortragsfolgen Mittwoch 1. September

3.30 nm.

Jugendbühne
(Unterhaltungsstunde)

Die Funkprinzessin erzählt:

"Von Engeln und Teufelchen"

Die Funkprinzessin: Gertrud Nube

4.30-6 nm.

Nachmittagskonzert der Berliner Funk-Kapelle
Leitung:
Konzertmeister Franz v. Szpanowski

1. Immer fesch, Marsch..........Ellenberg
2. Immer oder nimmer, Walzer....Waldteufel
3. Vier Menschenalter..........Lachner
4. a) Loreley-Paraphrase........Nesvadba
   b) Blumengeflüster..........v. Blon
5. Fantasie a. d. Oper "Martha"....Flotow
6. a) Passion Flowers..........Sommerville
   b) Ständchen..............Heykens
7. Potpourri aus der Operette "Die lustige Witwe"..........Lehár
8. Pearl of Malabar, Foxtrot......Nicholls

Anschließend: Ratschläge fürs Haus – Theater- und Filmdienst

Inhaltsangabe von Grabbes Tragödie "Herzog Theodor von Gothland"

An der schwedischen Küste landen die finnischen Scharen unter Führung ihres Oberfeldherrn, des wilden Negers Berdoa, der einst vom Herzog von Gothland ausgepeitscht wurde und seitdem auf Rache sinnt. Er weiß mit Hilfe des schwächlichen Dieners Rolf den Herzog zu umgarnen; er verdächtigt den Kanzler Friedrich, des Herzogs Bruder, des Mordes an seinem dritten Bruder, Manfred, und bringt in dessen Grabkapelle ein, um der Leiche die Zeichen eines gewaltsamen Todes zuzufügen. Durch den Augenschein überzeugt, klagt Herzog Theodor vor dem König Olaf seinen Bruder des Meuchelmordes an; der aber erkennt die Verblendung des Herzogs und beschuldigt ihn selbst des Hochverrats, weil er sich mit dem Erbfeind der Schweden, dem Neger, verbunden habe. In der folgenden Schlacht kämpft Herzog Theodor auf der Seite der Finnen. Sein Vater, der alte Gothland,

Walter Franck
Aufn. Baro v. Tuchotsta, Charlottenburg

8 nm.

SendeSpiele
"Das deutsche Drama aus zwei Jahrhunderten"
(in Gegenüberstellungen)

I. Grabbe — Wedekind

"Herzog Theodor von Gothland"

Tragödie in fünf Akten von Chr. Dietrich Grabbe
Für den Rundfunk bearbeitet von Klabund und Alfred Braun
Musik von Kurt Weill
Dirigent: Bruno Seidler-Winkler
Regie: Alfred Braun

Personen:

Olaf, König der Schweden..........Theodor Loos
Der alte Herzog von Gothland......Arthur Kraußneck
Theodor, Herzog von Gothland, Kronfeldherr....Werner Krauß
Friedrich, Herzog von Gothland, Reichskanzler....Lothar Müthel
Graf Skiold....................Ferdinand Gregori
Cäcilia, seine Tochter, Gemahlin Theodors von Gothland....Johanna Hofer
Gustav, ihr Sohn................Veit Harlan
Graf Holl......................Oscar Ingenohl
Graf Arboga....................Robert Müller
Björn, ein schwedischer Hauptmann....Gert Briese
Erik, Burgvogt Theodors von Gothland....Otto Eggert
Rolf, Diener Friedrichs von Gothland....Bruno Fritz
Berdoa, ein Neger, Oberfeldherr und Oberpriester der Finnen....Walter Franck
Usbek, Feldherr der finnischen Reiterei....Meinhart Maur
Rossan } Feldherren der finnischen Infanterie....Amandus Grohmann
Irnak } ....Stefan Lux

Volk; schwedische Große; schwedische und finnische Hauptleute und Soldaten; russische, norwegische und deutsche Krieger usw.

Der Ort der Handlung ist Schweden
Berliner Funk-Orchester

Anschließend: Wetterdienst, Zeitansage, dritte Bekanntgabe der neuesten Tagesnachrichten, Sportnachrichten

6.30 nm. Kriminalschriftsteller Ernst Engelbrecht: "Kriminalistische Streifzüge durch süddeutsche Städte"

Vortragsreihe anläßlich der Großen Deutschen Funk-Ausstellung Berlin 1926

7 nm. Dr. Michel: "Die große Deutsche Funk-Ausstellung, die größte Funk-Ausstellung der Welt"

7.30 nm. Dr. Alfred Kerr: Einführung zu dem Sende-Spiel "Herzog Theodor von Gothland"

schwört ihm Rache. Rolf, der die Wahrheit gesteht, wird von dem wütenden Herzog ins Meer geschleudert. Viele Stämme der Finnen fallen von Berdoa ab und wählen Theodor von Gothland zu ihrem König. Seine Gattin, die edle Cäcilia, verstößt der grimmige Herzog. Sein jugendlicher Sohn Gustav gerät in die Fallstricke des Negers. Cäcilia und ihr greiser Vater suchen Gothland in seinem Zelt auf, werden jedoch von ihm in die kalte Winternacht hinausgejagt. Sie finden in einer Hütte Unterschlupf; Cäcilia stirbt. Der alte Gothland trifft mit Theodor in der Hütte zusammen. Der Herzog erbleicht im Angesicht der Zeugen seiner Missetaten. Berdoa ist gefesselt worden, entspringt aber und läßt nun den entkräfteten Herzog binden. Doch auch er zerreißt seine Fesseln und verfolgt nun den Neger, der ihm Gustavs Leiche in den Weg wirft. Der Herzog fühlt die alte Rache in dem Blute des Negers, wird aber von einem betrogenen Fürsten erstochen. Der siegreiche König Olaf findet das stolze Haus Gothland verwaist.

Theodor Loos
Aufn. Becker & Maaß, Berlin

Dr. Alfred Kerr
Aufn. Dührkoop, Berlin

111. Weill wrote incidental music for a radio production of *Herzog Theodor von Gothland*, Christian Dietrich Grabbe's play adapted by Klabund and Alfred Braun. The music is lost. This program appeared in *Die Funkstunde*, 29 August 1926.

Weill (in Berlin) to Peter Bing, 3 September 1926: You would have taken pleasure in my incidental music to Grabbe's *Herzog Theodor von Gothland*. Rarely have I written such colorful, dramatic, and original music, and—most of all—everything now actually sounds the way I had imagined it. I especially succeeded with a little Turkish march, a song with harp and saxophone, a stirring battle song, war music, choral effects, and a big funeral march. Musically the performance was very good, but the staging was a total failure and the performance as a whole did not leave much of a mark, except my own 1,000. Otherwise there is little news. Jarnach keeps silent after our heart-to-heart talk, which proved me right in all respects. Hertzka is coming some time soon. He is dripping with charm. How are things with Papa's concert? He can have the first performance of *Orpheus*. Give him my regards!

ROYAL PALACE

Opera [-ballet] in one act; text by Iwan Goll

1927   Berlin, Staatsoper (2 March)
Erich Kleiber, conductor; Franco Aravantinos, designer, Max Terpis, choreographer. Presented with a film directed by F. L. Hörth and produced by Phoebus-Film AG. The triple bill included a concert performance of Der neue Orpheus *and closed with Manuel de Falla's* Meister Pedros Puppenspiel

1929   Essen, Städtische Bühnen (27 June)

KURT WEILL
ROYAL PALACE
OP. 17
KLAVIERAUSZUG MIT TEXT

UNIVERSAL-EDITION
No. 8690

112. Cover of vocal score of *Royal Palace* published by Universal Edition.

Verkaufspreis 50 Pf.

STAATS-THEATER
Staats-Oper
am Platz der Republik

Berlin, Sonnabend, den 5. März 1927
29. Abonnements-Vorstellung

Royal Palace
Oper in einem Akt von Kurt Weill / Text von Iwan Goll
Musikal. Leitung: General-Musikdirektor Erich Kleiber / In Szene gesetzt von Fr. L. Hörth

Dejanira . . . Delia Reinhardt	Der alte Fischer . . . Rudolf Watzke
Der Ehemann . . . Leo Schützendorf	Sopran-Solo . . . Gitta Alpar
Der Geliebte von gestern . . . Leonhard Kern	Oberkellner . . . Rudolf Kölling
Der Verliebte von morgen . . . Carl Jöken	Boy . . . Harald Kreutzberg
Der junge Fischer . . . Marcel Noé	Portiers, Boys, Kellner / Zeit: Gegenwart

Choreographie: Max Terpis / Tänze ausgeführt von: Elisabeth Grube, Melanie Lucia, Gertrud Berghoff, Lina Geisel, Gertrud Schröder, Edith Moser, Harald Kreutzberg, Willi Wtorczyk, Walter Junk, Rudolf Kölling und das gesamte Ballettpersonal

Vorher als Prolog:
Der neue Orpheus
Kantate für Sopran-Solo, Solo-Violine und Orchester (Uraufführung) von Kurt Weill, nach der Dichtung von Iwan Goll / Delia Reinhardt, Professor Rudolf Deman

Meister Pedros Puppenspiel
Oper in einem Akt von Manuel de Falla / In Szene gesetzt von Fr. L. Hörth
Große Marionetten:

Meister Pedro . . . Waldemar Henke	Sancho Pansa . . . Willi Wtorczyk
Sein Junge . . . Genia Guzzalewicz	Der Wirt . . . Walter Junk
Don Quixote . . . Theodor Scheidl	Der Student . . . Kurt Krüger
	Der Mann mit Lanze und Hellebarde
	Ewald Ludewig

HOTEL ADLON
Die neue Restaurant-Terrasse
ist der Treffpunkt der eleganten Welt
Kapelle Marek Weber

113. Program for *Royal Palace* and *Der neue Orpheus*.

114. The notice in the *New York Times* of the premiere of *Royal Palace* records the audience reaction of "wild applause and a few scattering [sic] hisses." (3 March 1927, p. 23)

115. These excerpts from a copyist's manuscript of the women's chorus part illustrate Karl Holl's review from the *Frankfurter Zeitung*, 4 March 1927, in which he comments on the woman's chorus singing of "Dejanira, Janirade, Rajedina, Nirajade."

116. Dejanira (Delia Reinhart) is pampered by the hotel staff in a scene from *Royal Palace* at the Berlin Staatsoper. Pictured with Dejanira are Tomorrow's Lover (Carl Jöken), her Husband (Leo Schützendorf), and Yesterday's Lover (Leonhard Kern). Photo: Zander & Labisch.

117. An advertisement published in the May-June 1927 issue of *Pult & Taktstock* indicates the forthcoming performance of *Mahagonny*. Neither the libretto nor vocal score are yet available.

KURT WEILL

Tonkünstlerfest in Krefeld

op. 9 Quodlibet
Eine Unterhaltungsmusik
Vier Orchesterstücke aus einem Kindertheater
U. E. Nr. 8348 Partitur . . . . Mk. 40·—

Musikfest in Baden-Baden

Mahagonny
Ein Songspiel nach Texten von Bert Brecht

op. 8 Streichquartett I
U. E. Nr. 7699 Partitur . . . . Mk. 1·50
U. E. Nr. 7700 Stimmen . . . . Mk. 6·—

op. 10 Frauentanz
Sieben Gedichte des Mittelalters
Für Sopran mit Flöte, Bratsche, Klarinette, Horn und Fagott
U. E. Nr. 7599 Partitur . . . . Mk. 7·—
U. E. Nr. 7600 Stimmen . . . . Mk. 5·—
U. E. Nr. 7748 Ausgabe für Gesang und Klavier . . . . Mk. 2·—

op. 12 Konzert
Für Violine und Blasorchester
U. E. Nr. 8339 Ausgabe für Violine und Klavier . . . . Mk. 9·—

op. 16 Der neue Orpheus
Kantate für Sopran, Solo-Violine und Orchester
Text von Iwan Goll
U. E. Nr. 8471 Partitur . . . . Mk. 40·—
U. E. Nr. 8472 Ausgabe für Gesang, Violine und Klavier . . . . Mk. 4·50

Bühnenwerke

Der Protagonist
Ein Akt Oper von Georg Kaiser
U. E. Nr. 8387 Klavierauszug mit Text . . . . Mk. 15·—
U. E. Nr. 8388 Textbuch . . . . Mk. —·50

Royal Palace
Oper in einem Akt von Iwan Goll
U. E. Nr. 8690 Klavierauszug mit Text . . . . Mk. 15·—
U. E. Nr. 8691 Textbuch . . . . Mk. —·50

Universal-Edition A. G., Wien — New York

Weill (in Berlin) to Universal Edition, 4 April 1927: It [*Na und?*] is the first operatic attempt to throw light on the essence of our time from within, rather than by recourse to the obvious externals. The theme is the actions and reactions of contemporary man. . . . It is a type of light-hearted opera that has not been developed since *Der Rosenkavalier.* . . . not grotesque or parody, but cheerful and *musikantisch*. The form is: seventeen closed numbers, linked by recitatives or melodramas accompanied by piano or chamber ensembles.

Weill (in Berlin) to Universal Edition, 2 May 1927: In haste, a note that I have changed my mind about Baden-Baden. I have suddenly had a very good idea on which I am working at the moment. Title: *Mahagonny*, a Song-Spiel on texts by Brecht. I hope to finish this short work by the middle of May. Then I can send the parts and piano score to you for production. You'll also have a use for it outside of Baden-Baden.

Weill (in Berlin) to Universal Edition, [26 May 1927]: The rest of the *Mahagonny* score is being sent to you today. I have just received your letter of the 23rd and am sending you a copy of the *Hauspostille*, which I would like to have *returned*. These texts, however, are intended *only* as orientation for the copyist. The final text with the intermediary titles, finale, and stage instructions will be sent off to you in the next few days to be used in preparing the libretto. Perhaps you could make this little libretto especially attractive by including illustrations of the five sets which the well-known set designer Caspar Neher will be making for Baden-Baden.

Weill (in Berlin) to Universal Edition, 22 June 1927: Iwan Goll just wrote from Paris to say that he has spoken at length with Diaghilev about *Royal Palace* and *Orpheus* and has given him both piano scores. The situation looks good and Goll suggests that together with you we begin a kind of "general offensive" on Diaghilev. I urge you to write Diaghilev an emphatic letter right away (current address: S. de Diaghilev, Director of Russian Ballet, Princess Theater, London). *Royal Palace* can be performed as a ballet without any changes, since it was conceived as such.

118. Bertolt Brecht, ca. 1927.

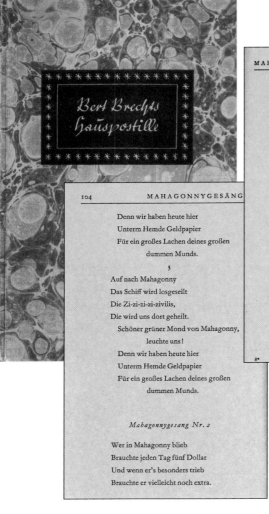

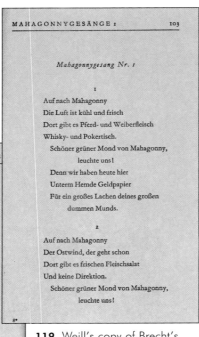

119. Weill's copy of Brecht's *Hauspostille* (1927) includes the texts and Brecht's melodies for the five *Mahagonny* songs.

120. Weill with Ernst Toch in Baden-Baden, July 1927.

Weill (in Berlin) to Lotte Lenya, [3? June 1927]: Now I can give you a blow-by-blow account, so you'll have some idea of what I've been up to. The flight was magnificent. One actually feels amazingly safe, and much less nervous than on a train. The most beautiful moment is when the airplane very slowly lifts itself into the air. On Monday afternoon we [Brecht and Weill] had a preliminary talk with the Essen officials, and in the evening when we walked every which way through the factories, some overwhelming acoustic impressions suddenly gave me an entirely new concept of sound for the play. Tuesday we drove ten hours through the entire Ruhr region up to the Rhine. Koch knows the territory very intimately and could comment on everything. Coming out of the poisonous fumes of the Ruhr valley to the Rhine we immediately thought: Never go back into the poisonous gases! And we realized how beautiful it would be to recreate the colorful liveliness of this river instead of the gloomy gray factories that lie beyond it. The next day by noon we again emerged from the mines into daylight; then it became clear—the terrible horror down there, the boundless injustice that human beings have to endure, performing intolerably arduous labor seven hundred meters underground in complete darkness, in thick, smoldering air, just so that Krupp can add another five million to their 200 million a year—this needs to be said, and in such a way, indeed, that no one will ever forget it. (But it will have to come as a surprise, otherwise they'll shut our mouths!) We spent four hours in the mines, six to seven hundred meters deep; we walked for two hours, then climbed on all fours through two levels, then down ladders a hundred and fifty meters into the depth—and afterward went pitch-black into the bathtub. All my bones still hurt today. Thursday we took another plane ride over the Ruhr region, then we spent hours in the Krupp steelworks. This was quite refreshing and soothing after those terrible impressions. In between we went to city hall, to Bochum and Duisburg, to museums and archives. We have drafted a very favorable contract; let's hope it will happen. We get paid 5,000-7,000 marks (each), but the play will belong to us. The title will probably be "REP" (Ruhrepos, Essen Documentarium). They have paid decently for expenses; I still have 30 Marks left over.

Weill (in Berlin) to Universal Edition, 6 June 1927: The question is: Do you want to print only the text of the five songs from *Hauspostille* or (which of course would be better) the entire thing with the scenario, texts between numbers, and finale)? In the latter case, you would first have to get in touch with Bert Brecht (Berlin W., Spichernstr.16). I think it best if you would print the entire *Mahagonny* text with Neher's pictures in a *special* small volume, since the piece has very good possibilities for different usages—it could be inserted into revues, etc. Please send me a piano-vocal score as soon as it has been finished, since I need it here for coaching the part of "Bessie."

121. Weill and Brecht often ironically invoke well-known works. Two excerpts from Weill's full score of the *Mahagonny Songspiel* show quotations from Weber's *Der Freischütz* (at the words "Schöner, grüner") and the famous workers' song *Die Internationale*.

122. Sheet music from the "shimmy" "Komm nach Mahagonne" from 1922, which probably provided the name of Brecht's imaginary land and the repeated syllable device ("Zi-zi-zi-zi-ziehharmonika") that he would parody in "Mahagonnygesang Nr. 1." The song was also available on at least two popular recordings.

123. Otto Griebel's painting *Die Internationale*.

124. The Revelers, an American vocal quartet with pianist (and forerunner to the Comedian Harmonists), recorded extensively with Columbia Records and toured Germany in the 1920s. Their singing style may have inspired Weill's male-quartet writing in *Mahagonny*, as Lenya recalled that she and Weill were fans.

125. Brecht (right) with the German boxer Paul Samson-Körner.

MAHAGONNY
Songspiel after texts by Bertolt Brecht

1927   Baden-Baden, Deutsche Kammermusik (17 July)
Ernst Mehlich, conductor; Bertolt Brecht, director (with Walther Brügmann); Caspar Neher, designer

1932   Hamburg, Schilleroper (13 October)
Paris, Salle Gaveau (11 December) [+ 4 songs from the opera]

1933   London, Savoy Theatre (18 July) [+ 4 songs from from the opera]
Rome, Sala di Santa Cecilia (29 December) [+ 4 songs from the opera]

1949   Venice Festival (September) [+ 4 songs from the opera]

The chamber opera which aroused the most discussion was Kurt Weill's *Mahagonny* (accent on the third syllable, please!). A pupil of Busoni's, Weill is the new *enfant terrible* of Germany. But it is not so easy to be an *enfant terrible* as it used to be and nothing is more painful than the spectacle of a composer trying too hard to be revolutionary. Weill, in writing *Mahagonny*, cannot escape the accusation. It is termed a "songspiel" and is, in effect, a series of pseudo-popular songs in the jazz manner. (One remembers particularly Jessie and Bessie repeatedly singing in English "Is here no telephone.") Weill is not without musical gifts but these are too often sacrificed for the sake of questionable dramatic effectiveness. **Aaron Copland, "Baden-Baden 1927," Modern Music 5 (Nov.-Dec. 1927): 32.**

126. Walther Brügmann assisted Brecht with the stage direction of *Mahagonny*. He later directed the premieres of *Aufstieg und Fall der Stadt Mahagonny* and *Der Zar lässt sich photographieren* in Leipzig.

Mahagonny

Ein Songspiel nach Texten von Bert Brecht
von Kurt Weill

Personen:

Jessie	Lotte Lenja
Bessie	Irene Eden
Charlie	Erik Wirl
Billy	Georg Ripperger
Bobby	Karl Giebel
Jimmy	Gerhard Pechner

Dirigent: Ernst Mehlich
Regie: Bert Brecht
Bühnenbilder: Caspar Neher
Kostüme entworfen von Caspar Neher, ausgeführt von Emilie Walut-Franz Droll
Musik. Einstudierung: Otto Besag
Orchesterbesetzung: 2 Violinen, 2 Klar., 2 Tromp. Saxophon, Posaune, Klavier, Schlagzeug.

Kurt Weill, geb. 2.3.1900 in Dessau, badischer Abstammung. 1918 Hochschule in Berlin. 1919—1920 Theaterkapellmeister. 1921 Schüler Busonis. Weill lebt in Berlin. Werke u. a. Streichquartett op. 8. Quodlibet op. 9. Frauentanz Op. 10. „Recordare" (a capella-Chorwerk) op. 11. Violinkonzert op. 12. „Der neue Orpheus" op 15. Opern: „Der Protagonist," „Royal Palace."
In seinen neueren Werken bewegt sich Weill in der Richtung jener Künstler aller Kunstgebiete, die die Liquidation der gesellschaftlichen Künste voraussagen. Das kleine epische Stück „Mahagonny" zieht lediglich die Konsequenz aus dem unaufhaltsamen Verfall der bestehenden Gesellschaftsschichten Er wendet sich bereits an ein Publikum, das im Theater naiv seinen Spass verlangt.

13

127. Festival program for Deutsche Kammermusik 1927, at which *Mahagonny* was premiered.

Weill (in Berlin) to Universal Edition, 4 August 1927: The sensational success of *Mahagonny* in Baden-Baden has resulted in an abundance of excellent reviews which I'll be sending you in the next few days since (as we discussed) you plan to begin a major publicity campaign for the work. You have no doubt received the piano and full score back from Baden-Baden. Perhaps you could have the "Alabama Song," which you wanted to publish separately, arranged by one of your popular music specialists for voice, piano, and violin and then sent to me for inspection. For salon orchestra editions one could rely heavily on the original.

Weill (in Prerow, Germany) to Universal Edition, 16 August 1927: Several days ago I entered negotiations for a production of *Mahagonny* as part of an elaborate revue. I was evasive since the matter wasn't terribly urgent.

Yesterday I received a similar offer, only in a decidedly more favorable setting. It is likewise a revue, but of a more serious artistic character with outstanding participants and excellent opportunities (a well-known Berlin theater, a famous director and with *consecutive performances*—not a one-sided agreement as with Piscator!). I think this would be the only possibility to exploit the Baden-Baden success effectively without hurting the chances of a later, longer Mahagonny oper(ett)a. On the contrary, I am convinced that incorporating the Baden-Baden piece into this kind of major commercial revue would be excellent preparation for the opera. (In addition, there is the following possibility: after we premiere the large *Mahagonny* opera in a provincial theater, the same theater director would also produce it in Berlin as a series performance.) You can easily see the possibilities for music sales ("Alabama Song"!!) with such a revue performance.

128. From rehearsals of *Mahagonny*. Lenya and Irene Eden are in the boxing ring. Weill and Hindemith are visible on the left; Brecht is on the right. Photo by Kühn & Hitz.

130. Rehearsal of the finale of *Mahagonny*, where the singers wield placards; in the boxing ring, left to right: Karl Giebel, Georg Ripperger, Irene Eden, Gerhard Pechner, Erik Wirl, and Lotte Lenya. Weill and Brügmann are at the left; Brecht is on the right. Lenya's placard reads, "Für Weill!" Photo by Kühn & Hitz.

129. Review of *Mahagonny* by Eberhard Preussner in *Die Musik* 19, no. 12 (September 1927): 887-88.

PREUSSNER: DEUTSCHE KAMMERMUSIK 1927   887

hier so lebendig, wie sie kurz ist, einfach und klar und dabei voller Witz. Die musikalische Charakterisierung der Personen ist überaus fein, die Melodie prägnant und die Verwendung selbst der einfachsten Akkorde zur Schilderung grotesker Situationen stets spannend — nämlich akkord-spannend. Wer bei diesen Tonbewegungen nicht von der ganzen Heiterkeit eines Singspieles erfaßt wird, muß geradezu die tauben Ohren der Tante haben, die Hindemith am Anfang des Stückes haapschü und zum Schluß Pschühaa niesen läßt. Den von der Sinnlosigkeit des menschlichen Lebensablaufes überzeugten Menschen und den von der Wichtigkeit ihres eigenen Lebens durchdrungenen Persönlichkeiten wird dieser Sketch gleich lehrsam sein. Möge er bald durch Deutschland »hin und zurück« gehen!

Das Enfant terrible des Musikfestes war entschieden das *Songspiel »Mahagonny«*, durch das sich *Bert Brecht* und *Kurt Weill* lebhaft zum Worte meldeten. Wie stets bei den vorlauten Kindern der Muse versteckte sich hinter dem allgemeinen Kopfschütteln und der Mißbilligung der leidtragenden Angehörigen alias Publikum nur die grenzenlose Verwunderung über die Nacktheit solcher offenen Aussprache. Bert Brecht, zeitgemäßer Dichter, Sänger von Balladen, Songs und Dramen, die bereits zur Hälfte musikalisch sind, hat diese Mahagonny-Gesänge seinem Gedichtband »Die Hauspostille«*) entnommen. Brecht muß den Musiker besonders anregen und fesseln. Er ist ein Volkssänger im Zeitalter des Wolkenkratzers, der eben nur das Pech hat, kein aufnahmefähiges Volk oder Publikum hinter sich zu haben. Denn sonst wäre manches von Brechts Gesängen, sicher aber seine Legende vom toten Soldaten**) längst Allgemeingut des Volkes. Während wir emsig auf der Suche nach neuen und alten, am liebsten aber ältesten Volksliedern sind, liegen hier zeitgebundene Lieder vor.

Daß ein Komponist auf die Texte Brechts stoßen mußte, war vorauszusehen. Kurt Weill, zeitgemäßer Musiker, Schöpfer von bühnenwirksamen Opern, aufnahmebereit für die Ideenwelt der Dichter, ist der glückliche Finder. Was Brecht erfand, deutet er klanglich mit großem Geschick aus; das eigentlich Schöpferische liegt in diesem Fall aber beim Dichter, nicht beim Musiker. Konnte man in Hindemiths Sketch noch den Umriß einer »Handlung« feststellen, die allerdings durch die Umkehrung sich selbst ad absurdum führt, so gibt es in den Mahagonny-Gesängen keinerlei dramatische Fortentwicklung. Es herrscht das reine *Spiel* von Gesängen zu deutschen und englischen Versen. Da es in dieser Welt nichts gibt, woran man sich halten kann, schafft Brecht einen Idealstaat Mahagonny mit den Gestalten der Männer von Mahagonny, die jenseits von Gut und Böse so singen, wie sie gerade gelaunt und gestimmt sind. Gelaunt sind sie aber! Als Gott ihnen mitten im Whisky erscheint, streiken die Männer von Mahagonny:

*) Erschien 1927 im Propyläen-Verlag. Brecht gibt am Schluß des Gedichtbandes selbst »Gesangsnoten«.
**) Auch in der »Hauspostille« enthalten.

888   DIE MUSIK   XIX/12 (September 1927)

»An den Haaren
Kannst du uns nicht in die Hölle ziehen,
Weil wir immer in der Hölle waren.«

Verhüllung und Sentimentalität gibt es in Mahagonny nicht mehr. Die Sänger klettern in den Boxring, die Welt der Seile erobert die Opernbühne; hinter sich die Filmleinwand singen sie von Pferd- und Weiberfleisch, von Whisky- und Pokertisch.

Wie musikgetränkt die Verse an sich sind, höre man an diesem Beispiel:

Schöner grüner Mond von Mahagonny, leuchte uns!

Und daß hier der amerikanische Schlager künstlerische Durchdringung erfahren hat, ohne etwas an Schlagkraft zu verlieren, erkenne man am Benares Song:

»There is no whisky in this town
There is no bar to sit us down   *Let's go to Benares*
Oh!   *Where the sun is shining*
Where is the telephone?   *Let's go to Benares!*
Is here no telephone?   *Johnny, let us go.«*
Oh, Sir, God damn me:
No!

Gewiß mag in all diesem die Opernbühne bereits verlassen sein und das Kabarett seinen fröhlichen Einzug halten, aber dennoch lebt im ganzen ein neuer, ernster Zug. Zunächst scheint es mir, als sei es in diesem Maße bisher überhaupt noch nicht gelungen, eine Aneinanderreihung von Gesängen, also etwa die Form einer Kantate so auf die Bühne zu stellen, daß sie lebendig, spannend und fast dramatisch geladen wirkt. Rein musikalisch ist Weill einmal nachzurühmen, daß er das, was wir unter zeitgemäßer Musik vor allem in rhythmischer, aber auch in melodischer Hinsicht verstehen, zum mindesten ideal in sich aufgefangen hat und nun in einer großen Bilderfolge abrollen läßt. Dann aber ist erkennbar, daß der Sänger als einzelner Virtuose hier entthront ist, dafür ein voll ausgenutztes Ensemble von zwei Frauen- und vier Männerstimmen musiziert, wobei jede Stimme zu größter Selbständigkeit geführt wird. Eine neue Form bühnenmäßigen Geschehens ist angedeutet. Und wenn noch so sehr dem Zeitgeist geopfert wird, die Opfer sind nicht ganz umsonst gebracht. Das Baden-Badener Pfeifkonzert, das den Männern von Mahagonny gewidmet wurde, tat diesen anscheinend wohl; denn — sie waren ja immer in der Hölle.

Die beiden übrigen Kammeropern, die in Baden-Baden uraufgeführt wurden, stoßen nicht so weit in Neuland vor. Merkwürdig, welche Bedeutung die griechische Mythologie als Textvorwurf für den modernen Musiker wieder erlangt hat. Von Peris und Caccinis »Euridice« geht eine große Linie bis hin

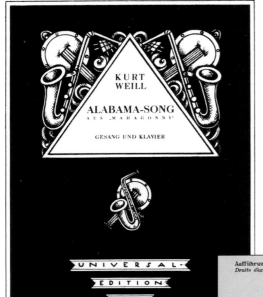

Weill (in Berlin) to Lotte Lenya, [25 August 1927]: By the way, you don't have to feel too sorry for me. After those few days in Grünheide I now feel very frisky, and I don't look quite as bad anymore. I rather think that it won't take me long to recuperate entirely. . . . Mami [Margarethe Kaiser] really is a dear, and I like being with her just because she's so fond of you. The children are now all at a good age—nice, intelligent, and decent. Anselm is slender and attractive. Last night I was at the Wurms' to play *Mahagonny* for them. [Hans] Salter and Papi [Georg Kaiser] were there. Everyone was simply knocked out. I had to play it three times. They now want to put a lot of pressure on Haller, and Salter will try to get the "Alabama Song" away from U.E. [Universal Edition] for America, because he thinks he can do terrific business with it over there. . . . Dear, there is a wonderful American movie, *Die Rivalen* [*What Price Glory*, screenplay by Maxwell Anderson] (I saw it with Mami). I liked it because of its pacifist stance and its artistic realization.

132. Olin Downes reviewed *Mahagonny* in the *New York Times*, 14 August 1927. Weill called it "the most detailed and substantial" review and encouraged Universal Edition to publish it in *Anbruch*.

By OLIN DOWNES.

BADEN-BADEN, July 20.

A PIECE done at Baden-Baden, a fifteen-minute chamber opera, or "song-spiel," by a bold and bad young man, Kurt Weill of Berlin, should properly have been given in Vienna. It was a little out of the frame in a fashionable watering place, having something to do, to paraphrase a line in "The Mikado," with that kind of modern dissatisfaction which recently culminated in the cutting up of policemen by the proletariat.

This piece is "Mahagonny," a clever and savage skit on the degeneration of society, the triumph of sensualism, the decay of art. It is done by a young composer who knows his business. They say that Weill, a pupil of Busoni, born in 1900, has had a hard time of it and that his life has unfortunately colored his social and artistic ideas. Be that as it may, his was the triumph of the festival, and it is a pity that others could not be as witty, as accomplished in the manipulation of material, and, even, save for some offensive and insurrectionary placards shown on the stage, as cognizant of the line between farce and satire.

His show is a series of songs in the form of quartets, duets and ensembles of six singers who jump over the ropes of a construction which suggests a prize-ring or the deck of a boat, and proceed to do their stuff. The quartet of men, "Charley," "Billy," "Bobby" and "Jimmy," look like vaudevillians out of a job, going, for want of a better place, to "Mahagonny." This fabulous locality does not exist, a fact eventually yelled through a speaking trumpet from the stage; but it has suspicious resemblance, according to fantastic geographical maps which are shown as backdrops, to New York. The songs sung by the men are in German, the two girls rejoin in English. The girls are in tight black dresses and red stockings. Those on the stage behave lackadaisically with a professional carelessness and sangfroid. The men in shirt-sleeves and derby hats chant of

Mahagonny
Das Schiff wird losgeseilt
Die Zi-zi-zi-zivilis.
Die wird uns dort geheilt.
Schoener gruener Mond von Mahagonny, leuchte uns!
Denn wir haben heute hier
Unterm Hemde Geldpapier
Fuer ein grosses Lachen deines grossen dummen Munds.

The girls howl in cabaret fashion about whisky, telephones and love; the two groups performing in turn. The quartet "numbers" have the character of the coon-song with barber-shop chords gone wrong. The girls, sitting on their suit-cases, parody the lilt and sentimentality of the jazz ditty. There is no development of a particularly concrete kind, but the music has a slangy twist and a sardonic sting admirably contrived. The climax comes when the vaudevillians, seeking relief from their boredom in the newspapers, bend forward in intense excitement. An earthquake in Benares! Sensation. They jump to their feet, placards with unmentionable texts are brought forward, and the bunch shuffle from the stage.

In this composer's wit there is a thrust. As a craftsman he can afford to stick his tongue in his cheek. Musically speaking, his bitterness is under perfect control and the audience has good reason to laugh at various vocal and orchestral ingenuities. But Weill's ideas are not for the drawing room, and those who planned the stage must have been considerably restrained for the Baden-Baden production. We saw the original sketches of "Mahagonny" made in Berlin, and they were not pleasant. Judging by them the stage production at Baden-Baden was skeletonized. Quite enough was done under the circumstances. But how do they achieve such a performance on a stage set up for a moment in a concert hall, and an "opera" rehearsed between other jobs for a single performance at a three-day musical festival? The quartet of men, Eric Wirl, Georg Ripperger, Karl Geibel, and Gerhard Pechner, and the girls, too, Lotte Lenja and Irene Eden, were immense in make-up, in action and in song. With lesser interpreters, who visualized as well as made audible the spirit of the piece, it would have been far less fortunate. The question of the worthiness of the subject can go begging here. Composer and interpreters most emphatically achieved their ends.

131. The publication of Weill's first popular sheet music edition prompted both composer and publisher to discuss how the accompaniment should be simplified. Universal Edition wrote to Weill: "We have had one of our arrangers look at the 'Blues' in *Mahagonny* and asked him to bring it into a more suitable form for a 'popular' edition. We are sending you the manuscript of this edition at this time with the request to look at it and let us know how you feel about it. As far as we are concerned, we feel that the first part (up to the refrain) should be made simpler and more playable, especially in the left hand, since the second in the chords of the first and third quarter-notes sounds bad throughout. We would suggest doing without the sharp dissonances on the first and third beats in these bars and possibly having only the first tone played an octave lower. The grotesque character of this part still comes through, the remaining harmony is sufficiently expressive, and the whole thing will sound much better on the piano." (23 August 1927)

Weill (in Berlin) to Universal Edition, 25 August 1927: The reason I am drawn to Brecht is, first of all, the strong interaction of my music with his poetry, which surprised all those in Baden-Baden who were competent to judge. But further I am convinced that the close collaboration of two equally productive individuals can lead to something fundamentally new. There can certainly be no doubt that at present a completely new form of stage work is evolving, one that is directed to a different and much larger audience and whose appeal will be unusually broad. This movement, whose strongest force in the spoken drama is Brecht, hasn't had any effect upon opera to date (except in *Mahagonny*), although music is one of its most essential elements. In long discussions with Brecht I have become convinced that his idea of an operatic text largely coincides with my own. The piece we are going to create won't exploit topical themes, which will be dated in a year, but rather will reflect the true tenor of our times. For that reason it will have an impact far beyond its own age. The task is to create the new genre which gives appropriate expression to the completely transformed manifestation of life in our time.

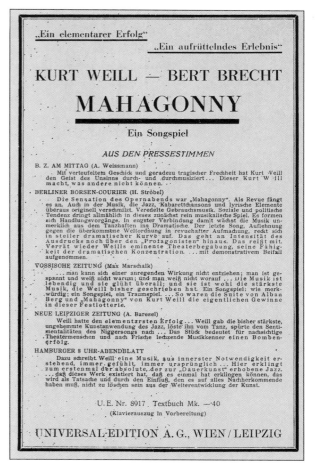

134. A summary of the positive reviews appeared in the September-October 1927 issue of *Pult und Taktstock*.

135. Autograph score for the incidental music to Strindberg's play *Gustav III*, performed October-November 1927 in the Theater an der Königgrätzer Straße, Berlin. Weill contributed incidental music to several plays produced in Berlin between October 1927 and November 1928.

133. Marek Weber, whose band often played at Berlin's fashionable Adlon Hotel, recorded a dance orchestra arrangement of "Alabama-Song." Electrola released the record in early 1928 with "Tango Angèle" on the reverse side. (See page 69.)

Weill (in Berlin) to Universal Edition, 8 December 1927: I am enclosing a synopsis of *Mahagonny*. From it you will see that in this work—which, I'd like to emphasize, establishes a totally new operatic style with real potential for development—we have succeeded in laying a solid foundation for a genuinely popular success, mainly through the extremely exciting plot, the "popular numbers" as well as in the revue scenes (Mahagonny-Idyll, Boxing Match, Trip to Bilbao, Courtroom Scene). I would very much like to hear what you say about it.

Emil Hertzka of Universal Edition (in Vienna) to Weill, 16 December 1927: Having received your letter of the 8th with the synopsis of *Mahagonny* I must candidly confess that I was a little disappointed by this outline. I had believed that it would be possible for you and Mr. Brecht to make the Mahagonny theme the basis for a symbolically conceived opera plot. What I see in the synopsis may well be a new opera style, but it is still just a series of scenes, admittedly sometimes very exciting and original, which could be the basis for a certain new kind of "opera revue." No doubt a good and interesting opera revue can be infinitely more worthwhile than a bad opera, but I believe it would have been possible to shape the Mahagonny theme and idea—which we have discussed often—into a plot that would surely have paved the way for the work without eliminating what you find so lively and attractive. The overemphasized wild west realism of this plot should be balanced with a measure of positive human qualities—whether friendship, love, or loyalty—and the lyrical effect which accompanies such things. Even if you write of a Mahagonny idyll and maybe have planned such a scene, boxing, murder, violence, drunkenness, and the like still predominate, and that might well prove hard to take for an entire evening. A few days ago I was in Wiesbaden for the performance of *Romeo and Julia auf dem Dorfe* (after a novella by Keller). There was nearly two and a half hours of practically nothing but lyricism without any dramatic explosions to speak of and held together by only the thread of a plot. In spite of the wonderful music by Delius, the work is impossible as an opera. It seems to me that *Mahagonny*, with its blood-red, bloodthirsty, but likewise single-thread plot, is the mirror image of this pale, colorless and harmless series of scenes. . . . Naturally I have no desire to influence the two of you in your creative work; if you are both set on writing an opera revue and accept the joys and sorrows of this new genre without laying particular value on material success, then there isn't much I can add. Of course even in this form I'll accept the work with great interest and will do my best for it. But if you keep in mind that the work must be performed in opera houses by personnel involved with other kinds of works and that you are appealing to an audience which, when it comes to the opera still brings with it certain (shall we say) traditional preconceptions, then all these things must somehow be taken into consideration. You cannot forget that there is a tremendous difference between producing a modern opera and a modern prose stage work. The theaters that perform the dramatic works of Brecht, whom I very much admire, not only have actors familiar with and capable of communicating Brecht's radical expressionistic style, but also an audience that has in part been prepared for this style.

Weill (in Berlin) to Universal Edition, 27 December 1927: I never expected that you would find *Mahagonny* even in this form "lacking in action." If you consider that in Baden-Baden I succeeded in holding the audience in rapt attention for twenty-five minutes *without a trace of plot* I would think that an opera with a plot so logical and direct and with such a wealth of exciting individual incidents would seem enough. I have worked with Brecht day after day for three months on shaping this libretto, and I directed my very substantial share of the work almost entirely toward achieving the most logical, straightforward and easily comprehensible plot possible. The comparison with Delius's *Romeo and Julia* somewhat frightened me; the great shortcoming of this opera lies in the fact that it is—forgive the harsh word—boring. And I can tell you this much already: there won't be so much as one moment of boredom in *Mahagonny*. However, in the operatic style I am establishing here, music has a much more fundamental role than in the purely plot-driven opera, since I am replacing the earlier bravura aria with a new kind of popular song. As a result I can completely allay any fears you may have that this work is somehow derived from a spoken play. With great difficulty I have succeeded in getting Brecht to the point that he was actually challenged by the task of writing a text to suit musical requirements, and I have examined every word with an eye to the demands of the opera stage. It is the first libretto in years that is fully dependent upon music, indeed upon my music. I found it very interesting that you detected a preponderance of raw, grim elements over simpler, human emotions. That made me stop and think, and I am already busy with a change by which the Jimmy-Jenny love story will be given greater emphasis.

Weill (in Berlin) to Universal Edition, 10 November 1927: I have just returned from Leipzig and wanted to report to you right away. I worked a long time with Brecher [on *Der Zar lässt sich photographieren*]. He is incredibly pedantic and completely committed to a certain theory of declamation, which he applies without exception to all operas. That makes working with me particularly difficult since I am far removed from any kind of declamatory style. By being persistent I have in most cases succeeded in satisfying him with minor displacements of the vocal line, often simply with a change of text which alters nothing of the structure of the work. In a very few instances (four or five) the repetition of a measure will be necessary. All of the changes, which I can endorse (without finding them absolutely necessary from an artistic point of view), have one practical advantage: they will greatly facilitate and simplify rehearsal of the work. For that reason I would suggest incorporating them, as far as possible, into the piano score.

Universal Edition (in Vienna) to Weill, 24 November 1927: We would like to discuss another important question with you. In addition to the usual musical materials for the *Zar*, we also have to provide the gramophone discs of the Tango. Since Berlin has the best possibilities for having recordings done, we would appreciate your getting in touch with the leading recording companies there in order to open negotiations.

Weill (in Berlin) to Universal Edition, [1 December 1927]: With reference to my discussions with Director Hertzka I spoke with Georg Kaiser again today about the title *Der Zar lässt sich....* In the meantime he, too, has heard from several quarters that this title might be somewhat offensive and suggests that we leave it with *Der Zar lässt sich photographieren* after all. I don't know if it is still possible to make this change in the piano score.

DER ZAR LÄSST SICH PHOTOGRAPHIEREN

Opera buffa in one act; libretto by Georg Kaiser

1928   Leipzig, Neues Theater (18 February)
Gustav Brecher, conductor; Walther Brügmann, director and set designer

Dusseldorf, Stadttheater (27 March)
Dessau, Friedrichtheater (4 April)
*Altenburg, Landestheater (8 April)
Gera, Landestheater (22 April)
Dortmund, Stadttheater (10 May)
Stettin, Stadttheater (25 May)
Hagen, Stadttheater (11 June)
Breslau (Germany, now Poland), Stadttheater (14 June)
*Frankfurt, Städtische Bühnen (19 June)
Chemnitz, Städtisches Theater (3 September)
Magdeburg, Städtisches Theater (28 September)
Bremen, Stadttheater (3 October)
*Berlin, Städtische Oper (14 October)
Prague, Deutsches Landestheater (11 November)
*Stuttgart, Landestheater (15 December)
Braunschweig, Landestheater (16 December)

1929   Kaiserslautern, Stadttheater (1 February)
Koblenz, Stadttheater (2 February)
Ulm, Stadttheater (14 February)
Freiburg, Stadttheater (23 February)
*Hannover, Städtische Bühnen (26 February)
Beuthen (Germany, now Poland), Landestheater (10 March)
Lübeck, Stadttheater (15 March)
Augsburg, Stadttheater (28 April)
Osnabrück, Stadttheater (30 April)
Nuremberg, Stadttheater (30 May)
Mainz, Stadttheater (12 November)

1930   Coburg, Landestheater (3 October)
Danzig (Germany, now Poland), Stadttheater (26 November)

1931   Bamberg, Stadttheater (14 January)

1949   New York, Juilliard School (27 October)

*performed with *Der Protagonist*

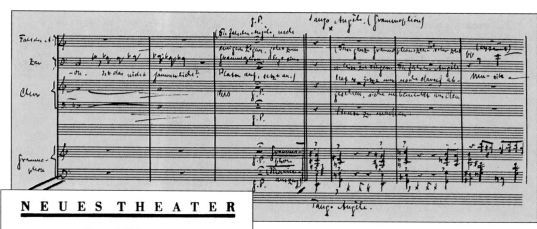

136. In the full score of *Der Zar lässt sich photographieren*, Weill indicates that the "Tango Angèle" is played on a gramophone, one of the earliest uses of recorded music in opera. He provides only a piano reduction of the music. The publisher provided the recording to opera companies.

137. Program for *Der Zar lässt sich photographieren*.

138. The recording of "Tango Angèle," performed by Saxophon-Orchester Dobbri, was offered for sale to the general public by Parlophon-Beka (Lindström AG) as well as used in performances of the opera.

---

1 9 2 8

MUSIC + THEATER:

Eugen d'Albert *Die schwarze Orchidee*

Maurice Ravel *Bolero*

George Gershwin *An American in Paris*

LITERATURE + FILM:

Stephen Vincent Benét *John Brown's Body*

Aldous Huxley *Point Counterpoint*

The first Mickey Mouse films (Walt Disney)

SCIENCE + SOCIETY:

Alexander Fleming discovers penicillin

H. Geiger and W. Müller construct the Geiger counter

Amelia Earhart is first woman to fly across the Atlantic

POLITICS:

Italy signs twenty-year treaty of friendship with Ethiopia

Kellogg-Briand Pact, outlawing war, signed in Paris by 65 states

Herbert Hoover elected U.S. President

Weill (in Berlin) to Erwin Stein, Universal Edition, 5 January 1928: Now that I have the piano reduction of my *Zar* opera, I do not want to neglect thanking you sincerely for the excellent execution of this score, or telling you how happy I am especially about the clarity and playability of the piano part. I do so hope that it will be possible for you to do the reduction of *Mahagonny* as well.

Weill (in Berlin) to Universal Edition, 23 February 1928: I find the plan for performing a chamber orchestra version of the *Zar* in America especially noteworthy. That should be relatively easy since Kaiser is very popular in America and they really like this sort of thing over there. Perhaps you could start on this plan soon so that if a performance is arranged I could begin an arrangement for small orchestra. Such an acceptance would have an incredible impact over here. I also think it should be possible to do the *Zar* in Russia, where they've long been interested in the *Protagonist*. In a Russian version (and also in any possible outline made for the Russian theaters), the character of the Czar would have to be made still more ludicrous than we were permitted to do here.

139. Cover, title page, and first page of the first edition vocal score of *Der Zar lässt sich photographieren*, inscribed by Weill to his parents.

140. A caricature of Weill drawn by B.F. Dolbin was published with a short interview with Weill in the *Neue Leipziger Zeitung*, 18 February 1928.

141. Scene from the premiere of *Der Zar lässt sich photographieren* at the Neues Theater, Leipzig, with the male chorus standing in the orchestra pit.

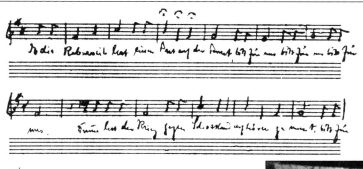

142. Weill may have sketched this song for the March 1928 Leipzig production of Brecht's and Feuchtwanger's play *Leben Eduards des Zweiten von England* (based on Marlowe) while in Leipzig working on *Der Zar lässt sich photographieren*. The song was written for Act I, scene 1, to be sung by the ballad-seller. The text reads:

Edis Kebsweib hat einen Bart auf der Brust
Bitt für uns, bitt für uns, bitt für uns
Drum hat der Krieg gegen Schottland aufhören gemusst
Bitt für uns, bitt für uns, bitt für uns.

143. Cast and creative team of *Der Zar lässt sich photographieren*, including (seated) Theodor Horand (Zar) and (standing, left to right) Walther Brügmann (director), Ilse Koegel (Angèle), Gustav Brecher (conductor), Maria Janowska (False Angèle), and Weill.

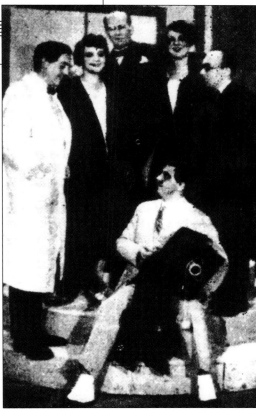

144. Alfred Baresel's review of the premiere of *Der Zar* in the 17 February 1928 issue of *Neue Leipziger Zeitung*.

145. Leading director Erwin Piscator, ca. 1927.

Weill (in Berlin) to Universal Edition, 8 March 1928: As far as I know, Piscator's theater has cabled you about the *Zar*, asking for the option. Piscator wants to do the piece in a consecutive run at the Lessing Theater. I am eager to learn your thoughts on this plan. Piscator will travel on the 14th to Leipzig, and decide immediately after the performance. I am not unaware of the difficulties inherent in this project (orchestra, singers, etc.), but, on the other hand, I see great financial potential and a welcome break with traditional opera house routine.

Weill (in Berlin) to Universal Edition, 15 March 1928: The Piscator people still seem to be undecided. For reasons of scheduling they would have to open the *Zar* by the middle of April and that seems to me virtually impossible. In a few days I'll have a detailed conference with Piscator, whose results I will report to you. The prospects with Klemperer look better and I hope to have a decision there by the end of the week. They are thinking about coupling the *Zar* with Ravel's *L'heure espagnole* in May—an excellent combination, by the way. However, it is not at all certain whether this plan can be realized, and I would like to suggest that you write to Hörth on your own with reference to the negotiations with Klemperer and Piscator and recommend to him the combined performance of *Protagonist* and *Zar*. All in all, I think a Berlin performance of the *Zar* this season would be very advantageous, but if Hörth coupled the work with the *Protagonist* we could wait until the beginning of next season.

146. The Stadttheater Düsseldorf mounted the second production of *Der Zar lässt sich photographieren* on 27 March 1928 in a double bill with *Oedipus Rex* by Stravinsky. Weill attended the performance.

Universal Edition (in Vienna) to Weill, 29 March 1928: You will be interested in the response from one of our Russian representatives. The person in question, a legal advisor of the Moscow State Opera, writes: "Kurt Weill's opera is an outstanding work. I would also like to get to know his other works. It is, to be sure, very amusing, but the ideology of this opera makes a performance in Soviet Russia out of the question. The composer is only satirical. He doesn't take any sides. He sees the Czar just as satirically as the revolutionaries; indeed the latter play the comic role in the opera, and we are not at all pleased with the sight of comic revolutionaries on the stage. However, I will report on the opera in our papers and will give some thought as to how one could modify the contents for our situation."

Weill (in Berlin) to Universal Edition, 20 March 1928: The Berlin *Zar* situation has changed once again as a result of my discussion today with Dr. Curjel. He does not believe that Klemperer will let the piece get away and in Klemperer's absence would rather reach a decision with him by telephone than abandon the work to Walter. Since Klemperer is doing *Cardillac*, Zemlinsky might be called upon to do *Zar* and in this case it wouldn't be at all out of the question to add the *Protagonist*, which suits Zemlinsky especially well. That would naturally be a splendid solution, and I would like to urge that you bring all your influence to bear upon Klemperer and also upon Zemlinsky to try and achieve it. The people here have apparently forgotten the great success of the *Protagonist* premiere and can't grasp the strong audience appeal of the work. They were quite surprised when I told them about the forty-six curtain calls at the Dresden premiere.

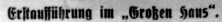

Universal Edition (in Vienna) to Weill, 20 March 1928: Electrola Berlin has sent us the following telegram: "If 'Tango Angèle' from Weill's *Zar*, set for jazz or salon orchestra, has already come out, please send it immediately to Electrola via air-mail."

We have written to the gentlemen that we do not as yet have the materials for "Tango Angèle" and that they should contact you since the parts for the original recording are in your possession. We beg you to be so kind and immediately get in touch with Electrola. We have made no exclusive arrangements with Lindström, so that there is no reason to refuse Electrola another recording. By the way, you have taken care of the negotiations with Lindström yourself, so that you will know best whether a new recording with Electrola is possible. We beg you to inform us about the result of your negotiations with Electrola.

147. A recording of Marek Weber's dance arrangement of "Tango Angèle," issued by Electrola (E.G. 853) testifies to the popularity of the number.

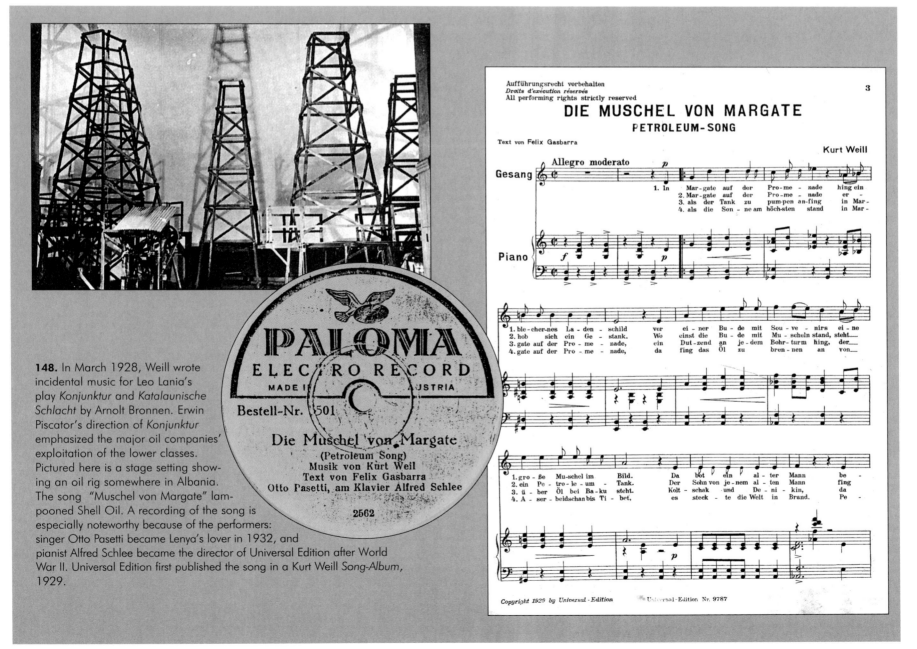

148. In March 1928, Weill wrote incidental music for Leo Lania's play *Konjunktur* and *Katalaunische Schlacht* by Arnolt Bronnen. Erwin Piscator's direction of *Konjunktur* emphasized the major oil companies' exploitation of the lower classes. Pictured here is a stage setting showing an oil rig somewhere in Albania. The song "Muschel von Margate" lampooned Shell Oil. A recording of the song is especially noteworthy because of the performers: singer Otto Pasetti became Lenya's lover in 1932, and pianist Alfred Schlee became the director of Universal Edition after World War II. Universal Edition first published the song in a Kurt Weill *Song-Album*, 1929.

> *Morgen 11⁰⁰ Arrangierprobe*
> **Katalaunische Schlacht**
> *Damen: Carola Neher*
> *Herren: Müthel, Frank, Grätz*
> *Wäscher, Weber*

149. None of Weill's music survives from Arnolt Bronnen's play *Katalaunische Schlacht*, first performed at the Berlin Staatstheater on 25 April 1928. Production photos feature a gramophone as a prominent prop. Weill is shown here supervising the moving of a gramophone into the theater.

150. This addendum to the contract between Weill, Brecht, and Felix Bloch Erben for publishing and licensing *Die Dreigroschenoper*, signed 26 April 1928, also clarifies Universal Edition's rights. Royalties were split 62½ percent for Brecht, 25 percent for Weill, and 12½ percent for Elisabeth Hauptmann.

FELIX BLOCH ERBEN
BERLIN·WILMERSDORF I

VERLAG DRAMATISCHER UND
MUSIKALISCHER WERKE
REDAKTION UND VERLAG
DES „CHARIVARI"

Anhang zum § 5.

Der vorliegende Vertrag tritt erst dann in Kraft, wenn das vorgesehene Abkommen bezüglich des in § 1 genannten Werkes mit der Direktion des "Theater am Schiffbauerdamm" in Berlin endgültig zustande kommt oder wenn die Firma Felix Bloch Erben innerhalb von drei Tagen nach Ablieferung des Buches durch die Autoren die Erklärung abgibt, dass sie den Bühnenvertrieb des Werkes übernimmt.

Herr Bert Brecht verpflichtet sich, das fertige Buch des Werkes rechtzeitig für die Aufführung abzuliefern, während Herr Kurt Weill verpflichtet ist, die vollständige Partitur innerhalb von sechs Wochen nach Uebergabe des fertigen Buches mit allen Texten an ihn abzuliefern.

Im Falle der endgültigen Vertriebsübernahme des in § 1 genannten Werkes durch die Firma Felix Bloch Erben stellt diese den Herren Bert Brecht und Kurt Weill einen Tantièmen-Vorschuss von Rmk. 5.000.-- (fünftausend Reichsmark) zur Verfügung, der mit 1% über dem Bankdiskont verzinslich ist. Der Tantièmen-Vorschuss ist wie folgt zahlbar: M 3000.-- am Tage der endgültigen Vertriebs-Uebernahme und M 2000.-- bei Ablieferung der vollständigen Partitur.

Die Firma Felix Bloch Erben ist berechtigt, sämtliche auf Grund des vorliegenden Vertrages bei ihr eingehenden Beträge bis zur Deckung des Tantièmen-Vorschusses nebst den aufgelaufenen Zinsen zurückzubehalten.

Hinsichtlich des Musikverlages an dem in § 1 genannten Werke besteht Einverständnis darüber, dass durch die vertraglichen Bindungen

FELIX BLOCH ERBEN
BERLIN·WILMERSDORF I

VERLAG DRAMATISCHER UND
MUSIKALISCHER WERKE
REDAKTION UND VERLAG
DES „CHARIVARI"

-2-

des Herrn Kurt Weill Musikverlag der Universal Edition A.-G., Wien, zu übertragen ist. Hinsichtlich des Buches und der von ihm verfassten Texte ist Herr Bert Brecht verpflichtet, den üblichen Musikverlags-Vertrag mit der Universal Edition abzuschliessen.

Die Universal Edition, die das Material des Werkes für die Bühnen-Aufführungen herstellt, hat sinngemäss auch das Recht, ein Regie-Buch zu drucken, während sich Herr Brecht das Druckrecht für sein Buch mit Texten für den Buchhandel vorbehält, und zwar in der Weise, dass nach zwanzig Bühnen-Annahmen des Werkes die Firma Felix Bloch Erben selbst oder durch einen Dritten das Erscheinen in Buchhandel veranlassen muss. In der Zwischenzeit kann Herr Bert Brecht über das Erscheinen des Buches im Buchhandel selbst verfügen, ist jedoch verpflichtet, der Firma Felix Bloch Erben vorher davon Mitteilung zu machen, um ihr Gelegenheit zu geben, schon vor den zwanzig Bühnen-Annahmen das Erscheinen selbst oder durch einen Dritten zu veranlassen.

Die Bühnen-Tantièmen des Werkes werden zwischen Herrn Bert Brecht, Herrn Kurt Weill und Frau Elisabeth Hauptmann, die an dem Buch mitarbeitete, wie folgt verteilt:

Herr Bert Brecht erhält: .... 62½ %
Herr Kurt Weill erhält: .... 25 %
Frau Elisabeth Hauptmann erhält: .... 12½ %

Die Ludenoper
The Beggar's Opera
ein altenglisches Balladenstück
von
JOHN GAY
Übersetzt v. ELISABETH HAUPTMANN
Deutsche Bearbeitung
von
BERT BRECHT
Musik von
KURT WEILL
Uraufführung im Theater am Schiffbauerdamm
unter der neuen Direktion von
Ernst Josef Aufricht
im September 1928
Musikverlag: Universal-Edition, Wien

151. Soon after the contract was signed, Felix Bloch Erben began advertising in its magazine *Charivari* Brecht's forthcoming German adaptation of John Gay's *The Beggar's Opera* in a translation by Elisabeth Hauptmann and with original music by Weill.

152. Weill and Lenya on the French Riviera, where they went with Brecht, Helene Weigel, and Elisabeth Hauptmann to work on *Die Dreigroschenoper*, May or June 1928. Weill, an avid swimmer, enjoyed the Mediterranean coast as a favorite escape from Berlin.

153. Silhouettes of Weill and Brecht by artist and filmmaker Lotte Reiniger. Reiniger was married to Karl Koch, who reportedly filmed large portions of a performance of *Die Dreigroschenoper* in September 1928. The film has not been found.

Kurt Weill
Charlottenburg
Luisenplatz 3
Tel. Wilhelm 8025

Berlin, 26. 7. 1928

Sehr geehrter Herr Dr.,

anbei sende ich Ihnen die gewünschten Angaben für das Lexikon:
Kurt Weill (mit zwei l!), badischer Abstammung, geboren 2. März 1900 in Dessau, erster Unterricht bei dem damaligen Dessauer Kapellmeister Albert Bing. 1918 Berliner Hochschule für Musik, aber nur für ein Semester, dann Theaterkapellmeister, zuerst in Dessau, dann am Stadttheater Lüdenscheid (Westf.). 1921 Rückkehr nach Berlin, Schüler von Busoni, bis zu seinem Tode persönlich eng befreundet. Lebt in Berlin.
Veröffentliche Werke: (alle: Universal-Edition, Wien)
op. 8 Streichquartett, op. 9 "Quodlibet" für Orchester, op. 10 "Frauentanz", 7 Lieder nach mittelalterlichen Texten für Sopran und Bratsche, Flöte, Klarinette, Horn, Fagott. op. 12 Konzert für Violine und Blasorchester (Paris 1925). op. 15 "Der neue Orpheus", Kantate für Sopran und Orchester.
Bühnenwerke: "Der Protagonist", ein Akt Oper, Text von Georg Kaiser (Dresdener Staatsoper 1926). "Royal Palace", Oper in einem Akt, Text von Iwan Goll. "Der Zar lässt sich photographieren", Opera buffa in einem Akt, Text von Georg Kaiser. "Mahagonny", Songspiel, Text von Bert Brecht (Baden-Baden 1927). Das letztere ist eine Studie zu der demnächst erscheinenden dreiaktigen Oper "Mahagonny", Text von Bert Brecht. Ferner erscheint soeben eine neu komponierte Musik zu "Des Bettlers Oper", einer deutschen Bearbeitung der altenglischen Balladenoper "The Beggars Opera" (Textbearbeitung Bert Brecht).
Unveröffentlicht: Neben einer Anzahl von Frühwerken (darunter eine

Symphonie, ein Orchesterwerk "Fantasia, Passacaglia und Hymnus", ferner Kammermusik und Lieder) ein a capella Chorwerk "Recordare", Orchesterlieder nach Rilke, eine Ballade "Vom Tod im Wald" für Bass und 10 Bläser. Ausserdem mehrere Schauspielmusiken, u.a. zu Strindbergs "Gustav III.", Bronnens "Katalaunische Schlacht", Brechts "Leben Eduards II.". Eine unveröffentliche zweiaktige Oper "Na und?!" (geschrieben 1926)

Mit den besten Grüssen

Ihr sehr ergebener

Kurt Weill.

154. In a letter to music critic Alfred Einstein, Weill summarized his career and compositions up to July 1928.

155. Caspar Neher's sketches for *Die Dreigroschenoper*: the brothel in Act II (left) and Macheath's reprieve in Act III (below).

156. Caspar Neher's costume design sketch for Polly Peachum.

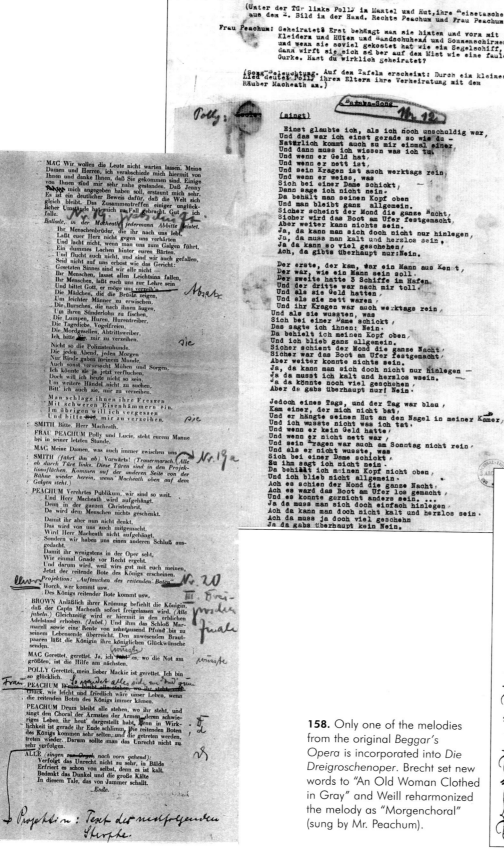

157. A diverse group of sources is required to reconstruct the changes made to *Die Dreigroschenoper* during a frantic rehearsal period. It includes a typescript of the libretto with Weill's annotations showing a reordering of the songs and a set of printer's proofs for Universal Edition's published libretto, also annotated by Weill. Universal Edition provided the printed libretto to theaters as rental material.

158. Only one of the melodies from the original *Beggar's Opera* is incorporated into *Die Dreigroschenoper*. Brecht set new words to "An Old Woman Clothed in Gray" and Weill reharmonized the melody as "Morgenchoral" (sung by Mr. Peachum).

. MAC'S MERRY MACS .

160. Weill orchestrated *Die Dreigroschenoper* for a jazz band of seven musicians. Many such bands were playing in Berlin at the time, including Mac's Merry Macs (pictured here), Alex Hyde and His New York Jazzband, Eddie Woods and His Kentucky Serenaders, and Eric Borchard's Jazz Band.

161. Three songs were cut from *Die Dreigroschenoper* before opening night: According to Lenya, Rosa Valetti objected to the risqué lyrics in Mrs. Peachum's "Ballade von der sexuellen Hörigkeit." The song was omitted from the published vocal score and did not appear in print until 1929, in the *Kurt Weill Album* (U.E. 9787). Jenny's only solo number, "Salomonsong," was also deleted before opening night, as was "Lucy's Aria" (see page 81). The English titles were added to Weill's manuscript by Marc Blitzstein in 1952.

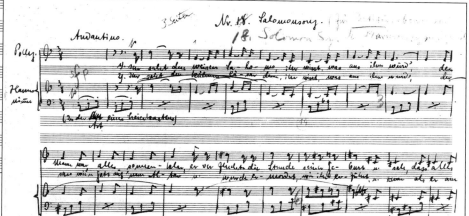

Weill (in Berlin) to Universal Edition, 21 August 1928: I am very glad that the parts for the *Beggar's Opera* will be prepared here since otherwise it would be very tight. The orchestra rehearsals begin on the 25th, the premiere is on the 31st. Today I would like to ask a favor of you. Now that I've finished work on the *Bettleroper*, I think I've written a good piece and that several numbers in it, at least musically, have great prospects for becoming popular very quickly. For that to happen, however, it is absolutely necessary that the music be given its due in all the promotional activity surrounding the premiere. Theater people (like all literary types) seem to be a bit frightened by the power of music, and I fear that in the announcements and notices in the press, etc., the score will be treated more as incidental music, although with its twenty numbers it goes far beyond the scope of the usual theater music. I'd like to ask that you categorically insist that the Theater am Schiffbauerdamm (NW 6 Schiffbauerdamm 4a) give my name as co-author in all publications, notices, posters, and advertisements, that my picture be printed in the program, etc.; otherwise, for purely business reasons, you cannot grant performance rights for the music. You know that I myself don't set any great store by such things, but if it isn't given enough attention at the premiere we may well lose all commercial potential for this music.

162. One of the most obvious parodies of opera comes in the Finale, when police chief Brown enters dressed as a mounted messenger to deliver the Queen's pardon in recitative.

159. Weill and Brecht wrote "Moritat von Mackie Messer" ("Mack the Knife") at the last minute for the street singer to set the tone for the entrance of Harald Paulsen (playing Macheath). Weill had the accompaniment of the strophic, sixteen-measure song adapted for barrel organ, which was played by the street singer.

DIE DREIGROSCHENOPER

Play with music; text by Bertolt Brecht,
after John Gay's *The Beggar's Opera* in a
German translation by Elisabeth Hauptmann

1928   Berlin, Theater am Schiffbauerdamm (31 August)
        Theo Mackeben, conductor; Erich Engel, director; Caspar Neher, designer

        Frankfurt, Neues Theater (20 October)
        Hamburg, Deutsches Schauspielhaus/Thalia-Theater (21 November)
        Breslau (Germany, now Poland), Lobetheater (1 December)
        Leipzig, Städtisches Theater (25 December)
1929   Augsburg, Stadttheater (13 January)
        Dresden, Albert Theater (17 January)
        Zurich, Neues Theater (29 January)
        Erfurt, Stadttheater (2 February)
        Oldenburg, Landestheater (4 February)
        Moscow, Kammertheater
        Hannover, Deutsches Theater (12 February)
        Stuttgart, Schauspielhaus (21 February)
        Königsberg (Germany, now Russia), Schauspielhaus (2 March)
        Vienna, Raimund Theater (9 March)
        Aussig (Czechoslovakia, now Czech Republic), Stadttheater
        Lübeck, Stadttheater (23 March)
        Nuremberg, Intimes Theater (30 March)
        Magdeburg, Städtisches Theater (12 April)
        Mannheim, Nationaltheater (17 April)
        Bremen, Schauspielhaus (19 April)
        Bonn, Stadttheater (23 April)
        Halle, Städtische Bühnen (24 April)
        Cottbus, Stadttheater (27 April)
        Graz (Austria), Städtische Bühnen (30 April)
        Brno (Czechoslovakia, now Czech Republic), Deutsches Theater (30 April)
        Basel, Stadttheater (31 May)
        Hagen, Stadttheater (13 June)
        Carlsbad (Czechoslovakia, now Czech Republic), Stadttheater (7 July)
        Wiesbaden, Staatstheater (25 August)
        Munich, Kammerspiele (1 September)
        Dusseldorf, Schauspielhaus (21 September)
        Riga (Latvia), Schauspiele (25 September)
        Darmstadt, Landestheater (29 September)
        Dusseldorf, Stadttheater (2 October)
        Frankfurt an der Oder, Stadttheater (12 October)
        Stettin, Stadttheater (19 October)
        Kassel, Staatstheater (26 October)
        Liegnitz (Germany, now Poland), Stadttheater (4 November)
        Heilbronn, Stadttheater (14 November)
        Zurich, Stadttheater (22 November)
        Prague, Neues deutsches Theater (1 December)
        Greifswald, Neues Theater (9 December)

1930-33, in the following cities: Amsterdam, Bad Oeynhausen, Bad Kudowa
(Kudova), Bern, Beuthen (Byton), Brandenburg, Braunschweig, Brieg (Brzeg),
Budapest, Bunzlau (Bolesławiek), Coburg, Cologne, Copenhagen, Danzig (Gdańsk),
Dessau, Dortmund, Eger (Cheb), Elberfeld, Gera, Görlitz, Hanau, Helsinki,
Hildesheim, Karlsruhe, Kiel, Koblenz, Leningrad, Ljubljana, M.-Ostrau (Ostrava),
Meiningen, Memel (Klaipeda), Münster, New York, Olmütz (Olomouc), Oslo, Paris,
Pforzheim, Philadelphia, Pilsen (Plzeň), Potsdam, Reichenberg (Liberec), Remscheid,
Rostock, Salzburg, Stockholm, Talinn, Tel Aviv, Teplitz-Schönau (Teplice-Lázně),
Troppau (Opava), Ulm, Zittau, Zwickau

1934-45 Amsterdam, Antwerpen, Johannesburg, Moscow, Paris

1945-50 Berlin, Evanston, Flensburg, Hamburg, Hannover, Munich, Stuttgart,
Urbana-Champaign, Zurich

163. The opulent, baroque interior of the Theater am Schiffbauerdamm
in Berlin provided an ironic setting for an "opera for beggars."

164. Program of the premiere of *Die Dreigroschenoper*. Now a 20th-
century classic, the success of this play with music provided Weill with a
renewed artistic confidence and the financial freedom to quit teaching
and stop writing criticism for *Der deutsche Rundfunk*.

165. Scene from *Die Dreigroschenoper* showing Caspar Neher's stage design, in particular the much-praised half-curtain and banners carrying narrative inscriptions. Visible top center are the organ pipes and two members of the Lewis Ruth Band.

166. The seven-member Lewis Ruth Band is positioned at the back of the stage. The leader and keyboard player, Theo Mackeben, was also a composer and arranger.

167. Three photos from the original production (clockwise from upper left): Filch joins the ranks of the beggars in Mr. Peachum's shop; Mr. Peachum bemoans Macheath's escape from jail; the messenger delivers the Queen's pardon of Macheath and a happy ending.

„Die Dreigroschenoper."

Uraufführung im Theater am Schiffbauerdamm.

Da gibt es nun nichts — das war ein großer Sieg.

[Fraktur review text by Walter Steinthal, Berlin — full article]

Walter Steinthal.

168. Caricatures by Erwin Goltz of the original cast of *Die Dreigroschenoper*: Erich Ponto (Peachum), Kurt Gerron (Brown, Moritat Singer), Harald Paulsen (Macheath), Roma Bahn (Polly), Rosa Valetti (Frau Peachum), published in *12-Uhr Blatt* along with a review by Walter Steinthal.

169. Unknown artist's rendering of the five principal cast members published in *Berliner Zeitung am Mittag*, 1 September 1928.

Die Hauptdarsteller der „Dreigroschen-Oper": Ponto, Valetti, Paulsen, Bahn, Gerron

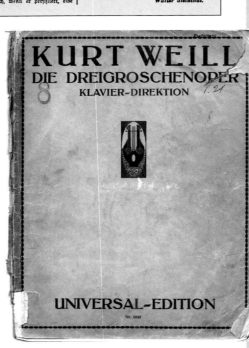

170. The full score of *Die Dreigroschenoper* was never published during Weill's life. Instead, Universal Edition provided a minimally cued piano-conductor score to theaters. Weill protested that it was full of errors and failed to give an accurate impression of the piece.

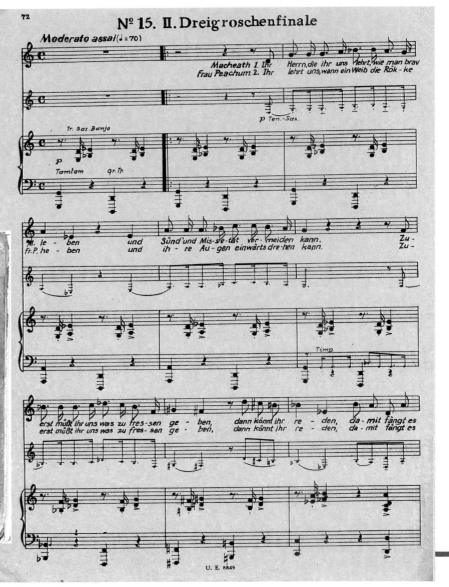

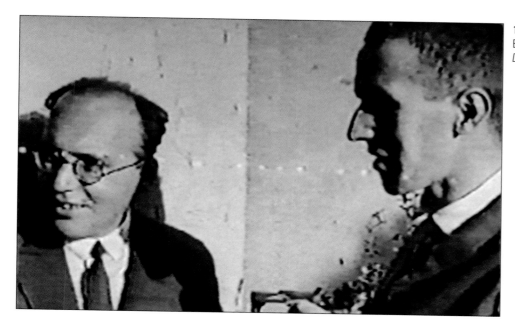

171. A frame taken from film footage of Brecht and Weill together at the time of *Die Dreigroschenoper*.

172. An advertisement in *Charivari* placed after the successful premiere of *Die Dreigroschenoper*, with reprinted reviews.

173. Weill autographed this copy of "Kanonen-Song" to Otto Klemperer: "True, only a three penny song—but good."

Universal Edition (in Vienna) to Weill, 8 September 1928: Now to the question of the dance orchestra editions. These exquisite pieces must be exquisitely arranged, and of the specialists here there is unfortunately no one who has enough imagination or originality for the job. In Berlin, on the other hand, there are a number of excellent modern arrangers, and we would like to suggest that you yourself get in touch with a qualified person and commission arrangements of the most important songs. You already have the parts there and could discuss the technique with the arranger on the spot. We have already sent in the portions of the score we have received to be photoprinted so that these too, should you need them, will be available in a few days. We ask for your help in this important matter so that we can do everything possible to produce the piano score, libretto, individual numbers for piano, solo orchestra editions and printed orchestral score as quickly as possible for theaters.

In Berlin the following arrangers should be considered:
Jerzy Fitelberg, Berlin-Halensee, Westfälische Strasse 58;
Nico Dostal, Berlin W. 30., Hohenstaufenstr. 33;
Hermann Krome, Berlin S.W. 48, Verl. Hedemannstr. 5/III;
Hartwig v. Platen, Berlin-Wilmersdorf, Prinz Regentenstr. 65.

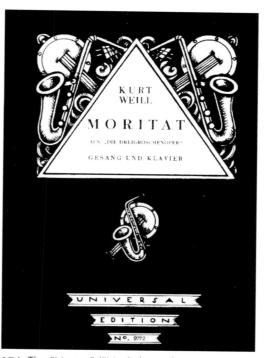

174. The "Moritat" ("Mack the Knife") was one of six songs from *Die Dreigroschenoper* issued as sheet music by Universal Edition. Kiepenheuer also published a volume of Brecht's and Hauptmann's lyrics. The "Moritat" was not the most popular number initially; it did not obtain "hit" status until recordings of it were made by American popular musicians in the 1950s after Weill's death.

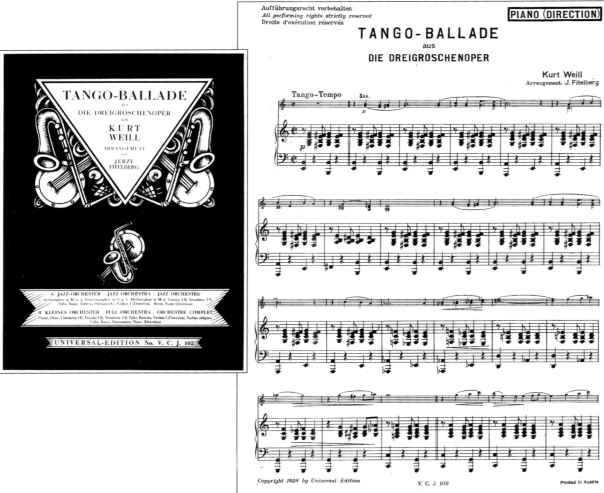

175. Several songs from *Die Dreigroschenoper* were arranged for jazz band or dance band and played in Berlin's fashionable hotels. This version of "Tango-Ballade" ("Zuhälterballade") was arranged by Jerzy Fitelberg.

177. The Adlon, an opulent hotel in Berlin where Marek Weber and his orchestra played tunes from *Die Dreigroschenoper*, held daily tea dances at 5 o'clock.

176. Marek Weber and his orchestra at the Hotel Adlon, 1927.

Weill (in Berlin) to Universal Edition, [received 24 September 1928]:
Mr. Karl Koch, one of our best film producers, filmed large segments of the *Dreigroschenoper* during a performance. From this material one could select and enlarge about fifty excellent photos showing all the important scenes and position changes for a performance and include them on four pages of the piano score. This would be an entirely modern, unprecedented innovation that would enhance the value of the piano score not only for the theaters, but also for the consumer, especially since this Berlin production of the *Dreigroschenoper* already enjoys a great reputation. I could get you the necessary material right away. According to Mr. Koch's preliminary estimate the cost of these photo pages would be about 250 Marks. Please wire me about it immediately.

178. A piece of *Dreigroschenoper* wallpaper.

179. "Lucy's aria" was cut from *Die Dreigroschenoper* because Kate Kühl (who played Lucy) was unable to sing the mock-operatic number. It was first printed four years later in *Die Musik* 25, no. 2 (November 1932). Weill never orchestrated it. Shown here are the first and third pages.

Weill (in Berlin) to Universal Edition, 11 October 1928: Incidentally, I hear from Frankfurt that they already want to start making all kinds of orchestra reductions in the *Dreigroschenoper*. I consider that very dangerous and ask that you forbid Director Hellmer from making any changes in the music or instrumentation without my permission.

Weill (in Berlin) to Universal Edition, 2 October 1928: First to the question of the essay: I was very pleased, Dr. Heinsheimer, that in the latest *Anbruch* issue you take such an energetic stand on a movement that I, as you know, feel is absolutely trend-setting. It is also very exciting that you want to take the lead along this line. I just don't know whether it would be tactically wise if I myself now attempted to give a theoretical foundation to this movement, of which I am so far the only exponent. In such an essay I would have to talk almost exclusively about what I have done in the *Dreigroschenoper*, for in *Mahagonny* I will already be a good deal further. Also, as you know, I've always been a little reluctant to write about what I am doing because to date these remarks have always been misinterpreted. Don't you think that another could say what absolutely has to be said more easily and precisely than I myself? For someone else could also establish one of the most essential points, which is that my music in the *Dreigroschenoper* (and thereby the entire tendency of this work) is enjoying the broadest possible popular success. Perhaps it is possible to find a form for me to say all that, maybe with you writing above: "From a letter from Weill to his publisher," and then the entire thing would actually seem as if it had been excerpted from a letter.

180. Dolbin's caricature of the five composers who contributed to the Berlin im Licht festival: Tiessen, Toch, Butting, Weill, and Hindemith.

181. Weill contributed the title song to "Berlin im Licht," a festival of lighting displays throughout the city that could be seen by car, rail, and on foot. Composer Max Butting and other members of the November Group organized the music component of the festival as a way to bridge the gap between popular and serious music. Ten simultaneous outdoor concerts took place at busy plazas and meeting areas during the evening of 15 October 1928. Weill's "Berlin im Licht" is scored for military band. Universal Edition also published a song version, the text for which is credited to Weill but may have been written with Brecht's help.

Weill (in Berlin) to Universal Edition, 17 October 1928: I telegraphed you about the favorable outcome of the Charlottenburg performance. After the *Zar* the response was extraordinary and all the whistling forced the cast to come out for twenty curtain calls. You have no doubt read the excellent reviews by Kastner, Schrenk (especially good!), Pringsheim, Bie, among others (if not, I can send them). I was especially pleased with Weissmann's complete turnaround. In any event, given the circumstances, I believe that we could hardly have expected a more favorable result from this performance.

I am enclosing the article [for *Anbruch*] in the form of an answer to your letter. I hope it arrives in time. I would only ask that in your letter, which you will also print, you leave out the sentence: "Weill as Humperdinck" since I have a very personal aversion to this composer. Perhaps you could write instead something along the lines: "From Offenbach to Weill," or the like.

182. Program for a performance of a double bill of *Der Protagonist* and *Der Zar lässt sich photographieren* at the Städtische Oper Berlin, October 1928. These were the first performances of either opera in Berlin.

183. Scene from *Der Zar lässt sich photographieren* in Berlin, sets designed by Gustav Vargo.

184. Climactic scene from *Der Protagonist* as staged in Berlin.

KORRESPONDENZ ÜBER DREIGROSCHEN-OPER

Lieber Herr Weill!

Der sensationelle Erfolg der „Dreigroschenoper", der ein Werk eines ganz neuartigen, in die Zukunft weisenden Stiles plötzlich zum Kassenschlager werden läßt, bestätigt aufs erfreulichste die Prophezeiungen, die in diesem Blatte wiederholt geäußert wurden. Die neue, volkstümliche Opern-Operette, die aus den artistischen und sozialen Voraussetzungen der Gegenwart den richtigen Schluß zieht, ist da in einem schönen Musterbeispiel gelungen.

Dürfen wir Sie, der Sie unseren soziologischen und ästhetischen Ableitungen die eindeutige Legitimation praktischer Leistung und bewiesenen Erfolges voraushaben, bitten, über den hier beschrittenen Weg nun auch theoretisch sich in unserm Blatt zu äußern?

Lieber Anbruch!

Ich danke Ihnen für Ihren Brief und will Ihnen gern einiges sagen über den Weg, den wir, Brecht und ich, mit diesem Werke eingeschlagen haben und den wir weiterzugehen gedenken.

Sie weisen in Ihrem Brief auf die soziologische Bedeutung der „Dreigroschenoper" hin. Tatsächlich beweist der Erfolg unseres Stückes, daß die Schaffung und Durchsetzung dieses neuen Genres nicht nur für die Situation der Kunst im rechten Moment kam, sondern daß auch das Publikum auf eine Auffrischung einer bevorzugten Theatergattung geradezu zu warten schien. Ich weiß nicht, ob unsere Gattung nun an die Stelle der Operette treten wird. Warum sollen nicht, nachdem nun auch Goethe durch das Medium eines Operettentenors wieder auf Erden erschienen ist, noch eine weitere Reihe geschichtlicher oder zumindest fürstlicher Persönlichkeiten am zweiten Aktschluß ihren tragischen Aufschrei von sich geben? Das erledigt sich von selbst, und ich glaube gar nicht, daß hier eine Lücke frei wird, die es auszufüllen lohnt. Wichtiger für uns alle ist die Tatsache, daß hier zum erstenmal der Einbruch in eine Verbrauchsindustrie gelungen ist, die bisher einer völlig anderen Art von Musikern, von Schriftstellern reserviert war. Wir kommen mit der „Dreigroschenoper" an ein Publikum heran, das uns entweder gar nicht kannte, oder das uns jedenfalls die Fähigkeit absprach, einen Hörerkreis zu interessieren, der weit über den Rahmen des Musik- und Opernpublikums hinausgeht.

Von diesem Standpunkt aus gesehen, reiht sich die „Dreigroschenoper" in eine Bewegung ein, von der heute fast alle jungen Musiker ergriffen werden. Die Aufgabe des l'art pour l'art-Standpunktes, die Abwendung vom individualistischen Kunstprinzip, die Filmmusik-Ideen, der Anschluß an die Jugendmusikbewegung, die mit all dem in Verbindung stehende Vereinfachung der musikalischen Ausdrucksmittel — das alles sind Schritte auf dem gleichen Wege.

Nur die Oper verharrt noch in ihrer „splendid isolation". Noch immer stellt das Opernpublikum eine abgeschlossene Gruppe von

24

Menschen dar, die scheinbar außerhalb des großen Theaterpublikums stehen. Noch immer werden „Oper" und „Theater" als zwei völlig getrennte Begriffe behandelt. Noch immer wird in neuen Opern eine Dramaturgie durchgeführt, eine Sprache gesprochen, werden Stoffe behandelt, die auf dem Theater dieser Zeit völlig undenkbar wären. Und immer wieder muß man hören: „Das geht vielleicht im Theater, aber nicht in der Oper!". Die Oper ist als aristokratische Kunstgattung begründet worden, und alles, was man „Tradition der Oper" nennt, ist eine Betonung dieses gesellschaftlichen Grundcharakters dieser Gattung. Es gibt aber heute in der ganzen Welt keine Kunstform von so ausgesprochen gesellschaftlicher Haltung mehr, und besonders das Theater hat sich mit Entschiedenheit einer Richtung zugewandt, die man wohl eher als gesellschaftsbildend bezeichnen kann. Wenn also der Rahmen der Oper eine derartige Annäherung an das Zeittheater nicht erträgt, muß eben dieser Rahmen gesprengt werden.

Nur so ist es zu verstehen, daß der Grundcharakter fast aller wirklich wertvollen Opernversuche der letzten Jahre ein rein destruktiver war. In der „Dreigroschenoper" war bereits ein Neuaufbau möglich, weil hier die Möglichkeit gegeben war, einmal ganz von vorn anzufangen. Was wir machen wollten, war die Urform der Oper. Bei jedem musikalischen Bühnenwerk taucht von neuem die Frage auf: Wie ist Musik, wie ist vor allem Gesang im Theater überhaupt möglich? Diese Frage wurde hier einmal auf die primitivste Art gelöst. Ich hatte eine realistische Handlung, mußte also die Musik dagegensetzen, da ich ihr jede Möglichkeit einer realistischen Wirkung abspreche. So wurde also die Handlung entweder unterbrochen, um Musik zu machen, oder sie wurde bewußt zu einem Punkte geführt, wo einfach gesungen werden mußte. Dazu kam, daß uns dieses Stück Gelegenheit bot, den Begriff „Oper" einmal als Thema eines Theaterabends aufzustellen. Gleich zu Beginn des Stückes wird der Zuschauer aufgeklärt: „Sie werden heute abend eine Oper für Bettler sehen. Weil diese Oper so prunkvoll gedacht war, wie nur Bettler sie erträumen, und weil sie doch so billig sein sollte, daß Bettler sie bezahlen können, heißt sie die ‚Dreigroschenoper'". Daher ist auch das letzte Dreigroschenfinale keineswegs eine Parodie, sondern hier wurde der Begriff „Oper" direkt zur Lösung eines Konfliktes, also als handlungsbildendes Element herangezogen und mußte daher in seiner reinsten, ursprünglichsten Form gestaltet werden.

Dieses Zurückgehen auf eine primitive Opernform brachte eine weitgehende Vereinfachung der musikalischen Sprache mit sich. Es galt eine Musik zu schreiben, die von Schauspielern, also von musikalischen Laien gesungen werden kann. Aber was zunächst eine Beschränkung schien, erwies sich im Laufe der Arbeit als eine ungeheure Bereicherung. Erst die Durchführung einer faßbaren, sinnfälligen Melodik ermöglichte das, was in der „Dreigroschenoper" gelungen ist, die Schaffung eines neuen Genres des musikalischen Theaters. Ihr ergebener

Kurt Weill.

25

185. Weill's article about *Die Dreigroschenoper* appeared as a letter to the editor in *Anbruch* 11, no. 1 (January 1929): 24-25.

Weill (in Berlin) to Universal Edition, 25 October 1928: I would like once again to speak with you at length about the potential impact of my popular compositions. I am very disturbed about the success of the pieces to date and about their immediate prospects. Every day I hear from all sides, from all public quarters, that these pieces have a popular appeal unlike any music in years. Everyone assures me that with the five or so pieces of this genre I have written to date one could easily make a small fortune. But at the moment I don't see any prospect at all of earning any appreciable sums with these pieces. I urge you not to take this as a reproach. I am quite certain and am firmly convinced that you are working on my behalf with the greatest industry and with all the means at your disposal. The only reason I bring this matter up is because I'm really afraid that by underexploiting these popular numbers I may miss a good opportunity to assure my financial well-being for years to come. I am convinced that my gift for writing a completely new kind of popular melody is absolutely unrivaled today. If this were ingeniously promoted on large scale there is no doubt that my popular compositions could take the place of American jazz music, which is already somewhat passé. That is also the unanimous conclusion of all the foreigners who have seen the *Dreigroschenoper*. I would therefore like to suggest that we get together as soon as possible to discuss in detail the possibilities presented here, preferably on Director Hertzka's next visit to Berlin. I would especially like to urge that we consider giving the best numbers from the *Dreigroschenoper* to a popular music publisher in America, since I don't see any other way of exploiting the incredible potential for my music in America. Music dealers here in Berlin aren't doing anything at all. I haven't heard anything from Mr. Huebner in weeks. Not one music store has displayed the two numbers. The papers are printing inquiries from the public asking why there is no music or any recordings of the *Dreigroschenoper*. It would be such a shame if the energy and prompt attention you invested in publishing these pieces were to go to waste in this way. And I don't know how many more pieces I'll be able to write with the impact of the "Alabama Song," the "Kanonensong," the "Tango Ballade," the "Ballade vom angenehmen Leben," and the "Moritat."

Weill (in Berlin) to Maurice Abravanel, [late 1928]: Please don't be angry about our long silence. Thank God you aren't among those who take offense at such things. All I can say is that gradually I am getting sick and tired of this fame of mine. I don't think that I have to elaborate to you the extent of this *Dreigroschenoper* success. All at once I have gotten the kind of things I had expected to achieve, at the earliest perhaps in another ten years or so. Of course, this offers lots of advantages—not only of a material kind, but also because my name (which right now is worth a lot of money!) will enable me to do all kinds of other things. I can assure you that I'll be taking full advantage of all possibilities.

By the way, have you seen the *Dreigroschenoper* yet? If at all possible, you should try to see it in Berlin. It really is a good piece and surely the best thing I have done so far. And musically, the Berlin performance is definitely worth hearing. At the moment the piece is a tremendous success in Leipzig and many other cities.

You can well imagine what an endless chain of various business opportunities this sudden world fame of mine has attracted. Sometimes I simply don't know how to cope anymore. On top of that, I've been doing all kinds of new things, among them a small cantata, *Das Berliner Requiem*, which is supposed to be done by the Frankfurt radio at the beginning of February. I'm working on *Mahagonny* again, but I won't bring it out before the beginning of next season. . . .

Lenja has become a famous actress and right now she is playing one big role after another at the Berlin Staatstheater. We now have a very charming apartment of our own and a small Fiat.

Weill (in Berlin) to Universal Edition, 29 December 1928: I went to the premiere of the *Dreigroschenoper* in Leipzig, where the work had an especially big success of Berlin proportions. For the time being it has been scheduled for daily performances for the next two weeks and the first performances sold out long ago. Enclosed are two reviews, which are especially good for me.

I have now finished the cantata for Frankfurt radio and believe that it is one of my best and most original pieces. It is called *Das Berliner Requiem* and consists of a series of seven pieces, part solemnly tragic, part ironic in character. Performance time 20-25 minutes. Scoring: three men's voices and fifteen instruments (winds, banjo, percussion and organ). I am quite convinced that thanks to its simplicity and similarity to my present stage style, this work will find its way into the concert halls. . . .

To the extent that I have connections, I am having the radio stations perform the songs from the *Dreigroschenoper*, which will naturally contribute a great deal to the dissemination of the pieces. . . . The record by the Deutsche Grammophon Corporation has appeared. It is very effective, though technically not quite up to the mark. Unfortunately I wasn't able to get a properly sung performance of the songs.

In returning most heartily your New Year's wishes, I wish all of U.E. a wonderful and "fruitful" 1929!

186. The first recording of music from *Die Dreigroschenoper* appeared on the Grammophon label. Paul Godwin and his "Jazz-Symphonikern" issued "Kanonen-Song" and "Tango-Ballade," recorded in September 1928.

187. Program of performance at the Theater am Schiffbauerdamm about three months after the opening. The cast has already changed significantly, although Paulsen, Valetti, Kühl, and Gerron remain.

188. Program and photo from Lion Feuchtwanger's play *Petroleuminseln*, for which Weill supplied the song "Das Lied von den braunen Inseln" ("Song of the Brown Islands"). Eugen Klöpfer (H.B. Ingram) played the male lead and Lenya played Charmian Peruchacha.

1929 – 1933

Every text I set looks entirely different once it's been swept through my music.

Kurt Weill

1929

Recordings of music from *Die Dreigroschenoper*, including songs and salon orchestra arrangements, are issued for the popular market.

February 7
Kleine Dreigroschenmusik für Blasorchester (December 1928–January 1929). Staatsoper am Platz der Republik (Krolloper), Berlin, Preussische Staatskapelle; Otto Klemperer, conductor.

March 6
Supervises the first production of *Die Dreigroschenoper* in Vienna. In 1929, the work has forty-six new productions in Germany as well as productions in Italy, Switzerland, Poland, Hungary, Finland, and the USSR.

April-May
Composes the first version of *Der Lindberghflug*. Weill and Paul Hindemith each set roughly half of Brecht's text.

Hopes to form a touring troupe for the purposes of presenting *Mahagonny Songspiel*, *Das Berliner Requiem*, and *Der Lindberghflug* in a new form between concert and theater.

May 22
Das Berliner Requiem (1928, Bertolt Brecht). Südwestdeutscher Rundfunkdienst Frankfurt; Ludwig Rottenberg, conductor.

May-June
Vacations at Hostellerie de la Plage, St. Cyr sur Mer, and works on *Happy End*.

June
Hindemith's *Neues vom Tage* is played at the Krolloper. Throughout the summer and fall, Weill and Universal Edition attempt to convince Klemperer and the Krolloper to produce *Aufstieg und Fall der Stadt Mahagonny*.

July 27
Der Lindberghflug (1929, original version with Paul Hindemith, text by Bertolt Brecht). Kurhaus, Baden-Baden, Frankfurter Rundfunkorchester; Hermann Scherchen, conductor. Neither Weill nor Hindemith is pleased with the result. Weill had already decided to set the entire text himself.

September 2
Happy End (June–August 1929, lyrics by Bertolt Brecht; play by Elisabeth Hauptmann and Brecht). Theater am Schiffbauerdamm, Berlin; Theo Mackeben, conductor; Erich Engel, director. The success of *Die Dreigroschenoper* is not repeated, and the play closes after three performances. Universal Edition does not publish a vocal score or libretto. The work is not revived until 1958.

September
Universal Edition publishes the *Song Album*, which contains six previously unpublished songs.

Early October
Considers writing songs for "Apollo-Brunnenstraße," a play by Stefan Grossmann with lyrics by Franz Hessel. Hans Heinsheimer of Universal Edition discourages him, and Weill drops the project.

November
Die Legende vom toten Soldaten and *Zu Potsdam unter den Eichen* (1929, Bertolt Brecht). Berliner Schubertchor; Karl Rankl, conductor. (*Zu Potsdam unter den Eichen* is arranged for men's chorus from the orginal version written for *Das Berliner Requiem*.)

December
Attempts to get the rights to Jaroslav Hašek's novel *Good Soldier Schweik* to set as an opera with a libretto by Brecht. Difficulties in dealing with Hašek's heirs doom the project; by June 1930 Weill has given up the idea.

December 5
Der Lindberghflug (September–November 1929, second version with music entirely by Weill). Staatsoper am Platz der Republik (Krolloper); Otto Klemperer, conductor.

1930

February
Travels to Leipzig two weeks before the premiere of *Aufstieg und Fall der Stadt Mahagonny*. Lenya records two songs from the opera for Ultraphon, conducted by Theo Mackeben.

March
The Deutsches Theater, run by Max Reinhardt, takes an option to give the first Berlin performance of *Aufstieg und Fall der Stadt Mahagonny*. Despite Weill's high hopes, it becomes clear by the end of October that the opera will not be performed there.

March 9
Aufstieg und Fall der Stadt Mahagonny (1927–30, Bertolt Brecht). Neues Theater, Leipzig; Gustav Brecher, conductor; Walther Brügmann, director. The premiere performance is interrupted by Nazi demonstrations, and subsequent performances continue under close police supervision.

March 28
American premiere of the Konzert für Violine und Blasorchester, op. 12 under Fritz Reiner in Cincinnati with violinist Emil Heermann.

April
Universal Edition publishes "Sieben Stücke nach der *Dreigroschenoper*," arranged for violin and piano by Stefan Frenkel. Weill presents a *Mahagonny* radio program in Berlin.

June 23
Der Jasager (January–May 1930, Bertolt Brecht). Live broadcast, with the stage premiere the following day. Zentralinstitut für Erziehung und Unterricht, Berlin; Kurt Drabek, conductor, with singers taken from the Staats-Akademie für Kirchen- und Schulmusik and other Berlin schools. After the Festival for New Music rejects Brecht and Eisler's *Die Maßnahme*, Weill withdraws *Der Jasager* in protest. It is premiered independently of the festival as a "counter-event." The work is immensely successful and is subsequently performed in schools all over Germany. In November, Weill discourages a performance at the Krolloper with Klemperer until the work is firmly established in the school setting.

Summer
Temporary end of Weill's collaboration with Brecht because of growing aesthetic and political differences.

July 21
Travels to London and stays at the Bushy Hall Hotel; the reason for this visit is unknown.

July 26
Travels to Unterschondorf (Ammersee) to work with Brecht, possibly on the film version of *Die Dreigroschenoper*.

August
Considers settings of Jack London and an opera based upon an unspecified work by Franz Kafka. Begins work on a new opera libretto with Caspar Neher, which becomes *Die Bürgschaft*.

Autumn
Der Jasager "Neue Fassung" (autumn 1930). Two new interpolations are included in a performance at the Karl-Marx School, Berlin-Neukölln.

October
The Frankfurt performances of *Aufstieg und Fall der Stadt Mahagonny* are accompanied by Nazi disturbances.

October–November
Weill and Brecht take legal action against the Nero-Tobis company for breach of contract arising from unauthorized changes made to *Die Dreigroschenoper* in the film version to be directed by G. W. Pabst. Weill's complaint is upheld; Brecht's is rejected, but the film company settles with him anyway; both collect damages.

189. Secret meeting of Nazi storm troopers in a forest, before their movement was made legal in 1932.

December	Ultraphon records songs from *Die Dreigroschenoper* with Kurt Gerron, Erich Ponto, Willy Trenk-Trebitsch, Erika Helmke, Lenya, and the Lewis Ruth Band conducted by Theo Mackeben. Despite the fact that they were made more than two years after the premiere and involved several new performers, these recordings have frequently been misidentified as original cast recordings.

1931

February 6	*Mann ist Mann*, incidental music for the 1931 Berlin production of Bertolt Brecht's play. Partly missing. Berlin Staatstheater; Brecht and Ernst Legal, directors.
February 6?	Signs a final settlement agreement with Nero-Tobis Films.
Mid-February	Spends a couple of weeks at the Hotel und Terrassen Wang, Brückenberg, to recuperate after his lawsuit against Nero-Tobis.
February 19	Premiere of *Die Dreigroschenoper* film directed by G. W. Pabst, in Berlin.
April	Considers a large-scale choral composition for David Joseph Ball, pioneer of the Austrian Workers' Music movement. Proposes a collaboration with Brecht for a piece inspired by Jack London's *General Strike*. Lack of time and quarrels with Brecht put an end to the project.
April 4	American premiere of *Der Lindberghflug*, performed by the Philadelphia Orchestra under Leopold Stokowski.
May–June	Vacations with Lenya at the Provence Hotel, Le Lavandou, France. They travel by car through Spain, meeting Caspar Neher for ten days in Zaraux (near San Sebastian) for work on *Die Bürgschaft*. Returning to Berlin via Paris, they stay at the Hotel Astor. Weill, concerned by the worsening political situation, opens a Swiss bank account.
August–November	Lenya travels to Russia to act in a film directed by Erwin Piscator. By this time Weill is romantically involved with Erika Neher (Caspar Neher's wife).
October	Buys a house as a birthday present for Lenya at Wissmannstraße 7 (now called Käthe-Kollwitz-Straße) in Kleinmachnow, a fashionable suburb in southwest Berlin. Finishes orchestrating *Die Bürgschaft*.
December 21	Weill's revised version of *Aufstieg und Fall der Stadt Mahagonny* opens for a commercial run at Theater am Kurfürstendamm, Berlin. Revises some numbers to accommodate Lenya and other singing actors in the cast. Quarrels with Brecht in the course of rehearsals.

1932

January	Electrola records "Querschnitt aus der Oper *Aufstieg und Fall der Stadt Mahagonny*," conducted by Hans Sommer.
January 11	Karl Kraus presents a lecture about *Aufstieg und Fall der Stadt Mahagonny* in his series "Theater der Dichtung." Weill plays excerpts on the piano.
March 11	*Die Bürgschaft* (1930–31, Caspar Neher). Berlin Städtische Oper; Fritz Stiedry, conductor; Carl Ebert, director. The opera premieres in the spotlight of direct political attack from the Nationalist and Nazi press. Weill's most ambitious work to date, it becomes a rallying point for the remaining defenders of the Republic's artistic freedom.
March	Moves into the new house in Kleinmachnow (Berlin-Zehlendorf). Lenya and Weill are now estranged, but Weill registers the deed in Lenya's name.
April–May	Discusses with Caspar Neher and Universal Edition three project ideas: a cantata for workers' choirs, a new genre of opera for amateurs, and small-scale operas without chorus for commercial theaters.
April 26	Attends the first Viennese performance of *Aufstieg und Fall der Stadt Mahagonny*, with Lotte Lenya as Jenny. During rehearsals Lenya meets a singer named Otto Pasetti (who plays Jimmy) and stays in Vienna to live with him.
June	Proposes four projects to impresario and director Erik Charell for a series of international productions intended for Vienna, Paris, London, and Berlin. The plan, which eventually involved Caspar Neher and Georg Kaiser, never materialized.
August	Begins composing *Der Silbersee* to a text by Georg Kaiser.
December 11	Acclaimed performance at the Salle Gaveau in Paris of *Mahagonny Songspiel* (with four additional numbers from the opera) and *Der Jasager* conducted by Maurice Abravanel with Lenya and Pasetti performing. The concert is sponsored by Vicomte Charles de Noailles and Vicomtesse Marie-Laure de Noailles. Weill investigates possible commissions while in Paris.

1933

Early 1933	Lenya begins divorce proceedings in Germany.
January	Composes the first movement of Symphony no. 2.
January 30	Hitler becomes chancellor.
February 18	*Der Silbersee* (August 1932–33, Georg Kaiser). Altes Theater, Leipzig; Gustav Brecher, conductor; Detlef Sierck [Douglas Sirk], director. Simultaneous premieres in Erfurt and Magdeburg.
February 22	Nazis demonstrate at the second performance of *Der Silbersee* in Magdeburg. Weill is subjected to anti-Semitic attacks and is asked to resign from a film project for Tobis.
February 27–28	The burning of the German parliament building (Reichstag) signals Hitler's rise to absolute power.
March 4	The last public performance of any work by Weill (*Der Silbersee*) in Germany until 1945. In early March Lenya and Louise Hartung pack some of Weill's belongings from the house on Wissmannstraße and drive Weill to Munich, where they presumably went to await the outcome of the 5 March elections. Lenya proceeds to Vienna and Weill returns to Berlin, where he first stays in a hotel in Charlottenburg and then moves to the Nehers' house.
March 21	Potsdam Day. Weill flees Berlin by car with Caspar and Erika Neher, arriving in Paris on 23 March. Stays first at the Hôtel Jacob and the Hôtel Splendide, and soon moves to the home of Charles and Marie-Laure de Noailles, 11 place des États-Unis.

April	Receives a commission from Edward James to write a ballet for the troupe Les Ballets 1933. Weill tries to interest Jean Cocteau in writing a libretto for a *ballet chanté*. When Cocteau declines, the financier Edward James suggests Brecht as author, and Weill agrees. Weill and Cocteau decide to collaborate on a Faust opera in a modern setting.
April 3	Universal Edition cuts Weill's monthly stipend in half.
April 5	Meets Lenya in Nancy and offers her and Pasetti parts in *Die sieben Todsünden*.
Mid-April	Brecht arrives in Paris from Carona, Switzerland; together he and Weill write the text of *Die sieben Todsünden* to a scenario by Edward James, after which he composes the music
April 13	American premiere of *Die Dreigroschenoper* in an English translation by Gifford Cochran and Jerrold Krimsky, Empire Theater, New York. The production closes on 24 April after only twelve performances.
June	Baron Florian von Pasetti tries to get some of Weill's money out of Germany. Members of Hitler Youth burn Weill's music in public demonstrations.
June 7	*Die sieben Todsünden* (Bertolt Brecht). Théâtre des Champs-Elysées, Paris, and 30 June–15 July 1933, Savoy Theatre, London; Maurice Abravanel, conductor; George Balanchine, choreographer. This is the first work by Weill to be produced in England. Weill left Paris for Italy a week after the opening. A concert of the "Paris version" of *Mahagonny* and *Kleine Dreigroschenmusik* is presented on 20 June at the Salle Gaveau.
June 13–August	Vacations in Italy (Alassio, Positano, Rome, Florence) while *Die sieben Todsünden* plays in London.

June 18	Asks Universal Edition to send copies of his published vocal scores to his brother Hanns in Mannheim.
September	*Es regnet* (after Jean Cocteau) and *Der Abschiedsbrief* (Erich Kästner), Paris. Written for Marlene Dietrich in response to a request for revue and recording material.
September 3	Stays again at the Hôtel Splendide, Paris.
September 18	Divorce from Lotte Lenya is finalized in Potsdam.
Late September	Universal Edition begins to negotiate a release from Weill's contract.
October 31	Signs a new publishing agreement with Heugel, Paris, which guarantees an advance of 4,000 French francs per month.
November 3	*La grande complainte de Fantômas* (Robert Desnos). Radio Paris; Alejo Carpentier, conductor; Antonin Artaud, director. Largely missing.
November 19	Weill and Universal Edition come to agreement on the termination of his contract. Universal Edition retains rights in the works they have published to date.
November 23	Writes to Lenya from his new apartment: 9 bis place Dreux, Louveciennes (outside of Paris).
November 26	In Paris, Weill is subjected to a pro-Hitler, anti-Semitic demonstration led by composer Florent Schmitt, after a performance of three songs from *Der Silbersee* conducted by Maurice Abravanel. Lenya sells the house in Berlin and sends Weill some furniture in Paris.
December 24	Travels to Rome for a production of the "Paris version" of *Mahagonny* and *Der Jasager* (December 29).

1 9 2 9

MUSIC + THEATER:	LITERATURE + FILM:	SCIENCE + SOCIETY:	POLITICS:
Franz Lehár *Das Land des Lächelns*	Alfred Döblin *Berlin Alexanderplatz*	Airship "Graf Zeppelin" flies around the world	Trotsky expelled from USSR
Max Brand *Maschinist Hopkins*	Erich Maria Remarque *Im Westen nichts Neues*	Alexander Fleming discovers penicillin	Lateran Treaty establishes independent Vatican City
Elmer Rice *Street Scene*	Richard Hughes *A High Wind in Jamaica*	Kodak introduces 16mm color movie film	U.S. stock market crash on "Black Friday"

190. The list of January 1929 nominees to the Preußische Akademie der Künste includes five names under the heading "Einheimische" (native to Prussia) and eleven names under "Auswärtige" (from other places). Weill, number four on the "native" list, was not elected. Schoenberg first nominated Weill for membership the previous year but after *Die Dreigroschenoper* no longer supported his candidacy. Max Trapp, Ermanno Wolf-Ferrari, and Julius Weismann were elected in 1929.

191. Shortly after the success of *Die Dreigroschenoper*.

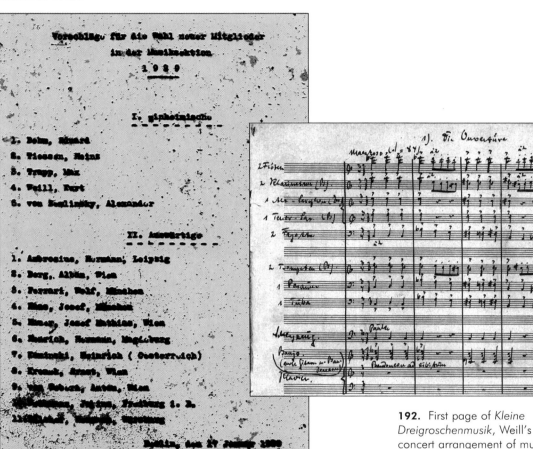

192. First page of *Kleine Dreigroschenmusik*, Weill's concert arrangement of music from *Die Dreigroschenoper*, and the program from the premiere conducted by Otto Klemperer, 7 February 1929. The piece has become Weill's most performed concert work.

Weill (in Berlin) to Universal Edition, 5 February 1929: I heard the *Kleine Dreigroschenmusik* (I have intentionally avoided the word suite) at the rehearsal yesterday and am very satisfied with it. There are eight numbers in an entirely new concert arrangement, including some new interludes and a completely new instrumentation for 2 flutes, 2 clarinets, 2 saxophones, 2 bassoons, 2 trumpets, 1 trombone, 1 tuba, banjo, percussion, piano. I believe that the work can be played very often since it is exactly what conductors are looking for: a rousing final number.

ÜBER DEN GESTISCHEN CHARAKTER
DER MUSIK

VON

KURT WEILL-BERLIN

Der Komponist Kurt Weill, der typische Gebrauchsmusik für unsere Zeit geschaffen hat, äußert sich in diesem Aufsatz über konstruktive Grundlagen seiner Opernwerke. Die Schriftleitung

Bei meinen Versuchen, zu einer Urform des musikalischen Bühnenwerkes zu gelangen, habe ich einige Beobachtungen gemacht, die mir zunächst als völlig neue Erkenntnisse erschienen, die sich aber bei näherer Betrachtung durchaus in die geschichtlichen Zusammenhänge einordnen ließen. Während ich mich bei meiner eigenen Arbeit immer wieder über die Frage: »Welche Anlässe gibt es für Musik auf der Bühne?« zur Entscheidung gezwungen habe, tauchte bei der rückwärtigen Betrachtung eigener oder fremder Opernproduktion eine andere Frage auf: »Wie ist die Musik auf dem Theater beschaffen, und gibt es bestimmte Eigenschaften, die eine Musik zur Theatermusik stempeln?« Es ist ja oft festgestellt worden, daß eine Reihe bedeutender Musiker sich entweder gar nicht mit der Bühne beschäftigt hat oder vergebliche Versuche angestellt hat, sich die Bühne zu erobern. Es muß also bestimmte Eigenschaften geben, die eine Musik für das Theater geeignet erscheinen lassen, und ich glaube, daß man diese Eigenschaften unter einem Begriff zusammenfassen kann, den ich als den gestischen Charakter der Musik bezeichnen möchte.

Ich setze dabei jene Form des Theaters als gegeben voraus, die mir für eine Oper in unserer Zeit die einzig mögliche Grundlage zu bieten scheint. Das Theater der vergangenen Epoche war für Genießende geschrieben. Es wollte seinen Zuschauer kitzeln, erregen, aufpeitschen, umwerfen. Es rückte das Stoffliche in den Vordergrund und verwandte auf die Darstellung eines Stoffes alle Mittel der Bühne vom echten Gras bis zum laufenden Band. Und was es seinem Zuschauer gewährte, konnte es auch seinem Schöpfer nicht versagen: auch er war ein Genießender, als er sein Werk schrieb, er erlebte den »Rausch des schöpferischen Augenblicks«, die »Ekstase des künstlerischen Schaffensdrangs« und andere Lustgefühle. Die andere Form des Theaters, die sich heute durchzusetzen beginnt, rechnet mit einem Zuschauer, der in der ruhigen Haltung des denkenden Menschen den Vorgängen folgt und der, da er ja denken will, eine Beanspruchung seiner Genußnerven als Störung empfinden muß. Dieses Theater will zeigen, was der Mensch tut. Es interessiert sich für Stoffe nur bis zu dem Punkt, wo sie den Rahmen oder den Vorwand menschlicher

‹419›

---

420   DIE MUSIK   XXI/6 (März 1929)

Beziehungen geben. Es legt daher größeren Wert auf die Darsteller als auf die Mittel der Bühne. Und das Genießertum, auf das sein Publikum verzichtet, ist auch seinem Schöpfer versagt. Dieses Theater ist im stärksten Maße unromantisch. Denn »Romantik« als Kunst schaltet das Denken aus, sie arbeitet mit narkotischen Mitteln, sie zeigt den Menschen nur im Ausnahmezustand, und in ihrer Blütezeit (bei Wagner) verzichtet sie überhaupt auf eine Darstellung des Menschen.

Wenn man diese beiden Formen des Theaters auf die Oper anwendet, so zeigt sich, daß der Komponist heute seinem Text gegenüber nicht mehr die Stellung des Genießenden einnehmen darf. In der Oper des 19. und beginnenden 20. Jahrhunderts bestand die Aufgabe der Musik darin, Stimmungen zu erzeugen, Situationen zu untermalen und dramatische Akzente zu unterstreichen. Auch jene Form des musikalischen Theaters, die den Text nur als Anlaß für ein freies, ungehemmtes Musizieren benutzt, ist schließlich nur eine letzte Konsequenz aus dem romantischen Opernideal, weil sich hier die Musik noch weniger als im Musikdrama an der Durchführung der dramatischen Idee beteiligt.

Die Form der Oper ist ein Unding, wenn es nicht gelingt, der Musik im Gesamtaufbau und in der Ausführung bis ins einzelnste eine vorherrschende Stellung einzuräumen. Die Musik der Oper darf nicht die ganze Arbeit am Drama und seiner Idee dem Wort und dem Bild überlassen, sie muß an der Darstellung der Vorgänge aktiv beteiligt sein.

Und da es sich im Theater von heute um die Darstellung des Menschen handelt, so muß auch die Musik einzig auf den Menschen bezogen sein. Nun gehen der Musik bekanntlich alle psychologischen oder charakterisierenden Fähigkeiten ab. Dafür hat sie eine Fähigkeit, die für die Darstellung des Menschen auf dem Theater von entscheidender Bedeutung ist: sie kann den Gestus wiedergeben, der den Vorgang der Bühne veranschaulicht, sie kann sogar eine Art von Grundgestus schaffen, durch den sie dem Darsteller eine bestimmte Haltung vorschreibt, die jeden Zweifel und jedes Mißverständnis über den betreffenden Vorgang ausschaltet, sie kann im idealen Falle diesen Gestus so stark festzulegen, daß eine falsche Darstellung des betreffenden Vorgangs nicht mehr möglich ist. Jeder aufmerksame Theaterbesucher weiß, mit wieviel falschen Tönen, mit wieviel verlogenen Bewegungen oft die einfachsten und natürlichsten menschlichen Handlungen auf der Bühne dargestellt werden. Die Musik hat die Möglichkeit, den Grundton und den Grundgestus eines Vorgangs soweit festzulegen, daß wenigstens eine falsche Auslegung vermieden wird, wobei dem Darsteller immer noch reichlich Gelegenheit zur Entfaltung seiner persönlichen Eigenart bleibt. *Natürlich ist gestische Musik keineswegs an den Text gebunden, und wenn wir Mozarts Musik überall, auch außerhalb der Oper, als »dramatisch« empfinden, so kommt das eben daher, daß sie nie ihren gestischen Charakter aufgibt.*

WEILL: GESTISCHER CHARAKTER DER MUSIK   421

Wir finden gestische Musik überall, wo ein Vorgang zwischen Mensch und Mensch in naiver Weise musikalisch dargestellt wird. Am auffallendsten: in den Rezitativen der Bachschen Passionen, in den Opern Mozarts, im »Fidelio« (»Nur hurtig fort und frisch gegraben«), bei Offenbach und Bizet. »Dies Bildnis ist bezaubernd schön« — die Haltung eines Mannes, der ein Bild betrachtet, ist hier durch die Musik allein bestimmt. Er kann das Bild in der rechten oder linken Hand, nach oben oder unten halten, er kann durch einen Scheinwerfer beleuchtet sein oder im Dunkeln stehen — sein Grundgestus ist richtig, weil er von der Musik richtig diktiert ist.

Wie sind die gestischen Mittel der Musik beschaffen? Sie äußern sich zunächst in einer rhythmischen Fixierung des Textes. Die Musik hat die Möglichkeit, die Akzente der Sprache, die Aufteilung der kurzen und langen Silben und vor allem die Pausen schriftlich zu notieren und dadurch die schwersten Fehlerquellen der Textbehandlung auf der Bühne auszuschalten. Man kann übrigens einen Satz auf die verschiedensten Arten rhythmisch interpretieren, und auch das Entscheidende bleibt nur, ob der richtige Gestus getroffen wird. Diese rhythmische Fixierung, die vom Text her erreicht wird, bildet aber nur die Grundlage einer gestischen Musik. Die eigene produktive Arbeit des Musikers setzt erst dann ein, wenn er mit den übrigen Ausdrucksmitteln der Musik den Kontakt zwischen dem Wort und dem, was es ausdrücken will, herstellt. Auch die Melodie trägt den Gestus des darzustellenden Vorgangs in sich, aber da der Bühnenvorgang bereits ausgesprochen ist, bleibt für die eigentlichen musikalischen Ausdrucksmittel, für die formale, melodische und harmonische Gestaltung ein viel größerer Spielraum als etwa in einer rein schildernden Musik der Gefahr, zugedeckt zu werden. Die rhythmische Festlegung von seiten des Textes ist also für die Opernkomponisten keine schlimmere Fessel als zum Beispiel das Formschema der Fuge, der Sonate, des Rondos für die klassischen Meister. Im Rahmen einer solchen rhythmisch vorausbestimmten Musik ist jede Art der melodischen Ausbreitung, der harmonischen und rhythmischen Differenzierung möglich, wenn nur die musikalischen Spannungsbögen dem gestischen Vorgang entsprechen. So ist etwa ein koloraturartiges Verweilen auf einer Silbe durchaus angebracht, wenn es durch ein gestisches Verweilen an der gleichen Stelle zu begründen ist.

Ich gebe ein Beispiel aus meiner eigenen Praxis. Brecht hatte früher aus dem Bedürfnis einer gestischen Verdeutlichung heraus zu einigen seiner Dichtungen einige Noten aufgezeichnet. Hier ist in Grundgestus rhythmisch in der primitivsten Form festgelegt, während melodisch die durchaus persönliche und nicht nachzuahmende Gesangsweise festgehalten ist, in der Brecht seine Songs vorträgt. Der Alabama-Song sieht in dieser Fassung so aus:

---

422   DIE MUSIK

Man sieht: das ist nicht mehr als eine Aufzeichnung des Sprachrhythmus und als Musik überhaupt nicht zu verwenden. In meiner Komposition desselben Textes ist der gleiche Grundgestus gestaltet, nur ist er hier erst mit den viel freieren Mitteln des Musikers wirklich »komponiert«. Der Song ist bei mir ganz breit angelegt, schwingt melodisch weit aus, ist auch rhythmisch durch die Begleitungsformel ganz anders fundiert — aber der gestische Charakter ist gewahrt, obwohl er in einer ganz anderen Erscheinungsform auftritt:

WEILL: GESTISCHER CHARAKTER DER MUSIK   423

Es ist noch zu sagen, daß keineswegs alle Texte gestisch zu gestalten sind. Die neue (oder: erneuerte) Form des Theaters, die ich meinen Ausführungen zugrunde lege, wird ja heute nur von sehr wenigen Dichtern gehandhabt, und nur diese Form erlaubt und ermöglicht eine gestische Sprache. Daher ist das hier angeschnittene Problem in gleichem Maße ein Problem des modernen Dramas. Aber für die Bühnenform, die vom Menschen aussagen will, ist die Musik durch ihre Fähigkeit einer gestischen Fixierung und Verdeutlichung des Vorgangs unentbehrlich. *Und nur eine Form des Dramas, für die die Musik unentbehrlich ist, läßt sich vollkommen auf die Bedürfnisse jenes rein musikalischen Kunstwerkes umstellen, das wir Oper nennen.*

Lotte Reiniger:
Kanonensong aus der Dreigroschenoper von Kurt Weill

193. "Über den gestischen Charakter der Musik" appeared in *Die Musik* 21, no. 6 (March 1929): 419-23.

KURT WEILL

BLUES-POTPOURRI

(TANZPOTPOURRI I)

AUS

DIE DREIGROSCHENOPER

ARRANGEMENT FÜR SALONORCHESTER MIT JAZZSTIMMEN
VON

HARTWIG von PLATEN

BESETZUNG

Violino I (Dir.) / Violino obligat
Cello / Basso / Flauto / Oboe
Clarinetto I / Trombe I und II
Tromboni I und II/III / Batteria
Banjo / Saxophon I Mi♭ (Es)
Saxophon II Si♭ (B)
Saxophon III Mi♭ (Es)
Harmonium / Piano (Dir.)

ERGÄNZUNGSSTIMMEN

Violino II / Viola / Clarinetto II
Fagotto / Corni I/II

**UNIVERSAL
EDITION**
WIEN / LEIPZIG
V. C. J. 110

194. Universal Edition continued to issue arrangements of Weill's songs for dance orchestra, including a "Blues-Potpourri" by Hartwig von Platen. This 1930 announcement (published on the back of the sheet music for "Alabama-Song") shows the current catalogue of UE's "Vindobona-Collection."

Neue Jazzmusik

Vindobona-Collection Jazz-Serie

V.C.J.Nr.		Preis Mk. Sàlon-orchester / Kleines Orchester mit Jazz
	BENATZKY R. Aus „Die fünf Wünsche"	
106	TANGO MACABRE	2.— 3.—
107	FLIRT (Slow-Fox)	2.— 3.—
108	L'HEURE BLEUE	2.— 3.—
	DOUCET C.	
112	CHICKEN PIE, Foxtrot (H. PLATEN)	3.— 3.50
113	A SIX CYLINDER RAG-TIME (H. PLATEN)	3.— 3.50
	FOX-JUREK	
101	DEUTSCHMEISTER SLOW-FOX Jazzparaphrase über W. A. Jureks Deutschmeister-Marsch von Frank Fox	
	Kleines Orchester mit Jazz	3.—
	KŘENEK E. Aus „Jonny spielt auf"	
109	„LEB' WOHL, MEIN SCHATZ", Blues (J. RISSELIN)	2.— 2.50
	WEILL K.	
104	BERLIN IM LICHT-SONG (O. LINDEMANN)	3.— 4.—
114	BILBAO-SONG (H. PLATEN)	3.— 3.50
	Aus „Die Dreigroschenoper":	
102/03	TANGO-BALLADE UND KANONENSONG (J. FITELBERG)	3.50 4.—
110	BLUES-POTPOURRI (H. PLATEN) (Tanzpotpourri I) Salonorchester mit Jazzstimmen	3.50 4.50
111	FOXTROT-POTPOURRI (H. PLATEN) (Tanzpotpourri II) Salonorchester mit Jazzstimmen	3.50 4.50
	Aus „Aufstieg und Fall der Stadt Mahagonny":	
115	ALABAMA-SONG (R. ETLINGER)	3.— 3.50

KLAVIERMUSIK IM JAZZSTIL, JAZZLIEDER, U. A.

SIEHE SPEZIALPROSPEKT

Universal-Edition A. G. Wien—Leipzig

No. 140

195. This copyist's score of *Berliner Requiem* includes "Können einem toten Mann nicht helfen" as the second movement. The premiere took place at the Frankfurt radio on 22 May 1929. Weill removed this movement from the work and used it for the finale of *Aufstieg und Fall der Stadt Mahagonny*.

196. Brecht behind the wheel of his car, an Austrian Steyr, ca. 1928.

Weill (in St. Cyr) to Universal Edition, 25 May 1929: After a lovely six-day auto trip I arrived here on Thursday. Brecht, who came along in his car, had an accident near Fulda, where we were to meet for a meal, and I had to have him taken back to Berlin with a broken kneecap. Unfortunately that has delayed all my plans since we wanted to come here together to work. We wanted to write the song texts for *Happy End* and discuss new plans. But above all I wanted to discuss and work out a change for *Mahagonny* that had occurred to me in the last few days. The only passage that might conceivably undermine the work's success—Klemperer, for instance, also thinks it's dangerous—is the Portrayal of Love in the 2nd Act, the scene with the long line of men in front of the bordello. I now have an idea for transforming this scene into "Statistics on Love Life in Mahagonny," which would have to be presented partly sung and partly with projections or animation. The "Song of Mandelay," which is part of the scene as it stands now, would have to be included in some new fashion. If Brecht agrees to this change I will try to get the necessary text from him as soon as possible. . . . More difficult will be realizing my plan for subjecting the text and stage directions of the finished portions of the piano score to a thorough revision with Brecht. Since there should be no delay in printing the piano score, the finishing touches on the text will have to be done on the proofs in July, when I am together with Brecht.

198. In summer 1929, Ullstein Verlag issued a popular songbook of eleven numbers from *Die Dreigroschenoper* as number 274 in its *Musik für Alle* series.

199. Poster advertising the one-hundredth performance of *Die Dreigroschenoper* at the Raimund Theater in Vienna, June 1929.

197. The first page of Weill's autograh score for *Der Lindberghflug* in the Baden-Baden version; Weill composed 7½ parts and Hindemith composed 5½. Three additional parts were spoken, without music. Brecht's text was first published in *Uhu* (April 1929). A few months later Weill composed all the sections.

Weill (in St. Cyr) to Universal Edition, 4 June 1929: The *Berliner Requiem* seems to have had a very big success in Frankfurt. I ask you, however, not to allow the work to be done until after the *Mahagonny* premiere since the song "Können einem toten Mann nicht helfen" plays an important role in *Mahagonny*. I would then suggest the following: I am writing the *Lindberghflug* for Baden-Baden together with Hindemith. The sections I have done (more than half of the whole) are so successful that I will set the whole text myself, including the sections Hindemith is doing now. We could then publish a very nice volume: 3 *Songspiele* by Weill and Brecht. 1. *Mahagonny-Songs* (i.e., the Baden-Baden version of *Mahagonny*), 2. *Das Berliner Requiem*, 3. *Der Lindberghflug*. I also plan to have these three works performed together in a new form between concert and theater, with sets, etc., and in Berlin I want to put together a troupe which I can then send on tour, not to theaters, but to concert organizations or cabarets.

Weill (in St. Cyr) to Hans Curjel, 13 June 1929: Meanwhile I have received many of the Berlin reviews of the Hindemith opera [*Neues vom Tage*]. It was clear to me that a topic so stupid would not be a success in Berlin. But I never expected it to turn out to be a washout of these dimensions. I believed that, just once, people might fall for this kind of pseudo-humor. . . . I have learned one thing about *Mahagonny:* the instinct not to conceive *Mahagonny* as "comic opera" has been the right one, and we must see to it that the entire performance will proceed in deadly earnest throughout. The so-called "buffo" character really makes me want to puke. That over-the-top style of acting has finally played itself out.

200. Weill, Ernst Hardt, Hindemith, Hans Flesch, and Brecht at the 1929 Baden-Baden festival.

201. Weill coaches tenor Josef Witt, who sang the part of Charles Lindbergh in *Der Lindberghflug*, Baden-Baden, 1929.

202. Dolbin's caricature of Weill, Hindemith, and conductor Hermann Scherchen at a rehearsal of *Der Lindberghflug* in Baden-Baden, 1929.

Weill (in St. Cyr) to Universal Edition, 25 June 1929: In putting together the Baden-Baden program some things have happened (in my absence) that have only confirmed my earlier unpleasant impressions of this entire event. I will fill you in on the details in person, but today would like to ask you to place the following notice in the papers: "The newest composition by Kurt Weill is a cantata, the *Lindberghflug*, on a text by Bert Brecht. The work will be given its premiere in the fall. Several movements from this composition will be performed at this year's Baden-Baden music festival." For tactical reasons it is very important that this notice appear soon.

Weill (in Berlin) to Hans Curjel, 2 August 1929: Baden-Baden was really shitty. Hindemith's work on *Lindberghflug* and on the *Lehrstück* was of a superficiality that will be hard to beat. It has clearly been proven that his music is too tame for Brecht's texts. What's amazing is that the press has discovered this as well, and they now present me as the shining example of how Brecht should be composed.

203. ca. 1929.

204. Producer Ernst Josef Aufricht expected *Happy End* to follow in the successful footsteps of *Die Dreigroschenoper*, but it closed after three performances. In spite of this initial failure, the score contains some of Weill's most popular and enduring songs, including "Surabaya-Johnny," "Matrosen-Tango," "Bilbao Song," and "Song of Mandelay." Shown here is a sketch for "Surabaya-Johnny" dating from summer 1929, a fair copy prepared for publication, and the cover of the sheet music issued by Universal Edition.

205. Caspar Neher's sketch of Bill Cracker, the leading male character in *Happy End*.

206. Lilian Holliday (Carola Neher) sings "Surabaya Johnny" to Bill Cracker (Oskar Homolka) in the original production of *Happy End*.

HAPPY END

Play with music in three acts; book by "Dorothy Lane"
[Elisabeth Hauptmann]; lyrics by Bertolt Brecht

1929   Berlin, Theater am Schiffbauerdamm (2 September)
*Theo Mackeben, conductor; Erich Engel and Brecht, directors;
Caspar Neher, designer*

Theater am Schiffbauerdamm
Direktion: Ernst Josef Aufricht

Happy End

Eine Magazingeschichte von D o r o t h y L a n e
Deutsche Bearbeitung: E l i s a b e t h H a u p t m a n n
Songs: B r e c h t u n d W e i l l
Regie: E r i c h E n g e l u n d B r e c h t
Musikal. Leitung: T h e o M a c k e b e n
Kapelle: L e w i s R u t h B a n d
Bühnenbilder: C a s p a r N e h e r
Techn. Leitung: H a n s S a c h s

P e r s o n e n :

Lilian Holliday, genannt „Hallelujah-Lilian"	Carola Neher
Bill Cracker, genannt „Ballhaus-Bill"	Oskar Homolka
Die Dame in Grau, genannt „Die Fliege"	Helene Weigel
Sam Worlitzer, genannt „Mammy"	Kurt Gerron
Jimmy Dexter, genannt „Reverend"	Theo Lingen
Dr. Nakamura, genannnt „Governor"	Peter Lorre
Johnny Dutch, genannt „Das Baby"	Albert Hoerrmann
Bob Merker, genannt „Professor"	Karlheinz Carell
Major der Heilsarmee	Paul Günther

Leutnant Jackson	Sigismund v. Radecki
Leutnant Brown	Werner Maschmeier
Jane	Erna Schoeller
Mary	Marianne Oswald
Kommissar Hawkins	Erich Harden
Zwei Männer aus Dakota	{ Ernst Rotmund { Hugo Bauer
Polizist	Hans Brandes
Mirjam	Veronika Nitschmann
Arme und Bedürftige	{ Wanner-Kirsch, { Richrad, Tilgner usw.

207. This drawing of the cast of *Happy End* by the Berlin caricaturist Linne appeared in *Tempo* (4 September 1929). From left to right: Peter Lorre (the Governor), Helene Weigel (Die Fliege), Oskar Homolka (Bill Cracker), Carola Neher (Lilian Holliday), Kurt Gerron (Mammy).

„Happy end"?

Schiffbauerdamm.

I.

Ein Spielmeister, der (wie Erich Engel) wirklich in der Spieltönung ein Meister ist, kann manches für den, also, Autor tun — bloss eines kaum: für ihn auch noch dichten. Daran hapert's. Wenn ein Stück schliesslich nicht zu leben und nicht zu sterben vermag; deshalb nimmer aufhöret bis um halb zwölf; gleichsam ein Radfahrer, der nur sitzen und treten gelernt hat, wenn ihm jemand Fremdes raufhilft, aber nicht absteigen kann, und immer weitertritt, immer weiter, bis zur Langweile der Zusehenden: dann hilft ihm kein Engel.

II.

Das Eindrucksergebnis, wenig vor Mitternacht, am Telefon war: „In diesem Stück, das unter Brechts Firma und unter der Firma einer nicht sicher existierenden Dame geht, hat Brecht bei sich selber abgeschrieben. Ein paar nette Einfälle. Eine schmeichelnde Musik. Aber manchmal ein Gipfel der Stupidität. Der Beifall kam vor einem bestimmten Teil der Zuschauerschaft. („Bestimmt" ist hier nicht ein Partizipium.) Zum Schluss Theaterskandal."

III.

Warum pfiffen sie mitten hinein? Weil ein als Zeitdramaticus Maskierter bisher die Zuflucht zu Verstorbenen wie Marlowe, dreihundertfünfzig Jahr, John Gay, zweihundert Jahr, Rimbaud, heute siebzig, Büchner, hundert Jahr, Villon, fünfhundert Jahr, Tauchnitz-Verlagsjubiläum, nahm — jedoch diesmal auf etwa „Miss Helyett" zurückgriff.

IV.

Eine Helyett von der Heilsarmee rechts; der schneidige Verbrecherisch, Mackie Messer nochmals, Geschäft ist Geschäft links: zum Schluss ergibt es ... ein Paar. Mancher hatte das, in der revolutionären Gegenwartsdichtung oder Reform der Operette, vorausgesehn. Nicht vorausgesehn: die Verbrecher werden Soldaten der Heilsarmee. Unter Brechts Motto: „Happy entlehnt".

V.

Die glänzend artikulierende Frau Weigel sprach, nein: las am Schluss des versandenden Abends von einem Zettel rasch noch ein bisschen Sozialkritik. Angepappt. Worin das versuchte Helyettgeschäft schandenhalber dem Kommunismus fix was hinwarf;

einer Zeitsehnsucht mit unmeinen Mitteln flüchtig den Mund zu stopfen. Dies war das Uebelste. Dies war das Allerübelste. Verlesene Worte — dazu schwerlich auf Brechts Acker gewachsen. (Sie könnten, wären sie geistreicher, von Tucholsky sein.)

VI.

Rast für einen Rundblick. Diese Angelsächseleien mit dem Moderduft für neue Zeitdramatik auszugeben: — Schluss! Die Ausflucht, Abgetragenes sei „Parodie", geht als ganz selbstverständlich zu den Akten. Aber ja doch. Parodie — auf wen? Zeitdramatik ist: Pump mit Gesangseinlagen.

VII.

Eine Gesangseinlage hat als Kehrreim: das Wort „geschi ... en". Mehrmals. Immer nochmal. Ich bin kaum zimperlich; aber die hinreissend-liebe, zaubersüsse, volkseinfache Menschenblume, Neher-Carola genannt, eine künftige Dorschin vielleicht, schien sich bei so geistlosem Dreck zu schämen. Ein anderer Kehrreim: „In die Fresse!" Immerfort: in die Fresse. Ein dritter: „Ihr könnt mich ..." Wiederholt; wiederholt. Wenn etwas dahintersteckte: man lässt ja mit sich reden. Aber der Kampf gegen den Schmutz- und Schundkampf wird hier blossgestellt, in Verruf gebracht — so blossgestellt, so in Verruf gebracht, wie zugleich hier die Kritik am sozialen Elend; wie aller Emporwühler der Umschatteten blossgestellt. Es bleibt an dem Geschäftsversuch das Niederste. Rast für den Rundblick: Schluss! (Die Zeit wird hier bemogelt.)

VIII.

Homolka wirkt kostbar, wuchtverkommen, saftvoll neben der himmlischen Klabundfrau. Der Musiker Weill ... Also: Brecht hatte sich weg von der neueren Dramatik (die er nach Behauptungen, nie in der grünen Wirklichkeit getätigt) abgewandt zu Brecht. Wozu Weill Melodien, die schon längere Zeit bestanden, komponierte. Das Publikum stimmte diesen freundlichen Erinnerungen, erlöst von Weills anderem Versuch, vierhundertmal in der „Dreigroschenoper" zu. Was dem verstorbenen John Gay komischerweise zu Kopf stieg, während sich Brecht im Sarg umdrehte.

IX.

So hat Weill durch ältere, vorhandene, zuverlässige Melodien, wenn auch in der Jazzmaske, das Publikum von der neuen Musik weggelockt. Aber Weill ...,

Schmeichler! Er setzt wenigstens entzückend, was das Volk (gegen Entree) singt. Er ist ein sehr Aparter im Ungeparten. Herzenspitzbub! mit Programm. Soll man erst noch versichern, dass er es einmal „angetau" hat?

X.

Caspar Nehers Halbgardine. Inschriften, mühevoll im Film abgeschafft. (Parodie, selbstverständlich.) Lorre, Günther, Hoerrmann, Radecki, Carell, Schöller, Lingen, Oswald. Von Zeit zu Zeit seh' ich den alten Gerron.

XI.

Schauspielende Durchbildung (soweit das Vielermannsstück fertig ist) meisterhaft; im Einschnitt; in der Stufung; im Wechsel. Bloss nicht im Dichten. Wann, Engel, schreiben Sie das nächste Drama selbst?

Alfred Kerr.

208. Brecht's nemesis Alfred Kerr wrote this review for the *Berliner Tageblatt* (3 September 1929). The show closed after three performances. Helene Weigel stopped the show cold with an improvised Marxist speech towards the end of the last scene.

209. A press announcement of *Happy End*, with photos of the principal cast members.

„Happy End."

Oscur Homolka

Carola Neher

Kurt Gerron

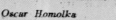

Die Hauptdarsteller in „Happy-End" im Theater am Schiffbauderdamm.

Heilsarmeemädchen und Verbrecher wandeln auf dem Pfad der Dreigroschenoper im dunkelsten Chicago und singen Songs von Brecht und Weill. Carola Neher, Homolka und Kurt Gerron übertreffen einander. Das Ganze eine Magazingeschichte aus dem Amerikanischen, deutsch dramatisiert von Elisabeth Hauptmann, wird voraussichtlich ein Erfolg stark zweiten Aufgusses.

E. M.

210. Kurt Gerron (Sammy/Mammy Wurlitzer) dresses in drag.

211. Rudolf Arnheim's review of *Happy End* appeared in *Die Weltbühne* 30, no. 37 (10 September 1929): 406–407.

Krankenkost von Rudolf Arnheim

„Brecht und Weill" — die Vornamen werden burschikos unterdrückt (nächstens wird es wohl im Programmheft heißen: „Brecht, genannt the Shiffbowerdammbert") — Brecht und Weill dekorieren ihr neues Werk „Happy end" als eine Magazingeschichte von Dorothy Lane. Mag es mit dieser Quelle stehen, wie es wolle, die Wahl ist charakteristisch: man bedient sich einer Literaturgattung, die eindeutig nicht Literatur ist, man nennt, um der Firma weiterhin einen unseriösen Anstrich zu geben, als Verfasserin eine Frau und als Ursprungsland vollends jenes beneidete Amerika, wo die Leute Kunstwerte mit der Stoppuhr messen und sich unter Sophokles einen europäischen Zeitgenossen von unbestimmter Nationalangehörigkeit vorstellen. Es ist dies das beliebte und schon nicht mehr originelle Bekenntnis zum Albernen und Ordinären, das Kokettieren mit dem Offenbarungseid, die Desertion der Künstler, die unter dem Schlachtruf: „Wer will denn das noch wissen!" ins feindliche Lager übergehen, wo breitbeinige Männer einander in die Fresse hauen, wo man einen Groschen in den Musikautomaten steckt, wenn man ein Bedürfnis nach Kunstgenuß verspürt, wo man mit dem Messer ißt und diskutiert, und wo jene Stammtischphilosophie zuhause ist, die wir aus den Chansons von Brecht kennen: daß nichts mehr los ist mit dem lieben Gott, daß alles kommt, wie es kommen muß, und daß es traurig auf der Welt ist heutzutage.

Der Regisseur Erich Engel entwickelt die erstaunlichsten Hausfrauentugenden, um uns den Aufenthalt in Bill Brechts Ballhaus behaglich zu machen. Er schnitzt die Figuren scharf, macht sie koboldhaft, gibt ihnen aber dabei doch einen Schuß Diesseits, der verhindert, daß sie zu Marionetten werden. Nur die intellektuell verhärtete Schauspielerin Helene Weigel ist Granit, auf den jeder Regisseur vergeblich baut. Diese energische Dame liebt es, mit hochgezogenen Schultern, den Unterkiefer wie einen Sturmbock nach vorn gestoßen, über Bühnen zu laufen, auf denen grade Theater gespielt wird; sie sollte endlich von dieser hysterischen Liebhaberei lassen —

Theaterspielen ist keine Privatsache. Oskar Homolka gegen löst sich ohne Hemmung oder kritischen Vorbehalt in seiner Rolle wie ein Stück Zucker in Wasser Vor seinen blanken Augen schwimmen selige Fuselträume, die Lippen heben sich durstig saugend empor, und an diesen Lippen scheinen Kopf und Körper, Wille und Verstand hilflos zu hängen, von ihnen scheinen sie vorwärtsgeschleift, einem Ziel zu, das ihre trunkenen Augen nicht sehen — unübertreffliche Verkörperung tierischen Triebmenschentums. Und aus Carola Neher holt Erich Engel als ein zartfingriger Gynäkologe das Kind, das in ihr steckt, das schroffe, verstockte und wiederum verwegen fabulierende, liebliche Kind.

Viel gutes Fleisch um kein Skelett. Das Stück ist aufgezogen als eine Parodie auf die Kriminalgeschichten, weil es zu schludrig erdacht ist, um sich als ernsthafter Reißer hervorwagen zu dürfen. Edgar Wallace würde, wenn ihm seine Exposéabteilung einen Entwurf vorlegte, in dem eine Dame vorkäme, die Tod bringt, wenn sie um Feuer bittet, und die vermittels einer komplizierten Lautsprecheranlage ihren Komplizen fernmündlich mitteilt, was sie ihnen auch persönlich sagen könnte, mit der Zigarettenspitze um sich hauen und die schuldigen Unterdichter fristlos entlassen. Im letzten Akt landen die Spießgesellen, von der Macht der Religion jäh gebrochen, auf dem Bußbänkchen der Heilsarmee, und nun brauchte nur noch Wasser in die Manege zu laufen und Verbrecher und Heilgehilfen in den Wellen zu ertränken, und das Ganze wäre eine Ausstattungspantomime von Paula Busch.

Warum kommt ein solches Stück zustande und warum wird es aufgeführt? Schuld ist gewiß jener verbreitete Snobismus, der Geist darin sieht, keinen zu haben, aber auch Dummheiten fallen nicht vom Himmel. Diese hat ihren Grund in der Müdigkeit der Menschen. So wie mancher Arzt, Jurist, Wissenschaftler abends „Das blutige Dreieck" oder „Die drei Lieben der Mabel Savage" braucht, um sich abzuspannen, so spektakelt auf unsern Bühnen eine minderwertige, wenn auch oft raffiniert servierte Parterreakrobatik, weil die Menschen diesseits und jenseits der Rampe müde sind, weil Krieg und Inflation ihnen die Nerven verdorben haben und sie nicht den Elan und vor allem nicht die Lust aufbringen, Werte zu schaffen oder zu genießen. Wir alle stecken in dieser Krise, aber es kommt viel darauf an, wie man sich ihren Auswirkungen gegenüber verhält: ob man sich die Ärmel aufkrempelt und geräuschvoll mitmacht und Beifall klatscht oder ob man unruhig und traurig beiseite geht.

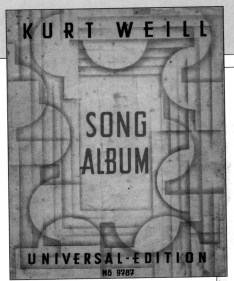

KURT WEILL

SONG ALBUM

UNIVERSAL-EDITION

N⁰ 9787

INHALT

1. **MUSCHEL VON MARGATE (PETROLEUMSONG)**
   WORTE VON FELIX GASBARRA   Seite 3
2. **DAS LIED VON DEN BRAUNEN INSELN**
   AUS LION FEUCHTWANGERS „PETROLEUMINSELN"   Seite 6
3. **MARTERL (AUS „BERLINER REQUIEM")**
   WORTE VON BERT BRECHT   Seite 8
4. **ZU POTSDAM UNTER DEN EICHEN (AUS „BERLINER REQUIEM")**
   WORTE VON BERT BRECHT   Seite 11
5. **BALLADE VON DER SEXUELLEN HÖRIGKEIT**
   WORTE VON BERT BRECHT   Seite 15
6. **VORSTELLUNG DES FLIEGERS LINDBERGH (AUS DEM „LINDBERGHFLUG")**
   WORTE VON BERT BRECHT   Seite 18

212. In 1929, Universal Edition published six songs originally written for larger stage or concert works. Although not credited in the table of contents, "Muschel von Margate" was written for the play *Konjunktur* and "Ballade von der sexuellen Hörigkeit" for *Die Dreigroschenoper*.

213. This page from the piano-vocal score of *Aufstieg und Fall der Stadt Mahagonny* shows the beginning of the love duet (also known as the "Crane Duet") inserted into Act II by Weill and Brecht to make the scene less racy. Weill wrote to his publisher: "I am sending you the new version of the 14th scene (Love Scene), ready to print in the libretto and piano score. It is a completely novel and, I believe, very successful piece. We have intentionally fashioned it into the opposite of the previous version and in the new version have written a long conversation between two lovers in a strict style. I believe that the scene in this form will assume an important position within the entire work. . . . I am also finishing the *Lindberghflug* which will go off to you in full score in about two weeks. It is very important to me to have the *Lindberghflug* performed as often and as prominently as possible this winter since before *Mahagonny* I absolutely must have a serious work of this kind as a contrast to my song works." (1 October 1929)

214. Members of Bill Cracker's gang attend a Salvation Army meeting.

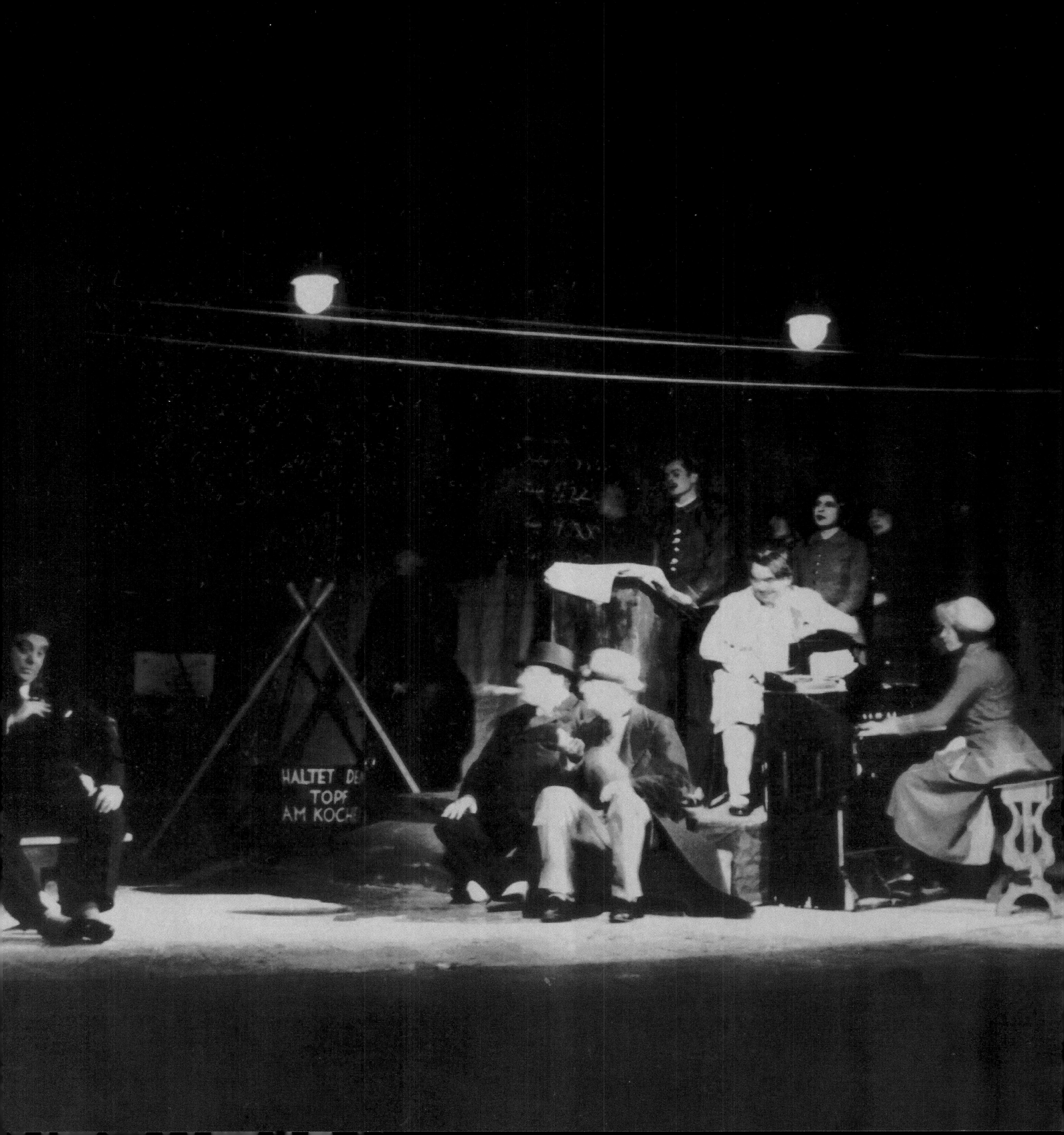
HALTET DE
TOPF
AM KOCH

Universal Edition (Hans Heinsheimer) in Vienna to Weill, 10 October 1929:
We spoke in Baden-Baden in great detail about principles and tactics, and I would like to add the following: the situation in which you find yourself right now is not simple. The style established in *Die Dreigroschenoper* and *Happy End*, which is also continued in *Mahagonny . . .* cannot be copied indefinitely. If I assess its place in your development correctly, it is, as it were, the breakthrough to a popular, simple musical style that radically liberated you from the confines of the style evident in, say, *Frauentanz*. But in the long run this song style can serve only as a springboard for you to find your way back to more profound and substantial musical creations, and I want to say at this point that I received a joyous shock when I played through the new scene ["Crane Duet"] from *Mahagonny*. Here, dear friend Weill, is what I've been expecting and frequently calling for, namely, the synthesis between the melodic and rhythmic wealth of your fantasy, which was freed by the song technique and made broadly accessible, and the shaping and forming which bear the mark of artistic responsibility on a truly high plane. For that reason I consider this scene in *Mahagonny* so especially important. Here you are bringing the style of 1928 to a close, here the new sound of the coming years becomes audible, that sound which I believe is created out of a new romanticism, a new longing, a new search for the "unattainable," in short, an emotional sphere which must fully embrace [*begreifen*] the *neue Sachlichkeit* in order to overcome it. . . .

I'm not the least bit surprised by the strong resistance evident everywhere in Germany against the dominance of Berlin. Indeed, it is quite in keeping with a development that is inevitable. The German provinces have their own strong and admirable intellectual life. I am absolutely convinced that the vital forces active throughout Germany will define the intellectual and artistic character of the coming years. . . . So if in closing I were to clearly formulate my view, it would be: you should and must free yourself once and for all from the kind of commercialized artistic activity practiced in Berlin.

Weill (in Berlin) to Hans Heinsheimer of Universal Edition, 14 October 1929: Thank you very much for your lengthy letter. I was extremely pleased that you wrote about my present situation with such understanding, with such care and genuine friendship, and what you say is so true and so in keeping with my own views. . . . Since your letter addressed such fundamental issues and since I find your position so appealing, you will also allow me to add something to these statements of principle. Above all, I was pleased that you were so accurate in recognizing the essence of the stylistic transformation I am undergoing. (For there are not many who notice it.) But one must date the beginning of this stylistic transformation much earlier than you do. By far the greater part of *Mahagonny* is already entirely independent from the song style and reveals this new style, which in seriousness, "stature," and expressive power surpasses everything I have written to date. Almost everything that has been added to the Baden-Baden version is written in a completely pure, thoroughly responsible style, which I am convinced will endure longer than most of what is produced today. *Happy End*, too, has been completely misunderstood in this regard. Pieces like the great "Heilsarmeemarsch" and the "Matrosenlied" go far beyond the song character and the music as a whole represents a formal, instrumental, and

melodic development so far beyond the *Dreigroschenoper* that only helpless ignoramuses like the German critics could miss it. At issue here is a major evolution which hasn't stood still *for one moment* and which, as you correctly note, has made another new advance in the new *Mahagonny* scene and in *Der Lindberghflug*. We must not be misled into trivializing what was achieved through the *Dreigroschenoper*—achieved not only for my music, but for musical life in general—just because some of my new work happens to be badly mounted in a bad play. From our standpoint the fact that my *Dreigroschenoper* music has been commercialized doesn't speak against it, but for it, and we would be falling back into our old mistakes if we were to deny certain music its importance and artistic value simply because it found its way to the masses. You are right: *I* cannot copy this song style indefinitely and with the works since *Mahagonny* I have demonstrated that I have no intention of copying it. But we cannot deny that this style has become a model, and that today more than half the younger composers from the most diverse backgrounds make their living from it. That's why it's very easy for the general public to overlook the fact that I myself, who defined this style only a year ago, have in the meantime quietly continued on my own path. So you see that your arguments are essentially in complete agreement with my own views.

On one point, however, I cannot concur with you: regarding your remarks about Berlin and the German provinces. I know the German provinces. I grew up there. These days I often travel to provincial cities and I read the papers. The "spirit of the German provinces" as portrayed in the papers is deeply reactionary, and it is absolutely inconceivable that a new, forward-looking artistic movement could emerge from one of these cities. In any case, opposition to Berlin's theater life cannot be that strong if the *Dreigroschenoper*, the most daring and revolutionary product of this much maligned Berlin spirit, is enjoying full houses everywhere. No, dear friend Heinsheimer, the battle against Berlin being waged in certain prominent provincial circles is part of that great offensive which reactionary forces have launched in recent years in hopes of exerting influence over the artistic sphere as well. The provincial intellectuals of whom you speak want nothing more than to come to Berlin. The developments within the German theater over the last decade have come exclusively and entirely from Berlin, from Brahm, from Reinhardt, from Jessner and Piscator, and finally from the Theater am Schiffbauerdamm. Do you really believe one can dismiss the achievements which make Berlin today's unrivaled theatrical capital of Europe with the expression "commercialized artistic activity"? And do you really believe one can apply this description to what I do? For years now I have been the only creative musician who has worked consistently and uncompromisingly in the face of opposition from the snobs and aesthetes toward the creation of fundamental forms of a new, simple, popular musical theater. Even the least significant of my music theater works during this time have been written with this sense of responsibility, in a continuing effort to further what I consider the only possible development. Is that commercialized artistic activity? Wouldn't it be much easier (and commercially much more profitable) if, like most of the others, I were to continue making minor variations on the traditional opera style and adapt myself from the outset to the taste and mentality of the provincial operagoer? No one knows the dangers of Berlin's literary scene as well as I do. But I have demonstrated that in precisely this atmosphere, as long as one doesn't fall victim to its pitfalls, the most substantial and the purest artistic accomplishments are possible.

Weill (in Berlin) to Universal Edition, 19 November 1929: I must add a few words about the question of my GEMA rating. This time I was given a rating of 125 points and at first I thought I'd have to be satisfied with that. Now I have learned to my surprise that other colleagues who are neither as well known as I am nor have as many overall performances have been given decidedly more favorable ratings. Just to cite a few examples, d'Albert and Hindemith have exactly twice as many (!) points as I do. In rating me they apparently missed the fact that I have to be rated for serious music as well as for popular music. Naturally I am performed in fewer concerts than, say, Hindemith, but on the other hand the "Kanonen Song," "Tango Ballade" and *Dreigroschenoper*-Potpourris are performed in the programs of countless restaurants, cinemas, radio broadcasts, etc. In any event it is unjust to give me exactly half the rating of colleagues of equal stature.

Weill (in Berlin) to Universal Edition, 16 December 1929: You will have received the reviews of the *Lindberghflug* from Mr. Loewy and found much in them that can be used well to propagate this work. The performance generated a great deal of interest here and is still being discussed everywhere because of the novelty of this experiment. At any rate I am pleased that my (and your) plan for premiering a bona fide concert work could be so successfully realized, and I am convinced that a great number of concert institutions both here and abroad will perform the work. Independent of that I will see if we can't get some sort of performance in the schools. That is a favorite idea of mine, and I am aware that its realization will initially meet with great obstacles.

215. In his essay "Whither Opera?" Weill tries to define *Gebrauchsmusik*, a concept he had made his own, and which, to him, represented music that is "capable of satisfying the musical needs of broad strata of society without forfeiting its artistic substance." In composing for the musical stage, this meant giving up opera's rigid and thus limiting formal aspects in order to employ innovations coming from the spoken theater.

216. Program of the first performance of Weill's workers' choruses with texts by Brecht, "Die Legende vom toten Soldaten" and "Zu Potsdam unter den Eichen," sung by members of the German Workers' Singing Club in late December 1929.

217. Cover of the first edition of the vocal score of *Der Lindberghflug*, published by Universal Edition. Weill provided the publisher with the cover photos.

Das Verdienst der guten Ausführung des Konzertes lag vorwiegend bei dem begabten Kapellmeister Karl Rankl. Jedenfalls lassen sich einige Bedenken zum Thema »Arbeitermusik« erheben, denn die musikalischen Auffassungskräfte der wirklichen Arbeiter reichen nicht aus für die vielfach zu hoch gespannten Bildungsexperimente ihrer intellektuellen Wortführer. Der Arbeiter ist infolge seiner abhängigen Wirtschaftslage stets auf Klassenkampf und Klassenhaß eingestellt und für reinen, über den äußeren Unterhaltungszweck hinausgehenden Kunstgenuß erst dann empfänglich, wenn er besser situiert, also quasi mehr bürgerlich geworden ist.

Wie sehr dagegen tendenziöse Kunst den Arbeiter interessiert, konnte man an einem Konzertabend des Berliner Schubertchors beobachten. Es kamen nämlich neue Chöre von Kurt Weill und Hanns Eisler zur Uraufführung: ganz zeitkritisch gehaltene, im Textinhalt stark aggressive, direkt revolutionäre Chorgesänge. Von Eisler hat derselbe Verein schon im Vorjahre höchst wirkungsvolle neue Chöre herausgebracht (z. B. »Bauernrevolution«). Diesmal gefiel besonders das da capo verlangte Stück »Auf den Straßen zu singen« neben »Streikbrecher« und »An Stelle einer Grabrede«. Eislers Chorton ist balladesk und von realistischer Ausdruckskraft, im Stimm- und Satzgefüge durchaus eigenartig und von persönlicher Eingebung zeugend. Kurt Weill, der etwas stark gepfefferte Gedichte von Bert Brecht technisch ebenfalls interessant vertont hat, eine »Legende vom toten Soldaten« und die Satire »Zu Potsdam unter den Eichen«, ist vielleicht nicht so originell wie Eisler, aber dafür stärker in der Kunst persiflierender Zuspitzung des Effektes. Auch dieses Konzert stand unter der Leitung des mitreißenden Dirigenten Karl Rankl, der übrigens Opernchorleiter in der Staatsoper am Platz der Republik ist.

218. The piano-vocal version of "Zu Potsdam unter den Eichen" published by Universal Edition in the *Song Album* in 1929 included a musical reference to the song "Üb immer Treu und Redlichkeit," which was played hourly on the Garnisonskirche carillon in Potsdam and thus linked clearly to German militarism.

219. "Zu Potsdam unter den Eichen" for unaccompanied four-part male chorus.

220. Review of the German Workers' Singing Club concert in *Die Musik* (January 1930) by Karl Westermeyer, p. 299.

For every age and part of the world, there is a place about which fantasies are written. In Mozart's time it was Turkey. For Shakespeare, it was Italy. For us in Germany, it was always America. You have no idea how little we knew about America. We had read Jack London and we knew absolutely all about your Chicago gangsters, and that was the end. So of course when we did a fantasy, it was about America.

When the hurricane was coming, I got out a map and looked for places for it to hit. I found Pensacola. It has a marvelous name for a city to be hit by a hurricane in a musical. I built up the whole chant around it—Pensacola, Pensacola, Pensacola, *wham!* Kurt Weill, "Pensacola Wham," *New Yorker*, 10 June 1944.

Weill (in Berlin) to Universal Edition, 31 December 1929: By the way, something very important came out of my recent discussions with Brecher. Already after *Happy End* my friends pointed out that the use of American names for *Mahagonny* might be dangerous since the Jimmys, Jackys, Bills, etc. have already appeared in many works and might tend to establish completely misleading concepts of Americanism, wild west, or the like. I have been worrying for weeks about these old and confusing names, and I am very happy that together with Brecht I have now found a very good solution—and just when Brecher, too, brought this danger to my attention. So in Leipzig and in other cities we will perform *Mahagonny* with largely German names, and I ask that you paste in a notice with the following text in the piano score (where the orchestra scoring is given), as well as in the libretto:

Since the human pleasures which are to be had for money are everywhere and always the same and since the pleasure city Mahagonny is international in the widest sense, the names of the protagonists can be altered to suit the appropriate locale. It is therefore recommended, for instance, that for the German performances the following names be used:

Instead of		
Fatty	Willy	
Jim Mahoney	Johann Ackermann (or Hans)	
Jack O'Brien	Jakob Grün	
Bill	Sparbüchsenheinrich (or Heinz)	
Joe	Josef Lettner, called Alaskawolfjo.	

I urge you to make this small change since I am convinced that we can thereby sidestep a serious criticism, especially in the press.

221. Weill's "Vorwort zum Regiebuch der Oper *Aufstieg und Fall der Stadt Mahagonny*," first appeared in *Anbruch*, the magazine of Universal Edition (*Anbruch* 12, no. 1 (January 1930): 5-7).

VORWORT
ZUM REGIEBUCH DER OPER „AUFSTIEG UND
FALL DER STADT MAHAGONNY"
Kurt Weill

Kurt Weill arbeitet gemeinsam mit Caspar Neher und Bert Brecht an einem „Regiebuch" zur Oper „Mahagonny", das genaue Vorschläge für die szenische Aufführung des Werkes enthält und das zusammen mit dem musikalischen Aufführungsmaterial und mit den Projektionstafeln Nehers an die Bühnen gegeben wird. Wir bringen hier die prinzipiellen Ausführungen des Vorworts.

Phot. Atelier Jacobi

In der „Dreigroschenoper" wurde die ursprüngliche Form des musikalischen Theaters zu erneuern versucht. Die Musik ist hier nicht mehr handlungstreibend, sondern der jeweilige Einsatz der Musik ist gleichbedeutend mit einer Unterbrechung der Handlung. Die epische Theaterform ist eine stufenartige Aneinanderreihung von Zuständen. Sie ist daher die ideale Form des musikalischen Theaters, denn nur Zustände können in geschlossener Form musiziert werden, und eine Aneinanderreihung von Zuständen nach musikalischen Gesichtspunkten ergibt die gesteigerte Form des musikalischen Theaters: die Oper. In der „Dreigroschenoper" mußte zwischen den Musiksätzen die Handlung weitergeführt werden; daher ergab sich hier ungefähr die Form der „Dialogoper", einer Mischgattung aus Schauspiel und Oper.

Der Stoff der Oper „Aufstieg und Fall der Stadt Mahagonny" ermöglichte eine Gestaltung nach rein musikalischen Gesetzen. Denn die Form der Chronik, die hier gewählt werden konnte, ist nichts als eine „Aneinanderreihung von Zuständen". Es wird daher jedesmal der neue Zustand in der Geschichte der Stadt Mahagonny durch eine Überschrift eingeleitet, die in erzählender Form den Übergang zur neuen Szene herstellt.

Zwei Männer und eine Frau, auf der Flucht vor den Konstablern, bleiben in einer öden Gegend stecken. Sie beschließen, eine Stadt zu gründen, in der den Männern, die von der Goldküste her vorüberkommen, ihre Bedürfnisse erfüllt werden sollen. In dieser „Paradiesstadt", die hier entsteht, führt man ein beschauliches, idyllisches Leben. Das kann aber die Männer von der Goldküste auf die Dauer nicht befriedigen. Es herrscht Unzufriedenheit. Die Preise sinken. In der Nacht des Taifuns, der gegen die Stadt heranzieht, erfindet Jim Mahoney das neue Gesetz der Stadt. Dieses Gesetz lautet: „Du darfst alles". Der Taifun biegt ab. Man lebt weiter nach den neuen Gesetzen. Die Stadt blüht auf. Die Bedürfnisse steigen — und mit ihnen die Preise. Denn: man darf zwar alles — aber nur, wenn man es bezahlen kann. Jim Mahoney selbst wird, als ihm das Geld ausgeht, zum Tode verurteilt. Seine Hinrichtung wird zum Anlaß einer riesigen Demonstration gegen die Teuerung, die das Ende der Stadt ankündigt.

Das ist die Geschichte der Stadt Mahagonny. Sie wird dargestellt in einer lockeren Form von aneinandergereihten „Sittenbildern des 20. Jahrhunderts". Es ist ein Gleichnis vom heutigen Leben. Die Hauptfigur des Stückes ist die Stadt. Sie entsteht aus den Bedürfnissen des Menschen, und die Bedürfnisse des Menschen sind es, die ihren Aufstieg und ihren Fall herbeiführen. Wir zeigen aber die einzelnen Phasen in der Geschichte der Stadt lediglich in ihrer Rückwirkung auf den Menschen. Denn so wie die Bedürfnisse der Menschen die Entwicklung der Stadt beeinflussen, so verändert wieder die Entwicklung der Stadt die Haltung der Menschen. Daher sind alle Gesänge dieser Oper Ausdruck der Masse, auch dort, wo sie vom einzelnen als dem Sprecher der Masse vorgetragen werden. Die Gruppe der Gründer im Anfang steht den Gruppen der Ankommenden gegenüber. Die Gruppe der Anhänger des neuen Gesetzes kämpft am Schluß des ersten Aktes gegen die Gruppe der Gegner. Das Schicksal des einzelnen wird nur dort vorübergehend geschildert, wo es beispielhaft für das Schicksal der Stadt ist.

Außerhalb dieses Grundgedankens psychologische oder aktuelle Zusammenhänge zu suchen, wäre falsch.

Der Name „Mahagonny" bezeichnet lediglich den Begriff einer Stadt. Er ist aus klanglichen (phonetischen) Gründen gewählt worden. Die geographische Lage der Stadt spielt keine Rolle.

Es ist dringend abzuraten, die Darstellung des Werkes nach der Seite des Ironischen oder Grotesken zu verschieben. Da die Vorgänge nicht symbolisch sondern typisch sind, empfiehlt sich größte Sparsamkeit in den szenischen Mitteln und in dem Ausdruck des einzelnen Darstellers. Die schauspielerische Führung der Sänger, die Bewegung des Chors, wie überhaupt der ganze Darstellungsstil dieser Oper, wird bestimmt durch den Stil der Musik. Diese Musik ist in keinem Moment illustrativ. Sie versucht die Haltung des Menschen in den verschiedenen Situationen, die den Aufstieg und Fall der Stadt herbeiführt, zu realisieren. Die Haltung des Menschen ist in der Musik

bereits so fixiert, daß eine einfache, natürliche Interpretation der Musik schon den Darstellungsstil angibt. Daher kann sich auch der Darsteller selbst auf die einfachsten und natürlichsten Gesten beschränken.

Bei der Inszenierung der Oper muß stets berücksichtigt werden, daß hier abgeschlossene musikalische Formen vorliegen. Es besteht also eine wesentliche Aufgabe darin, den rein musikalischen Ablauf zu sichern und die Darsteller so zu gruppieren, daß ein beinahe konzertantes Musizieren möglich ist. Der Stil des Werkes ist weder naturalistisch noch symbolisch. Er könnte eher als „real" bezeichnet werden, denn er zeigt das Leben, wie es sich in der Sphäre der Kunst darstellt. Jede Übersteigerung nach der Seite der Pathetik oder der tänzerischen Stilisierung ist zu vermeiden.

Die Projektionstafeln Caspar Nehers bilden einen Bestandteil des Aufführungsmaterials (sie sollen daher auch gemeinsam mit dem Notenmaterial an die Bühnen verschickt werden). Diese Tafeln illustrieren selbständig, mit den Mitteln des Malers, die szenischen Vorgänge. Sie liefern ein Anschauungsmaterial zur Geschichte der Stadt, das nacheinander während oder zwischen den einzelnen Szenen auf eine Wand projiziert wird. Vor dieser Wand spielt der Darsteller seine Szenen und es genügt vollständig, wenn hier die nötigsten Requisiten aufgestellt werden, die der Darsteller zur Verdeutlichung seines Spiels braucht. Es ist in dieser Oper unnötig, eine komplizierte Bühnenmaschinerie in Tätigkeit treten zu lassen. Wichtiger sind einige gute Projektionsapparate sowie eine geschickte Anordnung der Projektionsflächen, die es ermöglicht, daß sowohl die Bilder wie hauptsächlich die erklärenden Schriften von allen Plätzen deutlich zu erkennen sind. Der Bühnenaufbau soll so einfach sein, daß er ebenso gut aus dem Theater heraus auf irgendein Podium verpflanzt werden kann. Die solistischen Szenen sollen möglichst nahe an die Zuschauer herangespielt werden. Daher ist es ratsam, den Orchesterraum nicht zu vertiefen, sondern das Orchester in der Höhe des Parkettes zu postieren und von der Bühne ein Podium in den Orchesterraum hineinzubauen, so daß manche Szenen mitten im Orchester gespielt werden können.

222. Orchestra of the Leipzig Opera in the late 1920's, with Gustav Brecher at the podium.

223. ca. 1930.

Weill (in Berlin) to Lotte Lenya, 27 January 1930: Yesterday I was on the go the whole day: at noon at Hanns's for lunch, then to the theater, where I spoke with Stravinsky, then to the café with [Ernst Josef] Aufricht [the producer of *Die Dreigroschenoper*], and in the evening to a radio concert [of *Le baiser de la fée*], which Stravinsky conducted. He was really enthusiastic about *Die Dreigroschenoper* and said that in foreign countries it is the best-known and most talked-about contemporary German work of art. It's seen as a play that could have originated only on German soil, but just the same an entirely new mixture of Shakespeare and Dickens. The music, he said, is perfect. I'm supposed to send him all the recordings and music immediately, because he wants the play to be with him always.

Weill (in Berlin) to Lotte Lenya, [31 January 1930]: I was so busy all the time in Leipzig that I could hardly spend an hour with my parents. We worked only with Brügmann. At first he seemed really dumb, so that first evening we were quite desperate. Then he suddenly got excited when the word "masks" came up. Finally he saw the light (insofar as he could, being such a jackass). The outcome: we'll play the entire piece with masks, completely rigid ones made to fit the facial form of each performer. Of course, that will be a great advantage. Since we're committed to going through with this, it could actually turn out to be the most modern theatrical performance; for years everyone has talked about using masks, but nobody has done it. And they will really hamstring those over-emoting singers. I had a marvelous idea right away: at the end, the "Gott in Mahagonny" must tear the masks off the men's faces. After that the revolution starts. (Isn't that beautiful?)

1 9 3 0

MUSIC + THEATER:

George Antheil *Transatlantic*

Leoš Janáček *From the House of the Dead* (posth.)

Igor Stravinsky *Symphony of Psalms*

LITERATURE + FILM:

Robert Musil *Der Mann ohne Eigenschaften*

Robert Frost *Collected Poems*

Der blaue Engel (film by Joseph von Sternberg)

SCIENCE + SOCIETY:

Planet Pluto discovered

Walter Reppe makes artificial fabrics from acetylene base

Photo flashbulb comes into use

POLITICS:

Heinrich Brüning forms right-wing coalition in Germany

Last Allied troops leave Germany

In the German elections Nazis gain 107 seats from the center parties

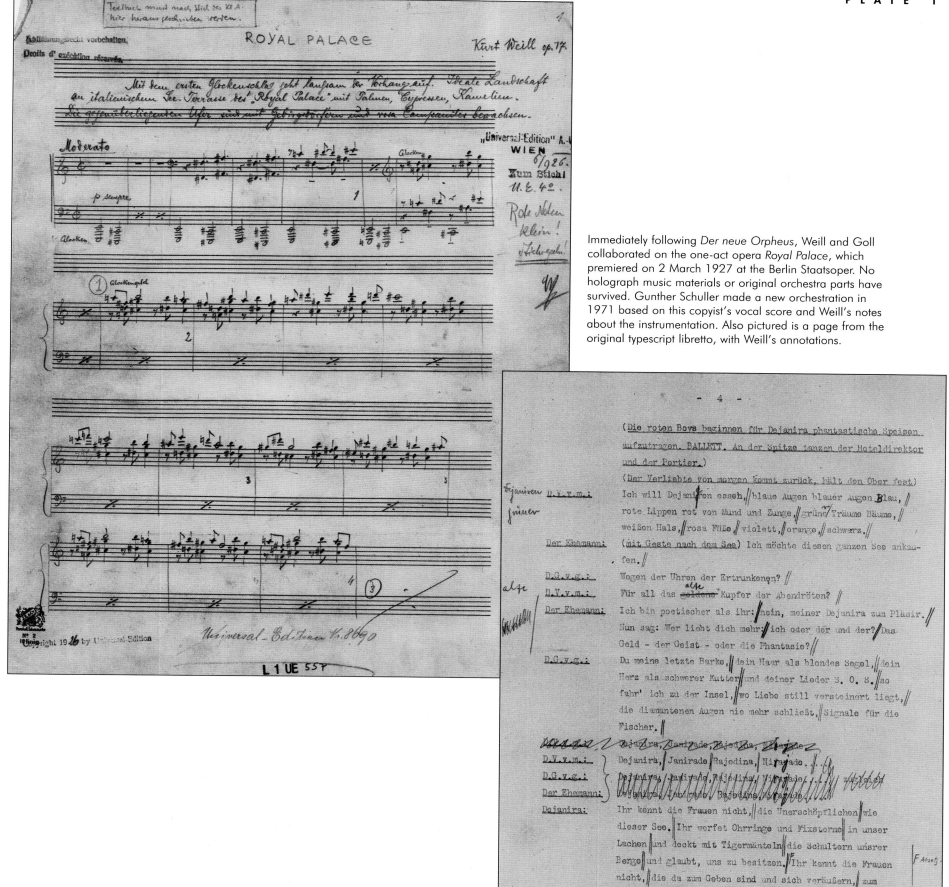

Immediately following *Der neue Orpheus*, Weill and Goll collaborated on the one-act opera *Royal Palace*, which premiered on 2 March 1927 at the Berlin Staatsoper. No holograph music materials or original orchestra parts have survived. Gunther Schuller made a new orchestration in 1971 based on this copyist's vocal score and Weill's notes about the instrumentation. Also pictured is a page from the original typescript libretto, with Weill's annotations.

PLATE 2

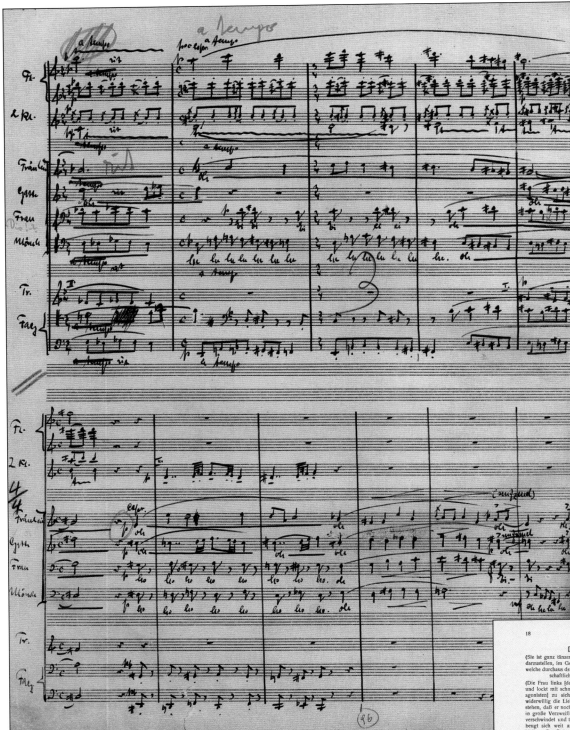

Weill and Kaiser included two pantomimes in *Der Protagonist*. The first pantomime is represented here by a page of Weill's full score (showing nonsense syllables in the voice parts) and the synopsis of the action that appeared in the published libretto (Universal Edition Nr. 8388).

PLATE 3

Scene and costume designs by Adolf Mahnke for the first production of *Der Protagonist* at the Dresden Staatsoper.

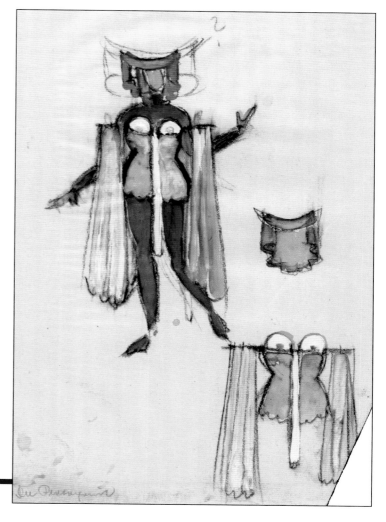

PLATE 4

Hein Heckroth designed a production of *Royal Palace* for Essen that opened in June 1929, two years after the Berlin premiere. (He also designed *A Kingdom for a Cow* in London, 1935.) Pictured here are sketches for the hotel, the hotel lobby (also showing a location for the film projections), and a group of sculptures. The opera is set on Lake Como in Italy, but Heckroth apparently used a photo of Lake Leman near Montreux, Switzerland for inspiration.

PLATE 5

"The Reckoning"

It's fine to have a blow-out in a fancy restaurant,
With terrapin and canvas-back and all the wine you want;
To enjoy the flowers and music, watch the pretty women pass,
Smoke a choice cigar and sip the wealthy water in your glass.
It's bully in a high-toned joint to eat and drink your fill,
But it's quite another matter when you
. . .   Pay the bill.

Time has got a little bill—get wise while yet you may,
For the debit side's increasing in a most alarming way;
The things you had no right to do, the things you should have done,
They're all put down; it's up to you to pay for every one.
So eat, drink, and be merry, have a good time if you will,
But God help you when the time comes, and you
                                                        Foot the bill.

"The Spell of the Yukon"

They're making my money diminish;
I'm sick of the taste of champagne.
Thank God! When I'm skinned to a finish
I'll pike to the Yukon again.
I'll fight—and you bet it's no sham-fight;
It's hell!—but I've been there before;
And it's better than this by a damsite—
So me for the Yukon once more.

An early edition of Robert Service's *The Spell of the Yukon* with excerpts from two poems: "The Reckoning" and "The Spell of the Yukon" (New York: Barse, 1916). Perhaps neither Brecht, Elisabeth Hauptmann, nor Weill knew Robert Service's poems or his novel *The Trail of Ninety-Eight*, or the 1928 silent movie based on the novel, but the characters and plot outlines in these works are uncannily similar to those of *Mahagonny*.

A gambling scene from the film *The Trail of '98*, featuring Dolores Del Rio as an innocent turned prostitute. Robert Service's novel on which the film is based chronicles the Gold Rush experiences of a quartet of miners, each of whom had descriptive nicknames such as "Salvation Jim" and "the Prodigal," and where the city of Dawson was "a giant spider, drawing in its prey."

The city of Dawson in the Yukon Territory was like a real-life Mahagonny, a place where entrepreneurs set up shop to make quick money and then moved on. Photo: Clarke and Clarence Kinsey, ca. 1898.

"The Gold Diggers' Saloon" by George Grosz, 1915-16.

PLATE 6

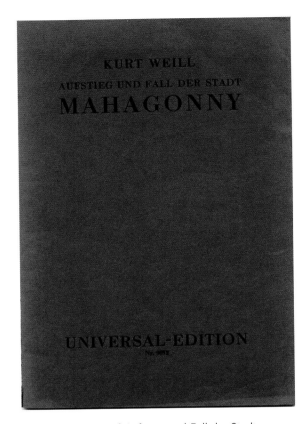

Published libretto of *Aufstieg und Fall der Stadt Mahagonny*.

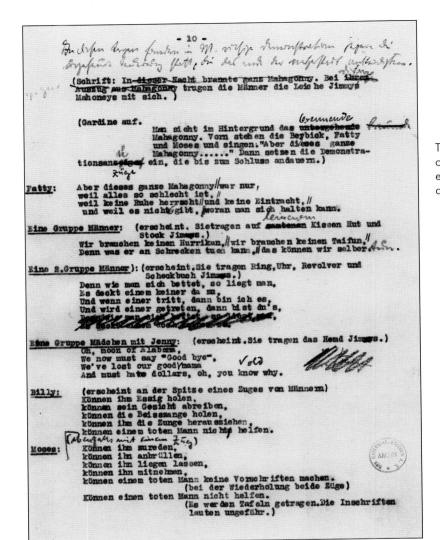

This page from the third act of the typescript libretto bears emendations by both Weill and Brecht.

This first edition of the piano-vocal score belonged to Weill's brother Nathan.

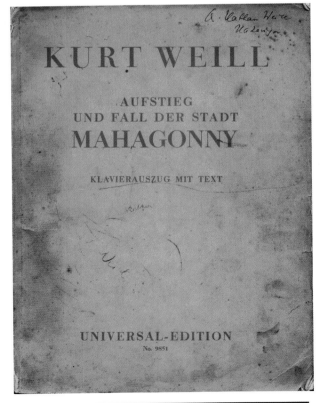

This insert into the published libretto reflected Weill's request to replace the American names with German ones.

Weill's instructions to Universal Edition on how to lay out the title page for *Aufstieg und Fall der Stadt Mahagonny:* "not 'Brecht-Weill,' but opera by Weill, text by Brecht."

PLATE 7

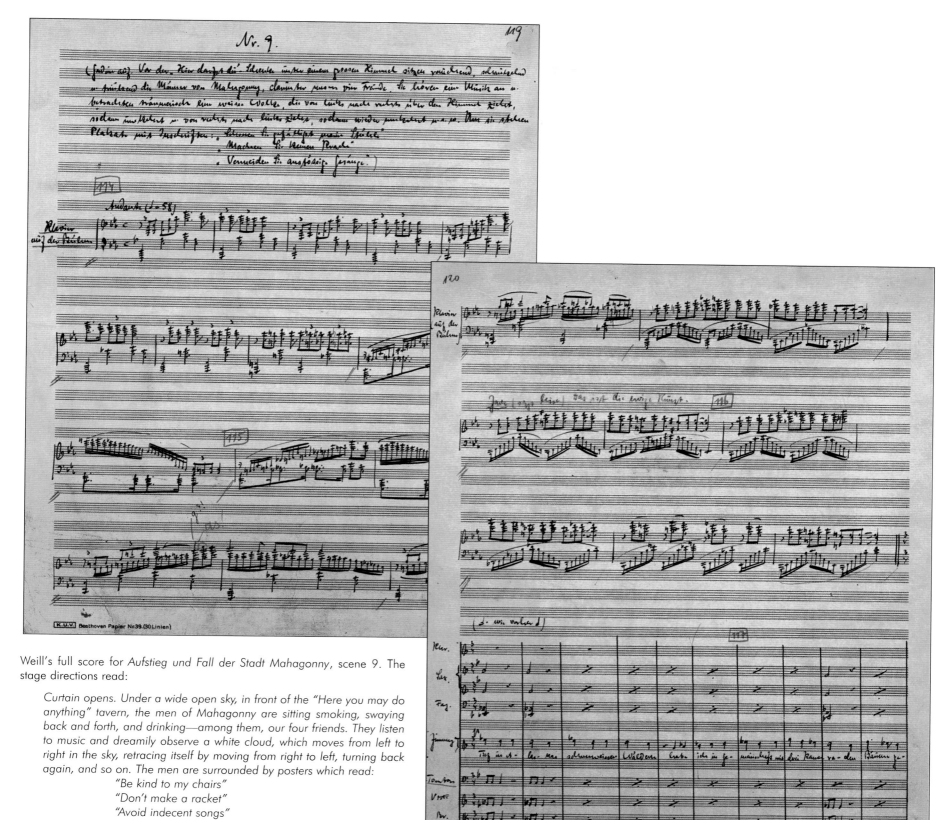

Weill's full score for *Aufstieg und Fall der Stadt Mahagonny*, scene 9. The stage directions read:

> Curtain opens. Under a wide open sky, in front of the "Here you may do anything" tavern, the men of Mahagonny are sitting smoking, swaying back and forth, and drinking—among them, our four friends. They listen to music and dreamily observe a white cloud, which moves from left to right in the sky, retracing itself by moving from right to left, turning back again, and so on. The men are surrounded by posters which read:
> > "Be kind to my chairs"
> > "Don't make a racket"
> > "Avoid indecent songs"

In this scene Weill interweaves the very popular parlor piano piece, "Gebet einer Jungfrau" ("The Maiden's Prayer") by Tekla Badarzewska, with Jimmy's aria "Tief in Alaskas schneeweißen Wäldern." Above the second system he has written Jack's line of dialogue, "Das ist die ewige Kunst" ("This is eternal art").

PLATE 8

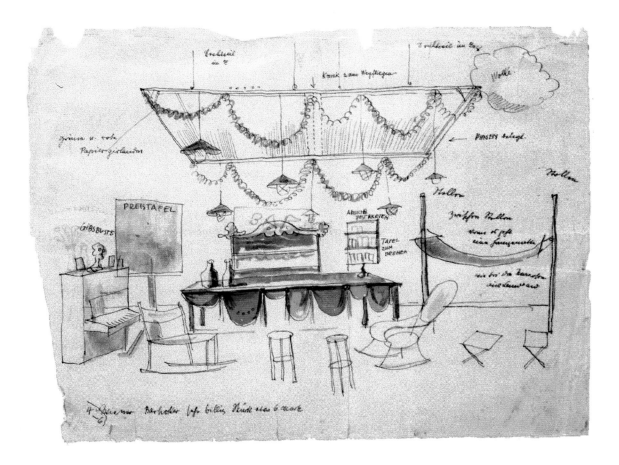

Caspar Neher's set designs for Begbick's tavern
(Act I) and the "eating" scene (Act II).

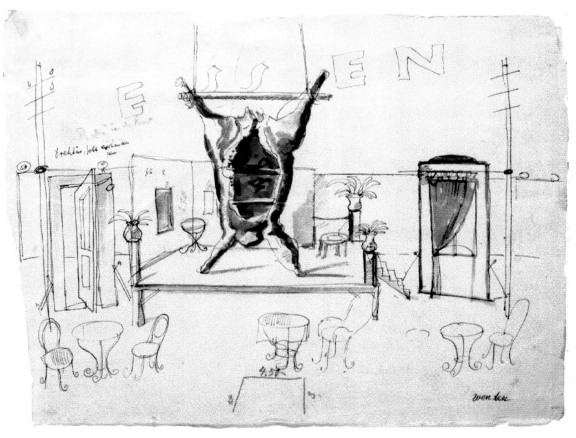

AUFSTIEG UND FALL DER STADT MAHAGONNY

Opera in three acts; text by Bertolt Brecht (with Kurt Weill)

1930	Leipzig, Städtisches Theater (9 March)
	Gustav Brecher, conductor; Walther Brügmann, director;
	Caspar Neher, designer
	Braunschweig, Landestheater (12 March)
	Kassel, Staatstheater (12 March)
	Essen, Städtische Bühnen (cancelled)
	Oldenburg, Landestheater (cancelled)
	Dortmund, Stadttheater (cancelled)
	Prague, Deutsches Landestheater (12 July)
	Frankfurt, Städtische Bühnen (16 October)
1931	Berlin, Theater am Kurfürstendamm (21 December)
1932	Vienna, Raimund Theater (26 April)
1933	Copenhagen, The New Theatre (31 December?)

224. Artistic team at the Leipzig Opera: Gustav Brecher, intendant Barthol, director Walther Brügmann, director Kronacher, technical director Dobra, assistant intendant Köppen.

225. This advertisement for a recording of two songs from *Aufstieg und Fall der Stadt Mahagonny* appeared in the program of the premiere. The recording, made 24 February 1930, featured Lotte Lenya.

NEUES THEATER

Sonntag, den 9. März 1930
Außer Anrecht
Uraufführung

Aufstieg und Fall der Stadt Mahagonny

Oper in drei Akten — Musik von Kurt Weill — Text von Bert Brecht
Bühnenbilder und Projektionen: Caspar Neher
Musikalische Leitung: Gustav Brecher — Spielleitung: Walther Brügmann

Leokadja Begbick	Marga Dannenberg
Willy, der „Prokurist"	Hanns Fleischer
Virginia-Moses	Walther Zimmer
Jenny	Mali Trummer
Johann Ackermann	Paul Beinert
Jacob Schmidt	Hanns Hauschild
Heinrich (genannt Sparbüchsenheinrich)	Theodor Horand
Josef Lettner (genannt Alaskawolfjoe)	Ernst Osterkamp
Tobby Higgins	Alfred Holländer
Ein Liebespaar	Ilse Koegel / Hans Lißmann

Acht Mädchen von Mahagonny, Männer von Mahagonny
Chöre: Konrad Neuger
Kostüme nach Entwürfen von Caspar Neher angefertigt in den Werkstätten
für Theaterkunst Hermann J. Kaufmann, Berlin
Lautsprecher: Radiohaus Fritz Meyer & Co., Leipzig
Technische Einrichtung: Oswald Ihrke

Größere Pause nach dem 1. Akt   Änderungen vorbehalten
Rückgabe von Eintrittskarten wegen Umbesetzungen ausgeschlossen
Einlaß 19 Uhr   Anfang 19½ Uhr   Ende nach 22 Uhr

226. Weill with his mother in Leipzig, around the time of the premiere of *Aufstieg und Fall der Stadt Mahagonny*.

No. 4. "Auf nach Mahagonny."

No. 6. Seduction scene between Jimmy and Jenny.

No. 12. The hurricane scene.

227. Caspar Neher made drawings for projections for three different productions of *Mahagonny*: the Songspiel in Baden-Baden (1927), *Aufstieg und Fall der Stadt Mahagonny* in Leipzig (1930), and *Aufstieg und Fall der Stadt Mahagonny* in Berlin (1931). The descriptions found in the 1929 vocal score and the libretto published in volume 2 of Brecht's *Versuche* (1930) are useful starting points for determining which drawings were indeed used as projections for the Leipzig production, even though the sources are incomplete or contradictory. Each drawing below is identified with the musical number from the 1929 vocal score that it probably illustrates.

No. 14. The crane duet.

No. 16. The trial scene.

According to Weill's theory, the soloists in a work of this kind should be brought as close as possible to the audience. Therefore, a small stage had been erected over the orchestra pit, on which all the solo action took place.

As for the stage settings to this "*hintertreppen*" potpourri, they were simple to the point of primitiveness. They were dominated entirely by the Caspar Neher pictures which were projected on a backdrop during and between the scenes, and clearly emphasized the Billingsgate tone of the whole. It is understood that these drawings, as well as the explanatory texts which preceded each episode like the captions to a moving picture, form an integral part of the work and must be included in the decor. The actors all wore short white masks, which was an effective idea in its way and quite in keeping with the general style. Geraldine de Courcy, "Opera Satire on Modern Life Creates Uproar," *Musical America*, 10 April 1930): 5.

No. 19. Benares song.

228. First scene of *Aufstieg und Fall der Stadt Mahagonny* at the Leipzig premiere, 9 March 1930.

230. A drawing of the trial scene, Act III, rendered by Dolbin.

229. This photo of a scene from Act I shows the singers wearing white masks.

232. Weill's and Neher's typescript of "Suggestions on staging the opera *Aufstieg und Fall der Stadt Mahagonny*."

231. Final scene of *Aufstieg und Fall der Stadt Mahagonny* at the Leipzig premiere.

Here and there, above and below in the electrically charged room opposition flared up, inciting opposition against the opposition which in turn ignited a third source of opposition. The woman on my left was seized by spasms of the heart and wanted out; only the suggestion that she might miss a historic event kept her from leaving. The old Saxonian on my right clasped the knee of his own wife in his excitement! A man behind me was talking to himself, "I can't wait for Brecht to get here!" He was licking his chops. Preparedness is everything. Belligerent shouts, hand-to-hand fighting at some place, hissing, applauding that sounded grimly as if the hissing people had been symbolically slapped in the face, enthusiastic fury mixed with furious enthusiasm. Finally, a demonstration en masse by the complainers crushed by a hail of applause. Alfred Polgar, "Krach in Leipzig," *Das Tagebuch* 12, no. 12 (22 May 1930): 465-67.

233. Maurice Abravanel, Weill, director Jakob Geis, and intendant Max Berg-Ehlert at the Kassel Staatstheater, where *Mahagonny* opened three days after the Leipzig premiere.

234. Production photo from the trial scene in Kassel. Left to right: Annelies Jolowicz (Jenny), Georg Buttlar (Bill), Viktor Mossi, (Dreieinigkeitsmoses), Barbara Clema (Begbick), and Laurenz Hofer (Jim Mahoney).

Weill (in Berlin) to Maurice Abravanel, 2 February 1930: Between you and me: I am afraid that Geis wants to bend the performance strongly toward the literary side. I hope you people won't make the very mistake you criticized in the Leipzig performance of the *Zar*! *Mahagonny* is an opera, an opera for singers. Casting it with actors is as good as impossible. Only where I have notated it specifically can there be spoken words, and any kind of changes are possible only with my consent.

It is a long time since a dramatic work has met with such passionate opposition; a long time too, probably, since the first performance of a new work has been awaited with such tense excitement. For if a way out of the present crisis in the realm of opera is to be found, the only hope lies in the quarter where Brecht and Weill are carrying out their ideological renovation of traditional genres. . . . We have come to the point of decision: the decision that there must be a new form of opera, a radically different kind of theater. Kurt Weill, now 30 years old, has been aiming at this new form ever since his musico-dramatic beginnings. In *Die Dreigroschenoper* he achieved it for the first time. These are its characteristics: a total and uninhibited revolution in theme; a complete avoidance of pomposity and false heroics; a ruthless excision of all "narcotic" elements; and a thoroughgoing adoption of the techniques of the film and cabaret. In addition, a pronounced emphasis on social issues. . . . And here the music comes into its own: the widest mass effects are possible. One may lean on the popular song, and the memory of a familiar strain becomes a vigorous artistic stimulus. It is not the originality of the means which is decisive, but their power of suggestion.

The primitive and rough grandiosity of these incidents, linked by the subtitles of traditional balladry, demands an elemental type of music. Weill abides by the principles which made the success of *Die Dreigroschenoper*. He dissolves the action into song-type episodes and thus creates hauntingly melodic operatic numbers. Not only the most attractive high point—such as the "Alabama-Song," the ballad "Wie man sich bettet, so liegt man," or the magnificent "Cranes" love duet—but also linking passages have been worked with loving detail and are often modeled directly on pre-classical (Handelian) example. . . . The ninth scene, which contains the piano variations on "A Maiden's Prayer," is a virtuoso showpiece of modern operatic style, in color and power comparable to the Tavern Scene from Berg's *Wozzeck*.

The work stands at the forefront of the historical development of modern day musico-dramatic production. For all its occasional beery humor, its adolescent romanticism, it effectively supports the justification for the New Theater, and for this very reason it should receive enthusiastic acclaim. It proves plausible the possibilities of opera for the present and the future while at the same time breaking through its boundaries.

Any liberal-minded criticism had to founder on this piece. Here the pretext of "on the one hand—on the other" was no longer possible, as even the most flexible commentators were forced to admit. And that is also of incalculable importance: Thus the work (whose particular qualities do not matter for this purpose) became a point of orientation for modern opera and, moreover, for the theater of the future as well as for new music. H.H. Stuckenschmidt, "Mahagonny," *Die Scene* 20, no. 3 (March 1930): 75-77.

Weill (in Berlin) to Universal Edition, 18 March 1930: In the meantime here in Berlin another major project has come up, which is, however, strictly confidential. [Erik] Charell is extremely interested in *Mahagonny* and would like to try to do it as soon as May in the Großes Schauspielhaus (3,500 seats!), perhaps as a guest appearance of the Leipzig opera. . . . Aufricht doesn't know anything yet about this plan.

Weill (in Berlin) to Universal Edition, 20 March 1930: I am very pleased that you have already begun the publicity for *Mahagonny*. What would you think about putting an appendix in the pamphlet that deals with the Leipzig scandal, laid out as a string of newspaper notices? In this way one could totally isolate the *Leipziger Neueste Nachrichten* and those few nationalist papers that also urged censorship and demonstrate to the theater directors, which would be very important, that it is only a matter of the conspiratorial machinations of elements of the radical right (which was clear in Braunschweig).

In the meantime I have heard indirectly that in Essen and Dortmund they are thinking of postponing *Mahagonny* "indefinitely." We must do everything we can to fight this plan. Apparently it is the result of urging from the Zentrum circles which, if permitted, would mean lasting damage to every modern theatrical endeavor. I therefore ask you to use every legal means at your disposal (breach of contract, compensation), to see that the performances take place. The work is now available in a version that can be performed for a Catholic audience, and it is blind prejudice if they are agitating against the performance even before they've seen this version.

Weill (in Berlin) to Universal Edition, 25 March 1930: You will see that with our changes (which are now final) it is quite explicit and clear that *Mahagonny* is nothing other than Sodom and Gomorrah. We show clearly that anarchy leads to crime and crime to ruin. You can't get any more moral. Dramaturgically the whole thing has been significantly improved. In particular, the close of the second act is much more effective because now Jim's aria is at the beginning of the 3rd act and the effective choral piece "Lasst euch nicht verführen" is placed at the close of the 2nd act. "Gott in Mahagonny" is now in no way provocative since it isn't directed toward the audience, but rather toward the condemned. I now find the changes that Mr. Brecher and Dr. Heinsheimer wanted after the premiere, and which have in the meantime been relayed to the other stages, went too far. The sentence with the underwear (page 62) didn't offend anyone in Kassel, likewise the first part of Jim's song "Wenn es etwas gibt," page 139, was received with absolute calm. I have therefore only made such changes as seemed necessary after quiet deliberation and in light of my experiences in Kassel.

| 292 | ZEITSCHRIFT FÜR MUSIK | April 1930 |

Der 2. Teil wurde ebenso wie der 1. durch Handzeichen bestimmt und an die Tafel geschrieben. — Zum Schluß wurde das Gedicht im ganzen noch einmal mit verteilten Rollen durchgenommen, und an den richtigen Stellen setzte der Elfenchor nun mit dem Liede ein, und das Fingerhütchen sang ebenfalls seine Zeile dazu.

Aufstieg und Fall der Stadt Mahagonny. Uraufführung in Leipzig.

Halloh, meine sauberen Herren B r e c h t und W e i l l, Ihre Tage dürften wohl ebenfalls so gezählt sein wie die Ihrer Abschaumstadt M a h a g o n n y! Setzte es doch bei der Uraufführung dieses denkbar übeln, hundsgemeinen und vor allem künstlerisch impotenten Stücks einen derart ehrlichen, prächtigen Theaterskandal bei reinlichster Scheidung zwischen anständigen und, sagen wir, gegenteilig gearteten Zuhörern ab, wie er, zur Zeit wenigstens und gerade in Leipzig, eindeutiger nicht gewünscht werden kann. Ein so kräftiges, innerlich berechtigtes Pfeifen, dazu mit Rufen wie: Pfui Teufel! Schluß! untermischt, hat es im Neuen Theater sicher noch nie abgesetzt, und so entspann sich hernach ein wohltuendster Kampf zwischen Klatschenden und Pfeifenden, der — und darüber besteht wohl kein Zweifel — eine entscheidende Wendung in der Stellung zu der Schmutz-Poesie des Herrn Brecht wie auch der gleichgesinnten Maschinen-Jazzmusik Herrn Weills herbeiführen wird. Der Abend war nichts anderes als ein Volksgericht und ging ganz erheblich über einen gewöhnlichen Theaterskandal hinaus, mochte der modische Kunstpöbel, wozu wir ihm schönstens gratulieren, auch noch äußerlich stärker sein und Hervorrufe auch der Autoren erreichen. Was steckt aber alles hinter dieser Theaterschlacht? Daß der vorläufig noch kleinere Teil des Publikums zur Selbsthilfe griff, greifen mußte, weil es Würde und Ansehen der Kunst erstens von einer skrupellos auch das Gemeinste in den Himmel erhebenden, modernen und tonangebenden Großstadtpresse, zweitens aber von städtischen und staatlichen Kunstbehörden verraten und in den Staub getreten sieht. Selbsthilfe des besseren Teils des Publikums völligen Versagens von Presse und Behörden wegen, das ist's, was hinter diesem Theaterkampf steckt. Und wenn nunmehr die teilweise ganz gleiche Presse, die nicht nur einen Jonny, sondern auch eine Dreigroschenoper mit einem Glorienschein umgeben hatte, sofort umfällt und sich selbst Ohrfeigen erteilt, so ist dies die unmittelbare Folge dieses Volksgerichts. Denn wir stellen nur noch in letzter Redaktionsstunde fest, daß „Mahagonny" keineswegs wesentlich gemeiner ist als die Drei-Groschenoper, als deren Fortsetzung sie gewissermaßen zu gelten hat. Hieß es dort: Zuerst das Fressen, dann die Moral, so lautet hier das Leitmotiv: „Erstens, vergeßt nicht, kommt das Fressen, / Zweitens kommt die Liebe dran [unter solcher versteht Herr Brecht lediglich das Bordell], / Drittens das Boxen nicht vergessen, / Viertens saufen, solang man kann. / Vor allem aber achtet scharf / Daß man hier alles d ü r f e n darf." Was man aber noch 1928 d u r f t e, darf man 1930 nicht mehr! Das ist des Rätsels Lösung! Wir müssen abwarten, welche Folgen diese Theaterschlacht für Leipzig im besonderen hat. Aber davon abgesehen, der 9. März bedeutet sicherlich auch über Leipzig hinaus einen S e l b s t b e s i n n u n g s t a g erster Ordnung; die goldene Zeit für Dichter des Zuhältertums ist um!

235. This right-wing attack on *Aufstieg und Fall der Stadt Mahagonny* which foreshadows Nazi cultural politics was published in the *Zeitschrift für Musik* 97, no. 4 (April 1930): 292.

236. A production of *Die Dreigroschenoper* was staged at the Kamerny Theatre, Moscow in 1930 by Alexander Tairov and designed by Vladimir and Georgy Stenberg.

237. "Asleep in the Deep," the original English-language version of "Seemannslos." Music by H. W. Petrie; words by Arthur J. Lamb. Below, the first two measures begin with the words "Stormy the night." The passage as used by Weill can be found on p. 234 of the 1929 vocal score.

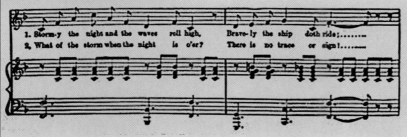

Weill (in Berlin) to Universal Edition, 5 April 1930: I've just received your letter regarding "Seemannslos." First of all I am utterly amazed by your strange position in this matter. Your remark that you had "no inkling of this matter" is absolutely false. You have had the libretto of the *Mahagonny* opera for a year, the score for two years, and I am amazed that you want to admit to knowing so little about an opera whose libretto, full score, piano score and orchestral parts you have printed. . . . Besides, it was as a result of our discussion of this point that with the appearances of "Gebet einer Jungfrau" I added the footnote "with use of the 'Gebet einer Jungfrau.'" [See plate 7.] With "Seemannslos" it seemed unnecessary to us, since the spoken text clearly reads:

"The best thing is to sing: 'Stormy the Night,' in order not to lose our nerve."

"'Stormy the night' is excellent, if one loses one's nerve. In any event we want to sing right away."

From that it is quite clear that it is a simple quotation, clearly intended as a caricature and parody. That is above all evident in the musical arrangement: in the introduction (p. 234) and the refrain of the song I have added counterpoint and in addition added a rhythm which underlies the whole scene. Musical quotations of this sort are quite frequent. If I were to file a suit every time my *Dreigroschenoper* songs were parodied I would soon be a rich man.

238. The vocal score of *Der Jasager* includes two key non-autograph changes: the dedication to Gustav Brecher and the notation that the text was "reworked" by Brecht.

239. First page of the autograph full score of *Der Jasager*.

DER JASAGER

School opera in two acts; text by Bertolt Brecht after the Japanese play *Taniko*

1930 Berlin, Zentralinstitut für Erziehung und Unterricht (23 June)
Live broadcast on Berlin radio; Kurt Drabek, conductor

More than seventy productions between 1930 and 1936 in cities in Austria, Belgium, Czechoslovakia, Denmark, France, Germany, Japan, Sweden, Switzerland, and the United States. More than 300 productions in German schools before 1933.

[*Der Jasager*] is extremely important just now because it shows an undeniable departure from the song style and counters the constant attempts to stereotype me with the *Dreigroschenoper*. Also the completely apolitical, purely humane nature of the text is very propitious at the moment. Weill to Universal Edition, 14 April 1930.

NEUE MUSIK UND SCHULE

Uraufführung der Schuloper „Der Jasager" von **Brecht-Weill**

Chöre und Liedsätze aus dem Staatlichen Liederbuch für die Jugend

Veranstaltung der Musikabteilung des Zentralinstituts für Erziehung und Unterricht, Berlin. Montag, den 23. Juni 1930, 20 Uhr

240. *Der Jasager* was first performed as a live broadcast on Berlin radio, 23 June 1930; the stage premiere took place the following day. The first half of the program was devoted to choral and solo singing.

Vortragsfolge

Liedvorträge aus dem staatl. Liederbuch für die Jugend

Chorlieder:
Wach auf, wach auf mit heller Stimm' . Satz von Kurt Thomas
  vierstimmig mit Flöte, Violine und Violoncello
Maria durch ein Dornwald ging . . . . . Satz von Heinrich Kaminski

Ein- und zweistimmige Lieder mit Begleitung:
Die Brünnlein, die da fließen . . . . Satz von Philipp Jarnach
Ich armes Maidlein klag' mich sehr . . . Satz von Philipp Jarnach
Wach auf mein Hort . . . . Satz von Ernst Křenek
Rätselaufgeben . . . . Satz von Hermann Zilcher
  für Sopran, Bariton, Flöten und Violine

Chorlieder:
Ein Knäblein ging spazieren . . . . Satz von Waldemar von Baussznern
  zweistimmig mit Violine
Rosestock, Holderblüh . . . . Satz von Heinrich Kaspar Schmid
  zweistimmig mit Violinen, Lauten, Violoncello

Ausführende: Jugendchor und Instrumentalgruppe der Staatlichen Akademie für
  Kirchen- und Schulmusik unter Leitung von Prof. Heinrich
  Martens
  Sopransolo: Eva Duffing   Studierende der Aka-
  Baritonsolo: Herbert Rungenhagen   demie für Kirchen-
  Klavier: Karl Riehm   und Schulmusik

P A U S E

Uraufführung der Schuloper „Der Jasager"
Text nach einem alten japanischen Stück bearbeitet von Bert Brecht.
Musik von Kurt Weill

Personen: Der Knabe
  Die Mutter
  Der Lehrer   Kräfte des Jugendchors
  Die drei Studenten
  Der große Chor

Ausführende: Jugendgruppe und Instrumentalgruppe der Staatlichen Akademie
  für Kirchen- und Schulmusik
  Sämtliche Ausführende sind Schüler Berliner Lehranstalten

8

Über meine Schuloper „Der Jasager"
Von Kurt Weill

Die Absicht, eine Schuloper zu schreiben, liegt bei mir etwa ein Jahr zurück. Das Wort „Schuloper" umfaßte für mich von Anfang an mehrere Möglichkeiten, den Begriff „Schulung" mit dem Begriff „Oper" zu verbinden. Eine Oper kann zunächst Schulung für den Komponisten oder für eine Komponisten-Generation sein. Gerade in dieser Zeit, wo es sich darum handelt, die Gattung „Oper" auf neue Grundlagen zu stellen und die Grenzen dieser Gattung neu zu bezeichnen, ist es eine wichtige Aufgabe, Urformen dieser Gattung herzustellen, in denen die formalen und inhaltlichen Probleme eines vorwiegend musikalischen Theaters auf Grund neuer Voraussetzungen neu untersucht werden. In diesem Sinne könnte man auch Busonis „Arlecchino", Hindemiths „Hin und Zurück", Milhauds „Armer Matrose" und die „Dreigroschenoper" als Schulopern bezeichnen, da jedes dieser Werke eine Urform der Oper herzustellen versucht.

Eine Oper kann auch Schulung für die Operndarstellung sein. Wenn es uns gelingt, die gesamte musikalische Anlage eines Bühnenwerkes so einfach und natürlich zu gestalten, daß wir die Kinder als die idealen Interpreten dieses Werkes bezeichnen können, so wäre ein solches Werk auch geeignet, die Opernsänger (oder solche, die es werden wollen) im Gesang und in der Darstellung zu jener Einfachheit und Natürlichkeit zu zwingen, die wir in den Opernhäusern so oft vermissen. In diesem Sinne könnte die Schuloper etwa als „Etüde" für Opernschulen und Opernbetriebe dienen (täglich vor Beginn der Probe einmal aufzuführen).

Die dritte Interpretation des Wortes „Schuloper" ist diejenige, die die beiden ersten in sich einschließt: es ist die Oper, die für den Gebrauch in den Schulen bestimmt ist. Sie ist einzureihen unter die Bestrebungen zur Schaffung einer musikalischen Produktion, in der die Musik nicht mehr Selbstzweck ist, sondern in den Dienst jener Institutionen gestellt wird, die Musik brauchen, und für die gerade eine neue Musikproduktion einen Wert darstellt. Zu den älteren Absatzgebieten (Konzert, Theater, Rundfunk) sind jetzt hauptsächlich zwei neue hinzugekommen: die Arbeiterchorbewegung und die Schulen. Eine lohnende Aufgabe für uns besteht darin, für diese neuen Gebiete nun auch Werke größeren Umfangs zu schaffen, die aber doch in den äußeren Mitteln so weit einschränken, daß die Ausführungsmöglichkeit an den Stellen, für die sie bestimmt sind, nicht behindert ist. Ich habe daher den „Jasager" so angelegt, daß er in allen Teilen (Chor, Orchester und Soli) von Schülern ausgeführt werden kann, und ich kann mir auch denken, daß Schüler zu diesem Stück Bühnenbilder und Kostüme entwerfen. Die Partitur ist entsprechend den Besetzungsmöglichkeiten eines Schülerorchesters eingerichtet: als Stammorchester Streicher (ohne Bratschen) und zwei Klaviere, dazu ad libitum drei Bläser (Flöte, Klarinette, Saxophon), Schlagzeug, Zupfinstrumente. Ich glaube aber nicht, daß man den

Schwierigkeitsgrad der Musik bei einer Schuloper zu weit herabsetzen soll, daß man eine besonders „kindliche", leicht nachsingbare Musik für diese Zwecke schreiben soll. Die Musik einer Schuloper muß unbedingt auf ein sorgfältiges, sogar langwieriges Studium berechnet sein. Denn *gerade im Studium besteht der praktische Wert der Schuloper*, und die Aufführung eines solchen Werkes ist weit weniger wichtig als die Schulung, die für die Ausführenden damit verbunden ist. Diese Schulung ist zunächst eine rein musikalische. Sie soll aber mindestens ebensosehr eine geistige sein. Die pädagogische Wirkung der Musik kann nämlich darin bestehen, daß der Schüler sich auf dem Umweg über ein musikalisches Studium intensiv mit einer bestimmten Idee beschäftigt, die sich ihm durch die Musik plastischer darbietet und die sich stärker in ihm festsetzt, als wenn er sie aus Büchern lernen müßte. *Es ist daher unbedingt erstrebenswert, daß ein Schulstück den Knaben außer der Freude am Musizieren auch Gelegenheit bietet, etwas zu lernen.* Das alte japanische Stück, das wir (Brecht und ich) als Textunterlage der ersten Schuloper auswählten, schien uns zwar seiner ganzen Grundhaltung nach sofort für den Gebrauch in Schulen geeignet, aber den Vorgängen fehlte noch jene Begründung, die erst eine pädagogische Verwertung berechtigt erscheinen läßt. Wir fügten daher den Begriff „Einverständnis" hinzu und änderten das Stück danach um: der Knabe wird jetzt nicht mehr (wie im alten Stück) willenlos ins Tal hinabgeworfen, sondern er wird vorher befragt, und er beweist durch die Erklärung seines Einverständnisses, daß er gelernt hat, für eine Gemeinschaft oder für eine Idee, der er sich angeschlossen hat, alle Konsequenzen auf sich zu nehmen.

Aus unserer Arbeit am Jasager
Von Heinrich Martens

In erfreulicher Stetigkeit wächst mit der Hineinstellung der Musik in den Gesamtorganismus der Schule, mit dem Wiederaufnehmen der Verbindung zum Haus- und Privatmusikunterricht der kritische Sinn der Jugend auch in musikalischen Dingen. Wo Anregung, Auswertung und Befruchtung dieser willkommenen jugendlichen Eigenkräfte unterbleibt, kommt der Musikerzieher in Gefahr, von der Jugend zum alten Eisen geworfen zu werden. Unter der Oberfläche entwickeln sich dann Wildlinge und Schädlinge, die zur Gefahr für Jugend und Schule werden können.

Als man versäumte, das starke Hindrängen der Jugend zur Jazzmusik rechtzeitig einzufangen und in gesunde Bahnen zu lenken, entstanden die Schülertanzkapellen. Mancher Musiklehrer übersieht oder ignoriert auch heute noch die häufig unter der Oberfläche wirkenden Kräfte in musikalischen Dingen.

Problematisches, Reibungen und Spaltungen der Meinungen können, richtig gesehen, eminente Kraftquellen des Schaffens werden. Nur müssen alle guten Willens sein.

241. Weill's essay "Über meine Schuloper *Der Jasager*" appeared in the program.

2

3

242. Weill and director Heinrich Martens consult the score.

243. A brief review of *Der Jasager,* with photos, appeared in the German radio magazine *Die Funk-Stunde,* July-August 1930.

244. Hans Heinsheimer of Universal Edition. Photo: E. Marcus.

245. Stefan Frenkel recorded selections from his own arrangement of seven numbers from *Die Dreigroschenoper* for violin and piano.

Hans Heinsheimer of Universal Edition (in Vienna) to Weill and Brecht, 1 July 1930: We would like to report briefly on the results of the Berlin *Jasager* performance and about our future publicity plans. The critical response has been quite extraordinarily favorable. It is especially interesting to note that the work has been unanimously praised by papers of all political persuasions. There were especially good reviews in *Vorwärts, Deutsche Tageszeitung, Tempo, Deutsche Allgemeine Zeitung, Berliner Tageblatt, Berliner Börsencourier, B.Z. am Mittag, 8 Uhr Abendblatt, Frankfurter Zeitung,* etc. It is also important that a certain Dr. Arno Huth, who writes for about thirty provincial papers, wrote a truly enthusiastic review that could have a very significant impact on the provinces. We are now in the midst of preparing what we hope will be an especially effective pamphlet directed particularly at the schools. This pamphlet will also include the articles from the program.

Weill (in Berlin) to Universal Edition, 6 August 1930: With the help of a lawyer we have finally succeeded in securing satisfactory contractual assurances that we will be given effective collaboration rights on the *Dreigroschenoper* film. Nero, purely commercial in orientation and curiously disorganized, apparently wanted to make a harmless operetta film out of the *Dreigroschenoper.* We had, and have, to use every means at our disposal to guard against that. The work on the script is now underway. In the meantime I am busy carefully studying the technical and acoustic requirements and adjusting the instrumentation accordingly. . . . As for my new plans, at the moment I'm thinking a lot about Jack London, whose works have given me all kinds of new ideas. Furthermore, a plan for a Franz Kafka opera is taking shape (all this naturally in confidence). I hope that in the course of the next weeks something concrete will emerge from all these plans so that I can begin a big new project in the fall.

246. ca. 1930.

247. Ludwig Scheer, head of an association of German cinema owners, had objected to the filming of *Die Dreigroschenoper*, which he regarded as immoral. This ad, sponsored by Warner-Tobis, celebrates the strong reaction of the German press against Scheer.

248. Scene from the Frankfurt production of *Aufstieg und Fall der Stadt Mahagonny*, October 1930. Photo: Gabor Hirsch.

Weill (in Berlin) to Universal Edition, 24 August 1930: All the papers were very prompt in taking our side in the Scheer matter and from the right to the left there was a real storm of outrage. Nevertheless the Nero people don't understand that they would be better off just letting us work in peace without constant jostling, rather than being in a constant state of confrontation with us. An atrocious industry!

Weill (in Berlin) to Universal Edition, 27 August 1930: I have been working with Caspar Neher on an opera libretto for about two weeks. The results of this work so far are surprisingly good. We have constructed a very strong and simple plot and have now written the prologue. I think it quite possible that this collaboration can produce the libretto I need now. The title of this full-length opera will probably be *Die Bürgschaft*.

Weill (in Berlin) to Universal Edition, 28 September 1930: I am a bit unsettled about the Frankfurt *Mahagonny* matter. A few days ago I got the enclosed letter from Dr. Graf, which, quite frankly, doesn't sound very promising, and I fear that the gentlemen are pursuing the same tactics with me as they did with Schoenberg. You'll remember that they didn't invite him to the rehearsals and then asked him to leave when he tried to give his opinion at the dress rehearsal. Concerning "Gott in Mahagonny," I replied that the proposed change to "Glück" (I hope Dr. Graf hasn't misunderstood the entire work the way he did this scene) is completely out of the question, but that I would agree to having the whole scene cut, as would Brecht. However, that would be very difficult since the entire musical climax would be removed from the conclusion. So they have to let me know how they want to solve this difficulty. . . . I believe the greatest danger lies in their watering down or diluting the work out of pure fear so that absolutely nothing remains of the exciting or shattering effect so readily apparent in Leipzig.

Weill (in Berlin) to Universal Edition, 6 October 1930: As you have heard, we will have to go to court over the *Dreigroschenoper* film. It is unbelievable the way these people have behaved and after the latest events there is no doubt that our every attempt to protest against this manufactured kitsch will be suppressed by use of deliberate force and methods one only thought possible in wild west novels. When I tried for the first time to exercise my contractual right of co-determination and objected to a scene that seemed especially harmful, my employment contract was canceled for no reason at all. My attorney, Otto Joseph, thereupon filed suit. The date (together with Brecht's case) is set for 17 October.

Weill (in Berlin) to Universal Edition, 21 October 1930: Because of the trial I've been unable to write you until today. The Frankfurt premiere, as you could see from the papers, was a tremendous, unanimous success. Prof. Turnau, the city fathers [*Dezernenten*], and all involved agreed that there would be a run like *Das Land des Lächelns*. The premiere was completely sold out, with the seats full of dinner and smoking jackets. After only a quarter hour, you could feel the resistance (which was artificially fanned) completely disappear. There was frequent applause during scenes, then twelve curtain calls after the first act and twenty-three at the end (only 5-6 curtain calls at the Frankfurt Opera is considered a success!). So it has been absolutely proven (with the most stolid, old-fashioned opera audience in Germany at that), that in the present version *Mahagonny* has extraordinary potential for success and can pass the test with any audience (see the *Frankfurter Zeitung*). By the way, this version has great dramaturgic advantages over the earlier version; the whole thing is clearer and more cohesive. However, I don't want there to be any question that the somewhat lessened impact was in any way the result of our arrangement (which in reality is none at all), but rather due to the somewhat apprehensive, indecisive, and (between us) underwhelming performance in Frankfurt. . . . Of course, it was a real stroke of bad luck that the second performance in Frankfurt was disturbed by the Nazis. This scandal was naturally not in any way directed against the work.

Nationalſozialiſtiſche Theaterſtandale

Eigene Meldung der Voſſiſchen Zeitung

Frankfurt a. M., 20. Oktober

Zu ſchweren Krawallen kam es in der zweiten Aufführung der Oper „Mahagonny", die im Rahmen der 50-Jahr-Feier der Frankfurter Oper uraufgeführt wurde. Während der erſten Pauſe erſtürmten etwa 150 Nationalſozialiſten das Veſtibül, wo ſie einen ohrenbetäubenden Krach machten. Pfeifen, Geſchrei und Gejohle dröhnte durch das ganze Haus, während auf dem Platz vor der Oper ihre Verbündeten ihren Schlachtruf „Deutſchland erwache" brüllten. Nachdem die Polizei mit einiger Mühe die Ruhe wieder hergeſtellt hatte, konnte der zweite Akt beginnen. Es dauerte jedoch nicht lange, als ſich über das Publikum im Parkett ein wahrer Hagel von Stinkbomben ergoß. Feuerwerkskörper explodierten und die Aufführung mußte wieder unterbrochen werden. Das japaniſche Prinzenpaar Takamatſu, das die Vorſtellung grade beſuchte, verließ entrüſtet die Oper. Nach der Aufführung ſetzten die Nationalſozialiſten ihre Radaugelüſte in Form einer Demonſtration durch die Frankfurter Straßen fort, die jedoch von der Polizei bald auseinandergetrieben werden konnte. Verſchiedene Verhaftungen wurden vorgenommen.

249. Reacting to press coverage of the Frankfurt performances of *Mahagonny*, Weill wrote to Universal Edition on 25 October 1930: "It becomes apparent what kind of people (butchers and train robbers) will now decide the fate of art works in Germany. The democratic press placidly follows these goings on. They print sensational reports about the scandal but have no opinion about it. Everyone knows that this situation is intolerable, but no one dares to say anything, much less write about it."

250. Several essays by prominent German artists were published in the 21 December 1930 issue of the *General-Anzeiger für Dortmund* to combat the growing Nazi threat. Weill's essay (to the left) called for active resistance to the Nazis; he wrote, "We will accomplish nothing by intellectual means."

General-Anzeiger für Dortmund und das geſamte rheiniſch-weſtfäliſche Induſtriegebiet

Dortmund, Sonntag, 21. Dezember 1930. Nr. 352 (5. Blatt)

Deutschland, erwache!

Zu den Kundgebungen gegen die Vergewaltigung der geiſtigen und künſtleriſchen Freiheit in Berlin — Aufruf zu einer gemeinſamen Front im Kampf gegen die kulturelle Reaktion

[Multi-column German newspaper text with the following section headings:]

Die Dramatiker!

Weimars Ruhm läßt München nicht schlafen

Die „Verbotenen" und „Aus-gewiesenen" haben das Wort

Der Komponiſt

Schließt die Reihen gegen die Kultur-Reaktion!

Mit geiſtigen Mitteln nichts zu machen!

Kurt Weill

Frick über Deutſchland!

Der bildende Künſtler

Bilderſturm in Weimar

Erziehung zur Barbarei

Nur Schildbürgerei . . .?

Alfred Döblin

Oskar Schlemmer
Professor an der Kunstakademie Breslau.

Gegen die Vernichtung ewiger Werte

Max Pechstein

Der Regisseur

. . . deshalb bekämpft er den Paragraphen 218

Erwin Piscator

Helene von Nostiz-Wallwitz
v. Benedendorf a. d. Hindenburg.

Carl Zuckmayer

Harry Graf Keßler

Unser Bild zeigt Ivan Lebedoff, der der bestangezogene Mann der Filmstadt Hollywood sein soll.

TELEFUNKEN

Aus der „3-Groschen-Oper"
1. Teil — Kurt Weill
Begleit.: Lewis Ruth Band, Dirig.: Theo Mackeben
Ouvertüre (Lewis Ruth Band)
Moritat (Kurt Gerron), Ballade vom angenehmen
Leben (Willy Trenk-Trebitsch)
Verbindende Worte: Kurt Gerron
Umseitig: 2. Teil

Bestell-Nr.
A 752
Seite 1

BIEM
15 907-50

251. Side one (of eight) of Telefunken's recording of selections from *Die Dreigroschenoper*, realized two years after the premiere, in December 1930. These recordings have come to be regarded as documentation of the original production at the Theater am Schiffbauerdamm, but only three members of the original cast were represented: Erich Ponto, Kurt Gerron, and Lotte Lenya. Lenya sang songs that she did not perform in the original production, and many songs and orchestrations were modified.

252. "Barbarischer Marsch," incidental music contributed by Weill for a production of Brecht's play *Mann ist Mann* in Berlin, February 1931. Weill also used this music in *Die Bürgschaft*, Act III, number 18.

254. Universal Edition released a *Dreigroschenoper* songbook, timed to take advantage of the opening of the film in early 1931.

253. Theo Mackeben conducted the score for the *Dreigroschenoper* film, having also conducted the premiere in the theater. Photo: Casparius.

1 9 3 1

MUSIC + THEATER:	**LITERATURE + FILM:**	**SCIENCE + SOCIETY:**	**POLITICS:**
Prussian government closes Berlin's Krolloper	William Faulkner *Sanctuary*	Max Planck *Positivismus und reale Außenwelt*	Bankruptcy of German Danatbank leads to closure of all German banks; 5 million Germans unemployed
Hanns Eisler *Die Mutter*	*M* (film by Fritz Lang)	Jehovah's Witnesses formed	Largest Nazi demonstrations to date in Braunschweig
Carl Zuckmayer *Der Hauptmann von Köpenick*	*City Lights* (film by Charlie Chaplin)	The Empire State Building is completed in New York City	British Commonwealth of Nations formed

255. The program for the German version of the *Dreigroschenoper* film shows the creative team and principal cast members. The film opened at the Atrium Theater on 19 February 1931; a week later Nazis picketed the opening in Nuremberg. It opened on 5 March in London and on 15 May at the Warner Theatre in New York.

A French-language version was also made, featuring Albert Préjean (Mackie Messer), Odette Florelle (Polly), Gaston Modot (Tiger Brown), Margo Lion (Jenny), Jacques Henley (Peachum), Lucy de Matha (Frau Peachum), and Vladimir Sokolov (Smith). It opened in Berlin on 8 June at the Atrium and in Paris at the Studio des Ursulines in October 1931.

256. Scene from the shooting of the *Dreigroschenoper* film: sound engineer Adolf Jansen, director G.W. Pabst, Rudolph Forster (Mackie Messer), Reinhold Schünzel (Tiger Brown), and Carola Neher (Polly). Photo: Casparius.

257. Mackie Messer (Rudolph Forster) in the brothel; Lotte Lenya is visible to the right. Photo: Casparius.

258. Ernst Busch as the Street Singer. Photo: Casparius.

259. The French and German Pollys, Odette Florelle and Carola Neher, prepare for shooting. Photo: Casparius.

260. The *Dreigroschenoper* film led to popular editions of Weill's music in France. Florelle (who played Polly in the French version of the film) recorded the "Barbara-Song" for Polydor. Seven songs were issued in French sheet music arrangements by Editions Max Eschig.

Weill (in Berlin) to Universal Edition, 5 March 1931: No doubt you will have followed all the newspaper scribblings about the outcome of my trial. All of a sudden they didn't want to let me end this lawsuit, which was actually beginning to get on my nerves and keep me from my more important work and which I had fought to the end with more courage and consistency than you are likely to find among the gentlemen at the newspapers. Then they simply tried to obscure or distort the extraordinary result of this suit: that a musician has received the chance to do independent film work, insulated from studio pressures. In fact, a contract has been signed according to which Tobis grants me for my future film work the greatest artistic concessions, unlike those any author has ever received.

Weill (in Berlin) to Erwin Stein of Universal Edition, 7 August 1931: I am very pleased that, as UE tells me, you are preparing the piano score of *Die Bürgschaft*. . . . As far as the piano reduction goes, I would like to suggest that this time it be arranged not like *Mahagonny*, solely with playability for the general public in mind, but rather so as to reproduce exactly the structure of the music with all important subsidiary voices, rhythmic, harmonic and voice-leading variants, while still reflecting the transparency of the full score, which for me is the most essential thing.

Weill (in Berlin) to Universal Edition, 19 November 1931: We must do everything to see that the *Mahagonny* performance doesn't take precedence over *Die Bürgschaft*. It ought to be stressed in various places with absolute clarity that *Mahagonny* represents the end of a creative period which began with the Baden-Baden *Mahagonny*, and which I have already superseded, while *Die Bürgschaft* is the first major product of a new style, which began with *Der Lindberghflug* and above all *Der Jasager*. I would be very pleased if you could expand upon these thoughts in some sort of public form in the weeks before the opening of *Mahagonny*.

Weill (in Berlin) to Universal Edition, 1 December 1931: The rehearsals for *Mahagonny* are now in full swing. . . . I am making a series of changes and am also re-composing some pieces.

Should *Mahagonny* be a great success we must have parts for café and dance bands ready very quickly. In this case I would think it best if we could concentrate on one number and give it a big build-up. The best one for that (text and music) would be "Wie man sich bettet," which could be made into an interesting and easy-to-play number by a first-class arranger (who would only have to simplify the introduction somewhat).

Hans Heinsheimer of Universal Edition (in Vienna) to Weill, 7 December 1931: I just want to tell you today that yesterday's Vienna premiere of *Jasager* received an excellent, especially well rehearsed orchestral and choral performance by the worker's chorus "Stahlklang" and enjoyed a very great success and made a profound and moving impression upon the audience. I myself heard the work for the first time in performance and would like to tell you how extraordinarily strong my personal impression was. The effect on the public was much stronger than one could have anticipated, in particular the farewell scene ("Seit dem Tage, da uns der Vater verliess") had such an incredibly staggering effect that one could hardly hear the music for all the sobbing.

264. Universal Edition published song selections from *Aufstieg und Fall der Stadt Mahagonny* in time for the Berlin premiere on 21 December 1931 of a commercial run at the Theater am Kurfürstendamm. Weill wrote to Universal Edition on 9 December 1931: "Neher has absolutely no time to give me anything for [the] cover. I have therefore taken my nice "Begbick" picture by Neher out of its frame and sent it to you yesterday (unfortunately somewhat late). It is a very nice title picture for the *Mahagonny* album."

261. Weill adapted the opera *Mahagonny* to accommodate Lenya and the other singing actors in the cast. Shown here is a new setting of the song "Ach bedenken Sie, Herr Jakob Schmidt," which Weill composed for Lenya to sing in the role of Jenny.

262. Linne's caricature of the principal cast of the Berlin production of *Aufstieg und Fall der Stadt Mahagonny*, with Lenya (Jenny) and Harald Paulsen (Jim Mahoney) to the left and Trude Hesterberg (Begbick), Franz Forrow (Dreieinigkeitsmoses) and Maris Wetra (Willy) to the right.

263. Weill gives conductor Alexander Zemlinsky a helping hand.

265. Impresario Ernst Josef Aufricht, who had staged the premiere of *Die Dreigroschenoper* in 1928, also produced *Happy End* at the Theater am Schiffbauerdamm and *Aufstieg und Fall der Stadt Mahagonny* at the Theater am Kurfürstendamm.

PROBEN ZUR OPER
„AUFSTIEG UND FALL DER STADT MAHAGONNY"
(KURFÜRSTENDAMMTHEATER) VON WEILL & BRECHT
(A. E. I. Aufricht Produktion)
Musik. Leitung v. Zemlinsky / Inszenierung Casper Neher

Weill, v. Zemlinsky, Brecht

266. A publicity shot of Weill and Brecht rehearsing with Zemlinsky. Weill wrote to Universal Edition: "Zemlinsky is really first-class!"

267. Lenya and the prostitutes sing "Oh, moon of Alabama."

268. Trude Hesterberg as Begbick presides over the trial scene in Act III.

269. Demonstrators make their stage entrance during the finale.

270. Caspar Neher.

Weill (in Berlin) to Universal Edition, 2 February 1932: We have been working together uninterruptedly for a week now [on *Die Bürgschaft*]: Ebert, Stiedry, Neher and I. It has been a very enjoyable and intense collaboration. In addition, at the beginning of March I will be moving into my new little house in Zehlendorf.

Weill (in Berlin) to Universal Edition, 2 March 1932: Many thanks for your various letters regarding *Mahagonny* [in Vienna] which naturally interest me very much. However, I would first like to talk with you about this plan at length, dear Dr. Heinsheimer, since it seems that you want to alter the work quite extensively. The instrumental changes indicated by Mr. Simon surely represent a complete shift in my usual sound, and the *Mahagonny* score in particular is so carefully worked out in its completely unique timbral quality that simply subsuming missing instruments into other groups is not at all possible. We must talk about all of this at length.

Heute hat Geburtstag
Kurt Weill

Er wird heute irgend etwas um die Dreißig herum, irgend so ein indiskutables Jungensalter. Er sieht aus wie ein höllisch gewedter Abiturient hinter einer großen blinkenden Griechenbrille — und er repräsentiert den Stand der Bühnenmusik im 20. Jahrhundert. Er hat die moderne Musik aus der Vergitterung des Zunftmäßigen befreit. Ein Schöpfer höchsten Niveaus — der zugleich ein Volkstümlicher ist. Allein diese Synthese gibt es nur alle 300 Jahre einmal. Seine Entwicklung setzt ein, wo die radikalsten Vorgänge aufhören — und hat trotzdem das Publikum für sich. Die Dreigroschenoper war, was ihr Name bedeutet, das Beste, aber für die Masse. In der eine Zeit lang glückhaften Verbindung mit Brecht war dieser Grundsatz — gegen die Creme, für das Volk — zum Prinzip, zu einer Art Kunstphilosophie. Die Musik Weills, atemlos und voll tiefster Rhythmik, agressiv und voll tiefster Melodie, kalt und voll tiefster Theaterkraft, zurückhaltend und dennoch aufwühlend, vermochte auch schwächere Werke Brechts in die Höhe zu reißen. Diese Periode liegt hinten. Die rationierende Aufteilung der Wirkung zwischen zwei zeitweilig homogenen Autoren ist vorbei. Weill kann jetzt nur sich selbst gebrauchen, steht mitten in der Umformung der deutschen Oper. Er wird heute irgend etwas um die Dreißig herum, irgend so ein indiskutables Jungensalter, und er sieht aus wie ein höllisch gewedter Abiturient hinter einer großen blinkenden Griechenbrille.

272. Unidentified clipping, probably from March 1932.

271. Caricature of Weill and Caspar Neher, authors of the opera *Die Bürgschaft*.

1 9 3 2

MUSIC + THEATER:
Schoenberg *Moses und Aron*
Schreker *Der Schmied von Gent*
Eubie Blake *Shuffle Along of 1933*

LITERATURE + FILM:
Hans Fallada *Kleiner Mann—was nun?*
Aldous Huxley *Brave New World*
Kuhle Wampe (film by Brecht and Eisler)

SCIENCE + SOCIETY:
Six million people unemployed in Germany
Famine in the USSR
The Lindbergh baby is kidnapped and murdered

POLITICS:
Franz von Papen named German chancellor
Hitler refuses Hindenburg's offer to become vice-chancellor
Austrian-born Hitler receives German citizenship

273. Weill bought this house at 7 Wissmannstraße (now Käthe-Kollwitz-Straße) in the Kleinmachnow section of Berlin as a birthday gift for Lenya in October 1931. He moved into it in the spring of 1932. Lenya lived there only briefly, if at all. Photo by Louise Hartung.

274. Weill's maid Erika at Kleinmachnow, with his beloved German shepherd Harras.

DIE BÜRGSCHAFT

OPER IN DREI AKTEN UND EINEM VORSPIEL

VON

KURT WEILL

TEXT VON

CASPAR NEHER

Nr. 1527

UNIVERSAL-EDITION A. G.
WIEN   COPYRIGHT 1938 BY UNIVERSAL-EDITION   LEIPZIG
Printed in Austria

275. The published libretto for *Die Bürgschaft* included a parable written by Johann Gottfried Herder in the late eighteenth century on which the opera is based. Including the parable may have allowed Weill and Neher to avoid identifying the Talmudic source.

Für den mittleren Teil dieser Oper wurde folgende Parabel von Herder verwendet:

Alexander aus Mazedonien kam einst in eine entlegene goldreiche Provinz von Afrika. Die Einwohner gingen ihm entgegen und brachten ihm Schalen dar voll goldener Früchte. „Esset ihr diese Früchte bei Euch!" sprach Alexander. „Ich bin nicht gekommen, eure Reichtümer zu sehen, sondern von eueren Sitten zu lernen." Da führten sie ihn auf den Markt, wo ihr König Gericht hielt.

Eben trat ein Bürger vor und sprach: „Ich kaufte, o König, von diesem Mann einen Sack voll Spreu und habe einen ansehnlichen Schatz in ihm gefunden. Die Spreu ist mein, aber nicht das Gold; und dieser Mann will es nicht wieder nehmen. Sprich ihm zu, o König, denn es ist das Seine."

Und sein Gegner, auch ein Bürger des Orts, antwortete: „Du fürchtest Dich, etwas Unrechtes zu behalten; und ich sollte mich nicht fürchten, ein solches von Dir zu nehmen? Ich habe Dir den Sack verkauft, nebst allem, was darinnen ist. Behalte das Deine. Sprich ihm zu, o König!"

Der König fragte den Ersten, ob er einen Sohn habe. Er antwortete: „Ja". Er fragte den Andern, ob er eine Tochter habe und bekam „ja" zur Antwort. „Wohlan!" sprach der König, „ihr seid beide rechtschaffene Leute; verheiratet eure Kinder untereinander und gebet ihnen den gefundenen Schatz zur Hochzeitsgabe — das ist meine Entscheidung."

Alexander erstaunte, da er diesen Ausspruch hörte. „Hab' ich Unrecht gerichtet," sprach der König, „daß du also erstaunst?" — „Mitnichten", antwortet Alexander, „aber in unserem Lande würde man anders richten", — „Und wie denn?" fragte der afrikanische König.

„Beide Streitende", sprach Alexander, „verlören die Häupter, und der Schatz käme in die Hände des Königs."

Da schlug der König die Hände zusammen und sprach: „Scheinet denn bei Euch die Sonne und läßt der Himmel noch auf euch regnen?" Alexander antwortete: „Ja". — „So muß es", fuhr der König fort, „der unschuldigen Tiere wegen sein, die in euerem Lande leben; denn über solche Menschen sollte keine Sonne scheinen, kein Himmel regnen!"

276. Shortly before the premiere, Weill and Neher revised a scene in the second act of *Die Bürgschaft*; the first page of the copyist's score is reproduced here.

DIE BÜRGSCHAFT

Opera in three acts; libretto by Caspar Neher and Kurt Weill

1932   Berlin, Städtische Oper (10 March)
       Fritz Stiedry, conductor; Carl Ebert, director; Caspar Neher, designer

       Wiesbaden, Staatstheater (16 March)
       Dusseldorf, Stadttheater (12 April)
1935   Brno (Czechoslovakia, now Czech Republic), Deutsches Theater (25 March)

277. At rehearsals for *Die Bürgschaft*: director Carl Ebert, conductor Fritz Stiedry, and Weill. Photo: Walter Israel.

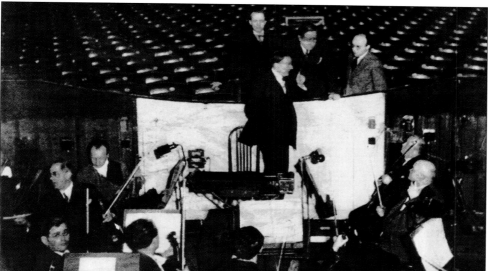

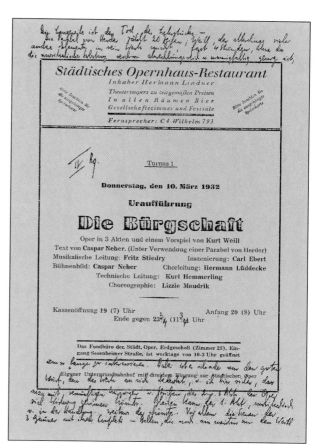

278. Program for opening night of *Die Bürgschaft*, extensively annotated by an unknown spectator.

279. Wilhelm Rode (Orth) and Hans Reinmar (Mattes) rehearse the final scene of *Die Bürgschaft*. Photo: Walter Israel.

280. In the final scene Orth leaves Mattes to be finished off by the angry crowd.

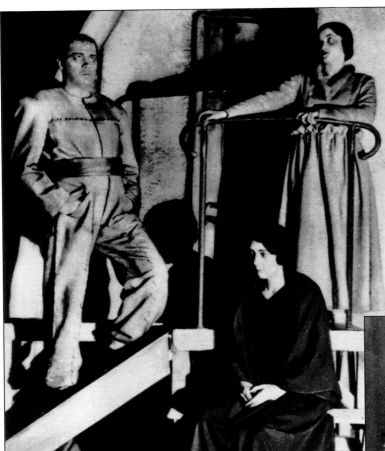

281. The Mattes family was played by Hans Reinmar (Mattes), Irene Eisinger (his wife), and Charlotte Müller (his daughter) in the original production.

Links: Die Erpresser auf der Lauer aus der Oper „Die Bürgschaft" (Wilhelm Gombert, Rudolf Gonszar, Eduard Kandl).

282. Act 1 (no. 5). The blackmailers wait to ambush Mattes. Left to right: Wilhelm Gombert, Rudolf Gonszar, Eduard Kandl.

283. Act 2 (no. 16), in the city marketplace. At the second trial, both Orth and Mattes are jailed and their money is confiscated by the new regime. Photo: Zander & Labisch.

284. Act 3 (no. 17). Rising prices, hunger, and sickness descend on the mythical town of Urb.

Weill (in Berlin) to Universal Edition, 30 March 1932: You can tell the theaters with which you are negotiating that *Die Bürgschaft* is already being performed in a severely cut version. Yesterday's Berlin performance, in which we cut out the entire bureaucrat scene, no. 14, lasted three hours and twenty minutes in all, and in Dusseldorf I hope through further cuts to bring it down to three hours (including intermissions). Beyond that I am working with Neher on a complete revision of the 2nd act, which we want to make into a short dramatic act (of at most twenty minutes in length) so that the opera with one intermission will last hardly over two hours and fifty minutes.

Weill (in Berlin) to Maurice Abravanel, 3 May 1932: I just got back after two weeks in Vienna where *Mahagonny*, very well performed by a group of young people, has been a great success. Meanwhile I have worked actively in your behalf, but I have to tell you quite honestly that all of my efforts have been unsuccessful. Iltz [the intendant in Dusseldorf] who has to hire someone for Martin's position, told me right off the bat: "I know you are going to recommend Abravanel to me and I don't know anyone whom I would rather engage than him. But I am already having enormous difficulties keeping Horenstein here, so that I can't burden myself with yet another Jew with a French name." That's the kind of answer I get everywhere: Ebert, Brecher. It's driving me to despair.

Weill (in Berlin) to Universal Edition, 4 May 1932: Having returned to Berlin, I would like to say above all how especially interesting this Vienna visit was for me. I believe that at present Vienna is more receptive to new musical impulses than most German cities. I am therefore very pleased that the clear, lively, and really youthful spirit of the *Mahagonny* performance assured a success for this work in Vienna that it has never really had elsewhere. Beyond that I would like to reiterate that the "Wiener Opernproduktion" seems to have taken a very impressive course and, especially considering the progressive calcification of the major state-run opera houses, I would welcome it if it were possible to build up a new, young opera culture from the ground up.

Hans Heinsheimer of Universal Edition (in Vienna) to Weill, 14 May 1932: I finally received the following word from Coburg, where I am also in especially close contact with the intendant:

> Considering the special constellation of the audience in Coburg, I will hardly be able to do *Die Bürgschaft*. As you know, the entire right-wing press has made a particularly solid front against the work, and it would be senseless to try to force the work on a city like Coburg.

Then a letter from Hamburg, where I was particularly energetic on behalf of *Die Bürgschaft* recently. Dr. [Karl] Böhm writes the following:

> Unfortunately I cannot do *Die Bürgschaft* at the moment. I have not been permitted. Since, as you know, we have to reckon with certain influences at present, I simply have to bow to these pressures.

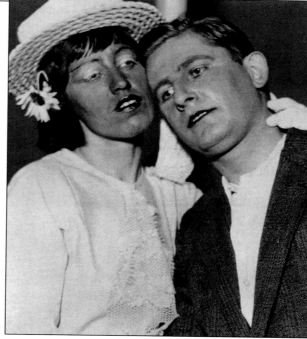

286. Program of the first production of *Aufstieg und Fall der Stadt Mahagonny* in Vienna, with Lenya as Jenny and Otto Pasetti as Jimmy (above). Their work together on this production led to a protracted affair.

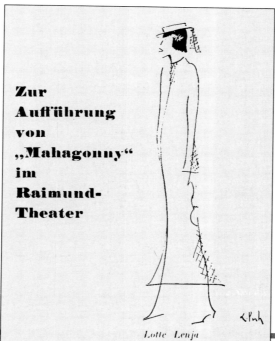

285. Caricature of Lenya by the designer of the Vienna *Mahagonny* production, Lizzi Fisk.

Zur
Aufführung
von
„Mahagonny"
im
Raimund-
Theater

Lotte Lenja

Weill (in Berlin) to Walter Bruno Iltz, intendant of the Dusseldorf Opera, 16 May 1932: I would like to return today to our discussions in Dusseldorf and here in Berlin. Your position regarding the theater politics of right-wing circles seems to be of an importance and significance so far beyond your activity there that I consider it absolutely vital to make your action more widely known. As you know, for years now most German theater intendants have been submitting themselves to the rule of a censor that doesn't even exist. For years now, that is, at a time when there wasn't the slightest reason to do so, the vast majority of the theater directors have shied away from any decision out of cowardice. In that way they have precipitated the situation in which we find ourselves now. On the other hand, your affair shows that it wasn't at all necessary then and isn't necessary today. You have always had enough personal conviction and courage to carry out what you consider artistically correct and necessary. The importance of your current action resides therein, that whenever you have found any right-wing demand unreasonable you have attempted to make clear to these circles that they are misapplying their slogans and that to implement their demands would bring shame both to those who make those demands and those who accept them.

It is really incredible what I have experienced in this regard yet again with *Die Bürgschaft*. The directors of almost all the German theaters are more than positive about the work and are convinced of its artistic importance; most are also in favor of performing it. But they don't dare. No one forbids them. But hints are enough to undermine their resolve. It would be very important to show these people once and for all that it is possible to do it differently. I therefore ask you to be so kind as to describe in a few sentences the events preceding the premiere of *Die Bürgschaft* (the protest of the right-wing Kulturbund, your explanatory reply and the loyal acceptance of this answer by the Kulturbund) and give me the permission to have this report distributed by U.E. to encourage or shame the other theater directors.

In addition I will ask a leading Berlin journalist (say, Kerr, Stefan Grossmann, or Manfred George), to make your report the point of departure for an essay on the same theme I have touched upon in this letter. I am convinced that whether or not we will have anything like a theater culture in Germany in the coming years will be decided in these next few months. For that reason, concerted action is necessary now.

Weill (in Berlin) to Universal Edition, 17 May 1932: I never seriously expected *Die Bürgschaft* could be done in Coburg, the Nazi-Burg. . . . It is certain that one must become very active now. I will try to get together a group of people with the resolve to defend themselves.

Weill (in Berlin) to Universal Edition, 3 June 1932: I have gotten people at least to begin to see the necessity for decisive opposition. Today I have a meeting with [Eberhard] Preussner, next week with [Leo] Kestenberg. First I would like to arrange for a group of progressive artists to gather material on the progressive barbarization of the German provincial theaters and make it available to their allies in the press with complete disclosure of the names of all involved. A new example: in Dresden, Mr. Reucker prevented Lopatnikoff from *auditioning* his Danton opera for his friend Busch!! I will ask you to give me all your material on this subject from the last few years (*Wozzeck, Totenhaus, Hahnrei, Mahagonny, Bürgschaft*, etc.). . . . All kinds of projects are taking shape, which, if they are realized, could be of the greatest interest for you as well. In any event, given the course of developments, the large public art institutions scarcely come into question. But there are enough possibilities outside these institutions. I am thinking not only of organizations for which I want to develop the "layman's opera" genre, but also the private theatrical enterprises for which I want to write a kind of opera of very reduced means and no chorus that would be very easy to perform and could be played everywhere independent of the public institutions. I am now trying to stake out the boundaries between this genre and the genre of the "layman's opera" and to explore the possibility of combining them.

Weill (in Berlin) to Universal Edition, 29 June 1932: A few days ago [Erik] Charell had a decisive idea for his next production and this idea is solely inspired by the thought of working with me. It's supposed to be a 90% musical piece based on *Das Kabinett des Dr. Caligari*. . . . He plans (all this under the seal of absolute silence!) to open the work in Vienna, then take it to Paris and London and finally to Berlin.

All that sounds very nice. Now for the difficulties which, however, all lie in the purely artistic area. Yesterday Charell, Neher, and I took a look at the film. Aside from the title I don't think this film offers anything that could be appropriated for a theater piece. Charell sees it purely from the atmospheric point of view. He sees fairgrounds, hypnosis, sleepwalking, mystics—all private, abnormal, bourgeois phenomena which I can't make the basis of a work now after having spent years taking the most adamant stand that theater must be devoted to the great ideas of the time. The ensuing six-hour debate on both sides left the impression that there is a great gulf between his and my idea of theater. It won't be very easy to bridge this gulf.

Weill (in Berlin) to Universal Edition, 29 July 1932: In the meantime a very nice new project has developed from the discussions I had with Georg Kaiser in conjunction with the Charell plan. Kaiser wants to write a musical folk play [*Der Silbersee*] with me. He has come up with a very nice, truly Kaiserian idea on which we have been working for several days. I believe that we will have an outline for this play by the beginning of next week. It isn't to be an opera, but a work between genres. It remains up to me whether it is a "play with music," that is, with simple songs sung by plain actors, or whether I want to make greater musical demands and write music of the length and difficulty of, say, an Offenbach *musiquette*. I would be more attracted to the latter because I could go beyond the genre I created in the *Dreigroschenoper*.

Weill (in Berlin) to Hans Heinsheimer of Universal Edition, 20 September 1932: The political situation has changed decisively during these last weeks. Places which were already openly following Nazi policies in deference to the anticipated dawning of the Third Reich are now quite plainly and openly disassociating themselves from Hitler. The whole so-called "*Generalanzeiger*" press in the provinces is now speaking out against Hitler as fiercely as they had damned all Hitler enemies a few weeks ago. The anti-Semitic question doesn't play any role at all since now it's just the trouble-making goyim fighting against each other. Even the theaters must have heard by now that Hitler is done for and it is high time the theater directors left their mouse holes, since otherwise they won't notice that a few things have changed.

Weill (in Berlin) to Universal Edition, 24 November 1932: It is naturally *quite impossible* to use a piano score for conducting [*Der Silbersee*]. This isn't an operetta, where the instrumentation doesn't matter, but a fully formed, very carefully crafted score. The work is intended for a theater's principal conductor who would surely be justified in refusing to conduct such an extensive and carefully worked-out score from a piano reduction. I remind you, dear Dr. Heinsheimer, that when you were in Berlin I *explicitly* rejected the idea of having a so-called conductor's reduction made for this work. Even with the *Dreigroschenoper* (where there are only seven instruments) the conductor's reduction didn't work because no one could get any idea about the tone color, which is always especially important with me.

Weill (in Berlin) to Universal Edition, 26 December 1932: Naturally the "Sérénade" will do everything possible to mount another production of the short version of *Mahagonny* in the spring, after having been encouraged to do so by the press. The Marquise de Casa-Fuerte, the director and founder of the Sérénade, is especially interested and even Curjel is working full steam on the plan. That leaves only one big problem: what does one couple with this *Mahagonny*? (Aufricht asked me the same question before he spoke with you about a tour—by the way, use extreme caution!—Aufricht shows up wherever he smells a good deal, and now he has learned the ropes, so one must be very careful, especially about royalties.) Of course it would be very desirable for this tour to couple one of my other works with *Mahagonny*, and for Paris it is absolutely indispensable. I would also be prepared to write or arrange something for this purpose. Naturally the most obvious would be (an old plan of mine) to arrange the songs from *Happy End* as a similar kind of Songspiel with short spoken scenes, etc., something along the lines of "scenes from the life of a Salvation Army girl." Naturally Brecht could do that, but I dread the thought of taking upon ourselves the difficulties of working with Brecht for such a small and simple matter. . . . In any event I will pursue this plan since in this way one might be able to have a very nice theater evening for six performers and an eleven-man orchestra.

288. Many of the Parisian composers and artists in Marie-Laure de Noailles's circle undoubtedly attended Weill's 11 December 1932 concert. Pictured here are: Henri Sauguet, Nikolai Nabokov, Marie-Laure de Noailles, Yvonne de Casa-Fuerte (head of La Sérénade concert society), Igor Markévitch, Charles Koechlin, Roger Desormières, and Francis Poulenc.

287. Weill composed his last work in Germany, *Der Silbersee*, between August 1932 and January 1933. This excerpt of his autograph score is from Frau von Luber's number, "Lied vom Schlaraffenland."

289. Program from the concert sponsored by La Sérénade, 11 December 1932. A major success for Weill, the concert featured performances of *Der Jasager* (with the student cast from Berlin) and *Mahagonny* conducted by Maurice Abravanel and directed by Hans Curjel. On 14 November 1932, Weill reported to Universal Edition: "The Paris matter looks good. Noailles approved a respectable increase so that we can bring Martens' Berlin *Jasager* performance to Paris (assuming the school vacation is approved). At the moment we don't want to have it publicized in order to keep the Cultural Ministry from butting in" (14 November 1932).

290. Headline from a review by André Cœuroy published in *Paris Midi*, 19 December 1932.

Weill (in Berlin) to Lotte Lenya, 7? January 1933: I'm trying to make this kind of life bearable for me. But that is very, very hard to do, because it's so totally different from what I'm used to. I'm happy to have talked to you—and then again, not happy at all. I can only hope that you believe everything I've told you.

291. Lotte Lenya. Photo by Lotte Jacobi.

Weill (in Berlin) to Lotte Lenya, 9 January 1933: Bidi [Bertolt Brecht] has pestered Aufricht for days to get me together with him. Finally I suggested that Aufricht should arrange it. That took place on Friday, but nothing really came of it. I was quite cool and restrained, while he was sedulous, submissive, shit-friendly. He wants to write a shorter play as a supplement to *Mahagonny*, with a wonderful role for you. He claims to have good material for that. After I got home, he called me at two o'clock in the morning with a proposition. Well, what do you think? You'll never guess: he wants to "dramatize" *Der Lindberghflug* for this purpose. Isn't that insane? Now he's calling me all the time; I should meet with him, but I don't want to yet. This time he will hear things from me that so far no one has ever told him. . . . Now the latest: I have a big movie offer. Gab Frank is really a big wheel in the movies. In just six months he has built up "Europa-Distribution," which already is the only rival of UFA. He suggested that I do four films with him in the next two to three years. I've made extensive demands to have a decisive voice, especially as far as the director, the property, the screenwriter, etc., are concerned. The first film is to be done right away, and indeed it's a subject I can accept in good conscience: *Kleiner Mann—was nun?* by [Hans] Fallada.

There are also personal reasons why I want to accept the film. In the last few weeks I've seen once again how I completely fall apart when I'm not working. This film, which is already supposed to be in the studio by March, together with the premiere of *Der Silbersee*, would throw me into such a whirl of work that I would no longer have time for bouts of depression.

How is it with you, *Tütilein*? I thought you might write to me after the telephone call. But most likely you're not allowed to. I've thought of you a lot these past days and wished so much for my sake that someday it could again be the way it used to be.

Weill (in Berlin) to Lotte Lenya, 28 January 1933: Life is funny: seven years ago today at about this time we met [Martha] Gratenau, [Emil] Lind, and Caña in front of city hall in Charlottenburg. Now Gratenau is a happy housewife and mother, Lind probably has become an old woman, and Caña is dead; you're far away from me, and I sit in my little house and brood over whether someday love will bloom again for me too.

How are you, Linerle? Are you well and happy? When I don't hear from you for such a long time, I just can't imagine whether you actually think about me or, even more, about the two of us. When are you coming? I'm so delighted that you'll be coming to Leipzig with me.

1 9 3 3

MUSIC + THEATER:
Roy Harris *Symphony No. 1*
Aaron Copland *Short Symphony*
Richard Strauss *Arabella*

LITERATURE + FILM:
Maxwell Anderson *Both Your Houses*
André Malraux *La condition humaine*
King Kong (film by Cooper and Schoedsack)

SCIENCE + SOCIETY:
Prohibition is repealed in the U.S.
Philo Farnsworth develops electronic television
Artists, scientists, politicians who oppose Nazism are forced to leave Germany

POLITICS:
Hitler becomes German Chancellor; first concentration camp opens (Dachau)
Franklin D. Roosevelt becomes U.S. President, introduces the "New Deal"
Germany and Japan withdraw from League of Nations

Weill (in Berlin) to Erika Neher, 29 January 1933: I also believe that the only way to achieve any kind of inner development in times like these is to become a stoic, but not to lose that great emotion within your heart. That's why I am always filled with gratitude toward you, my dearest, sweetest, most tender, richest little angel, because without you I could never have survived all this but would have perished by now.

292. Erika Neher with Weill.

293. "The Ballad of Caesar's Death" from *Der Silbersee* is generally considered to be a satiric attack on Hitler. Weill had feared that this song would not appear in the published songbook, but at the last minute Universal Edition included it at Weill's insistence, replacing "Auf jener Strasse."

V. CÄSARS TOD

Kurt Weill

Rom hieß ei - ne Stadt und al - le Rö - mer hat-ten in den A-dern hei-ßes

Blut, als sie Cä-sar einst ty-ran-nisch reiz - te, koch-te es so-fort in Sie-de-

glut. Nicht die War - nung konn-te Cä-sar hin-dern: „Hü - te vor des Mär-zen I-den

Copyright 1933 by Universal-Edition   U. E. 10471

294. Film director René Clair, ca. 1930. Photo by Lotte Jacobi.

Weill (in Berlin) to Hans Heinsheimer of Universal Edition, 6 February 1933: I am working full time to establish a basis on which, despite all obstacles, I can continue working on the film, and it now appears again that the matter might come off. I don't know whether you have any idea how much patience, caution, and fortitude is required just to establish conditions under which one can work in peace with these people. They are in constant fear of nothing more than my firm intention of producing an artistically worthwhile film. That is enough. But I am in tight with the major financial backers and therefore hope to be successful. I have been able to get [Berthold] Viertel as a collaborator. This is a very auspicious combination. But for the moment neither he nor I have a contract. In spite of that we are now working 8-10 hours a day on the script.

Hans Heinsheimer of Universal Edition (in Vienna) to Weill, 8 February 1933: I cannot agree that the course in Germany might only be a nightmare lasting a few months. I am filled with the deepest pessimism because I believe that only now will we pay the price for underestimating the opponent, that only now will we see that they will maintain a better, firmer, and more ruthless hold on everything than the Republicans ever dared to do over fifteen years. So how will this situation concretely affect *Silbersee*? I think that evasive action now—for example, a postponement of the premiere until after the elections—is useless. However, we could discuss it. We must simply let it happen and then see what the new official papers and authorities say about Weill now that their fight has been won. In any event it will be a very important and revealing measure of your current reputation in these circles. So I believe that we should be prepared for anything and just let fate take its course.

DER SILBERSEE

Musical play in three acts; text by Georg Kaiser

1933 Leipzig, Altes Theater (18 February)
Gustav Brecher, conductor; Detlef Sierck, director;
Caspar Neher, designer

Magdeburg, Städtisches Theater (18 February)
Erfurt, Stadttheater (18 February)
Berlin, Deutsches Theater (cancelled)

ALTES THEATER

Sonnabend, den 18. Februar 1933
Außer Anrecht

Uraufführung

„Der Silbersee"

Ein Wintermärchen von Georg Kaiser — Musik von Kurt Weill
In Szene gesetzt von Detlef Sierck
Musikalische Leitung: Gustav Brecher
Leipziger Sinfonie-Orchester

Olim	Erhard Siedel
Severin	Alexander Golling
Frau von Luber	Lina Carstens
Fennimore	Gretl Berndt
Laur	Ernst Sattler
Der dicke Landjäger	Wilhelm Engst
Alter Arzt	Karl Huth
Junger Arzt	Walter Kiesler
Krankenschwester	Gert Riederer
Erster	Max Noack
Zweiter	Martin Flörchinger
Dritter } Bursche	Joachim Gottschalk
Vierter	Hans Tenhoff
Ein Diener	Artur Nicklas
Lotterieagent	Albert Garbe
Eine Zofe	Irmgard Fischer
Ein Sänger	Hans Lißmann

Chöre gesungen von Mitgliedern des Opernchores, Leitung Konrad Neuger
Bühnenbilder: Caspar Neher

Änderungen vorbehalten
Kleinere Pause nach dem vierten Bild
Größere Pause nach dem zweiten Akt (sehsten Bild)
Rückgabe von Eintrittskarten wegen Umbesetzungen ausgeschlossen

Einlaß 19½ Uhr   Anfang 20 Uhr   Ende 23 Uhr

Preis des Programms 30 Pfg.

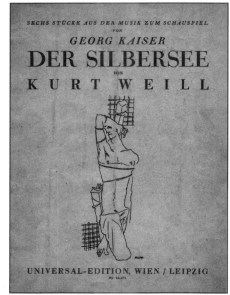

SECHS STÜCKE AUS DER MUSIK ZUM SCHAUSPIEL VON
GEORG KAISER
DER SILBERSEE
VON
KURT WEILL

UNIVERSAL-EDITION, WIEN / LEIPZIG
Nr. 14.471

300. Cover of the Universal Edition songbook containing six songs from *Der Silbersee.*

299. Program of the premiere of *Der Silbersee* in Leipzig, 18 February 1933, nine days before the Reichstag fire which precipitated Hitler's seizure of absolute power. It opened on the same day in Magdeburg and Erfurt.

295. Scene sketch for Olim's castle, drawn by Caspar Neher, depicting Fennimore's arrival and approach to Frau von Luber.

296. Olim's castle, as seen in the Leipzig production. Fennimore (Gretl Berndt) is on the left of the staircase and Severin (Alexander Golling) is on the right. Olim (Ethard Siedel) and Frau von Luber (Lina Carstens) are in the center.

298. In Act I, scene 2 of the Magdeburg production, Severin and his gang (left) prepare to rob the shop.

297. Ernst Busch (standing) played Severin in the Magdeburg production.

Hans Heinsheimer of Universal Edition (in Vienna) to Weill, 24 February 1933: We mustn't kid ourselves: as nice as the Leipzig success was, the situation is just as grave as we have felt all along. The fact that they have been so successful in attacking this harmless play in Magdeburg means that the attack isn't against the play itself, but against you personally. Have you read the review in the *Leipziger Tageszeitung* (Nazi)? Once again, dear friend, I urge you to think carefully about our conversation and to consider the options, such as films, emigrating to Paris, a trip to America, or simply adjusting yourself to an indefinite vacuum with German theaters, schools, and the radio, and to make your decisions in a new pitiless situation.

Weill (in Berlin) to Universal Edition, 26 February 1933: After the *Silbersee* success the film matter naturally looked very favorable. The contract was drawn up, the points I discussed with you were altered as you wished, the contract was all ready for signing, and then suddenly everything ground to a halt on some sort of pretext that the contract wasn't delivered. Then yesterday I was suddenly told that on the basis of the Magdeburg events (which were terribly blown up in the *Nachtausgabe* here), one can't help but fear that a film with music by me could also cause disturbances, which would endanger their investment of approximately 300,000 Marks. They are still undecided, but they will probably have to ask me to withdraw from the project in the next few days. I immediately declared that I wouldn't do that and that I would be forced to insist on the contract since it is completed and only lacks a signature. Perhaps they will offer me the next René Clair film as compensation. I would very much welcome such a solution.

BIG KAISER-WEILL SUCCESS

. . . Kurt Weill's music binds Kaiser's work together and drives it forward. It is marvelously compact and impressive. It does not consist of isolated musical numbers, but it is a virtuoso feat of exciting, compelling sharpness which ties the action together like a huge painting. Weill's music comes to the aid of Kaiser's language; it supports it, guides it to the end. A brilliant score for a beautiful libretto. The sound of these clear, meaningful, soaring tones is the foundation and the strength of the success of this evening. The Leipzig Symphony Orchestra, conducted by Gustav Brecher, played with admirable discipline and buoyancy and brought out Weill's music with sparkling effect. Rolf Nürnberg, "Großer Kaiser-Weill-Erfolg," *Leipziger Feuilleton*, 20 February 1933.

URAUFFÜHRUNG IN LEIPZIG

Detlef Sierck has rendered the Jewish literati . . . a service that he may pay for dearly. . . . One must treat a composer like Weill with distrust, especially when he, as a Jew, allows himself to use a German opera stage for his un-German purposes. . . . The most shameful thing is that the general music director of the city of Leipzig, Gustav Brecher, has lent himself to such a performance! A man with any sensitivity—and of all times five days after the fiftieth anniversary of the death of Richard Wagner, in the middle of the commemorations by the opera house that is unfortunately still entrusted to him!—would have rejected this kind of presentation! Recently, at the commemorative celebrations, Mister Brecher scrutinized our Führer rather closely in the Gewandhaus. I had the opportunity to observe this. Now he will come to know the Führer and the . . . power that emanates from him much better! F. A. Hauptmann, "Uraufführung in Leipzig," *Völkischer Beobachter*, Berlin edition, 24 February 1933.

301. Ernst Busch's recording of two songs from *Der Silbersee* is the last surviving recording of Weill's music made in Germany before 1945.

302. The burning of the Reichstag, 27–28 February 1933, signalled the end of the Weimar Republic.

FUNK-STUNDE
G. M. B. H.
BERLIN

PRESSE-INFORMATIONSBÜRO
EILIGE PRESSE-NOTIZ

Berlin-Charlottenburg 9 · Haus des Rundfunks
Drahtanschrift   Ruf: J 3
Funkstunde Berlin   Westend 9000

Keine Jazzmusik mehr im Programm der Berliner Funk-Stunde
- -

In der "Jazzmusik" lernte Deutschland in den ersten
Jahren nach dem Krieg eine Art von Tanzmusik kennen, die von
einem hemmungslosen, übermässig scharf akzentuierten Rhythmus
beherrscht wurde, und in der grelle Klangfarben der Bläsergruppen
und ein vielfältiger Komplex von Schlag- und Geräuschinstrumenten
den Charakter kennzeichneten.

Diese musikalische Entartung wurde zuerst von Amerika
eingeführt, wo die Volksmusik der nordamerikanischen Neger die
Anregung zur Entstehung des Jazz gegeben hatte. In der Entwicklung der letzten Jahre aber ist der Jazzmusik vieles Unschöne,
grotesk und aufreizend Wirkende genommen worden. Die krassen Klangfarben sind gemildert, die rhythmische Grundierung ist dezenter
geworden, willkürliche Improvisationen sind ausgeschaltet und eine
melodische Linie ist entstanden. In den Tänzen im Dreivierteltakt
und im Tango tritt die Violine wieder in ihr Recht, und eine Melodie schwingt sich wieder im ruhigen Ablauf aus.

Die Berliner Funk-Stunde verbannt alle fragwürdige, vom
gesunden Volksempfinden als "Negermusik" bezeichnete Tanzmusik,
in der ein aufreizender Rhythmus vorherrscht und die Melodik ver-
gewaltigt wird. Die Funk-Stunde wird aber auch weiterhin moderne
Tanzmusik pflegen, soweit sie in ihren musikalischen Elementen
nicht unkünstlerisch ist oder deutsches Empfinden verletzt. Die
blosse Verwendung von Instrumenten, die der Jazz bevorzugt, wie
z.B. Saxophon und Banjo, kennzeichnen eine Musik noch nicht als
Jazzmusik.

Berlin, den 8. März 1933
Mi/Bu.

303. An announcement from Funkstunde Berlin (Berlin radio), dated 8 March 1933, states that jazz will no longer be programmed.

304. At the beginning of March, Weill was warned by Walter Steinthal, on behalf of Hans Fallada (who had already been arrested), to leave Berlin. Lenya and photographer Louise Hartung gathered some of Weill's belongings from his house in Kleinmachnow and together they drove to Munich. Shortly before 14 March, Weill returned to Berlin to settle his affairs, where he stayed first in a hotel and then with the Nehers.

On Potsdam Day, 21 March 1933, Weill fled Germany in a car driven by Caspar Neher. That evening a torch-light procession at the Brandenburg Gate in Berlin (pictured at right) celebrated the reopening of the Reichstag at the Potsdam Garnisonskirche and Hitler's ascent to power. Weill's passport shows him entering France on 22 March, and he arrived in Paris on 23 March. Very few details are known about the exact circumstances and events surrounding his departure from Germany.

Weill (in Berlin) to Hans Heinsheimer of Universal Edition, 1 March 1933: Now, in order to make my plans as soon as possible, I have pressured them for an immediate decision, and I will sign a contract today withdrawing from the film *Kleiner Mann—was nun*? The distributor Europa, together with the German, French, and English Tobis will do another film with me in the course of the year.

Weill (in Berlin) to Hans Heinsheimer of Universal Edition, 14 March 1933: I get the impression you've already thrown in the towel and, probably under the influence of the numerous Berlin alarmists you've met there, have fallen into a lethargy which is unwarranted, especially now. I find it quite wrong and indefensible to have all of you sitting in Vienna and moping instead of doing the only thing possible under today's circumstances: to go abroad and to explore all the possibilities for finding new markets for your works; to establish new contacts, to track down or create new performance possibilities. Why aren't you in Paris now, dear Dr. Heinsheimer? You have seen how the enormous success I had there hasn't been exploited at all, as there's no one really working on it there. . . . It's a real shame that the incredible opportunities that Paris now offers me (and no doubt Křenek and Alban Berg, as well) have remained entirely untapped. I myself am doing what I can. For months now I've been carrying on negotiations instead of saving my nerves for my work.

Hans Heinsheimer of Universal Edition (in Vienna) to Weill, 15 March 1933: Wreede sends word today that you and he have come to an agreement that you won't be going to America for the time being. I would be very grateful for news about your plans for the immediate future. I've actually been expecting for some time to see you here; Mr. Renoir also thought you would have come to see him. I am extremely surprised by your change of plans and find it inexplicable. Please send us word soon.

Sonderheft   Berliner   20 Pf.

Illustrirte Zeitung

Verlag Ullstein Berlin SW 68

SONDERHEFT

Der 21. März 1933

Die Staatsfeierlichkeiten bei
der Reichstagseröffnung

This chart provides a chronological listing of the stamps entered into Weill's German passport (Reisepass 287/124/31), which was valid from April 1931 to 21 April 1936. His entry into France on 22 March 1933 is highlighted.

B = Boarding; E=Entry; L=Landing; X=Exit.

1931.04.24-?	Cinvalde	Czechoslovakia
1931.04.25-?	???	Czechoslovakia
1931.05.01-E	Coccau	Italy
1931.05.04-X	Ponte San Luigi	Italy
1931.05.30-E	La [...Sor(?)]quera	Spain
1931.06.17-?		
1931.10.21-E	Thayngen	Switzerland (Schweiz)
1932.04.16-?	Oinvalde	Czechoslovakia
1932.04.17-?	??	Czechoslovakia
1932.05.01-X	Salzburg	Austria
1932.12.07-E	Jeumoit	France
1933.03.22-E	**Lon[?]lle [Longueville?]**	**France**
1933.06.13-X	Monte Cenis	France?
1933.06.13-E	Colle del Moncenisio	Italy
1933.08.20		Switzerland (Svizzera)
1933.08.22-X	Piaggio Valmara	Italy
1933.??.24-X		France?
1933.12.24-E	Bardonecchia	Italy
1933.12.31-X	Tarvisio [railway]	Italy
1933.12.31-E	Arnoldstein	Austria
1934.01.01-X	Freistadt-Summerau	Austria
1934.01.01		Czechoslovakia
1934.01.06-X	Břeclav	Czechoslovakia
1934.01.06-E	Břeclav	Austria
1934.01.10-E		France?
1934.05.10	Dover	UK
1934.05.15-?	Boulogne sur Mer	France
1934.06.14-E	Basel	Switzerland (Schweiz)
1934.06.16-E	Chia??	Italy
1934.06.27-E	Brigue	Switzerland (Suisse)
1934.06.28-E		France?
1934.07.06-L	Boulogne sur Mer	France
1934.07.25	Dover	UK
1934.07.??-?	Calais	France
1934.08.01-E		Italy
1934.08.12-X	?? di Chiavenna	Italy
1934.08.13-E	Schalklhof	Austria
1934.08.18	Schaanwald	Switzerland/Liechtenstein
1934.10.??	Bruxelles [Transit]	Belgium
1934.10.12	Gare du Nord, Paris	France
1934.12.30-E	Basel	Switzerland (Suisse)
1935.01.02?-E		France
1935.01.22-B	[Die(?)]ppe	France
1935.01.22-L	Newhaven	UK
1935.03.01-L	Boulogne sur Mer	France
1935.03.05-L	Folkestone	UK
1935.03.21-L	Boulogne sur Mer	France
1935.03.25-L	Folkestone	UK
1935.05.11-L	Le Bourget [French airport]	France
1935.05.12-B	Le Bourget [French airport]	France
1935.05.12-L	Croydon [British airport]	UK
193?.05.16.-L		France
1935.05.17-L	Folkestone	UK
1935.07.09-L	Calais	France
1935.07.16	??	Italy
1935.07.17-E	Prato alla Orava	Italy
1935.07.17-X	Prato alla Orava	Italy
1935.07.25-X	Ponte Eneo	Italy
1935.07.25-E	Sušak	Yugoslavia
1935.07.31-X	Sušak	Yugoslavia
1935.07.31-E	Ponte Eneo	Italy
1935.08.05-X	Brennero	Italy
1935.08.05-E	Gries-Brenner	Austria
1935.09.04-B	Cherbourg	France
1935.09.10-L	New York	USA

305. Weill's passport documents his travels between 1931 and 1936. The second page reproduced here shows his entry into France (at Lon[?]lle) on 22 March 1933 (bottom, right-hand side). Another page (not pictured) shows his withdrawal on 18 March of the equivalent of 500 Marks in French francs from his Dresdner Bank account for travel in France.

Vereinbarung zwischen Herrn Kurt Weill und Dr. Kalmus für Universal-Edition:

[handwritten contract document]

Paris 30/III 1933

[signature] Alfred Kalmus

306. Notice of changes in Weill's contract with Universal Edition, dated Paris, 30 March 1933, and signed by Alfred Kalmus.

307. Weill in the country, ca. 1933.

Weill (in Paris) to Hans Heinsheimer of Universal Edition, 3 April 1933: Many warm thanks for your letters. You can't imagine what a joy and reassurance such a friendly greeting meant to me in my current situation. Now is the time where true friendship and true solidarity are put to the test. We must take note of those who stand by us. One day things will once again be reversed.

Naturally it would have been wonderful to have had the opportunity to talk at length. You know of the faith I have in you and how gladly I follow your advice. But my presence here was urgently needed and you see from the most recent events how right my instinct was to come here.

In the ten days I've been here I have already achieved a good deal. It is apparent everywhere how fortunate I was to have had the *Mahagonny* evening here in December. The negotiations for the Renoir film are going well. There are three possibilities for financing this film: one with Pathé-Nathan (the largest French film company) and two others with smaller firms, of which one especially (Braunberger) would be extremely favorable because it would guarantee the greatest artistic freedom. In the course of this week we hope to get to the point that we have a firm commitment from one of these three so that we can begin the script. For this purpose I wanted to go south with Renoir around the 10th of April. Now, however, another matter seems to have changed that.

The best and youngest dancers of that Russian ballet, which is made up of the remaining students of Diaghilev, have formed an excellent ballet troupe under the artistic direction of Balanchine and the financial direction of Boris Kochno, which will open a season here on 27 May and thereafter go to London for a full season. Kochno has pestered me ever since I got here to write something for him. He has already premiered original ballets by Milhaud and Sauguet. I held back since I wasn't fully confident of the whole business. Then yesterday an English financier showed up, Mr. [Edward] James, husband of Tilly Losch, who wants to finance the whole thing on the condition that I write something. I negotiated with him yesterday. He seems ready to agree to my financial demands (30,000 francs). Artistically, I have requested collaboration with a poet of equal stature. I have a plan for which I need good texts, since under no circumstances do I want to write the kind of ballet others do. I have suggested Cocteau. I am now going to enter into serious negotiations in this matter and will write you more when I return.

I have just spoken with Mr. James alone. Now it's just a matter of whether he can find a suitable theater in London since the Alhambra theater, which was offered to him, is too large. He doesn't want to pay me more than 25,000 francs. I told him I could only do it at this price if he were actually to produce both *Mahagonny* (in the Paris form) and *Jasager* in London during the same season (which has long been his intention). On this basis it actually seems possible to reach an agreement. He is speaking with Cocteau today and by tomorrow noon the matter should be finalized.

Hans Heinsheimer of Universal Edition (in Vienna) to Weill, 3 April 1933: We received your telegram and have sent you 500 Marks. As far as future amounts are concerned, we must ask you to be a bit patient. The last eight days have seen such a catastrophic worsening of the situation, that for the time being we are not at all certain about the continuation of the German business. Director Winter has gone to Berlin to gather information and to find out what possibilities actually still exist there. Under these circumstances we must ask you to be satisfied with 500 for April. After Director Winter gets back we should have a better overview of the situation and then we will give you further news.

308. Program of the first American performance of *The 3-Penny Opera*, which opened 13 April 1933 at the Empire Theatre on Broadway after an out-of-town tryout at the Garrick Theatre in Philadelphia. Francesco von Mendelssohn directed the cast in an English translation by Gifford Cochran and Jerrold Krimsky. The production lasted only about two weeks and met generally unfavorable reviews. Weill's emigration to France forced him to abandon plans to attend rehearsals and the premiere.

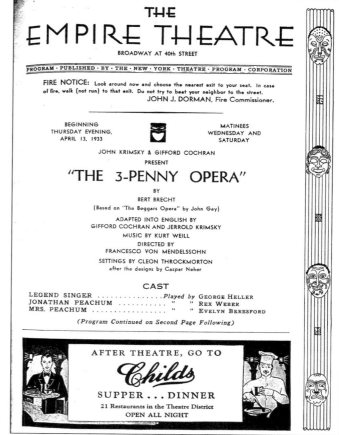

309. Lucy (Josephine Huston) and Polly (Steffi Duna) sing the "Jealousy Duet" while Macheath (Robert Chisholm) looks on amused from his prison cell in *The 3-Penny Opera*, Empire Theatre, New York, 1933.

310. The night after *The 3-Penny Opera* closed at the Empire Theatre, the Music School of the Henry Street Settlement in the Lower East Side section of New York City gave the American premiere of *Der Jasager*, conducted by Lehman Engel and directed by Sanford Meisner. Alice Mattullath prepared the English translation. The program was a double bill with Hindemith's *We're Building a City* (*Wir bauen eine Stadt*).

311. Scene from the New York premiere of *Der Jasager*, 1933.

312. In April 1933, the writer, artist, and prominent British art patron Edward James commissioned Weill to compose *Die sieben Todsünden* for George Balanchine's company Les Ballets 1933. Together they decided on a ballet with singing and James wrote a scenario. Weill first approached Jean Cocteau to collaborate on the project, but he declined. Weill then asked Brecht to write the lyrics and Caspar Neher to design the production. Photo by Cecil Beaton.

Weill (in Paris) to Director Hugo Winter of Universal Edition, 9 May 1933: Many thanks for your news and for your efforts in the matter of the transfer of my personal funds. I hope you have undertaken the right method of doing it, and that I won't have any difficulties as a result. Frankly, I hadn't expected that my name would have to be given at all in this matter. But let us hope that everything goes smoothly.

Weill (in Paris) to Erika Neher, May 1933: The worst thing is the fact that neither of you (how terrible that I have to include both of you in this) has any confidence whatsoever in me; otherwise you'd realize that every text I've set looks entirely different once it's been swept through my music. . . . But no, darling, let's be honest. The reasons lie elsewhere. C[aspar] has been putting me off for weeks because of his indecisiveness. You have now confirmed by telephone (and in writing) something I had suspected all along, that for completely understandable reasons, Cas is now reluctant to work with B[recht] and myself. . . . This is the same Cas who never dared to say anything against B., who kept quiet whenever there was a complaint, who left me completely in the lurch in my battle against B. during the Berlin *Mahagonny*, who always got together with him even after B. and I had become enemies. . . . Little angel, dearest, most beloved, sweetest angel, don't be angry that I'm writing all this. But I do have to carry this burden alone. Since six o'clock yesterday I've been pacing this room, brooding over the matter, and now your letter has arrived. . . . I'm in one hell of a situation. I have to find another designer, right when I'm working day and night on the full score—to say nothing of my problems with the divorce lawyers, problems with the Dresden bank, problems with the ballet rehearsals, and the continuing effect of the serious dizzy spells I suffered on Sunday afternoon. But I should not close this letter without telling you that, despite everything, the thought of you makes me quiet and happy, and my thoughts of you are sad but very beautiful.

313. Weill stayed for a time at the Paris townhouse belonging to the Vicomte de Noailles, 11 place des États-Unis. (Photo taken in 1998.)

314. Weill's request for asylum in France, dated 23 May 1934. The official who filled out this form gave Weill a favorable recommendation ("avis favorable").

315. The report of a Hitler Youth bookburning in Bretten appearing in a June 1933 issue of *Süddeutsches Volksblatt* listed the names of authors whose works were destroyed. The composers listed are: Alban Berg, Hanns Eisler, Berthold Goldschmidt, Alois Hába, Erich Katz, Erich Korngold, Ernst Křenek, Arnold Schoenberg, Franz Schreker, Alexandre Tansman, and Kurt Weill. *Wozzeck* and *Die Dreigroschenoper* are specifically mentioned.

316. A Nazi bookburning in front of the Berlin Opera, May 1933.

Kampfwoche gegen Schmutz und Schund

Hitler-Jugend Gefolgschaftsbann 2 Bez. Bretten, Unterbann 172

Der derzeitige Kameradschaftsführer der Kameradschaft H.J. Bretten

Lehrer Heiner Groß

ist beauftragt in der Kampfwoche für deutsche Kultur gegen Schmutz und Schundliteratur die Sammlung der Bücher und Schriften in der Stadt Bretten vorzunehmen!

Wir ersuchen den Sammlern das nötige Verständnis entgegenzubringen und unnötige Zwischenfälle zu vermeiden.

Heil Hitler!

H. Riegler, Kreispropagandaleitung.

Bücherliste:

A. Unterhaltungs-, Theater- und Musik-Literatur

Sämtliche Werke nachstehender Verfasser:

Asch Nathan	Koestner Erich	Ludwig Emil	Schnitzler Arthur
Asch Schalman	Kerr Alfred	Mann Klaus	Toller Ernst
Brodt Max	Raun Irmgard	Mann Heinrich	Thomas Adrienne
Barbusse Henry	Haus Gina	Ullbrecht Iwan	Bassermann Jakob
Brecht Berthold	Klaeber Kurt	Neumann Robert	Tucholsky Kurt
Doeblin Alfred	Kollontan W.	Remarque Erich M.	Werfel Franz
Feuchtwanger Lion	Lampel Peter	Renn Ludwig	Strindberg
Glaeser Ernst	(nur: Verratene	Schirokauer Alfred	Zweig Arnold
Hasenklever Walter	Jungen)	Ottwald Ernst	Zuckmayer
Holitscher Arthur		Sinklai Upton	Zweig Stefan

Sämtliche Monatszeitschriften:

Das Leben	Das Magazin	Dr. Markuse — Hans
Die Revue des Mo-	u. ähnl. Klabund	Heinz Ewers
nats	Baum Bicky	Joachim Ringelnatz

Musikwerke von:

Berg Alban (Oper	Haba Alois	Schönberg Arnold	Tansmann Aleg.
Wozzeck) u. a.	Katz Erich	Schreker Franz	Weill Kurt (Drei
Eisler Hans	Korngold Erich	Tauber Richard	Groschenoper)
Goldschmidt Berth.	Krennek Ernst		

Politische und wissenschaftliche Werke:

Aber Max	Gumbel C. J.	Landsberger A.	Preuß Hugo
Bauer L.	Hegemann Werner	Fürst Lichnowsky	Rathenau Bauer
Bebel August	Heuß Th.	Lenin	Schoenaich Frhr. v.
Bernstein Eduard	Hifferding R.	Lichtenberger Henri	Wolff Theodor
Blos A.	Hirschfeld Magnus	Liebknecht Karl	Urbantschitsch
Deutsch Otto	Hillquitt R.	Mann Thomas	Beide Th. H. van de
Diehl Karl	Kautsky K.	Marx Karl	Wehberg Claus
Engels Friedrich	Krakauer S.	Roelling E.	Windegg B.
Foerster F. H. W.	Lassalle	Rippold Otto	Wolf Julius
Freud Sigmund	Kaesterer Erich	Otto Berthold	

Gottlosen-Literatur:

Brenner Th.	Hartwig (Vorf. des	Hobam Dr. Max	Siemsen A. Dr.
Brugbacher R	Freid.-Verb.)	Moslowsky S.	Siewers H.
Cerwin R	Höllein Emil	Löwenstein R.	Wendel Fr.
Dunker	Hoernle Edwin	Roßt H.	Senß H.
Essenroth H.	Krisch E.	Menken J.	Zapp A.

Agitationsbibliothek d. Freidenkerverbandes	Monistische Bibliothek
Leninsbibliothek	Neuland — Antireligiöse Zeitschrift
Monistische Monatshefte	Volkstümliche Freidenker Schriften

317. Weill's letter to Bertolt Brecht dating from sometime in May 1933 brings him up to date on the progress of *Die sieben Todsünden*. Brecht had been involved in the work for only ten days in April.

Paris, Donnerstag
11. Place des Etats Unis.

Lieber Brecht,

es ist das übliche Durcheinander. Natürlich hat sich unter den Anhängern des alten Russenballetts eine kleine Partei gebildet, die unser Ballett zu wenig "reine Choreographie". Dadurch hat es in den letzten Tagen grosse Kräche gegeben, und ich habe durchgesetzt, dass ein Mann kaltgestellt worden ist. Balanchine steht zwar zwischen den Parteien, hat aber ausgezeichnet gearbeitet und tatsächlich einen Darstellungsstil gefunden, der zwar sehr tänzerisch, aber doch real ist. Lenja und die Familie werden sehr gut, ebenso natürlich die Bühne von Caspar und die Musik. Das übrige hängt davon ab, ob Balanchine seine angeborene und durch die Gegenpartei noch geschürte Faulheit überwindet und seine Tänze präzis ausarbeitet oder nicht. Dabei kann man ihm weder helfen noch dreinreden.

Wir würden uns natürlich alle sehr freuen, wenn Sie kommen würden. James, mit dem ich darüber gesprochen habe, hat das gleiche gesagt (er ist schon wieder mit anderen Dingen beschäftigt und an Tilly ganz uninteressiert), er hat mir schon halb und halb versprochen, Ihnen die Reise zu zahlen, wenn Sie kommen, und ich glaube, ich kann versprechen, 1000.-francs für Sie herauszukriegen, wenn Sie kommen wollen.

Die Hauptprobe ist Montag, die Generalprobe Dienstag (Zeiten noch unbekannt), die Premiere Mittwoch, die zweite Aufführung Sonnabend. Sie können es sich also einrichten, wie Sie wollen, da Sie das Ganze ja wahrscheinlich doch mit Ihrer Uebersiedlung nach Dänemark verbinden würden.

In der Dreigroschenoper-Sache habe ich nichts wieder gehört. Dagegen beschäftige ich mich mit dem Plan betr. Spitzköpfe und Rundköpfe, den ich Ihnen vorgeschlagen hatte, und zwar in Verbindung mit Steinthal, der hier ev. in enger Zusammenarbeit mit mir Theater machen will. Dazu wäre allerdings folgendes zu klären: Sie wissen, dass ich mich seit längerer Zeit mit dem Gedanken trage, aus diesem Stück eine Art "Operette" zu machen, und dass dieser Gedanke ausschliesslich von mir stammt. Nun scheint Aufricht mit Steinthal geäussert zu haben, dass Sie von Eisler die Musik zu dem Stück schreiben lassen wollen. Da ich auf keinen Fall Ihre gemeinsamen Pläne mit Eisler tangieren möchte und nur unter ganz klaren und eindeutigen Verhältnissen arbeiten könnte, möchte ich Sie bitten, diese Frage zunächst aufzuklären, bevor ich mich mit dem Plan weiter beschäftige.

Uebrigens mache ich jetzt zunächst einmal 2 Monate vollkommene Ferien, die ich dringend nötig habe. Ich habe eine sehr angenehme Einladung nach Italien und werde wohl gegen 12.Juni hier abreisen.

Viele herzliche Grüsse
von Ihrem
Weill

318. Weill's second letter to Brecht before the opening of *Die sieben Todsünden*, dated 1 June 1933, invites Brecht to attend the premiere on 7 June.

Paris, 1.6.33
11 PLACE DES ETATS UNIS XVI
TROY 46-05

Lieber Brecht,

James ist endlich zurück u. ich habe ihn sofort gebeten, Ihnen das Geld zu schicken. Er hat versprochen, es gleich zu tun. Tilly ist auch hier, ich habe sie noch nicht besichtigt, aber Abravanel sagt, sie macht einen begabten Eindruck. Uebrigens ist James von der Dichtung vollkommen begeistert u. es wird alles so gemacht werden, wie wir es wollen.

Im arbeite wie ein Pferd, aber es macht mir großen Spaß. 5 Nummern sind fertig. Ich glaube, es wird sehr schön. Sonst nichts neues, außer dass Sie die Photographie auf dem Abtransport bald bekommen werden!

Herzlich Ihr Weill

319. Weill's list of names and addresses in Paris, including Honegger, Sauguet, Mauprey (translator of *Die Dreigroschenoper*), and Brecht.

Universal Edition (in Vienna) to Weill, 7 June 1933: As things stand now, with the complete collapse of the German market for your works, the income from your compositions is reduced to a minimum scarcely worth mentioning, especially since even abroad we have virtually no returns from the large majority of your works because there are no stage performances of any material significance to be had. As a result, this year's receipts will scarcely reduce your debit balance of over 15,000 Marks, and, from this point of view, increasing the debt through further monthly payments is a heavy burden upon our financial management. Therefore we would have been very happy if—in spite of your current situation, which we hope will continue to improve—you had shown some understanding for the publisher, which the whole time has been going to the limit for you. Considering the current situation in Germany, we hoped that you would have allowed the contract to continue for the next few months even without monthly payments. If you are not prepared to accept this solution, we will make a proposal that is surely in your interests; that is, that we return to you the full rights for all the works you compose during the next year. You would then be in a position to exploit freely your next compositions and receive separate publishing income from them as well. Three months before the end of that year a new agreement would be reached regarding the continuation of our contract.

320. Neher's set design for *Die sieben Todsünden* shows seven doors surmounted by seven banners. The family is shown at a table to the right.

321. Caspar Neher designed seven banners for *Die sieben Todsünden*; one for each sin. This one depicts "Ira" (anger).

DIE SIEBEN TODSÜNDEN

"Spectacle in nine scenes";
scenario by Edward James; text by Bertolt Brecht

1933   Paris, Théâtre des Champs-Elysées (7 June)
        London, Savoy Theatre (1 July)
        Maurice Abravanel, conductor; George Balanchine, choreographer;
        Caspar Neher, designer

1936   Copenhagen, Kongelige Teater (12 November)

Leaning against a door frame, a small man with an ironic gleam behind his glasses, an intelligent, somewhat sardonic expression, responds with cheerful imprecision to the questions which fall on him like hail. It is Kurt Weill, of *Threepenny Opera* fame, who has written the score of *The Seven Deadly Sins*, a work which will be premiered by the Ballets 1933.

Has he been in France long?
Three months.
Are there any prospects?
Of course!
Which?
Well, for instance, visiting the south of France.
And the movies?
Ah, the movies . . .
But here's something definite:
I am in negotiation with several French motion picture studios. Perhaps something will come of it. I would like to make a musical film, but . . . Eloquent gesture . . . Yvon Novy, "Lorsque Tilly Losch, Balanchine et Kurt Weill parlent des Ballets 1933 entre un cocktail et d'exquises tartes aux fraises," *Comoedia*, 22 May 1933.

322. First page of the program
for Les Ballets 1933.

323. Left to right: Anna II (Tilly Losch) and Anna I (Lenya) are two sides of the same personality. Weill also invited Otto Pasetti to sing in the production.

324. Production
photos from *Die
sieben Todsünden.*

The Seven Deadly Sins brings us into tangential contact with an aesthetic of despair, or at least disappointment, which flourished in Germany after the war, and against which the broad masses of that nation are currently rebelling through romanticism, exoticism, expressionism. We note all these trends as instructive phenomena, to be sure, but we must regard them as relics of the past. We in Paris have no particular reason to grant them asylum, to be perfectly frank. Our eyes also are trained on the future, and therefore we refuse to take responsibility for these errors which do not even have the excuse of being widespread. In this regard, we will add that the score of Mr. Kurt Weill, which is more of a cantata than a ballet, reveals to us nothing that we did not already know. It has a remarkable sound, but its sonorities are already familiar. Ferroud, *Paris-soir*, 12 June 1933.

325. Jean Cocteau sent Weill one of his personal postcards (pictured above) the day after the premiere of *Die sieben Todsünden*. He wrote: "You must have felt how much I suffered from the tragic frivolity of the hall last night. But you owned the place; you imposed your will on it. In a way it was superb—how the piece depicts the struggle between comfort and selfishness on the one hand and discomfort and altruism on the other. The two women were astounding, creating a superhuman atmosphere about themselves. I've been living in this tempo of your work—tender and cruel—for the last two days. I embrace you."

Certainly "The Seven Deadly Sins" turned out to be less a ballet than an immorality play, with Lotte Lenja (Weill's wife) singing the plot in German for Tilly Losch (James' wife) to dance to, which she did, unfortunately, in the language of Wigman rather than Taglioni. The two ladies, by cynical symbolism, were supposed to represent the Good or Material-minded Side and the Bad or Spiritual-souled Version of the same girl, named Anna. They were supported in their mixed mutual endeavors by a male Teutonic quartet which sang that its Vaterland was in Louisiana, plus a masculine *corps de ballet* in straw boaters and tights, jumping through seven paper doors all of which, so far as Bad Anna was concerned, could have been marked "Gentlemen," since 'twas they who led her to her downfall each time, but which were more ecclesiastically marked "Sloth," "Greed," etc., instead. Herr Weill, who is always reported an intellectual Communist and who, with his wife, was on this trip to Paris a houseguest of the Vicomte de Noailles and *his* wife, took his bow and his boos for the premiere while standing in the door marked "*Luxure*." Gênet, "Paris Letter," *New Yorker*, 8 July 1933, p. 41–2.

326. Envelope addressed to Boris Kochno, the artistic director of Les Ballets 1933. Weill wrote to him from Italy, where he vacationed after the premiere of *Die sieben Todsünden*.

327. Weill (in Alassio, Italy) to Boris Kochno, 20 June 1933: "I want to tell you once more how much I enjoyed our collaboration during these last few weeks. I believe that our show has been altogether successful, and a large part of it is due to your intensity, your energy and your work's precision. I do so hope that we will have the opportunity to work together again soon.

I am quite pleased with the success of *The Seven Deadly Sins*. My musical theater is meant to incite discussion rather than amusement. I believe that it was not only important, but absolutely essential to introduce my philosophical ideas—a humane attitude—into the ballet. That for me was a task well worth the effort.

May I ask you most cordially to give your best attention to the performance in London and see to it that it will be as good as the one in Paris? Perhaps you could arrange something so that the English public, which doesn't yet know me very well, could get an idea about my music and my kind of musical theater."

328. From left, Boris Kochno; Marie-Laure, Vicomtesse de Noailles; and artist Christian Bérard, who designed "Mozartiana" for Les Ballets 1933.

SALLE GAVEAU, 45, RUE LA BOÉTIE, PARIS

MARDI 20 JUIN 1933
A 21 HEURES
••

HUITIÈME CONCERT
DE

LA SERENADE
• • •

AVEC LE CONCOURS DE MMES
LOTTE LENJA
ROMANITZA
MARIE CHACKO

ET DE MM.
ALFREDO CASELLA   OTTO DE PASETTI
Maurice de ABRAVANEL   ALBERT PETERS
JEAN FRANÇAIX   ERIK FUCHS
HEINRICH GRETLER

The Seven Deadly Sins, Weill's latest work, marks as great an advance on *Mahagonny* as *Mahagonny* did on the *Beggar's Opera*. The line is more varied and more continuous, the construction far firmer, and the once disparate German and American traits are blended into a homogeneous and highly personal style.

There are at present no records of this music, which is a pity, as it gives Lotte Lenja her greatest opportunity as a singer. At the same time it is possible that the music would lose much of its savor without the ironic counterpoint of the stage action. For example, the churchy four-part chorus "Here is a wire from Philadelphia" with the unctuous solo "But our Anna really is quite sensible; she will know a contract is a contract" would lose its point without the visual accompaniment of the wretched Anna doing slimming exercises and being kept away from the dish of fruit at the point of a revolver.

In spite of the superficial bustle of much of it, the music to *The Seven Deadly Sins* is remarkable for the extraordinary weariness, a neurasthenic fatigue which, though sterile in a way, reaches in the finaletto a certain grandeur.

Even those who do not find Weill's music sympathetic must realize that he symbolizes the split that is taking place not between highbrow and lowbrow, but between highbrow and highbrow. In the 19th century the split would have been that between a follower of Liszt and a follower of Johann Strauss or [Joseph] Gungl.

But today Weill stands nearer to Ellington than he does to a fellow pupil of Busoni like Jarnach. He and Alban Berg represent the two extremes of Central European aesthetic, and in their widely different ways are the most successful exponents of their respective styles. Constant Lambert, *Times* of London, August 1933.

329. Following the run of *Die sieben Todsünden*, La Sérénade's eighth concert featured an encore performance of *Mahagonny*, which had been performed the previous December.

330. Lenya, photographed for *Vogue* by George Hoyningen-Huene.

331. This excerpt from the copyist's piano-vocal score shows an English translation by Edward James, which he prepared in consultation with Lenya for the London performances. None of the music from *Die sieben Todsünden* was published during Weill's lifetime.

332. A handbill advertising the London performances of Les Ballets 1933.

Weill (in Positano, Italy) to Lotte Lenya, 16 July 1933: The reports about *Die sieben Todsünden* from Germany are shameless and mean. They're simply making up lies about a failure and maintain that Paris, too, does not want to hear any more about these botched pieces of work, which the "new Germany" rejected long ago. In retrospect I've come to realize that Paris too has quite an active anti-Weill contingent and that they are agitating against me furiously. Sometimes I wonder whether I really need to put myself into a another witch's cauldron and use up my nerves fighting this dung heap of intriguers. If I move to Paris, I'll certainly live way out of the city and do nothing but work. Or maybe it would be better to live very simply somewhere in Ticino, Lake Garda, or some place like that and go to Paris only when it's necessary.

Weill (in Italy) to Emma and Albert Weill, 23 July 1933: Many thanks for your letter, dear Hanns. I'm happy that you had a good rest and that you all are well. I'm fine, too. The rash is completely gone now and one can assume that the psoriasis has practically been cured as well. To be sure, I've been baking under a blazing sun for four weeks. But now it's getting so hot that one can barely stand it. We're leaving here on Tuesday, will stay for awhile in Rome and Florence and then spend a couple of weeks in the Dolomites. I'm not entirely sure about the future course of my life yet, but I'm not worrying about it, which is a sign that I'm somewhat recuperated. Lots of plans for new works are gradually surfacing—also a good sign. The 7 *Deadly Sins* were *the* great success of the season in London and Lenya especially has made a big hit.

Could you possibly send me the following books to Trento (Italy) general delivery:

1). The Reclam edition of *1001 Nights*.
2). All Reclam Calderon volumes (except *The Judge of Zalamea*)
3). The works of Sholem Asch which have been published in German.
4). A German edition of *Tales from the Talmud*.

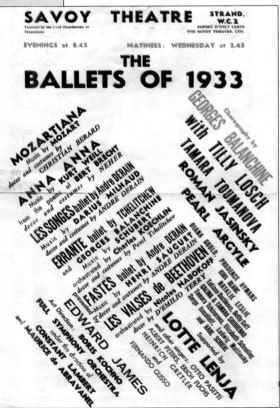

Lotte Lenya (in Berlin) to Weill, [September 1933]: The divorce matter is in order. There's no longer any need to rush it (I don't think). It's good enough for now. I only hope that you'll find something soon, so you'll have your peace and get out of those hotel rooms. . . . I, too, think it best to let a real estate agent handle the house [in Berlin]. . . . I'll do whatever can be done to get rid of it as soon as possible.

334. Newspaper advertisement for the broadcast of the radio play *Fantomas* (3 November 1933), for which Weill supplied the music for a moritat-type song. The text was written by Robert Desnos, and Antonin Artaud directed.

333. Letter from Weill to his lawyer Engelhardt, transferring the balance of his account in a Berlin bank to Lenya as an alimony payment.

335. On 18 November 1933, Weill informed Jean Cocteau that he had finished setting Cocteau's poem "Es regnet."

On a crié
"Vive Hitler!"
à la Salle Pleyel...

...pour protester
contre quelques... « chansons »
de Kurt Weill

Hier après-midi, au cours d'un concert donné à la Salle Pleyel et dont notre collaborateur Paul Le Flem rend compte par ailleurs, Mme Madeleine Grey interprétait, en première audition, trois chansons de Kurt Weill, l'auteur de L'Opéra de Quat-Sous, qui a quitté l'Allemagne depuis quelques mois à la suite du mouvement antisémite. La première chanson, La Vendeuse, fut accueillie avec un certain succès, ainsi que la seconde, La Parente pauvre. Mais la troisième, intitulée prétentieusement, Ballade de César, ne fut pas du goût de deux spectateurs qui, lorsqu'elle fut terminée, crièrent d'une voix forte: « Vive Hitler! »

Le cri surprit. Des applaudissements y répondirent. Mais les protestataires s'entêtaient: « Vive Hitler! Vive Hitler! » répétaient-ils; et l'un d'eux ajouta exactement:

— Nous avons assez de mauvais musiciens en France sans qu'on nous envoie tous les Juifs d'Allemagne.

Mme Madeleine Grey, prenant pour un encouragement les applaudissements de la salle, amusée par l'incident, bissa sa « ballade césarienne ».

Les protestataires firent entendre à nouveau leur cri de: « Vive Hitler! » dont les spectateurs, cette fois, un peu interloqués, comprirent l'intention. Des applaudissements récompensèrent le mérite de l'interprète. Des agents parurent. Il y eut un léger remous dans le fond de la salle, les protestataires sortirent et la discussion se poursuivit dans le hall et jusque sur le trottoir du faubourg Saint-Honoré.

L'incident a pu sembler badin. Il est indicatif: c'est la première fois qu'un Français crie: « Vive Hitler! » dans un endroit public. Et ce Français — qu'il nous permette de le nommer — c'est M. Florent Schmitt, un maître de la musique française, qu'accompagnait un de ses amis, lequel, du reste, s'est associé à ses protestation.

Qu'on ne s'y trompe pas: c'est la première goutte d'eau qui annonce l'orage.

Si encore M. Kurt Weill nous avait vraiment apporté quelque chose! Mais jugez par vous-mêmes; voici le « corps du délit »:

Rome est une ville où les Romains ont du sang
　　　　　　　　[bouillant dans les veines
La tyrannie de César les agaçant, aussitôt leur
　　　　　　　　[colère se déchaîne.
« Garde-toi des Ides de Mars » Et malgré cet
　　　　　　　　[avertissement
César se crut maître de Rome et poursuivit tous
　　　　　　　　[ses buts insolents (bis)
Ébloui par cette réussite, on n'entendait que lui
　　　　　　　　[au Capitole.
Il raillait les conseils des sénateurs se moquant de
　　　　　　　　[leurs bonnes paroles.
Le fier sang des Romains ne fit qu'un tour, pour
　　　　　　　　[César plus d'amis fidèles!
Les amis ne pouvant lui servir qu'à poursuivre son
　　　　　　　　[but personnel (bis)
En cachette, les conspirateurs se concertent la nuit
　　　　　　　　[pleins d'ardeur
Et le jour des Ides de Mars, de César, Brutus
　　　　　　　　[perça le cœur.
Hébété, César s'écroula à terre. Sans comprendre,
　　　　　　　　[fixant son assassin
« C'est toi, Brute crie-t-il en latin, car c'est la
　　　　　　　　[langue de tous les Romains.
Que personne ne se laisse mener par l'ambition
　　　　　　　　[ou la folie.
Par le glaive César voulut régner c'est le poignard
　　　　　　　　[qui lui ôta la vie.
Par le glaive César voulut régner c'est le poignard
　　　　　　　　[qui lui ôta la vie.

Vraiment, comme l'a dit un homme qui avait de l'esprit, c'est « de la musique que c'est pas la peine ». Et les paroles, donc!

Paul ACHARD.

---

336. An announcement of a concert by the Orchestre Symphonique de Paris at which three songs from *Der Silbersee* were performed by Madeleine Grey. Madeleine Milhaud made the French translations. The concert produced a demonstration led by composer Florent Schmitt, who cried "Vive Hitler!" and condemned Weill's music. This report appeared in the 27 November 1933 issue of *Comoedia*.

ORCHESTRE SYMPHONIQUE DE PARIS
Dimanche 26 novembre, à 17 heures, salle Pleyel,
sous la direction de M. DE ABRAVENEL.

Ouverture pour l'inauguration de la maison. . . . . BEETHOVEN.
Concerto en sol majeur . . . . J.-CH. BACH.
　　(Clavecin et orchestre.)
Aquarelles . . . . M. ROESGEN-CHAMPION.
　　Clavecin : M⁻ᵉ Roesgen-Champion.
Première Symphonie. . . . . SCHUMANN.
Trois Airs du Silbersee . . . . KURT WEILL.
　　(Première audition.)
　　Mˡˡᵉ Mad. Grey.
Don Juan . . . . R. STRAUSS.

Weill (in Paris) to Lotte Lenya, [29? November 1933]: I'm glad to have news from you. I can imagine how it bugs you that those bourgeois people are now living in that beautiful house. I feel the same way, but then I tell myself that it would have hardly been possible for you to live in that environment, and nothing that we gave up there is irreplaceable. You can see what they're doing to the likes of us: without cause GEMA [the German performing rights society] has reduced me from 125 points to 5, which means from 4,000 Marks to 150. This is practically expropriation; one could also call it highway robbery. . . . I've had a very upsetting experience: the three songs [from *Der Silbersee*] were a great success at the concert. Caesar ["Ballade von Cäsars Tod"] had to be repeated because a French composer, Florent Schmitt (approximately as talented as Butting), got up and screamed: "Heil Hitler! Enough music by German refugees," etc. The audience acted quite decently and soon shut him up, and the song was sung once more and was again a success. But almost the entire French press is siding with this "French master" against me. The same people who a year ago jumped with enthusiasm for *Mahagonny* are now cool and reserved. [Darius] Milhaud is being remarkably decent. This matter seems to be going entirely too far for him. For a few days I was very angry, although it shouldn't matter to me, because my publisher [Heugel] told me this Schmitt is a lunatic and completely irresponsible.

Felix Weingartner to Florent Schmitt, [November 1933]: A hearty bravo for your bravery! You have found just the right word to characterize a certain kind of music which is not music at all, but an unconscionable imposition on the good faith of the public, which has forgotten to trust its ears and fears that it will be condemned if it does not admire this wretched stuff. Art groans everywhere beneath the tyranny of this so-called modernism, which is really nothing but impertinent dilettantism. My dear sir, I shake your hand. Quoted in Yves Hucher, *Florent Schmitt: l'homme et l'artiste: son époque et son oeuvre* (Paris: Plon, 1953), 99.

337. The Princesse de Polignac commissioned Weill's Symphony no. 2. She was an heiress of the Singer family, whose fortune came from manufacturing sewing machines.

338. Lenya playing Anna I in *Die sieben Todsünden.*

339. Weill sent his song "Der Abschiedsbrief" (text by Erich Kästner) to Marlene Dietrich as a New Year's greeting. (17 December 1933)

340. Weill's autograph score for his Symphony no. "1" bears a dedication to the Princesse de Polignac. This work is now known as Symphony no. 2. Weill's first symphony, written during his apprenticeship with Busoni, was not performed by an orchestra until 1956.

341. Program for the first Italian performances of *Mahagonny* and *Der Jasager*, 29 December 1933. Lenya and her lover, Otto Pasetti, both sang, and Weill's old friend Hans Curjel staged both works, as he had for the performance in Paris one year before.

A [theater] composer cannot content himself with the creation of music, but assists in the construction of every scene of the action to the point where his music becomes an integral part of the whole.

Kurt Weill

1934 – 1940

1934

January 1–5   Visits parents in Carlsbad, Czechoslovakia.

February   Begins work on *Der Kuhhandel*, an operetta with libretto by Robert Vambery. During January–May 1935 the collaborators adapt it for a production in England under the title *A Kingdom for a Cow*. (The original German version is not performed until 1994.) Weill looks for a French publisher and transfers his performing rights from the German society (GEMA) to the Italian society (SIAE).

May 5   Reports to Hans Heinsheimer that Josef von Sternberg has invited him to write the music for Marlene Dietrich's next film. The project never materializes.

May 10   Spends a few days in London staying with Edward James at his residence at 35 Wimpole Street. At the end of the month both Caspar and Erika Neher visit Weill for a week in Louveciennes.

     Complainte de la Seine (M. Magre) and *Je ne t'aime pas* (M. Magre). Numerous cabaret performances by Lys Gauty.

June 16   Spends ten days in Venice and sees Lenya before traveling on to Salzburg for negotiations with Max Reinhardt and Franz Werfel over *Der Weg der Verheißung*.

July 6   Returns to London and stays again with Edward James for about two and a half weeks.

August   Takes a summer vacation in Italy with Caspar and Erika Neher before arriving on 14 August in Salzburg for meetings with Reinhardt and Werfel. Weill begins setting Werfel's text. On returning to Louveciennes, Weill finds that he is obliged to write on very short notice the songs and incidental music for *Marie galante*, a stage adaptation by Jacques Deval of his best-selling novel.

October   Lenya moves to Weill's house in Louveciennes.

October 11   *Symphony no. 2* [billed as "*Symphonische Fantasie (Symphonie no. 1)*"] (January 1933–February 1934). Concertgebouw Orchestra, Amsterdam; Bruno Walter, conductor. Weill attends rehearsals and the performance. Walter conducts the symphony again in New York, 13 December 1934. Both times critical reception is very poor.

December 22   *Marie galante* (Jacques Deval). Théâtre de Paris; Edmond Mahieux, conductor; H. Henriot, director. The production runs for three weeks.

December 30   Travels to Switzerland for three days, presumably to meet his parents, who were still living in Germany.

1935

     Youkali (Roger Fernay). An instrumental tango from *Marie galante* is given lyrics by Roger Fernay, son of Paul Bertrand of Heugel.

January   Travels to London to work on *A Kingdom for a Cow* and searches for film work. Stays at the Park Lane Hotel in Piccadilly until March, when he rents an apartment at 7 Bramham Gardens, Earls Court.

April   Lotte Lenya comes to London, presumably to study English. A performance of Symphony no. 2 conducted by Désiré-Emile Inghelbrecht in Paris is well reviewed.

May–June   Stays at Edward James's residence, probably without Lenya.

June 28   *A Kingdom for a Cow* (January–May 1935, English lyrics by Desmond Carter; English book adapted from Vambery by Reginald Arkell). Savoy Theatre, London; Muir Matheson, conductor; Ernst Matray and Felix Weissberger, directors.

Summer   Parents move to Palestine.

July 9   Returns to Louveciennes; Lenya stays in London and receives her mail care of Gerty Simon, the photographer.

July 13   Travels to Switzerland, where he meets the Nehers before vacationing with them in Italy and Novi, Yugoslavia. Spends three weeks in Salzburg working with Werfel and Reinhardt before returning to Louveciennes at the end of August.

August   Finishes work on *Der Weg der Verheißung* in Louveciennes and Salzburg. The work is not performed in the original German version, but it is revised October 1935–December 1936 for an American production under the provisional title *The Road of Promise*.

Mid-August   Further discussions with Reinhardt, Werfel, and Weisgal. The premiere is planned for January 1936 in New York. Weill invites Lenya to go to New York with him.

September 4   Sails aboard the S.S. *Majestic* from Cherbourg with Lenya and Meyer Weisgal. Eleanora and Francesco von Mendelssohn travel with them.

September 10   Arrives at New York Harbor. Weill and Lenya stay at the St. Moritz Hotel, Central Park South, New York, until February 1936.

October   Attends a rehearsal of George and Ira Gershwin's *Porgy and Bess*.

November   Meets with Brecht and Marc Blitzstein to consider a version of *Mahagonny* for Broadway.

December 17   The League of Composers sponsors a concert of excerpts from *Mahagonny*, *Die Dreigroschenoper*, *A Kingdom for a Cow*, and *Die Bürgschaft*, with Lenya singing some numbers; it is coolly received.

1936

January   The production company for *The Eternal Road* is declared bankrupt, and the production is postponed. Werfel returns to Europe, Reinhardt goes to California, and Weill remains in New York.

February   Weill and Lenya move to a less expensive hotel, the Park Crescent, at 150 Riverside Drive. Weill obtains a new passport from the German consulate and explores various opportunities in the theater, notably the offer of a commission from the American Ballet and a performance of *Aufstieg und Fall der Stadt Mahagonny* in Hartford. He hopes to set Wedekind's two-act pantomime *Die Kaiserin von Neufundland*, but he cannot secure the rights.

March	Heugel gives notice of termination of Weill's publishing contract. Weill meets Cheryl Crawford, a theater producer and co-founder of the Group Theatre, who will be instrumental in helping Weill establish himself in America.
May 3	Cheryl Crawford arranges for Weill to travel to Chapel Hill, North Carolina, to work with Paul Green on a new musical.
June 4	Spends a day at Maxwell Anderson's home in New City, Rockland County. The two had met at a theatrical party during the previous winter after a performance of Anderson's *Winterset*.
June–August	Weill, Lenya, Paul Green and Crawford join the Group Theatre at Pine Brook in Trumbull, Connecticut to work on *Johnny Johnson*. Weill lectures the cast about the nature of musical theater and introduces them to music from *Die Dreigroschenoper*. Marc Blitzstein is in attendance.
Summer	*The Fräulein and the Little Son of the Rich* (Robert Graham). A "song drama" written for Lenya, unperformed.
August	Weill and Lenya live at Crawford's house in Bridgeport, Connecticut, and in September move to her apartment at 455 East 51st Street, where they live for the next year.
November	Signs a contract with music publisher Chappell for publication of new works, beginning with *Johnny Johnson*. The production team for *The Eternal Road* is reassembled.
November 19	*Johnny Johnson* (June–November 1936, Paul Green). 44th St. Theatre, New York; Lehman Engel, conductor, Lee Strasberg, director. 68 performances.

1937

January 7	*The Eternal Road* (1934–36, Franz Werfel, English translation by Ludwig Lewisohn and additional lyrics by Charles Alan). Manhattan Opera House, New York; Max Reinhardt, director; Norman Bel Geddes, designer; Isaac van Grove and Leo Kopp, conductors. 153 performances. Weill's contribution is praised, but press coverage of the music is dominated by the celebrity of Max Reinhardt and the size of the spectacle. (The original German version, *Der Weg der Verheißung*, is not performed until 1999.)
January 9	Delivers a lecture, "Music in the Theatre," sponsored by the International Ladies' Garment Workers' Union.
January 19	Weill and Lenya remarry in a civil ceremony in Westchester County, north of New York City.
January–June	Travels to Hollywood to work with writer Clifford Odets and director Lewis Milestone on *The River Is Blue* and pursue other opportunities. Stays at the Roosevelt Hotel, moves to 6630 Whitley Terrace on 18 February, and on 14 May moves to 686 San Lorenzo Drive in Santa Monica. (Lenya stays at Cheryl Crawford's New York apartment.) Weill makes further contacts with George and Ira Gershwin and George Antheil. He also plans a series of radio operas with Howard Dietz and tries to obtain the rights to adapt Ferenc Molnár's *Liliom*.

March–June	Begins working with Sam and Bella Spewack, and E.Y. (Yip) Harburg on a musical play ("The Opera from Mannheim") about German refugee actors. Presumed lost.
March–April	*The River Is Blue*, film score commissioned by Walter Wanger, Hollywood. The film's working title, *Castles in Spain*, is changed to *The River Is Blue*, then to *The Adventuress* and *Rising Tide* before finally becoming *Blockade*. Weill explores film scoring and recording techniques. Both George Antheil and Charlie Chaplin are impressed with his music, but the score is eventually discarded by Wanger and replaced with one by Werner Janssen.
April 17	A performance of Symphony no. 2 under Bruno Walter is relatively well received in Vienna.
May	Accepts an offer to write music for a Fritz Lang film, *You and Me*, hoping that the money will enable him to continue his theater work.
May 27	Supervises a performance of *Der Lindberghflug* at the Antheil Gallery in Hollywood. The next day he attends the successful Los Angeles premiere of *Johnny Johnson* at the Mayan Theatre, produced by the Federal Theatre Project.
July	Returns to New York.
August	Returns to North Carolina to work with Paul Green on *The Common Glory*, a musical pageant sponsored by the Federal Theatre Project. After working for four months they cannot agree on a story line and abandon the project.
August 27	Applies for American citizenship after reentering the U.S. from Canada on an immigrant visa. Madeleine Milhaud arranges to send Weill's belongings from Louveciennes to New York.
September	Moves to duplex apartment at 231 East 62nd Street, New York. Actor Burgess Meredith encourages Weill to collaborate with H. R. Hays on a play about American folk hero Davy Crockett for production by the Federal Theatre Project.
September 29	Ernst Josef Aufricht's production of *L'opéra de quat'sous* opens in Paris. Weill has composed two additional songs for Yvette Guilbert, "Pauv' Madam' Peachum" and "Tu me démolis" (texts by Guilbert), but she probably does not sing them in the production.
November	*Albumblatt für Erika*, New York. Unpublished piano transcription of a section from *The Eternal Road* for Erika Neher.
December 13	Travels to Hollywood with Lenya to work on the film score for *You and Me*, directed by Fritz Lang. They rent a cottage at 940 Ocean Front Street in Santa Monica.

1938

	Two Folksongs of the New Palestine. "Havu l'venim" and "Baa m'nucha" (traditional texts; melodies by Mordecai Seira and Daniel Sambursky, respectively). Arranged for voice and piano and published by Nigun Press, New York, 1938.
January–April	*Davy Crockett* (H. R. Hays). An unfinished show for the Federal Theatre Project.

February Returns with Lenya to New York.

April-May Travels to Hollywood to attend recording sessions for *You and Me*. Address: Villa Carlotta, 5959 Franklin Avenue, Hollywood. Lenya stays in New York and performs a nightclub act at Le Ruban Bleu on West 56th Street.

Spring *You and Me*, film score, lyrics by Sam Coslow and Johnny Burke, directed by Fritz Lang. Only nine of twenty-three music cues are credited to Weill alone. First screened in New York, 1 June 1938. "The Right Guy for Me" is published as sheet music by Famous Music Corp, 1938. Weill also begins work on *Railroads on Parade* for performance in the railroad pavilion at the 1939 World's Fair.

May Attempts to locate German recordings of *Die Dreigroschenoper* to give to Maxwell Anderson.

Summer Begins writing *Knickerbocker Holiday* with Maxwell Anderson and helps his brother Hanns's family immigrate to the U.S.

Rents a country house three and a half miles outside Suffern, New York: "Eastman Estate," Sky Meadow Road, Route 202, Ramapo, New York. From here he has easy access to Maxwell Anderson's and Burgess Meredith's homes in New City.

October 19 *Knickerbocker Holiday* (June–September 1938, Maxwell Anderson). Barrymore Theatre, New York; Maurice Abravanel, conductor; Joshua Logan, director. 168 performances.

November 9–10 "Kristallnacht": Nazi storm troopers ransack Jewish-owned shops and set synagogues ablaze across Germany and Austria.

1939

January Vacations with Lenya and the Andersons in Naples, Florida.

April 30 *Railroads on Parade* (Spring 1938–Winter 1939, Edward Hungerford). New York World's Fair; Isaac van Grove, conductor; Charles Alan, director. Revised and performed again at the 1940 World's Fair.

June Accepted as an "active member" of ASCAP, the predominant performing rights organization in the United States. Throughout his career in America, Weill makes periodic petitions to the organization requesting an increase in his ranking.

June 6 Leaves with Lenya by car for California, where he works during July with Maxwell Anderson on *Ulysses Africanus*, a musical based on Harry Stillwell Edwards's *Eneas Africanus* (1919). Anderson had offered the title role to Paul Robeson, who declined it, and now the show is conceived for Bill Robinson. When Robinson has scheduling conflicts, Weill and Anderson abandon the project. They later adapt and incorporate four songs from the show into *Lost in the Stars*.

September 1 Germany invades Poland. Two days later Britain and France declare war on Germany.

November 13 *Madam, Will You Walk?* Music for the Night Court scene in Act III of Sidney Howard's play. The play is poorly reviewed in Baltimore and Washington and does not move to New York.

December *Nannas Lied* (Bertolt Brecht), New York. Written for Lenya, Christmas, 1939.

Stopping by Woods on a Snowy Evening (Robert Frost), New York. Manuscript missing; a portion of a copyist's manuscript has survived.

1940

January 20 *Two on an Island* (December 1939, incidental music to the play by Elmer Rice). Broadhurst Theatre, New York. Lost.

February 3 In an interview published in the *New York Sun*, Weill unreservedly commits himself to the development of Broadway's musical theater.

February 4 *The Ballad of Magna Carta* (radio cantata, Maxwell Anderson). Columbia Broadcasting System, New York; Mark Warnow, conductor. Commissioned by Norman Corwin for his series *The Pursuit of Happiness*.

---

1 9 3 4

MUSIC + THEATER:	LITERATURE + FILM:	SCIENCE + SOCIETY:	POLITICS:
Paul Hindemith *Mathis der Maler*	Robert Graves *I, Claudius*	Albert Einstein *My Philosophy*	Hitler and Mussolini meet in Venice
Virgil Thomson *Four Saints in Three Acts*	*The Last Millionaire* (film by René Clair)	Marie Curie dies	Austrian Chancellor Dollfuss assassinated by Nazis
Cole Porter *Anything Goes*	*It Happened One Night* (film by Frank Capra)	The Grossglockner Alpine Road (Austria) opened to traffic	U.S. Congress grants Roosevelt additional powers

Weill (in Paris) to Lotte Lenya, 11 January 1934: It was very enjoyable at my parents'. They were terribly happy that I'd come. They're really nice once they are away from the rest of the family. They're quite content and don't complain at all. For a mere 100 marks I had a very attractive winter suit made. In addition, a Carlsbad doctor gave me a bloodletting to cure that rash. It's completely gone from my head and almost all gone from my hands, but there's still some on my body. Now I don't know what actually helped: the diet, the tea, the injections, the ultraviolet rays, the ointment, or the bloodletting. Probably none of it. In any case, I'll stay on the diet, because I notice that it's better for me. I was in Vienna for only a day and a half. When you see the refugees hanging around there, you're really glad you're not one of them. I find it all the more unpleasant because the worst mob of literati has simply clumped together there, which is so totally unproductive. I had made an appointment with [Karl Heinz] Martin, and there they were, all huddling together: [Max] Pallenberg (the most repulsive of the lot), the [Alfred] Polgars, the Martins, [Curt] Bois, and all the other hypocrites. They're complaining and wailing, but they're still far too well off. They all harbor a hatred for Paris, because there's no use for them there. By contrast, thinking about how nice and jovial it was when we were all together in Rome, I realize that we've done the right thing after all. Of course, they all send their regards to you. The nicest of the bunch was [Fritz] Stiedry, who had just come back from Russia. He saw [Georg] Kaiser in Berlin; things are terrible. He's completely at his wits' end and talks only of suicide; Stiedry seriously believes it might end in catastrophe if they don't get him out.

Weill (in Louveciennes) to Lotte Lenya, 25 January 1934: I stayed out here all last week and got a lot of work done. The full score [of the Second Symphony] is two-thirds done. This week I'm busy with some very important negotiations that are almost settled (knock on wood). Here's what they're about: Jacques Deval, the season's most in-demand and most frequently performed French playwright, whose play *Tovarich* is the biggest international theatrical hit of the year, wants to do his new play with me. We want to dramatize his most successful novel, *Marie galante*. An excellent, serious subject: a French peasant girl runs off with a man and ends up somewhere in Panama, but once there she wishes only to go home again; she earns money in a whorehouse, and when she has saved up enough and has already bought her steamship ticket, she dies. If at all possible, the play is supposed to open as soon as May at the most beautiful theater in Paris, the Théâtre Marigny, and then in the fall in London and New York. It looks as if this might be the big international opportunity I've been waiting for.

343. 11 January 1934 letter to Lenya in San Remo, where she was still staying with Otto Pasetti. The date written on the envelope is in Lenya's hand.

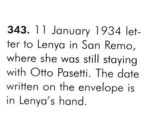

344. With Natasha (Natalie) Paley, a Russian princess who was very close to Marie-Laure de Noailles and later a friend of Cocteau.

345. Robert Vambery, who had been assistant dramaturg at the Theater am Schiffbauerdamm at the premiere of *Die Dreigroschenoper*, wrote the libretto for the operetta *Der Kuhhandel*.

346. Weill began composing *Der Kuhhandel* in early 1934 with the hope of having it performed in Paris or Zurich. This number, "Das Erlebnis im Café," written for the General, was cut from the English version performed in London the following season.

Weill (in Louveciennes) to Lotte Lenya, 20 February 1934: The events in Austria are really terribly depressing for anyone who has some sense of justice left. Animals are more merciful than these people. Politically we have come to a most dangerous turning point. Not since 1914 have we been as close to war as we are now. I for one don't believe that it'll come to that, but the wartime spirit is growing more and more, and those vandals won't rest until they finally have their way.

Weill (in Louveciennes) to Lotte Lenya, 3-6 March 1934: Today was an exciting day. Last night I got a call asking me to wire my address to Marlene [Dietrich], which I did right away, and by this morning there was the following telegram: "Would you be interested in coming here and working with Sternberg and me on a musical film. Time required approximately six months. Wire me whether you want to and whether you can. Everything else taken care of by Paramount. Warmest regards. Marlene." Now you're raising your eyebrows. You're surprised, aren't you? . . . Sternberg and Marlene and six months of work—that doesn't come up often.

Weill (in Louveciennes) to Hans Curjel, 19 April 1934: There are three different plans which have begun to crystallize and which are developing with a slowness that is so typical nowadays—still, they are definitely moving ahead: *Marie galante* with Deval will definitely be done here in October, but I won't be able to write any of it this summer because Deval is in Hollywood (it is quite possible that I'll be there as well). The big plans for a staged oratorio on the Old Testament with which Reinhardt—in contact with me—has occupied himself for some time, are making good progress but will hardly be definite before the end of next season. It's supposed to come out in London in big style. The third plan, which I'm having the most fun with and which also has progressed the furthest, is the operetta which I am writing with Vambery . . . It is an excellent libretto, drawing on the best tradition of operetta, but far removed from Viennese operetta-trash. The structure is complete; I have already set the lyrics for twelve musical numbers, which have turned out brilliantly. The libretto will be finished in May. I'm already in negotiations with a big theater here as well as with Cochran in London. But we would really love to have a German performance before the French and English one.

Weill (in Louveciennes) to Hans Curjel, 23 April 1934: I am enclosing the outline for the operetta. Naturally, the title won't be retained. I ask you to consider this outline as nothing more than what it is meant to be: a basis for my music. Up to now, everything I have composed has caused a sensation wherever I have shown it—especially a very popular "Marching Song" for the General, a barcarolle; a hit, "Auf Wiedersehn"; a song about the great Pharaoh and the "Song of the Cow," with the very beautiful text:

> Ich habe eine Kuh gehabt, [I once owned a cow;
> Ich hab die Kuh nicht mehr, But I don't have it any more.
> Ich hab dafür, Instead—may God help me—
> Gott helfe mir, I have a machine gun now.]
> Jetzt ein Maschinengewehr.

The main characters are: the General (brilliant part for a comedian),

Juanita (a good actress who can sing or a good singer who can act), Juan (lyric tenor), The President (good actor). If you cast the General with a star, [Otto] Wallburg would be an excellent choice, but from another point of view, it could also be done by [Max] Pallenberg, for whom it might be something very different from what he's done up to now. In that case, we could cast Juanita according to our own taste, i.e., probably best with Lenja, who could make something big out of the "Ballade vom Räuber Esteban." Or we could cast Juanita with a star; for that it would be worth considering either a talented operetta singer, preferably Novotna or Lizzie Waldmüller, or a movie star, possibly Renate Müller or Magda Schneider. In this case, I would cast the General according to our own taste, meaning Gretler. One would have to find a young, good-looking tenor with acting talent. Everything else is easy to cast. I could probably make do with an orchestra of seventeen, if I can put the orchestra together my way. I'm writing the chorus parts easy enough, but—as in every decent operetta—one would still need approximately fifteen-twenty people. . . . The great advantage of the piece is that it takes up the best traditions of operetta, which have been buried alive for decades, and represents a very skillful mix of the serious and the gay, the lyric and the dramatic, with great topicality (much more topical than the Third Reich), and all portrayed in a kindly and comical fashion.

Naturally Paris must become my new home. I know that here new battles await me, battles that at home are already old hat but still have to be waged here, and I feel I'll be able to do some good. It's hard, but at the same time, nice to begin anew with such a change of direction. In my heart of hearts I have never left Germany. Interview with Ole Winding in the Danish newspaper *Aften-Avisen*, 21 June 1934.

347. Stopping for gas near Salzburg, where he began work on *Der Weg der Verheißung* in 1934 with Franz Werfel and Max Reinhardt. Photo by Reimann.

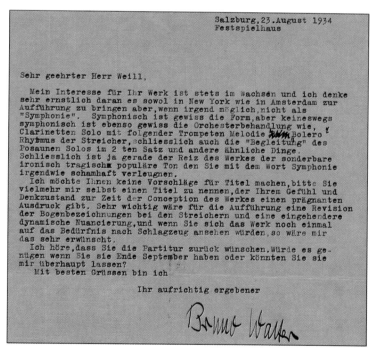

Weill (in Louveciennes) to Lotte Lenya, 16 September 1934: Musically this Bible thing is becoming very beautiful and very rich. It makes me see how far I've developed since *Die Bürgschaft*. It's just as serious, but in expression much stronger, richer, more varied—Mozartian.

Weill (in Louveciennes) to Lotte Lenya, 23 September 1934: [Odette] Florelle is going to play Marie galante. That's a brilliant choice because she's a box-office draw here and will sing the chansons decently (by local standards). Inkijinoff (from *Sturm über Asien*) will play the Japanese man, and for the third lead we want to have Harry Baur. That would be a fantastic cast.

348. In a letter dated 23 August 1934, Bruno Walter requests another title for Weill's Symphony no. 2.

349. From left: Franz Werfel, Max Reinhardt, and Weill at Reinhardt's home, Leopoldskron, in Salzburg, 1934.

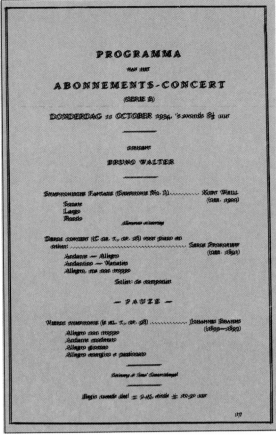

350. Program of the premiere of Weill's Second Symphony, billed as "Symphonische Fantasie," played by the Concertgebouw Orchestra in Amsterdam. Weill attended the premiere and wrote to Lenya, "The rehearsal was wonderful. Walter does it marvelously and everyone is really enthusiastic, especially the *entire orchestra!* It's a good piece and sounds fantastic." (10 October 1934)

Weill (in Louveciennes) to Max Reinhardt, 6 October 1934: Ever since I returned from Salzburg I've been working literally day and night on our project [*Der Weg der Verheißung*] with an enthusiasm I haven't felt for quite some time. I believe (and so does everyone else to whom I've shown some of it) that it's the best music I've written up to now. Most important, I think I've succeeded in solving the technical questions, in that I've been able to create large-scale musical forms—interrupted by spoken dialogue—without changing any text. Thus the whole thing gets the scaffolding it needs, and the danger that it all might melt away (which frequently comes to mind when you read the libretto) is eliminated. . . . I am using original Jewish motifs very sparingly, i.e., only when there's a connection to the liturgy. The Jewish liturgy is rather poor in melodies—it's mostly composed of melodic turns and short motifs, which at times could serve as background to the rabbi's readings. . . . Werfel has sent me all four parts of the work now. I greatly admire what he's done. . . . I'm most pleasantly surprised with the end of the piece. The vision of the Messiah has true greatness in its genuine naïveté and simplicity, and all questions about the work being tendentious have thus been laid to rest, since a light has been shed upon its full meaning. . . . I'm convinced more than ever that it'll be necessary to cast some of the roles with singers, but those singers of great stature that you had in mind. You will hardly find actors able to forget their naturalism and able to act in "elevated" style, whereas singers are accustomed to acting in elevated style, and it will be easier to wean them from their false pathos than actors from their naturalism and false pitches. . . . I think it's essential that we bring a conductor with us, one who understands this kind of musical theater, who can get to work immediately without long discussions, and who will collaborate enthusiastically on the project without thinking of himself. I think Jascha Horenstein, the most talented and committed among the young German conductors and also known in America, is the ideal man for the job.

351. Sheet music cover for individual numbers from *Marie galante*, the ill-fated collaboration with Jacques Deval. In spite of the play's short run, some of the songs became well-known through recordings by Florelle and Lys Gauty.

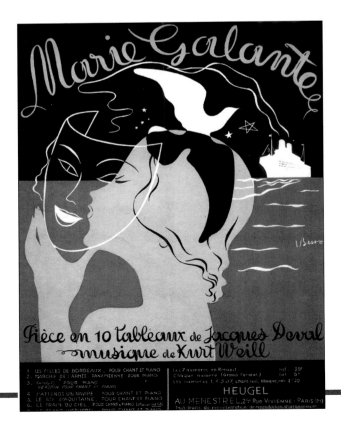

352. Cover of the sheet music for "Complainte de la Seine," published by Heugel. The popular singer Lys Gauty had success with several of Weill's songs.

MARIE GALANTE

Play with music in ten scenes by Jacques Deval,
adapted from his novel of the same name; lyrics by Deval

1934   Paris, Théâtre de Paris (22 December, three-week run)

Edmond Mahieux, conductor; H. Henriot, director; André Lefaur, designer

353. Scene from the original production of *Marie galante*,
with Alcover (as Staub) and Florelle (as Marie).

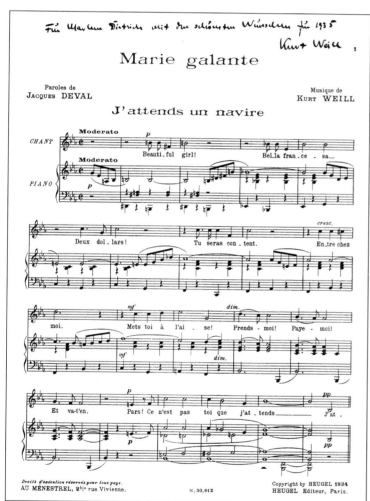

354. Scene 3, in a Panamanian dance hall, features an
on-stage dance band and at least three musical numbers:
"Introduction," "Scène au dancing," and one or two tangos.

355. Weill autographed this copy
of "J'attends un navire" to Marlene
Dietrich in 1935. During World
War II, he learned that this song
had become an anthem of the
French Resistance.

1 9 3 5

MUSIC + THEATER:

George Gershwin *Porgy and Bess*

Charles Ives *The Unanswered Question*
(rev. version)

Maxwell Anderson *Winterset*

LITERATURE + FILM:

John Steinbeck *Tortilla Flat*

Sinclair Lewis *It Can't Happen Here*

Mutiny on the Bounty (film by Frank
Lloyd)

SCIENCE + SOCIETY:

Radar equipment built to detect aircraft

Alcoholics Anonymous organized in
New York City

Committee for Industrial Organization
(CIO) formed

POLITICS:

Hitler revokes citizenship rights of Jews

Roosevelt signs Social Security Act

Italy under Mussolini invades Ethiopia

356. Identity card for 1935-1936 issued by the police prefect of Louveciennes.

357. In Chiddingfold, England, with Connie Lutrell Wollheim and her son Richard, April 1935. Producer Eric Wollheim had taken an interest in *Der Kuhhandel* in 1934, but he did not directly assist in the 1935 London production.

Weill (in Louveciennes) to Maurice Abravanel, 21 January 1935: Meanwhile the whole passion play about *Marie galante* has taken place. Deval revealed himself to be the nastiest pig I have met in my entire life. One after another he has betrayed, lied to, conned anyone who had anything to do with this thing; and on top of it all, without gaining anything for himself. Because the publisher has made him live up to his contractual obligation to write the piece and has pushed through the performance by the Théâtre de Paris, he has systematically sabotaged the performance with maneuvers I never even knew existed. Because of this it was a horrid performance, but the music made a tremendous hit, getting brilliant reviews, in contrast to the play, which was roasted. The success of the music could have swept the whole thing off the ground, but behind my back Deval used every trick in the book to bring it down, and so finally it was canceled after a three-week run. A disgraceful flop.

Walter did a brilliant job with the symphony. He was honestly enthusiastic, conducted it from memory, and rehearsed it fabulously. The orchestra played with a kind of dedication I have never seen with a brand new piece. Big success with the audience—catastrophe in the press ("banal," "worn out," "empty," "Beethoven in the beergarden," etc.). Despite all that, Walter played it again in Rotterdam and The Hague, and then in New York on 13 December. He sent me a telegram: "Big success. Congratulations." After that the reviews arrived: catastrophic—not one friendly word. Apparently this work has

unleashed the experts' opposition to me, which had always been latent before. Until now they always allowed that someone who writes for the theater can write the kind of music which reaches the audience directly, without interference from the experts. But the idea that a concert work can catch on and have an immediate impact on the listener is too hard for them to swallow.

As you see, what's been happening to me in the meantime is not exactly gratifying or encouraging, and it takes a hell of a lot of self-confidence and strength to deal with this kind of *Dreck*. Thank God, my work gives me pure and undisturbed pleasure, and I am convinced that I am on a very good track. The symphony sounds excellent, Walter was ecstatic about my ability to orchestrate only what's essential while being able to retain a full and beautiful sound. By the way, he is really a marvelous guy; we understood each other very well.

The operetta is finished. Right now I am writing both piano-vocal scores at the same time—the one for the Bible and the one for the operetta—the two full scores after that. Tomorrow I am going to London to start a major offensive for the performance of the operetta. It won't be easy to accomplish, because the whole thing is on a very high level—a true comic opera, with two big, colorful, well-constructed finales. If I succeed in bringing out this work, which I believe to be my very best, I will be over the worst. But will anyone allow this? In any case, once you are the *Generalmusikdirektor* of Melbourne, be kind enough to reserve the job of orchestra manager for me.

DER KUHHANDEL / A KINGDOM FOR A COW

Operetta in two acts / Musical play in three acts; German book and lyrics by Robert Vambery, English libretto adapted by Reginald Arkell, lyrics adapted by Desmond Carter

1935   London, Savoy Theatre (28 June; two-week run)
Muir Mathieson, conductor; Ernst Matrai and Felix Weissberger, directors; Hein Heckroth, designer

359. The program cover for *A Kingdom for a Cow* features a drawing by Hein Heckroth. In its transformation for an English music-hall audience, the two-act German operetta became a three-act musical play.

SAVOY THEATRE — STRAND, W.C.2

Licensed by the Lord Chamberlain to ... ... RUPERT D'OYLY CARTE
Proprietors ... ... THE SAVOY THEATRE, Ltd.
Manager ... ... (For Savoy Theatre) ... ... F. C. POOL
Licensees ... ... CHARLES KILLICK and VICTOR PAYNE-JENNINGS

EVENINGS at 8.30 p.m.
MATINEES: TUESDAY and THURSDAY at 2.30

A
KINGDOM
FOR A COW
A Musical Play

Composed by
KURT WEILL

Adapted from the Book and Lyrics of
ROBERT VAMBERY

REGINALD ARKELL (Libretto)   DESMOND CARTER (Lyrics)

Play produced by ERNEST MATRAI and FELIX WEISSBERGER

Decor designed by **H. HECKROTH**

358. Hein Heckroth designed the sets for the London production of *A Kingdom for a Cow* (the English adaptation of *Der Kuhhandel*) in 1935.

360. From the program: a map of the two fictitious Caribbean nations, Ucqua and Santa Maria, whose arms race makes up the plot of *A Kingdom for a Cow*.

361. A souvenir fan, given to customers at performances.

THE PLAYBILL   9

SYNOPSIS OF SCENES

ACT I.

Scene 1. A hilltop in a small town. April, 1917.
          ("How sweetly friendship binds.")
Scene 2. The Tompkins home. Several nights later.
          ("Keep the home fires burning.")
Scene 3. Recruiting Office No. 596,673. The next day.
          ("Your country needs another man—and that means you.")
Scene 4. A camp drill-ground. A week later.
          ("Pack up your troubles in your old kit bag.")

ACT II.

Scene 1. A front-line trench. Several weeks later.
          ("There is one spot forever England.")
          During this scene the stage is darkened to denote the passage of several hours.
Scene 2. A churchyard. An hour later.
          ("If thine enemy hunger—")
Scene 3. The hospital. A week later.
          ("'Tis not so deep as a well—but 'tis enough. 'Twill serve.")
Scene 4. The Chateau de Cent Fontaines, somewhere behind the lines. The same night.
          ("In the multitude of counsellors there is safety.")
Scene 5. The edge of a great battlefield. The same night, just before dawn.
          ("Still stands thine ancient sacrifice.")
Scene 6. No Man's Land.
          ("Dulce et decorum est pro patria mori.")

ACT III.

Scene 1. Superintendent's office, State Hospital. A month later.
          ("Is there no balm in Gilead, is there no physician there?")
Scene 2. The forensic arena in the House of Balm. Ten years later.
          ("Out of the mouth of babes and sucklings.")
Scene 3. A street. Today.
          ("Whither have ye made a road?")

CREDITS
Scenery constructed by William Kellam. Painted by Bergman Studios. Properties by Moe Jacobs.
Hammond Organ used. Lighting equipment by Century Lighting Co. Costumes by Eaves. Furs by
Jaeckel. Bags by Goldsmith Bros. Initials by Monocraft. Shoes for Miss Brand and Miss Miller by
I. Miller.

STAFF FOR THE GROUP THEATRE, INC.
Business Manager .... Philip Adler
Press Representative .... Emanuel Eisenberg
Production Committee .... Stella Adler, Elia Kazan, Sanford Meisner
Stage Manager .... Michael Gordon
Assistant Stage Managers .... Alfred Saxe, Bess Eitingon, Judson Hall
Technical Director .... Isaac Benesch
Master of Properties .... Moe Jacobs
Master Carpenter .... William Kellam
Master Electrician .... George Gebhardt
Audience Manager .... Helen Thompson

For information regarding theatre parties and benefits, communicate with
Helen Thompson at 246 West 44th Street, PEnn. 6-1793.

The Deodorizing Air Purifiers and the Creco Liquid Soap Dispensing System used in this theatre are
manufactured by the Creco Company, Inc.

362. The Savoy Theater opened in 1881 as a home for Gilbert and Sullivan operettas. It was redesigned in art deco style during a 1929 renovation.

363. Alan Bott's review, "A Cow of the Stars," from *The Tatler*, no. 1777, 17 July 1935.

364. In Louveciennes, with his German shepherd Harras.

Weill (in Louveciennes) to Lotte Lenya, 10-11 July 1935: I think of London only as far as you are concerned. Everything else I have to forget first. But I was especially pleased with you again this time; I think you are a grand *Pison* and that your qualities as a human being keep developing parallel to my own, so that (after ten years!) you are still giving me things that no one else can give me, things that are crucial. On my way back I was thinking that we've really solved the question of living together, which is so terribly difficult for us, in a very beautiful and proper way. Don't you think so? I have a very good feeling about England and America as far as you and your work are concerned. We'll make it, won't we?

Weill (in Novi, Yugoslavia) to Lotte Lenya, 26 July 1935: I still haven't gotten over this London flop, and I stay awake at night brooding about it for hours. My only consolation is the Verdi letters, which I'm reading again. The analogies are startling.

365. *A Kingdom for a Cow* was covered in the 5 July 1935 issue of *The Illustrated Sporting and Dramatic News.*

July 5, 1935   THE ILLUSTRATED SPORTING AND DRAMATIC NEWS

"A KINGDOM FOR A COW"

The New Musical Play
at the Savoy

A DANCER OF EXCEPTIONAL GRACE
La Jana (above and right), so easily familiar to many London playgoers for her combination of good dancing and good looks, is one of the most decorative features of "A Kingdom for a Cow"

VILLAGE WOOING: Juan (Webster Booth) with Juanita (Jacqueline Francell) and her attendants in "A Kingdom for a Cow." The music is composed by Kurt Weill, and the libretto has been adapted by Reginald Arkell from the original of Robert Vambery. The story is a satire on armaments and dictators. A review by "Play Bill" is published on page 40

366. In Salzburg, 1935.

Weill (in Salzburg) to Lotte Lenya, [26 August 1935]: We're in the middle of negotiations with Weisgal. . . . If it comes out the way I hope it will, then I'm supposed to sail with Weisgal on the *Majestic* on 4 September. . . . Now we can start thinking about your trip. Naturally it would be great if we could sail together, and I've reserved a double cabin, just in case. . . . Farewell, *Kleene*. I'm looking forward to seeing you. If only you haven't gotten too fresh!

367. Weill and Lenya departed on 4 September 1935 from Cherbourg aboard the SS *Majestic* and arrived six days later in New York Harbor (pictured here). Francesco and Eleonora von Mendelssohn (on the left) and Meyer Weisgal (on the right) traveled on the same boat.

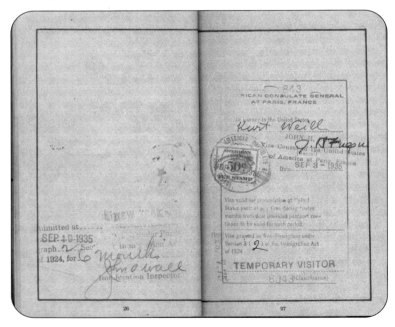

368. Weill enters the U.S. on a temporary, one-year visa.

Weill (in New York) to Max Reinhardt, 27 November 1935: Since you announced yesterday not only the deletion of the Solomon and Temple scenes in their entirety, but also that Moses' big farewell song might be a possibility, I would like, once more, to clarify where I stand on this matter.

From the first day of our collaboration I have, as you know, always stuck to my position that I wouldn't write incidental music, but rather a kind of music in which song—i.e., a new, looser kind of singing—should play a prominent role. Not only has my music been constructed according to this basic principle, but Werfel's book too, the intensity of which consistently leads into the music, so that any deletion of musical climaxes would be tantamount to deleting the climaxes of the work as a whole.

These musical climaxes, in light of your wishes and Werfel's wishes, and after much hard work, have been shaped into thorough and carefully designed musical structures that cannot be tinkered with without completely destroying them. I believe structure not only to be the most essential part of artistic work, but also the most important factor for success; in my own career, when I have allowed my structure to be compromised, I have experienced failure. "The Sacrifice and Redemption of Isaac," "The Farewell Song" and "The Death of Moses," "The Book of Ruth," "The Building of the Temple and Solomon's Consecration of the Temple" and "The Choruses of Jubilation"—all these were artistic forms which have been shaped according to musical and theatrical rules and would be robbed of their effect if one starts cutting them up.

369. Publicity photo taken shortly after Weill and Lenya arrived in the U.S. Photo: Louise Dahl-Wolfe.

Kurt Weill's music suits [Virgil] Thomson's public even better that Thomson's does; it is much more ordinary, and as cunning in detail. The hand-picked public at the Cosmopolitan Club, determined to pull no gaffes for the amusement of Parisian tea-drinkers and relatives (Weill was "made" in Paris by the *Sérénade* ladies), applauded all the numbers with equal fervor. Both the music and Lotte Lenja were worth a more discerning response. Parts of *Mahagonny* are stunning music of the faux-populaire school; on the other hand the new "J'attends un navire" is about rock-bottom in melodic cheapness. . . . Marc Blitzstein, "New York Medley, Winter, 1935," *Modern Music* 13, no. 2 (January–February 1936): 36-7.

"American jazz has influenced modern music undoubtedly," [Weill] answered in careful English that bore the faintest foreign accent, "Rhythmic and harmonic freedom, simplicity of melodic material, directness—saying things as they are—these are the contributions of jazz. . . . I do not mean the jazz of today, but the jazz of the time of the 'St. Louis Blues' and other pieces of that period. Today it is much more complicated and it has been influenced in turn by Debussy, Rimsky-Korsakoff, and so on. I wish to make it clear that modern composers did not go to jazz to borrow its idiom. It was not the actual taking of material. It was an influence you did not feel. Freedom, directness, simplicity, that's what jazz had." R.C.B., "Kurt Weill has Secured Niche of His Own at 35," *New York World Telegram* (21 December 1935).

Weill (in New York) to Mr. Voigt, 7 January 1936: May I repeat again what I told you this morning on the telephone. . . . I would absolutely agree to the performance of the short *Mahagonny* by the League of Composers, with whom I am in the best and most friendly relations.

On the other side, I think we should not give away this version of *Mahagonny* for several performances in connection with a ballet season, for even a short run of this work would be a serious blow to our project of a Broadway performance of the opera *Mahagonny*.

370. The League of Composers welcomed Weill to the U.S. with a concert on 17 December 1935. Neither Weill's music nor Lenya's performance was well received.

371. Throughout the winter of 1935-36, the authors of *The Eternal Road* helped the producers raise money for the production. Here, Weill poses with two unidentified society women. Photo by Paul Parker.

1 9 3 6

MUSIC + THEATER:	LITERATURE + FILM:	SCIENCE + SOCIETY:	POLITICS:
Richard Rodgers *On Your Toes*	Margaret Mitchell *Gone With the Wind*	J. M. Keynes *General Theory of Employment, Interest, and Money*	Spanish Civil War begins
Samuel Barber *Symphony No. 1*	Dylan Thomas *Twenty-five Poems*	Hoover Dam completed	Mussolini and Hitler proclaim Berlin-Rome Axis
Robert E. Sherwood *Idiot's Delight*	*Modern Times* (film by Charlie Chaplin)	Olympic Games held in Berlin, Jesse Owens wins four gold medals	Anti-Comintern pact signed by Germany and Japan

372. The libretto of *The Eternal Road*, translated into English by Ludwig Lewisohn, was published by Viking in 1936.

FRANZ WERFEL

Author of

MAX REINHARDT'S

First American Stage
Production in English

''THE
ETERNAL
ROAD''

A New Play With
Music by Kurt Weill

PRESENTED BY
MEYER W. WEISGAL

◆ ◆

NEW MANHATTAN
OPERA HOUSE
Eighth Avenue at 34th Street

WORLD PREMIERE
JANUARY 1936

373. A promotional bookmark advertises the opening of *The Eternal Road* in January 1936, but after delays the production went bankrupt in February and the premiere was postponed indefinitely. Reinhardt went to Hollywood and Werfel returned to Vienna. Weill started developing other projects.

Weill (in New York) to Heugel, 31 January 1936: The rehearsals are practically finished and in two weeks the piece could be ready for performances. But it seems that the theater management is in financial difficulties, which will have to be overcome before the show can go on. The reconstruction of the theater has cost much more than had been anticipated. They have already spent more than $250,000, and the backers of the show have refused to give more money before a definite budget has been established. They are preparing such a budget and have found out that they will need another $200,000. Over here, the sum of $450,000 is perfectly normal for such a huge spectacle, especially in case of a complete reconstruction of the theater. But it isn't easy to find that kind of money. . . . They have stopped working for ten days in order not to run up unnecessary expenses and to give Mr. Weisgal a chance to straighten out the financial situation. . . . I now have a little time to occupy myself with new theater projects through my American friends. There is a very good chance of having a show opening here next season. I'm in discussions with Ben Hecht and Charles MacArthur. These are the famous authors of *Jumbo*, which is New York's biggest theatrical success. They want to do a musical with me, and we're in the process of finding a subject. I'm also having discussions with the Group Theatre, the youngest and most modern theater in New York. They are also very interested in me. Finally, I'm having discussions with two film studios in Hollywood (Metro-Goldwyn-Mayer and Paramount). I've proposed that they sign me for three films.

It would be marvelous if Yvonne Printemps would do *Marie galante*. I'm sure it would be a great success and I would certainly come to Paris if this should materialize.

374. An article in the 20 February 1936 issue of the *New York Herald Tribune* paraphrases Weill's explanation of how the prerecorded orchestral accompaniment for *The Eternal Road* will be played "from an ultra-violet recording, and will be broadcast from amplifiers hidden in the proscenium arch, in the walls, and in the back of the theater to produce a more complete illusion of reality in sound." Five months earlier, Weill consulted with Leopold Stokowski about the feasibility of this experiment.

Films Test Sound Device To End Fuzzy High Notes

Use Ultra-Violet Light in Recording, Instead of White Ray

A new method of recording sound for motion pictures, which eliminates the fuzziness of high-pitched and sibilant sounds by using ultra-violet light instead of ordinary white light, was demonstrated for the first time yesterday by the Radio Corporation of America at its sound studio at 411 Fifth Avenue. The demonstration, arranged for motion picture producers in the afternoon, was followed by a technical report on the new development delivered by Glenn L. Dimmick, R. C. A. sound engineer who helped to perfect the new device, before the Society of Motion Picture Engineers at its monthly meeting last night at the same address.

The lisping and hissing effects of many motion picture actors will be eliminated by the new method of recording, officials of the company asserted. The blurring or distortion on the sound track of the upper frequency tones recorded by ordinary light have been eliminated, they explained, by the sharper delineation on the negative emulsion of light rays restricted to the narrow band in the ultra-violet range.

One of the selections used for yesterday's demonstration was an explanation of the new method given without pictorial accompaniment from a screen by Kurt Weill, exiled German musician who has written the score for the forthcoming production by Max Reinhardt of "The Eternal Road." The production, he said, when it opens in New York, will have no orchestra in the theater. The music will be played instead, he said, from an ultra-violet recording, and will be broadcast from amplifiers hidden in the proscenium arch, in the walls and in the back of the theater to produce a more complete illusion of reality in sound.

375. One of Weill's first publicity photographs taken in New York, autographed to songwriter Ann Ronell.

376. Paul Green. Cheryl Crawford, a theater producer and one of the founders of the Group Theatre, encouraged a collaboration between Weill and Green, who had won a Pulitzer Prize in 1927 for his play *In Abraham's Bosom*. Photo by W. Moulton.

377. A page from Paul Green's notes for *Johnny Johnson* contains ideas for the ending.

Weill (in Chapel Hill, North Carolina) to Lotte Lenya, [3 May 1936]: It's wonderful here. I'm a completely different person when I'm away from the city. I slept quite well on the train; looking out the window this morning, I found myself in the midst of a really green summer landscape with a fragrance reminiscent of the south of France: the heat combined with the flowers. . . . America's oldest university is here. The whole place looks very English; you can see green trees and meadows from every window. I have a charming room with a shower, and I'm living the high life. This peace is heavenly. You see only young people here, and you realize for the first time what America is really like and how unimportant New York is for this country. Paul Green makes a very good impression: refreshing, young, easy-going, almost like Zuckmayer. I think he's going to be a good man for me. We've already worked very well all afternoon and evening.

Weill (in New York) to Heugel, 4 June 1936: It is with the greatest regret that our [publishing] collaboration is finished, at least for the time being. This collaboration has always been one of great joy for me, since at all times I have felt that you had confidence in me and my work. Therefore I don't have any doubts that one day—and I hope soon—we will be able to continue our very friendly relationship. Right now I am trying to create a place for myself in American theatrical life. That will be very difficult, and I will need all of my patience and all of my energy. Once I have found my place over here, I will be able to return to the kind of work which corresponds to my talents and ambition, and that would be the time to offer you operatic works of international caliber, which, I am sure, would be of interest to you.

I will make every effort to find performances for the works which I have written for you over here. The outlook for *Eternal Road* is not bad. An excellent Broadway producer, Mr. Crosby Gaige, has taken the whole matter into his hands. He is very optimistic about finding the money for a fall production and believes that it will be a great success.

378. Marc Blitzstein inquires if Weill would like to have *Die sieben Todsünden* performed in a small series of chamber operas, 22 June 1936.

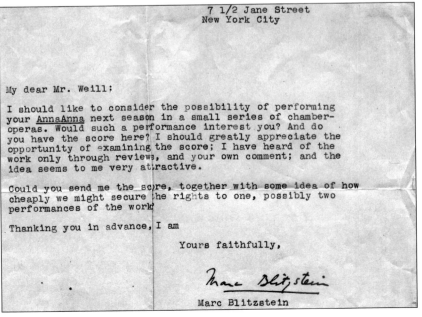

7 1/2 Jane Street
New York City

My dear Mr. Weill:

I should like to consider the possibility of performing your AnnaAnna next season in a small series of chamber-operas. Would such a performance interest you? And do you have the score here? I should greatly appreciate the opportunity of examining the score; I have heard of the work only through reviews, and your own comment; and the idea seems to me very attractive.

Could you send me the score, together with some idea of how cheaply we might secure the rights to one, possibly two performances of the work?

Thanking you in advance, I am

Yours faithfully,

Marc Blitzstein

Marc Blitzstein

Weill (in Nichols, Connecticut) to Erika Neher, 28 July 1936: For days I've been carrying those two dreadful letters of yours around with me. I knew immediately how I should respond, I'm afraid—after all, this will have a profound impact on my life. . . . But could I have offered you anything that might have kept you? A vagabond, pursued by bad luck, involved in eternal struggles against injustice, without a home and without rights. . . . You have forgotten what I have said and written to you a thousand times: that you are the only human being capable of making me happy and content, that for me there is not and never will be any good fortune other than the one I have found in you. . . . All that is left to me is cutting out the part of my life called love, feeling, tenderness, happiness, and trying to carry on without any of that. This has happened to others before me, and they have been able to survive. . . . Please, my dearest, do everything necessary in order to keep yourself happy and calm and then it will again be beautiful between us—even if in quite a different way.

380. The three directors of the Group Theatre: Cheryl Crawford, Lee Strasberg, and Harold Clurman. Photo by Ralph Steiner.

379. When faced with working on *Johnny Johnson* with the actors in the Group Theatre, Weill realized that he had to teach them how to sing. To prepare them, he gave a lecture in which he addressed the question, "what is musical theater?" These notes, prepared in advance of the lecture, provide a number of insights into Weill's opinions about his career and what he was trying to achieve at different steps along the way. He also distinguishes singing in the theater from opera singing (or, "music as opiate") and discusses the function of music in a theater piece.

```
                                    August 12, 1936


    Dear Meyer,

          I am deeply disgusted about what happened last night.
Never in my life I had to go through such a degradation, such a
prostitution of my art. This is entirely your fault. You
continue your method of bluffing, you put people in the most
embarrassing situations and you don't even know how you hurt the
feelings of an artist who has made every sacrifice to bring about
this show.

          I don't want to be connected in any way with these
methods. I would rather drop the whole "Eternal Road" than to
have dragged my name again through all this mess. This evening,
which had been arranged for Mr. Keo to hear my music and which
turned into the most terrible humiliation for me, makes me feel
that your eagerness to put through this "business", makes you
entirely forget the "ethical" background of this enterprise and
its artistic value.

          After this new experience I have to insist that the
most important point of the whole enterprise has to be cleared
up: Who is the producer of this show? Who has the right to offer
parts to persond who are absolutely unfit, and to discuss with
them changes of the play and of the music? Without a clear and
definite solution of this question I am convinced that - in spite
of all your efforts - the fate of the show will be the same or
worse than in the last season.

                                    Sincerely yours,
```

Weill (in Nichols, Connecticut) to Franz Werfel, 3 August 1936: The longer I am here, and the more I get to know this country, the better I like it—and there is not much to draw one back to Europe these days.

I saw Reinhardt in New York on his way to Europe. I hadn't heard anything about *The Eternal Road* for several months, except that Weisgal hadn't given up his attempts to rescue the whole thing (when anyone else in his position would have). Weisgal gave Reinhardt and me a report on what he had achieved, in the presence of a very well-known and sought-after lawyer (Louis Nizer), who made an extremely positive impression on both Reinhardt and me. Weisgal actually achieved the impossible and organized the whole thing in a completely new way, wiped out all the misdeeds of the old partnership, and got a new partnership with new money and new financing up on its feet. . . . There are three things, from my point of view, that still need to be taken care of: 1) The question of dates, which rests with Reinhardt alone. . . . 2) Reinhardt has to insist that Geddes make changes necessary for the success of the show, including a permanent synagogue, simpler sets which are easier to change, and better costumes. . . . 3) I believe that we still need to do some work on the piece itself. I have lived here almost one

381. An angry letter to Meyer Weisgal, probably in response to a fundraising event to attract more backers for *The Eternal Road*.

Excerpt from

THE ALCHEMY OF MUSIC
BY KURT WEILL

One of the most difficult form problems of contemporary playwrights is the balancing of the opposed values of humor and tragedy without having one destroy the other. I have seen numerous plays where I was unable to rise sympathetically to the dramatic climaxes of the story because the previous humorous scenes had not prepared me for them at all. In a musical play the author can mingle these elements with far greater freedom; his comic scenes can be more comic, his tragic more tragic, since music creates the balance.

The final scene in Mozart's *Don Juan* is the classic instance of how a single scene can change from the most abandoned gaiety into the most appalling horror with only one chord. All experiments in musical theater have unanswerably proven that true theater music is a great driving force, that it can lead a scene to its climax with unparalleled speed and directness, that it can establish the atmosphere of a scene instantaneously, where the playwright so often needs great stretches of dialogue. Music can do what the greatest performer can do at the height of his playing; it can win over the spectator with passion, it can create an exalted mood, which makes the poet's fantasy so much easier to follow and accept.

It would be wrong to conclude that the form of musical theater which we are here considering could be brought into existence by turning out some incidental music and then leaning back, or by using music as a marginal sensual stimulant. A play must be conceived from the very beginning as a musical play, if the demands of musical theater are to be at all fulfilled; the form of the play must be created from the musical point of view; the action of the musical play must be more pliable than that of sheer drama, so that lyrics can be planted; the suspense is created not so much through the progress of the action as through the dynamics of the epic tale; and psychology, which has been such an intrinsic feature of drama during recent decades, is replaced by simple, human, universal elements.

The aim and meaning of musical theater is the binding of speech and music, the most thoroughgoing fusion of the two. Only when speech and music truly combine in song can one speak of musical theater. Song is not a simple interruption of action, which could proceed very well without it. It is an indispensable aid to comprehension of the play and its nature; it projects the actions of the play to a different and higher level; over a stretch of scenes it provides a commentary on the action from a human, universal point of view; it lifts the characters out of the frame of the play and makes them express, directly or indirectly, the philosophy of the author. The power of music makes it possible to extend the movement of a word and its operation so that the values of speech find their complement in the values of music.

The common task of poet and composer is to see to it that the song is not inserted into the text as a number, but that it rises naturally and inevitably out of the scene and that it sinks back just as unobtrusively. Thus, in the ideal musical theater, the dialogue has a musical quality even when there is no actual music, so that the transition can be entirely simple and unforced when the actor switches from speech to song. Of course it is never singing in the sense of pure singing art, like opera. The actor sings with his natural voice, the voice he would use to give speech its highest intensity. This makes it imperative for the composer to produce a clear, simple melodic line so that the performer will not be faced with any unnatural burdens. But in general I have found (and my collaboration with the Group Theatre has sharply confirmed it) that actors work with great excitement and devotion on musical problems, and that they are astonishingly musical, and that one can impose greater musical difficulties upon them than anyone imagines.

Once song has been acknowledged as an exalted medium of expression and as an intrinsic feature of dramaturgy, we begin to glimpse infinite possibilities for its use in solos, in small groups, and in a chorus. One can cover (as I did with Max Reinhardt for *The Eternal Road*) all the middle tones of the scale from pure speech to song-speech, recitative, half-singing, and even pure singing. And with the aid of music one can enter the realm of fantasy and give speech to "superhuman" qualities which can only be referred to in the realistic theater. This occurs twice in *Johnny Johnson*: when song is understood as coming from a statue and then from a machine.

But all this is possible only on the basis of intimate collaboration between author and composer from the day the play is conceived to the night it achieves its first performance, so that the composer cannot content himself with the creation of music, but assists in the construction of every scene of the action, to the point where his music becomes an integral part of the whole. *Stage* (November 1936): 63-4.

year and have studied American theater and its audience meticulously, and after all that I have seen and learned, I believe we should do everything to make the synagogue scene into a unified, compelling plot that begins in the first scene and carries through the whole piece to the end, and which holds the biblical scenes together better than it does now.

Alma Maria Werfel (in Vienna) to Weill, 20 August 1936: Werfel sends many thanks for your letter. It's too bad that you haven't come to Europe, although *I too* would prefer living over there to living over here.

Werfel is not in favor of building up the synagogue scene. He thinks this could easily turn into a potboiler with musical hits from the Bible inserted here and there. Even if the producers are not capable of artistic integrity, it is our obligation to retain it. The ordinary Jewish audiences of New York would probably react positively to a popular treatment, but that sort of plot would definitely overwhelm the essence and the purpose of the whole: the Bible.

Up to now *I* always had the feeling that there were too many Galician-Jewish elements. This synagogue action has to take a back seat, so that the real poetry and the music will retain the purity with which they have been conceived.

JOHNNY JOHNSON

Musical play in three acts; book and lyrics by Paul Green

1936   New York, Forty-Fourth Street Theatre (19 November; 68 performances)

Lehman Engel, conductor; Lee Strasberg, director; Donald Oenslager, set designer; Paul DuPont, costume designer

1937   Cleveland, Play House (10 March, with reduced score)
Federal Theatre Project productions in Los Angeles, Boston, and New Orleans
Chapel Hill, Carolina Playmakers (29 October)

382. Program for the premiere of *Johnny Johnson* with a list of scenes.

According to the Group, which is producing *Johnny Johnson* at the Forty-Fourth Street Theater, the piece in question is a "legend." That phrase will serve well enough in its place on the program, but it will hardly do to describe the curious fantasy, half musical and half dramatic, which Paul Green and Kurt Weil [*sic*] have concocted between them. The matter is as serious as possible, the manner often so broad as almost to suggest vaudeville or a revue, and yet the whole is somehow strangely effective. I am, in general, no great partisan of the experimental techniques, but *Johnny Johnson* is both amusing enough and moving enough to justify itself very handsomely indeed.

The hero is a sort of fool of God, an innocent young man who finally gets into the Great War because he believes it to be really a war to end war, and then baffles everyone from the drill sergeant into whose hands he falls first to the high command itself because he is too simple and too good to be understood by any person even normally complex or normally corrupt. Finally, he is sent to a hospital for mental cases, and there, in what is perhaps the best scene of all, a psychiatrist diagnoses the case. Johnny is suffering from a rare disorder—the St. Francis complex. Joseph Wood Krutch, "Fool of God," *The Nation* (5 December 1936): 674-76.

No. 13 - Song of the Guns

383. *Johnny Johnson*, Act II, scene 1. In the "Song of the Guns," the cannons (voiced by the men's chorus) sing to the sleeping soldiers. Weill explained his intentions for the scene in an interview. "My idea was this: instead of doing what most composers would do—make the music grim and stark, with timpani and such devices—I wanted it to be seducing, almost sweet, as if sung perhaps by prostitutes. For cannons are like prostitutes; their metal could have been used to better purposes, and moreover they do anybody's bidding, right or wrong. They say to the soldiers: 'you sleep, we do the work for you.' The music should [be] almost a lullaby." ("Composer of the Hour: An Interview With Kurt Weill," *Brooklyn Daily Eagle*, 20 December 1936.)

385. Minny Belle Tompkins (Phoebe Brand) and Johnny Johnson (Russell Collins).

384. Lyrics to "Song of the Guns," as they were published in *Out of the South*, a collection of Paul Green's plays (New York: Harper, 1939). The piano-vocal score was published by Samuel French in 1940.

386. The French Nurse (Paula Miller, behind the bed) sang "Mon ami, my friend" in Act II, scene 4.

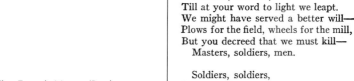

Soldiers, soldiers—
Sleep softly now beneath the sky,
 Soldiers, soldiers—
Tomorrow under earth you lie.
We are the guns that you have meant
For blood and death.—Our strength is spent
Obedient to your stern intent—
 Soldiers, masters, men.

Masters, masters,
Deep dark in earth as iron we slept,
 Masters, masters,
Till at your word to light we leapt.
We might have served a better will—
Plows for the field, wheels for the mill,
But you decreed that we must kill—
 Masters, soldiers, men.

Soldiers, soldiers,
Sleep darkly now beneath the sky,
 Soldiers, soldiers,
No sound shall wake you where you lie,
No foe disturb your quiet bed
Where we stand watching overhead—
We are your tools—and you the dead!—
 Soldiers, masters, men!

Weill (in New York) to Max Dreyfus of Chappell Music, 20 December 1936:

I cannot quite understand the way things are going with my music for *Johnny Johnson*. Maybe it is the difference between American and European music business which makes the whole thing so difficult to understand for me, and I would be glad if you could explain it to me.

Here is a musical play running in its fifth week, with growing success, after an excellent, partly sensational reception. The music was better received by critics and audience than any music on Broadway this season. The audience simply loves the show. There are between eight and twelve curtains every night, and people are humming the music in leaving the theater (which is, I think, internationally the best test for the success of a music).

And yet it seems not possible to have these songs sung over the radio, played in dance orchestras, in nightclubs, on records etc. I admit that we had difficulties in the beginning because we did not have the right material. But now Edward Heyman has written a very good commercial lyric for the most popular tune of the show—and yet there is not the least sign of a real activity on the part of Chappell. There are numbers of important dance bands in town who did not get the orchestration of "To Love You and to Lose You." Musicians, singers, radio stations, record firms don't even know the existence of this song. We (i.e., the Group Theatre and myself) got interested the WNEW sender [radio station], we also got a few band leaders to see the show and they are very enthusiastic about the music. That's how Leo Reisman and Benny Goodman are going to play the music. But a young band leader, whom I know, called up Chappell on Friday and asked for *Johnny Johnson* music. He got the answer: "We are not pushing this show, but we have a couple of other hits, why don't you play those?" Frankly, things of this kind never happened to me before.

387. The Adelphi Debating Society scene in the mental hospital (Act III, scene 2) contains "Asylum Chorus" and "Hymn to Peace."

388. An advertising flyer for *Johnny Johnson*.

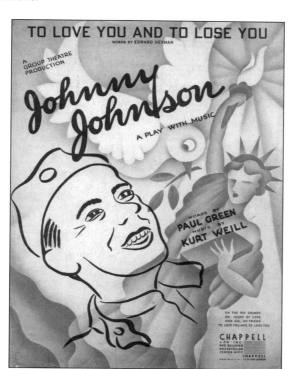

389. Cover of one of the four numbers from *Johnny Johnson* printed as sheet music. Originally titled "Johnny's Song," this number was given new lyrics by Edward Heyman in an effort to reach a wider market.

"The best play of the season.

A great many plays have been written against war since the big dirty business in France and this is the jolliest, the gentlest, the friskiest. It even has songs, sweet smiling songs. There are scenes in it funnier, much funnier, than the Marx Brothers or Bobby Clark or Jimmy Durante. You will want to see it. It is a play you cannot help but be fond of."
—ARTHUR POLLOCK
Brooklyn Daily Eagle

JOHNNY JOHNSON

A GROUP THEATRE PRODUCTION
PLAY BY PAUL GREEN • MUSIC BY KURT WEILL

"The Group's most ambitious production—a marriage of musical comedy and picaresque story telling. They have done an extraordinary job of dramatic expression. A sincere and generally exalting attempt to put on the stage an imaginative portrait of recent history. People who believe that plays should be written about intelligent themes have something to be thankful for. *Johnny Johnson* is an original and deeply moving piece of work."
—BROOKS ATKINSON
N. Y. Times

"A hilarious medley of satire, musical comedy, melodrama, farce, social polemic and parable. A delectable score by that brilliant German exile, Kurt Weill. It is to the eternal credit of *Johnny Johnson* that in its high moments it has a way of recalling to you the quality of Charlie Chaplin's greatest comedy *Shoulder Arms*."
—RICHARD WATTS
N. Y. Herald Tribune

44TH ST. THEATRE
West of Broadway
Telephone: LAckawanna 4-4337
Eves. 8:40. Prices 55c to $2.75. Mats. 55c to $2.20

390. Weill in 1936. This photo was used in the souvenir program of *The Eternal Road*.

391. With conductor Isaac van Grove at a rehearsal for *The Eternal Road*.

392. Caricature by B.F. Dolbin of the authors, Werfel and Weill, flanking director Max Reinhardt.

Score for THE ETERNAL ROAD

"Setting to work, in the fall of 1934, I proceeded to put down all the Hebraic melodies I had learned from childhood on. I had an abundance of material. For my father, who is a cantor and composer, had set great store upon my learning this heritage. With about 200 songs, which I had written in several days' memory seeking, I began work at the Bibliothèque Nationale to trace their sources as far as possible.

Many I discovered had been written in the eighteenth and nineteenth centuries, some borrowed from the most surprising sources—from opera, 'hit-songs' of the time, street tunes, concert music, symphonies. Those I dismissed, retaining only the traditional music. With that as my guide, I attempted to create music that would communicate naturally and inevitably the stories of the Old Testament." *New York Times,* 27 December 1936.

393. These excerpts from Weill's final rehearsal score for *Der Weg der Verheißung*, in four acts, which he completed before coming to America, show a sample of the Rabbi's recitative (from the beginning of Act II, "Moses in Egypt") and the main theme for the double chorus "Das ist ein Gott," featured in the Dance around the Golden Calf (also in Act II). The English translation for *The Eternal Road* has been inserted in an unknown hand.

THE ETERNAL ROAD

Biblical drama in three parts by Franz Werfel;
American version by Ludwig Lewisohn with
additional lyrics by Charles Alan

1937   New York, Manhattan Opera House
        (7 January; 153 performances)

*Isaac van Grove, conductor; Max Reinhardt,
director; Benjamin Zemach, choreographer;
Norman Bel Geddes, designer*

394. This page from the souvenir program and a sketch by Harry Horner illustrate the construction of the expansive, five-level set by Norman Bel Geddes. The set appropriated the orchestra pit for the staging of the synagogue scenes, thus requiring the score to be prerecorded using a new sound-on-film process developed by RCA. A small ensemble of musicians located in a remote room played the musical numbers added to the score after the recordings were made. The sound from the live ensemble was apparently played back electronically in the theater so that it sounded to the audience just like the prerecorded parts. The small band may have also satisfied a musicians' union requirement for the use of live musicians.

THE ETERNAL ROAD

In Construction

To the theatrical genius of Max Reinhardt has been added a vast engineering and construction project to install one of the world's largest stages and the most advanced technical equipment in the Manhattan Opera House. On these two pages are photos of various sections of the stage and several scenes of the preparation of costumes and properties for the production. In the lower right corner of this page are Norman Bel Geddes, the noted stage designer, Professor Reinhardt, and Franz Werfel, author of "The Eternal Road," surveying the progress of the reconstruction of the theatre. The sketch at the left is by Harry Horner, art adviser to Mr. Reinhardt.

395. Some time before the premiere Reinhardt decided to cut the fourth act. The program shows the final arrangement of scenes in three acts and the extensive cast.

396. *The Eternal Road.* In the opening musical scene of Act I, Abraham (Thomas Chalmers) makes a covenant with God, accompanied by the heavenly host.

397. Next page: in Act II of *The Eternal Road*, Moses (Samuel Goldenberg) kills the Egyptian taskmaster (Raymond Miller).

398. In Act II, the Alien Girl (Elene Lynn) and Jesse (Herbert Rudley) embrace in the synagogue while the Rabbi (Myron Taylor) looks on.

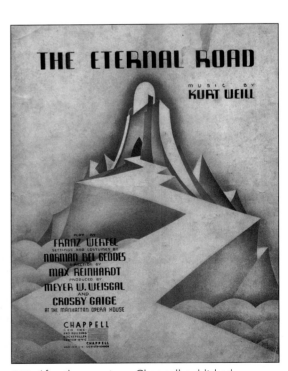

399. This photo depicts the final march out of the synagogue, initially conceived by the authors as the finale of Act IV. Photo: Lucas-Pritchard.

"The Eternal Road" Is Staggering

Greatest of Reinhardt Spectacles in the Greatest of Bel Geddes Settings

"The Eternal Road," Biblical spectacle, by Franz Werfel, adapted by Ludwig Lewisohn; music by Kurt Weil; setting by Norman Bel Geddes. Produced by Meyer W. Weisgal and Crosby Gaige at the Manhattan Opera House, New York, Jan. 7, 1937.

★ ★ ★ ★

PRINCIPALS:

Adversary ————Sam Jaffe	Ruth ————Katherine Carrington
Bath-Sheba ————Rosamond Pinchot	Miriam ————Lotte Lenja
Abraham ————Thomas Chalmers	Sarah ————Bertha Kunz-Baker
Hananiah ————Joseph Macaulay	King David ————Earl Wetherford
Rabbi ————Myron Taylor	Jacob ————Ralph Jamison
Timid Soul ————Mark Schweid	Premiere Danseuse ————Florence Meyer
Musa ————Samuel Goldenberg	Rachel ————Sarah Halvey

By BURNS MANTLE.

I have a feeling that "The Eternal Road," which was finally revealed at the Manhattan Opera House last night, epitomizes the peak of several distinguished careers.

It certainly must be physically the most staggering of all the Max Reinhardt spectacles. In magnitude it is two "Miracles," a "Midsummer Night's Dream," a "Tales of Hoffman" and a "Danton's Tod" rolled into one enormous panorama.

It must also bring to actual visualization practically all the Norman Bel Geddes dreams of platform stages and seemingly limitless vistas made possible in one location surrounded by four walls and capped by a roof.

For Franz Werfel, who did the original text, it probably represents the height of one ambition or another, and for Kurt Weil, who composed the incidental score, it must stand as the most expansive of his musical creations to date.

Max Reinhardt
He passes another miracle.

World's Greatest.

It is, so far as we may believe the record, an achievement beyond comparison with any that has previously been realized in a world that has rather gloried in the competition of sheer magnitude and visual impressiveness.

Stories that the Manhattan Opera House was being practically rebuilt to house this particular spectacle were accepted as a part of an elaborate ballyhoo. Now they may be repeated as demonstrated fact.

Being doubtful you will have a chance to verify the truth of these statements between now and mid-Summer.

I have no idea just how long "The Eternal Road" will run, but I should say at least a million Jews and half a million Gentiles will want to see it at least once.

As for the Werfel-Lewisohn text, that would seem to be a simple rendering of the Old Testament legends into straightforward prose without striving for literary flourishes or poetic flights. In narrative this is the retelling of the trials and triumphs, of the persecutions and prophecies that have alternately exalted and depressed the Jewish people from the birth of Abraham to the troubled present.

Story of the Scroll.

It is a reading of the sacred scroll in a synagogue illustrated by a March of Time duplication of the principal episodes of Old Testament history on stages that stretch to either side, as well as above and below, the Manhattan stage.

Or what was the Manhattan stage before Mr. Geddes tore it asunder and put a mountain there. A mountain that leads straight up to the portals of Heaven itself and reveals a choir of angels singing; it may be, on some distant roof, but within St. Peter's gates so far as this impressed spectator is concerned.

On this mountain side, which is rolling and earth-colored and soft to the tread, like unto no other stage mountain you have ever had foisted upon your too receptive imagination, nomad bands pitch their tents and Joseph, doing well by himself in Egypt, stages a dinner attended by dancing servitors.

Wheat fields grow up in the dark, are bathed in a blinding sun in the morning and disappear in the dark of the night following. The enslaved Israelites bend be-

neath the whips of their Egyptian masters and pass building stone from hand to hand from the depths that were once an orchestra pit to a building site that might be the other side of Ninth Ave.

Last of Spectacle.

It is all tremendously effective. Though I saw but little more than half of it, last night, that was enough to convince me that we never have seen its like before, nor are likely to see it again. At half a million dollars a spectacle, "The Eternal Road" is quite likely to be a spectacle to end spectacles. Promoters of the Meyer Weisgal capacity arise not oftener than once every generation or so. He is the money-raising genius who has given three years to this amazing enterprise.

There is no time for detailed report. Reinhardt has never, so far as we have seen his work, handled crowds with such clarity of movement and impressiveness of grouping. Nor kept his central theme moving more comprehendingly.

Much of the text is intoned, some of it is sung. The ensembles are agreeably soft and illuminative without ever forcing a consciousness of crashing effects upon you. Incidental songs are gentle and melodious.

Principals are admirably chosen, both for voice and type. But these meld so completely into the picture that few individuals stand out.

401. Burns Mantle's review of *The Eternal Road* from the New York *Daily News*, 8 January 1937.

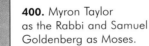

400. Myron Taylor as the Rabbi and Samuel Goldenberg as Moses.

THE ETERNAL ROAD

MUSIC BY
KURT WEILL

PLAY BY
FRANZ WERFEL
SETTINGS AND COSTUMES BY
NORMAN BEL GEDDES
DIRECTION BY
MAX REINHARDT
PRODUCED BY
MEYER W. WEISGAL
AND
CROSBY GAIGE
AT THE MANHATTAN OPERA HOUSE

CHAPPELL
CO INC
RKO BUILDING
ROCKEFELLER
CENTER N Y C

CHAPPELL

402. After the premiere, Chappell published simplified arrangements of six songs from *The Eternal Road*: "Promise," "Song of Miriam," "The Dance of the Golden Calf," "Song of Ruth," "David's Psalm," "The March of Zion." Weill dedicated the publication to his father.

Ralph Austrian of RCA (in New York) to Meyer Weisgal, 11 January 1937: Now that *The Eternal Road* has opened and is well under way, there are a few points in connection with the handling of the sound film that I would like to call to your attention. It is most necessary that these suggestions be followed closely in order that any breakdown in the sound shall be avoided.

1. At the conclusion of each performance the reels of film should not be rewound but they should be placed immediately in fireproof and dust proof containers and stored in a safe, cool place until an hour before the next performance, at which time they should be rewound and while rewinding, they can be cleaned and each patch carefully inspected to see that it is good shape and in no danger of opening at the next showing. Your operators have been instructed as to this procedure.

2. At all times when the film machines are not in use, they should be completely and carefully covered with dust proof, moisture proof covers.

3. The film machines should be constantly inspected to make sure that they are free from dust and dirt.

4. It is recommended that if it has not already been done that the floor of the generator room and the film machine room be painted with a rubberized paint, and at all times this floor should be kept free from dust.

5. With good care and careful handling, the two prints with which we have supplied you should run quietly for at least four weeks each. When you desire new prints made up from the negative, we ask that you give us at least one week's notice as all these prints must be made with infinite care and precision.

6. It is suggested that immediately prior to curtain time that the film machines which are selected for use at that particular performance, be run without film for at least five minutes so that they may be thoroughly warmed and lubricated. The amplifier racks should be lit at least five minutes before each performance.

403. Two days after the premiere of *The Eternal Road*, Weill presented a lecture-discussion at the International Ladies' Garment Workers' Union. (This group commissioned *Pins and Needles* from Harold Rome; the show opened in November 1937.)

Weill (in New York) to Hanns and Rita Weill, 15 January 1937: Many thanks for your telegram, which made me terribly happy. The success of the play [*The Eternal Road*] is really extraordinary, only the box office so far is not what we had expected after those reviews, and the show's weekly running expenses are outrageous. But we hope it will pull through—even financially.

In any case, it's wonderful for me, since I now have a big name here and I can finally start to improve my sadly deranged finances a little bit. That's why I've accepted an offer to do a movie [*The River Is Blue*], and I'm going to Hollywood for 8-10 weeks at the end of next week. Lenja will stay here for as long as she's performing [in *The Eternal Road*]. Of course, I'm very much looking forward to this trip and the new surroundings, although in my present condition I can hardly imagine how I'm supposed to start working on something new. But I hope that before the actual work starts I can recuperate somewhat in the lovely climate out there.

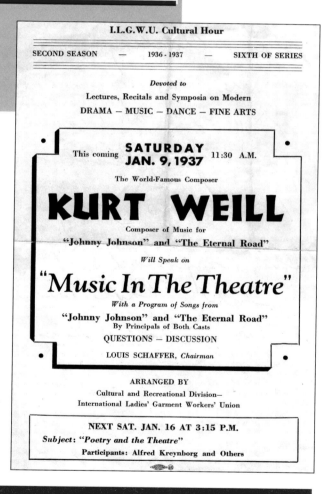

I.L.G.W.U. Cultural Hour

SECOND SEASON — 1936 - 1937 — SIXTH OF SERIES

Devoted to
Lectures, Recitals and Symposia on Modern
DRAMA — MUSIC — DANCE — FINE ARTS

This coming **SATURDAY JAN. 9, 1937** 11:30 A.M.

The World-Famous Composer

KURT WEILL

Composer of Music for
"Johnny Johnson" and "The Eternal Road"

Will Speak on

"Music In The Theatre"

With a Program of Songs from
"Johnny Johnson" and "The Eternal Road"
By Principals of Both Casts

QUESTIONS — DISCUSSION

LOUIS SCHAFFER, *Chairman*

ARRANGED BY
Cultural and Recreational Division—
International Ladies' Garment Workers' Union

NEXT SAT. JAN. 16 AT 3:15 P.M.
Subject: "Poetry and the Theatre"
Participants: Alfred Kreynborg and Others

---

1 9 3 7

MUSIC + THEATER:	LITERATURE + FILM:	SCIENCE + SOCIETY:	POLITICS:
Harold Rome *Pins and Needles*	John Steinbeck *Of Mice and Men*	Insulin used to control diabetes	Roosevelt signs U.S. Neutrality Act
Carl Orff *Carmina Burana*	Jean-Paul Sartre *La Nausée*	Golden Gate Bridge opens	Italy withdraws from League of Nations
Richard Rodgers *Babes in Arms*	*Snow White and the Seven Dwarfs* (film by Walt Disney)	Explosion of German dirigible "Hindenburg" at Lakehurst, New Jersey	Strike against Republic Steel, Chicago— 4 killed, 84 injured

Let This Certify That,

in the _Town_ of _North Castle_
County of _Westchester_ and State of _New York_
I, _Julius O. Rauer_, Justice of the Peace
did by virtue of the power in me vested, on the _19_
day of _January_ 19 _37_

Unite In Marriage

Mr. _Kurt Julian Weill_
of _Berlin_ of _New York City_
and _Charlotte Blamauer Weill_ of the
of _Paris France_ according to the laws of the State of _New York_

Daisy B. Lewis Witnesses _Julius O. Rauer_
Armonk N.Y.

404. Weill and Lenya did not remarry until 19 January 1937, although they had passed as husband and wife since arriving in the U.S.

405. In Hollywood, early 1937.

406. Weill was in a constant struggle to get the producers to pay royalties for *The Eternal Road*. To justify their non-payment, they provided a budget of operating costs and requested a reduction in author's royalties, which then amounted to a total of fourteen percent for all authors and creative personnel. Weill's royalty was 2½ percent. Accountant John Pinto prepared a statement of royalties earned as of 13 February 1937.

Weill (in Hollywood) to Lotte Lenya, 28 January 1937: So I drifted in here yesterday, January 27 (!). There was nobody at the train station except one of the agency employees, who took me straight to the Walter Wanger office, where Milly [Lewis Milestone] and Cliff [Odets] were waiting for me. I started working on the script immediately, and after one hour I had already succeeded in writing a song that will work into the story line brilliantly. It'll be a kind of revolutionary song, but at the same time a love song. . . .

My first impression of this place is rather awful. It's a miserable village; you can't take five steps without meeting someone you know. The scenery is magnificent, with mountains in the background, like Salzburg. But what they've built into it! It looks exactly like Bridgeport—except New York is three thousand miles away. So far the climate doesn't agree with me. It isn't warm and it isn't cold, and I have constant headaches. But that's probably only for the first few days. . . . I think I have great opportunities here, and it's entirely possible that I'll get a very big contract, because everyone says I have no competition, and they really need people like me. . . . Today marks eleven years since we married for the first time, and now you are a Weillchen for the second time. You just have to have everything double, you *Ameisenblume*.

Weill (in Hollywood) to Lotte Lenya, 1 February 1937: Work on the movie is slow, but it's quite interesting to learn the techniques of screenwriting. So far I haven't had any inspirations; it's really an entirely new medium for me, and I still feel quite insecure.

Weill (in Hollywood) to Lotte Lenya, 4 February 1937: I bought a classy Max [Weill's nickname for a car]. After I had almost decided on a new Ford on the installment plan, I suddenly got the idea to take a look at used cars—in the price range of our Buick—which are much cheaper here, and I actually found a 1934 Oldsmobile in excellent external and mechanical condition, a green two-seater coupe, very elegant, with a fantastic motor. It rides like a Buick, and of course it will look much better here to be driving around with a gorgeous car—and it's also $350 cheaper than a Ford. I only paid $200 down and then it'll cost $30 a month, including insurance and taxes.

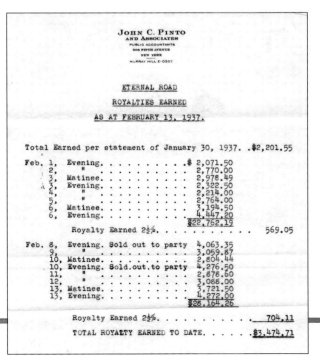

THE ETERNAL ROAD

Feb.4/37   ESTIMATED BUDGET OF OPERATING COSTS BEGINNING FEB. 8th

Number	Salaries		
59	Principal Actors	5,972.50	
35	Dancers	1,050.-	
13	Singers	475.-	
100	Extras	1,500.-	
1	Company Manager	95.-	
8	Stage Managers	385.-	
3	Technical Staff	225.-	
2	Production Directors	175.-	
221			9,877.50
3	Orchestra Conductors	360.-	
16	Men	1,600.-	
19			1,960.-
	Stage & Mechanical Crew		
14	Wardrobe	458.00	
3	Sound	300.-	
10	Road Men	992.50	
13	Electrical Dept.	789.-	
18	Carpenter Dept.	954.-	
15	Property Dept.	874.-	
73			4,347.50
	Make up, by contract		400.-
56	Theatre Employees		1,010.-
7	Administrative Staff		220.00
9	Exploitation Staff		385.00
385			18,200.00

ADVERTISING
English Speaking Newspapers   2,500.-
Yiddish   "   300.-
Promotion Sales,etc.   300.-
Photographs,Frames,Cards,etc.   100.-   3,200.-

R.C.A.   Payment a/c Equipment   828.-
Century Lighting Co. "   714.-
Insurance   100.-
Tickets   60.-
Miscellaneous Theatre Charges,
Fire Alarm Service,Supplies,etc.   500.00
Theatre Rent   1,500.-
"   Light and Heat   35,252.-
    4,060.-
    29,312.-

Royalty on $23,500 week

JOHN C. PINTO
AND ASSOCIATES
PUBLIC ACCOUNTANTS
505 FIFTH AVENUE
NEW YORK
MURRAY HILL 2-0557

ETERNAL ROAD

ROYALTIES EARNED

AS AT FEBRUARY 13, 1937.

Total Earned per statement of January 30, 1937. .$2,201.55

Feb. 1,	Evening.	. . . .	$ 2,071.50	
2,	"	. . . .	2,770.00	
3,	Matinee.	. . . .	2,978.49	
3,	Evening.	. . . .	2,322.50	
4,	"	. . . .	2,214.00	
5,	"	. . . .	2,764.00	
6,	Matinee.	. . . .	3,194.50	
6,	Evening.	. . . .	4,447.20	
			$22,762.19	
	Royalty Earned 2½%.			569.05

Feb. 8,	Evening.Sold out to party	4,063.35	
9,	"	3,059.87	
10,	Matinee.	2,804.44	
10,	Evening. Sold out to party	4,276.50	
11,	"	2,676.60	
12,	"	3,066.00	
13,	Matinee.	3,721.50	
13,	Evening.	4,272.00	
		$28,164.26	
	Royalty Earned 2½%.		704.11

TOTAL ROYALTY EARNED TO DATE. $3,474.71

PLATE 9

Poster for the original production of the Weill-Anderson musical, *Knickerbocker Holiday*.

Knickerbocker Holiday costume design by Frank Bevan for General Poffenburgh.

Set design sketch by Jo Mielziner, featuring the scaffold on the wharf.

Railroads on Parade, New York World's Fair, 1939.
Cover of the souvenir program
Architectural rendering of the three-tier stage
Cover of a promotional brochure
Sheet music for "Mile After Mile," with words by Charles Alan and Buddy Bernier.

PLATE 11

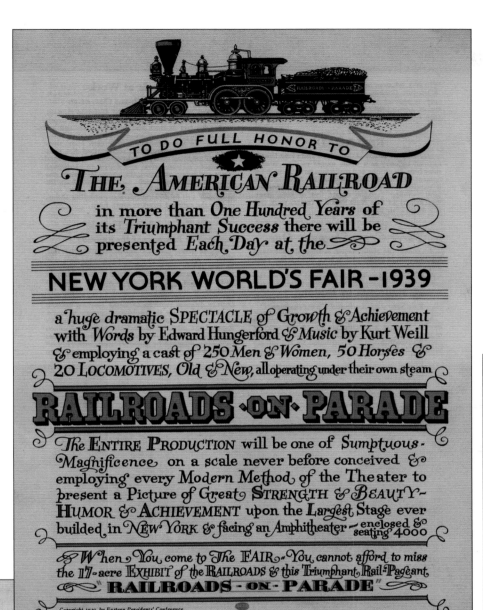

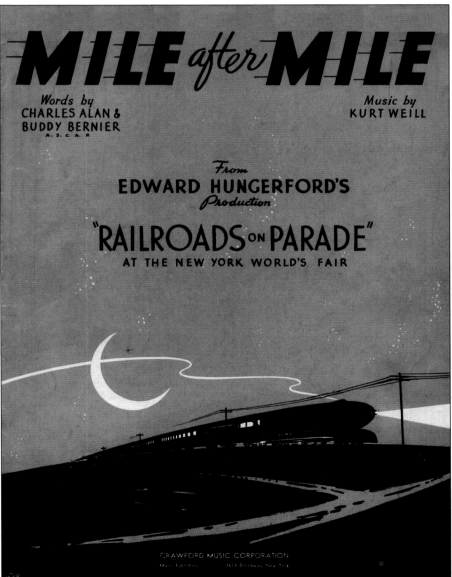

PLATE 12

The first page of "September Song" in Weill's autograph full score. To save time, he rarely wrote the vocal parts into his Broadway scores. The viola part on the bottom staff is in another hand and was added later.

PLATE 13

The souvenir program for *Lady in the Dark* (book by Moss Hart and lyrics by Ira Gershwin), which opened 23 January 1941 at the Alvin Theatre on Broadway. The star, Gertrude Lawrence, returned to the show for a second season, reopening at the same theater on 2 September 1941 with many new cast members in the supporting roles. *Lady in the Dark* was Weill's first unqualified Broadway success, spawning sheet music editions, radio broadcasts, a Hollywood film, and even a commercial line of dresses and hats based on Hattie Carnegie's designs.

PLATE 14

The American Theatre Wing sponsored a series of entertainments for factory workers called *Lunch Hour Follies* for which Weill served as chairman of the production committee. This is the cover of a promotional brochure.

In addition to producing the *Follies* shows, Weill also wrote songs for these and other events to support the war effort. One was "Schickelgruber," an anti-Hitler propaganda song with words by Howard Dietz. (Hitler's father was illegitimate and used his mother's name, Schicklgruber, until the age of 39.)

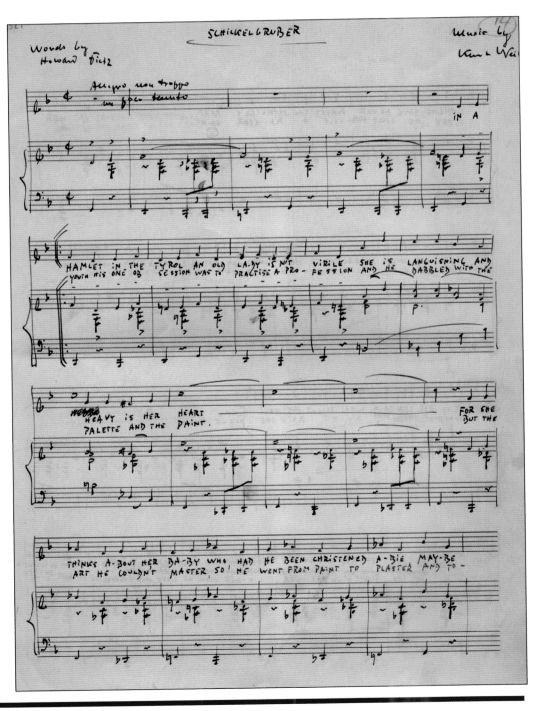

PLATE 15

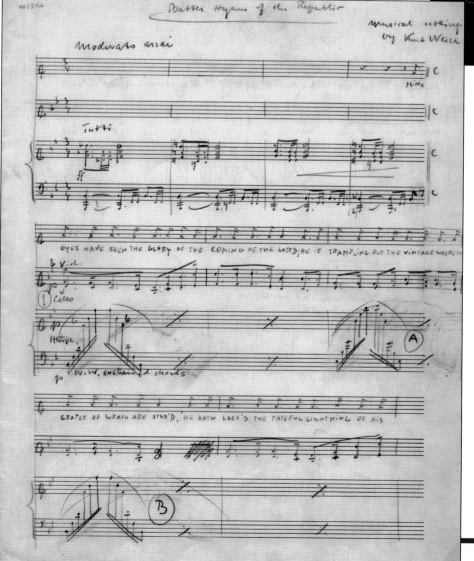

Helen Hayes asked Weill to make musical settings for a recording of patriotic recitations issued under the title *Mine Eyes Have Seen the Glory* (Victor M 909). The two-disc album includes three patriotic songs ("Battle Hymn of the Republic," "The Star-Spangled Banner," and "America") and an arrangement of Weill's setting of Walt Whitman's poem "Beat! Beat! Drums!". Hayes is accompanied by the Victor Concert Orchestra and a male chorus conducted by Roy Shields. Ted Dreher made the orchestrations based upon Weill's short scores. Weill went to Chicago to supervise the recording sessions on 30-31 March 1942. Pictured here is the first page of Weill's musical setting of "Battle Hymn of the Republic."

PLATE 16

"ONE TOUCH OF VENUS"

MARY MARTIN

One Touch of Venus (book by S.J. Perelman and Ogden Nash, lyrics by Ogden Nash) opened on 7 October 1943 at the Imperial Theatre after a tryout in Boston. It represents Weill's only attempt at traditional musical comedy. The show's star, Mary Martin, had made her name singing "My Heart Belongs to Daddy" in the 1938 production of Leave It to Me! by Cole Porter.

407. Posing with his new "Max," a 1934, two-seater Oldsmobile coupe.

Weill (in Hollywood) to Lotte Lenya, [25 February 1937]: Monday I was at the studio the entire day until four in the morning and watched how the musical director (who's very capable) recorded the music for a new Wanger film (*History Is Made at Night* with Charles Boyer and Jean Arthur, charming). I learned a lot. The atmosphere in this studio is marvelous: upbeat, matter-of-fact, no fights but lots of whiskey.

Weill (in Hollywood) to Lotte Lenya, [3 March 1937]: Wanger decided not to produce the movie for the time being but to wait until he finds the right all-star cast. The whole production has been called off. You can imagine how upsetting this was—but not for this little smarty. I get all the money as soon as I deliver the music. Therefore, tomorrow I'll begin working out the music, scene by scene. I hope to have everything ready by 1 April. That will be advantageous for me, because payment corresponds to the length of time I work on the film. The agent is now trying to find another job for me after 1 April. If he hasn't found anything by the day I deliver my music, I'll leave right away.

Weill (in Hollywood) to Cheryl Crawford, 5 March 1937: Don't worry, Hollywood will not get me. A whore never loves the man who pays her, she wants to get rid of him as soon as she has rendered her services. That is my relation to Hollywood. (I am the whore.) Most people try to mix the whore-business with "love"—that's why they don't get away.

Weill (in Hollywood) to Lotte Lenya, [10 March 1937]: I saw [George] Antheil recently. He has a hell of a lot of respect for me and apparently has made me a lot of publicity (which everyone has confirmed)—most likely because he wants to act the great Weill connoisseur. His wife—who, by the

Weill to Write Wanger Music

B'way Composer Will Pen Tunes for Odets' Movie, 'Loves of Jeanne Ney.'

Kurt Weill, who composed the music for "Johnny Johnson" and "The Eternal Road," has been signed by Walter Wanger to supply the musical background for the new Clifford Odets screen play, "The Loves of Jeanne Ney," which Lewis Milestone will direct, with Madeleine Carroll in the starring role.

The composer will leave shortly for the Coast to confer with the playwright and the director prior to preparation of the script, thereby establishing a screen precedent. It is customary for the musical score to be adapted to the completed script, but in this case Mr. Weill has insisted upon ample time to complete an original score—to be an essential part of the dramatic movement.

This is not Mr. Weill's first experience with the screen. His world-famous "Three-Penny Opera" was made into a film, in 1932, and is still being played in Paris. The following year he was assigned by a German company to write both the script and the music for "Little Man, What Now?" but the advent of the Hitler regime caused the producers to break their contract and led to Weill's flight from Germany. Mr. Weill was born in Dessau, Germany, and studied in Berlin under the great Busoni. Originally a conductor and composer of numerous concert works, he turned to the theater in search of a more popular musical medium.

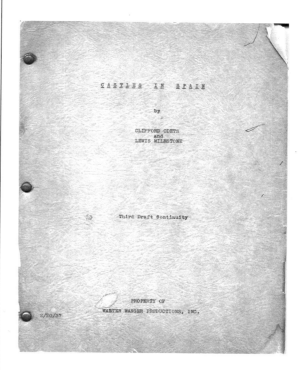

408. Weill went to Hollywood to compose music for a screenplay by Clifford Odets and Louis Milestone based on Ilya Ehrenburg's novel *The Loves of Jeanne Ney*. The working title for the film, "Castles in Spain," was later changed to "The River Is Blue." It was to be directed by Milestone and to be cast principally with actors from the Group Theatre. When the producer Walter Wanger fired Milestone from the project, Weill realized that his music would probably not be used, but he finished his score so that he would receive his fee.

409. Lewis Milestone and Clifford Odets working together in Hollywood, 1936.

410. The copyist's short score for *The River Is Blue* comprises about forty numbers. This excerpt shows the section that Weill describes to Lenya as "wild Spanish music with a lot of castanets which suddenly gives way to the clatter of machine guns."

way, is pregnant—has opened a modern art gallery here, which is very much in style, since snobbery plays a big part around here (she's preparing a big Max Ernst exhibit and expects it to be a great success). As the first social event at their gallery they'd like to hold a reception for me, with a performance of the *Jasager* and a screening of the *Dreigroschenoper* film. I think that would be very good for me, because I'm still too little known here, and everyone would come to that. If you were here, you could do some songs, but it would be easy in any case to arrange a song evening for you.

Weill (in Hollywood) to Lotte Lenya, [13 March 1937]: In the afternoon I was with Wanger; I played some recordings for him and was just starting to play some of the music for Cliff's film (which belongs to Wanger anyway), when the door opened and—in came Charlie Chaplin. He is truly the most enchanting person I've ever seen; you can sense his genius ten miles away. We hit it off right away. You can't imagine how enthusiastic he was about the music, jumping up all the time and saying, "play that again," and everything he said showed extraordinary understanding. He was beside himself about the opening of the film, where I start with some wild Spanish music with a lot of castanets which suddenly give way to the clatter of machine guns, while the wild music continues. "That's one of the greatest ideas I've ever heard," he said. We were together for an hour and a half, saw color tests for the new Wanger film (*Vogues of 1938*), and he talked only to me. You can imagine how that impressed Wanger. Before Chaplin showed up, Wanger was saying he didn't know whether I was American enough for the film *52nd Street*, but then when I was about to leave, he said, "Let's get together on *52nd Street*," and yesterday he called [Bert] Allenberg and said I should get together with the man who's writing the script. All of this, of course, does not mean I'll get the film. I would really love to do it, because it's a real musical with a brilliant idea behind it and great possibilities. So keep your fingers crossed.

Weill (in Hollywood) to Lotte Lenya, [15 March 1937]: Wanger has doubts whether I'm "American" enough for this picture [*52nd Street*]. I responded that the "most American" composer, Irving Berlin, is a Russian Jew—and I'm a German Jew; that's the only difference.

Weill (in Hollywood) to Lotte Lenya, [28 March 1937]: I spent the entire afternoon and evening with the Spewacks [Sam and Bella]. They're charming people; you'll like them a lot. The wife has something of Madeleine Milhaud. We worked out a wonderful plot, and all three of us are very enthusiastic: a play about the refugees. It starts in the Mannheim Opera during an opera rehearsal, which suddenly is interrupted by a Nazi who fires everyone because they are non-Aryans. They all immigrate to New York, and we will show their adventures there, with a lot of humor, of course, but, for example, there's also a scene in which they receive a letter from one of their friends in Mannheim who is no longer alive when the letter arrives. In the end, one of their friends from Germany comes to tell them that everything has been arranged so they can come back, but they tell him they do not want to return, and at the very end they perform the opera they once had rehearsed in Mannheim in a little movie theater in some small town in America. Isn't that a marvelous subject?

Volume XIV   May-June, 1937   Number 4

Modern Music

MINNA LEDERMAN, Editor

THE FUTURE OF OPERA IN AMERICA

KURT WEILL

The development of opera in Europe, which had a sudden upsurge after the war, has been stagnant for many years. I was therefore greatly interested in discovering the state of the theater when I came to America about twenty months ago.

What we have known for years in Europe is even more applicable here. The concept of opera cannot be interpreted in the narrow sense that was prevalent in the nineteenth century. If we substitute the term "music theater," the possibilities for development here, in a country not burdened with an opera tradition, become much clearer. We can see a field for the building of a new (or the rebuilding of a classical) form.

The music theater is as old as the theater itself. Those cultures from which our theater has descended (the Greek theater, the Japanese theater, the medieval mysteries) attempted and accomplished, each in its own way, the union of word, tone and movement from which sprang the later opera form. Since the theater was originally a folk-art, it needed music, always the most natural, most "popular" form of artistic expression. Opera arose in the sixteenth century with the attempt to revive the ancient theater, and the first operas were "musical theater" in the best sense, achieving a logical union of music and drama, and bringing the drama into complete balance with the musical form.

Thereafter, opera pursued its own road. It became an independent art-form, going further and further away from the theater, because the music subordinated the drama. A typical European phenomenon, it developed in correspondence with social necessities in Europe. For a long time it was produced for private enjoyment at the courts of princes and aristocratic patrons and so was a typically subsidized art. Not having to fight for its life, it grew spoiled, over-refined, exigent, following whims and disregarding general laws. The great operatic masterpieces—*Don Juan, Figaro, Fidelio*—were the results of successful battles against this danger of isolation by composers striving toward a universally applicable form against the intentions of their patrons.

So-called artistic freedom is something special. The creative artist seeks independence, he wants to conceive his work freely, unaffected by outer compulsion. On the other hand, he needs some restraining influence to prevent his wandering in abstract spheres. He must know for whom he is creating. Only by considering his objective will he find the necessary spiritual background that prohibits an empty play with forms. Most great works of art were produced as commissions, for a definite purpose and audience, that is, between the millstones of outer compulsion and inner freedom, between "must" and "will."

The existence of opera was endangered because it was too well safeguarded, because it was intended for a too narrowly prescribed public. Its production demanded great subsidies which in the course of time had a detrimental effect on inner structure. The contents of the librettos drew farther away from the realities of life, from the simple natural relations between people, and lost themselves in artificial, false emotions, in a meaningless world of kings, knights and princesses, or in pure symbolism. Coincidentally, the means of musical expression became increasingly complicated. Melody, always the most expressive element of the music theater, was threatened by over-emphasis on harmony and by orchestral effects. In an almost diseased passion for musical originality, the central problem of the music theater—to bring words and tones together in equilibrium—was lost to sight. In the process of extending its musical structure, making it more fine-spun, opera presentation was so neglected as to become almost ridiculous. The stiff, unnatural movements of singers, the old-fashioned scenery, the meaningless interruptions by ballets, these are the tragic signs of an age in which opera lost contact with the theater and led the existence of a museum piece, toilsomely preserved by its devotees.

Paralleling the subsidized product was a different kind of opera, reared on a far healthier basis as part of the amusement business by entrepreneurs who recognized and tried to satisfy the need of the masses for a music theater. The artistic value of such operatic works is often underestimated, because they are popular, completely comprehensible, and have a direct effect on the public. Mozart's *Zauberflöte* was written on commission and in collaboration with a commercial theater impresario; it is an ideal example of the union of popular music and the highest degree of artistic power. The flowering of Italian opera in the nineteenth century brought forth in Verdi a new peak of popular opera. The melodic invention of its music and the technical mastery of the means of expression rank it with the great masterpieces. At the same time its public reception was such that it could stand on its own feet. The circumstances under which Verdi wrote his operas provided the healthiest condition of the theater. There was a group of impresarios who were commissioning operas. Each had several prominent singers under contract, and from Verdi's letters to his librettists we know that

with each work there was a consultation about which singers had to be provided with roles. A direct motive for the creation of opera existed, and each one was awaited by an enthusiastic public.

It is noteworthy that the resurgence of a new opera culture in Europe after the war went hand in hand with a great Verdi renaissance, long proclaimed by Busoni. This reached its climax in the *Masked Ball* presentation of the Berlin Municipal Theater (staged by Carl Ebert with scenes by Caspar Neher). Musicians, critics, and the public suddenly discovered the treasures hidden in this music, its original solution of the problem of opera form. The influence of the Verdi revival on post-war composers was accompanied by a realization that opera must again find a union with the theater, and return to a simplified, clear, and direct musical language. Already, during the war, Busoni had written an opera (*Arlecchino*) which used an actress in the principal role. In Stravinsky's *L'histoire du soldat* a speaker carried the action; the *Dreigroschenoper* was written for an actress who could sing.

The great dramatists of the day began to interest themselves in opera. Jean Cocteau, André Gide, Paul Claudel, Georg Kaiser, Bert Brecht wrote librettos. Modern ideas of stage craft found their way into the music theater, the singers received dramatic training and discovered a simple, human manner of presentation that threw a new light on classical opera. The composers of this period found their strongest form of expression in the theater.

In the selection of themes we attempted to employ current ideas and events of the day in an operatic form—though this did not prove a permanent direction. The effort to use great, timeless materials in relation to great contemporary ideas developed a series of important choral operas. Attempts were also made to penetrate into the most diverse fields and groups of audiences outside the traditional opera theater. We recognized that just in those circles where music was really needed, where music had a "market value," second-rate matter was used almost exclusively. Thus we tried to break into the entertainment industry (musical comedy, night club, popular song.) The *Stück mit Musik* proved one of the most successful theater forms of the day. Composers also wrote works for radio, operas for schools, scenic choral pieces for mass meetings, and began to tackle the problem of musical films.

Suddenly this whole development was interrupted by political events in Central Europe. And under the existing situation in the Old World, there is scant hope that it will be resumed in a reasonable time. I do not believe that America can simply take up this music theater development right where Europe left off. The prerequisites for artistic construction here are quite different. But I do believe that a movement has already begun which runs parallel to the European and which will come closer to the goal we set in Europe, even though—or because—it develops on a new plane fixed by conditions in this country.

America stands near Russia; it is the only country in which the theater forms an active, vital part of cultural life. There is a genuine interest in the theater not only in New York but in other cities. Every season sees a number of outstanding successes of widely discussed theater evenings. American dramatists today hold first place for ability and ideas, and the plentiful "second-growth" of young writers is also a favorable sign. Everywhere we find a tendency to break away from the realistic scene of the last decade, to find an elevated, poetic level of theater, which can survive alongside the movies.

This tendency is especially important because the poetic is very close to the music theater. At the same time there is an unusually strong interest on the part of the American public in every form of music. From my own experience I can testify that I have seldom found so large, so direct a reaction to music in the theater as in New York. The musical taste of the general public is better here than in many other countries.

All these signs indicate that the soil is favorable for development. What will grow on it is hard to say, for there is no sort of tradition. The general public outside of the large cities knows little or nothing about opera, but they tell me that traveling troupes giving Verdi performances have had great success, and I am convinced that the radio, which is an important influence in this country, will do profitable preparatory work. Whether the growth will be opera in the European sense or music theater in a broader sense, a new amalgam of word and tone bearing a new idea, it is certain that it will be an active, vital part of the modern theater, that dramatists and composers will cooperate in its creation, that from the plentiful supply of young singers a generation of singer-performers will emerge.

It may be that a music theater will rise out of Broadway. There are already many starting points for a new kind of musical comedy here, and Gilbert and Sullivan in England, Offenbach in Paris, and Johann Strauss in Vienna have proved that a musical theater culture of high merit can arise from the field of light music. It is also possible that the few existing operatic institutions will take the lead and start a development similar to that of the German opera theaters in the post-war period. Perhaps the resurgence that the Metropolitan has experienced in recent years is the first indication that American composers will be able to create operas in the spirit of our own time for the great group of singers in that institution.

The best possibility for the birth of a new form of music drama, it seems to me, lies in the Federal theater. This young organization, which in a short time has become one of the most important and most promising factors in the theater and the music of the country, possesses not only the outer essentials but the inner compulsion to undertake the solution of this problem. A generously supported undertaking, which arose out of necessity, it rests in the hands of youth, and has a progressive spirit such as distinguishes few theater enterprises in the world. Spreading all over the country, it has the practical means to bring dramatists, composers, actors, singers, chorus and orchestra together for one great, unified work of art.

And perhaps even all these ideas are still too steeped in tradition. In America the new musical art work may after all develop from the medium of the movies. For nowhere else has the film attained that technical perfection and popularity which can smooth the way for a new art form.

PHILHARMONISCHE KONZERTE
77. SAISON 1936/37

Sonntag, den 18. April 1937, präzise ¼12 Uhr mittags
im Großen Musikvereins-Saale

8. Abonnement-Konzert

(Öffentliche Generalprobe: Samstag, den 17. April 1937, 3 Uhr nachm.)

Dirigent: BRUNO WALTER*

PROGRAMM:

Kurt Weill ... ... Symphonische Fantasie
    1. Sostenuto — Allegro molto —
    2. Largo — 3. Allegro vivace
    (1. Aufführung in den philharm. Abonnementkonzerten)

Rich. Strauß* ... ... Don Juan, Tondichtung für großes
    Orchester (nach Nicolaus Lenau)
    op. 20

Joh. Brahms ... ... Symphonie Nr. 4, E-moll, op. 98
    1. Allegro non troppo
    2. Andante moderato
    3. Allegro giocoso
    4. Allegro energico e passionato

* Ehrenmitglied der Wiener Philharmoniker

Streichinstrumente: Ateliers Anton Poller — Karl Haudek
(Gegründet 1840 von Gabriel Lemböck)

Außerordentliches Konzert

Sonntag, den 9. Mai 1937, ¼12 Uhr mittags, im Großen Musikvereins-Saale

Dirigent: BRUNO WALTER*

Programm:

Cherubini . . . . Ouverture „Anakreon"
Mozart . . . . Klavierkonzert D-moll
    vorgetragen von Bruno Walter
Bruckner . . . . Symphonie Nr. 7

* Ehrenmitglied der Wiener Philharmoniker

In diesen Konzerten spielten Liszt, Rubinstein, Bülow,
Brahms und alle lebenden Meister stets nur

Bösendorfer-Klaviere

411. Program of the Vienna Philharmonic concert of 18 April 1937, with Weill's symphony (referred to in the program as "symphonic fantasy") conducted again by Bruno Walter.

Weill (in Hollywood) to Bella and Sam Spewack, 30 April 1937: I am working every morning from 10 to 1 with Gip [E.Y. "Yip" Harburg]. He is a very intelligent boy, and I think he understands what we need. We have a great number of very good ideas for songs and musical scenes and we can see every day how good this theme of our play is. Gip will send you a complete description of our ideas in a few days and then you write us which ones of these ideas you like. Here are only a few of them: a song of this kind

> My little home in Heidelberg
> I wonder who lives in it,

with a very touching, sentimental melody. A very funny musical scene with the Nazi:

> The question is if Wagnerian
> Is aryan or not-aryan.

Two lyrical songs: "Tomorrow is Forever" and "Five Minutes of Spring." A ballet at night in the park, called "Midsummernight in Manhattan," with all the statues of the park dancing around Mendelssohn's statue (as a dream of the hero who is sleeping on a bench) with very good opportunity of using some of Mendelssohn's (or other persecuted) music. A strip-dance with a coloratura aria. A song with a little bird: "Tell Me Little Sparrow" in which he talks to his companion and asks him if he also has the same troubles. Etc., etc. . . .

I am starting today to work out a few of the definite hit-numbers. Of course, we would not start to work on the musical scenes before we know if you like them. But all what we do now is very flexible and will serve as good material to work on when we all get together. We are very excited about the whole thing and I hope you feel the same way.

Weill (in Hollywood) to Lotte Lenya, [8 May 1937]: It looks very much like the Fritz Lang movie at Paramount will work out. They've agreed to pay $10,000 for the whole job. I would have to work about four weeks on the movie and try to do as much as possible within that time. At the same time I would have to write the most important numbers for the show ["Mannheim Opera"]. Then I would be in New York around 10 June and could work for three months on the show. During this time Lang will prepare the movie and begin shooting, and I'll come back only when he needs me. . . . They have Sylvia Sidney and George Raft for the leads, and I think it could turn out to be a very interesting movie. It certainly won't be an easy nut to crack with Lang, who is a really miserable guy (although for the time being he is nice as pie to me), and we'll have the craziest fights. . . .

Blumi, we want to be very careful with money, because all I'm doing right now will ultimately be justified only if I can save enough to enable me finally to do something really significant again, by my former standards. I don't want to make the mistake everyone here makes (Cliff and all the others)—of spending all the money one makes and then be forced to take on another job and little by little become a complete slave to Hollywood. I know this is your point of view as well. If we're careful we could have approximately $16,000 dollars in the bank by this fall, when the movie is done, and could rent a small house near New York, have a maid and a car, and give up this gypsy life, where you never get a chance to collect your thoughts. . . . If money has any use at all, it's to give us independence.

In last Sunday's *Times* there was a report from Vienna that [Bruno]

Walter performed my symphony there. It was the first time that Toscanini went to another conductor's concert. The article says the audience reacted more positively to the work than to any other modern one. That makes me happy, especially as I sit here in Hollywood fighting with Boris Morros.

I spent one evening with Stokowski, who was very nice to me.

Weill (in Santa Monica) to Lotte Lenya, [29 May 1937]: Thursday we did *Der Lindberghflug* in the Antheil Gallery with just a few singers and two pianos. It's amazing how good that music is and how fresh an effect it still has after almost ten years. We also showed the *Dreigroschenoper* film, but we could get only the French version, which is rather poor and—in contrast to *Der Lindberghflug*—unfortunately feels quite old-fashioned already, which proves that it never was any good in the first place. Everybody in Hollywood who's interested in modern works was present: the Gershwins, Miriam Hopkins, [Anatole] Litvak, the Milestones, Lang, Luise [Rainer] and Cliff, and many more. . . . Yesterday was the Los Angeles premiere of *Johnny Johnson*. I went to a few rehearsals and helped them a little bit. It's the biggest project the WPA has undertaken up to now; of course, it has inferior actors—but a charming, very young Johnny (the play works quite differently with a young Johnny), a big (lousy) orchestra and chorus, and very interesting sets. That the second act received the strongest reaction by far demonstrates how greatly the performance differed from the New York one. They included the "French Wounded" chorus and did the "Dance of the Generals" in its entirety, which proved most effective.

412. In Act II, scene 7 of the Federal Theatre production of *Johnny Johnson* at the Mayan Theatre in Los Angeles, Johnny (Brian Morgan) poses as a messenger from the generals but fails to stop the inevitable slaughter. Under the scene the German and English priests sing the prayer, "In Time of War and Tumults."

While in Hollywood during the first half of 1937, actress Sylvia Sidney helped to get Weill hired to write the music for her upcoming movie for Paramount, *You and Me*, to be directed by Fritz Lang. He wrote his ideas about the musical treatment in May 1937. The concept of the "knocking song" was of particular interest to him.

Excerpt from:

About the music for "You and Me."
by Kurt Weill

In the scene in the elevator we hear for the first time the rhythm of the knocking song, this time not the melody but only the rhythm which should be so typical that the audience recognizes it immediately when it comes back. The rhythm and the tune of this knocking song (which is built on the knocking of the walls in prison, used as a mean for communication between the prisoners) is one of the two "Leitmotifs" of our picture and is carried through the whole picture. It indicates the former life of these people and the danger which results out of their past for their present life. The second time we hear it is when Raft teaches Sylvia how to say "I love you" in the knocking language. This time we hear also the tune which is built on the knocking rhythm. Raft should "sing" it, but it can be almost spoken to music—and, may be tap-danced. The knocking song is a question-and-answer-song, perhaps with the following idea:

> Do you hear me?
> I hear you.
> Do you know who it is?
> It's you.

> Do you love me?
> I do.

Raft teaches Sylvia how he sings the questions, and she has to sing the answers—and she learns it very fast (a little too fast). Then we hear the knocking song again in the scene on Christmas evening. The gang is sitting together, they are thinking of the good old times in prison when life still was dangerous and adventurous. They imitate the knocking, using tables, chairs, glasses, whistles, radiators, keys as instruments and so forming a strange orchestral sound without any orchestra instruments. Out of this knocking symphony grows the song, but this time it is not a sweet love song, this time it really shows the dangerous background of their [*sic*], it describes a kind of revolt, a rebellion in prison, each prisoner in his cell, and yet together with the others through the sound of the knocking which they all understand:

> Do you hear us?
> We hear you!

And it builds up to a wild, savage, rude song, changing these people who had tried to go straight back into criminals. And on the high spot of this song Raft enters, he is first bewildered, but then it gets him too and he joins the knocking orchestra with a wild tap dance. Kurt Weill, "About the Music for 'You and Me'," 24 May 1937, unpublished typescript, Weill-Lenya Research Center, Ser.31, box 2.

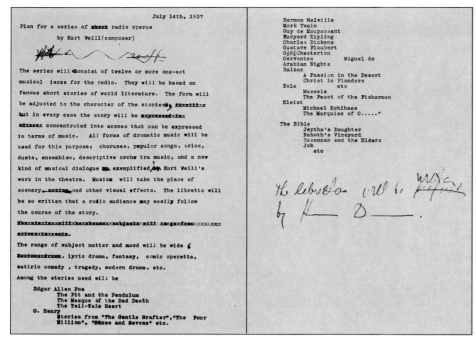

413. From the beginning of his time in the U.S., Weill concerned himself with the state of American opera. Less that two years after he arrived, he and Howard Dietz drafted a plan for a series of radio operas based on literary classics.

415. The second song added for Ernst Josef Aufricht's Paris production of *Die Dreigroschenoper,* "Pauv' Madam' Peachum." Press accounts indicate that Guilbert did not sing either of the songs in the production.

414. Scene from *Die Dreigroschenoper* in Paris, 1937: from left, Yvette Guilbert (Mrs. Peachum), René Bergeron (Mr. Peachum) and Renée St. Cyr (Polly).

Madeleine Grey (in Paris) to Weill, 29 June 1937: I hope that you still remember my name, because I am very faithful—better still: I have had great success with your songs.

I should tell you, that in front of both Italian and Swiss audiences, I had the good fortune of a public success with the song of the "poor relation" from *Silbersee* ["Ich bin eine arme Verwandte"]. As for "Roi d'Aquitaine" from *Marie galante,* in the three years that I have been singing it, it has become almost as popular in Naples as *Sole mio.* I believe that I have perfected these songs and must continue to be your interpreter. Therefore, I beg you to write a cycle of songs with some character for me so that I can premiere them in my recital in the coming season.

I just gave one on 11 June, also with great success, and I believe that Madeleine Milhaud has sent you my program.

Hurry up, Kurt Weill, I need to have new things written for me very badly. I remind you that I am a mezzo-soprano.

Weill (in New York) to Alfred Kalmus of Universal Edition, 28 July 1937: After such a long time, my main reason for writing to you today is—first of all—to ask you to have them send me as soon as possible several copies of all of my works that Universal Edition has published. As far as a recognition of my talent here in America is concerned, I have by now established myself to the point that I can be thinking about making my earlier works better known over here than they are now, as I am beginning to get requests for my former concert and theater works from several different quarters. Lots of new opera companies are coming into existence and I would like to interest them in *Die Bürgschaft,* as well as the other operas, but unfortunately I do not have any scores to show to people who might take them into consideration.

Weill (in New York) to Ernst Aufricht, 18 August 1937: Enclosed I send you the two songs for Yvette Guilbert. Both texts are excellent, and I think two very good *Threepenny* songs have been created. The first song ("Ah, Polly, Polly, tu me démolis") has to be taken rather fast, the rhythm has a slightly Spanish color; the third stanza (where she is already quite drunk) has been composed like a funeral march, but then—in the chorus—suddenly changes again into the merry tempo. The second song I have composed as a minuet. It is very much in the style of the *Threepenny Opera* to sing this somewhat obscene text to very graceful and charming music. I have built the song upon the question "Qui?" and want this "Qui?" spoken in between certain spots in the song, something that should be done each time with a different expression, of course. The answer, "C'est moi" each time must be like an outbreak of desperation and sorrow. In case the songs lie too high, they could easily be transposed a few tones down. . . .

I am very happy with your report. Naturally, I am very enthusiastic that La Guilbert is playing Mrs. Peachum, and I am sure that if the rest of the performance is as good, it should be a big success. Please do not imitate the Berlin performance, but try to make it as French as possible. And do not forget that our Berlin performance is now almost ten years old and may already seem old-fashioned.

416. American visa issued when Weill re-entered the U.S. from Canada in August 1937, the first step to becoming an American citizen.

Weill (in New York) to Paul Green, 19 August 1937: I am very impressed by Roosevelt's speech on Roanoke Island. I think a few things he said could give exactly the idea for our play. You remember that I said in Chapel Hill, I have the feeling that most people who ever came to this country came for the same reasons which brought me here: fleeing from the hate, the oppression, the restlessness and troubles of the Old World to find freedom and happiness in a New World. It is exactly this idea which the President expressed in his speech:

> "Most of them—the men, the women and the children, came hither seeking something very different—seeking an opportunity which they could not find in their homes of the old world. . . .
>
> "The opportunity they sought was something they did not have at home—opportunity freely to exercise their own chosen form of religion, opportunity to get into an environment where there were no classes, opportunity to escape from a system which still contained most of the elements of feudalism," etc.

But some lines further down he gives the complete ideological outline of our play:

> "I fear very much that if certain modern Americans who protest loudly their devotion to American ideals were suddenly to be given a comprehensive view of the earliest American colonists and their methods of life and government, they would promptly label them socialists. They would forget that in these pioneer settlements were all the germs of the later American Constitution."

It is this "comprehensive view" which we have to give—a picture of early America completely different from the one we are used to reading in schoolbooks and chronicles: the socialist idea in early America, its fight against the followers of European feudalism and its final triumph in the Constitution. . . . At the present moment I could see our play in three parts: an introduction in the form of a chorus-symphony, showing in broad *al fresco* painting, with a chorus reporting the great events which shake the old world, wars, revolutions, persecutions, etc. which bring new masses of people to this country who want freedom and a new social order. This should be a very exciting choreography, leading from the early days up to the seventeenth century. Then our main story (the second part) starts, showing the birth of the Constitution as the drama of an idea. The third part continues the symphonic report of the first part, showing the world-events of the nineteenth and twentieth centuries which bring new people to the shores of this country, more and more, black, white, and yellow men and women, carried by the same idea: to find a new world of freedom and equality. And that should go right up to Hitler and Mussolini.

417. After *Johnny Johnson*, Weill and Paul Green worked together on a musical based on the American Revolution, *The Common Glory*. This choral hymn, "Almighty and Everlasting God," represents the only surviving musical material. By December 1937 Weill and Green had developed divergent ideas about the story line, and they gave up the collaboration. Green later rewrote and completed the show without original music.

419. Weill and Boris Morros at a Hollywood dinner with an unidentified man and woman.

418. In December 1937, Weill returns to Hollywood and stays until early February working on *You and Me*. Lenya accompanies him, making her first trip to California. He is pictured here with Boris Morros, the head of the music department for Paramount.

420. Weill's friends Burgess Meredith and Charles MacArthur suggest that Weill and H.R. Hays collaborate on a musical version of Hays's play *The Ballad of Davy Crockett* for the Federal Theatre. The script bears the working title "One Man from Tennessee." Weill abandons the project in June 1938 when he learns that his planned collaboration with Maxwell Anderson on *Knickerbocker Holiday* is scheduled for production in late September. This page from the libretto of *Davy Crockett* and Weill's draft rehearsal score show the lyrics and music for "Oh I'm a Rolling Stone." Weill and Anderson later adapted this song for *Knickerbocker Holiday* as "There's Nowhere to Go But Up."

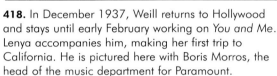

SCENE I

An open spot in the woods. The foliage is heavy and suggests a close grown virgin forest.

At rise music and sound of Josh's voice singing:

Song
Oh I'm a rolling stone,
There isn't no moss on me,
The world is my friend
And I'm never alone
Wherever I happen to be.

Chorus
Just keep right on agoing,
Never slacking, never slowing,
    There's a bright star shining on the hill.
If you never look behind you,
Hard luck can't never find you,
    There's a bright star shining on the hill.

(JOSH HAWKINS and DAVY CROCKETT enter.
JOSH is a lean, seasoned woodsman in his
forties, amiable and slow-spoken. DAVY
is a well grown youngster in his teens
but with a boyish manner. DAVY is downcast,
JOSH sings to put up a cheerful front)

Josh
I'm not for settling down,
A wife is just as bad.
I may die in a ditch
From a crack on the crown
But look at the fun I've had.

Chorus
(JOSH stops singing and examines a tree)
Well here's the split in the trail. I'm heading South.

Davy
How long'll take you to git to Texas.

Josh
About a month, I figure.

Davy
Let me go a little further with you, just till sundown....

AN OUTSTANDING CONTRIBUTION TO JEWISH MUSIC
FOLK SONGS of the NEW PALESTINE

composed by the true builders, the pioneers; and arranged by a group of eminent Jewish composers, including several of the leading musical personalities of our time; edited and annotated by Dr. Hans Nathan, with English translations by Harry H. Fein.

First Series

No.	title	arrangement by	composer
No. 1.	DANCES OF PALESTINE — Horas		
	Rise, O Brethren! *Kuma Echa*	Erich Walter Sternberg	Postolski
	We've Come *Banu*	Aaron Copland	Wellah
No. 2.	SHEPHERD'S SONGS		
	Lo, I Play Upon My Flute *Hinne Achal'la Bachalili*	Paul Dessau	Seira
	On a Hill in Galilee *Ale Giva*	Paul Dessau	Rabbinovitz
No. 3.	THE BUILDERS — Habonim		
	Bring the Bricks *Havu l'venim*	Kurt Weill	Seira
	Also Today *Gam Hayom*	Darius Milhaud	Postolski
No. 4.	SONGS IN SUMMERTIME		
	A Watermelon *Avatiach*	Ernst Toch	Rabbinovitz
	Our Baskets On Our Shoulders *Salenu Al K'tefenu*	Stefan Wolpe	Gorochov
	The Almond Tree is Blooming *Hashekdiya Porachat*	Menashe Rabbinovitz	Rabbinovitz
	Tel Aviv	Stefan Wolpe	
No. 5.	GUARDIANS OF THE NIGHT — Hashomrim		
	There Comes Peace Unto the Weary	Kurt Weill	Samburski
	Song of the Emek (*Baa M'nucha*)		
	My Step Resounds in the Dead of Night	Darius Milhaud and Stefan Wolpe	Seira
	Holem Tsaadi		
No. 6.	CHILDREN'S SONGS		
	Who Shall Build *Mi Yivne*	Lazare Saminsky	Nardi
	A Dunam Here and a Dunam There	Frederick Jacobi	Rabbinovitz
	Dunam Po V'dunam Sham		
	An Orange *Tappuach*	Ernst Toch	Rabbinovitz

Second Series

No.	title	arrangement by	composer
No. 1.	KINNERET		
	Maybe *V'ulay* text by Rachel	Paul Dessau	Shertok
	Kinneret, Kinneret	Leon Algazi	Seira
No. 2.	LITTLE LAMBS		
	Ascend My Well *Ali B'er* text by Bialik	Paul Dessau	Levi
	A Lamb and a Kid *Se Ugedi*	Ernst Toch	Matityahu
No. 3.	WORKERS IN THE FIELD		
	We Beheld Our Toil *Rainu Amalenu*	Arthur Honegger and Stefan Wolpe	Postolski
	When Ye Come to the Land *Ki Tavo'u*	Lazare Saminsky	Seira
	The Sun Is Blazing *Shemesh T'lahet*	Frederick Jacobi	
No. 4.	IDYLLS		
	On the Banks of the Kinneret *Al S'fat Yam Kinneret*	Paul Dessau	Karczevski
	I Planted a Tree *Natati Etz*	Leon Algazi	Esznchi
No. 5.	MORE CHILDREN'S SONGS		
	Tma	Max Ettinger	Rabbinovitz
	Alef Eretz *The Palestinian Alef Bet*	Ernst Toch	Postolski
	Tiny, Tiny Child *Yeled Kat*	Ernst Toch	Chitrik
No. 6.	CAMEL SONGS		
	The Camel Is Walking *Holech Haggamal*	Frederick Jacobi	Rabbinovitz
	O Camel, My Camel *Gamal, Gamali*	Paul Dessau	Gorochov

The songs, thirty in number are to be issued in twelve separate folders, amply and attractively prepared, at monthly intervals (excluding the summer months). Each contains two or more songs arranged for voice with piano accompaniment, annotations, Hebrew text, and English translations.

SUBSCRIPTION FOR BOTH SERIES $5.00
PRICE PER FOLDER .... $ .40

NIGUN   one eleven Fifth avenue, n.y.c.   room 607

Kurt Weill (in New York) to Hans Nathan, 30 May 1938. Immediately after my return from Hollywood, I began the arrangement of the two folk songs. I have just finished them and sent them to "Masada" [the organization that supported their publication].

I believe the two arrangements have turned out well. "Havu l'venim" has been provided with a brief introduction, and the whole song has been based on a restrained march rhythm which seems to me quite effective. The entire song can be repeated, the *prima volta* directly leading into the introduction.

For "Baa m'nucha" I have chosen a sort of through-composed form, without destroying the verse structure. The initial twelve measures in the three stanzas have been treated in diverse ways corresponding to the diverse character of the texts. The refrain remains the same in the three stanzas; only in the last stanza it has been treated freely in favor of the "night atmosphere."

421. Weill contributed twice to a "postcard project" organized by musicologist Hans Nathan, in which numerous composers were asked to provide settings for Jewish folk songs.

422. Weill's arrangement of "Baa m'nucha." A published version of this arrangement has not been traced.

423. First page of Weill's arrangement of "Havu l'venim" as published by the Nigun Press in 1938.

1 9 3 8

MUSIC + THEATER:

Richard Rodgers *The Boys from Syracuse*

Anton Webern *String Quartet, op. 28*

Thornton Wilder *Our Town*

LITERATURE + FILM:

Richard Wright *Uncle Tom's Children*

Ernest Hemingway *The Fifth Column*

The Lady Vanishes (film by Alfred Hitchcock)

SCIENCE + SOCIETY:

40-hour work week established in the U.S.

20,000 television sets are in service in New York City

Orsen Welles broadcasts *War of the Worlds*

POLITICS:

Germany annexes Austria, Hitler enthusiastically received in Vienna

Germany occupies Sudetenland, Czechoslovakia

House Un-American Activities Committee formed in the U.S.

BEGINNING THURSDAY APRIL 7th

LOTTE LENYA

WILL APPEAR NIGHTLY IN A REPERTOIRE

of **KURT WEILL SONGS**

at LE RUBAN BLEU

4 EAST 56th STREET   ELdorado 5-9787

424. Lenya performed for three weeks at the New York nightclub Le Ruban Bleu, named after the Paris club, in the spring of 1938 while Weill was in Hollywood.

425. Madeleine Carroll and Henry Fonda starred in *Blockade*, the final title of the film project Weill worked on for Walter Wanger. William Dieterle directed. Shortly before the release of *Blockade* by United Artists, Weill learned that his score had been discarded and replaced with a new one by Werner Janssen. Weill's friend Ann Ronell is credited with lyrics.

Weill (in New York) to Boris Morros, 17 March 1938: Thanks a lot for your letter from March 7. I was very interested to hear that the rehearsals for the knocking sequence were coming along fine and that you were going to shoot the scene last week. Of course, I am dying to hear how it worked out.

I also was very glad to hear that you as well as Walter Wanger were pleased with the temporary recordings for the Wanger picture [*The River Is Blue*]. Wanger promised me to send a copy of the score together with the final script so that I can prepare the new arrangement of the music according to the new script. But I never got a script or a score. Would you please have it sent to me? I have very definite ideas for the treatment of this score and I think we can do a very interesting job with this picture.

Telegram from Weill (in New York) to Walter Wanger, 8 April 1938: Being for weeks without news from you or Allenberg learn suddenly from today's morning papers that another composer is doing score to picture. This is hard to believe after your, Dieterle's and everybody's enthusiasm about my score. At least let me know the reasons for this strange change of mind.

Bert Allenberg (in Hollywood) to Weill, 9 April 1938: The entire matter came up rather suddenly. On the very day that I was wiring you about your return, Werner Janssen, who is an old and intimate friend of Wanger's, arrived in town. Wanger was very anxious for him to see the picture and hear the music. One thing led to another, and finally Wanger asked Janssen to come in and do the job for him.

Wanger's explanation to me was that after seeing the picture together, with the music in it, that it did not seem effective enough, and did not have enough power; that it meant a complete new score and that he certainly could not ask you to do a new score for nothing, inasmuch as you had already been most cooperative, and that inasmuch as Janssen was right there, and was willing to do it for him for a most reasonable sum, far less than what you received, he thought he might as well go ahead.

It was all done quickly and the deal with Janssen was arranged even before Wanger told me about it. There was absolutely nothing which could have been done to preclude or prevent it.

I am very sorry that it happened, because I was very anxious to have you have this credit. These things do happen and there is no sense in being too upset about it, as it's really not that important.

Weill (in Hollywood) to Lotte Lenya, 19 April 1938: This morning at 8:30 Fritz [Lang] showed me about two thirds of the movie [*You and Me*]. It's very beautiful, at times excitingly so, but *zu lang* [i.e., too long and too Lang], often very draggy and very German, but of a much higher standard than anything they're doing here. The songs are definitely the highlights, and one could just cry (or laugh) to think that in this movie all my ideas have again proved to be right and new and exciting—and nobody will ever know they were my ideas. "The Right Guy" is terribly effective; "Song of the Lie" [which was ultimately dropped] comes through much better than I had thought. The best thing is the cash register in the beginning, but of course they won't understand it (except for Lang), and I'm sure they'll cut it. Oh well, I've decided not to get upset, and I'm more convinced than ever that it isn't worth it getting irritated, because you're dealing with the lowest human scum. I've asked that Boris to his face what happened with Wanger, and from his stammering it became very clear that he had his dirty fingers in it. When it comes to making a real *Schweinerei*, then they all band together.

Weill (in Hollywood) to Lotte Lenya, 5 May 1938: I'm taking advantage of the first free minutes I've had to write you a few lines. For over a week I haven't slept more than four hours a night: I've been working until three, then up again at seven. Just working wouldn't be bad, because I always enjoy that, but it's these annoyances, these squabbles, and this horrendous stupidity and lack of culture I have to struggle against, and on top of that the secret conniving of Boris and, of course, our beloved Fritz, who opposes me at every opportunity and is so incredibly unmusical it makes you want to tear your hair out. I've found there is only one remedy that's effective here: to be incredibly brazen and tell them all to their faces what is on your mind. It's suddenly going much better since I started using this technique; they have more respect for me than for anyone else they've worked with up to now, and I was able to force through all kinds of things the way I wanted them.

428. Weill, Fritz Lang, and Boris Morros supervise the recording of the score of *You and Me*, April 1938.

426. An advertisement for *You and Me* from the pressbook for the film.

427. A selection from Paramount's publicity forecasts a new era in music for films.

"Musical Revolution" Forecast by Leading Hollywood Composers

The year 1938 will see a "musical revolution" in the film industry that will give composers and their works more importance than ever before in the history of the screen.

That's the consensus of Hollwood's musical directors as a result of the introduction of "uncuttable music" to the scoring of movies.

In the current Sylvia Sidney-George Raft film, "You and Me," which opens .... at the .... Theatre, the score is interwoven with thematic strains that are vital to the life and advancement of the plot, and, according to producer-director Fritz Lang, cannot be cut without causing the audience to lose "dramatic content."

Kurt Weill, European composer, who created a sensation in the musical world a few seasons ago by his original scoring of Max Reinhardt's "The Eternal Road," composed the theme music for "You and Me," working closely with Director Lang and Scenarist Virginia Van Upp.

Lang had marked success with this "musical scenarization" when he employed it experimentally, to a lesser degree, in "Fury" and "You Only Live Once," his two previous productions.

The story of "You and Me" is a drama of paroled convicts in love but forbidden by law to marry. Miss Sidney and Raft are supported by an excellent cast that includes Warren Hymer, Barton MacLane, Robert Cummings and George E. Stone.

429. The "Knocking Song" from *You and Me*: Weill's autograph score, a photo of music advisor Phil Boutelje rehearsing the number with Fritz Lang (on the right), and a photo of the scene from the film.

430. In *You and Me*, Joe Dennis (played by George Raft) confronts Helen (Sylvia Sidney) about her past.

Weill (in Hollywood) to Maxwell Anderson, 14 May 1938: The more I think about our play [*Knickerbocker Holiday*] the more I get enthusiastic about the whole idea, the characters, the background and the period. I am sure we can do something very original, and in using music, you can express your philosophy with great bite and irony. I am thinking a lot about the musical style of the play, and I have started to work out a style which would give a feeling of the period and yet be very up-to-date music. This combination of old and new gives great opportunity for humor in music, and my idea is that the music in this play should take [an] active part in the humorous as well as in the sentimental parts, because the more we can say in fun the better it is. For instance if we have the fight between the flute and the trumpet, I want our audience to laugh as much about the music itself as they'll laugh about the situation and the dialogue.

432. Sheet music was published for one number from *You and Me*, "The Right Guy for Me."

431. After the gang is caught robbing the department store in which they worked, the store owner allows them to go free. Helen, a reformed criminal, shows the gang that crime literally does not pay.

433. In 1938, the Nazis mounted an exhibition in Dusseldorf under the title "Entartete Musik" (degenerate music), in which Weill's works were prominently denounced along with those of George Antheil, Ernst Křenek, Darius Milhaud, Arnold Schoenberg, Franz Schreker, Ernst Toch, Anton Webern, and others. This was the logo of the exhibition.

434. These pages showing Weill's "offensive" work appeared in a booklet accompanying the exhibition: *Entartete Musik: Eine Abrechnung* von Staatsrat Dr. Hans Severus Ziegler (Dusseldorf: Völkischer Verlag, 1938).

435. This American report on the Entartete Musik exhibition published in the journal *Musical America* contained an abundance of wrong information and many misspellings. (*Musical America* 58, no. 12 (July 1938): 7)

DÜSSELDORF EXHIBITS 'DEGENERATE MUSIC'

'Reichs Week' Festival Displays Atonalists' Works and Books of 'Cultural Bolshevism'

BERLIN, June 20.—Besides the musical performances reported in another letter in this issue of MUSICAL AMERICA, the Düsseldorf Festival, officially designated as a "Reichs Music Week" (May 22-29), held an exhibition of "Degenerate Music." This contained representative works of the atonalists as well as books and articles preaching the tenets of "cultural Bolshevism" which were arranged in a room partitioned off into a series of open alcoves, each equipped with a gramophone playing one of the exhibits, which could be turned on by simply pressing a button. The jazz section contained Alfred Baresekk's 'Jazzbuch', miscellaneous articles by Bernhard Sekles and Paul Stefan and a formidable collection of music for the theatre associated with the names of the Rotter Brothers, Max Reinhardt, Viktor Hollaender, Erich Korngold, Richard Tauber and others. The department devoted to educational music included articles and press criticisms by Paul Bekker, Theodor Wiesengrund-Adorno, Ernest Bloch, Adolf Weissman, Alfred Einstein, and Hermann Scherchen, as well as a list of 75 composers backed by the former Berlin concert agents Wolff & Sachs, and prominently featured in the Baden-Baden and Donaueschingen music festivals. Besides other exhibits in this department there were Weill's school opera, 'Das Neue Werk', edited by Jöde, Hindemith and Mersmann, a choral collection by Erich Katz, stage settings, and so on.

A third division covered the "theorists" of atonality and embraced Arnold Schönberg's 'Harmonielehre', Hermann Erpf's 'Studien zur Klangtechnik der Modernen Musik', Hindemith's 'Lehre vom Tonsatz', Weissmann's 'Musik der Sinne', Mersmann's 'Musik der Gegenwart', Gerhard Frommel's 'Neue Klassik in der Musik' and works by Josef Hauer, Alban Berg and Paul Bekker. The musical exhibits contained the following:

Stravinsky: 'Geschichte vom Soldaten', and the autobiography 'Chronique de ma Vie'.

Hindemith: Three one-act operas, 'Cardillac', 'Neues vom Tage', the 'Brecht Lehrstueck', 'Das Unaufhoerliche', the 'Lindbergflug', 'Die junge Magd', a piano suite and a viola concerto.

Kurt Weill: 'Dreigroschenoper', 'Jasager', 'Mahagonny', 'Johnny', 'Der neue Orpheus', 'Der Sprung ueber den Schatten', 'Die Zwingburg', Second and Third Symphonies, songs.

Franz Schreker: 'Die Gezeichneten', 'Irrelohe', 'Der Ferne Klang'.

Hans Eisler: Ballade from the film 'Kuehle Wampe'.

Alban Berg: 'Wozzek', 'Lulu', violin concerto, three pieces for orchestra.

Karol Rathaus: Second Symphony, four dance pieces.

Josef Hauer: Sixth and Seventh Orchestral Suites.

Ernst Toch: The opera, 'Prinzessin auf der Erbse', the 'Doeblin' Cantata, symphony for piano and orchestra, piano pieces.

Hermann Reutter: 'Der neue Hiob'.

GERALDINE DE COURCY

The Paris Opéra-Comique is preparing a revival of Gounod's 'Le Médecin Malgré Lui', a setting of Moliere's play of the same name.

WESTMINSTER THEATRE

Third Series of Dances by:-

AGNES GEORGE de MILLE
Antony Tudor and Hugh Laing

1. Pavane ... ... *Anon. arr. Norman Franklin*
   Charlotte Bidmead and Hugh Laing

2. Ballet Class
   Agnes de Mille

3. Joie de Vivre ... ... *Offenbach-Weston-Stra u*
   Charlotte Bidmead and Therese Langfield

4. The Parvenues ... ... *Waldteufel-Strauss*
   Agnes de Mille and Hugh Laing

5. Hunting Scene ... ... *J. C. Bach*
   Antony Tudor, Charlotte Bidmead, Therese Langfield

6. Forty-Niner Cowboy Songs ... ... *arr. D. W. Guion*
   Hoe-Down: A dance competition between two partners in which the first to miss a step is forced to abandon his place to a successor. The dancer who survives the longest without once getting off-beat or missing step is, naturally, the winner. *Virginia Reel:* The most popular of the square dances, based on the English tradition, and still performed in the remote towns of the West, the southern mountains, and the fishing villages of New England.
   Agnes de Mille

7. The Judgement of Paris ... ... *Kurt Weil*
   The Company

436. A program for one of the earliest performances of Antony Tudor's ballet, *The Judgement of Paris*, which used music from *Die Dreigroschenoper*.

438. Weill and Maxwell Anderson (on the right) rehearse Walter Huston and Jeanne Madden for *Knickerbocker Holiday*. The authors based the show on Washington Irving's *The History of New York* by Diedrich Knickerbocker.

437. The five founding members of the Playwrights' Company. Clockwise from the bottom: Robert Sherwood, Sidney Howard, Elmer Rice, S.N. Behrman, and Maxwell Anderson. The Playwrights' Company produced *Knickerbocker Holiday* and *Lost in the Stars,* and coproduced *Street Scene.*

439. *Knickerbocker Holiday* yielded "September Song," Weill's first American "standard," or song that became part of the "standard repertory." These illustrations show three manifestations of the song: a compositional sketch, Weill's rehearsal score, and a popular, sheet music version. (The full score is reproduced on plate 12.) Weill borrowed the beginning motive of the refrain from the arietta "Seit ich in diese Stadt gekommen bin" from *Der Kuhhandel.*

KNICKERBOCKER HOLIDAY

Musical play in two acts; book and lyrics by Maxwell Anderson

1938   New York, Ethel Barrymore Theatre (19 October; 168 performances)

Maurice Abravanel, conductor; Joshua Logan, director;
Carl Randall and Edwin Denby, choreographers;
Jo Mielziner, set designer; Frank Bevan, costume designer

Tour (9 weeks): Philadelphia, Buffalo, Cleveland, Pittsburgh, Detroit,
Columbus, Cincinnati, Chicago

1948   Essen, Städtische Bühnen (25 November)
1949   Göteborg, Stadsteatern (1 January)
        Boston, Copley Theatre (3 January)
1950   Helsinki, Suomen Kansallisteateri (4 January)

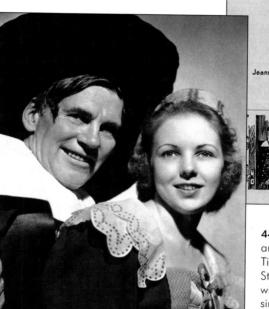

440. Opening night program for *Knickerbocker Holiday*, with the star's name above the title.

441. Walter Huston (Stuyvesant) and Jeanne Madden (Tina Tienhoven). The much older Stuyvesant almost succeeds in winning Tina's affection by singing "September Song" to her.

442. Act I: Brom (Richard Kollmar), the rebellious ne'er-do-well, sings "There's Nowhere to Go But Up" after having hit rock bottom. He wants to start a business as a knife sharpener so that he can marry Tina.

443. Act II, scene 1: Brom, jailed by Stuyvesant for being the "first American" (i.e. being unable to take orders), pulls his fiancée Tina into his cell. With Brom's sidekick Tenpin (Clarence Nordstrom), they conspire to escape, a plan thwarted by the arrival of Tina's father, the leader of the city council. Photo: Lucas-Pritchard.

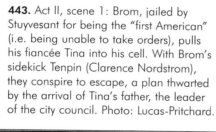

444. Although the city council has backed the totalitarian regime of Stuyvesant, at the end they refuse to hang Brom. The enraged governor is about to start a bloodbath when the narrating author Washington Irving intervenes as *deus ex machina*, convincing Stuyvesant that posterity would want to see him in a good light, a sort of patron saint of New York City.

I think calling the New Deal fascist is a poor sort of joke, and I consider labeling Roosevelt the American Hitler a vicious perversion. Mr. Anderson is too clever to damn the New Deal by calling it Red. Instead he has his Peter Stuyvesant paraphrase Roosevelt, even to the "my friends"—and then call in Storm Troopers. *Knickerbocker Holiday* is no crude, slambang attack on progressive America. Mr. Anderson makes his points by indirection. His lyrics are suave. His jokes disarming up to the stinger on the end. . . .

It seems a shame to have to add to this review of Mr. Anderson's attack on democracy in America the words, "With Music by Kurt Weill." And Mr. Weill's score for *Knickerbocker Holiday* is delightful. Many of the songs are hauntingly beautiful, and one at least, "September Song," will surely become a classic. Mr. Weill shows a new power in *Knickerbocker Holiday*, and a new variety of expression. I think it is nothing short of a catastrophe that this Kurt Weill music should illuminate Mr. Anderson's book. Ruth McKenney, *New Masses*, 1 November 1938.

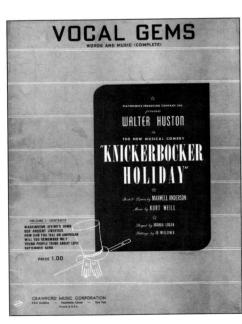

[From Final Edition of Yesterday's Times.]

THE PLAY

Walter Huston in Maxwell Anderson's Musical Comedy, 'Knickerbocker Holiday'

KNICKERBOCKER HOLIDAY, a musical comedy in two acts. Book and lyrics by Maxwell Anderson. Music by Kurt Weill. Staged by Joshua Logan; settings by Jo Mielziner; costumes designed by Frank Bevan; dances arranged by Carl Randall and Edwin Denby; produced by the Playwrights' Company as its second offering. At the Ethel Barrymore Theatre.

Washington Irving.............Ray Middleton
Anthony Corlear..............Harry Meehan
Tienhoven ....Mark Smith
Vanderbilt ....George Watts
Roosevelt....................Francis Pierlot
DePeyster ....Charles Arnt
DeVries ....John E. Young
Van Rensselaer ....James Phillips
Van Cortlandt Jr............Richard Cowdery
Tina Tienhoven..............Jeanne Madden
Brom Broeck.................Richard Kollmar
Tenpin......................Clarence Nordstrom
Schermerhorn................Howard Freeman
Pieter Stuyvesant...........Walter Huston
General Poffenburgh.........Donald Black
Mistress Schermerhorn.......Edith Angold
Citizens of New Amsterdam—Helen Carroll, Jane Brotherton, Carol Dels, Robert Arnold, Bruce Hamilton, Ruth Mabel, William Marel, Margaret MacLaren, Robert Rouneaville, Rufus Smith, Margaret Stewart, Erika Zaranova, William Wahlert.
Soldiers—Albert Allen, Matthias Ammann, Dow Fonda, Warde Peters.
Fighters—The Algonquins.

By BROOKS ATKINSON

Out of the early history of Manhattan, Maxwell Anderson has written the book and lyrics for a cultivated musical comedy, "Knickerbocker Holiday," which was staged at the Ethel Barrymore last evening, and Kurt Weill has written the music. It is an antic exercise in mummery and political satire, unlike anything Mr. Anderson has attempted before. With Walter Huston giving a salty performance as Peg-Leg Stuyvesant, the first dictator of this island, "Knickerbocker Holiday" is beautifully staged by the incipient Playwrights' Company under the versatile direction of young Joshua Logan, and there is much to recommend it in the way of intelligent showmanship and excellent music. But Mr. Anderson's style of writing leans toward the pedantic in a brisk musical setting. He cannot trip it quite gayly enough for the company he is keeping.

* * *

He is telling a fable of seventeenth century New York as Washington Irving might write it in his facetious history book. It depicts the knavery of the Dutch council government before stormy old Peg-Leg arrives and the tyranny of his personal administration when he stumps across the Battery mall. Under the conventional pattern of musical comedy making, Mr. Anderson has some general observations to make—about democracy as government by amateurs, which is superior to the practiced corruption of professionals, and about the anarchic spirit of the true American, who is constitutionally unable to take orders. At the opening of the second act Mr. Anderson takes a poke at the arbitrary economics of government by decree, which is doubtless inverted comment on the New Deal.

* * *

As a book-maker, Mr. Anderson's touch is a heavy one. He is at his best in his collaboration with Mr. Weill, whose music is lively and theatre-wise. In "How Can You Tell an American," which is the theme of this Knickerbocker festival, Mr. Anderson's rhymes have the subtlety of good lyric writing as well as the authority of a poet. Mr. Weill is a versatile fellow. He did the score for "Johnny Johnson" and "The Eternal Road." In his current work there is no style he cannot assimilate and compose. He writes dance tunes with modern gusto, romantic duets, comic pieces and a funeral march. Although it may not go far toward evoking the spirit of early America, it is vigorous composing for the modern theatre, superior to Broadway songwriting without settling in the academic groove.

* * *

As for the acting and staging of "Knickerbocker Holiday," they are both superb. Casting Walter Huston as Governor Stuyvesant is a stroke of genius. For he is an actor in the grand manner with a homely brand of native wit, bold in his gestures, commanding in his periods, yet purely sardonic and mischievous in spirit. After one of Mr. Anderson's bawdiest songs in im-peccable English, Mr. Huston brings the house down with a peg-leg dance at the end of a line of Dutch chorus girls. Mr. Huston is a great fellow to have in town again.

* * *

Mr. Logan has surrounded him with new faces, fresh voices and youthful enthusiasm for the stage. As Washington Irving, a sort of commentator on the scene, Ray Middleton is a congenial actor with a good voice. Richard Kollmar and Jeanne Madden as the romantic pair are gifted young people who act and sing exuberantly. A comic chorus of obese Dutch councilors, amusingly costumed by Jo Mielziner, includes Mark Smith, whose sense of humor is out of the old theatre, and Harry Meehan, the venerable Irish thrush who can blow the top off any theatre.

* * *

Although the stage at the Barrymore is a small one to include both Mr. Mielziner's handsome view of the Battery and a group of dancing Dutch maidens, Mr. Logan has discovered how to keep the performance breezy in style. But Mr. Anderson's book, which is a little arbitrary in craftsmanship, is unwieldy. The light, fantastic vein of musical comedy does not become his serious mind—or vice versa, as the case may be.

A Preface to the Politics of
Knickerbocker Holiday

✧ ✧

KNICKERBOCKER HOLIDAY was obviously written to make an occasion for Kurt Weill's music, and since Mr. Weill responded by writing the best score in the history of our theatre, and since the public has voted an emphatic approval at the box office, the whole venture would seem to justify itself without further comment.

But there has been a good deal of critical bewilderment over the political opinions expressed in the play, and not a little resentment at my definitions of government and democracy. I should like to explain that it was not my intention to say anything new or shocking on either subject, but only to remind the audience of the attitude toward government which was current in this country at the time of the revolution of 1776 and throughout the early years of the Republic. At that time it was generally believed, as I believe now, that the gravest and most constant danger to a man's life, liberty and happiness is the government under which he lives.

It was believed then, as I believe now, that a civilization is a balance of selfish interests, and that a government is necessary as an arbiter among these interests, but that the government must never be trusted, must be constantly watched, and must be drastically limited in its scope, because it, too, is a selfish interest and will automatically become a monopoly in crime and devour the civilization over which it presides unless there are definite and positive checks on its activities. The constitution is a monument to our forefathers' distrust of the state, and the division of powers among the legislative, judicial and executive branches has succeeded so well for more than a century in keeping the sovereign authority in its place that our government is now widely regarded as a naturally wise and benevolent institution, capable of assuming the whole burden of social and economic justice.

✧ ▽ ✧

445. The plainspoken politics of Anderson's text became somewhat controversial, so much that he felt it necessary to write an essay explaining his opinions for the *New York Times*. He used the essay as a preface to the libretto published by Anderson House, the first page of which is shown here.

446. Brooks Atkinson's review of *Knickerbocker Holiday* in the *New York Times*, 21 October 1938.

447. Publicity shot taken shortly after the opening of *Knickerbocker Holiday*.

448. Crawford Music Corporation released two "vocal gems" albums from *Knickerbocker Holiday*, which contained between them about half of the songs.

449. Weill inscribed a copy of the "vocal gems" song collection to Maurice Abravanel, conductor of *Knickerbocker Holiday*, using a phrase from *Die Bürgschaft*. Weill viewed Abravanel as "his" conductor on Broadway; Abravanel conducted all of Weill's Broadway musicals-from *Knickbocker Holiday* through *Street Scene*. The text, changed slightly from the original, reads, "Wir sind dieselben, die wir immer waren. Du bist mein Freund seit vielen Jahren." ["We are the same as we've always been. You've been my friend for many years."]

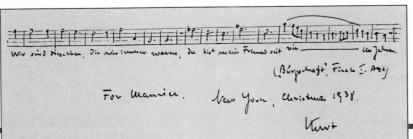

NO WORD UTTERED!!

For upon what other stage does the actor move and (seemingly) speak his lines, *without one word actually uttering from his lips*? The result is most baffling to the audience. Long ago we realized that dialogue spoken from the floor of the great unroofed stages could not by any possibility reach the far corners of our amphitheater, with its four thousand seats. But in these days of sound audition it was not necessary to have such an old-fashioned way of acting. The men and women upon our stage are merely mimes. Their acting is *pantomime*, exquisite gesturing. Their voices come from far away, from a concrete soundproof room just underneath the amphitheater. Within that hidden room and through a slender window of plate glass, the voice of each mime watches its master and speaks for him or her. Thus Abraham Lincoln on our stage is enacted by a young actor of just the correct build and type; *his voice* is that of another actor, who in his physique more closely resembles Taft than Lincoln. And so it goes, throughout the entire cast.

This technique used for individual members of the cast is also used for the chorus and for our twenty-five piece orchestra—under the baton of a distinguished conductor, Dr. Isaac van Grove—who are also assembled in the subterranean *sound room*. Closely adjacent to this room are two switchboards—the one for sound and the other for light—between them the control board for the entire production. Edward Hungerford, *Setting History to Music*, New York: Newcomen Society, 1939, pp. 14-15.

Railroads on Parade, the elaborate show which partakes of both the revue and the historical pageant, has a score by Kurt Weill. . . . Though it incorporates parts of possibly a dozen old American songs, there is no lack of original composition. At the close is a song by Weill, "Mile after Mile," that would have been a real hit in an earlier time. It may turn out to be one now. When the composer goes jazzy in the contemporary episodes of the pageant, he inclines, perhaps, to what the swing experts call "corny," but his music has animation and tune.

For a European, Mr. Weill has shown sympathy as well as skill and good judgment in his handling of various snatches of Americana. Inevitably, "O, Susanna" attends the travelers of covered wagon days and it could scarcely be expected that tracks could be laid across the continent without "I've Been Workin' on the Railroad." Nor could engines puff into view without some reference to "Casey Jones."

But it is in his use of still older songs, like "John Handy," "Erie Canal," "Heave Away," and the spiritual "This Train is Bound for Glory," that Mr. Weill has contrived to give the visual action precisely the right musical background. His own music is consistently apt. The use of the whistles of the locomotives for a colloquy between them when the first trains from the East and the West meet in Nevada is amusingly worked out.

For the benefit of those who will argue that some of the stage personages either speak or sing, let it be said that save for the utterances of the two narrators, every note and syllable originates in sound rooms under the audience and is carried from microphones to loud speakers on the stage. The actors merely mime their parts throughout. Isaac van Grove, the conductor, has under his direction a group of twenty-five picked singers and an orchestra of about the same size. The performance is amazingly well synchronized and the staging of Charles Alan deserves some sort of prize. Incidentally, composer Weill has called the show "a circus opera," which, so far as the music dictionaries go, is entitled to be considered a new form. Oscar Thompson, "New Roles for Music at Fair," [publication unknown].

RAILROADS ON PARADE

1939-40   New York World's Fair, Railroad Pavilion; multiple performances per day

*Isaac van Grove, conductor; Charles Alan, director;
Bill Matons, choreographer; Harry Horner, set and costume designer*

450. The program of *Railroads on Parade*. Three members of *The Eternal Road* production team participated in *Railroads on Parade*: Isaac van Grove, Charles Alan, and Harry Horner. Employing sound playback techniques similar to those used *The Eternal Road*, the music created by the live singers and musicians is played back in the amphitheater from a remote sound room.

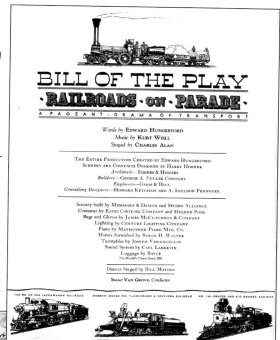

451. The first page from Weill's autograph score of *Railroads on Parade*.

452. Act IV, scene 3, set in a new, large, busy train station, begins with a modern-day, syncopated theme, "Oh mister, mister, where's the train?" Historian Edward Hungerford wrote the words to the pageant.

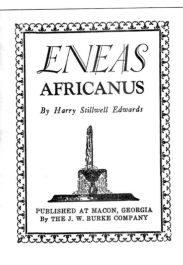

454. *Railroads on Parade* is featured in *Life* magazine (3 July 1939, pp. 62-63).

455. Frontispiece and title page of *Eneas Africanus*, an epistolary novella which Weill and Anderson tried to turn into a musical, following on the success of *Knickerbocker Holiday*. The work, retitled *Ulysses Africanus*, was never performed, though some of the songs were later incorporated into *Lost in the Stars* (1949).

453. Weill was finally elected to ASCAP (American Society of Composers, Authors, and Publishers) in May 1939, almost two years after receiving his formal immigration papers.

1 9 3 9

MUSIC + THEATER:

Aaron Copland *Billy the Kid*

Cole Porter *DuBarry Was a Lady*

Lillian Hellman *The Little Foxes*

LITERATURE + FILM:

John Steinbeck *The Grapes of Wrath*

The Wizard of Oz (film by Victor Fleming)

James Joyce *Finnegans Wake*

SCIENCE + SOCIETY:

Otto Hahn succeeds in nuclear fission

Edwin H. Armstrong invents frequency modulation (FM)

Pan-American Airways begins commercial flights between U.S. and Europe

POLITICS:

Roosevelt asks Congress for $552 million for defense

England and Poland sign a treaty of mutual assistance

Germany invades Poland, starts World War II

Arthur Lyons (in Hollywood) to Weill, 17 October 1939: As you probably know by this time, Aaron Copland has been set to do the music for *Of Mice and Men.* Both I and Abe Meyer worked very hard on this but unfortunately they have decided on Aaron Copland.

On Saturday I had lunch with Milestone and at that time I told him that both you and I were disappointed over the fact that you did not get to do the music for *Of Mice and Men.* Milestone explained that he, too, was very anxious to have you but Frank Ross insisted on Copland because they were able to get him for very little money. Whether or not this is the reason, I don't know, but I do know that it is a true fact that they were able to get him for very little money and with the economic wave at its height, it might have been a great influence. . . . Presently you are up for three pictures on which we are awaiting decisions.

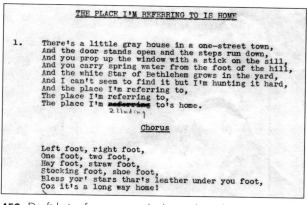

458. A portion of Weill's sketches for *Ulysses Africanus.* This upbeat song, "Hi-yo, Discernible Today," would have been sung by Homer, a character in a minstrel show that Ulysses was to stage within the play and in which his famous namesake was portrayed. (Anderson reworked the lyrics into a poem published in the *New Yorker* in 1948.)

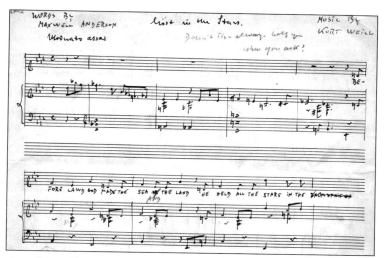

456. Originally written for *Ulysses Africanus,* "Lost in the Stars" became one of Weill's most popular American songs.

457. Bill Robinson. Anderson first offered the leading role in *Ulysses Africanus* to Paul Robeson, who declined. Bill Robinson, who was appearing on Broadway in *The Hot Mikado,* expressed interest in the part, but then was unavailable during the upcoming 1939–40 season.

THE PLACE I'M REFERRING TO IS HOME

1. There's a little gray house in a one-street town,
    And the door stands open and the steps run down,
    And you prop up the window with a stick on the sill,
    And you carry spring water from the foot of the hill,
    And the white Star of Bethlehem grows in the yard,
    And I can't seem to find it but I'm hunting it hard,
    And the place I'm referring to,
    The place I'm referring to,
    The place I'm referring to's home.

Chorus

    Left foot, right foot,
    One foot, two foot,
    Hay foot, straw foot,
    Stocking foot, shoe foot,
    Bless yor' stars thar's leather under you foot,
    Coz it's a long way home!

459. Draft lyrics for a song which was later fitted into *Lost in the Stars* under the title "The Little Gray House."

460. Painter Arthur Kaufmann made this portrait study of Weill to prepare for his triptych "Arts and Sciences Finding Refuge in the U.S.A."

461. Weill provided incidental music for Sidney Howard's play, *Madam, Will You Walk,* which closed after its tryout in Baltimore

George M. Cohan
in
"MADAM, WILL YOU WALK"
Week of Nov. 13, 1939

FORD'S THEATRE

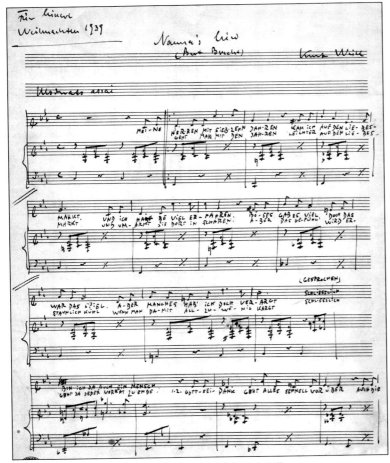

462. As a Christmas present for Lenya in 1939, Weill set Brecht's "Nannas Lied," a lyric from *Die Rundköpfe und die Spitzköpfe* previously set by Hanns Eisler.

I'm convinced that many modern composers have a feeling of superiority toward their audiences. Schoenberg, for example, has said he is writing for a time fifty years after his death. But the great "classic" composers wrote for their contemporary audiences. They wanted those who heard their music to understand it, and they did. As for myself, I write for today. I don't give a damn about writing for posterity.

And I do not feel that I compromise my integrity as a musician by working for the theater, the radio, the motion pictures, or any other medium which can reach the public which wants to listen to music. I have never acknowledged the difference between "serious" music and "light" music. There is only good music and bad music. . . .

After all, music can only express human sentiments. I'd never write a single measure for purely aesthetic reasons, in an effort to create a new style. I write only to express human emotions. If music is really human, it doesn't make much difference how it is conveyed. And as long as it is able to reach its audience emotionally, its creator should not worry about possible sentimentality or banality. William G. King, "Composer for the Theater—Kurt Weill Talks about 'Practical Music,'" *New York Sun*, 3 February 1940.

463. Cover of the published vocal score of the cantata *The Ballad of Magna Carta*, another collaboration with Maxwell Anderson, set for singing narrator, tenor and bass soloists, chorus, and orchestra. The work was commissioned by the Columbia Broadcasting System for a radio series produced by Norman Corwin called *The Pursuit of Happiness*.

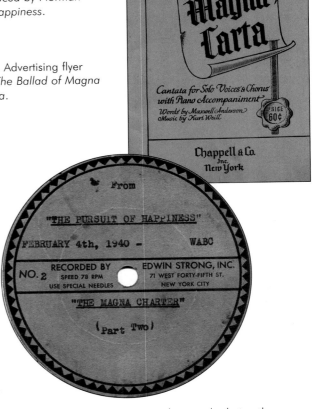

464. This excerpt from *The Ballad of Magna Carta*, where King John strikes down the Seneschal, is parallel musically to the section in *Aufstieg und Fall der Stadt Mahagonny* where Joe is killed in the boxing ring (*cf.* piano-vocal score, 1969 edition, p. 202).

THE BALLAD OF MAGNA CARTA

was produced for the first time on February 4th, 1940 on the "Pursuit of Happiness" program of the Columbia Broadcasting System, with Burgess Meredith in the role of the narrator.

This Cantata has been written so that it may be performed with or without scenery or costumes, although the use of the latter might heighten the effect. The writers have included suggestions for staging in the vocal score.

The text by the well known playwright, Maxwell Anderson, is most timely, and the music is impressive, but not too difficult for schools or colleges.

The rendition time is fifteen minutes.

The score and parts of Kurt Weill's original orchestration,—2 Flutes, 1 Oboe, 4 Saxaphones, 1 Bassoon, 3 Trumpets, 2 Trombones, Piano, Harp, Guitar, Drums and Strings, are available on rental, also special String Orchestra arrangement.

465. Advertising flyer for *The Ballad of Magna Carta*.

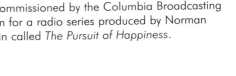

466. Label of an instantaneous recording made during the first performance of *The Ballad of Magna Carta*, broadcast on CBS Radio, 4 February 1940. Burgess Meredith, Weill's and Anderson's friend and neighbor in New City, was the narrator.

AMERICA CALLING

1940 – 1945

I wrote some orchestra music, but I threw it away.
It seems so silly to write music at a time like this.

Kurt Weill

1940

February — Begins to collaborate with Ira Gershwin and Moss Hart on *Lady in the Dark*.

July 15 — Weill and Lenya welcome close friends Darius and Madeleine Milhaud on their arrival in New York.

August — Takes a short vacation in Maine with Maxwell and Mab Anderson.

1941

January 23 — *Lady in the Dark* (February–November 1940, lyrics by Ira Gershwin, book by Moss Hart). Alvin Theatre, New York; Maurice Abravanel, conductor; Moss Hart, director. 545 performances over three seasons. The premiere marks Weill's first unqualified success on Broadway and solidifies his career in America.

May — The film rights to *Lady in the Dark* are sold to Paramount for $285,000, the highest price to date for a Broadway musical.

May 28 — Purchases Brook House in New City (Rockland County), New York, a home that Lenya keeps until her death in 1981. Their neighbors are Maxwell Anderson, actor Burgess Meredith, artist Henry Varnum Poor, cartoonist Milton Caniff, actress Helen Hayes, playwright Charles MacArthur, author Bessie Breuer, and publisher William Sloane.

Summer — Tries to set up a collaboration between himself, Ruth Page, and John Latouche for a show based on Bible stories and the evangelist Billy Sunday.

September — Meets with Ben Hecht to discuss a possible collaboration, but Weill advises that his play, *Lily of the Valley*, does not need music.

October 5 — *Fun to Be Free* (pageant by Ben Hecht and Charles MacArthur). Madison Square Garden, New York; Simon Rady, conductor; Brett Warren, director. Sponsored by Fight for Freedom, Inc.

December 7 — U.S. enters World War II after Japan attacks Pearl Harbor.

1942

January–June — While searching in vain for new collaborators and meaningful projects, Weill uses his talents to support the war effort.

January — *Walt Whitman Songs*: "Oh Captain! My Captain!" "Beat! Beat! Drums!" "Dirge for Two Veterans," New York. (A fourth song, "Come Up from the Fields, Father," is composed in 1947.) Weill hopes that Paul Robeson will record them. "Beat! Beat! Drums!" is recorded as a spoken song in March by Helen Hayes. All four songs are recorded in 1947 by tenor William Horne.

January 26 — The producers celebrate the first anniversary of *Lady in the Dark* by giving away defense bonds at the performances.

February — Tries to find a play for Lenya and suggests George Bernard Shaw's *Caesar and Cleopatra* with Walter Huston as the co-star.

February–April — [*Songs for the War Effort*], New York.

> "Schickelgruber" (Howard Dietz)
> "One Morning in Spring" (St. Clair McKelway, lost)
> "The Good Earth" (Oscar Hammerstein)
> "Buddy on the Nightshift" (Oscar Hammerstein)
> "Song of the Inventory" (Lewis Allan)
> "We Don't Feel Like Surrendering Today" (Maxwell Anderson)
> "Oh Uncle Samuel!" (Maxwell Anderson, melody by Henry C. Work)
> "Toughen Up, Buckle Down, Carry On" (Dorothy Fields)

February 14 — Registers for the draft (military service). Writes to Lenya that the songs for the war effort are going well, but he wishes he had an opera to work on.

February 28 — *Your Navy* (incidental music for a radio program by Maxwell Anderson). Score is missing. Norman Corwin, director; Don Vorhees, conductor; Frederic March and Douglas Fairbanks, Jr., narrators. Produced by NBC Radio, New York, the show aired on all four national radio networks.

March 31 — [*Four Patriotic Melodramas*]. Recorded by Helen Hayes; Roy Shields, conductor; Victor M 909. "Battle Hymn of the Republic," "The Star Spangled Banner," "America," and "Beat! Beat! Drums!"

Spring — Becomes chairman of the production committee for "Lunch Time Follies," presented by the American Theatre Wing. The "Follies" are performed in defense plants, but Weill, being an alien, is frequently denied admittance to the factories.

Corresponds with Clarence Muse, Paul Robeson, Brecht, and Adorno regarding an adaptation of *Die Dreigroschenoper* for an all-black cast in California. Angered by a proposal to reorchestrate the work for a jazz band and a proposed contract that would cede rights in perpetuity and pay him almost nothing, Weill agrees only to a one-time production in California, which never happens.

April — Works on *The Pirate*, a musical based on Ludwig Fulda's play *Der Seeräuber*, adapted by S. N. Behrman for production by the Playwrights' Company and Alfred Lunt. The collaboration never solidifies, and Weill withdraws from the project.

June — Cheryl Crawford, now an independent producer, agrees to back Weill's proposed collaboration with Sam and Bella Spewack on a musical adaptation of F. Anstey's novella *The Tinted Venus*, for which Ogden Nash will write the lyrics. Weill offers the title role to Marlene Dietrich.

June 4 — *Song of the Free* (Archibald MacLeish). Roxy Theatre, New York, Bob Hannon, vocalist.

August — *Russian War Relief* (J. P. McEvoy). Nyack, New York. The piece is performed in a revue, *Rockland Riot*, to benefit Rockland for Russia.

September 30	In California, Weill and Brecht meet for the first time since 1935. Weill discusses with Marlene Dietrich the lead role in *One Man's Venus*, the show he is working on with Bella Spewack. After Dietrich declines, Tilly Losch is considered.
November	Resumes work for "Lunch Time Follies."

1943

	Arranges six songs for Lenya to record on Bost Records (BA 8): "Surabaya Johnny," "Denn wie man sich bettet," "J'attends un navire," "Complainte de la Seine," "Lost in the Stars," and "Lover Man." Weill supervises and perhaps plays the piano accompaniment.
February	Ben Hecht calls a meeting of thirty Jewish authors and one composer (Weill) to discuss a concerted reaction to the killing of Jews in Germany. Only Weill and Moss Hart pledge support.
March 9	*We Will Never Die* (Ben Hecht). "A memorial dedicated to the Two Million Jewish Dead of Europe." Madison Square Garden, New York; Isaac van Grove, conductor; Moss Hart, director. The production travels to Washington, D.C., Philadelphia, Chicago, Boston, and Hollywood; it is also widely broadcast.
April	Finally despairing of the Spewack *Venus* script, Cheryl Crawford engages the celebrated humorist S. J. Perelman to write an entirely new book.
April 3	*Und was bekam des Soldaten Weib* (March 1942, Bertolt Brecht). Hunter College, New York. Lenya performs this song and three from *Die Dreigroschenoper* in a concert entitled "We Fight Back," a promotional event to sell war bonds to a German-speaking audience.
May	Brecht and Ruth Berlau visit Weill at Brook House, where the three begin work on an operatic version of *The Good Soldier Schweik* and a "half-opera" adaptation of *The Good Woman of Sezuan*. Neither project materializes and no music survives.
June	Works on film versions of *Lady in the Dark* and *Knickerbocker Holiday* in Hollywood. Weill is approached by MGM to write a film score, and tries to persuade Marlene Dietrich to star in *One Touch of Venus*. He returns to New York in July via St. Louis.
August 27	Becomes a U.S. citizen.
October 7	*One Touch of Venus* (June–September 1943, lyrics by Ogden Nash, book by S. J. Perelman and Ogden Nash). Imperial Theatre, New York; Maurice Abravanel, conductor; Elia Kazan, director. 567 performances over two seasons.
November	Works with Ira Gershwin on the film *Where Do We Go from Here?* in Hollywood, where he and Lenya take an apartment at 881 Moraga Drive in Bel Air. It becomes Weill's most ambitious film score, even including a 'mini-opera' for the Columbus sequence.

1944

January	The cast album for *One Touch of Venus* is released by Decca.
January–March	Further negotiations with Brecht regarding *Der gute Mensch von Sezuan*, resulting in a collaboration agreement.
February	The film version of *Lady in the Dark* starring Ginger Rogers is released by Paramount. Weill returns to New York in late Feburary.
Mid-April	The film version of *Knickerbocker Holiday* is released by United Artists, starring Nelson Eddy and Charles Coburn.
Spring	*Wie lange noch* (Walter Mehring). Recorded by Lenya for the Office of War Information, intended for broadcast in Germany behind enemy lines. Lenya also records *Und was bekam des Soldaten Weib* for the OWI.

Producer Billy Rose invites Weill to write a ballet score for Anton Dolin to be included in the revue *The Seven Lively Arts*. Weill declines but suggests Stravinsky, who composes *Scènes du ballet* for the production. |
April–May	*Salute to France* (Maxwell Anderson). Music for a propaganda film starring Burgess Meredith, directed by Jean Renoir and Garson Kanin and produced by the U.S. Office of War Information. The film is released in both English and French versions.
Late June	Travels to Hollywood for collaboration with Edwin Justus Mayer and Ira Gershwin on *The Firebrand of Florence*. Rents a house at 10640 Taranto Way, Bel Air, and attends recording sessions for the film *Where Do We Go from Here?* Lenya joins him in mid-September.
October	Completes the rehearsal score of *The Firebrand of Florence* and reluctantly renounces the Brecht project, having failed to find a Broadway producer for it. He and Lenya return to New York.

1945

March 22	*The Firebrand of Florence* (July–December 1944, lyrics by Ira Gershwin, book by Edwin Justus Mayer). Alvin Theatre, New York; Maurice Abravanel, conductor; John Murray Anderson, director. 43 performances. The show opens to poor reviews and is Weill's only flat-out Broadway failure.
April	Travels to Hollywood, staying at the Bel Air Hotel to work on the film score of *One Touch of Venus*. Considers other projects, including an adaptation of *Un chapeau de paille d'Italie* with René Clair, while hoping that his next project will be an opera. Meets Brecht on 18 April and corresponds with Paul Robeson concerning a "black Oedipus" opera. Other operatic project ideas include *Gone with the Wind*, *The Grapes of Wrath*, *Winterset*, and *Moby Dick*. Weill attends a screening of the final version of *Where Do We Go from Here?* (20th Century-Fox) on 29 April.

Playwright-Combine Offers 60 Air Shows

Sixty plays, written by members of the Playwrights Producing Co., are being made available to radio through the Playwrights Radio Co., an affiliate of the Playwrights Producing Co. Associated in the new venture are all members of the PPC, Elmer Rice, S. N. Behrman, Maxwell Anderson, Robert Sherwood and Sidney Howard's Estate.

Group will also invite well-known radio writers, including Arch Oboler, Irving Reis, and other writers. Staff of producers, directors and adaptors are associated with the new company, while an acting group is being organized. Dwight Cooke, Norman Corwin, Carlo DeAngelo, George Faulkner and Clyde North have been named as directors and adaptors. Kurt Weill is musical director, while Henry Souvaine will handle production and business activities.

468. A 7 February 1940 report in the trade paper *Radio Daily* announces plans by the Playwrights' Company to produce radio plays. Weill is named as music director, but the series never materializes.

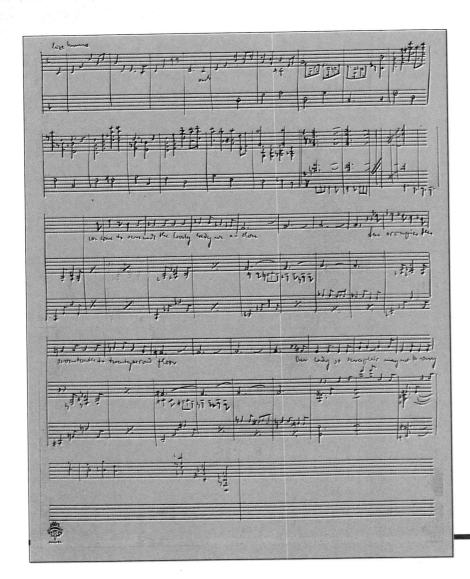

Weill (in Suffern) to Frank Cahill, 6 June 1940: This is just a reminder that we are thinking of you a lot during these dark days. I wanted to write to you for a long time, but things were moving at such a breathtaking tempo that it seemed silly to write letters, and now when there is so little to say for an onlooker, except that we are with you, that your fears are our fears and your hopes our hopes, and that we all have an enormous admiration for what you are doing over there and that we all know that you are fighting the last battle for civilization. This sounds like big words, but you know it is the simple truth.

But at the moment I am more interested to know how you are, if you are doing service and where. And how is your family? Where are the kids? Please, if you have a moment, write us a line, just to let us know how you are.

The news from us is less interesting. I wrote a new show with Maxwell Anderson, but we couldn't put it on because we could not cast it. Therefore I had no show last season. Now I have written a new musical play with Moss Hart and I am working on the score now. Ira Gershwin is writing the lyrics. The whole thing looks very promising. It is scheduled for a November opening, with Sam Harris as producer.

We are living in the country since last October, an hour from New York, a lovely old house at the foot of a hill, very isolated, with a beautiful garden. It is wonderful in times like this to live with trees, flowers and animals—they seem to have so much sense. That sounds rather "escapist," doesn't it? But I guess our turn will come before long, and then we need our nerves.

Weill (in Suffern) to Erika Mann, 17 June 1940: I guess I am not the only one who is trying to figure out what our, the refugees', position will be in this country in the coming months and years. What can we do to help America in her inevitable fight against Nazism? What can we do to avoid being mixed up with Fifth Column elements when anti-alien feeling grows stronger? What can we do to prove to our American friends that we are loyal citizens of this country? . . .

My idea is to form immediately an organization called something like "Alliance of Loyal Alien Americans" with the purpose of convincing the authorities and the public in this country that we are strongly anti-Nazi, that they can count on us in every effort to save American democracy, and that they can consider us in every way to be faithful American citizens. This organization could be of service to the authorities in investigations of Fifth Column activities because we would have a complete record of the activities of all of our members. We could also provide the press with material about the contributions of our friends to the economical, cultural, and educational life in the U.S.A.

469. Weill and Ira Gershwin began collaborating on *Lady in the Dark* in February 1940. This score shows Weill's draft for the beginning of the first extended dream sequence, the "Glamour Dream." The melody for "My Ship," which serves as a kind of leitmotif throughout the work, opens the section.

William Saroyan (in San Francisco) to Weill, 6 August 1940: I have assembled and arranged material for a musical revue, which is tentatively entitled *American Handicap*. I shall be in New York by the end of this month, August, and hope to begin production immediately upon arriving. I am writing to ask if you will be free to do the music for this show. Among the material needing music is a fifteen-minute spoof-opera, a ballet-poem, two song sketches, a sideshow (which will need musical accompaniment), a lecture (which will need some comic solos for accompaniment), and so on. A five-minute overture, also. If you like the idea and are free to do the music, will you write me immediately, so that I can send you the material, and give you an idea as to the scheme of the whole revue.

Benjamin Britten (in Owl's Head, Maine) to Elizabeth Mayer, 22 August 1940: We came into dinner the other evening and heard some pretty sophisticated talk going on and recognized Kurt Weill! He was spending a few days here with Mr. and Mrs. Maxwell Anderson (*Key Largo* fame—or infame!). We saw quite a lot of him and he was really awfully nice and sympathetic, and it was remarkable how many friends we had in common, both in Europe and here. He tells me that Werfel was not shot and may be coming here, and that Goland [i.e. Golo] Mann apparently has been contacted with—other news not so good.

Kurt Weill
Suffern, N.Y.   August 24, 1940

Dear Miss Lawrence,

        I was on a little fishing trip in Maine and when I
came back Moss told me that you would like to have some
of the songs. So I made a copy of "My Ship" for you and
also one of "One life to live". I hope you'll find a good
pianist to play them, and I hope you can read the words.

        If the two F's at the end of "My Ship" are too
difficult please try the whole song one tone lower (in
e flat) and let me know which key is better for you.
The verse of "One life to live" is written as a kind of
monotone because it is supposed to be done in the style
of a soap box orator on Columbus Circle.

        Ira went back to the coast last week. About 90%
of the score is finished. I am working out a complete
piano score now and then I start orchestrating. We are
all very excited about the show. In the second dream
you'll sing a charming Fairy tale "The Princess of Pure
Delight" and a kind of Hollywood song "Unforgettable"
(with Randy). In the third dream you have a little waltz
and a song "No matter under what star you're borne" which
leads into an "Habanera" and in the last dream you have
a duett "Our little home in San Fernando Valley". All
this I'll have to show to you before you can work on it.
Maybe, when your road will bring you closer to New York
we can get together.

        I hope you're having a nice time on the road and are
not working too much.

                                        With my best regards
                                        Yours truly,

                                        Kurt Weill

470. Letter to Gertrude Lawrence from 24 August 1940, with which Weill sent copies of two songs, "One Life to Live" and "My Ship."

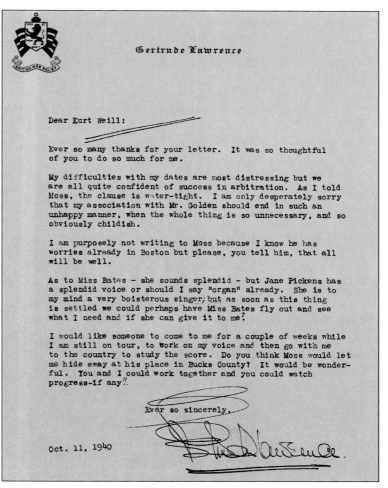

Gertrude Lawrence

Dear Kurt Weill:

Ever so many thanks for your letter. It was so thoughtful
of you to do so much for me.

My difficulties with my dates are most distressing but we
are all quite confident of success in arbitration. As I told
Moss, the clause is water-tight. I am only desperately sorry
that my association with Mr. Golden should end in such an
unhappy manner, when the whole thing is so unnecessary, and so
obviously childish.

I am purposely not writing to Moss because I know he has
worries already in Boston but please, you tell him, that all
will be well.

As to Miss Bates - she sounds splendid - but Jane Pickens has
a splendid voice or should I say "organ" already. She is to
my mind a very boisterous singer; but as soon as this thing
is settled we could perhaps have Miss Bates fly out and see
what I need and if she can give it to me?

I would like someone to come to me for a couple of weeks while
I am still on tour, to work on my voice and then go with me
to the country to study the score. Do you think Moss would let
me hide away at his place in Bucks County? It would be wonderful. You and I could work together and you could watch
progress-if any!".

                        Ever so sincerely,

Oct. 11, 1940

471. Gertrude Lawrence's reply to Weill's letter of 7 October 1940, reprinted below.

Weill (in New York) to Gertrude Lawrence, 7 October 1940: I am awfully sorry that this road tour is so strenuous for you and in reading your letter I realized that it would really be very difficult for you to start rehearsals on our play the same day you are closing *Skylark*. As you know I talked immediately to Sam Harris and Moss [Hart] about this matter. We had all hoped that you could quit this road tour a little earlier, but since that does not seem possible we all agreed that we should make it possible for you to get two weeks' rest, and we decided therefore to postpone rehearsals, for your sake, until December 2nd, although you can imagine how tough that is for us. Your husband told us that you would like to have someone check up on your voice during your two weeks' vacation in November. . . . I am always somewhat afraid of singing teachers because I have seen them spoil the individual qualities of natural voices in many cases (and I think you have a wonderful natural voice). I think what you want is somebody who would help you to relax your voice after the hardships of this road tour. I got very good reports about Clarissa Bates (222 Central Park South) who has done just this kind of work with very good results. I hear that she has prepared Jane Pickens for the Ed Wynn show and that everybody was very satisfied. Do you want me to talk to her?

Ira Gershwin remembers . . .

I met Kurt Weill at a party given by my brother, George, in 1935, shortly after Kurt had arrived in America. We hadn't exchanged more than a few sentences when Kurt said he would like to collaborate with me. Little did I think then that one day we would be working together.

In 1940, Kurt approached Moss Hart, another Pulitzer Prize winner, and kept after him for a possible play; a libretto to be made into a musical. But Moss kept responding that he was too busy with, among other matters, his psychoanalysis. So Kurt said, "Well, how about doing the play about psychoanalysis?" Moss said he'd think about it, and then they had several more meetings, until Moss thought he had something.

Some time after, I received a telegram from Moss asking whether I could work with him and Kurt on a musical play based on psychoanalysis to be called *I Am Listening*, which title, of course, he later changed to *Lady in the Dark*. Being free at the time, my answer was that I'd be delighted, and early in May, nineteen forty, I went to New York. Kurt and I worked in my hotel suite at the Essex House for sixteen weeks during the hottest summer I'd ever known, and no air conditioning, either. *Lady in the Dark* called for an unusually varied score; with serenades, fairy tales set to music, a great deal of recitative and, among other numbers, a simple childhood song which wound up as "My Ship." "My Ship," the song [that] ran through the play, was so brilliantly orchestrated by Kurt that it became a sort of *mysterioso* motive, keeping the audience in suspense about its meaning until the very end of the show when, finally, Liza suddenly remembered the lyric that had been haunting her and sang it with its words, which helped her and the analyst to solve her problem.

472. Ira Gershwin, New York, probably in 1945.

Kurt was receptive and responsive to almost any notion, and there were several times when he came up with excellent suggestions for lyrics. "A Living Liner" issued with "Two Worlds of Kurt Weill," RCA LSC-2863.

Weill (in Suffern) to Ira Gershwin, 2 September 1940: I met with Moss and Hassard at Moss' house to talk about the dreams. Moss had read the play to the boys in the office the night before. They were crazy about the whole show. Their only objection was that the bar scene and the Hollywood dream had nothing to do with the play. Moss suggested to throw both the bar scene and the Hollywood dream out. He first talked only about cutting out the Hollywood dream and I refused flatly. Then, when he said he would cut out the bar scene, I began to see certain advantages. It is obvious that this change would be very good for the play itself because it would mean that we go from the flashback scene directly into the last scene of the play. The decision which Liza makes in the last scene would be an immediate result of the successful analysis. The balance between music and book would be very good in the second act because we would make the flashback scene a completely musical scene, with a new song for the high school dance we'll have to write (I thought it should be a kind of early Irving Berlin song) and we have opportunity for a very nice dance production for this song, and then "My Ship" will become the big song of the second act. Another advantage would be that, with this cut, the show would be twenty-five to thirty minutes shorter and we save two sets and about 20,000 dollars. I could see all these advantages pretty soon, but on the other hand I saw that we would lose an entire musical scene and some very good material. That's why I didn't want to make any decision before I had heard your opinion. But Moss and Hassard had already made up their minds that they would make this cut. . . . Another thing which came up in my session with Moss and Hassard was the question of "material" for Gertie. Hassard seems to have the impression that Gertie hasn't got a really funny song. What he means is a show-stopping song with laugh lines, etc. He seemed sure that Gertie will not be satisfied if we don't give her material of this kind, and I'm afraid he might be right about that.

Weill (in New York) to Maurice Abravanel, 8 November 1940: Well, the conductor situation for my show is getting more critical than you think. The Sam Harris office insists that the conductor has to be there from the *first day of rehearsals*. They are very proud that they are the only producer organization on Broadway which always has their conductor for full rehearsal time, and they say that in the case of my show it is absolutely necessary because it is a difficult score, it is to a great part chorus work and we have only three weeks rehearsals before we go to Boston. They say it would be alright for them if I would do the complete rehearsal job for you, but that is physically impossible because I have to be at the dance rehearsals to work out the ballets, compose and orchestrate them and watch the rehearsals of the play for the incidental music which has to be written/orchestrated. All I can do is to work with the soloists.

1 9 4 1

MUSIC + THEATER:	LITERATURE + FILM:	SCIENCE + SOCIETY:	POLITICS:
Dmitri Shostakovich *Symphony No. 7*	F. Scott Fitzgerald *The Last Tycoon*	"Manhattan Project" of intensive atomic research begins in the U.S.	Germany invades Russia
Olivier Messaien *Quatuor pour la fin du temps* (composed as German POW)	*The Two-Faced Woman* (film by George Cukor)	Rudolf Bultmann "Neues Testament und Theologie"	Rommel retreats in North Africa
Bertolt Brecht *Mutter Courage und ihre Kinder*	*Suspicion* (film by Alfred Hitchcock)	Joe DiMaggio hits safely in 56 consecutive baseball games, establishing a major league record	Japan attacks Pearl Harbor

LADY IN THE DARK

Play in two acts by Moss Hart; lyrics by Ira Gershwin

1941 New York, Alvin Theatre, 23 January; 545 New York performances over three seasons; a national tour (September 1942–February 1943) and a west coast tour (May–July 1943).

Maurice Abravanel, conductor; Moss Hart and Hassard Short, directors; Albertina Rasch, choreographer; Harry Horner, set designer; Irene Sharaff, costume designer; Hattie Carnegie, gown designer for Gertrude Lawrence

1945 Berkeley, Wheeler Auditorium
1949 Sea Cliff, Summer Theatre
Long Beach, Crest Theatre

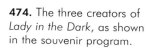

473. Title page of the *Lady in the Dark* souvenir program.

475. Lobby card for *Lady in the Dark*'s February 1943 return to Broadway.

474. The three creators of *Lady in the Dark*, as shown in the souvenir program.

476. A full score page from near the end of the first act of *Lady in the Dark*. Weill ultimately controlled the dramatic nuance of his Broadway works by orchestrating nearly all the music in his shows.

*Moss Hart * Kurt Weill * Ira Gershwin*

477. Maurice Abravanel: I remember I met Copland; I was doing his *Salon Mexico* which was brand new in New York, 1940 or something like that—'41. And we had luncheon together, and he said he saw *Lady in the Dark*. He said, "It's very interesting how Kurt goes from those straight play scenes into the musical scenes. What's the orchestration there?" There were two notes. I said "Clarinet." He said, "Yes, clarinet, what else?" I said, "Clarinet." "Well, what else?" I said, "Nothing else." He said, "Goddammit, we slave for months to find a thing like that. Kurt does that with one clarinet and two notes." (Interview with Maurice Abravanel by Alan Rich, Fall 1981, WLRC series 60.)

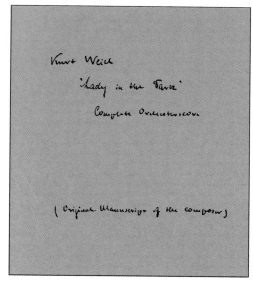

478. *Lady in the Dark* is the only Broadway work for which Weill left a carefully prepared and bound full score.

479. *Lady in the Dark*, Act I. Liza Elliott (Gertrude Lawrence) greets movie star Randy Curtis (Victor Mature) in the posh Manhattan office of *Allure* magazine.

480. The Glamour Dream. By decree of the President of the United States, a Marine (Macdonald Carey) paints Liza's portrait for a new 2-cent postage stamp while the chorus sings "Girl of the Moment."

481. The Wedding Dream. Liza's wedding to Kendall Nesbitt (Bert Lytell, in front of the stained glass window) is interrupted by the appearance of Randy Curtis.

483. The sheet music covers for seven songs from *Lady in the Dark* featured a photo of Gertrude Lawrence.

482. The Circus Dream. Liza stands trial for failing to make up her mind. On the left: Prosecuting Attorney Charley Johnson (Macdonald Carey), the defendant Liza Elliott (Gertrude Lawrence), and the Defense Attorney Randy Curtis (Victor Mature). On the right: Witness Kendall Nesbitt (Bert Lytell) and the Ringmaster (Danny Kaye).

Weill (in Suffern) to Ira Gershwin, 20 February 1941: The show is going very big. Standees all the time. Over 32,000 last week going again. Gertie is in very good spirits and the whole show is in very good shape. Gertie (or her husband) tried to lay off during holy week but Moss talked her out of it. She is doing the Victor recording on Sunday, at last. She kept postponing it from Sunday to Sunday till she found out that Hildegarde had made an album for Decca. Then she got all excited and finally agreed to make them. The first records are coming out now. The "Jenny" record of Mitchell Ayres is musically very bad. I hope the Duchin record is better. The people at Chappell's told me the biggest demand is for "My Ship," next is "This is New," and there is quite a demand for the fairy tale. "Jenny" doesn't seem to do too good. Some small radio stations who wanted to broadcast the record couldn't do it because of the word "gin" and the husband who wasn't hers.

Weill (in Suffern) to Ira Gershwin, 8 March 1941: It is lots of fun to have a smash hit. The show is doing wonderful business (as you know from your statements). We have between 20 and 100 standees at every performance and the audience reaction is wonderful. Even "My Ship" gets a good hand, probably because the song is getting a little more popular. I go about twice a week to check on the music and lyrics. It is in very good shape. I guess you've got most of the records (Benny Goodman excellent!, Reisman good, Sammy Kaye not so good, Hildegarde very good). I haven't heard the Duchin record yet. It came out yesterday. The Lawrence album is musically very good, but her voice sounds a little bit shaky. I hear Danny Kaye's records are wonderful, but it seems he has changed quite a lot; they'll probably go very big with the jitterbugs. I like very much the way Hildegarde sings the songs. She takes them very relaxed and that is good for the lyrics and the music. All the record shops have big signs in the windows "The song hits from *Lady in the Dark*." Max Dreyfus says the sale of records (especially Hildegarde) is far above average.

Reprinted from NEW YORK TIMES, January 24, 1941

Gertrude Lawrence Appears in Moss Hart's Musical Drama, 'Lady in the Dark,' With a Score by Kurt Weill and Lyrics by Ira Gershwin

By BROOKS ATKINSON

ALL things considered, the American stage may as well take a bow this morning. For Moss Hart's musical play, "Lady in the Dark," which was put on at the Alvin last evening, uses the resources of the theatre magnificently and tells a compassionately story triumphantly. Note the distinction between "musical play" and "musical comedy." What that means to Mr. Hart's mind is a drama in which the music and the splendors of the production rise spontaneously out of the heart of the drama, evoking rather than embellishing the main theme.

Although the idea is not new, since "Cabin in the Sky" and "Pal Joey" have been moving in that direction this year, Mr. Hart and his talented associates have carried it as close to perfection as any one except an academician can require. Eschewing for the moment his blistering style of comedy, Mr. Hart has written a dramatic story about the anguish of a human being. Kurt Weill has matched it with the finest score written for the theatre in years. Ira Gershwin's lyrics are brilliant. Harry Horner's whirling scenery gives the narrative a transcendent loveliness. As for Gertrude Lawrence, she is a goddess: that's all.

What brings this about is the emotional confusion of the woman editor of a smart women's magazine. Up to now she has been contented, living happily with a married man whose wife would not divorce him, and absorbed in work at which she is conspicuously successful. But suddenly everything has gone awry. Frightened by the jangle of her nerves, she goes to a psychoanalyst. "Lady In the Dark" is the drama of the strange images he draws out of her memories. In the end the analyst resolves her confusion into an intelligible pattern—proving, incidentally, that you never know whom you love, which is a terrifying prospect, but that is neither here nor there.

If that sounds like a macabre theme, you can rely upon Mr. Hart's lightness of touch and his knack for tossing in a wise-crack to keep the narrative scenes buoyant. And the long, fantastic interludes when the editor is exploring her memories carry "Lady in the Dark" into a sphere of gorgeously bedizened make-believe that will create theatrical memories for every one who sees them. Mr. Weill's score is a homogenous piece of work, breaking out in song numbers over a mood of dark evocation—nostalgic at times, bursting also into humor and swing. And Mr. Gershwin, in turn, has written his lyrics like a thoroughbred. Uproariously witty when the time is right, he also writes in impeccable taste for the meditative sequences.

To carry the burden of such a huge production, Mr. Horner has set his scenery on four revolving stages that weave naturalism and fantasy into a flowing fabric; and Hassard Short, as usual, has lighted it regally. The production is a rhapsody in blue and gold, giving reality in unreal size, shape and color, and Irene Sharaff's costumes are boldly imaginative. As the mistress of the choreography, Albertina Rasch has resigned vivid lines of dance movement, and the staging is full of grace and resourcefulness.

No one but Miss Lawrence could play a virtuoso part of such length and variety. She is on stage almost at curtain-rise, and she is never off it long—leaping from melancholy to revelry with a swiftness that would be bewildering if she could not manage caprices so well. She sings, she dances. After playing a scene as a mature woman, she steps across the stage to play a scene as a schoolgirl without loss of enchantment. Sometimes Miss Lawrence has been accused of overacting, which is a venial sin at most. But no one will accuse her of being anything but superb in "Lady In the Dark." She plays with anxious sincerity in the narrative scenes and with fullness and richness in the fantasy. For good measure, she sings "The Saga of Jenny" like an inspired showgirl.

The cast, under Mr. Hart's direction is excellent throughout. As a comic fashion photographer, Danny Kaye, who was cutting up in "The Straw Hat Revue" last year, is infectiously exuberant. Macdonald Carey, who played in the Globe Shakespeare at the World's Fair, acts the part of an aggressive magazine man with a kind of casual forthrightness. As a glamorous movie hero, Victor Mature is unobjectionably handsome and affable. Margaret Dale has an amusing part as a fashion editor and plays it with dry humor, and Natalie Schafer has some fun with a supermodish gadabout. In the unwelcome part of the sympathetic lover, Bert Lytell gives a good performance, and Donald Randolph, as the analyst, also behaves like a gentleman.

All these actors and variegated items of a show have been pulled into place by a theatre that has been put on its mettle by an occasion. "Lady in the Dark" is a feast of plenty. Since it also has a theme to explore and express, let's call it a work of theatre art.

484. Brooks Atkinson's review of the opening night of *Lady in the Dark*, from the *New York Times*, 25 January 1941.

485. Gertrude Lawrence's recordings of six songs from *Lady in the Dark* were preceded, and perhaps upstaged, by those of pop singer Hildegarde.

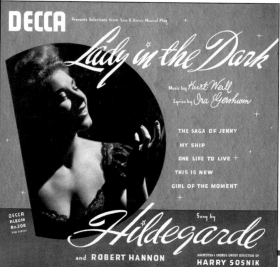

486. *Lady in the Dark* was the cover story of the 3 February 1941 issue of *Time*.

LEXIKON DER JUDEN IN DER MUSIK

Mit einem Titelverzeichnis jüdischer Werke

Zusammengestellt im Auftrag der Reichsleitung der NSDAP, auf Grund behördlicher, parteiamtlich geprüfter Unterlagen

bearb[...]

Dr. The[...]

Referent in der [...]

in Verbi[...]

Dr. habil. H[...]

Leiter der Hauptstelle Musik [...] für die Überwachung der gesamt[...] Schulung und Erz[...]

BERNHARD HAHNEF[...]

Weill, Kurt (Curt) Julian, * Dessau 2. 3. 1900, Komp, KM — früher Berlin. Der Name dieses Komponisten ist untrennbar mit der schlimmsten Zersetzung unserer Kunst verbunden. In Weills Bühnenwerken zeigt sich ganz unverblühmt und hemmungslos die jüdisch-anarchistische Tendenz. Nach verschiedenen Werken auf dem Gebiet der Kammer-, Chor- und Unterhaltungsmusik, des Liedes, der Kantate und Oper, errang er mit seiner gemeinsam mit Bert Brecht (Text) geschriebenen „Dreigroschenoper" (1928) einen sensationellen Erfolg (in einer Berliner Spielzeit über 200 Aufführungen). Als Bearbeitung und Umformung, z. T. mit handgreiflichen Plagiaten nach der alten Bettler-Oper von Gay und Pepusch geschaffen, wurde dieses Werk mit seiner unverhohlenen Zuhälter- und Verbrechermoral, seinem Song-Stil und seiner raffiniert-primitiven Mischung von Choral, Foxtrott und negroidem Jazz von jüdischer und judenhöriger Seite als revolutionärer Umbruch der gesamten musikdramatischen Kunst gepriesen. So schrieb z. B. der Vorkämpfer der musikalischen Dekadenz und Herausgeber der Zeitschrift „Melos", Hans Mersmann, noch 1934 in seiner „Deutschen Musikgeschichte": „Es ist eine in jeder Beziehung neue Form des Theaters, weder billige Unterhaltung noch ethische Moral, sondern eine Konsequenz — (wie es die beiden Autoren an einer anderen Stelle formulieren) gezogen aus dem unaufhaltsamen Verfall der bestehenden Gesellschaftsschichten. Hier liegt die Bedeutung des Textes, der statt eines Helden nur um das nackte Leben kämpfenden Menschen auf die Bühne stellt und den Hörer an den triebhaften Grundkräften seines eigenen Daseins zu packen versucht, hier auch die Kraft der Musik, die, scheinbar nur aus Einlagen bestehend,

lose mit der Handlung verknüpft, die Sentenzen des Textes dem Hörer mit der Kraft des Schlagers einhämmert."

Das nächste Werk in dieser Richtung war „Aufstieg und Fall der Stadt Mahagonny". (1929) Hier finden sich u. a. die Verse:

„Wenn es etwas gibt,
Was du haben kannst für Geld,
Dann nimm dir das Geld.
Wenn einer vorübergeht und hat Geld,
Schlag ihn auf den Kopf und nimm dir sein Geld:
Du darfst es!"

An einer anderen Stelle singt der Chor:

„Erstens vergeßt nicht, kommt das Fressen,
Zweitens kommt die Liebe dran,
Drittens das Boxen nicht vergessen,
Viertens saufen, solang man kann.
Vor allem aber achtet scharf,
Daß man hier alles dürfen darf!"

Da sich jedoch hier der musikalische Leerlauf Weills allzu deutlich zeigte und der Proteststurm aller künstlerisch gesund empfindenden Menschen gegen diese Verhöhnung der primitivsten Begriffe von Anstand auf der Bühne immer stärker wurde, wandte sich Weill von der klassenkämpferischen Verherrlichung des Untermenschentums und der Gosse zur Schuloper, zum Lehrstück und zur Funkkantate: „Lindbergh-Flug", „Der Jasager" (1930), die trotz aller jüdisch-marxistischen Grundhaltung offiziell gebilligt und propagiert wurden: Der Hochschulchor des Instituts für Kirchenmusik reiste 1931 sogar mit dem „Jasager" nach Paris.

Weinbaum, Alexander, * Berlin 4. 5. 1875, ChDgt, Org, ML (G) — Berlin.

Weinberg, Henriette (H), * Berlin 24. 8. 1910, MLn (K) — Berlin.

Weinberg, Joachim, * Lemberg 8. 10.

---

487. Weill received a fairly extensive entry in the 1941 edition of the Nazi reference book, *Lexikon der Juden in der Musik: Mit einem Titelverzeichnis jüdischer Werke* (Berlin: Hahnefeld, 1941).

OFFICE OF
SAM H. HARRIS
MUSIC BOX THEATRE
239-247 West 45TH Street
NEW YORK CITY

April 25th, 1941

The American Consul
Jerusalem
Palestine

Dear Sir:

This is to advise you that Mr. Kurt Weill is the composer of the music for the attraction, "Lady In The Dark", starring Gertrude Lawrence and currently playing at the Alvin Theatre, West 52nd Street, New York City.

The play, "Lady In The Dark" is an enormous success, now playing in its fourteenth week at capacity business, which indicates a run of at least two full years.

Mr. Weill receives three (3%) percent of the weekly gross receipts, which assures him of a weekly income of over $900., as long as the play is doing capacity. Mr. Weill is also a participant in the movie rights of this production which have already been sold to the Paramount Pictures Corporation for the sum of $285,000, and according to the present contractual agreements between the manager and the authors of the aforesaid production, Mr. Weill's share of the proceeds of the sale of the motion picture rights to the aforesaid production amounts to $42,750.

I wish to add that the play, "Lady In The Dark" is one of the most successful musical plays to have been produced in New York for the last ten years.

Yours very truly,

[signature]

The above statement sworn and attested to in my presence this 25th day of April, 1941

[signature]

IRIS JACOBS, NOTARY PUBLIC
N.Y. Co. Clerk's No. 15, Reg. No. 31 EO
Commission Expires March 30, 1943.

TELEPHONE CIRCLE 6-6767 | CABLE ADDRESS: SAMHAR

488. Letter from *Lady in the Dark* producer Sam Harris, testifying to Weill's financial ability to support immigrating family members. Weill's parents considered emigrating to the U.S. several times when they felt their safety threatened in Palestine.

490. View of Brook House from the back. This photo, taken by Ken Diego, dates from the late 1970s.

489. Weill (on the porch) and Lenya (below) posing in front of their new home at 100 South Mountain Road, New City, New York.

Weill (in Suffern) to Ira Gershwin, 28 May 1941:
I have written some orchestra music, but I threw it away. It seems so silly to write music at a time like this. . . . In the meanwhile I might write that ballet for Ruth Page I have been thinking about for a long time, and I might do some radio work during the summer.

Today I signed the deed for the new house. We have been busy with carpenters, plumbers, painters, etc. for about four weeks, but it is going very slowly. Lenya is dashing around all day and we are having lots of fun buying furniture, etc. and I think it will be very nice. We'll probably move in next week, even if it is not quite finished yet. It will probably take all summer to get it really finished, but we are in no hurry.

Weill (in New York) to Ruth Page, 22 May 1941: Well, I had lunch with [playwright and lyricist John] Latouche, at last. He seems to be a nice guy, very busy with twenty different projects, but apparently quite versatile. He likes the idea, but I don't think he has given it much thought. So I'm sending him the two books, and then I'll get together with him and try to work out a scenario which we will submit to Your Grace after which we should talk it over in detail.

My idea is that the whole thing should be a sermon by Billy Sunday, so that we still hear his voice through the Bible stories which he tells in his funny bizarre speech and which at the same time form our ballet. We should select from the Bible only the famous women stories, and the theme of the sermon should be: Temptation—and that's where you come in! I'll let you know as soon as I've had my first conference with L.

Weill (in New City) to Ruth Page, 28 June 1941: Latouche was in the country all this time. I finally managed to have lunch with him yesterday. Every time I meet him he has a terrible hangover, but he says that is purely accidental. Of course, he hasn't written a line yet, but his ideas, though rather vague, sound very nice and I think if we ever get him to write it, he'd probably do a good job. I told him all the ideas I had about it. I also offered to write the whole script together with him, because that is the way I'm used to working with my librettists and I get the best results that way. But he wants to start alone and then get together with me. So I guess we have to wait, and I hope he will not be so late that I get involved with a new show before he finishes. . . .

No news from [my parents in] Palestine, except one cable which indicated that they are alright. Their only and last hope is that Russia holds out, otherwise—well, I hate to think of the otherwise.

Arthur Lyons of A. and S. Lyons Agency (in Hollywood) to Weill, 21 June 1941: The industry has a Kurt Weill picture in *Lady in the Dark* and insofar as an original picture is concerned, there hasn't been one yet although we have searched for it in every possible place, studio, etc. This condition doesn't prevail only for Kurt Weill. Have you seen any studio assignments given this year to Jerome Kern, Ira Gershwin (with the exception of "The Life of Gershwin"), Rodgers and Hart, Emmerich Kálmán, Sigmund Romberg, Friml, or any other important composers?

That in itself should convince you, Kurt, that the studios have not been making deals for composers and lyricists to create properties for them. They prefer buying "tried and true" properties. As an illustration, the following are some of the properties the studios have bought this year: *Pal Joey, Panama Hattie, Dubarry Was a Lady, Louisiana Purchase, Lady in the Dark*, aside from many remakes of pictures made several years ago such as: *Girl Crazy, Lady Be Good, Strike up the Band, Sunny*, etc.

Weill (in New City) to Winifred Lennihan, 16 June 1941: When I met you with Burgess Meredith in front of the Algonquin the other day, you made a remark to the effect that I was "surrounded by communist friends." In the meanwhile I have heard from other sources that you are circulating the report that I am a communist.

I think it is very unwise of you to make a statement of this kind before you investigate the facts. It would have been very easy for you to find out that I am not and never have been a communist, that I am in complete disagreement with the communist attitude and that I have been very careful not to sign any literature which is openly or disguisedly communistic—not because it could be of personal disadvantage but because I am convinced that it is just as bad to be a communist as to be a Nazi.

I would be very interested to know on what facts you based your remarks about me.

Weill (in New City) to Arthur Lyons, 1 July 1941: In your letter of June 21st you don't say anything about what I was most interested in: what has become of the Goldwyn-Disney project and the Jeannette Macdonald proposition. I also think you are rather optimistic in calling *Lady in the Dark* a "Kurt Weill picture." You know that the industry usually doesn't use much more than the title and the basic idea of the play properties they are buying and I suppose there will not be much of our score left in the picture unless they are going to use our services for the score—and there are no indications as yet that they will do just that.

But let's forget about that for the time being. Here is another proposition which I want you to work on. I had several conversations with Robert Hakim in the last weeks. He had bought in France the story of a musical show which I had done in Germany in 1929 under the title of *Happy ending* [*sic*] and for which I had written a number of very good songs, one of which ("Surabaya Johnny") became a hit in Germany and France. I didn't even know that the author of the play (Bert Brecht) had sold the story and I suppose that any studio that would want to do the picture would have to settle with me first because I was co-author of the show. But Hakim told me that he would like to do this picture in collaboration with me, or, if he would sell it, to cut me in on the sales price. In France he had planned to make this picture with Danielle Darrieux and a very good French script writer had adapted our story into a movie outline. Then he had to leave France and he brought the property over here and would like to do it as an independent production for one of the major studios. He admits that he wants to use my reputation and the fact that I had written the music for the original in order to get a first class set-up in Hollywood. I read the script (it is the story of a salvation army girl and a gangster) and I thought it had good possibilities for a musical picture of my type provided that he gets a first-class director and cast. I told him that I would be interested if he would get a really first rate set-up. He told me that George Raft likes the script very much and would like to do it, and I suggested Deanna Durbin for the girl.

491. Program of the pageant, *Fun to Be Free*, by Ben Hecht and Charles MacArthur, for which Weill provided music. Performed once, on 5 October 1941 (two months before the attack on Pearl Harbor), the show was intended to increase support for the entry of the United States into World War II. The pageant was narrated by Tallulah Bankhead, Melvyn Douglas, Burgess Meredith, and Franchot Tone.

Weill (in New City) to Robert Sherwood, 12 December 1941: Like everybody else, I have the ardent desire to serve the country in some capacity. I would take any job. But it seems to me I could really be of some help if I would be allowed to use my connections and reputation among Americans of German descent and refugees from Nazi Germany to organize an effective "cultural attack" on Germany by short-wave radio.

Hitler's speech yesterday seems to me the first real sign of growing unrest among the German people and now seems to be the moment to give those people, by all available means, the answers to all those questions which they must ask themselves and which Hitler's speech left unanswered. . . .

There are in this country now the greatest German writers, poets, playwrights, composers, musicians, actors, and directors. What I would like to do is to mobilize all this talent for a cultural attack on the German people. We would write radio plays, pamphlets, songs, and comedy scenes. We would send them the great literature and music of all countries which is *verboten* to them. In word and music we would tell them the truth about their leaders, the hopelessness of their fight, the power of democracy, and the beauty of life in a free country.

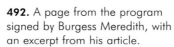

II

"FUN TO BE FREE"

A Pageant

By Ben Hecht *and* Charles MacArthur

Directed by Brett Warren

Music by Kurt Weill

Scenery and Technical Direction by S. Syrjala

Narrators: Tallulah Bankhead, Melvyn Douglas,
Burgess Meredith, Franchot Tone
I.L.G.W.U. Choruses, *conducted by* Simon Rady

★

492. A page from the program signed by Burgess Meredith, with an excerpt from his article.

493. Weill prepares for *Fun to Be Free* with Tallulah Bankhead.

494. An illustration from the program depicts the German "threat to America."

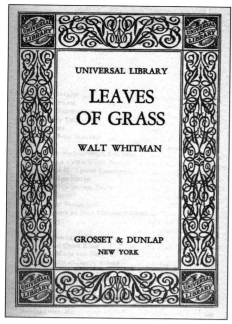

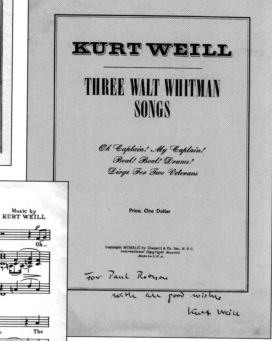

497. First page of "Oh Captain! My Captain!"

495. Title page of Weill's copy of Walt Whitman's *Leaves of Grass*, given to him by Paul Green in August 1937. Weill had written about Whitman in 1926, praising him as "the first to discover poetic raw material in the tempo of public life and in the landscape of the new world." (*Der deutsche Rundfunk*, 14 November 1926.)

496. In late 1941 and early 1942, Weill set three Whitman poems to music with the hope that Paul Robeson would sing them. In spite of receiving this autographed copy of the published edition, Robeson apparently never performed the songs.

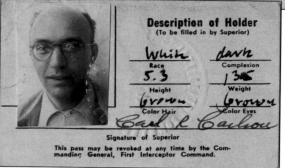

498. In addition to his artistic contributions to the war effort, Weill participated in U.S. civil defense. This was his identification card as an enemy aircraft spotter.

499. Maxwell Anderson (standing, center) and Weill (right) with two other spotters in Rockland County.

500. Brecht preserved this published photo of Anderson and Weill looking for enemy aircraft in his *Arbeitsjournal* from 1942.

---

1 9 4 2

MUSIC + THEATER:

Benjamin Britten *Sinfonia da requiem*

Irving Berlin *White Christmas*

Maxwell Anderson *The Eve of St. Mark*

LITERATURE + FILM:

Klaus Mann *The Turning Point*

Albert Camus *L'étranger*

To Be or Not To Be (film by Ernst Lubitsch)

SCIENCE + SOCIETY:

The first automatic computer developed in the U.S.

Magnetic recording tape invented in Germany

Sugar, coffee, and gasoline rationing begin in U.S.

POLITICS:

The murder of millions of Jews in the Nazi gas chambers begins

German Army defeated at Stalingrad

U.S. government imprisons over 100,000 Japanese-Americans

501. Weill and Lenya discuss agricultural prospects with their gardener.

Weill (in New City) to Emma and Albert Weill, 5 February 1942: Life here goes on rather normally, but everybody tries to help in his own way the gigantic war effort. I am alone now since four weeks because Lenya is traveling through the country with the play [*Candle in the Wind* by Maxwell Anderson] and she will stay until April. She hated to leave our beautiful house, but she had to go because it belongs to the duties of an actress here. We are having a very cold winter this year, and lots of snow. Today for instance it has been snowing all day and tomorrow morning I have to shovel the snow for several hours to get my car out of the garage. But I like to do that. I have bought already all the seeds for a big vegetable garden which I will start in the spring. I will have a big field with potatoes which still is my favorite food.

Weill (in New City) to Lotte Lenya, 5 February 1942: Yesterday I saw *Porgy*. They have done quite a good job. It is much more of a show now and less of an opera. They have a wonderful cast and the whole thing is very alive and refreshing. The songs are still magnificent, but the rest of the score pretty bad. I listened to the first dream of *Lady* in the evening and decided that it was much better music.

502. The published version *Your Navy* by Maxwell Anderson appeared in this collection along with other patriotic radio plays. Weill wrote to Lenya about *Your Navy*: "Max came back from Washington last night and just brought the script over. It is pretty dull and has very little opportunity for music. I am very disappointed because I had hoped I could do something exciting. But it is all talk and talk, just like a newspaper. So I am just writing what little music it needs." (19 February 1942)

THIS IS WAR!

A COLLECTION OF PLAYS ABOUT
AMERICA ON THE MARCH

By

NORMAN CORWIN   MAXWELL ANDERSON
STEPHEN VINCENT BENÉT   GEORGE FAULKNER
PHILIP WYLIE   RANALD MACDOUGALL
WILLIAM N. ROBSON   JOHN DRISCOLL

With an Introduction by
H. L. McCLINTON

DODD, MEAD & COMPANY
PUBLISHERS   NEW YORK

Weill (in New City) to Ruth Page, 26 February 1942: I have been working a lot. The song I did with Archibald MacLeish turned out exceedingly well and will come out shortly. Then I have done (with Maxwell Anderson) the third government program in the series "This Is War" which will go on the air this Saturday at 7. That was a lot of work and we had to be in Washington several times, but it was extremely interesting—and one is so glad to contribute something. I am working on another propaganda project now . . . it might turn out to be a very good show. I wrote with Howard Dietz a song "Schickelgruber," sung by Hitler's mother (staged like Whistler's mother) and I am working now with Hammerstein on a song, "The Good Earth," also for that show.

Your Navy

By MAXWELL ANDERSON

MARCH: You boys out there! You boys on blue water!

MUSIC: (*Gay music based on an old sea chanty.*)

MARCH (*continues over music*): Seamen! Marines! Gunners! Torpedomen! Machinists! Engineers! Aviators! Officers of the Staff and of the Line!

MUSIC: (*Stops abruptly.*)

SEAMAN (*in the distance but clearly*): Enemy sub off the port bow, sir. Submerging.

COMMANDER: Hard left. Come to course 155.

SEAMAN: Hard left, sir. Coming to course 155.

COMMANDER: Ahead full all engines.

ANNUNCIATOR: Both engines answer ahead full, sir.

COMMANDER: Are depth charges and Y-guns ready?

TORPEDOMAN: Depth charges and Y-guns ready, sir.

COMMANDER: Depth setting 100 feet.

TORPEDOMAN: Depth setting 100 feet, sir.

COMMANDER: Stand by.

[47]

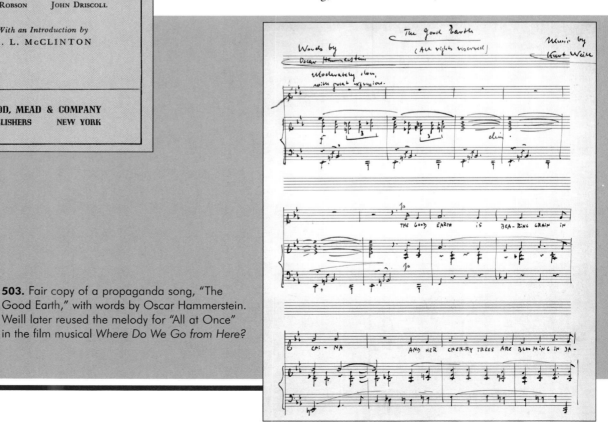

503. Fair copy of a propaganda song, "The Good Earth," with words by Oscar Hammerstein. Weill later reused the melody for "All at Once" in the film musical *Where Do We Go from Here?*

Weill (in New City) to Bertolt Brecht, 9 March 1942: Many thanks for your letter, which I found here—together with a telegram by Mr. Marton—when I came back from a trip to Washington and Detroit. . . .

I hope that you're not already too deeply involved in this deal, because I don't consider it to be a favorable one—not only from my own, but especially from your point of view. It's a shame that you didn't give me the opportunity to advise you at an earlier stage of negotiation. I believe I could have advised you better than most people in Hollywood, especially since in the matter of an American revival of *Die Dreigroschenoper* I am sort of an "expert," having been engaged with this problem continuously during the last seven years. Because of the overall nature of American theater, it is very tricky to revive a play that has failed once before, even if it has as good a reputation as *Die Dreigroschenoper*. But no doubt we will have a first-class revival of *Die Dreigroschenoper* if we wait for the best combination of translator (for the play and, what is especially difficult, for the lyrics), director, producer, and actors. In recent months I've had many negotiations with Charles MacArthur, one of the best young dramatists in America and a long-time collaborator with Ben Hecht. He was very interested, and my plan was to get a really first-class American adaptation either from him alone or together with Hecht, with whom I am very friendly. (We don't need a translation; what we need is an adaptation for the American theater, because one of the main reasons for the flop in 1933 was the fact that they used a literal translation). If I had such a worthwhile adaptation, it wouldn't be difficult for me to find a first class producer and a terrific cast. A performance of *Die Dreigroschenoper* as I envision it would not only be financially advantageous for you, but would also establish you as a theater author in America.

If we would allow *Die Dreigroschenoper* to be performed by a troupe of Negroes in California, then such a plan could probably never be realized—or at least not for the next ten years. As I wrote to you before, I worked on a Negro version of *Die Dreigroschenoper* with an American author a few years ago. At first we tried—as your people are apparently doing now—to have *Die*

Dreigroschenoper played by Negroes exactly the way it is. But it became clear that the idea of a German adaptation of an English ballad opera of the 17th century [recte: 18th century] played by American Negroes, was so sophisticated that it would leave the audience completely bewildered. Then we tried to adapt the piece in such a way that the problems would become Negro problems—but that meant writing a totally new piece. I don't know Clarence Muse and I don't know whether he could do a better job than the people I worked with. I do know that in the seven years I've been in America people have tried time and again to open plays in California and then bring them to New York (which, unfortunately, is still the only theater center in America)—but never successfully, for the simple reason that whatever they did in California just wasn't good enough. Which means that such a performance would be practically meaningless for you both from an artistic and a financial standpoint. It goes without saying that I can very well understand that you're eager to get something going here and also that your financial situation makes a quick theatrical success desirable. But I had hoped you would find a start in film through your friends in Hollywood so that we could wait with *Die Dreigroschenoper* until we could really take advantage of the best prospects this "property" holds for us. But you will probably say this is a typically capitalist viewpoint.

As far as I am concerned, naturally I would first of all have to see the translation of the play and the lyrics of the songs before I can make any decisions. The songs of *Die Dreigroschenoper* are well known and loved in knowledgeable circles. I've tried again and again to have translations of the lyrics done that would at least fit the music and come close to rendering the beauty of your original poetry. So far I haven't succeeded, and I do not want to release the music until the question of the translation has been absolutely resolved. So, please send me the book first. I can well imagine how my music would turn out if I were to agree to the theater's desire to do its own instrumentation. I have always, especially here in America, insisted that my music be played only in my own orchestrations in the theater, and I must hold to that principle in this case as well.

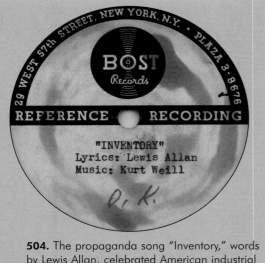

504. The propaganda song "Inventory," words by Lewis Allan, celebrated American industrial might. This test pressing is the only surviving recording; the performers are unidentified.

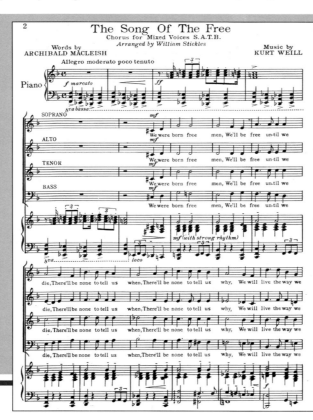

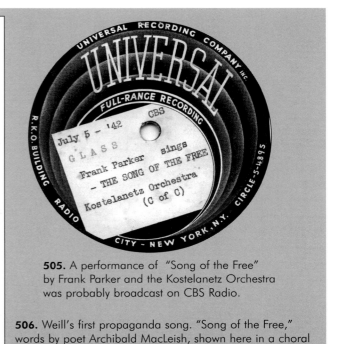

505. A performance of "Song of the Free" by Frank Parker and the Kostelanetz Orchestra was probably broadcast on CBS Radio.

506. Weill's first propaganda song. "Song of the Free," words by poet Archibald MacLeish, shown here in a choral arrangement by William Stickles.

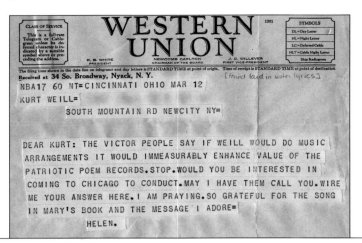

507. Helen Hayes asked Weill to arrange patriotic American songs and conduct her recording of them for RCA Victor. Weill supervised the recording but did not conduct. He explained his choice for the style of the musical settings in the liner notes.

508. Weill's parents, Albert and Emma, in Palestine, ca. 1942.

Weill (in New City) to Lotte Lenya, 12 April 1942: I also played the Helen Hayes records [for Archibald MacLeish]. He thought they are absolutely unique, and they should be spread all over the country, in schools, factories and private homes. He raved about Helen, said that she spoke these words so completely American, as they've never been spoken before and that he could listen for hours and hours to her reading. About the music he said it was miraculous what I had done. Well, all this is very important and very promising. He is [Franklin D.] Roosevelt's closest friend, and a wonderful man.

Weill (in New City) to Bertolt Brecht, 13 March 1942: Just now I received your second letter. First of all, many thanks for that beautiful song ["Und was bekam des Soldaten Weib?"]. I shall compose it, and if you wish, I'll offer it to the people who are doing those short-wave broadcasts to Germany. (By the way, it is possible that in the near future I'll be putting together my own radio program of a similar nature—for broadcast to Germany—and then I will need more material from you.)

As far as *Die Dreigroschenoper* is concerned, you must have gotten my letter in the meantime in which I explained my point of view to you. Of course I understand completely how important this performance is to you and you can be sure that I will completely support you in this matter as soon as I've determined that this performance is really a good opportunity for us. Look, Brecht, in my seven years in America I've seen again and again how people from over there have plunged heedlessly into this or that project which subsequently did them more harm than good. I'm thinking of your interests as much as my own when I use my experience in American theater to try to protect us from similar mistakes. Neither of us would want what happened to *Die Dreigroschenoper* here in New York in 1933 and later in Paris to happen again. With a little caution, we can prevent this. If these people are serious about their plans with *Die Dreigroschenoper*, they certainly won't object to showing me the book and informing me of the details of the performance.

Theodor Adorno (in Los Angeles) to Weill, 31 March 1942: After such a long time and a missed rendezvous in New York, it must be a surprise to suddenly be hearing from me. However, independent of the wish to keep alive a relationship which has meant a lot to me—and perhaps also in some ways to you—I am writing to you for a particular reason. And that is the problem of an American performance of *Die Dreigroschenoper*. . . . We are talking here about the founding of a Negro theater of national scope, backed by Paul Robeson and the so-called Negro lodges, which means considerable moral and financial backing and which, if successful, could lead to prospects for you and Brecht. . . . From the very beginning the performance practice of *Die Dreigroschenoper* has been based on the jazz arrangement. In my opinion there are only two possibilities for an appropriate performance: that is, the strict, note-for-note rendition of the original full score, a treatment toward which your own intention and Brecht's vision of montage were opposed. Or one has to give the work in an actual jazz adaptation. This, however, can only be successful over here if the principle of jazz variation would be applied in a far more radical way than would have been necessary in Europe. . . . One should strive for a economically self-sufficient performance—one in which the Negroes (whose sensibilities we never fully understand anyway) would largely be left to themselves to re-improvise the work in their own way.

Weill (in New City) to Lotte Lenya, 8 April 1942: Clarence Muse, that poor old Negro fellow who wants to do 3-Gr.-O. [*Dreigroschenoper*] wrote a desperate letter. I am sick and tired of this whole affair and wrote him I would be willing to make a contract for a production *in California only*, but that I don't allow to show it outside of California unless I have seen and passed it. That would be completely harmless for me because nobody cares anyhow what they are doing out there. If they don't accept this, to hell with them! But at least I have shown my good will. Muse writes me that Brecht had told him last summer he had written to me and I didn't answer! The good old swinish Brecht method. Well, I wrote Wiesengrund a letter which he won't forget for some time. I wrote him: It is a shame that a man of your intelligence should be so misinformed. Then I explained him that the American theater isn't as bad as he thinks and in the end I said: "maybe the main difference between the German and the American theater is the fact that there exist certain rules of 'fair play' in the American theater. Three cheers for the American Theater!"

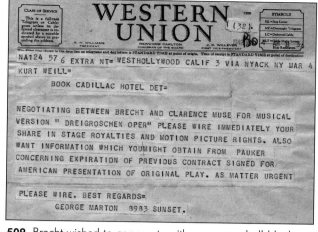

509. Brecht wished to cooperate with a proposed all-black production of *Die Dreigroschenoper* to be produced by Clarence Muse in California with the support of Paul Robeson and Theodor Adorno. Weill supported the notion of an all-black cast but rejected plans to rearrange his score for a jazz band. Brecht and other interested parties (such as his agent, George Marton) tried to persuade Weill to change his mind.

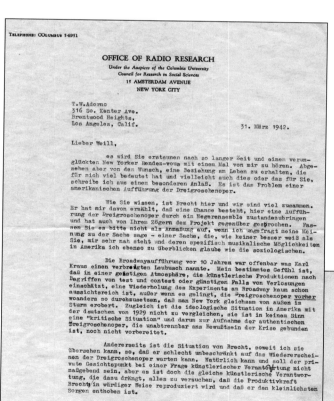

510. Facsimile of Theodor Adorno's letter to Weill on Brecht's behalf, urging Weill to permit the Clarence Muse production of *Die Dreigroschenoper*. He enclosed two essays on jazz with the letter. Weill's response has not been preserved, but he told Lenya that Adorno "won't forget it for some time."

511. In a letter from April 1942, Brecht provides Weill with more information about the proposed all-black production of *Die Dreigroschenoper*.

512. Sketch of Weill's setting of Brecht's poem, "Und was bekam des Soldaten Weib." Lenya premiered the song the following April at a concert in New York City to promote the sale of war bonds.

Scene XIII

Calypso Entertainment.

     The entertainment begins again. Seraphin sings the same Calypso song which he sang before, which is a pirate ballad. Now instead of being a failure, it is a tremendous success. Other entertainers appear. Other entertainers sing. Chorus of Calypso singers, also cas castanet dancers, etc. The entertainment is a complete success. Seraphin is highly delighted and they collect all the available cash in the town. Seraphin passes the hat. They throw money to the singers and they clean up. The audience disperses with a musical exit.

513. An excerpt from Weill's copy of a treatment of *The Pirate*, S.N. Behrman's play for Alfred Lunt.

Weill (in New City) to Lotte Lenya, 5 April 1942: They were both flabbergasted about my criticism of *The Pirate* script because it was the most exact and most constructive criticism anybody had made (it needs work in the 2nd act, but it can be the best play the Lunts have had in years). Alfred wants music "all through the play" and he said: "By the time you get through with it, the music will be just as important as the play." That means they realize that they have to pay me royalties (I'll ask 2%). It will be a much more interesting job than I expected because I will have seven Negro musicians *on stage*, playing, singing, dancing, etc. and that is something I always wanted to do. It is a difficult job because it has to sound like improvisation and I have to find a new style, half-Spanish, half-Negro. If they really want to do it in the spring I'll have to work like mad—but that's o.k. with me. Alfred was nice—but so stupid! Well, I think it will be a very nice thing for me to do next just because it is not a musical, and something original and high class. And would I be glad if this waiting period would be over.

Weill (in New City?) to Sam Behrman, 9 May 1942: I am somewhat puzzled, after a period of complete silence from you and Alfred, to see in the official newspaper statement of the Playwrights' Comp. that I am writing "incidental music" for the *Pirate*. I don't quite understand how such an announcement could be sent out without asking me if I want an announcement to be made and in what form. I happen to think that "incidental music" is the wrong description of what I am supposed to do for the play. Bill Fields, whom I asked for an explanation, told me that this phrase was chosen because you were afraid to give the impression that you had written a "musical comedy" or a "comedy with music."

You remember that in our first meeting with Alfred (and ever since) both you and Alfred insisted that the play should have a musical score "all through," and that my original idea of a Negro band of Calypso players and singers should be used extensively. During the following weeks I developed a number of ideas which you seemed to like enormously: the opening lullaby, the clarinet solo for Alfred, the street scene (as demonstrated in the audition which I arranged for you), the mysticism show in the third act, etc. All these ideas are part of a musical form which I have been interested in for a long time and which I have tried several times, a kind of improvised *commedia dell'arte* music. I think, and we all seemed to agree, that this would be the ideal musical treatment of your play and a valuable contribution to the success of the show, especially for an American audience which is not used to a stylized romantic period comedy.

But perhaps you have changed your mind about all this. You never sent me the revised script, and all I heard from Alfred was a message which he sent me through my servant (!!): I should write him some "hot numbers." If you would rather do the play without my ideas, as a straight play with some incidental music, you can tell me so quite frankly. I hope you know me well enough by now to realize that I don't want to impose myself or my music on your play. I am only trying to be helpful, and I thought I might be more helpful if I gave my showmanship as well as my musical talents. But maybe that was a mistake. I wonder.

Weill (in New City?) to Paul Aron, 15 May 1942: The rumor that I don't want to have anything to do with German musicians is very funny. As far as I remember, I didn't have much to do with them in Germany, and why should I change that in this country?

Weill (in New City) to Lotte Lenya, 27 May 1942: I just got notice that I am having my physical examination for the draft on Sunday at 2 p.m. . . . This is war—and we are all in it now. I was quite surprised that they called me already for the examination because nobody else has been called yet. But here in the country the draft boards are working much faster because they have fewer people. Of course, that doesn't mean yet that they'll take me, and there is nothing to worry about. Dr. Glass is doing the examination. If I pass the examination I will immediately try to get into Frank Capra's outfit in Washington.

Weill (in New City) to Archibald MacLeish, 9 June 1942: Do you remember that we talked some time ago about an idea of sending stage shows to the factories to help the morale of defense workers? I told you then that some members of the "American Theatre Wing" are working on a project of this kind. Yesterday I went with Moss Hart who is in charge of this project to see the first try-out of the "Lunch Hour Follies" at the Wheeler Shipyard in Whitestone, L.I. It was a 45-minute show—some songs, some dancing, a sketch, "Hitler in Russia" by Kaufman and Hart, and a pep talk by a naval officer. It was completely successful and a very exciting experience for everyone connected with it. At 12 o'clock sharp, about 1,200 men rushed from their place of work to a little square near the water where they had built a little stage. They took their seats on benches, on the floor and high up in the scaffolds and watched the show while they were eating their lunch. They had a wonderful time, and when it was all over we heard them saying, "We'll do twice as much work this afternoon." We all felt that here is the most natural field of activity for all those writers, musicians, and artists who are desperately looking for their place in the nation's war effort. But beyond that, we felt that this might become the birthplace of a real people's theater. I offered immediately to write one or several little musical plays of 30 minutes which could be performed by separate units of actors and singers all over the country.

514. Program cover for a revue held in Rockland County (Weill's and Lenya's home) to raise war relief money for Russia, 20 August 1942. Weill contributed a song, "Russian War Relief," for voice, guitar, and piano with words by J.P. McEvoy.

515. Weill and Lenya with a fellow resident of South Mountain Road, the painter Henry Varnum Poor.

No Fun in War Work? Broadway Has a Cure

With a makeshift wooden platform as a stage, a busload of Broadway talent played to standing room only Monday at the Todd Shipyards in Brooklyn. They were the sponsors and cast of *Lunchtime Follies*, the American Theater Wing's volunteer entertainment for war-production workers.

Four thousand Todd employes cut short their lunch hour to lampoon Hitler in pungent Brooklynese and whistle at Sunny O'Dea's flashy legs. Still wearing the steel helmets that are part of their war work, the men seemed to be having a good time.

Moss Hart, who serves with George Heller as co-chairman of the *Follies* committee, told them that the show was an experiment.

"If you like us, we'll be back to give you a show every week."

Loud and sincere applause gave Hart his answer. For this first edition of the *Follies* is a lively and professional review. It features both anti-Fascist highjinks and Broadway legs.

Sketches by George S. Kaufman and Moss Hart cut loose with low gags that are reminders of burlesque's palmier days, and Harold J. Rome reached for the boys in the back row with two songs that managed to be suggestive and patriotic at the same time.

While the men listened to a brief pep talk on production from Lt. J. D. Gessford, USNR, 3d Naval District, co-chairman Heller took time out to talk about the *Follies'* future plans.

The American Theater Wing, Heller says, expects to operate two regular units of the *Follies* within a few weeks. The units will visit six plants weekly and give both a noon and midnight show at each of them—if they are wanted.

James McGary, a Todd ironworker's helper who watched the show from a rooftop, said that he thought the *Follies* would be wanted, all right.

"I guess it's about the best performance I ever saw," McGary said. "The men know they're getting big-time entertainment. You can bet they appreciate it."

. . .

War Show: Dave Burns, playing Hitler, sang *Gee, But It's Cold in Russia* for 7800 workers at the Todd Shipyards, Brooklyn, last Monday noon in the first performance of the American Theater Wing's *Lunch-Hour Follies*. The idea came from England, where noontime shows have boosted afternoon production. Monday's showing was a tryout. Success of the half-hour of songs, dances and skits spurred plans for five touring troupes of paid actors to play noon and midnight shows at war plants in the East. ➡

516. A report on the first "Lunch Hour Follies" performance in Brooklyn, 22 June 1942, appeared in *PM* magazine. The name of the project is later changed to "Lunch Time Follies."

Weill (in Beverly Hills) to Lotte Lenya, 28 September 1942: Well, we had a six-hour session with Marlene yesterday. When I read the play on the train I knew that we would have difficulties with her because Bella [Spewack] had written all other parts much better than hers. Marlene found that out immediately. She was extremely intelligent about it and put her finger right on the wrong spots. She also was very constructive with suggestions how to improve the play. . . . Marlene liked the music, but started that old business about the different quality of my music here in America. I cut it short by saying, "Never mind those old German songs—we are in America now and Broadway is tougher than the Kurfürstendamm." That stopped her.

Weill (in Beverly Hills) to Russell Crouse, 30 September 1942: Thanks for your letter and the story outline. As Nell Gwynn story outlines go, this seems to me a good one, but, as you say we still haven't found that sparkling brilliant idea that would make this Nell Gwynn story different from all the others. I have made a thorough study of your material about Charles and the Melville book during my train ride and I consider myself some sort of Nell Gwynn specialist. I have made a lot of notes about incidents, characters, etc. but I haven't hit on that great modern idea that is hidden somewhere in this material.

Weill's notes for a musical with Russell Crouse based on the story of Nell Gwynn, a British actress and mistress of King Charles II. The show was intended as a vehicle for soprano Grace Moore.

Charles Hart—Charles Buckhurst [?]—Charles II.
Nell playing man's part because no women allowed on stage—gets in troubles
King speaks French—Nell teaches him to speak English. This is part of her effort to separate the King from his surroundings and bring him closer to the people of England.
Some deal with the Duke of York who is given New Amsterdam.
King gets Bombay and Tangier by marrying.
King was never in love, is completely cynical about women. Nell is the only one really devoted to him.
Violent card games   Lord Sandwich
Whole girls' chorus—the King's mistresses
Queen had no children
Story of La Belle Stuart
Lady Castelmaine (the Queen's rival had affair with Hart)
The Poor Whores' Petition (190-/
Nell played for King in Whitehall
Her acquaintance with the King was due to court intrigue against Lady Castelmaine   Duke of Buckingham
2 plays had to be postponed because she and Moll Davis were both pregnant from the King
She was first a poor evening's entertainment for the King, but she made him respect her by her frankness and impudence
WLRC, Ser.31, box 1.

Weill (in Beverly Hills) to Lotte Lenya, 1 October 1942: Marlene had tried to get me free from the night curfew. The result was that I was called to the police station where they told me I had no right to come to the military zone, and I should get out in forty-eight hours. That was fine by me and I made a train reservation for Friday. Of course, it was a misunderstanding and Marlene is arranging now that I can stay until Sunday or Monday, because we should have a few sessions with Bella whom we expect today. So this morning an army official called me and gave me permission to stay till Monday, but I cannot go out after 8:00. Yesterday I was free for a few hours and called [Richard] Révy. He came to see me, but he talked so much nonsense that I threw him out. Then I met Brecht. He was just as dirty and unshaved as ever, but somehow much nicer and rather pathetic. He wants badly to work with me and the way he talks about it sounds very reasonable but you know how long that lasts. Anyhow, I will try to see him once more before I leave. . . . If I don't have to go in the army I think I will do a show with Brecht *for you*. He has enough money now for two years and could come to N.Y.

Darius Milhaud (in Oakland) to Weill, [early November 1942]: I am very excited about the Offenbach business and I am going to accept to make this orchestration.

But as I have no experience of BROADWAY—please tell me exactly what they expect of me.

1.) Must I change the harmonies—put "pep" in it?

2.) What kind of orchestra can I use? What instruments?

Give me all sorts of good advice.

I can come (as Lewis asked me) for December but I must be here on January 11th.

I should like to know if this "affaire" has *already* a good financial backing. As I will have an awfully long job to do—I should like very much to have an advance of royalties as a *guarantee*. I wrote to Lewis about that but I should like to have your advice—you're *king of business*! I did not mention any amount in my letter to Lewis.

If I could have $1,000 in advance it would be "swell" and I could take Madeleine and Daniel with me in N.Y. You can talk to Russell Lewis of this question.

I hope you will help me for the contract as I am a dumkopf.

Weill (in New City) to Russell Lewis, 14 November 1942: Thanks for your letter. Darius wrote me last week and asked some questions about the *Belle Hélène* project. He seemed interested in doing it, but was not sure what exactly you wanted him to do. . . .

I saw *La vie parisienne* and was quite shocked how stale and how dated the Offenbach music sounded. It will take a great deal of musical showmanship to revitalize this music.

517. Letter from the Dramatists' Guild notifying Weill that he has been nominated for membership in the Guild's Council.

THE DRAMATISTS' GUILD
OF THE AUTHORS' LEAGUE OF AMERICA, Inc.
6 EAST 39th STREET, NEW YORK, N. Y.
Telephone MUrray Hill 5-6930

October 14th, 1942.

President
ELMER RICE

Vice-President
GEORGE KAUFMAN

Secretary
RICHARD RODGERS

Council
GEORGE ABBOTT
ROBERT ARDREY
PHILIP BARRY
CLARE BOOTHE
EDWARD CHILD CARPENTER
MARC CONNELLY
RACHEL CROTHERS
RUSSEL CROUSE
OWEN DAVIS
PHILIP DUNNING
DOROTHY FIELDS
ROSE FRANKEN
CLIFFORD GOLDSMITH
PAUL GREEN
LORENZ HART
LILLIAN HELLMAN
ARTHUR KOBER
MELVIN LEVY
HOWARD LINDSAY
GEORGE MIDDLETON
JOHN MONKS, JR.
EUGENE O'NEILL
ARTHUR RICHMAN
IRWIN SHAW
ARTHUR SCHWARTZ
ROBERT E. SHERWOOD
GEORGE SKLAR
LULU VOLLMER
VICTOR WOLFSON

Counsel
WILLIAM HAMILTON OSBORNE

Executive Secretary
LUISE M. SILLCOX

Assistant Secretary
DON ANGUS DOUGLAS

Mr. Kurt Weill
Brook House
So. Mountain Road
New City, New York

Dear Mr. Weill:

I tried to reach you last week to tell you that you had been appointed a member of the Nominating Committee to select new Council members for election at the Annual Meeting on November 9th, but found you were in California. Now that you are back, I want to give you a report of what took place at the meeting.

There are twelve vacancies on the Council -- ten for 1945; one for 1944; one for 1943. The Committee nominated twenty-five members from which will be elected these twelve Council members plus eight to serve as alternates. Following are the twenty-five nominees:

George Abbott   Sigmund Romberg
Robert Ardrey   Fred Finklehoff
Russel Crouse   John Van Druten
Owen Davis   Patricia Collinge
Lillian Hellman   Kurt Weill
Arthur Kober   Gladys Hurlburt
Lulu Vollmer   Howard Dietz
Johnny Green   Harold Rome
S. J. Perelman   John Cecil Holm
Joseph Fields   Frances Goodrich
Isabel Leighton   Thomas Job
Louis Weitzenkorn   Nancy Hamilton
                       Otto Harbach

We want to start getting the ballots ready very shortly so will you please call me if you have any objections to offer.

Sincerely yours,

Selma Rich

Selma Rich

My dear Kurt

I am very excited about the Offenbach business, and I am going to accept to make this orchestration.

But as I have no experience of BROADWAY, please tell me exactly what they expect of me.

1= must I change the harmonies, put "pep" in it.

2= what kind of orchestra can I use? what instruments?

Give me all sort of good advices.

I am come as Lewis asked me in December but I must be here on January 11th

I should like to know if this

518. Milhaud's self-portrait, enclosed in his letter to Weill.

519. The first page of Milhaud's letter to Weill about the prospect of adapting the music of Offenbach's *La belle Hélène* for a Broadway production. (The show eventually opened in 1944 under the title *Helen Goes to Troy* with musical adaptations by Erich Korngold.)

RECORDS: SONGS BY KURT WEILL

By HOWARD TAUBMAN

KURT WEILL is a versatile composer who has to his credit successful scores for opera, operetta, musical comedy and other theatre forms. He is adept at setting German, French and Italian so that the flavor of the words is complemented by the quality of the music. A new album, *Six Songs by Kurt Weill* (Bost 8, three ten-inch records) provides a view of his talents, but six songs out of so many are merely a glimpse.

Lotte Lenya sings these songs in the style that seems right, and since the recordings were made under the composer's supervision, it may be presumed that her approach has his blessing. Her voice is limited, but she uses it sensitively and insinuatingly; she manages to make the café-chanteuse technique of soft and softer singing sound as if it and the songs had integrity.

There are two songs in English, two in French, two in German. The English words are by Maxwell Anderson; the German by Berthold Brecht; the French by Jacques Deval and M. Magre. Mr. Weill writes music in a popular style, but his taste keeps it from becoming banal. Several of the songs are too obviously tearful, but works like *Lost in the Stars* and *Complainte de la Seine* project their emotion with restraint. *Lover Man, J'Attends un navire, Soerabaja Johnny* and *Wie man sich bettet* round out the album.

Lotte Lenya Sings Six Tunes — Other Releases

Lisa Perli and Stella Andreva, sopranos; Heddle Nash, tenor; John Brownlee and Robert Alva, baritones; Robert Easton, bass, and London Philharmonic Orchestra conducted by Sir Thomas Beecham (Columbia M-274, four twelve-inch records.) Another in Columbia's reissue of what it calls "rec-

Kurt Weill.

522. A review of the album by Howard Taubman.

Weill (in New City) to Lotte Lenya, 9 February 1942: There was a man who made all the records in Paris [Herbert Borchardt]. He is starting a recording firm here and would like to make a Kurt Weill album (which I would like to do). My idea is to have some German, some French, and some English songs of mine, the German and English to be sung by you.

521. The liner notes attempt to introduce an American audience to Weill's European works and to Lenya's distinctive voice: "Her style is absolutely a personal one—changing from childlike wistfulness to dramatic, from naive to cynical—yet always passionate and exciting."

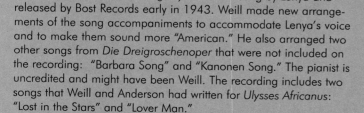

520. Album cover of *Six Songs by Kurt Weill* sung by Lenya and released by Bost Records early in 1943. Weill made new arrangements of the song accompaniments to accommodate Lenya's voice and to make them sound more "American." He also arranged two other songs from *Die Dreigroschenoper* that were not included on the recording: "Barbara Song" and "Kanonen Song." The pianist is uncredited and might have been Weill. The recording includes two songs that Weill and Anderson had written for *Ulysses Africanus*: "Lost in the Stars" and "Lover Man."

BOST ALBUM – BA8

SIX SONGS BY KURT WEILL

interpreted by LOTTE LENYA

KURT WEILL won his first acclaim in Europe at the age of twenty-four when he wrote his opera, "The Protagonist". This was followed by a great number of stage works amongst them Beggars Opera, Mahagony, Johnny Johnston, Knickerbocker Holiday, Lady in the Dark. Weill is one of those exceptional composers who sets his music to lyrics of different languages with equal success. His very individual musical style, never cheap or compromising, attracts innumerable followers who recognize and admire his sincere conceptions — be they tender or cruel.

In this album is a collection of six characteristic Weill songs, typical examples of his music to English, French and German lyrics. The texts for these songs were written by such famous playwrights and authors as Maxwell Anderson, Berthold Brecht and Jacques Deval.

LOTTE LENYA, equally as effective in English, French and German, is an ideal interpreter for these compositions, having created many Weill roles on the stage. Her style is absolutely a personal one — changing from child-like wistfullness to dramatic, from naive to cynical — yet always passionate and exciting.

LOST IN THE STARS   Record No. 5017A

A tender and imaginative tale of Negro influence. It seems that the Lord God, in his creation of the world, has let one little star slip through his fingers. He promised to look after that little lost star but somehow or other He has forgotten . . . even to look after us too when dark clouds roll by.

LOVER MAN   Record No. 5017B

Intensely dramatic monologue both in the music and in the stirring words by Maxwell Anderson in which a woman pleads with her lover who has gone away—almost to the point of trying to contact him telepathically to return to her.

J'ATTENDS UN NAVIRE   Record No. 5018A

From the music-drama "Marie Galante" was chosen this song. Jacques Deval wrote the play which had great success on the stage in France and was later filmed in Hollywood. It tells about a girl who has led a rather questionable life in the Panama Canal Zone and whose only idea is to return to her home in Bordeaux. As the title suggests, 'waiting for a boat' . . . whoever will contribute to her journey is welcome! The French have now given a new significance to this song, adopting it as a popular patriotic tune.

LOTTE LENYA
AND
KURT WEILL

COMPLAINTE DE LA SEINE   Record No. 5018B

The melancholy lament of the Seine River as it flows through Paris . . . with morbid contemplation on the jewels and pistols, corpses of drunkards, maniacs and suicides and all the tears which mix with the sands at the bottom of that River which gives refuge to all . . .

SOERABAJA JOHNNY   Record No. 5019A

The title is the nickname for the traditional roaming sailor with a girl in every port. This particular one hails from Soerabaja, Java. Bert Brecht is the author of the lyrics which tells about one of Johnny's romances — this time a young girl who has never loved before — until she met Johnny. It is she who is pleading with him throughout the song, embittered by his cruelty, his infidelity, his lies . . .

WIE MAN SICH BETTET   Record No. 5019B

In the philosophical mood, Bert Brecht's lyrics tells about a cynical and egoistic female whose actions in life are based on the principle of — "As you make your bed, so shall you lie in it".

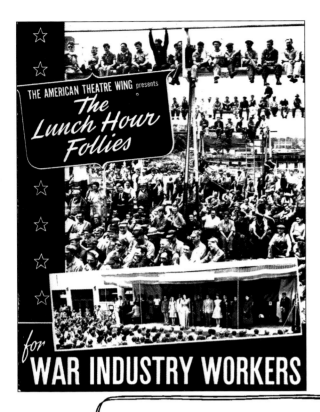

We are prepared to do shows to fit into any lunch hour, whether the "hour" lasts fifteen minutes or fifty minutes. We can present these shows during any lunch-hour shift, whether it occur at noon, midnight or early morning—regardless of time.

We will conform to all conditions of the plant, and will send a technician out ahead to adjust whatever facilities are available for presenting the show.

For information as to costs, arrangements and details, refer to Kermit Bloomgarden, c/o The American Theatre Wing Lunch Hour Follies, Lyceum Theatre Building, 159 W. 45th St.

523. Weill was chairman of the production committee for the "Lunch Hour Follies", a program of the American Theatre Wing that brought entertainment into U.S. defense plants to boost worker morale. As an alien, he was not permitted into the factories where the shows he produced were performed.

Aline MacMahon (in New York) to Herbert Wexler, 27 January 1943: This is to inform you that Mr. Kurt Weill, with whom you have had conversations, is a member of the Executive Committee, and Chairman of the Production Committee of the "Lunch Time Follies."

The Lunchtime Follies, like the Stage Door Canteens, is an operation of the American Theatre Wing War Service, Incorporated, which, as you know, is the non-profit war organization of the radio, screen, and stage people. . . .

As Chairman of our Production Department it is highly important that Mr. Weill gain access to the plants which we service. The fact that he has not obtained his final citizenship papers is a definite handicap to him in this work, inasmuch as admission to these plants is limited to United States citizens. Without Mr. Weill's services, the work of the Lunchtime Follies would be seriously jeopardized.

In view of the above, if it is at all possible to expedite the issuance of Mr. Weill's final citizenship papers, it would eliminate a problem which is a serious handicap confronting this important war effort.

Weill (in New City) to Herbert Wexler, 9 February 1943: Here is a short outline of my "personal history."

I was born in Dessau, Germany on March 2nd, 1900, started writing music at the age of ten and studied at the Berlin Academy for Music with Humperdinck, later with Busoni. My first operas were produced at the opera houses in Berlin, Dresden, Leipzig, etc. The "Three Penny Opera," a modern version of the old "Beggar's Opera," became the biggest theatrical success of pre-Hitler Germany, but my music became soon the object of violent attacks by the Nazis, and in March 1933 I had to leave Germany because I was in danger of being arrested by the Gestapo. A few months later, I was expatriated by the Nazi government and my property was confiscated.

In 1933 and 1934 I lived and worked in Paris and London and in September 1935 I came to New York to write music for Max Reinhardt's production *The Eternal Road* at the Manhattan Opera House. I have been in the United States ever since, with the exception of a few days in Canada in August 1937, when I took out my first citizenship papers.

My work in the American theater includes the music for *Johnny Johnson* (Paul Green), for *Knickerbocker Holiday* (Maxwell Anderson), for *Railroads on Parade* (New York World's Fair) and for *Lady in the Dark*.

I was one of the speakers on the government-sponsored radio program *I Am an American*. With Maxwell Anderson I wrote the cantata *The Ballad of Magna Carta* for the radio program *The Pursuit of Happiness*. Also with Maxwell Anderson I wrote the second program in the series *This is War*. I also wrote the music for Ben Hecht's and Charles MacArthur's pageant *Fun to Be*

1 9 4 3

MUSIC + THEATER:	LITERATURE + FILM:	SCIENCE + SOCIETY:	POLITICS:
Ralph Vaughan Williams *Symphony No. 5*	Betty Smith *A Tree Grows in Brooklyn*	Penicillin successfully used	German army defeated at Stalingrad and forced to retreat
Richard Rodgers *Oklahoma!*	Ernie Pyle *Here Is Your War*	U.S. Supreme Court rules that children need not salute flag in schools if it is against their religion	Allies land in Sicily, Mussolini is dismissed and arrested
Schoenberg *Ode to Napoleon*	*Casablanca* (film by Michael Curtiz)	U.S. takes over coal mines in response to miners' strike	Allied "round-the-clock" bombing of Germany begins

Free at Madison Square Garden, and *The Song of the Free*, which I wrote with Archibald MacLeish, was sung on the air on United Nations Day 1942.

Together with Moss Hart and Aline MacMahon I founded early in 1942 the "Lunch Time Follies," an entertainment service for workers in defense factories. This non-profit organization has been recognized by representatives of management and labor and by government officials as an important contribution to the war effort. In my capacity as chairman of the Production Committee, I am completely responsible for the programs of the "Lunch Time Follies," for the choice of material and talent and for the program policy. It is therefore necessary for me to attend a great number of our shows in the defense plants. As you know, the restrictions for entering defense plants are getting stronger every day, and I am having more and more difficulties in entering these plants because my final citizenship papers have not come through yet.

I filed my petition for final citizenship papers in July 1942, which was about five years after I had entered the country on an immigration quota (August 1937). My first papers were filed in November 1937. Since last July I have not heard anything about my papers except the letter of July 20, 1940, which I showed to you, but for reasons before mentioned I would appreciate it greatly if the issuance of my final citizenship papers could be expedited.

524. Exiled German artists presented "We Fight Back," a concert at Hunter College in New York, 3 April 1943, to aid in the war effort. Weill accompanied Lenya singing "Moritat von Mackie Messer," "Surabaya-Johnny," "Seeräuberjenny," and "Und was bekam des Soldaten Weib."

525. Ben Hecht's pageant, *We Will Never Die*, for which Weill provided the score (largely derived from his music for *The Eternal Road*) represented an early attempt to publicize the murder of two million Jews in Nazi-occupied Europe. The pageant premiered at Madison Square Garden on 9 March 1943 and was performed in five other cities: Washington D.C., Philadelphia, Boston, Chicago, and Los Angeles. A broadcast recording of the Hollywood Bowl performance has survived. The souvenir program cover drawing is by Arthur Szyk.

526. Hecht's script for *We Will Never Die*, with musical cues added by Weill.

527. Weill adapted "The Rabbi's Entrance" for *We Will Never Die* from music composed for *The Eternal Road*.

528. A photo from the New York performance of *We Will Never Die* at Madison Square Garden. Moss Hart directed a cast of more than 900 people. Fifty members of the NBC Symphony Orchestra, conducted by Isaac van Grove, accompanied the pageant.

Weill (in New City) to Ira Gershwin, 5 April 1943: As the weeks go by I feel more and more ashamed that I didn't answer yet your last letter. The only excuse I have is the fact, probably known to you, that I had terrible troubles with the Venus show. As everybody expected from the beginning, Bella [Spewack] became more and more difficult. . . . So we threw her out, and Sid Perelman, Ogden [Nash] and I sat down and worked out an entirely new story line, in complete disregard of Bella's script, with entirely new characters and no Olympus. Then Sid and Ogden started writing the dialogue which they just finished. Now it is a very fast-moving, very interesting show, witty and romantic at the same time, with good comedy situations and good parts. In the meanwhile, Ogden has developed into a good lyric writer and we have written some very good songs. But there is still some work to be done on the book and score and we decided to do the show in the early fall—with or without Marlene [Dietrich] (who, as you can imagine, is also quite a problem).

You can see what a headache this was during the last three months. But that wasn't all. I also had the "Lunch Time Follies" on my hands. Everybody had deserted me on that project, and practically all by myself I produced about fifteen shows for defense plants. Finally, I did the memorial pageant *We Will Never Die* at Madison Square Garden with Ben Hecht, Billy Rose, and Moss. It was a very effective show. Moss did a wonderful job of staging. I called him Moss Rein-Hart when I watched him directing the masses through a microphone—and did he like it! We will repeat it next Monday in Constitution Hall in Washington. . . .

We are having servant troubles, oil troubles, gasoline troubles and stomach troubles. Max Anderson is on his way to England. And, if you want some gossip, Gertie and Hugh Marlowe are what Winchell calls an item. People say that's why she wants to go on the road again. If I go on with this letter I might start telling jokes. So I'd better stop right here.

530. Around the time of *One Touch of Venus*. Photo by Vandamm.

531. Agnes de Mille, choreographer of *One Touch of Venus*. She had choreographed Rodgers and Hammerstein's *Oklahama!*, which opened on Broadway six months before *One Touch of Venus*.

532. A page from Weill's FBI file reveals that the U.S. Attorney General's office expedited Weill's final citizenship papers.

MOURN JEWISH DEAD IN EUROPE

'We Shall Never Die' Given as Memorial to Victims.

"We Shall Never Die," a spectacular memorial to the 2,000,000 Jews killed in Europe, was presented twice last night in Madison Square Garden, with an audience of 20,000 at each performance. The cast numbered more than 900.

The pageant included a plea to the Allied nations to rescue as many as possible of the 4,000,000 more Jews Adolf Hitler has promised to exterminate before the end of 1943.

Because of the advance demand for tickets, the second performance, beginning at 11:15 P. M., was arranged. The first ninety-minute presentation was at 8:45. Similar pageants are to be given in Philadelphia, Washington and Chicago.

The hall was decorated as a temple, with two forty-foot tablets inscribed with the Ten Commandments dominating the scene. Twelve-foot candelabra flanked the tablets. Draped around the tiers were 2,500 yards of crepe.

Paul Muni and Edward G. Robinson took leading parts in the pageant, which was sponsored by the Committee for a Jewish Army of Stateless and Palestinian Jews. It was written by Ben Hecht, produced by Billy Rose and directed by Moss Hart.

529. A review of the first performance of *We Will Never Die* from the *New York Sun*, 11 March 1943.

Many Collaborators.

Many actors, composers, producers, singers, directors and writers had a part in staging the spectacle. Among them were Kurt Weill, Kurt Baum, Luther Adler, Lemuel Ayers, S. Syrjala, Moe Hack, Jacob Ben-Ami, Herbert Rudley, Paul Lindenberg, Solvie Wiberg, William Malten, David Leonard, Margaret Waller, Edward Franz, Walter Kohler, Mark Schweid, Eleanora Mendlesohn and Sylvia Sidney. The NBC Symphony Orchestra was conducted by Isaac Van Grove.

Spotlights flashed upon the darkened stage brought each group of actors into sharp relief as they played their parts. Massed choirs sang from behind dark blue curtains.

Early in the pageant, Mr. Muni and Mr. Robinson alternately recited the names of the Jewish great in history, beginning with Abraham and Moses, and proceeding through the years to Colin Kelly's bombardier, Master Sergt. Meyer Levin.

The amplified sound of a telegraph key was used in the re-enactment of the surrender of Corregidor, news of which was flashed to the world by Irving Stobling, 22-year-old Jewish soldier from Brooklyn, now a prisoner of the Japanese.

'Killed According to Plan.'

In one case, the Allied and occupied nations meted out justice to the Axis, but no Jewish representative was present. The narrator explained: "There will be no Jews left in Europe for representation when peace comes. The 4,000,000 left to kill are being killed, according to plan."

Later, however, in a scene depicting the victims of the various Axis-dominated countries, a narrator said: "But we here tonight have a voice. Let us raise it. Perhaps the dying will hear it and find hope. Perhaps the Four Freedoms will hear it and find tongue. It is the voice of prayer."

The performance closed with recitation of the Kaddish, the prayer for the dead, with many in the audience joining in the chanting.

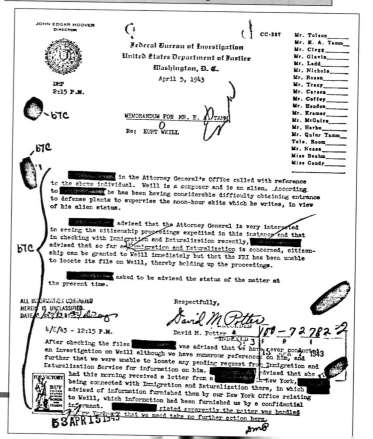

533. The Certificate of Naturalization confirming Weill's American citizenship, dated 27 August 1943.

Ogden Nash remembers . . .

Well, I could really talk indefinitely about my relationship with Kurt, because I had, [aside for] certain admiration and respect for him as a craftsman and a creator and, to use a too often used word, I think, really a genius of the theater. He was such a really darling man, who was hard as nails when need be, because he had to be after what he had been through. But he was essentially of great sweetness and patience. And I must have been a great trial to that, because I was an absolute greenhorn in the theater. I'd never done any theatrical work. In 1942, I was sitting quietly at my desk in Baltimore when the mail came in and there was a letter from Kurt up on the Hudson, asking me if I'd care to write the lyrics with him on an idea that he had, which at that time, he thought, would provide a starring vehicle for Marlene Dietrich. . . . And we started work and, never having worked with a composer before and, of course, I was amazed to find that, although there was a piano in the house, he didn't use it for writing his music that went on inside of that head of his. And most of the noise around the house was created by the mountain stream on the outside. And he taught me the values of quantity and stress which are so very different from those in my verse, which I had been accustomed to working with, where the writer supplies his own stress. And, of course, in songs, that is supplied by the music.

As far as our working together, the main thing that came out of it, really, was a song which we still hear a good deal today, "Speak Low," which I think has become one of the standards and one of Kurt's three or four best pieces. That was rather odd, because I was a lyric writer, and I was stuck for about eight weeks on what to do with it. It was a piece of music that Kurt had written. He had apparently been to the piano at least once, and he had this lovely, compelling, haunting melody. And we talked and talked. I thought and thought by myself, and then I talked and talked with Kurt, and then, finally, he came up with a quotation from Shakespeare that seemed to fit the situation and fit the meter of the thing which was "Speak low, when you speak love." Actually, I think the quotation is "Speak low, if you speak love," but we did take a certain amount liberty with Shakespeare, and changed the "if" to a "when." "A Living Liner" issued with "Two Worlds of Kurt Weill," RCA LSC-2863.

Agnes de Mille (in Hobbs, New Mexico) to Weill, 22 July 1943: On Tuesday at 3 p.m. I'm interviewing Sono Osato who wants to dance with us. Do you know her? Look up her pictures in any old Ballet Russe program and drop dead with joy. She'll lead the Bacchanale and make history.

534. Weill during rehearsals of *One Touch of Venus* with Mary Martin seated behind him. Producer Cheryl Crawford is seated at the rear right.

535. Authors and cast of *One Touch of Venus*, from left: Kenny Baker, director Elia Kazan, S.J. Perelman, John Boles, Kurt Weill (seated), Teddy Hart (standing), Ruth Bond, Paula Laurence, and an unidentified cast member.

536. First page of copyist's score of *One Touch of Venus*.

ONE TOUCH OF VENUS

Musical comedy in two acts; book by S.J. Perelman and
Ogden Nash; lyrics by Ogden Nash

Maurice Abravanel, conductor; Elia Kazan, director; Agnes de Mille,
choreographer; Howard Bay, set designer; Paul du Pont and Kermit Love,
costume designers; Mainbocher, gown designer for Mary Martin

1943   New York, Imperial Theatre (7 October; 567 performances over two seasons)
1947   Göteborg, Sweden
1948   Dallas, Starlight Operetta (5 July)

537. Opening night program
for *One Touch of Venus* at the
Imperial Theatre.

538. Theater poster for *One Touch of Venus*.

539 Paula Laurence sings the title number,
"One Touch of Venus," in the first act.

540. At the Artists' Ball,
the last scene in Act I,
Savory (John Boles)
recounts the grisly story
of "Dr. Crippen."

541. Teddy Hart, Harry Clark, John
Boles, and Kenny Baker perform
a humorous barbershop quartet,
"The Trouble with Women."

542. In Act II, scene 3, Mary Martin, as Venus,
sings "That's Him" directly to the audience.

543. In the "Venus in Ozone Heights" ballet, the goddess of love discovers the mundane life of a barber's wife, a prospect that causes her to flee back to her home among the gods.

544. A page from the souvenir program with photos and excerpts from reviews.

545. In addition to single numbers, Chappell issued this album of seven songs.

546. Shortly after *One Touch of Venus* opened, Mary Martin was featured on the cover of the 25 October 1943 issue of *Life.*

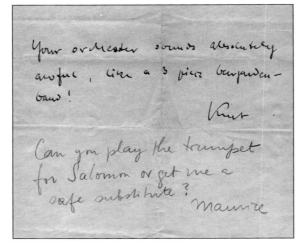

547. A humorous exchange between Weill and Maurice Abravanel, conductor of *Venus* and a former pupil of Weill's in Berlin. Abravanel refers to Weill's trumpet studies twenty-five years earlier, in case he would have been drafted during WWI.

548. A typical review of *One Touch of Venus* by the well-known theater critic Ward Morehouse (*New York Sun*), who considered the show "unconventional," a "musical show that breaks away from pattern and the accepted routine."

The New Play

'One Touch of Venus,' Musical Play, Brings Mary Martin Back to Broadway.

By WARD MOREHOUSE.

Broadway's theatrical season began on the torrid evening of August 1 but many New Yorkers waited until last night to start their playgoing. An audience that distinctly had that mid-season look turned out at the Imperial to greet "One Touch of Venus," a show that is smart, new-fangled and glossy, and in which Mary Martin distinguishes herself.

On the side of prophecy I suspect that this handsome and unconventional musical comedy will be a rousing success; certainly it comes as a welcome addition to a sparse and faltering season. On the side of perversity, I felt there were times when the new show is not up to the standard of its cast. Cheryl Crawford has given Miss Martin a delightful supporting company, and one that includes Kenny Baker, John Boles, Paula Laurence and Teddy Hart, in the role of a waggish undersized sleuth.

"One Touch of Venus" is a piece with women, some catchy songs, some devastating lyrics by Ogden Nash, a lot of S. J. Perelman's cockeyed subtleties and a story—a good story, too. That, indeed, of the quest for a millionaire art connoisseur for the statue of Venus, his importing it to his New York museum, and of the statue's coming to life when a young and starry-eyed barber happens to slip a ring on its finger. It's fantasy plot with a touching and affecting finish and in the role of Venus the red-headed Mary Martin from out of the plains of Texas gives Broadway her best performance.

The song numbers that are particularly effective are: "Foolish Heart," "Speak Low," "The Trouble With Women," "Way Out West in New Jersey" and "That's Him," fetchingly sung by Miss Martin. The book of S. J. Perelman holds up well but some of his dialogue falls rather flat. Lines that must have seemed enormously glib and funny in the script are surprisingly lifeless when spoken from the stage. The beginning of the show is very slow. Excellent comedy material is provided several secondary characters, such as those played by Ruth Bond and Helen Raymond, and the short scenes between Venus and the rasping Gloria, as done by Miss Bond, are grand.

Agnes de Mille, daughter of a hit-writing dramatist in the Broadway of another day, provides imaginative ballets for "One Touch of Venus." The dancing of Sono Osato is extraordinarily good. I could take a full evening of the lank, laconic and infectious Paula Laurence and I wish she had more to do. Kenny Baker, from out of the films and radio,

'ONE TOUCH OF VENUS.'
Musical play with music by Kurt Weill, book by S. J. Perelman and Ogden Nash, lyrics by Ogden Nash, staged by Elia Kazan, dances by Agnes de Mille; presented by Cheryl Crawford at the Imperial Theater Thursday evening, October 7, 1943. The cast:

Whitelaw Savory	John Boles
Molly Grant	Paula Laurence
Taxi Black	Teddy Hart
Stanley	Harry Clark
Rodney Hatch	Kenny Baker
Venus	Mary Martin
Mrs. Moats	Florence Dunlap
Store manager	Sam Bonnell
Bus starter	Lou Wills Jr.
Sam	Zachary A. Charles
Mrs. Kramer	Helen Raymond
Gloria Kramer	Ruth Bond
Police lieutenant	Bert Freed
Rose	Jane Hoffman
Zuvetli	Harold Stone
Dr. Rook	Johnny Stearns
Anatolian	Sam Bonnell
Premiere danseuse	Sono Osato

is an ingratiating performer and welcome he is to the domain of the Shuberts—and to that of Crawford & Wildberg.

It's really Miss Martin's show all the way, as it should be. She is handsomely gowned and is disconcertingly pretty and she can be assured that she has scored another personal success in the theater where she first came into Broadway's consciousness with "My Heart Belongs to Daddy."

Cheryl Crawford has performed Broadway a service in bringing along a musical show that breaks sharply away from pattern and the accepted routine. "One Touch of Venus" brings new and needed life to a season that has been fearfully meager. Notwithstanding my certain specified qualifications, I put "One Touch of Venus" down as a definite hit at the Imperial. The box office line has already begun forming.

Weill (in Los Angeles) to Emma and Albert Weill, 5 November 1943: Finally I've got some time to write you again. A few very difficult and aggravating months are now behind me, but, as you might have heard already, all this work has once again been rewarded and the new show has become a great success. It's been an especially difficult task because this time I didn't have a Moss Hart or an Ira Gershwin next to me, but had to rely entirely on my own judgment, had to make all decisions myself (often even against the wishes of my collaborators), and had to work on the libretto, the casting, the scenic designs, and the entire organization of a big Broadway show as well. During the seven weeks before the show's opening, I never slept more than two or three hours a night, because I had to be at rehearsals during the day and had to orchestrate at night. But one really doesn't notice it when one is "in the swing of things," and Lenya made sure that I ate regularly. The worst part was those three weeks in Boston, where at first it looked like the show would be a huge flop, and I had to pull things together in a very short time. But all of this is forgotten by now—thank God! . . .

Another important and joyful event: a few weeks ago I became an American citizen! I've been aspiring to this for years and I am very happy about it.

We arrived in Hollywood a few weeks ago, and I'll be working on a film for a few months and can relax a little bit at the same time. We've rented a charming little house, with a lovely garden, in which we can pick our own lemons from the trees, and a swimming pool. We've brought our maid along so we won't have to eat in restaurants, something I had to do constantly throughout the last few months. The climate here is wonderful at this time of year: cool during the night and pleasantly warm during the day. I think we'll be staying here until the beginning of February.

Weill (in Los Angeles) to Leah Salisbury, 17 November 1943: The next thing they [the producers] will try is to cut down the orchestra, and I'd better put down my own point of view now to you before anything happens. Before I started orchestrating I told Cheryl that my orchestration would be based on a good-sized string section and she heartily agreed with me (mainly because the same orchestra combination had been very successful in *Oklahoma!*). The figure of twenty-one pieces was mentioned in the contract only to make sure that, if the show is doing badly and they'd have to cut down, they never could play the show with less than twenty-one pieces. You know that the orchestration got great acclaim in the press and in the audience, and it would be a grave damage to the show if they would start fooling around with it. If they think they can cut down to twenty-one pieces they don't realize that this would mean a rearrangement of the whole score and an expense of about 3,000 dollars. Also I am sure that the Dramatists' Guild would protect me against any manipulations which would definitely damage my work, at a time when the show is doing smash business. I am perfectly willing to play the show, as originally planned, with twenty-five men (which is less than, for instance, *Oklahoma!*, *Merry Widow*, or *Carmen Jones*), if I have *my musicians*. It is not my fault that they have messed up the situation with the Shubert housemen, and I would be only too glad to cut out the housemen. I don't think you should mention this whole matter now before we have definite proof that they intend to do something. But I want you to be ready to take the necessary steps as soon as they try. Abravanel can give you all the information on this question.

549. A profile of Weill published in the *New York Post* on 20 October 1943.

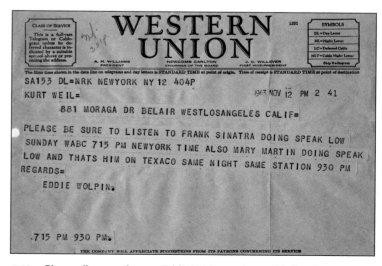

550. Chappell song plugger Eddie Wolpin advises Weill to listen to Frank Sinatra on the radio. Weill wrote to his agent, Leah Salisbury, "According to the latest reports from Chappell, 'Speak low' will probably be the most played song on the air early in December!!"

LIST OF BROADCASTS ON SPEAK LOW

FOR WEEK OF DEC. 4TH TO 12TH INCLUSIVE

- -

DEC. 4TH

3 SUNS	WEAF	6.30
BEASLEY SMITH	"	12.30
KOBBLERS	WJZ	6.15
COCA COLA	"	9.30
JAN GARBER	"	12.00
GUY LOMBARDO	WABC	11.15
BOB ALLEN	"	12.45
BOB STANLEY	WOR	5.30
TED LEWIS	"	11.30
JOHNNY MESSNER	"	12.45

DEC. 5TH

TH. PELUSO	WEAF	12.00
WHEELING STEEL	WJZ	5.30
FREDDY MARTIN	"	12.30
PRUDENTIAL	WABC	5.00
FRANK SINATRA	"	7.15

DECC 6TH

RUSS DAVID	WEAF	11.30
GRACE MORGAN	WJZ	9.55
LOU BREESE	"	11.30
SQUIBB	WABC	6.15
BALLANTINE	"	10.30
SHEP FIELDS	"	12.30
LANNY & GINGER	WOR	6.15
SONNY SKYLAR	"	10.15
JOSE MORAND	"	12.00

DEC. 7TH

ROY SHEILD	WEAF	12.00
DUFFY'S TAVERN	WJZ	8.30
RAY HEATHERTON	"	12.30
FUN WITH DUNN	WABC	5.00
BAYER	"	7.30
BENNY GOODMAN	"	12.00

DEC. 8TH

BOB REESE	WEAF	12.30
LOU BREESE	WJZ	11.30
JERRI SULLIVAN	WABC	6.30
CESAR PETRILLO	"	12.00
ABE LYMAN	WOR	12.30

DEC. 9TH

JACK MILLER	WEAF	8.30
GROOVER BOYS	"	12.30
REDD EVANS	WJZ	7.30
R. & H. BEER	"	7.45
COCA COLA	"	9.30
CHAS. SPIVAK	"	12.30
LANDT TRIO	WABC	5.30
DICK HAYMES	"	10.30
WAYNE MACK	"	12.00
ENRIC MADRIGUERA	WOR	11.30
COUNT BASIE	"	12.30

DEC. 10TH

LULU BATES	WJZ	10.15
JAN GARBER	"	12.15
BOB ALLEN	WABD	12.00
DON MC-GRANE	WOR	11.45

DEC. 11TH

JOS. GALLICHHIO	WEAF	6.15
ANDY RUSSELL	WJZ	6.30
BETTY RANN	"	11.45
FREDDY MARTIN	"	12.30
TUMS	WABC	10.30
BENNY GOODMAN	"	12.30

DEC. 12TH

GENERAL ELECTRIC	WEAF	10.00
FRANCIS CRAIG	"	12.30
FREDDY MARTIN	WJZ	12.30
RAY SINATRA	WABC	8.00
CAMPANA	WOR	5.45
COASTTO COAST	WJZ	10.00 A.M.
HORN & HARDART	WEAF	10.30 AM.
RUSS MORGAN	WUZ	11.00 AM.
SAMMY KAYE	WJZ	12.30
JOS. STOPAK	WJZ	4.00 PM

DEC. 5TH

PAULINE ALPERT	WOR	10.30 AM
FT. DIX	"	3.00 PM

551. The list of broadcast performances of "Speak Low" for the week of 4–12 December, 1943. At seventy total performances, it was the most-played song on the radio that week.

552. Telegram from Cheryl Crawford to Weill, 22 December 1943. She informs him of *Venus*'s forthcoming move from the Imperial Theater, and that *Venus* outsold *Oklahoma!* the previous week.

Russell Crouse (in New York) to Weill, 30 November 1943: It was very nice to hear from you again. In the meantime I've seen *One Touch of Venus* and enjoyed it very much. The freshness of approach warmed me, and your score is completely delightful—particularly "Speak Low," which, incidentally, broke my heart, for if I remember correctly the title came from our little plan to do *Much Ado* with music. It is a lovely number.

I still have hopes that we may one day do our Shakespeare—in fact I mentioned it to Terry Helburn one day last summer and she has been threatening to have lunch with me about it ever since. We may have to wait again, however, for someone has recently announced a Dawn Powell adaptation of *The Taming of the Shrew* with music. I still think our idea is better than any of the others.

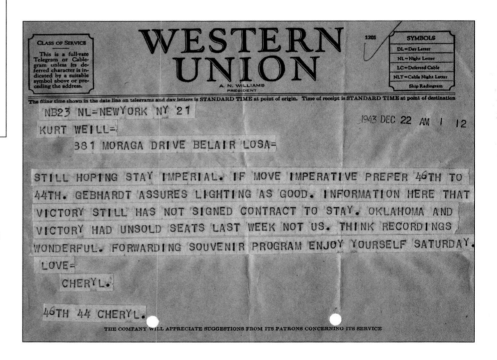

1	9	4	4

MUSIC + THEATER:	**LITERATURE + FILM:**	**SCIENCE + SOCIETY:**	**POLITICS:**
Aaron Copland *Appalachian Spring*	Lillian Smith *Strange Fruit*	Quinine synthesized	D-Day Allied landing in Normandy
Leonard Bernstein *On the Town*	John Hersey *A Bell for Adano*	Cost of living in U.S. rises almost 30%	U.S. troops land in Philippines
Tennessee Williams *The Glass Menagerie*	*Henry V* (film by Laurence Olivier)	William Beveridge *Full Employment in a Free Society*	Roosevelt elected to a fourth term

Weill (in Los Angeles) to Rita Weill, 12 January 1944: We're glad these holidays are over with because they're a real ordeal out here. We had to go to two of those awful Hollywood parties. I just can't have any fun when 60 or 80 people get together in a room and give you the order to have fun. . . .

My work for the movie [*Where Do We Go from Here?*] is progressing nicely, but without great excitement on my part. There is great enthusiasm in the studio about our score—so much so that they have decided to put one of the big comedians in the leading part. That makes the whole thing a little more interesting. We've written quite a lot of material and only about three songs are left to do, then I'll be through—I guess in about 3 to 4 weeks. . . .

Last weekend I was in San Francisco to see the [Darius] Milhauds. That is definitely the most beautiful city in this country, reminds me very much of Marseille because it is built on hills and you see the ocean from every corner of the town. . . .

Well, "Speak Low" has become a big hit now and is being played everywhere, even on the juke boxes. It's going to be back on the hit parade this Saturday as one of the most frequently performed songs. The record album will be out on February 1st. Bing Crosby just made a recording of "September Song." There will be two pictures out with my music in the next few weeks. *Lady in the Dark* and *Knickerbocker Holiday*. I haven't seen them yet, but I hear both are very good. People say that Ginger Rogers' singing of "Jenny" is terrific, and so is Charles Coburn's singing of "September Song."

553. The "original cast" recording of *One Touch of Venus* appeared in 1944 on five 10-inch records, with Mary Martin and Kenny Baker as the only soloists.

554. The inside cover of the *Venus* recording featured a number of photos from the recording session.

Ernst Aufricht (in New York) to Weill, 24 December 1943: Leo Kerz, a Berlin scenic designer whom I used to know, has offered to produce Brecht's play *The Good Woman of Sezuan* on Broadway. Brecht asked me to look into this man and his potential. I found out the following: He has $50,000 at his disposal. He has read the old as well as the new version. He wants to do the old version; he doesn't like the new one. He is prepared to acquire a three months' option right away in order to determine the possibilities for casting, a theater, etc. Under no circumstances would Brecht want to conclude any agreements before he knows if you are still interested in his play. Please send a telegram to either Brecht or me. Brecht would be glad to ignore this man if he could conclude a contract with you.

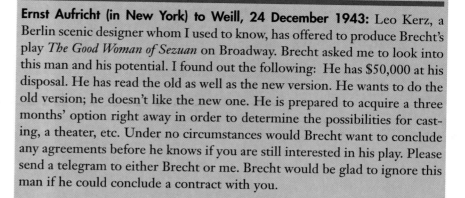

555. Brecht's typewritten synopsis for *Der gute Mensch von Sezuan* survives in Weill's archives.

Weill (in Los Angeles) to Maurice Speiser, 22 January 1944: You will have gathered from my wire that I feel a strong resentment against Brecht's attitude in the matter of *Sezuan*. I have known Brecht for years. He has always been the most difficult man to work with. Last spring, when he insisted on working with me again, I hoped that he had changed his attitude. I thought he realized that this was for him, for the first time, an opportunity to get a first-class Broadway production. Unfortunately, this proved to be a mistake. Instead of seizing his opportunity with both hands, he kept stalling, he made impossible demands and all kinds of difficulties. The last time I talked to him out here he seemed absolutely unwilling to sign our contract. The next thing I heard was the announcement in the newspapers that somebody else is doing the play. He is playing his old tricks again—and I just don't feel like going through all this again. Life is too short—and the finest American playwrights would be only too happy to give me their plays or to collaborate with me.

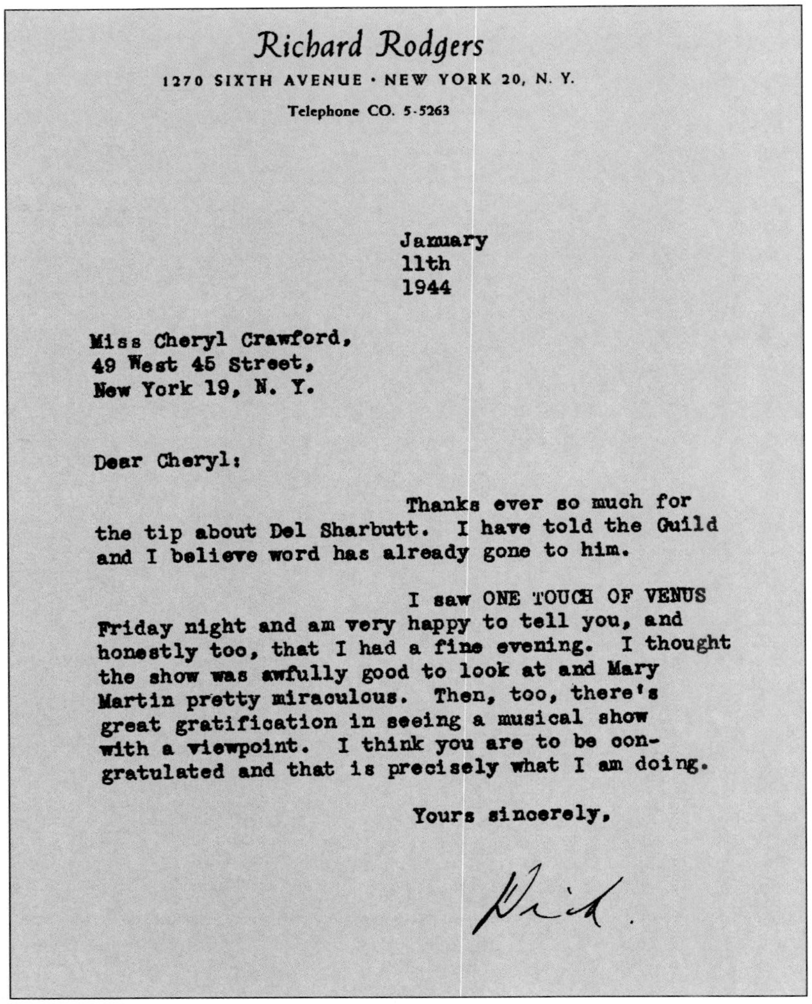

Richard Rodgers

1270 SIXTH AVENUE · NEW YORK 20, N. Y.

Telephone CO. 5-5263

January
11th
1944

Miss Cheryl Crawford,
49 West 45 Street,
New York 19, N. Y.

Dear Cheryl:

Thanks ever so much for the tip about Del Sharbutt. I have told the Guild and I believe word has already gone to him.

I saw ONE TOUCH OF VENUS Friday night and am very happy to tell you, and honestly too, that I had a fine evening. I thought the show was awfully good to look at and Mary Martin pretty miraculous. Then, too, there's great gratification in seeing a musical show with a viewpoint. I think you are to be congratulated and that is precisely what I am doing.

Yours sincerely,

Dick.

556. Richard Rodgers sent Cheryl Crawford a letter of congratulations on the success of *One Touch of Venus*.

Ogden Nash (in Baltimore) to Weill, 19 January 1944: Would you like to hear [a story] about our producers? . . . I tried to send a wire to the company for New Year's Day and the 100th performance but Western Union wouldn't accept it, so I thought I'd wait till I got to New York. When I arrived there Sid told me that the producers had not been going to do anything about New Year's at all; hadn't even planned to write a note. He finally shamed them, over their own screaming dead bodies, into sending a case of champagne which, when it arrived, turned out to be Portuguese, retailing, I think, at about eleven cents a bottle less than a domestic brand. This made me very sore, so I trotted out and ordered a case of Heidsieck sent to the theater for a surprise party. It was addressed to the *One Touch of Venus* company. By a fortunate chance I stopped by the Imperial that afternoon to check up on some tickets and ran into Nick [Holti], who informed me that Cheryl had seen the case of champagne a little while before and ordered it sent over to the Crawford-Wildberg office. I was just in time to countermand the order, so the kids got their champagne after all.

Weill (in Los Angeles) to Cheryl Crawford, 30 January 1944: The letters you sent me are very funny, especially the one from Dick Rodgers. What a stuffed shirt!

The report from David Lowe is very interesting. I knew about most of the "Speak Low" plugs from my Chappell reports, but the plugs for the other songs were new to me, and, as I wrote you in my last letter, there is a vast field for publicizing the show through those songs which haven't been touched yet and which are excellent radio material. When I get back to N.Y. I think I can be of some help. I will work out a rhythm version of "That's Him" and get somebody like Ginny Simms or Dinah Shore to do it. Then I'll write a complete waltz orchestration of "Foolish Heart" for Kostelanetz, and finally I'll write an orchestra suite from the music of the show (like the scenario from *Showboat*) which might be played a lot. If we place these things through Lowe we have a chance to get a plug for the show every time they are being played. Another approach for Lowe is to get, instead of single songs, the score of *One Touch of Venus* on the air. I don't know what happened with the "Hall of Fame." They were supposed to dedicate half of their program to our show in their second program, but then it was canceled and all they did was "Speak Low." Since they have done the same thing for *Oklahoma!* and *Carmen Jones* there is no reason they shouldn't do it for us. The same is true of the Kate Smith hour, the Kostelanetz hour and some other programs of the same type. On the whole, I think the employment of Lowe is a very good idea and I am sure you'll have good results.

Jack Kapp sent me the Decca album. It is very effective and beautiful to look at and one of the finest and most impressive recording jobs I have had. Unfortunately, the material of the disks is so bad that the records are a little scratchy, but with a good needle they sound alright. They are technically better than the *Oklahoma!* records, which are almost useless. I hope they'll sell as well! I heard that the Lombardo record sold already more than 200,000. By the way, did you hear Sinatra singing "Speak Low" on the President's birthday program?

Weill (in New City) to Ira Gershwin, 27 February 1944: In New York I found everything okay. *Lady in the Dark* is breaking all records at the Paramount. There is a line at the box office all around the block onto 43rd Street. I am sending you the notices, including the second reviews in today's Sunday papers. You'll see that the *Times* and the *Tribune* gave us (you and me) a break.

At Chappell's I saw the new covers for "Jenny" and "My Ship." They are beautiful. But that's all they did. As far as plugging is concerned, they take the usual "wait-and-see" stand. I will see Max Dreyfus tomorrow and will try to get some action.

Venus is in very good shape and plays better in the new house than at the Imperial. I was rather pleased to find, looking at it cold-bloodedly, that in spite of all the faults and mistakes it is a very good and interesting show and that it holds the audience all through once they sit through the first fifteen minutes, which are pretty awful.

558. In Hollywood, 1944.

557. The film version of *Lady in the Dark*, with Ginger Rogers and Ray Milland, appeared in February 1944. Very little of the music from the original stage work was retained in the movie. Even the signature song, "My Ship," was never sung; the melody was used only for underscoring.

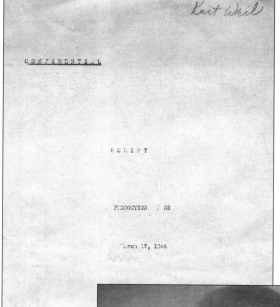

559. Script for a confidential government project to be entitled *Salute to France*, a film written by Maxwell Anderson, directed by Jean Renoir, and starring Burgess Meredith. Weill provided music for this propaganda film, which was one of a series of films produced by the U.S. Office of War Information prior to the opening of the "Second Front" in Western Europe in June 1944. The bilingual production was meant for American forces involved in the liberation of France and also for the French populace.

560. A shot from *Salute to France*: Joe Doakes (Burgess Meredith) with his mess kit. Weill's score incorporated some well-known French songs ("Le temps des cerises" and "Chant de Libération"), the "Horst Wessel Song," the "Marseillaise," and some music from *Johnny Johnson*.

561. Hollywood's version of *Knickerbocker Holiday* was released in April 1944, two months after *Lady in the Dark*. Again, very little of Weill's music survived in the film adaptation. Crawford Music Corporation issued the sheet music of "September Song" with a new cover to coincide with the film's release.

562. In his living room at Brook House with Wooly.

563. Weill and writer Walter Mehring borrowed the music from Weill's 1934 French song "Je ne t'aime pas" for their new propaganda song "Wie lange noch?" for broadcast in Germany by the U.S. Office of War Information.

Weill (in Los Angeles) to Lotte Lenya, 1 July 1944: It was only a week yesterday since I left New York, but it seems like much longer. . . . Ira as well as Bill got terrific reactions to our score for *Where Do We Go from Here?* It has become what they call "the talk of the industry." Bill played for us the Rodgers-Hammerstein movie score which they wrote for him (*State Fair*). It is very weak and Ira was refreshingly frank about it and told Bill that he didn't like it. Bill finally admitted that our score is "in a class by itself." . . . Ira and I played a lot of 16th-century music (madrigals, Italian folk-dances etc.) and got very good ideas for the style of the score. We are now really working well together.

W.C. Morck of the Office of War Information (?) to Weill, 3 July 1944: This organization wishes to express its deep appreciation and to thank you and Mrs. Weill for your very fine work on the song "Wie lange noch."

These recordings, which have a very definite place in the prosecution of the war, have been received, reshipped, and by the time this note reaches you, they will have reached their ultimate destination.

At some time in the future, we hope that it will be possible for us to show you more definitely how your song assisted in the total war effort. Until such time, however, we would appreciate your treating the song in a most confidential manner.

Weill (in Los Angeles) to Lotte Lenya, 14 July 1944: We have now a complete story outline, and a very good one. . . . We decided now definitely to treat great parts of the score in real opera style, without any attempt to write American popular songs. The part of Cellini will be treated in a kind of grandioso arioso style and, as I wrote you before, the whole thing might very well become an opera for Broadway—and you know how I would like that. I was so pleased with Ira yesterday. He knows so much about style in words and music and he plays up to all my ambitions as a musician. The next thing I have to do now is to find a musical style for this score which, if I find it, will be quite different from anything that I or anybody else has done.

Weill (in Los Angeles) to Lotte Lenya, 23 July 1944: The world news has been so exciting these last days that everything else seemed awfully small and silly compared with the events in Germany and Japan. For more than ten years we have been waiting for what is going on in Germany now. There is no doubt that this is the real thing. I don't believe that there was an attempt on Hitler's life. He staged another Reichstag fire to give himself a shabby excuse for the biggest mass murder in history. A desperate madman killing blindly. He might get away with it for another few months, and that is good for us because the greatest danger—a peace with the German generals—is now out of the question.

Weill (in Los Angeles) to Lotte Lenya, 9 August 1944:
They started recording the music for *Where Do We Go from Here?* and will start shooting in three weeks. Of course, they don't want us to interfere. Perlberg's secretary called in the last minute to ask if we want to come over for the recording of "Morale," but we were right in the middle of working, so I said no. The show is more important. They will do anyhow what they want with the picture score.

564. Poster from the film *Where Do We Go from Here?*, with music by Weill and lyrics by Ira Gershwin. Morrie Ryskind's screenplay about time travel was directed by Gregory Ratoff and produced for 20th Century-Fox by William Perlberg.

565. The plot of *Where Do We Go from Here?* is motivated by a genie who agrees to get Bill Morgan (played by Fred MacMurray) accepted into the army so that he can fight in World War II.

566. Condensed score for *Where Do We Go from Here?* Film composer David Raksin provided the continuity between Weill's songs. Maurice de Packh was one of several orchestrators.

567. Columbus (Fortunio Bonanova) faces down a mutiny in *Where Do We Go from Here?*

568. Weill and Gershwin conceived the Columbus sequence as a mini-opera inserted into the film. At ten minutes, in 1945 it was the longest musical sequence in the history of film. This short score is in Weill's hand except for the title and text underlay.

569. Chappell Music published three songs in popular sheet music arrangements: "All at Once," "If Love Remains," and "Song of the Rhineland."

570. *Where Do We Go from Here?* was completed in 1944 and released in spring 1945. Although reviews were generally favorable, the public's appetite for war movies of this type had waned with the war itself.

Fantasy Clever in Idea; Songs Amuse

BY EDWIN SCHALLERT

Clever ideas that bundle up and hit you with a skyrocketing effect—not to mix metaphors or anything — distinguish "Where Do We Go From Here?" which is a rather happy experiment in fantasy presently exhibited at Loew's State, Grauman's Chinese and Fox Uptown theaters. The picture is erratic in appeal, has boresome spaces, which are plot explanatory, but for most of those who go to see it will do pretty well. It is, at least, a distinct novelty.

Most amusing are the songs. Ira Gershwin and Kurt Weill, two experts, are responsible. They have hit a Gilbert and Sullivan mood, pleasantly modernized. The numbers are staged with spectacular emphasis, and naturally gain by the Technicolor. Costuming throughout this production is particularly picturesque.

Amusing Fantasy

"Where Do We Go From Here?" is dream stuff, with a jinni of sorts to help the illusion. He does an abracadabra with a watch, substitute for the legendary lamp. Fred MacMurray is the chap he seeks to help.

MacMurray portrays a 4-F who fails to impress his canteen sweetheart when he is turned down by the draft board. He visits her at the rendezvous of the servicemen, and finds that he isn't desirable for dancing, for food participation, or aught else. He ends up washing dishes, Kindler toward him is another girl. June Haver and Joan Leslie play these roles.

MacMurray's aims to be a hero are gratified by Gene Sheldon as the jinni, and he becomes part of a historical pattern including the Revolutionary War, the voyage of Columbus to America and New York under the Dutch rule. He is all but shot by a Hessian firing squad, protects the discoverer of America during a mutiny, and later is nearly tomahawked by an Indian, but buys the island of Manhattan for $24 instead. The Indian is Badger. So this is the original badger game.

Saved by Jinni

Subsequently MacMurray sells the island to the municipal governing board for 1,000,000 gulden, in order to save his sweetheart from an unhappy marriage, but finds that he owes more than the full amount in taxes comparable with those levied today. This means a jail term to cover the remaining 25 gulden, after his clothes are sold, for 25 years. He is saved once again, as is the heroine, by the jinni.

"Where Do We Go From Here?" will please those who get into its mood, and MacMurray with his easy naturalness is a great aid to that end, while both Miss Leslie, and Miss Haver, who is very glamorous in the Hessian and Indian sequences, embellish the plot.

Fine singing by Carlos Ramirez, especially, and by Fortunio Bononova in the Columbus scenes, and a good comedy performance by Anthony Quinn, as well as Alan Mombray's redoubtable impersonation of George Washington, lend to the agreeable impact of this movie event.

Gregory Ratoff directed and the story is credited to Morrie Ryskind and Sig Herzig.

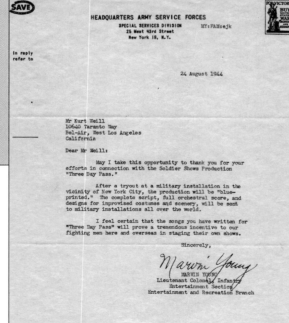

571. Letter of appreciation from the Entertainment and Recreation Branch of the U.S. Army recognizing Weill's work on a show entitled "Three Days' Pass." It is not clear which of Weill's songs were used in this production.

Weill (in Los Angeles) to Lotte Lenya, 12 August 1944: I really don't know why but it seems that I have become so sure now of my craftsmanship, of my theater knowledge and of my taste that I would take a dominating position in almost any combination. You can see clearly from the little samples of lyrics which I sent you that this will be more "my" show than anything I have done so far—even though I don't get credit for anything but the music. But I am sure that Verdi or Offenbach or Mozart contributed as much to their libretti as I do without getting credit for it. This is a part of a theater composer's job— to create for himself the vehicle which he needs for his music. . . . With Eddie I am having some troubles. He finally got through with the picture, but now he is tired. Yesterday he brought in a scene in which he just had copied the original play—so I tore it into pieces and gave him a detailed outline, almost word by word how to do it. As a matter of fact I had an idea last night of writing it myself (which I might do). Well, anyhow, Eddie was so overwhelmed by the accuracy and sharpness of my criticism that he accepted it without any hesitation. He really is an awfully nice guy—and so talented.

Kurt Weill, this Asiatic-European specimen. So far away from the Americans that he would be terrified if ever he would become fully aware of it. They like him, and to some degree he likes them. But they really don't know who he is. Excerpt from the diary of Richard Révy, 13 August 1944.

Weill (in Los Angeles) to Lotte Lenya, 18 August 1944: By the way, the combination Gershwin-Révy didn't work out so well and my little party would have been quite a flop if we wouldn't have gone to the ballet which made it a very short evening. The Révy's were so shy that they hardly talked, and confronted with Broadway-Americans, they are still quite European. The Gershwins, on the other hand, were a little impressed because I had told them that the R.'s have money and a wonderful picture collection. For me it was fun to watch.

Weill (in Los Angeles) to Lotte Lenya, 24 August 1944: I am terribly excited about France and the liberation of Paris. Who would have thought that the whole German fake would blow up so quickly? They just have nothing left, no fighting spirit and no gasoline. But Hitler doesn't allow them to quit until they are completely destroyed—and that is just perfect. What an exciting week! We will probably remember the events of these last days all our life.

Weill (in Los Angeles) to Lotte Lenya, 27 August 1944: Yesterday I spent four hours at the studio. . . . I saw a rehearsal of the opening number ("Morale") and the Hessian Drinking Song ["The Song of the Rhineland"] It looks terrific, real big production scenes, done with great taste and gusto, and the music comes out beautifully. If it works out the way it looks now, it will be a very important picture and a great thing for me. I am amazed how carefully they work. Every bar is worked out to the minutest detail. Yesterday they had a two-hour debate about the interpretation of one line, with an orchestra of fifty men waiting.

Weill (in Los Angeles) to Max Gordon, 17 October 1944:
We are working overtime this week to get as much as possible done before I leave. Tomorrow we are going to record parts of the score, with Ira singing and me at the piano.

I read your letter to Ira and I was surprised to find that you are still talking about Peggy Wood or Vivian Segal for the part of the Duchess. Both Ira and Eddie agree with what I had told you five months ago: that our conception of the Duchess is an entirely different one. Besides, neither of them would play the part because it is too small, and it would be fatal if we would have to build it up.

As you know, I've made it very clear to you and everybody concerned that I want Lotte Lenya (who happens to be Mrs. Weill) to play the part of the Duchess. I am sure that this is perfect casting, just as I was sure when I insisted on Mary Martin for Venus, or when I say that Walter Slezak should play the Duke.

572. In a letter to agent Leah Salisbury, Weill specified his conditions for working on the film version of *One Touch of Venus.*

10640 Taranto Way
Los Angeles 24, Cal.   Sept. 4, 1944

Dear Leah,

    here is the content of the non-interpolation clause as I want it in the contract for "Venus".

1. All the songs in the picture have to be taken from the score of the original show and the underscoring of the picture has to be based on themes from the original score.
2. The moving picture company has to call on me for the following services:
   a) to write any new songs or musical material as might be necessary for the moving picture treatment of the original show,
   b) to select and place the original songs for the requirements of the movie script and make necessary changes,
   c) to select themes and material from the original score for underscoring purposes.
3. The picture company has to advise me 10 weeks in advance as to when my services are required. If I am not available for the job we have to reach a mutual understanding as to who will replace me.
4. I have to paid for my services according to my Hollywood salary which was 2500.- a week for my last job at 20th Century. Transportation to and from Hollywood had to be paid by the company.
5. Billing. In the general contract we have to get a clause which gives us, the authors, a special frame with the following text:
        Based on the musical play
        "One Touch of Venus"
        Music by Kurt Weill
    Book by S.J.Perelman and Ogden Nash
        Lyrics by Ogden Nash.
If I am to do the special service job as outlined above I would have to get another frame with the text   Music by Kurt Weill
because I would be responsible for the entire music in the picture.

573. A letter from producer Max Gordon confirming that Melville Cooper (not Weill's first choice) was the most likely actor to play the Duke in *The Firebrand of Florence.*

574. In preparing *The Firebrand of Florence,* Weill made notes about his ideas for the casting of the leading roles.

MAX GORDON
149 WEST 45TH STREET
LYCEUM THEATRE BUILDING
NEW YORK 19, N. Y.

WISCONSIN 7-4204   CABLE MAXGORD

October 9, 1944

Mr. Kurt Weill
10640 Taranto Way
West Los Angeles, California

My dear Kurt:

Your letter to hand. I spoke to Ira Gershwin last night about Melville Cooper for 'The Duke.' I am very strong for this idea and since speaking to him last night, I had a talk with Cooper and find that he can sing songs. He did a comedy number in JUBILEE and that was a very great success. At present, Cooper is an enormous success in my new play WHILE THE SUN SHINES. I think this show will be through by the time we are ready, so let's figure on him for the part.

I wrote you regarding Wilbur Evans and Mike Todd and I will see Todd next week. Ira told me about Beverly Tyler, if you feel she is alright, let's sign her.

I am very excited about THE LATE GEORGE APLEY but I was even more excited when Ira told me what a wonderful score you had written and he was not in the least modest about the wonderful score and lyrics. Ira told me it was better than PORGIE and OF THEE I SING combined. I told him I would settle for half.

All best.

As ever,

MG:BS

575. Weill was nominated for an Academy Award for the score to the movie version of *Knickerbocker Holiday* in 1944.

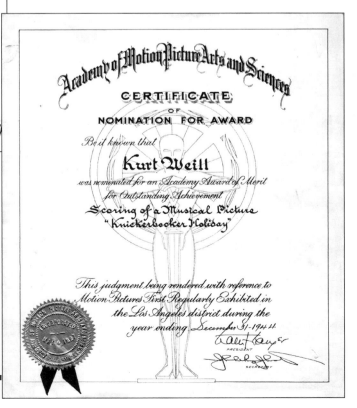

THE FIREBRAND OF FLORENCE

Operetta in two acts; libretto by Edwin Justus Mayer; lyrics by Ira Gershwin

1945   New York, Alvin Theatre (22 March; 43 performances)

Maurice Abravanel, conductor; John Murray Anderson, director; Catherine Littlefield, choreographer; Jo Mielziner, set and lighting designer; Raoul Pene DuBois, costume designer

577. A publicity photo for *The Firebrand of Florence*: from left, Kurt Weill, Ira Gershwin, Edwin Justus Mayer, and choreographer Catherine Littlefield.

578. Producer Max Gordon and Ira Gershwin study a lyric.

BEGINNING FEBRUARY 23, 1945
MAX GORDON
Presents
A New Musical

"MUCH ADO ABOUT LOVE"

by
EDWIN JUSTUS MAYER and IRA GERSHWIN
Music by KURT WEILL
With

| Melville COOPER | Earl WRIGHTSON | Beverly TYLER | Lotte LENYA |
| Ferdi HOFFMAN | Jean GUELIS | | Paul BEST |

Settings and Lighting by   Choreography by   Book Directed by
JO MIELZINER   CATHERINE LITTLEFIELD   JOHN HAGGOTT
Costumes by RAOUL PENE DuBOIS
Musical Director, MAURICE ABRAVANEL
All Musical Arrangements and Orchestrations by KURT WEILL
Staged by JOHN MURRAY ANDERSON

CAST
(In Order of Appearance)

HANGMAN	RANDOLPH SYMONETTE
TARTMAN	DON MARSHALL
SOUVENIR MAN	BERT FREED
MAFFIO	BOYD HEATHEN
MAGISTRATE	MARION GREEN
CELLINI	EARL WRIGHTSON
OTTAVIANO	FERDI HOFFMAN
ASCANIO	JAMES DOBSON
EMELIA	GLORIA STORY
ANGELA	BEVERLY TYLER
MARQUIS	PAUL BEST
CAPTAIN OF THE GUARD	CHARLES SHELDON
DUKE	MELVILLE COOPER
PAGE	BILLY WILLIAMS
DUCHESS	LOTTE LENYA
MAJOR-DOMO	WALTER GRAF
FIRST PETITIONER	FRANK STEVENS
SECOND PETITIONER	PAUL MARIO
ASTROLOGER	ERIC SANDER
THIRD PETITIONER	GAYNE SULLIVAN
FOURTH PETITIONER	MARJORIE COWEN
HARLEQUIN	JEAN GUELIS
COLOMBINA	NORMA GENTNER

APPRENTICES
John Cassidy, Lynn Alden, Walter Rinner, Frank Stevens

MODELS

The "Leonardo da Vinci" Model	Yvette Heap
The "Titian" Model	Doris Blake
The "Botticelli" Model	Marya Iversen
The "Raphael" Model	Gedda Petry
The "Veronese" Model	Rose Marie Elliot
The "Bronzino" Model	Perdita Chandler

SYNOPSIS OF SCENES
TIME: 1535
ACT I
SCENE   I—A Public Square in Florence.
SCENE   II—Before the Standards of Florence.
SCENE   III—Cellini's Workshop.

576. At the time of the Boston tryout in February 1945, *The Firebrand of Florence* was still called *Much Ado about Love*.

579. Two production photos from the Boston tryout of *The Firebrand of Florence*, one showing Beverly Tyler (seated) and Lotte Lenya.

1 9 4 5

MUSIC + THEATER:	**LITERATURE + FILM:**	**SCIENCE + SOCIETY:**	**POLITICS:**
Benjamin Britten *Peter Grimes*	George Orwell *Animal Farm*	Vitamin A synthesized	Yalta Conference between Roosevelt, Churchill, Stalin
Richard Rodgers *Carousel*	*Roma città aperta* (film by Roberto Rossellini)	First atomic bomb detonated near Alamogordo, New Mexico	Roosevelt dies
Richard Strauss *Metamorphosen*	*The Lost Weekend* (film by Billy Wilder)	Black markets for food, clothing, and cigarettes develop throughout Europe	Germany and Japan surrender

580. The first violin part from *Firebrand* lists the numbers from the show in order. The first page of "Sing Me Not a Ballad" shows a typical Broadway orchestra part from the 1940s.

581. As pre-opening publicity for *Firebrand*, *The New York Times* (18 March 1945) ran a caricature of the lead actors in the show. From left: Melville Cooper (the Duke), Beverly Tyler (Angela), Earl Wrightson (Cellini), Lotte Lenya (the Duchess), Ferdi Hoffman (Ottaviano), and Gloria Story (Emilia).

ALVIN THEATRE

OWNED AND OPERATED BY ALVIN THEATRE CORP.
Directors: Alexander H. Pincus   Norman Pincus

EMERGENCY NOTICE: In the event of an alert, remain in your seats. A competent staff has been trained for this emergency. Keep calm. You will receive information and instructions from the stage. F. H. La GUARDIA, Mayor.

FIRE NOTICE: The exit indicated by a red light and sign nearest to the seat you occupy is the shortest route to the street. In the event of fire please do not run—WALK TO THAT EXIT. Patrick Walsh, Fire Commissioner and Chief of Department

THE · PLAYBILL · A · WEEKLY · PUBLICATION · OF · PLAYBILL · INCORPORATED

Week beginning Sunday, March 25, 1945   Matinees Wednesday and Saturday

MAX GORDON
presents
A New Musical

THE FIREBRAND OF FLORENCE

By EDWIN JUSTUS MAYER and IRA GERSHWIN

Music by KURT WEILL
with

MELVILLE COOPER   EARL WRIGHTSON   BEVERLY TYLER   LOTTE LENYA
FERDI HOFFMAN   JEAN GUELIS   PAUL BEST   GLORIA STORY

Settings and lighting by Jo Mielziner
Costumes by Raoul Pene DuBois
Choreography and Singing Ensembles by Catherine Littlefield
Book directed by John Haggott
Musical Director, Maurice Abravanel
All musical arrangements and orchestrations by Kurt Weill
Staged by JOHN MURRAY ANDERSON

582. The program for *The Firebrand of Florence*. The show lasted only about five weeks on Broadway.

THE PLAYBILL
FOR · THE · ALVIN · THEATRE

THE FIREBRAND OF FLORENCE

Weill (in Los Angeles) to Albert and Emma Weill, 30 April 1945: Finally I'm finding a little time to write to you. As always when I'm bringing out a new work, the last few months have been full of vexations, and I was so completely wrapped up in my work that I didn't have time for anything else. This time it was particularly difficult because the dramatist [Edwin Justus Mayer], who had written the libretto, was a total failure, and I had felt a particular responsibility because it was a very big and expensive show and, of course, because Lenya performed in it. Musically it was the best I have written in years, a real opera with big choral and ensemble numbers, full of melodic invention, taking advantage of all the craftsmanship I have acquired through the years. Ira Gershwin, who wrote the lyrics, also surpassed himself. But the libretto was very weak and the performance left much to be desired. Outside of Lenya (who gave a magnificent portrait of the Duchess of Florence) the cast wasn't very good, and this time we didn't have any big names. The long and the short of it: this time it wasn't as big a success as were the last two shows. I personally scored a big success with my music, but otherwise the reviews were very bad. Not only that, but we opened right at a time

583. Attempting to hang Benvenuto Cellini is a frequent occurrence in *The Firebrand of Florence*, although somehow his enemies never quite succeed in doing him in.

584. The lecherous Duke (Melville Cooper) attempts to steal the heart of Cellini's model and consort Angela (Beverly Tyler).

585. Sheet music from *The Firebrand of Florence*. A couple of numbers were also released with the Boston title "Much Ado about Love" on the cover.

THERE'LL BE
LIFE, LOVE AND LAUGHTER

MAX GORDON
Presents

THE FIREBRAND
OF FLORENCE

Book by
EDWIN JUSTUS MAYER

Lyrics by   *Music by*
IRA GERSHWIN   KURT WEILL

Staged by
JOHN MURRAY ANDERSON
Musical Director
MAURICE ABRAVANEL

YOU'RE FAR TOO NEAR ME
THERE'LL BE
LIFE, LOVE AND LAUGHTER
SING ME NOT A BALLAD
A RHYME FOR ANGELA

CHAPPELL

Two on the Aisle

'Firebrand of Florence' Strikes Very Few Sparks

By Wilella Waldorf

As we remember Edwin Justus Mayer's play, "The Firebrand," it was very good fun. The musical version presented last night at the Alvin Theatre as "The Firebrand of Florence," however, is for the most part an elaborate bore, enlivened at odd moments by Melville Cooper as the nit-wit Duke, lavishly decorated with lovely Renaissance scenery and costumes designed by Jo Mielziner and Raoul Pene DuBois, and distinguished by one of Kurt Weill's finest scores, not always projected as it should have been.

It's book trouble again, of course, but that isn't the whole story. Edwin Justus Mayer and Ira Gershwin have managed to extract an extremely tiresome script from Mr. Mayer's play, and Mr. Gershwin's lyrics range from second to third, fourth and even fifth rate W. S. Gilbert.

But much of Mr. Weill's music is uncommonly fine and he has arranged some skillful and beguiling orchestrations that often sound very lovely as Maurice Abravanel and his musicians interpret them. It is a pity that poor casting in some of the leading roles puts a strain on both book and music that neither are quite able to bear.

586. One of many negative reviews, this excerpt by Wilella Waldorf from the *New York Post* praises Weill's score but condemns the show as an "elaborate bore."

Edwin Justus Mayer's famous *Firebrand* came back to town last evening. It did so in the guise of Max Gordon's latest musical, and this time it is called *The Firebrand of Florence*. Second things are usually not as good as first things, and in this the new show is no exception. Despite a Kurt Weill score, the original author's collaboration with Ira Gershwin on the book, and a lavish production, Benvenuto Cellini's return to the stage is not a happy one. *The Firebrand of Florence* lacks sparkle, drive, or just plain nervous energy; it is a little like an old-fashioned operetta, slowly paced and ambling.

The blame probably may be distributed more or less evenly on all sides, save Mr. Gordon's purse. The book is a simple one and there is not much of it, but wit has been kept carefully away and bright lines are absent. Mr. Gershwin's lyrics are not outstanding; his purest muse must have stood blindfolded at his side this time. Nor is Mr. Weill's score the best that has come from his piano. One or two of the songs have a good rhythm, and another has a tinkling, gay charm, but the rest are casual and not distinguished. The dancing is brief, and that, too, is not equal to the dances of a number of other musicals. The costumes, however, are colorful, and visually the Alvin stage is in order, even though it is not in other directions.

The company is a large one, and when he has a chance John Murray Anderson, the director, has been able to fill his stage with swirling figures. Too often the soldiers, promenaders and the courtiers depart, however, leaving one or two persons and something akin to a somnolent state of gloom. Melville Cooper, one of the most amusing actors in the business, manages to put a little comedy into the part of the duke; the evening could stand a great deal more of both Mr. Cooper and comedy. Earl Wrightson, a newcomer, is Cellini; he has a good voice and does well by the Firebrand. Beverly Tyler, as Angela, is attractive; Lotte Lenya, who in home life is Mrs. Weill, is miscast as the Duchess.

Mr. Weill did not stint in setting down his score, for there are all types of songs and there are many of them. Songs in musicals are meant to be hummed afterward, and for that purpose he has offered "There'll Be Life, Love, and Laughter" and "The Night Time Is No Time for Thinking." A tune named "My Dear Benvenuto" has a catchy air, and "Sing Me Not a Ballad" is nice, although Miss Lenya does not give it all she might. As lyricist, Mr. Gershwin is at his best in such a number as "You Have to Do What You Do Do," where complexities always keep up a poet's spirit—and that of an audience.

There can be no doubt, however, that the production itself is a beautiful one to see. Jo Mielziner has designed the settings, and Raoul Pene du Bois the brilliant costumes. If the book, music, and acting were up to their physical dressings, the return of the *Firebrand* would be a special event of the first order. They are not, however, so neither is *The Firebrand of Florence*. Lewis Nichols, *New York Times*, 23 March 1945.

when the tension about the events in Europe was so great that people didn't have much interest in going to the theater. Apart from the momentary irritations and annoyances which always go with these things, the failure of *The Firebrand of Florence* hasn't touched me very much, and you definitely shouldn't worry about it. I've long since gotten used to the ups and downs of success, and I've been very aware for sometime that after the two huge successes I've had in the last few years I was about due for a setback. In a way I'm even pleased that I'm not falling into the routine of a steady, successful career. The possibility of such reversals is always part of the bargain, as long as I try in each work to do something new, something in many cases ahead of its time. Of course it's easier now that I'm in a good financial position. So let's forget it—and on to new deeds! . . .

All of our personal experiences are overshadowed by the gigantic events which are playing themselves out on the world stage. One is filled with hope and confidence to be permitted to experience the victory of justice, to see that after only a short time that evil is punished and good is triumphant. I don't believe any nation in human history has ever suffered so terrible a defeat as Germany, or that any nation has ever deserved humiliation as much as these barbarians, who have presumed to destroy everything good and decent people have been building up through the centuries. If one remembers the courage and pride with which the English, the Dutch, the French, the Russians, the Yugoslavs, and, most of all, the Jews have endured their defeats, one can only be filled with a deep disgust witnessing the cowardice, the degradation, and the pathological rage for self-destruction that the so-called master race is exhibiting at the time of defeat. What the allied armies have accomplished in four short years borders on the miraculous and was possible only because it so obviously was a war of good against evil. Any day now, we are expecting the unconditional surrender, and we are sure that by the time you get this letter the war in Europe will be over. Lenya and I are already talking about coming to see you as soon as private trips are permitted—and if all goes well, it might be as early as next winter or next spring.

1945 – 1950

I seem to have a very strong awareness of the suffering of
underprivileged people; of the oppressed, the persecuted.
I can see that when my music involves human suffering, it is,
for better or worse, pure Weill.

Kurt Weill

1945

April — *Where Do We Go from Here?* (film score, 20th Century-Fox, 1944), lyrics by Ira Gershwin, screenplay by Morris Ryskind, directed by Gregory Ratoff.

May 8 — "V. E. Day" marks the end of the war in Europe.

June — Returns to New York from Hollywood and begins developing new projects, among them a musical based on the life of Joseph Jefferson with Maxwell Anderson and George Cukor.

August 14 — End of the war in the Pacific.

August 15 — First post-war performance of *Die Dreigroschenoper* in Germany, at the Hebbel-Theater, Berlin.

August–November — *Down in the Valley*, version for radio (Arnold Sundgaard). Maurice Abravanel conducted an audition recording, but it was never broadcast; revised April 1948.

November — Begins collaborating with Elmer Rice and Langston Hughes on *Street Scene* and starts composing music for it in January. Engages Irving "Swifty" Lazar to be his Hollywood agent, replacing Arthur Lyons.

December 30 — The Theatre Guild on the Air broadcasts a radio adaptation of *Knickerbocker Holiday* on ABC.

1946

May 10 — *Kiddush*, for cantor, chorus, and organ, completed 16 March 1946. Park Avenue Synagogue, New York; Cantor David Putterman, soloist.

July 31 — Elected as the first composer and new member in the Playwrights' Company since its inception in 1938. Spends all year working on *Street Scene*; the Playwrights' Company acts as co-producer.

September 5 — *A Flag Is Born* (August 1946, music for a pageant by Ben Hecht). Alvin Theatre, New York; Isaac van Grove, conductor; Luther Adler, director. Sponsored by the American League for a Free Palestine. The one-act show plays fifteen weeks in New York and then tours to five American cities.

November — *Die Dreigroschenoper* receives its first U.S. performance since 1933 in an English translation by Desmond Vesey at the University of Illinois. Weill does not attend.

1947

January 9 — *Street Scene* (1946, book by Elmer Rice, lyrics by Rice and Langston Hughes). Adelphi Theatre, New York; Maurice Abravanel, conductor; Charles Friedman, director. 148 performances.

March — Weill's brother Hanns dies of kidney disease on 1 March. First discussions with Alan Jay Lerner about a collaboration.

April 6 — Receives a "special" Antoinette Perry (Tony) Award for distinguished achievement in the theater during the inaugural year of the awards. Although there was yet no award category for "best score," the award was undoubtedly made for the score of *Street Scene*.

May 6 — Leaves New York on the S.S. *Mauretania* for London via Liverpool, traveling from there by plane or train to Paris, Geneva, Rome, Cairo, Palestine, back to Paris, London, and New York. This is his first trip to Europe since his departure from France in 1935 and the first meeting with his parents since January 1934. While in Paris and London he tries to arrange performances for several of his American works.

June — Discusses with Herman Wouk an adaptation of his novel *Aurora Dawn*.

June 12 — Returns to New York and holds an angry post-mortem with the Playwrights' Company on the closure of *Street Scene* (17 May), which in his view was unwarranted.

July — Begins work on *Love Life* with Alan Jay Lerner.

Late August — Brecht writes from Hollywood inviting Weill to write the music for the first production of *Schweyk im 2. Weltkrieg*. Brecht also mentions plans for a Swedish film version of *Die Dreigroschenoper*, which he hopes will pay for his upcoming trip to Zurich.

September — The production of *Love Life* is postponed until spring, and Weill declines Brecht's invitation to compose music for *Schweyk im 2. Weltkrieg*.

October 19 — The Theatre Guild on the Air broadcasts a 45-minute radio version of *Lady in the Dark* on ABC.

October 27 — Weill and Maxwell Anderson sign a protest against the House Committee on Un-American Activities hearings. Brecht testifies before the committee on 30 October and leaves for Switzerland the next day. Caspar Neher discusses a production of *Die Bürgschaft* with the Vienna Staatsoper.

November 25 — *Hatikvah* (Israeli national anthem), arranged for full orchestra. Waldorf-Astoria Hotel, New York; Serge Koussevitzky, conductor.

1948

Early spring — Hans Heinsheimer, now director of publications at Schirmer, approaches Weill with a request for a school opera in the tradition of *Der Jasager* for production by the opera department of the Indiana University School of Music; Weill offers to adapt his unpublished radio opera *Down in the Valley* with librettist Arnold Sundgaard.

July 15	*Down in the Valley* (stage version, revised 1948, Arnold Sundgaard). Indiana University, Bloomington; Ernst Hoffmann, conductor; Hans Busch (son of Fritz Busch), director. Weill and Lenya attend the premiere with Alan Jay Lerner. Lerner's wife, Marion Bell, plays Jennie.
August 7	*Down in the Valley* is broadcast on NBC Radio.
October 7	*Love Life* (July 1947–January 1948/July–August 1948, Alan Jay Lerner). Forty-Sixth Street Theatre, New York; Joseph Littau, conductor; Elia Kazan, director. 252 performances.
October 24	Universal Edition expresses an interest in representing *Street Scene* in Germany. Weill and Lerner write a treatment for a film musical called "Miss Memory." The film version of *One Touch of Venus* starring Ava Gardner, directed by William A. Seiter and produced by Lester Cowan for Universal-International, opens in New York on 28 October.
November	Hoping to sell the film rights to *Love Life*, Weill and Lerner travel to Hollywood for a rest and to pursue new projects, including "Miss Memory" and a film treatment by Weill himself called "I Married a King." Weill writes to Lenya that the movie business is almost dead, with only MGM and 20th Century-Fox still making musicals. He returns to New York on 29 November.
December	The Festival Musicale di Venezia contacts Weill about a possible production of the Paris version of *Mahagonny Songspiel*. Weill tries unsuccessfully to persuade them to do *Street Scene* instead.

1 9 4 9

January	Begins work on *Lost in the Stars* with Maxwell Anderson.
January–February	Disagrees with Brecht about updating the text and music for *Die Dreigroschenoper*. Demands clarification of the publishing rights.
February 6	Attends a concert performance of *Street Scene* at the 92nd St. Y in New York, conducted by Maurice Levine.
May–June	Discusses with Maxwell Anderson an adaptation of his play *The Wingless Victory* for baritone Lawrence Tibbett.

July	Collapses on Alan Jay Lerner's tennis court. He recovers quickly and swears Lerner to secrecy about the attack.
July 30	Maurice Abravanel conducts excerpts from *Street Scene* and a "Symphonic Nocturne" from *Lady in the Dark*, arranged by Robert Russell Bennett, at Lewisohn Stadium in New York City.
August 21	A concert performance of *Street Scene* is given at the Hollywood Bowl under conductor Izler Solomon.
October 27	Attends an English-language performance of *Der Zar lässt sich photographieren* conducted by Kurt Adler and staged by Dino Yannopoulos for the Metropolitan Opera Studio, Juilliard School of Music, New York.
October 30	*Lost in the Stars* (Maxwell Anderson). Music Box Theatre, New York; Maurice Levine, conductor; Rouben Mamoulian, director. 281 performances in New York; tours to ten American cities.

1 9 5 0

January	Writes to Brecht of his plans to visit Europe with Lenya in the spring.
January–March	Works with Maxwell Anderson on a plot outline and five songs for a musical adaptation of Mark Twain's *The Adventures of Huckleberry Finn*. Unfinished.
January 14	*Down in the Valley* is broadcast on NBC-TV, one of the first music theater works to be produced for television. Weill supervises the production.
March 17	Suffers heart attack at Brook House and two days later is taken by ambulance to Flower Hospital.
April 3	Dies, Flower Hospital, New York.
April 5	Buried, Mount Repose Cemetery, Haverstraw, New York.
July 10	Memorial concert for Weill in New York's Lewisohn Stadium with a eulogy by Maxwell Anderson.

588. Ann Ronell, mid-1940's. She prepared the score for the film version of *One Touch of Venus*.

589. Weill and Ronell wrote a new song, "The Picture on the Wall," for the film version of *One Touch of Venus* in the spring of 1945. It was not included in the movie.

Weill (in Los Angeles) to Lotte Lenya, 1 May 1945: My little dinner party at Chasen's was "*kurz und schmerzlos*" [short and painless]. Just the Andersons, the Perlbergs and the Gershwins. The picture [*Where Do We Go from Here?*] is excellent and comes over as something very fresh and completely original and utterly different from any musical they've made so far. The Columbus opera is really sensational and shows that it would be possible to do a film-opera. Of course, there are weak spots in the picture, especially in the end. They cut out the Indian number ["Woo, woo, woo, woo, Manhattan"] and "It could have happened" but on the whole I was very pleased. . . . My dinner with René Clair has been postponed. Max got suddenly all excited about the idea of doing an American version of *Dreigroschenoper*, laid in the Bowery around 1900, as a satire on Tammany and the election machine. We would use only a few songs from *Dreigroschenoper* and write new ones . . . Yesterday I had a letter from Paul Robeson, with two different ideas for an opera for him, and that's another thing I'll follow up because I feel more and more like writing opera again—opera for Broadway, of course. So you see, I am in no way discouraged and full of ideas.

Weill (in Los Angeles) to Lotte Lenya, 8 May 1945: Here is "Happy V-E Day!" for my Linnerl darling. I am thinking of you all day because this is the day we've been waiting for twelve long years, ever since that night when we drove to Munich, March 1933. You never gave up that firm belief that we'll live to see the end of this horror—and here it is. . . . When I got up in the morning (I heard Truman's and Churchill's speeches at 6 a.m.), I realized more than ever before what this meant—and when I drove down to the studio I felt like a million dollars because this happened at a time when we are still young and can enjoy what is considered the best part of our lives in a world without Nazis.

Weill (in Los Angeles) to Lotte Lenya, 18 May 1945: So [Richard] Rodgers "is defining a new directive [*sic*] for musical comedy." I had always thought that I've been doing that—but I must have been mistaken. Rodgers certainly has won the first round in that race between him and me. But I suppose there will be a second and a third round.

Weill (in Los Angeles) to Hanns and Rita Weill, 21 May 1945: It's strange how depressed everybody has been ever since the end of the war in Europe. It's appalling to think that not the slightest attempt is being made to solve any of the world problems, and [it] looks as if the world will be in worse condition after this war than after the last one. . . .

I'm glad to get back home soon and I hope we'll have a nice summer in New City. Physically I'm feeling well and I suppose my blood pressure is behaving alright.

Elmer Rice (in New York?) to William Schuman, 28 June 1945: I am not sure that it would be wise for me to allow *Street Scene* to be done as a musical play at this time. . . . What it really comes down to is that I have to weigh the chances of the success of a musical version as against that of a revival.

This brings me back to some of the things we discussed. I understand and am in sympathy with your criticism of some of the aspects of the Broadway theater, particularly on the musical side. However, the production of a musical play on a commercial basis presents many practical problems that can be met only by people who have experience in this field. I do not have this experience, and I gathered from our conversation that you do not either. So that I feel it would be essential to the success of the venture to set up a production under the auspices of someone who is thoroughly familiar with the production of musical plays. . . .

Besides all this, I have been talking to Kurt Weill, who has just returned from California. As I told you, Kurt spoke to me three or four years ago about the possibility of setting *Street Scene* to music. But, after some discussion, he decided that he was not quite ready to do it. Now, he would like to consider it again. Of course, the objections that I have set forth to the whole idea of a musical version would apply also to Kurt. But he is an old friend of mine and has had many years of experience in the theater. And, if we did get together on it, I am sure that we would not have any difficulty in seeing eye to eye as to how the whole thing should be handled.

J.P. McEvoy (in Paris) to Weill, 3 September 1945: I thought this might interest you. I saw this show [*Die Dreigroschenoper*] in Berlin last week. The house was crowded—sold out weeks ahead, and a good ten percent of the audience were Russian officers. It was an excellent performance.

You would have to see Berlin to see how appropriate a Beggar's Opera is there now. And when in the last act an appeal was made from the stage for food, the beggar's chorus shouted from the top balcony, but the audience shouted louder.

Arnold Sundgaard remembers ...

In the weeks that followed our first meeting we surveyed a rambling range of American folk songs in an effort to find one that might prove evocative for our purposes. Kurt brought to this search a fresh insight and a stimulating curiosity. He perceived in many of the songs a richness of language and melodic strength that neither Olin Downes nor I had noticed before. The familiar frequently became for him the fantastic. He told how in Germany he had loved the sound of the name "Alabammy" as Al Jolson had sung it. . . . He enjoyed the sound of "Shenandoah" and "Missouri" recurring in one of the songs under consideration. . . . He listened like an attentive schoolboy when I attempted an explanation for the pronunciation of "Arkansas" and laughed delightedly when my wits failed me.

As a result of these discussions we began to see the songs in a fresh light. I recalled one which I considered the most familiar of them all, so familiar, in fact, that for several days I hesitated mentioning it ["Down in the Valley"]. It was one of the oldest folk chestnuts in the book, and I knew it well.

[On rewriting *Down in the Valley* for the stage]: We rewrote it together, assuming now that the characters would be seen as well as heard, and extended it somewhat to fit the needs of the stage. But the fluidity of the radio technique remained, making it possible to move freely from scene to scene. In this way it could be performed on practically a bare stage. Arnold Sundgaard, "Portrait of the Librettist as a Silenced Composer," *Dramatists Guild Quarterly* (Winter 1980): 24-30.

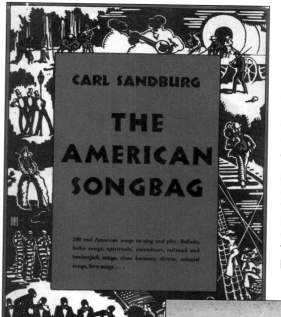

590. Weill and librettist Arnold Sundgaard consulted a number of books of American folk songs while developing *Down in the Valley,* including Carl Sandburg's standard collection *The American Songbag* (New York: Harcourt, Brace, 1927). Weill also owned a number of sound recordings of American folk songs, including *America's Favorite Songs,* volume 1 (Disc New York 607) which contained performances of "Down in the Valley," "Casey Jones," "Go Tell Aunt Nancy," "The Cowboy's Lament," "Buffalo Gals," and "Careless Love" by Bess Lomax, Tom Glazer, Pete Seeger, and Butch Hawes.

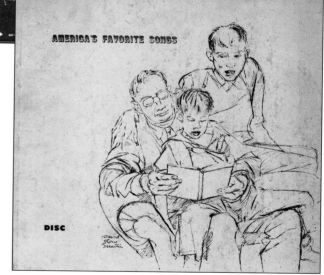

MUSIC: CHORUS:	RETURN TO If you don't love me, love whom you please, Throw your arms round me, give my heart ease. Give my heart ease, dear, give my heart ease, Throw your arms round me, give my heart ease.
SOLO:	He broke loose from jail down in Birmingham City To spend his last hours with Jennie near home, He swore that he loved her and needed her pity Before he could die on the gallows alone. Gallows alone, gallows alone Before he could die on the gallows alone.
MUSIC:	SWELLS UP SHARPLY AND THEN BREAKS TO DISTANT WAILING OF TRAIN. CONTINUES THROUGH.

591. Weill and Sundgaard wrote *Down in the Valley* for advertising executive Charles McArthur and music critic Olin Downes to launch a series of short radio operas called "Your Songs, America," each to be based on a folk song or popular ballad. The series did not find sponsorship. This fragment from the typescript libretto for the radio version of *Down in the Valley* includes a staging note added by Weill presumably when he and Sundgaard adapted the work for the stage in 1948.

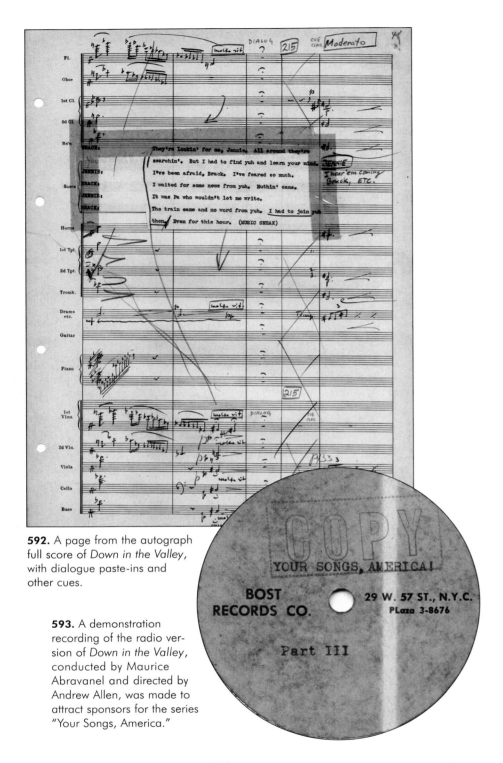

592. A page from the autograph full score of *Down in the Valley*, with dialogue paste-ins and other cues.

593. A demonstration recording of the radio version of *Down in the Valley*, conducted by Maurice Abravanel and directed by Andrew Allen, was made to attract sponsors for the series "Your Songs, America."

Weill (in New York) to Charles McArthur, 21 January 1946: Ever since we recorded our first radio program, *Down in the Valley*, I wanted to tell you how proud I am to be connected with this project because I am convinced that something very important will result from this first beginning.

I have been convinced for a long time that in a deeply democratic country like ours, art should belong to the people. It should come out of their thinking and their emotions, and it should become part of their lives. It should be "popular" in the highest sense of the word. Only by making this our aim can we create an American art, as opposed to the art of the old countries which belong to a selected class of aristocrats or "connoisseurs."

The natural basis for the creation of an American music is the American folk song which, not only in quantity but also in the quality of its texture, in the depth of its emotion, in the exuberance of its humor, in the beauty of its melody, and in the strength of its rhythm overshadows the folk songs of all other countries. There have been numerous attempts to exploit the wealth of American folk song for different forms of concert music, but in most cases these attempts followed traditional musical patterns which are not fundamentally American. For our radio program we have found a new way of making the folk song the basic element of an American art-form. We decided to dramatize the folk song itself, to exploit the old American habit of storytelling and to present the folk song in its most natural surrounding: in scenes from the American life. That means that in our folk-operettas, we create situations which allow people to sing their songs as they probably (or conceivably) were sung at the time when they came into existence: the lover yearning for his beloved; the working man singing in rhythm with his work; the congregation in church; a happy crowd in dance meetings—and always the wandering minstrel with his guitar, telling the stories he has seen and heard. The treasure of folk songs which can be used for these dramatizations is inexhaustible. There is a great variety of songs which have enough "story" in themselves to build a folk play around. Sometimes, like in the case of "Down in the Valley" there is only a line in the song which indicates a story, but there are always good dramatic situations and rich characterizations in these songs. There are heroic stories, love stories, comedies, murder stories, and tales from different parts of the country. And then there is another vast field for the production of these musical folk plays: instead of dramatizing the folk songs themselves, we can take stories from American history and legend (and there are libraries full of them) and build them around the folk songs of their periods.

What could be a more natural medium for the presentation of these modern "ballad operas" than the radio? There is a huge audience of American people. The melodies of our folk songs are in their blood, and the stories which we dramatize are taken right out of their lives or the lives of their fathers. These millions of listeners are waiting impatiently for a new popular art of radio entertainment that would speak their language and express their emotions. I have felt for a long time that the radio sponsor is the modern equivalent of the great art sponsors of

1 9 4 6

MUSIC + THEATER:
Irving Berlin *Annie Get Your Gun*
Gian Carlo Menotti *The Medium*
Arthur Miller *All My Sons*

LITERATURE + FILM:
Erich Maria Remarque *Arc de Triomphe*
The Best Years of Our Lives (film by William Wyler)
Die Mörder sind unter uns (film by Wolfgang Staudte)

SCIENCE + SOCIETY:
Isotope Carbon-13 discovered
Xerography process invented by Chester Carlson
Joe Louis defends heavyweight boxing title for twenty-third time

POLITICS:
Nuremberg trials
Churchill gives his "Iron Curtain" speech at Fulton, Mo.
Truman creates Atomic Energy Commission

the past. Just as the Catholic Church at the time of the Renaissance, the Protestant Church at the time of Bach, the aristocrats at the time of Mozart commissioned works of art for their respective places of worship or entertainment, the modern sponsor can become the mediator between creative artists and their audiences. Bach had to write a new cantata every week for the Sunday service in his church, and these cantatas, which were written "for a job" belong to the greatest works of art ever created. By the same token, a radio sponsor in our time can create a perfect medium for the development of a great American art—but, being an American art, it will be "by the people, of the people, for the people."

The new combination of the three elements music-drama-radio which we have found in our program is what we in show business call a "natural." To anybody who doubted it, we have proved that it can be done. I am sure that the American people will take it to their hearts.

Weill (in New City) to Rouben Mamoulian, 22 January 1946: Thank you very much for your wire. Both Elmer and I were very pleased to hear that you are interested in our *Street Scene* project. Let me tell you some more about it.

It had been one of my favorite ideas for years to do a musical play based on *Street Scene*, and when I talked to Elmer about it last fall, we both decided to go ahead with it. We agreed immediately to some important decisions for this show: to do it in one set like the original play (the whole form of the play, like in the ancient Greek tragedy, is based on unity of time, place, and action); to avoid the conventional musical comedy technique and to work it out as a kind of popular Broadway opera (the dialogue will be spoken, but underscored, so that the audience should never know where the dialogue ends and the song starts—and by "song" I mean arias, duets, trios, and all forms of musical ensembles, and some real songs too). No ballets, but some dancing wherever it comes naturally out of the action. The political element in the original play will be considerably toned down, the love story between Sam and Rose will be made more important and more passionate; Sam, instead of being always the beaten Jew, will be the young poet trying to adjust himself to the world and the hateful surroundings he is living in. The janitor of the house will be a Negro who will be alone on stage at the end of the first act, after everybody has gone to bed, with a song called "Great Big Sky." The three women (Mrs. Olsen, Mrs. Jones, and Mrs. Fiorentino) form a gossip trio all through the play. There will be a big musical ensemble about the "Melting Pot," leading into a dance, a sextet about ice cream at Lippo's entrance, a musical children's game scene at the beginning of the second act (the children imagining that they live in a Park Avenue house), a funny chorus of sightseers after the murder (opening third act). The curtain of the second act will be Mrs. Maurrant's death, then the house will remain darkened and a short orchestral interlude will lead into the third act, so that it is really a two-act show.

I am giving you these few examples of what we are doing, to show you how much this show is "up your alley." I know how much you always have been interested in this form of musical theater where music and drama are completely integrated, and I also know that you have the technique and the experience in staging this type of show like nobody else in this country. So I keep my fingers crossed, hoping that you will be available.

The Playwrights' Company, very enthusiastic about the project, is planning an early fall production. Elmer and I have worked out a blueprint for the musical treatment, and I am working now with Langston Hughes, the Negro poet, who is writing the verse. I have written about half the first act and am very excited about it. If you come to New York I want to show it to you. Please let us know as soon as possible if you can do the show—and please say yes.

594. Karsh, the noted fashion and celebrity photographer, took a series of stylized photos of Weill at Brook House in 1946. The one depicting a "successful composer at his desk" was printed in the souvenir program for *Street Scene* and became one of the most published photos of Weill. The music in the photo is Frank Maurrant's aria from *Street Scene*, "Let Things Be Like They Always Was."

595. With Elmer Rice, whose play *Street Scene* won the Pulitzer Prize in 1929 and was made into a movie directed by King Vidor in 1931.

596. *Street Scene* lyricist Langston Hughes was a major figure of the Harlem Renaissance, known for a large body of socially conscious poetry and other writings dealing with race and urban issues.

Weill (in New York) to Langston Hughes, 22 January 1946: Things are getting pretty hot with *Street Scene*. . . . Elmer finally gave in to my constant nagging about Mamoulian, and we wired him Thursday. He answered immediately very enthusiastically. He will know in a few weeks if he is available in the fall. . . .

My work is progressing very well now and I am very happy with some new things I have written. "Great Big Sky" is a peach—and will be the most impressive act-curtain, with a terrific lift at the end. "Wouldn't You Like to Be on Broadway" also worked out very well—a real seduction song. I also wrote the "heat" trio for the opening (very hot) and the pattern for the gossip trio. The new version of Kaplan's song is also finished. I have started now on Mr. Maurrant's aria. Then I'll get to the ice cream sextet.

Besides this I did quite a lot of work with Elmer. We went through the first act very carefully. Tomorrow we have another meeting, and then Elmer will start putting dialogue together. We also went over all the lyrics very carefully and we have a number of changes to suggest, mainly to make the lyrics more singable, smoother, and easier on the ear. We'll talk about that when you get back. Here are a few major suggestions we have to make.

1. Sam's Aria (unless you have a better idea) should be about the house (as Elmer lined it out the last time we all met—the house being a prison for the spirit, etc.). It could almost become a theme song for the show. It should be passionate and very moving, but as personal as we can make it, that means: not abstract!!!

2. We both feel that the Love Duet can be improved. Sam should start out (as you have it) in the mood of his aria, but then through Rose's optimism he should be more and more carried away. When Rose sings about the policeman in the park she should continue: but the lilac bush is there, it is ours, nobody can take it away from us—and that should build into a beautiful duet which reaches its climax (after a short interruption with Buchanan) when he asks her to kiss him, and here the lilac bush theme should sing out in the orchestra.

3. The Melting Pot scene we have worked out somewhat on the following line: it should start out with a very funny description of Columbus' trip by Lippo, always at the end of a stanza interrupted by Olsen's dry remark, "But Ericsson was first." Then we'll have a number of rather short songs of different nationalities, built on a refrain: "If it weren't for the Irish (German, Negroes, etc.), where would America be?" This would lead into a short fight. Then, we decided, Sam should come in and should give them the Melting Pot idea, and this leads to a big ensemble. This has the great advantage that Sam has a very strong entrance.

4. The ending of Mr. Maurrant's aria should be changed so that he speaks against the foreigners at the end. This allows us to go right into the Melting Pot scene.

These are a few of the things we have been talking about. You see there is quite a lot of work waiting for you. But I think it will be worth your while.

Weill (in New City) to Caspar Neher, 2 April 1946: Things are going well for me. I have truly found a home, friends, an interesting circle of colleagues, and, all in all, a much healthier atmosphere than anywhere in Europe. It is a wonderful country, this America, and I cannot imagine living anywhere else. I have worked without interruption, and my work has found great acceptance, especially the two theater successes *Lady in the Dark* (1941) and *One*

Touch of Venus (1943). Unfortunately, there is only one big theater institution in this country: Broadway, the commercial theater district in New York, and it is a very narrow field and a very hard struggle—but the audiences are great—naive, hungry for knowledge, and very eager to soak it up.

Weill (in New City) to Caspar Neher, 2 July 1946: Last night when I came home from the city, I found your and Erika's letter of 27 May. What a joy to finally hear from you again after all those years—to know that you have survived these catastrophic times and that you are safe, that you can work again and that you are beginning to make plans for the future. It is strange: when I saw your letters, it suddenly felt as if the eleven years since 1935 had shriveled up; it seemed like only yesterday that we had taken leave of each other for the last time, and all those wild, ugly, unspeakably cruel things which have occurred during those years suddenly seemed to have been wiped out, so that our old, good friendship could quietly resume as if it had never been interrupted. You can imagine the kind of revulsion I experienced over the events which took place in Germany during those years, and toward those who threatened to rush headlong into the destruction of not only their own people, but of the entire world. This feeling—along with a great sentiment of gratitude and affection for the new home I have found over here—created within me a sort of indifference and apathy toward the fate of the people I had once known in Germany. You and Erika were the only exceptions, and there hardly ever was a day when I didn't think of you in some kind of context—professionally, of course, when I ran into difficulties with my librettists and remembered our collaboration, or time after time when I had to compare stage designs with your work, only to conclude each time that nobody here can hold a candle to you. . . . Of course, the first few years over here were very difficult. The biblical stage work with Reinhardt was a failure but my music received high praises, and I discovered that there existed a fertile ground for my special talents as theater composer. Since there are no subsidized theaters over here (apart from the old-fashioned, inaccessible Metropolitan), and no other opera houses exist, I decided to develop a type of musical play which leans more and more toward opera, thereby gradually preparing the ground for something like an American opera. I have been very successful with this, and in the eleven years I've been here, the musical theater on Broadway has developed tremendously.

Weill (in New City) to Emma and Albert Weill, 9 September 1946: I am working incessantly on *Street Scene*. It is the biggest and most daring project I have undertaken over here so far, because this time I'm writing a real opera for the Broadway theater. If this succeeds, it will open up a large new vista for me, because today I'm almost without competition in the field of popular opera. Therefore I'm using all of my talent, ability and energy for this work, in order to make it as good as possible. The composition is approximately eighty percent finished and for four weeks now I've been busy with the orchestration, sitting at my desk from eight in the morning till late into the night, writing approximately fifteen pages a day. But Lenya sees to it that I don't overwork myself, and that I take time out to do something for my health—riding my bicycle, working in the garden, etc. . . .

Of course, we are continually concerned and agitated about the ongoing events in your area [Palestine], which is, after all, only one small part of this disquieting world. It seems more and more that we are living in a period

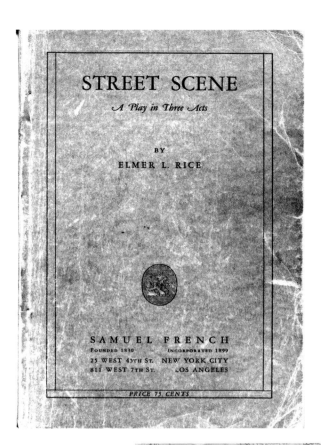

597. Weill made notes on how he planned to musicalize *Street Scene* in this copy of Rice's original play.

598. The first page of the full score of *Street Scene* shows the unifying theme from the song "Lonely House."

599. To open the second act, Weill borrowed from the Nocturne he wrote in 1928 for the play *Konjunktur* by Leo Lania.

600. The lead-in to Mrs. Maurrant's aria, "Somehow I Never Could Believe," demonstrates Weill's mixing of underscored dialogue and recitative-like passages.

which probably will go down in history as "The Hundred Years War." The ideological division in the world leads more and more toward a collision between the truly great powers, which fortunately has been prevented up to now, because secondary powers like Germany and Japan have tried to push themselves into the foreground. But now we seem to be approaching the real, fundamental conflict—and only the wisest, most ingenious statesmanship could preserve us from new catastrophes. Thank God nobody in the world right now is inclined toward or interested in a new war, and humankind's ancient instinct for self preservation will—as it has done before—find a way out of the mess.

I think I wrote you in my last letter that I've been elected to be a member of the Playwrights Producing Company. That is a high distinction, since this organization consists of the finest group of creative artists in the theater (besides myself, there are only three other members: Maxwell Anderson, Elmer Rice, and Robert E. Sherwood—all three of them are respected, first-rate dramatists).

Gertrude Lawrence (in Cape Cod) to Weill, 20 September 1946: First I want to congratulate the Playwrights for having taken you into their holy of holies!! It certainly was about time, and I hope you are happy about it.

Next—I wanted to let you know that like the proverbial elephant I "never forget," and having been inspired by your enthusiasm originally, I thought you would be interested to know that I have acquired an exclusive option from Sir Max Beerbohm and his family to the rights of *Zuleika Dobson* until 1947! . . .

Dear Kurt, are you still interested in working on the score for me as you were before, and what are your ideas in regards to a librettist?

Alfred Schlee (in Vienna) to Weill, 26 September 1946: I don't know if you remember me. During your last days in Berlin I visited you a few times as representative of Universal Edition and left behind a thoroughly bad impression.

After the liberation of Vienna I took over the management of Universal Edition, as you might have already heard from Heinsheimer. We reprinted the *Dreigroschenoper* right away, but we have not pushed for an immediate performance since the presently available stage directors seem dubious to us.

During the Nazi era, various employees of Universal Edition (especially Ms. Rothe and Mr. Decsey) tried very hard to save as much as possible of our properties. Unfortunately, we could not keep the Gestapo from confiscating and removing certain items. To my greatest regret, *Mahagonny* was among them. Since performances of this work would now be possible, especially in the first version, we want to ask you whether you might have some of that material. If so, please do send it to us as soon as possible.

Would you have any new orchestral or chamber music work which could be given over here? I hear that you are working very successfully on Broadway. Perhaps you have written something that could be performed in Europe?

KURT WEILL'S NOTES ON STREET SCENE, DEC. 21ST.

The most important job to be done on *Street Scene* is to decide on a definite *form* for the show and then to be consistent in carrying through this form. Ever since Elmer and I started talking about this show, we thought in terms of a "musicalized" *Street Scene*, a show that flows naturally from dialogue into music and back. We always were aware of the danger of falling into the conventional musical-comedy pattern of dialogue-number-dialogue-number. That's why we decided to have the numbers grow out of action and to have the dialogue underscored—to avoid the break between spoken word and sung word.

It is obvious now that whenever we stick to this formula we have a great show; and whenever we get away from it we confuse our audience; and it is no accident that the emotional parts are the high spots of the show because we have achieved a complete blending of music and words and action.

But in some parts, especially in the first act, we have not succeeded yet in blending the elements of the show. In some places we try to be too legitimate, in other places, too musical comedy. We are definitely using too much the number technique of musical comedy instead of the flowing technique we had in mind. There are far too many stops for applause, especially in the beginning of the show when we should establish the form of the show. So here are some suggestions:

Heat Number: Cut musical tag at end and start music of Willie's entrance on last note of Heat chorus.

1st Gossip Number: Make all movements of the women more natural, less deliberate, take out whispering into ear, replace by stronger expression of gossiping women. Take out pose for applause at the end.

Buchanan's Song: Take out business with oranges. Ending to be changed so that Buchanan runs into house without pause for applause.

Cut dialogue lines after Buchanan's Song and go directly into Maurrant's entrance. This can be done musically by interrupting the end of Buchanan's Song with Maurrant's music.

2nd Gossip: Pointing of fingers in the beginning to be toned down. Whole number should be less parodistic because action has progressed to a more serious point.

Ice Cream: To be cut and re-staged.

Sam's Entrance: Give Sam a few more serious lines to build up his character.

Kaplan Scene: Before fight spreads out so much that we have a hard time to get back into musical form. Should be cut.

Ribbon: There is a completely dead moment because Lippo does not cut in with his line. We should decide if we want to stop or not, and do it.

Broadway: Possibility of cut in second chorus, starting with release. Take out pose for applause at the end. We could also try to have Rose sing "What Good Would the Moon Be" after first chorus of "Broadway," as an answer to Easter's proposal, and then have Easter answer her with a shortened version of the second chorus. The movements in Easter's song can still be simplified so that he comes over as a real threat.

Moon-Face: First chorus should be simplified so that we don't tip off our dance number. Ending to be fixed.

Opening Second Act: There could be a little more life and activity of the wakening house. There are long pauses between entrances which should be filled in. Since we have taken out the relief material of the second act, we should do a little more with the opening, which is full of possibilities.

Technicolor: Unless we get a number which replaces the relief values of this number, it should be restored in the following way: In the dialogue before, Rose should talk about the Bay of Naples, Lippo should praise Hudson Bay so that we set immediately the idea of the song. The verse might be cut, the rhumba rhythm changed into an Italian rhythm, the song should not be danced but clearly express Rose's dream of "happy Italy" and Lippo's opposite view.

Trio: Mrs. Jones's dustpan has the same effect on this scene which her lines after the murder scene have on that one. Should definitely be cut.

Murder Scene: Here our audience, which has long since accepted the form of our show, gets completely confused because we play a long, drawn-out, detailed, naturalistic description of a murder scene. Scene needs cutting and enormous speeding-up, maybe underscoring. Weill (in Philadelphia) to Dwight Deere Wiman, Elmer Rice, Langston Hughes, and Charles Friedman, 21 December 1946.

601. Autograph vocal score of the climax of the first act, the duet between Rose and Sam, "Don't Forget the Lilac Bush."

602. Brian Sullivan (Sam) and Ann Jeffreys (Rose) in the original production of *Street Scene*.

603. The stars of the show, Norman Cordon (Mr. Maurrant) and Polyna Stoska (Mrs. Maurrant), chat with conductor Maurice Abravanel.

STREET SCENE

"An American Opera" in two acts; book by Elmer Rice; lyrics by Langston Hughes and Elmer Rice

1947   New York, Adelphi Theater (9 January; 148 performances)

   Maurice Abravanel, conductor; Charles Friedman, director; Jo Mielziner, set designer; Lucinda Ballard, costume designer; Anna Sokolow, choreographer

1949   Concert performances at the 92nd St. Y in New York, Lewisohn Stadium, and the Hollywood Bowl.

1950   Cincinnati, Music Drama Guild (2 March)

STREET SCENE

THE PLAYBILL
FOR THE ADELPHI THEATRE

606. *Street Scene* opened at the Adelphi Theater on 9 January 1947 after an out-of-town tryout in Philadelphia.

607. This tableau from the "Ice Cream Sextet" was featured as the center pages of the *Street Scene* souvenir program.

605. Opening night telegram from Ingrid Bergman, who was appearing at the time on Broadway in Maxwell Anderson's *Joan of Lorraine.*

604. Posters in New York's theater district.

OPERA ON BROADWAY
KURT WEILL TAKES FORWARD STEP IN SETTING IDIOMATIC AMERICAN TO MUSIC
BY OLIN DOWNES

We had long entertained the suspicion that American opera, in the vital, contemporaneous sense of that word, would be more likely to come from our popular theater than from our august temples of operatic art. After seeing and hearing *Street Scene* at the Adelphi Theatre we feel that this supposition was wholly justified. This piece is as idiomatic, American, direct, and unacademic in its approach to the musico-dramatic problem as the artificial and unrooted opera [*The Warrior* by Bernard Rogers], also of native authorship, given the week previous at the Metropolitan, was not. In fact, *Street Scene*, the drama by Elmer Rice, the score by Kurt Weill, with lyrics by Langston Hughes, is the most important step toward significantly American opera that the writer has yet encountered in the musical theater. *New York Times*, 26 January 1947.

1 9 4 7

MUSIC + THEATER:

Frederick Loewe *Brigadoon*

Burton Lane *Finian's Rainbow*

Tennessee Williams *A Streetcar Named Desire*

LITERATURE + FILM:

Albert Camus *La peste*

Thomas Mann *Doktor Faustus*

Diary of Anne Frank published

SCIENCE + SOCIETY:

Bell Laboratories scientists invent the transistor

Thor Heyerdahl sails on a raft from Peru to Polynesia to demonstrate prehistoric immigration

Over one million U.S. war veterans enroll in colleges under the "G.I. Bill of Rights"

POLITICS:

General George Marshall appointed U.S. Secretary of State; calls for European Recovery Program

Peace treaties signed in Paris

Initial statement of the "Truman Doctrine"

PLATE 17

While in the midst of writing *Street Scene*, Weill once again came to the aid of Ben Hecht and the American League for a Free Palestine by contributing music and lending his name to Hecht's pageant *A Flag Is Born*. Isaac van Grove, the music director for both *The Eternal Road* and *We Will Never Die*, arranged the score using traditional Jewish melodies and some of Weill's music from *The Eternal Road*. In the final scene of the play, David, a 16-year-old concentration camp survivor played by Sidney Lumet, is recruited by three Jewish freedom fighters to join their cause. David makes a flag from the prayer shawl of his dead friend Tevya, attaches a star of David to it, and marches into battle.

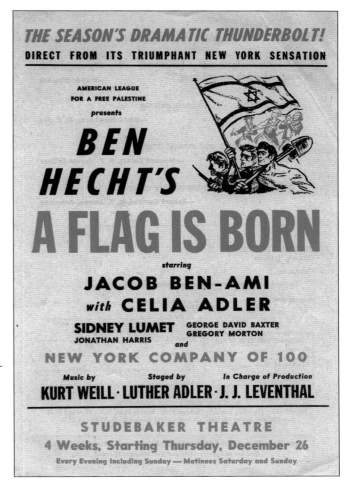

The pageant played for fifteen weeks on Broadway before embarking on a two-month national tour. Shown here is a handbill for the Chicago performances at the Studebaker Theatre.

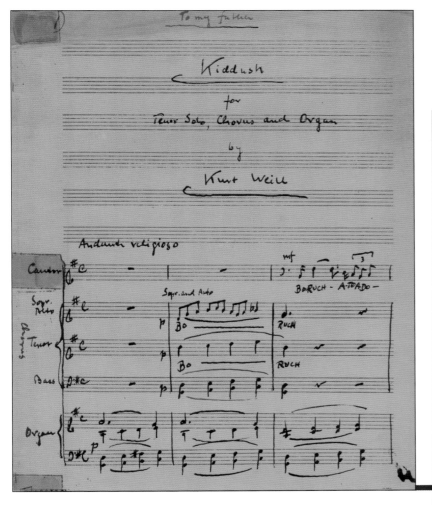

In March 1946, at the request of Cantor David J. Putterman, Weill composed the *Kiddush* [Sabbath prayer for blessing the wine] for the 75th anniversary of the Park Avenue Synagogue in New York. The work was published by Schirmer in a 1951 collection of synagogue music that included pieces by Leonard Bernstein, Henry Brant, Mario Castelnuovo-Tedesco, Paul Dessau, David Diamond, Morton Gould, Roy Harris, Darius Milhaud, and William Grant Still. Weill dedicated the work to his father.

PLATE 18

Street Scene most fully realized Weill's ambition to write "An American Opera," which is how he identified the work in the published vocal score. Much to Weill's dismay, the producers closed the show while he was out of the country visiting his parents in Palestine, after only 148 performances at the Adelphi Theatre. Pictured here is the "lobby card," (a small-sized poster), the cover of the souvenir program featuring a photo of the two nursemaids gossiping about the Maurrant murder, the sheet music for Sam's arietta, "Lonely House," and the label from a transcription recording of Bing Crosby singing "Moon-Faced, Starry-Eyed" on ABC radio.

PLATE 19

Columbia Records recorded the original cast album. Weill's liner notes explain how the work fulfilled two of his dreams: to achieve a complete blending of drama and music, and to write an American opera.

STREET SCENE

Excerpts from the Broadway Production
Music by KURT WEILL
Words by LANGSTON HUGHES
From the Book by ELMER RICE
Produced by Dwight Deere Wiman and The Playwrights' Company
ANNE JEFFREYS, POLYNA STOSKA, BRIAN SULLIVAN (Courtesy of MGM) and other members of the original company, with Orchestra conducted by MAURICE ABRAVANEL

COLUMBIA MASTERWORKS SET M-MM-683

Among all the theatrical works I have written, operas, operettas, musical plays, musical comedies, ballets, pageants — about twenty-five altogether — Street Scene occupies a niche of its own. It means to me the fulfillment of two dreams which I have dreamed during the last twenty years and which have become a sort of center around which all my thinking and planning revolved.

Dream No. 1. Ever since I made up my mind, at the age of 19, that my special field of activity would be the theatre, I have tried continuously to solve, in my own way, the form-problems of the musical theatre, and through the years I have approached these problems from all different angles. One of the first decisions I made was to get the leading dramatists of our time interested in the problems of the musical theatre. The list of my collaborators reads like a good selection of contemporary playwrights of different countries: George Kaiser and Bert Brecht in Germany, Jacques Deval in France, Franz Werfel, Paul Green, Maxwell Anderson, Moss Hart and Elmer Rice in America.

The obvious approach to the musical theatre for a young composer in the early twenties was, of course, grand opera. So I wrote three operatic works in short intervals and saw them produced in German opera-houses between 1926 and 1928. But soon I discovered that the special requirements of the opera-house, its performers and its audiences, forced me to sacrifice certain elements of the modern theatre, and it was at that time that I began to dream of a special brand of musical theatre which would completely integrate drama and music, spoken word, song and movement.

All the theatrical works I have written since then, have been stepping stones in this direction; in each of them I tried out certain elements of the musical theatre which I was dreaming about. In the *Three-Penny Opera*, which was my first musical play, I deliberately stopped the action during the songs which were written to illustrate the "philosophy", the inner meaning of the play. *Mahogany* was a sort of "dramatic review", using elements of the theatre from slapstick to opera. *The Silver Lake* was a serious musical which mixed realism and fantasy and

used actors together with a singing chorus and a symphonic orchestra. But not until fifteen years later, not until *Street Scene*, did I achieve a real blending of drama and music, in which the singing continues naturally where the speaking stops and the spoken word as well as the dramatic action are embedded in overall musical structure.

Dream No. 2. When I arrived in this country, in 1935, another dream began to get hold of me — the dream of an American opera. My first Broadway show, *Johnny Johnson*, was still a continuation of the formula which I had tried out in Europe. But through this show I learned a great deal about Broadway and its audience. I discovered that a vast, unexploited field lay between grand opera and musical comedy, although the ground was all ready well prepared. I discovered that there was a highly receptive audience with great sensitivity for music and a

Kurt Weill

great capacity for emotions. I discovered also that there was a rich collection of young singers with great acting talent, full of ambition and eager to work, but frustrated by the lack of outlets for their talents. The more I studied this situation the more I became convinced of the possibility to develop out of this material a musical theatre which could eventually grow into something like an American opera. But at the same time I made up my mind that such development could only take place on Broadway, because Broadway represents the living theatre in this country, and an American opera, as I imagined it, should be a part of the living theatre. It should, like the products of other opera-civilizations, appeal to large parts of the audience. It should have all the necessary ingredients of a "good show".

In the different Broadway shows which I wrote during the following years, I tried to make the music an integral part of the plays; especially in *Lady in the Dark*, with its three little one-act operas, I continued the story in musical fantasies when the realistic story stopped. In the meantime, the whole Broadway scene began to change in the same direction. *Porgy and Bess* became a big popular success, *Carousel* and *Carmen Jones* introduced operatic elements, and the American public became more and more opera-conscious. When I finally decided that the time was ripe for a real Broadway opera, I found in Elmer Rice's famous play, with its gripping story and its rich-

ness of characters, a perfect vehicle. The form I decided on as the best possible realization of an American opera-form was exactly that complete integration of drama and music which I had attempted in my earlier works. And that's how *Street Scene* became to me the fulfillment of two dreams.

* * *

The recording of the music from *Street Scene* offered a problem. The integration of music and drama has been carried so far in the case of *Street Scene* that the work has been regarded as an "operatic" event ever since it opened in New York, because "opera" is the form of theatre in which the dramatic action is expressed through music, and the emotional power of the original play is heightened and intensified through the use of singing voices and orchestra. Therefore, if we wanted to set down on discs the real values of the *Street Scene* score, we had to keep in mind that only some of the people who will listen to these records will have seen the show while many others will have to rely on this album to find out what sort of musical treatment I have given to Elmer Rice's famous play. That's why I was very happy when Goddard Lieberson, Vice President of Columbia Records, suggested an album of six twelve-inch records. This made it possible to show, in about fifty minutes of music, the variety of musical forms which I have used in this score, to include songs, arias, duets, ensembles, orchestral interludes and even dialogue which, in *Street Scene*, takes the place of the recitative in the classic opera. It also allowed me to work out a sort of continuity so that, in listening to these records, we can follow the action and the emotional up-and-down of this play about life in a street of New York.

We see, in the beginning, the women who live in the house, sitting on the steps, complaining about the heat ("Ain't it awful, the heat"), talking to the janitor who comes up from the cellar singing his blues song ("I got a marble and a star"), gossiping about Mrs. Maurrant's love life ("Gossip") and making fun of young Buchanan whose wife is having a baby ("When a woman has a baby"). Then we hear Mrs. Maurrant's aria ("Somehow I never could believe"), expressing her troubled mind and her secret desires; the song of the young girls coming home from the graduation exercises ("Wrapped in a ribbon and tied in a bow"); Sam Kaplan's song of adolescent melancholy ("Lonely House"); then Rose Maurrant's scene with her "boss", Mr. Easter, who is trying to lure her into a different sort of life ("Wouldn't you like to be on Broadway?"); Rose's decision to live her own kind of life ("What good would the moon be?") and the scene of young love between Rose and Sam, dreaming of lilac bushes and happiness ("Remember that I care").

The second act opens with the morning music, the awakening of the house and the "Children's Game", and goes on to Mrs. Maurrant's touching song to her little son ("A boy like you"), to a passionate duet of the two lovers, Sam and Rose, who have decided to take life in their own hands ("We'll go away together") and the horror-stricken death scene of Mrs. Maurrant ("The woman who lived up there"). In the last scene we see the two nursemaids trying to sing the babies to sleep, while at the same time gossiping about their parents ("Lullaby"); we see Rose meeting for the last time her father who has killed his wife and is being taken away by the police ("I loved her too"); and finally Rose saying goodbye to the one she loves ("Farewell Duet"). Of course, some important parts of the score, like the Ice-Cream Septet and the Trio in the second act, had to be omitted, but we offer enough material in this album to give a complete impression of the *Street Scene* score and its blending with the action of the play.
Notes by KURT WEILL

PLATE 20

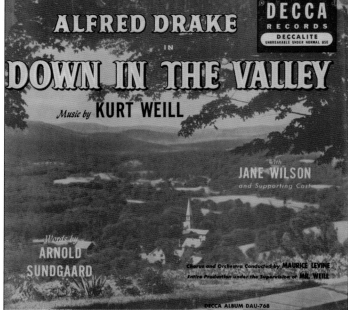

In some ways *Down in the Valley* became Weill's American counterpart to *Der Jasager*. After the successful premiere of the stage version at Indiana University in 1948, it had hundreds of performances in high schools and colleges throughout the U.S. The vocal score published by Schirmer features a painting by Grandma Moses. According to Hans Heinsheimer, Schirmer acquired the reproduction rights for the painting from Grandma Moses's agent for $100 and a page of autograph music by Weill.

Decca and RCA Victor released 78 rpm recordings of *Down in the Valley*. The RCA release featured the cast of the NBC television broadcast, which first aired on 14 January 1950.

Wolfgang Roth, the designer of the sets for the premiere production of *Down in the Valley*, was an assistant to Caspar Neher at the time of *Die Dreigroschenoper* (1928) and also worked at the Piscator-Theater in Berlin. This sketch shows the Shadow Creek Cafe, the setting where Brack Weaver murders Thomas Bouché.

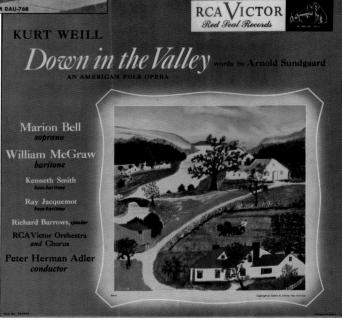

PLATE 21

Nanette Fabray won a 1949 Tony award for best actress in a musical for her portrayal of Susan. She was profiled in the 26 October 1948 issue of *Look* magazine.

Love Life, with book and lyrics by Alan Jay Lerner, is considered a show ahead of its time and has been dubbed the first "concept musical". The show ran for 252 performances on Broadway, but it did not have a national tour. Pictured here is the lobby card.

Chappell published nine songs from the show in sheet music editions. "Here I'll Stay" and "Green-up Time" were the most commercially successful songs.

Boris Aronson's design for the minstrel show, the show's climactic production number in which the characters search unsuccessfully for quick and easy answers about love and life.

PLATE 22

This photo of Susan (Nanette Fabray) singing "Women's Club Blues" appeared in the *Sunday News*, 27 February 1949. The original photo caption gave a good summary of the scene: "It's Sam and Susan Cooper's love life that's under discussion at the 46th St., and you get glimpses of it from 1791 to the present, interspersed with some of the most delightful music to be heard on Broadway. In the scene above, the early 1890s have been reached, and Ray Middleton, as Sam, has just finished singing "My Kind of Night," in that booming baritone that needs no artificial aid. Sam, quite content with his lot, is blissfully unaware that inside, Nanette Fabray, as Susan, is urging her neighbors to join in [the] struggle for woman suffrage."

PLATE 23

In Act II, scene 5 of *Lost in the Stars*, pastor Stephen Kumalo resigns from his ministry on the day before his son will be hanged for the murder of Arthur Jarvis. The scene ends with the chorus singing "A Bird of Passage," the music chosen by Maxwell Anderson to be engraved on Weill's tombstone.

PLATE 24

Lost in the Stars, Weill's last completed musical, had a book and lyrics by Maxwell Anderson based on Alan Paton's famous novel, *Cry, the Beloved Country*. Set in apartheid South Africa, the musical tragedy explored spirituality and the relationship between fathers and sons. The show ran for 281 performances before closing on 1 July 1950, three months after Weill's death. Afterwards it was taken on a fourteen-week national tour with an expanded orchestration. The touring company had difficulties because the black actors could not be accommodated in "white" hotels, and the cast resisted playing in segregated theaters or were picketed when they did.

Chappell issued sheet music editions of six songs from the show.

Decca recorded an original cast album on 7-8 November 1949 and released it on 19 December.

Set designer George Jenkins's drawing for Act II, scene 3, the courtroom in which Absalom Kumalo is found guilty of murder, even though his shooting of Arthur Jarvis was unintentional. The accomplices in the robbery are acquitted.

608. Weill orchestrated all his Broadway scores except when a specific number required a jazz-like or "hot" orchestration. An example of such a number from *Street Scene* is "Moon-Faced, Starry-Eyed," an upbeat song-and-dance sequence for the characters Dick and Mae. This excerpt shows the beginning of Ted Royal's orchestration.

Musical Hits CONTINUED

A SHOW-STOPPING INTERLUDE IN "STREET SCENE" IS THIS FRANTIC LOVE DANCE DONE BY SHEILA BOND AND DANNY DANIELS IN FRONT OF TENEMENT HOUSE

NEW VERSION OF "STREET SCENE" IS A MAJOR STEP TOWARD AMERICAN OPERAS

While nobody in the U.S. has yet written a great native opera, better attempts are made on Broadway than under the lofty banner of the Metropolitan Opera. This season a musical version of Elmer Rice's famous stage play, *Street Scene* (1929), prompted the New York *Times's* cautious music critic, Olin Downes, to call it "most important step toward significantly American opera that the writer has yet encountered in the musical theater."

In its new form, *Street Scene* was written again by Rice, with lyrics by Poet Langston Hughes, and music by German Composer Kurt Weill (*Knickerbocker Holiday*, *Lady in the Dark*). Its tragedy is enacted before a Manhattan tenement where a love-starved wife has a brief affair with a bill collector and is murdered with her lover by her husband. With excellent voices singing an eloquent score, *Street Scene* brings new stature to the U.S. stage.

609. This feature from the 24 February 1947 issue of *Life* magazine shows a sequence of photographs from "Moon-Faced, Starry-Eyed." The dancers are Sheila Bond and Danny Daniels.

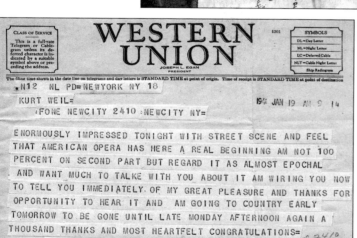

613. A congratulatory telegram from prominent music critic Olin Downes.

610. After the children's game that begins Act II, Willie Maurrant (Peter Griffith) gets into a fight with another boy.

612. Rose Maurrant attempts to speak to her mother after the shooting.

611. Just after shooting his wife and her lover Steve Sankey, Frank Maurrant (Norman Cordon) holds the crowd at bay.

Musical 'Street Scene' a Splendid And Courageous Sidewalk Opera

By JOHN CHAPMAN

(Reprinted from yesterday's late editions)

From Elmer Rice's bitter and compassionate drama, "Street Scene," Mr. Rice, Langston Hughes and Kurt Weill have made a moving, remarkable opera—a work of great individuality which makes no compromise with Broadway formula. It was presented last evening at the Adelphi by Dwight Deere Wiman and the Playwrights' Company, and it was sung and acted by a top-flight company.

The authors call their work a dramatic musical, but it may well be called a metropolitan opera—a work that catches in both score and story the feel of tenement house life. As was the play, it is set before a shabby warren into which are crowded the races, the lovers, the haters and the big and little events of city life. It is a grim Knickerbocker holiday.

Mr. Rice's story, so far as I can judge, remains intact. It tells of Sam Kaplan and Rose Maurrant, who are most tenderly in love—tenderly but, caught up by tragedy and imprisoned by poverty, with little hope. It tells of Rose's drunken father and of her gentle, affection-starved mother, and of the father's two murders. It is packed with the incidents of a night and a day on a steaming New York sidewalk.

Score a Story Itself.

Mr. Weill and Mr. Hughes have made this story into music and lyrics—excellent lyrics and richly colored, effective music. The score is no pushover to sing and no pushover to hear; it is, like the play it follows, a dramatic narrative. Mr. Weill has chosen to hew to the line and let the hits fall where they may.

I doubt if there are any hits in the juke box-radio sense, but there are some fine songs—songs of tenderness, of longing, of heartbreak and of humor; big songs like "Somehow I Never Could Believe," extraordinarily touching ones like "A Boy Like You," wry and cynical numbers like the lullaby two nurses sing to their infant charges as they gawk and gossip at the murder scene. The nearest thing to a musical comedy number is "Moon-Faced, Starry-Eyed," a jitterbug interlude delightfully sung and danced by Sheila Bond and Danny Daniels.

Fine Performances.

Mr. Weill's music matches the Rice story and the Hughes lyrics mood for mood, exhibiting a considerable range of style and being splendidly orchestrated by the composer. The drama moves inexorably toward the commission of the murders and the score sweeps right with it, building to a tingling climax.

The large company gives many fine performances. Polyna Stoska as Mrs. Maurrant, Norman Cordon as the evil Maurrant, Anne Jeffreys as their daughter and Brian Sullivan as Sam Kaplan carry the major vocal and acting burdens quite magnificently. Among those who contribute their vivid and often amusing bits to "Street Scene" are Hope Emerson, Lauren Gilbert, Sydney Rayner, Robert Pierson, Beverly Janis and Remo Lota. And a number of children make a rowdy passel of tenement brats.

"Street Scene" is a far from ordinary event in the theatre, and I salute the courage, imagination and skill of those who have made it.

Polyna Stoska
A tragic mother.

614. John Chapman's favorable review of *Street Scene* appeared in the *Daily News*.

616. A publicity flyer for *Street Scene* featured praise from several of New York's leading theater and music critics.

"Bravo!...'Street Scene' has an electric theatrical quality which has been too often wanting this season."
BARNES, *Herald Tribune*

"The producers of 'Street Scene' have found superb singers who have helped make this one of the memorable nights in theatre going. Mr. Weill, the foremost music maker in the American theatre, has found notes to express the myriad impulses of Mr. Rice's poem and transmuted it into a sidewalk opera; and Langston Hughes has set it to affectionate lyrics."
ATKINSON, *Times*

"Mr. Rice, Langston Hughes and Kurt Weill have made a moving, remarkable opera—a work of great individuality which makes no compromise with Broadway formula. 'Street Scene' is a far from ordinary event in the theatre, and I salute the courage, imagination and skill of those who have made it."
CHAPMAN, *News*

"Dwight Deere Wiman and The Playwrights' Company find themselves co-owners of a solid hit this morning. . . . It is tuneful, exciting and absorbing. It held the interest of the first nighters like a magnet does a piece of metal. And it won from the appreciative audience the robust applause it deserved."
COLEMAN, *Mirror*

"This is a great show, and, without reservations, a MUST for lovers of the lyric stage."
MUSICAL COURIER

" 'Street Scene' is the best contemporary musical production to grace any American stage."
MUSICAL AMERICA

"The most important step toward significantly American opera that the writer has yet encountered in the musical theatre."
OLIN DOWNES, *Times*

DWIGHT DEERE WIMAN
and
THE PLAYWRIGHTS' COMPANY
present

"STREET SCENE"
A Dramatic Musical
From the Pulitzer Prize Play by ELMER RICE

Music by **Kurt WEILL**   Book by **Elmer RICE**

Lyrics by **Langston HUGHES**   Directed by **Charles FRIEDMAN**

Scenery and Lighting by **JO MIELZINER**

Costumes by **LUCINDA BALLARD**   Dances by **ANNA SOKOLOW**

with

Norman CORDON   Anne JEFFREYS   Polyna STOSKA
Brian SULLIVAN   Sydney RAYNER   Hope EMERSON

Musical Director **Maurice ABRAVANEL**

ADELPHI THEATRE 54th Street East of B'way

MATINEES WEDNESDAY and SATURDAY

615. A publicity photo taken at Brook House. Photo by Karsh.

Weill (in New City) to Caspar Neher, 16 February 1947: I was so exhausted after the premiere of *Street Scene* that for weeks I couldn't even gather the strength to write a letter. It was a tough nut to crack this time around. I had made up my mind to really write an opera for Broadway, something I had been planning and preparing for years. If you knew Broadway a little better, you would have some idea of what a daring enterprise this was. . . . The great challenge for me was to find a form which translated the realism of the plot into music. The result is something entirely new and probably the most "modern" form of musical theater, since it applies the technique of opera without ever falling into the artificiality of opera. It is a type of number opera, but I composed right through the spoken dialogues between the musical numbers, like a recitative, so that the dialogue melts into the musical numbers and creates a unity of drama and music that I had never achieved before (among all of my former works, only the first act of *Bürgschaft* had this same kind of unity of drama and music). We had a great cast, with great acting talent, wonderful voices, and during rehearsals we all had the feeling we were onto something new. Here it's custom to try out a new piece a few weeks outside New York before presenting it on Broadway. We opened in Philadelphia on 16 December—a total fiasco. We never anticipated that these provincial cities would still be so far behind the times—the critics were uncomprehending and hostile; for three weeks the theater was empty every evening, general discouragement and doubts prevailed. But you know how I am in situations like this. I keep on working, calmly making cuts and changes. In New York the rumor had spread that we were a flop, and they were preparing for a first-class burial. But as soon as the music started at the premiere (9 January), the entire picture changed, and after ten minutes I knew that I had the audience in the palm of my hand. This evening and the next morning's newspapers surpassed all my expectations. The press greeted it as the first American opera and called me the foremost theater composer in America (which isn't such a great compliment, when I look at my competition). The important thing is that for six weeks an opera has been running in a Broadway theater without subsidies. The piano-vocal score will be printed in a few months and I will send it to you.

Ogden Nash (in Baltimore) to Weill, 11 March 1947: I must tell you that *Street Scene* overwhelmed and entranced three generations of my family, as Frances' mother was at the theater that same evening. Every time I glanced at the girls they were leaning forward, their eyes shining, really spellbound, as were Frances and I. I had not realized how much could be added to the original play, which I remember well, by the emotional richness, subtle suggestion, and dramatic impact of the music, the wonderful pacing of the transition from the trivial to the unbearably heart-breaking. It was an evening in the theater that we are still discussing, warm and cruel and disturbing and human. In other words, magnificent and important and please God it will eventually see more performances than *Oklahoma!* Thank you.

Weill (in New City) to Caspar Neher, 25 March 1947: Thank you for all your birthday wishes, they made me very happy. I have just been through several very difficult weeks. I was starting to recover somewhat from the trials and tribulations of this past winter, when Fate dealt me a powerful blow: my brother Hanns died one day before my birthday. Approximately two years ago, he began to suffer from blood pressure problems (as a result of kidney disease). His doctors had secretly warned me that he would not live long, but I tried on every front to fight this disease and seemed to be successful; first, a strict diet, then a major operation that he tolerated without complications, so that everyone thought he was safe—and suddenly, he had a heart attack. The great unknown is implacable; he takes his victims and we must keep still and grit our teeth. It is a hard blow because my brother and I were very close, especially during the years here in America. It is horrible for my parents (who don't know yet), and I have made up my mind to go to Palestine as soon as I have a visa and tickets for ship's passage. . . .

What you had to say about *Bürgschaft* interests me greatly because I have often thought about revising it. I believe it to be, alongside *Dreigroschenoper* and *Jasager*, the most important and enduring work I wrote in Germany. The second act must be totally rewritten, because it is confusing and musically weaker than the first and third acts. But first, we must examine the whole theme and possibly come up with a new design. It would be nice if we could discuss that, and much more, in the spring. All I have is the piano-vocal score. We must be careful with Klemperer because I'm not sure if he's cured. But those are questions for later, also the question of whether *Bürgschaft* still belongs to Universal Edition or not.

Weill (in New City) to Margarethe Kaiser, 1 May 1947: I am very happy that Martin wants to do *Silbersee* at the Hebbel Theater, and I don't have any objections to performances of *Der Protagonist* and *Der Zar lässt sich photographieren* in German opera houses. Unfortunately, however, it is very difficult for me to clear up the whole situation with the publisher from here. I received a letter from Universal Edition with the laconic statement that the Gestapo had confiscated and taken away all of my full scores. Of course, this is a case of unbelievable neglect of a publisher's obligation to its authors. I do not possess any full scores of my European works and therefore, I can't tell you how to get hold of them at this time.

Weill (in Nahariya, Palestine) to Lotte Lenya, 22 May 1947: So here I am in Nahariya and I must say it is much nicer than we thought it would be. . . . This is really a lovely place, very much like California, and beautifully built up by German Jews—the whole thing very impressive. Even more than in London and Paris I am sorry that you are not with me. I'm sure you would like it, especially the wonderful beach and ocean. The family is much more pleasant than we thought. The parents are amazing—no lamenting or complaining, but sheer happiness to see me. Father looks like a man of sixty, swims with me every morning, mother a little sickly, but nice and intelligent. Nathan is a swell guy, witty and more like me than anybody in the family. They are knocking themselves out, of course, to make everything nice for me. I live at Nathan's, eat lunch at mother's, go to the beach all morning, drive around with Nathan in Arab villages (very interesting), and talk to all friends of the family—which is the whole town. There is a great feeling of happiness, of youth and gaiety over this whole place. The papers are full of reports about my arrival and all theatrical and musical organizations want to give receptions for me. Next week I will spend two days to see Jerusalem and Tel Aviv, probably speak at the Radio and make a "personal appearance" with the Palestine Orchestra and the Habima [Theater].

Elmer Rice tries unsuccessfully to have Weill nominated to the American Academy of Arts and Letters.

Douglas Moore (in New York) to Elmer Rice, 24 March 1947: This is an awful spot to be on. Your play, *Street Scene*, has always been deeply moving to me. It is the sort of work that a composer prays for. I found Kurt Weill's music cold and perfunctory, contributing nothing to the drama, not because of its low-brow moments, surprisingly enough, but in the parts which aspire to be operatic. I had the same feeling about *Knickerbocker Holiday*. He has a marvelous technique and impressive facility, but heart and conscience I can't find anywhere.

Please forgive me for speaking plainly. It's my admiration for you as an artist and as a fellow member of the Institute that is responsible.

Aaron Copland (in Boston?) to Elmer Rice, 25 March 1947: Of course I'll be glad to second Kurt Weill's candidacy in the Institute. I expect strong opposition however. . . !

---

617. Weill replied to *Life's* review of *Street Scene* by pointing out that he did not consider himself a "German composer." The letter appeared in the 17 March 1947 issue, p. 17.

LETTERS TO THE EDITORS
—CONTINUED—

GENTLE BEEF

Sirs:

Thanks very much for the kind words about *Street Scene* ("Three Musical Hits," LIFE, Feb. 24). However I have a gentle beef about one of your phrases. Although I was born in Germany, I do not consider myself a "German composer." The Nazis obviously did not consider me as such either and I left their country (an arrangement which suited both me and my rulers admirably) in 1933.

I am an American citizen and during my dozen years in this country have composed exclusively for the American stage, writing the scores for *Johnny Johnson*, *Knickerbocker Holiday*, *Lady in the Dark*, *One Touch of Venus*, *The Firebrand of Florence* (ouch!) and *Street Scene*.

KURT WEILL
New York, N.Y.

---

618. Weill attempted to answer questions about musical theater in this article for *The Composer's News-Record*, May 1947.

The **Composer's** NEWS -- RECORD

Published by THE NATIONAL COMPOSER MEMBERS OF THE LEAGUE OF COMPOSERS

NUMBER 2   MAY, 1947

Broadway and the Musical Theatre

It has been my opinion for a long time that the Broadway stage can become an important outlet for the American composer and might even become the birthplace of a genuine American "musical theatre" or, if you wish, an American opera. That this theory has been widely accepted lately, is to me one of the most gratifying results of the success of "Street Scene." I never could see any reason why the "educated" (not to say "serious") composer should not be able to reach all available markets with his music, and I have always believed that opera should be a part of the living theatre of our time. Broadway is today one of the great theatre centers of the world. It has all the technical and intellectual equipment for a serious musical theatre. It has a wealth of singers who can act, excellent orchestras and conductors, music-minded directors, choreographers and designers. Above all, it has audiences as sensitive and receptive as any audiences in the world. In watching the audiences at "Street Scene" I noticed that, when the first vogue of "sensationalism" was over, we started building an audience of our own, and there seem to be enough people who like music and drama equally to support a musical play of operatic proportions like "Street Scene" (which, at the time of this writing, has played to more than 200,000 people.)

It is now up to us, the composers in America, to continue this movement which so far has expressed itself only in isolated efforts. There is no doubt that a great number of composers in this country have not only the ambition but also the talent to work for the theatre, but, since we still have not created a real "market" and since we are just beginning to establish a form convention for an American opera, it is natural that composers find it difficult to get their theatrical projects started. I will try to answer a few of the questions I am being asked in this connection.

How can we find a libretto? This, of course, has always been the biggest problem for the theatre composer, and I don't think it is more of a problem today than formerly. The easiest solution is the one which

worked so well with Mozart, Verdi and many other composers: to find a play which is adaptable to the kind of music you want to write. There is a wealth of material in English and American literature, from the Elizabethan theatre to O'Neill. The real problem is to find the right collaborator, and there is no doubt that the art of libretto writing has been very much neglected in America. But there are a number of highly talented playwrights who are vitally interested in the imaginative theatre and who would be willing to work with us if we succeed in developing the musical theatre into an important branch of the general theatre.

How can we find a producer? I don't think it is much more difficult to find a producer for a dramatic musical today than for any other play. Right now, at the end of the season 1946-47, we find on Broadway a definite trend away from the traditional musical comedy towards a more integrated form of musical theatre, and the big successes of the season have been shows which are unorthodox in form and content. Most producers are very conscious of this development. There are also indications that, before long, we might have some form of institutional outlet for a new musical theatre. But again, the pressure has to come from us. Do we have to make concessions to Broadway? Personally I don't think we have to do it, for the audiences are willing to accept any musical language so long as it is strong and convincing. On the other hand I cannot see any harm in making such concessions. Certainly it would be much healthier for an American musical theatre to make certain concessions to Broadway showmanship than to cater to a traditional opera form which is European in concept and purpose. The important concessions to Broadway are of a practical nature: limitation in the size of orchestra and chorus, and limitation in the size of leading singing parts. But in the history of the arts, such limitations have often brought very excellent results because they represent a challenge to the imagination and the skill of the creative artist.

KURT WEILL

619. Weill shows his parents the souvenir program for *Street Scene* at their home in Palestine, April 1947. It was his first reunion with them since January 1934, and it also turned out to be his last.

620. On the beach in Nahariya, Palestine.

THE PLAZA
FIFTH AVENUE AT 59TH STREET
NEW YORK

November 29, 1947

Mr. Kurt Weill,
Playwrights Co.,
630 Fifth Avenue,
New York City

My dear Mr. Weill:

We have not met since your visit to my house in Palestine and it was a great pleasure to see you again on the evening of the 25th of November and also to hear your beautiful orchestration of the Hatikvah, which I hope will be adopted by the Jewish State to be played on the occasion of the first opening of Parliament.

If I remember rightly, you said something about coming over to Palestine again. Perhaps your visit will coincide with the Passover season which, as you may know, is the most beautiful month in Palestine.

With all my good wishes, I remain

Gratefully yours,

Ch. Weizmann

621. A letter from Zionist leader Chaim Weizmann thanking Weill for his work on *Hatikvah*, which Weill orchestrated for a concert and dinner held on 25 November 1947 in New York to celebrate Weizmann's 75th birthday. Attended by 2,000 people, the event featured the Boston Symphony Orchestra conducted by Serge Koussevitzky. In addition to *Hatikvah* the orchestra performed "The Star-Spangled Banner," Mendelssohn's Symphony no. 4, Beethoven's *Egmont* Overture, and Beethoven's Symphony no. 3. News reports portrayed the event as a political rally in support of Weizmann as the first president of the proposed Jewish state in Palestine.

Weill (in Nahariya, Palestine) to Maxwell and Mab Anderson, 30 May 1947: It is less than four weeks since I left New York, but I have seen so much that it seems like much longer and we will have to sit together many evenings if I want to tell you all about it. London was very grim. They have very little to eat and drink and shelter, but the spirit is amazing and more than anywhere else I have found there a young intelligentsia of great determination and political wisdom. Paris is quite the opposite—as corrupt as a Balkan city, without belief or morale, with plenty of excellent food for the rich, but a very superficial philosophy, choking in tradition. Palestine is like fresh air after Europe—one sees happy faces everywhere, youth, hope, and the general theme is construction. The most fascinating aspect for me here is the mixture of civilizations. It is all basically Oriental and very colorful, but overimposed by the Christian civilization of the last 2000 years and now a new Jewish civilization which is very impressive. Yesterday, for instance, I visited some Jewish settlements in the north, bathed in the Lake of Gennesaret [Sea of Galilee] and dined in the house of an Arabian chief, a client of my brother. I could go on like this—but in two weeks I hope to be home. I am full of health and good spirits and very ready to start working.

Weill (in Nahariya) to Lotte Lenya, 31 May 1947: This is my last day in Nahariya, and I want to spend it as much as possible at the beach. My trip through the country was very interesting but quite tiring because it was as hot as Needles, California. Those Jewish settlements are very impressive indeed—but what fascinated me much more was the strangely beautiful, biblical landscape and the completely Oriental character of life and people, the mixture of colorful Arabs on their horses or camels, monks and churches, Jewish farmers on their Ford tractors, ancient and new, Christian, Mohammedan, Jewish—three civilizations together in a small piece of land. We bathed in the Sea of Galilee (Gennesaret, where Jesus went) and spent the night in an ancient town, Safed, and went up to the Syrian border the next day. Thursday afternoon I came back and went to the beach where your voice came from the loudspeaker singing the Pirate ballad ["Seeräuberjenny"]. That was very nice. I had a letter from Victor [Samrock] with a description of the last night of *Street Scene* which, he says, was something unheard of in the American theater—an ovation of ten minutes, then everybody singing "Auld Lang Syne" and then the public going on cheering.

Weill (in New City) to Maxwell and Mab Anderson, 22 June 1947: Judging from your letter, you really seem to have the Hollywood blues and I wish you could pack up and come home. The Road is absolutely lovely this time of year (or it seems so to me after six weeks' absence)—but it isn't quite real without you around. . . . The flight from London to New York was lovely (seven hours across the Atlantic), and coming home to this country had some of the same emotion as arriving here twelve years ago. With all its faults (and partly because of them), this is still the most decent place to live in, and strangely enough, wherever I found decency and humanity in the world, it reminded me of America, because, to me, Americanism is (or ought to be) the most advanced attempt to fill the gap between the individual and technical progress. Countries like France and Italy seem too far removed from this form of Americanism, while England, at the moment, seems to get a little ahead of us—and I have a suspicion that Russia could become, in this sense, "Americanized"—if we want it.

Weill (in New City?) to Lester Cowan, 26 June 1947: I feel I have to tell you once more how enormously enthusiastic I am about your idea of making *One Touch of Venus* into a Ginger Rogers-Fred Astaire vehicle. I am convinced it will make a perfect vehicle for them. Ginger Rogers (who had been our idea for Venus even before we sold the rights to Mary Pickford) as the goddess who falls in love with an average American boy and becomes very very mortal—and Fred Astaire as the little guy who somehow never had known what love is, but who learns fast and well and, in doing so, becomes the kind of man every woman wants.

I can imagine a scene where he begins to dance for the first time after Venus has touched him and I can see their first love scene done in the style of the unforgettable "Night and Day" sequence from *Gay Divorcee*.

The whole idea is so exciting that I would be very happy to spend some time on it and write some new material wherever Rogers and Astaire would feel they need it. Since I am free to work with any lyric writer on the picture score, we could all get together and pick the one we like (I am sure Ira would like to do it).

Weill (in New City?) to Max Dreyfus of Chappell, 9 October 1947: As I understand, you are now negotiating with Schirmer's for the English stage rights of the Menotti operas.

As you remember, I had great hesitations to have *Street Scene* published by Chappell's. I wanted to give it to Boosey & Hawkes because with them I could have been sure of the kind of standard exploitation which this score calls for, of an English production (Covent Garden), and of performances in European opera houses. You promised that all these things could be done by Chappell's as well as by any other publisher. But you did not keep your promises.

I am sure you will have all kinds of reasons why you did not keep your promises and why you and your affiliates are more interested in the property of another publisher than in my work, which, I am sure, is one of the most important properties in your catalogue. Personally, I don't agree with most of those reasons. All I can see is the negative result of my association with Chappell's.

I have been faithful to you for twelve years, in spite of many disappointments. But now I am convinced that I cannot continue my present publisher situation without doing serious harm to my work. That's why I have just accepted an offer from Schirmer's to publish a school opera which I have written this summer. And, in order to avoid any misunderstanding, I want you to now that I consider myself completely free with regard to the publication of my next show and any future works.

Weill (in New City) to Emma and Albert Weill, [November–December 1947]: The big event of the last few weeks was of course the "Partition" [of Palestine], and I can imagine the great excitement you must have felt during all these weeks. Of course, at the moment the consequences are still somewhat unclear and it will take some time before things calm down again. But the fact that the great nations could get together to help a powerless minority gain its rights is the first sign that we're heading toward better times. For Palestine, for Zionism, and the Jewish Agency it is a great victory, especially for Weizmann and [Moshe] Shertok. On 25 November there was a big gala dinner ($250 per person) for Weizmann, at which the Boston Symphony Orchestra (the best orchestra in the world) under Koussevitzky gave a concert in Weizmann's honor. Weizmann called me and asked me to orchestrate the *Hatikvah* for this occasion, which of course I did.

622. In 1947 Weill added a fourth song, "Come Up from the Fields, Father," to the three Whitman songs he had composed in 1942. Tenor William Horne recorded all four for a limited edition distributed by Concert Hall Records.

623. Chappell issued "My Week," with lyrics by Ann Ronell, as sheet music.

624. Universal Pictures released the film version of *One Touch of Venus* in October 1948, with Robert Walker and Ava Gardner in the principal roles (pictured here) along with Dick Haymes and Eve Arden. William A. Seiter directed, and Eileen Wilson dubbed Gardner's songs. Weill's score was reduced to a few adapted songs with revised lyrics.

Weill (in New City?) to Ann Ronell, 4 February 1948: As to the outline of the numbers, I thought that your end of it was very well done. Personally, I don't think there should be too much business going on during the numbers, but I suppose that is up to the taste of the director. I liked very much what you have done with "I'm a Stranger," especially the way you have treated the punch lines at the end. I think the new lines at the top of page three could stand a little clarification. "Speak Low" is fine as long as it stays with Venus, but I'm not so sure of the effect when it switches to the other characters. The "Heart Song" scene can be very effective and the new lyrics are very Ann Ronell-ish. The new ending seems all right for the different character you want to give the song, but I wrote on the music sheet a suggestion for a change of the last bars. According to your letter, these seem to be the only songs used in the picture. Do you think that is enough? I don't. But, who are we?

Ann Ronell (in Hollywood) to Weill, 6 February 1948: I have just finished the new statement of "West Wind," now called "My Week," which Dick Haymes requested as his choice for his number in the picture (please see attached memo). Not only was it very difficult to find a spot in the story that would stand the slowing of pace necessary for insertion of a song number for Dick, but also there was a distinct dislike of "West Wind" when I first suggested its use in the picture many weeks ago to Bill Seiter and Dick Haymes's manager, Bill Burton. I am sure you understand that the original lyric carries no significance now in our screenplay and could not be considered for Savory, in any event, since he is not a singer; the new lyrics, therefore, had to be contrived for the one character who could sing a solo, Joe, played by Dick Haymes, and these lyrics had to mean something to the progression of the story.

When I started writing new lyrics based on my conception of the character and the story cue, I found changes were necessary in the melody. Obviously, this number had to be compact and saleable, light and casual in treatment, and evolve as an entirely new number to accomplish being used at all. Thank goodness, the gorgeous melody was flexible enough for the above requirements. I have always loved the number but recognized why the others didn't—it was too special for general appeal both in lyric and in operetta flavor.

Traute von Witt of Universal Edition (in Vienna) to Weill, 5 July 1948: During the Nazi era the songs from *Die Dreigroschenoper* were a sort of hymn in certain private circles and served as spiritual refreshment for oppressed souls. You have no idea how beloved and honored you have been.

1 9 4 8

MUSIC + THEATER:	LITERATURE + FILM:	SCIENCE + SOCIETY:	POLITICS:
Cole Porter *Kiss Me, Kate*	Giovanni Guareschi *Mondo piccolo, Don Camillo*	Long-playing record invented by Peter Goldmark	The Jewish state comes into existence
Arnold Schoenberg *A Survivor from Warsaw*	W. H. Auden *Age of Anxiety*	Alfred C. Kinsey *Sexual Behavior in the Human Male*	Berlin airlift begins
Benjamin Britten *Beggar's Opera* (new version)	Alan Paton *Cry, the Beloved Country*	Federal rent control bill passed in U.S.	The Malan government announces apartheid policy for South Africa

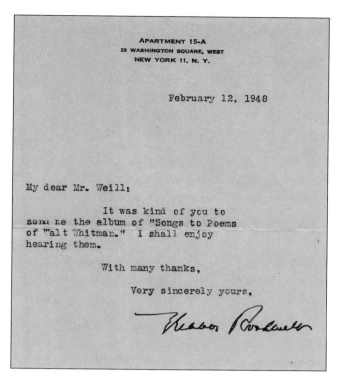

February 12, 1948

My dear Mr. Weill:

It was kind of you to send me the album of "Songs to Poems of Walt Whitman." I shall enjoy hearing them.

With many thanks,

Very sincerely yours,

Eleanor Roosevelt

625. A thank-you note from Eleanor Roosevelt for Weill's gift to her of the recording of his Whitman songs.

626. Weill began collaborating on *Love Life* with the 29-year-old lyricist and bookwriter Alan Jay Lerner in July 1947. Lerner had just scored a big success with his musical *Brigadoon*, which had a score by Frederick (Fritz) Loewe.

627. Lerner's draft of the lyrics for "Love Song," which was sung by a hobo in the fifth vaudeville act. *Love Life* is billed as a vaudeville, and it uses vaudeville-type musical numbers to comment on the action. As such it is often identified as the first "concept musical," a term coined by critics in the late 1960s to refer to musicals that replace the traditional story line with an overall theme or "concept" that the authors illustrate, often ironically, with songs, dances, and scenes. Some of the musicals often mentioned as being influenced by *Love Life* include *Cabaret*, *Company*, *Follies*, *Pacific Overtures*, and *Assassins*.

628. A fair copy of "Here I'll Stay," one of the hit songs from *Love Life*.

629. Weill looks on as Lenya and family friend Biff McGuire play with his sheepdog Wooly in the yard at Brook House.

DOWN IN THE VALLEY

A folk-opera in one act; libretto by Arnold Sundgaard

1948   Bloomington, Indiana University Players (15 July)

Ernst Hoffmann, conductor; Hans Busch, director; Wolfgang Roth, set and costume designer

1949   Zurich, Stadttheater (31 January)
New York, Lemonade Opera (6 July)

1950   New York, NBC studios: televised production (14 January)

In the first year after its publication *Down in the Valley* was performed by eighty different colleges and high schools, with many more to follow. Weill supervised the preparation of the television performance, which was first broadcast on 15 January 1950 by NBC. It was one of the first instances of a televised opera production.

630. *Down in the Valley*, an opera for school and amateur groups with a libretto by Arnold Sundgaard, premiered at Indiana University in July 1948. This publicity photo shows the principal cast members: the Leader (David Aiken), Jennie Parsons (Marion Bell, Lerner's wife and star of *Brigadoon*), Brack Weaver (James Welch), Thomas Bouché (Charles Campbell), and Jennie's father (Earl Jones).

631. The climax of *Down in the Valley* occurs when young Brack Weaver murders his rival in love, Thomas Bouché.

IU STUDENTS AGAIN PROVE TALENT IN
DOWN IN THE VALLEY
BY HENRY BUTLER

The greatest merit of *Down in the Valley* is its simplicity. With an admirably expressive libretto by Arnold Sundgaard, Mr. Weill, who was present last night and acknowledged deserved applause, has written an extended treatment of the well-known folk song from which the opera derives its title. . . . With skillful but unpretentious writing, Mr. Weill has made his brief music drama extraordinarily impressive.

He uses a chorus, Greek tragedy fashion, to comment on the action. The chorus members even help move some of the economical scenery.

In place of the elaborate, artificial, and cumbersome settings we've learned to expect from the Metropolitan and other big-time opera, *Down in the Valley* uses a valley picture projected on a screen in the background, plus such accessories as jail bars, a church door, and a cottage porch with a bit of fence and a mailbox.

Those things, symbolic and suggestive, rather than crudely realistic, plus excellent lighting and the marvelously directed, vigorous action of the principals and the chorus, give the opera tremendous effect. *Indianapolis Times*, July 16, 1948.

632. Weill, Lenya, Alan Jay Lerner, and director Hans Busch gather on the set of *Down in the Valley*. Weill waived his royalties for all amateur productions.

Weill (in New City) to Irving Sablosky, 24 July 1948: My teacher Busoni, at the end of his life, hammered into me one basic truth which he had arrived at after fifty years of pure aestheticism: the fear of triviality is the greatest handicap for the modern artist; it is the main reason why "modern music" got more and more removed from reality, from life, from the real emotions of people in our time. I lost this fear through years of working in the theater, and in doing so, my whole aspect towards musical composition changed. Instead of worrying about the material of music, the theory behind it, the opinion of other musicians, my main concern is to find the purest expression in music for what I want to say, with enough trust in my instinct, my taste, and my talent to write always "good" music, regardless of the style I am writing in. . . .You may have gathered by now that I don't quite recognize the existence of a "purely musical standpoint," especially in the theater. It is your right as a composer to say that you would give folk-tunes a less sophisticated treatment, but it would be wrong to develop this feeling into a general theory. The treatment I have used is not based on any musical theory but on the necessity for the particular moment within the musical-dramatic construction. Besides, what seems sophisticated to you might seem oversimplified to another composer. I am not sure either if there are really two different idioms of folk music—an instrumental and a vocal. If such a separation really exists, it seems to me a rather artificial one, and it might be a very good idea to mix them. I am sorry I offended your ears with the sixth in the last chord. But you can see in the piano score that I arrive at the sixth entirely out of "Stimmführung" (development of voices) [recte: voice leading], so it is not used as an "effect." But here again, it offends your ear because it is being used a great deal in popular music today. If you had lived in the 18th century, your ear would have been offended a thousand times listening to Mozart using over and over again the same cadenza which every other composer of his time used.

633. The first page of the score to "This Is the Life" from *Love Life*, a multi-part musical sequence that depicts Sam's frenetic insecurity apart from his wife and children. The 6½ minute scene is sometimes compared with Billy's "Soliloquy" from *Carousel*, which premiered on Broadway in April 1945.

634. Copy of the vocal score of "This Is the Life," evidently used by Chappell to prepare the printed sheet music.

635. Weill goes over the score with Joseph Littau, conductor of *Love Life*.

LOVE LIFE

"A Vaudeville" in two parts; book and lyrics by Alan Jay Lerner

1948   New York, Forty-Sixth Street Theatre (7 October; 252 performances)

Joseph Littau, conductor; Elia Kazan, director; Boris Aronson, set designer; Lucinda Ballard, costume designer; Michael Kidd, choreographer

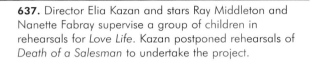

636. This mock conversation between Weill, Lerner, and a Boston theatergoer appeared in *The New York Times* on 3 October 1948, four days before *Love Life* opened on Broadway.

DRAMA—SCREEN   + +   X 3

TWO ON THE STREET

Collaborators Stage a Scene Aimed at Explaining Their Musical Play

By KURT WEILL and ALAN JAY LERNER
Composer and Librettist, respectively, of "Love Life"

SCENE: In front of Shubert Theatre, Boston. Lerner and Weill are standing breathing in the morning air. A man comes by and stares at the theatre marquee.
MAN: Pardon me. Do either of you know anything about this show?
LERNER: Yes, we saw it in New Haven.
MAN: What is it? I am a little confused. It says here on the sign it's a vaudeville.
WEILL: That's right, it is.
MAN: You mean it has vaudeville acts?
WEILL: Lots of them.
MAN: That's fine. Then I don't have to worry about following a plot. That's a relief.
LERNER: No. There's a plot.
MAN: I thought you said it was a vaudeville.
LERNER: It's a vaudeville with a plot.
MAN: How does that work?
WEILL: Well, the sketches and the vaudeville acts have a continuity and supplement each other.
MAN: (Scratching his head) Did you understand?
WEILL: I did.
LERNER: So did I.
MAN: Well, I guess it must be a very simple story.
WEILL: It is. It not only tells the saga of 150 years of American home life but also the love life of two people and the gradual changing of their personalities as life becomes more complex.
LERNER: Not to mention the disintegration of their home until divorce separates them.
WEILL: You see, it's very simple.
MAN: What holds it together?
LERNER: Vaudeville.
MAN: Vaudeville?
WEILL: Why not? If you want to tell an American story, isn't that the most typical form of American theatre?
MAN: I suppose so.
LERNER: After the minstrel show, it certainly is the most native form.
WEILL: Isn't that true?
MAN: (His brow tightening) I suppose so.
WEILL: Is it all clear now?
MAN: No. Let me ask you something else. If the play goes over a 150 years, in what generation does Nanette Fabray and Ray Middleton appear?
LERNER: In all of them.
MAN: You mean they live 150 years?
WEILL: That's right. And not only that, they don't grow any older.

MAN: But how is that possible?
LERNER: With vaudeville.
WEILL: Isn't that simple?
MAN (Wiping his forehead) I don't know. Is it like a lot of little plays strung together?
WEILL: Not exactly. One sketch is a musical play, one is an American ballad, one is a straight comedy, one is satire, one is danced, one is musical comedy, one is dramatic. All different styles.
MAN: How do they all fit together?
LERNER: With vaudeville.
WEILL: Isn't that simple?
MAN: No. You mean it all has a form?
WEILL: Yes, in a formless way.
LERNER: That gives it a very real form.
MAN: Now, look. Wait just a minute. You say that there's a lot of vaudeville in the show. Is there a comedian?
LERNER: No. But there is a lot of comedy.
MAN: Is there a crooner?
WEILL: No. But there are a lot of songs the crooners will sing.
MAN: But no crooners? That's a promise?
LERNER: It's a guarantee. You see, singing is an integral part of the development of the nation. As the plot of the play progresses by way of words and scenes, the music, too, progresses through the ages, so that, at the beginning, there are tunes reminiscent of the folksy home life.
MAN: Dances, too, the square dance, etcetera?
LERNER: Yes, dances, too. Songs and dances. Which change with the mood of the play, from the simplicity of 150 years ago, through the frenzy of the prohibition era and on into the frenetic and zany torchiness of today.
WEILL: Isn't that simple?
MAN: (Looking around wildly for a road to escape). I suppose so. But, anyway, there are no comics and no crooners but there IS vaudeville.
LERNER: That's right.
MAN: For instance?
LERNER: There's a magician.
WEILL: And a trapeze artist.
LERNER: And a male quartet.
WEILL: And a female trio.
MAN: And all this has a plot?
WEILL: That's right.
MAN: And it is easy to follow?
WEILL: It was for us.
MAN: This I've got to see! (He walks to the window to buy a seat. Lerner and Weill shake hands and walk down the street.)

638. The out-of-town tryouts for *Love Life* took place at the Schubert Theatre in New Haven and Boston, beginning 9 September 1948. This is the program cover from Boston.

637. Director Elia Kazan and stars Ray Middleton and Nanette Fabray supervise a group of children in rehearsals for *Love Life*. Kazan postponed rehearsals of *Death of a Salesman* to undertake the project.

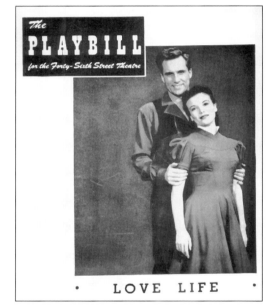

639. Caricaturist Al Hirschfeld documented the starring couples from four shows that opened or were playing in the fall of 1948 (*left to right*): Nanette Fabray and Ray Middleton in *Love Life*; Carol Stone and Jack McCauley in *High Button Shoes*; Bobby Clark and Irene Rich in *As the Girls Go*; and Alfred Drake and Patricia Morison in *Kiss Me, Kate*. (Carol Stone was Nanette Fabray's replacement in *High Button Shoes*, which had opened a year earlier, in September 1947.)

640. The cover of the opening night playbill on Broadway featured the stars Ray Middleton (Samuel Cooper) and Nanette Fabray (Susan Cooper).

641. The center pages of the *Love Life* souvenir program featured a medley of photographs, including several of the vaudeville acts. The songs heard in each of these scenes are (clockwise from top left): "Who is Samuel Cooper?", "Madame Zuzu," "Here I'll Stay," "Progress," and "Divorce Ballet."

642. Pictured below are: the bedroom scene, "Women's Club Blues" (two photos), children in "Mother's Getting Nervous," "Susan's Dream," the Cooper family, and the "Madrigal" that opens Act II.

Unless it is illegal to do so, this column would like to express a feeling of general disappointment over *Love Life*, which was put on at the Forty-Sixth Street last evening. Although billed as a "vaudeville," it is cute, complex, and joyless—a general gripe masquerading as entertainment.

This may be a thoroughly illegal opinion, since some of the most honored people in show business have worked at it. Kurt Weill has written one of his most flexible and idiomatic scores for it, and Ray Middleton and Nanette Fabray sing some of his best numbers rapturously. Alan Jay Lerner, the "Brigadoon" man of letters, has written the book and lyrics. Elia Kazan, the protean director, has staged it with one or two beguiling ballets by Michael Kidd. Scenery by Boris Aronson, the old maestro; costumes by Lucinda Ballard, the enchanted seamstress. This list, with Cheryl Crawford presiding justly at the top of it, includes quite a section of theater's hall of fame.

But to at least one discontented theatergoer *Love Life* is an intellectual idea about showmanship gone wrong. Vaudeville has nothing to do with the bitter ideas Mr. Lerner has to express about marriage. Although he is trying to be a philosopher, unhappiness keeps creeping in. He looks jocose on the surface, but he is full of anguish. . . .

As a matter of fact, most of the pleasures come out of Mr. Weill's music-box. He has never composed a more versatile score with agreeable music in so many moods—hot, comic, blue, satiric, and romantic. "Progress" and "Economics" are very literate satire. "Love Song" is a beautiful ballad that Johnny Thompson sings with genuine feeling. Mr. Middleton learned long ago how to sing Mr. Weill's music, and "This Is the Life," lanky and ruminative, is an especially stirring number. Miss Fabray, an uncommonly gifted music queen, makes something lively and gay out of "Mr. Right."

But those pleasant interludes are the result of a deliberate effort to find something beautiful or amusing in the lugubrious train of the story. The vaudeville sequences are generally inferior and contribute nothing at all to the theme. Brooks Atkinson, "At the Theater," *New York Times*, 8 October 1948.

Weill (in Los Angeles) to Lotte Lenya, 13 November 1948: The movie industry is practically dead, with those few executives and their relatives frantically holding on to the sinking ship. There are only two studios still making a few musicals. One is MGM—there the ruler is Arthur Freed who said, after reading "Miss Memory" [treatment for a film by Weill and Lerner]: "this is no time for sophisticated stuff; what we need is meat and potatoes." The other studio is 20th Century and there is a slight chance to get [Darryl] Zanuck interested. At Warner's the "front office" liked the story very much and they are giving it now to their producers to read. But I am pretty doubtful about the chances, not only for "Miss Memory" but for anything halfway good, in this town.

Weill (in New City?) to Alfred Schlee of Universal Edition, 11 December 1948: The situation concerning *Dreigroschenoper* seems to be rather confused. A few weeks ago I received a report from Munich that the music has been changed considerably and new music has even been added for a revival of the work there. I would be most grateful to you if you could find out whether this actually is the case. Of course, I would strictly forbid even the slightest change in this score, and in case of any repeat performances I would have to take legal action.

Weill (in New City) to Bertolt Brecht, 17 January 1949: Today I finally received the changes to *Die Dreigroschenoper* and I hasten to give you an answer.

I must confess that I don't understand what you intend to achieve with these changes. It's possible that I can't judge the situation in Germany sufficiently from over here, but it seems clear to me that from your point of view, as the lyricist of *Die Dreigroschenoper*, these new texts represent a weakening of the original text, since the more cabaret-style allusions to "current" events are simply not on the level of *Die Dreigroschenoper* (besides the fact that [Hermann] Göring, [Dr. Hjalmar] Schacht and [Wilhelm] Keitel are hardly current any more).

Perhaps you will say that this isn't any of my business since these changes do take the music into consideration. But since the music was written to your original lyrics and since this merging of words and music into one was one of the main virtues of *Die Dreigroschenoper*, I'm afraid that these drastic changes (e.g. in the "Kanonen Song") must have a disturbing effect on the public, who have been singing these songs for the last twenty years.

Bertolt Brecht (in Berlin) to Weill, 28 January 1949: Many thanks for your speedy reply. I've made these revisions for very simple reasons: Mr. Peachum's cripple-copies are not attractive in Germany right now, because too many real (war)-cripples, or their relatives, are in the audience. An alternative solution simply had to be thought of. Fortunately, these changes were so small that they didn't change the character of the piece. Here, as in the case of the additional lyrics, it is a question of temporary changes, valid *only* at this particular point in time (and not to appear in print).

I quite agree with your objection that adding two additional verses to the "Ballade vom angenehmen Leben" causes monotony; I will also revise the end of the final ballad, so it will fit the character of the music. I know nothing about prohibiting *Die Dreigroschenoper* in Munich. It's probably nothing but a net of intrigues.

I believe that I can arrive at a friendly agreement with Bloch Erben. They will no longer represent the work; before I get everything settled, you will, of

1 9 4 9

MUSIC + THEATER:	LITERATURE + FILM:	SCIENCE + SOCIETY:	POLITICS:
Richard Rodgers *South Pacific*	George Orwell *Nineteen Eighty-Four*	Philip Hench discovers cortisone	North Atlantic Treaty signed in Washington
Jule Styne *Gentlemen Prefer Blondes*	Eleanor Roosevelt *This I Remember*	USSR tests its first atomic bomb	German Federal Republic comes into being with Bonn as capital
Arthur Miller *Death of a Salesman*	*The Third Man* (film by Carol Reed)	Charlemagne Prize for European Understanding established at Aachen, Germany	Democratic Republic established in East Germany

course, receive the exact wording, so you will be able to add your own proposals. Meanwhile, I'd like to leave the representation and the overall supervision of the Albers performances to Jakob Geis, who would then forward your royalties to Universal Edition (in case you would want this). He is absolutely reliable. Naturally, these are only temporary measures and for final arrangements we simply would have to meet in person. You can take my word that I will undertake nothing, absolutely nothing, against your interests and will in every instance consult with you, if only because I'm still hoping for further collaboration between us. I would be very happy if you could give your consent to the Albers guest performance soon, so Albers can go ahead.

Weill (in New York?) to Karlheinz Gutheim, 31 January 1949: I am grateful for your comprehensive report concerning *Die Dreigroschenoper* matter. Right after receiving your letter, I sent you a cable in which I stated that I strictly forbid any changes in my music or in my orchestrations.

In case the management of the Kammerspiele wants to know the reasons for my objection, I will give you a short explanation, although I am confident that as a musician you will understand my position. In the twenty years of its existence, *Die Dreigroschenoper* has become a classic, and thousands of performances have rendered proof of its artistic strength as well as of its power over an audience. In music schools, the work's full score is being taught as an example of great orchestration achieved by modest means, and up to now, no one has ever gotten the idea that this full score should be improved on. If performances in German theaters have not been so successful lately, I can only say that either the music has been played badly (and probably also sung badly), or that under present circumstances German audiences are not receptive to a work like *Die Dreigroschenoper* (something I can easily imagine). To me this simply means that for the time being this piece cannot be performed in Germany. However, in no case would I allow my music to be changed arbitrarily just to bring it into line with present standards in Germany. By the way, I take the same attitude about the changes in the text that Brecht has sent me; I do not approve of his "updatings" at all.

Weill (in New City) to Alan Jay Lerner, 18 April 1949: I just read the first story in the collection "First Love" (Bantam Book No. 503). It is Stephen Vincent Benét's short story, "Too Early Spring," and it moved me very much. I think it is closer to the kind of young-love story we have been looking for than anything we have seen (I haven't read all the stories in the book yet, but the ones I did read were nothing compared to this one). I am sure it could make a very lovely, moving musical play of the kind we have been talking about, and could even include elements of the honky-tonk juke-joint background. Of course, the story would have to be developed, but the elements are all there—the first meeting when he looks down on her because she is too young, her difficulties at home because of her constantly quarreling parents, baseball games, drugstores, canoes on the lake, the lovely scene where they pretend they are married, finally the beautiful scene at night when they both fall asleep, and the following catastrophe. . . .

It was very good to talk to you yesterday. I know how lonely it can be out there. But, as I told you, it was a little depressing here too. The evening at Oscar's was pleasant until Dick [Rodgers] showed up—then suddenly everybody froze into a sort of pompous silence and it was impossible to discuss anything except the cheapest, most obvious kind of show

643. The famous German actor Hans Albers starred in the 1949 production of *Die Dreigroschenoper* in Munich. Directed by Harry Buckwitz, the production used Brecht's revised script and lyrics without Weill's permission.

644. Weill appeared on an NBC Television variety program called "The Swift Show" on 31 March 1949, hosted by Lanny Ross. Here, Ross sings a chorus of "September Song" with Weill accompanying him. The program also featured Ross singing "Here I'll Stay" in a duet with soprano Martha Wright.

talk. Obviously, Dick suffers from a terrible case of inferiority complex which he tries desperately to hide behind arrogance. It came out clearly in the expression of his face (and visible to everyone) when I played some of the music [from *Lost in the Stars*], especially things like the great lament "Cry, the Beloved Country," at the end of which he got so nervous that he couldn't sit in his chair any more and started walking around so that I almost began feeling sorry for him, and that three days after the opening of *South Pacific*! It was all very strange and weird.

Weill (in New City) to Heinz Jolles, 27 May 1949: Lenya and I came here in 1935 and immediately fell in love with this country, and my success here (which people usually ascribe to "luck") is mostly due to the fact that I took a very positive and constructive attitude towards the American way of life and the cultural possibilities in this country, of which most German intellectuals who came here at the same time were critical and doubtful. I found enormous latent possibilities in my special field, the musical theater. When I arrived here, the musical theater on Broadway consisted almost entirely of revues and light musical comedies and everybody thought I was crazy when I started with serious musical plays like *The Eternal Road* and *Johnny Johnson*. Both were financial failures, but they made a deep impression on Broadway and in the country. It was a hard struggle the following years (and still is), but through the work I have done the entire picture of musical theater in this country has changed: the musical play, as I have created it in Europe, is now the big vogue in America, and since I wrote my first American opera *Street Scene*, which ran for five months on Broadway in 1947, opera has become a major element of American culture. Of the ten theater pieces I have written since I came here, about half were successes, the other half failures. I am not rich, but I make a good living and I enjoy the work I am doing. We are living in a lovely house in the country, about an hour from New York. Lenya has tried to work here too, but it is too difficult for actors with her originality, and she has made a perfect adjustment and is contented taking a part in my work as she always did. My parents and my oldest brother (the doctor) are living in Israel since 1935, and I went to see them there two years ago. My sister is living here,

and my brother Hanns, whom you probably knew, died here two years ago.

That's about all I can tell you about myself, except that I am working now on a new musical play with Maxwell Anderson, based on a book about the Negroes in South Africa, called *Cry, the Beloved Country*.

Weill (in New City?) to Max Leavitt of the Lemonade Opera, 29 June 1949: I wanted to thank you once more for letting me see the rehearsal of *Down in the Valley* last night. I was greatly impressed with the spirit of youthful enthusiasm and the fine singing quality of your troupe, with the careful musical preparation which the work has been given, and the imaginative style which you have found for the staging.

Sundgaard and I, in discussing our impressions of the rehearsals, both agreed that we should explain once more where the style of your production differs from our conception, because we are sure that it won't be difficult to make some changes in the basic attitude. We know that the Lemonade Opera has been very successful at presenting opera in a highly formalized and stylized way, and since this is the accepted style of your performances we understand that you want to adhere to it (although it might be interesting from your standpoint to show that you can also do a different kind of musical theater). *Down in the Valley* is a red-hot piece of theater. It has been called an American *Cavalleria rusticana*—and we are not ashamed of that. Its effect has always been a highly emotional one. It has moved people and excited them through a mixture of melodrama and oratorio which is the basic style of the piece. In last night's rehearsal, the melodrama, the story of love and hate and jealousy and fight, was neglected in favor of the oratorio, and the result was a feeling of coolness and aloofness. The job that should be done now is to combine the beauties of your conception with the natural theatricality of the work and to make especially the love story more real and more passionate.

Weill (in New City) to Emma and Albert Weill, 11 July 1949: In the meantime I had a most pleasant surprise, which I want to tell you about. My folk opera *Down in the Valley*, which you have heard on the radio, has already been given in 100 American cities and now it has come out in New York in a small theater, where a group of young singers has been giving operas with great success for several years now. They call themselves "Lemonade Opera" because they sell lemonade during the intermission, and also to emphasize the contrast with pompous grand opera (just as we did back then with the *Dreigroschenoper*). It was a brilliant performance and an enormous success, but I did not expect what happened the next morning: the newspapers greeted my opera as the great event in America's musical life. The *Times* critic compares it to the *Beggar's Opera*, which became the origin of English opera, and says that *Down in the Valley* will go down in history as the "fountain-head" of American opera. Another critic starts his review: "Kurt Weill, who was born in Dessau and who came to our country to live, will some day be called the founder of American opera by later generations." You can imagine what this means to me, since this recognition allows me to work once more in the field of opera, which has really always been my proper field of activity. My next piece after the one I'm working on now will be an opera [*The Wingless Victory*], for which Maxwell Anderson will write the libretto and in which the famous American baritone Lawrence Tibbett will sing the leading role.

The American Opera Society of Chicago
national
hereby confers officially its **David Bispham Memorial Medal** upon the distinguished American composer

Kurt Weill

for his outstanding contribution to American art in his American folk opera "**Down in the Valley**"

May 19th 1949.

President *Helen A. Braud*

Ch. Med. Awards *Anita West Bills*

645. The American Opera Society of Chicago recognized Weill for his contribution to American opera with *Down in the Valley*.

Weill (in New City) to Emma and Albert Weill, 6 September 1949:
Yesterday I finished the musical composition and now I'm working under high pressure to finish as much of the orchestration as possible before rehearsals start on 19 September. The play's new title is *Lost in the Stars*, which in German means "In den Sternen verloren," which also is the most important vocal piece. All summer long we have worked on the casting of this play. It has been extremely difficult and sometimes we thought we would have to give up the whole thing, because we couldn't find the right performers. But now, after all our endeavors, we have an excellent cast, with the famous Negro baritone Todd Duncan in the leading role and the famous English actor Leslie Banks in an important role of a white man, along with a number of very good male and female Negro singers. This time we open directly in New York on 30 October. It's a very difficult task, but very interesting for just that reason.

In the meantime all kinds of things have happened with my earlier works and it almost looks like I am to reap some sort of reward after twenty-five years of heavy, tireless work—not in a financial, but in a purely idealistic sense. After the success of *Down in the Valley* and the *Street Scene* concert performance, which was also a big success in Hollywood, I've suddenly been promoted to the rank of "classical composer" and people are beginning to talk about the "historical significance" of my work. Now they want to perform my first American play, *Johnny Johnson*, in Los Angeles, and I just found out that the opera studio of the Metropolitan Opera will perform my old opera *Der Zar lässt sich photographieren* with young stars of the Metropolitan three days before the premiere [of *Lost in the Stars*].

646. From left: Alan Paton, author of *Cry, the Beloved Country*, Weill, and Maxwell Anderson discuss *Lost in the Stars.*

647. As a first step in adapting *Cry, the Beloved Country*, Anderson excerpted Paton's thirty-six chapters and structured them into seventy-nine scenes (the first sixteen are shown here).

648. To prepare for writing *Lost in the Stars*, Anderson and Weill procured some recordings of South African music from ethnomusicologist Hugh Tracey, though the score shows little influence.

649. Shortly before the beginning of rehearsals, director Rouben Mamoulian summarized previous discussions with the authors.

+ dog Voolly

Out of Trouble

By MARY BRAGGIOTTI

With the Broadway opening of his new show, "Lost in the Stars," only a matter of weeks ahead of him, composer Kurt Weill was as calm the other day as the cool green trees that surround his 150-year-old house in New City, N. Y., and the unhurried brook that flows quietly, below his terrace, towards the Hudson. While Lotte Lenya—Mrs. Weill—is not the placid type, her vivacity was due to natural exuberance—not pre-opening jitters.

Double Take

"Kurt is extraordinarily quiet for a composer," said Lenya (she's usually called Lenya instead of Lotte) in a Viennese accent which is charming to American ears. "There is only one moment when he is doing a show that he says, 'I'll never get through with that score. This time I'll never make it.' I never pay any attention—not the SLIGHTEST—because I know he is always ahead of time."

"It is the orchestration I worry about," said Weill, who is one of the few theatrical composers who does his own orchestrating. "I cannot do it before rehearsals begin because I have to hear the singers' voices and also work with the choreographer. It means I am at rehearsal all day long and must work on the orchestration at night. I get no sleep . . ."

"Don't feel sorry for him," his wife admonished. "He loves every minute of it. After opening night he always says, 'Now I am going to have a good rest.' The rest lasts exactly two days. Then he says 'NOW what am I going to do?'"

Lenya should know her husband's habits and idiosyncrasies by this time. They have been married 21 years, the last 14 of which they have spent in the U. S. The Weills have lived through more troubles and triumphs together than the average couple living peacefully in the rural suburbs of New York.

Kurt Weill, known in the U. S. for his excellent scores for "Johnny Johnson," "Knickerbocker Holiday," "Lady in the Dark," "One Touch of Venus," "Street Scene," "Love Life" and the American folk-opera, "Down in the Valley," which has had over 100 productions in semi-professional theatres throughout the country in the past year, was born in Dessau, Germany, in 1900. His father was a cantor (both his parents are now living in Israel) and Kurt's talent burgeoned in an atmosphere of music.

"There was never any doubt," he says, "about what I wanted to be."

Dessau had one of the finest little opera houses in Germany. Kurt grew up with it. He accompanied on the piano the singers who visited his home and wrote songs for them, and his first lessons in composition and harmony were with the opera's conductor. At 18 he went to Berlin, where he studied for six months with the venerable composer, Humperdinck. In the next three years he got his first real baptism of the theatre as conductor for a theatre in Westphalia. His duties included conducting operas, operettas and musical comedies; shifting scenery and arranging scores for a 25-piece orchestra.

"As soon as I started writing for the theatre," Weill recalls, "my music became direct and simple. I discovered I am really a theatre composer."

That was the year, too, in which Lenya and Kurt were married. Lotte Lenya was born in Vienna. When she was very young, she went to Zurich to study ballet and eventually danced, sang and acted in the Zurich State Theatre.

"Then I went to Berlin," she said. She turned to her husband who was sitting beside her on a couch by the old fireplace in the low-ceilinged living room which used to be the kitchen of their stone house. "Now you know the story better than I," she said with a smile.

"We were doing a children's ballet in Berlin," Weill said, "and we were looking for a girl 15 or 16 who could dance, sing and act. One day someone brought in a young lady who I thought was charming. I was playing the piano in the pit. After she'd tried out, she went away and I asked the director where she'd gone. 'She'll be back,' he said. I looked for her, but she didn't come back.

"A year later George Kaiser invited me to his house outside Berlin. He told me to take the train, then walk from the station through the woods to a certain place on the river where a boat would be waiting for me. Well, there was the boat and there was the girl in it that I'd seen in the tryout. She rowed me across the lake."

"And that was the end of him," Lenya said. "Love on second sight."

Lenya played leading parts in several of Weill's works, notably "The Three Penny Opera" and "The Rise and Fall of Mahogany," a musical play about, of all places, a mythical town in Alabama. The opening of the latter in Leipzig in 1930 was the occasion of one of the first Hitler scandals. The Nazis bought out part of the opera house and staged a riot. From then on Weill's professional life in Germany was a continuous battle.

The night of the burning of the Reichstag, he was warned that he was on a list of 120 intellectuals marked for immediate arrest. It was Lenya who insisted that they flee Berlin, leaving all their worldly possessions behind them. After long stops in Paris and London (Weill wrote a ballet-with-words in Paris, in which Tilly Losch and Lenya appeared, and a play-with-music with Jacques Deval), the Weills arrived in New York just 14 years ago this month.

"After 'Johnny Johnson,'" said the composer, "I decided this

MUSICAL SHOW composer Kurt Weill and his wife Lenya.

was the place I could continue what I'd tried in Europe—a form of musical play between opera on one hand and musical comedy on the other."

In America, too, Weill continued his habit of working only with the best writers, and working closely with them from the moment an idea for a new play is born. In this way he has collaborated with Paul Green, Moss Hart, Ogden Nash, Alan Lerner and, of course, his famous neighbor, Maxwell Anderson. Weill and Anderson have written several music-plays together, including the forthcoming "Lost in the Stars," which the playwright wrote from Alan Paton's best seller, "Cry, the Beloved Country."

And Lenya? Lenya has done some acting here, but comparably little. The spoken word, unfortunately, is not as international as music.

"I've given up acting," she explained, "because why should I sit around waiting for a part with a little Viennese accent? But I don't mind—I got it out of my system."

"She doesn't have to be analyzed," her husband smiled.

Lenya is not only vivacious and attractive but also chic. She patronizes only the top designers—or makes clothes for herself on a dressmaker's dummy she calls "Suzy." Since leaving Europe she has found she can cook. In fact, her husband says, she is good at anything manual, including repairs around the house.

The Weills swim a little, play a little tennis, ride bicycles a little and enjoy their intellectual and artistic neighbors a lot.

"America," said Weill, "always seemed a very romantic country to me. It still does."

LIVE peacefully in country.

MAKES clothes for herself.

SHE'S "GOOD at anything manual," he says.

---

650. On 18 September 1949, the *New York Post* ran a human interest story about Weill and Lenya.

651. Vocal score of "The Shadowy Glass," a number for the leader and chorus cut from *Lost in the Stars*.

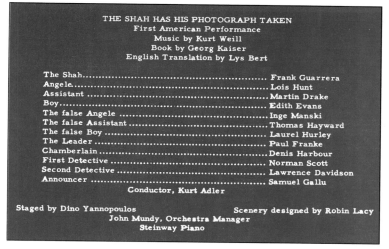

THE SHAH HAS HIS PHOTOGRAPH TAKEN
First American Performance
Music by Kurt Weill
Book by Georg Kaiser
English Translation by Lys Bert

The Shah .... Frank Guarrera
Angele .... Lois Hunt
Assistant .... Martin Drake
Boy .... Edith Evans
The false Angele .... Inge Manski
The false Assistant .... Thomas Hayward
The false Boy .... Laurel Hurley
The Leader .... Paul Franke
Chamberlain .... Denis Harbour
First Detective .... Norman Scott
Second Detective .... Lawrence Davidson
Announcer .... Samuel Gallu

Conductor, Kurt Adler

Staged by Dino Yannopoulos   Scenery designed by Robin Lacy
John Mundy, Orchestra Manager
Steinway Piano

655. The Metropolitan Opera Guild training program mounted an evening of *opera buffa* at the Juilliard School of Music that included the first American performance of the 1928 one-act opera *Der Zar lässt sich photographieren*, translated into English by Lys Bert Symonette and directed by Dino Yannopoulos.

653. *Lost in the Stars* does not have an overture. It opens with the unifying theme from the song "Cry, the Beloved Country" and segues immediately into the introduction of "The Hills of Ixopo."

652. The opening song in Act II for the leader and chorus, "The Wild Justice," explores the complex nature of human justice. It was not included in the cast recording issued on Decca.

654. Playing through the score with conductor Maurice Levine, who made his Broadway debut in *Lost in the Stars*.

LOST IN THE STARS

A musical tragedy in two acts; book and lyrics by Maxwell Anderson

1949   New York, Music Box (30 October; 281 performances and tour to ten American cities.)

Maurice Levine, conductor; Rouben Mamoulian, director; George Jenkins, set designer; Anna Hill Johnstone, costume designer

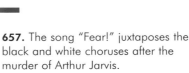

656. *Lost in the Stars* was Weill's last completed work.

Two plays in which music is employed copiously but incidentally are *Regina* (née *The Little Foxes* by Lillian Hellman), with text and music by Marc Blitzstein, and *Lost in the Stars* (a Maxwell Anderson play and lyrics based on Alan Paton's novel *Cry, the Beloved Country*) with music by Kurt Weill. . . .

Not quite so incidental is the composer's contribution to *Lost in the Stars*. Here there are solos, choruses, all sorts of set pieces. And they have form; they are "numbers." Even the passages of dialogue that separate them have a beginning, a middle, and an ending. The whole spectacle is therefore a series of forms, some spoken and some sung; and the sequence of these makes a continuity, too, a narrative nowhere lacking in variety or in movement towards its goal. It is not however, either purely or chiefly a musical narrative. It is a play with musical numbers, a *singspiel*. Whether you "like" Mr. Weill's numbers or not (I personally find the tunes weak but their scoring masterful), their relation to the play is a model of procedure. His music does all the right things at all the right times. Its layout is perfection. So is its performance, by the way. Virgil Thomson, "Music Written for the Theater, a Summary of the Early Season," *New York Herald Tribune*, 13 November 1949.

From my point of view Kurt was the perfect composer. He could find the right air for any lyric, and could find it instantly, could change it instantly if conditions changed—if, for example, there was an alteration in the cast that called for a different vocal or emotional setting. It has always been my custom to write a play from beginning to end, not in patches, and I wrote musicals for Kurt in the same fashion. The lyrics were written as they were needed, in the course of the story. Kurt took each lyric as it came along, set it to music, usually within an hour or two of first reading it, and brought it to me—so that I could hear it before I went further. Sometimes Kurt wrote more than one tune, sometimes several, and played them all for me to choose among. Usually, however, the first setting he made was so right, so perfect for the words, that there was [no] need to go further. Maxwell Anderson, unpublished manuscript, WLRC Ser.35, box 1, folder 5.

657. The song "Fear!" juxtaposes the black and white choruses after the murder of Arthur Jarvis.

658. Sheila Guyse as Linda sings "Who'll Buy" in a Johannesburg bar.

660. A few weeks before Absalom Kumalo (Julian Mayfield) is executed for murder, Stephen marries him in the prison to his long-suffering fiancée Irina (Inez Matthews).

659. In the climactic murder scene from Act I of *Lost in the Stars*, Absalom, in a panic, kills Arthur Jarvis. Photo by George Karger.

661. Stephen Kumalo pays a visit to the father of the murdered man, James Jarvis (played by Leslie Banks). At the end of the play, the fathers of the murderer and victim are reconciled.

662. *Lost in the Stars* by cartoonist Al Hirschfeld.

663. Howard Barnes's review of the show appeared in the *New York Herald Tribune*, 6 November 1949.

'Lost in the Stars' Brings to the Stage a Beautiful Tragedy, Developing a Difficult Theater Form to a High Degree

By HOWARD BARNES

The musical play is a strange form. It skirts the opera on one side and the hurly-burly musical comedy on the other. Although the connotation of the word has been completely altered, it should properly be called melodrama. It is one of the most difficult idioms of the theater, but when it is employed with clarity and eloquence it brings a stage to vibrant life.

"Lost in the Stars," which has opened at the Music Box, is melodrama in its original sense: a stage play in which songs are interspersed and in which orchestral music accompanies the action. Out of Alan Paton's fine book of racial tensions in South Africa, "Cry, the Beloved Country," Maxwell Anderson has designed a story line and lyrics which capture the full burden of a great tragedy. Kurt Weill has written a score which supplements the action at every turn of the plot and Rouben Mamoulian has staged a complicated show with rare vision.

There are those who relished the book who feel that the surging conflict between black man and white man has not been fully realized in the stern musical tragedy which has emerged at the Music Box. They are mistaken. For the theater employs its own terms in its particular fashion and needs no antecedent references for its magic. With Todd Duncan playing a Zulu Anglican minister with both vocal and acting authority and Leslie Banks reflecting his agony in a restrained climax, "Lost in the Stars" is a work of truth, beauty and immense artistry.

Anderson took on a challenging task in making over a valiant novel into a musical. One might have expected him to give the original the straight dramatic impact which has distinguished so many of his plays. Strangely enough, he was wise as well as wary in supplementing his adaptation with songs, dances and splendid choral renditions. The Negroes, who are so ably led by Frank Roane in what amounts to a Greek chorus, contribute enormous force to what might have been a straggling show. Both the lyrics and recitation are so neatly blended with straight drama that there is rare theatrical excitement at the Music Box.

With Integrated Score

Kurt Weill's score is no counterpart of George Gershwin's music for the classic musical tragedy, "Porgy and Bess," but it always carries the melodrama to its inexorable and moving conclusion. Moreover, he has written such lovely tunes as "The Little Grey House," "Trouble Man" and "Stay Well," which would be distinguished outside of the context of the show. His "Fear" brings principals and their performing assistants together in a terrible interlude, in which the police of Johannesburg are searching for the Negro minister's son who has unwittingly shot the white man who is the greatest benefactor of the Negro race.

However arduous their collaboration may have been, Anderson, Weill and Mamoulian have made it so simple and fluent that the book on which it is based is merely a jumping-off place for a triumphant piece of theater. The brilliantly terse settings of George

Jenkins shift the action back and forth between the small village of Ndotsheni and Johannesburg as the "Umfundisis," Stephen Kumalo, finds that his son has murdered his white friend and almost loses his faith. Twenty scenes unfold with scarcely any interruption in a production which groups large ensembles with astringent individual drama.

A Rich Cast

Although Duncan has the chief role, he is given ample support by a superb cast. Banks confronts him as an English planter, who turns from a frightened intolerance of the Zulus to a real friendship for the father of the boy who killed his son, with splendid intensity. Inez Matthews is equally fine as the common-law wife of the murderer, bringing rich dimensions to a part which might well have been a shadow in a music drama. Warren Coleman is excellent as the sinister brother of the man of God, who runs a tobacco shop in Johannesburg, and Julian Mayfield is altogether right as the son who precipitates a tragedy.

"Cry, the Beloved Country," was so superior in its own right that it is somewhat astounding to find its transmutation into musical terms so tremendously effective. The Messrs. Anderson, Weill, Mamoulian and their colleagues have composed an engrossing stage threnody which enriches the theatrical season immeasurably. Even in such bits as the number "Who'll Buy?" in which Sheila Guyse is torridly attractive, "Lost in the Stars" is a completely satisfying entertainment.

664. In late March 1950, Weill was correcting proofs for the piano-vocal score of *Lost in the Stars* in his hospital bed three days before he died. The score was published in August.

KURT WEILL
MAXWELL ANDERSON

LOST
IN THE
STARS

CHAPPELL & CO., Inc.

665. On 14 December 1949, Weill discussed two of his favorite subjects—musical forms and the American musical theater—in a letter to music critic Olin Downes. The letter is misdated.

The Playwrights' Company   630 FIFTH AVE., N.Y. 20, N.Y. CI. 5-7930

DIRECTORS
Maxwell Anderson
Elmer Rice
Robert E. Sherwood
Kurt Weill
John F. Wharton
BUSINESS MANAGER
Victor Samrock
PRESS REPRESENTATIVE
William Fields

November 14, 1949

Mr. Olin Downes
205 West 57th Street
New York, N.Y.

Dear Olin,

thank you very much for your kind letter. I am more than happy that you liked "Lost in the Stars", because I know that you have always been very honest with me. Of course, I was especially glad to find that you too consider this score another important step towards an American musical theatre. That is what I hoped it would be and what I find it to be every time I see what a deep effect it has on the audiences.

In this connection I was greatly interested in what you have to say about the formality of the song-form, because you have hit here on one of the basic problems of our musical theatre. It must be somewhat surprising indeed to find a serious subject treated in a form which (in this country at least) has been used so far only for a lighter form of entertainment. But that was exactly the nature of my experiment - to do a "musical tragedy" for the American theatre so that the typical American audience (not a specialized audience) can accept it; and the real success of the piece to me is the fact that the audience did accept it without hesitation, that they accepted a lot of very serious, tragic, quite un-Broadway-ish music of operatic dimensions, together with some songs written in a more familiar style. Personally I don't feel that this represents a compromise because it seems to me that the American popular song, growing out of the American folk-music, is the basis of an American musical theatre (just as the Italian song was the basis of Italian opera), and that in this early state of the development, and considering the audiences we are writing for, it is quite legitimate to use the form of the popular song and gradually fill it with new musical content. But I do agree with you that this infiltration of song in the musical theatre will gradually become more refined and more removed from its origines. (I am quite sure, by the way, that "Regina" could have been a better success if Blitzstein's attempts at writing songs would have been more successful). I hope we'll have a chance to discuss all this.

Olin Downes (in New York) to Weill, 9 December 1949: It's awfully interesting to me to watch your hand get firmer with each thing you are doing, and your new treatments and forms and new technical resources. It is wonderful that you've got such an opera over on the stage. This work, and the *Street Scene*, will be among the most significant steps which have so far been taken both to modernize and to popularize the operatic principle, and say something worthwhile in the artistic sense. But I am still waiting for the day when you get exactly the subject which you can treat without the faintest consideration of public taste or expediency of any sort, while in the meantime you are constantly developing a reputation for making it more and more possible for you to do exactly what you want to do ultimately in the musical field.

Excerpt from Weill's radio appearance on "Opera News on the Air," 10 December 1949. The host of the program is Boris Goldovsky.

Goldovsky: Tell me, Mr. Weill, as a composer yourself, are you conscious of any particular emotional appeal that brings forth the most characteristic in you; that brings out the Weill in Weill, so to say?

Weill: Well, I'm not conscious of it when I actually write music, but looking back on many of my compositions, I find that I seem to have a very strong reaction in the awareness of the suffering of underprivileged people; of the oppressed, the persecuted. I know, for instance, that in the music I wrote for *Lost in the Stars*, I consciously introduced a certain amount of South African musical atmosphere, and yet, in retrospect, I can see that when the music involved human suffering, it is, for better or worse, pure Weill.

666. A portion of Weill's and Anderson's outline for a musical version of *Huckleberry Finn*. The show was never completed.

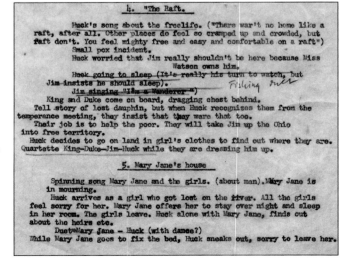

4. "The Raft.

Huck's song about the freelife. ("There war't no home like a raft, after all. Other places do feel so cramped up and crowded, but raft don't. You feel mighty free and easy and comfortable on a raft")
Small pox incident.
Huck worried that Jim really shouldn't be here because Miss Watson owns him.
Huck going to sleep (It's really his turn to watch, but Jim insists he should sleep).
Jim singing "I'm a Wanderer".
King and Duke come on board, dragging chest behind.
Tell story of lost dauphin, but when Huck recognizes them from the temperance meeting, they insist that they were that too.
Their job is to help the poor. They will take Jim up the Ohio into free territory.
Huck decides to go on land in girl's clothes to find out where they are.
Quartette King-Duke-Jim-Huck while they are dressing him up.

5. Mary Jane's house

Spinning song Mary Jane and the girls. (about men). Mary Jane is in mourning.
Huck arrives as a girl who got lost on the river. All the girls feel sorry for her. Mary Jane offers her to stay over night and sleep in her room. The girls leave. Huck alone with Mary Jane, finds out about the heirs etc.
Duet Mary Jane - Huck (with dance?)
While Mary Jane goes to fix the bed, Huck sneaks out, sorry to leave her.

Leah Salisbury
NEW YORK
234 W. 44TH STREET • LACKAWANNA 4-8633

To: S.Perelman, O.Nash, K.Weill, A.Collins, C.Crawford.

From: Leah Salisbury

Subject: ONE TOUCH OF VENUS - U.S.Govt.

November 7, 1949

As I have mentioned to you before, the U.S. Government, Department of the Army, wants permission to produce "One Touch of Venus" in Germany and Austria. After discussing this with Kurt some weeks ago and finding him in favor of such production I studied our contract with Anstey and found that we had no right to proceed in such territory without their consent. I then had Blackburn contact Dr. Miller, and have just received a letter from Blackburn saying Miller will consent, provided they get one percent (1%) royalty.

The government pays $300. advance "when the play is actually produced," against seven percent (7%) of the gross. The 1% to Anstey therefore would leave 6% for you. Also, the government would get the production rights "for four years from the date of the agreement, or the duration of the U.S. occupation of Germany, whichever is the shorter"; and they ask for permission to have typed or printed about 250 copies for their production use.

If you want to okay this production, please write "Yes" on this memo and return it to me at once. I will then send the contracts on to Ogden, Sid and Kurt for signature.

yes. K.W

Sincerely,

Leah

LS:BY MEMBER OF INCORPORATED SOCIETY OF AUTHORS' REPRESENTATIVES

667. The U.S. government, still occupying parts of Germany and Austria, sought permission to perform *One Touch of Venus* there late in 1949 (*Knickerbocker Holiday* had already been performed there under U.S. auspices, and *Lady in the Dark* would be staged in Germany after Weill's death, in 1951). Although Weill approved the production at first, he later revoked his permission, writing, "The more I think about it, the less sure I am that I want *One Touch of Venus* produced in Germany at this time. From all I know about the present status of the German theaters, my impression is that they are in no way equipped to do justice to a piece like *Venus*, and a bad production would do a lot of harm to me. My European reputation is worth more to me than the very negligible amount of money I can make with this production." (7 January 1950, to Leah Salisbury)

Weill (in New City) to Bertolt Brecht, 7 January 1950: I have not heard from you in a very long time. The last time you wrote to me was when you told me that the contract with Felix Bloch Erben had been dissolved and that you intended to hand over the stage representation of *Dreigroschenoper* to Suhrkamp Verlag. I answered you at the time that I would agree to such a solution, provided that I could come to terms with Suhrkamp about the conditions of the contract. I had asked you to see to it that Suhrkamp Verlag sent me a draft of the contract. Unfortunately, I have heard nothing at all either from you or from Suhrkamp. Now I think that we cannot let this situation drag on any longer. The entire legal situation of *Dreigroschenoper* remains unresolved, because I have given orders to Universal Edition not to license any further musical performances until the question of stage representation has been settled, and therefore any further performances of this work are illegal. Dr. Kurt Hirschfeld, who was here in the fall, asked me for the rights for Zurich, and I told him that the Zurich Schauspielhaus would have to make a contract with me personally. However, this could only happen concerning performances outside Germany, whereas performances in Germany have been put on ice altogether until we have contractually agreed on a stage representative.

At that time I had also asked you to let me know whatever happened to my royalties from Munich, and—in case it is still being given there—to whom these royalties are being paid on my behalf. I have never received an answer to this either.

668. A page from Weill's journal for 7–9 January 1950 records progress on *Huckleberry Finn* and notes a rehearsal for *Lost in the Stars* when Todd Duncan had to be replaced by Joseph James.

1 9 5 0

MUSIC + THEATER:	LITERATURE + FILM:	SCIENCE + SOCIETY:	POLITICS:
Frank Loesser *Guys and Dolls*	Ray Bradbury *The Martian Chronicles*	Margaret Mead *Social Anthropology*	Senator Joseph McCarthy advises Truman that the State Department is riddled with Communists
Gian Carlo Menotti *The Consul*	John Hersey *The Wall* (novel about the Warsaw Ghetto)	Albert Einstein *General Field Theory*	Britain recognizes Israel
Arnold Schoenberg *Modern Psalms*	*Sunset Boulevard* (film by Billy Wilder)	1.5 million TV sets in U.S. (one year later approx. 15 million)	Korean War starts

HUCKLEBERRY FINN WILL BE A MUSICAL
BY LAWRENCE PERRY

Confirming today a report that Mark Twain's famous novel, *Huckleberry Finn*, is to be adapted to the stage as a musical comedy, Kurt Weill, famous composer for *Lady in the Dark, One Touch of Venus, Street Scene*, and the current hit, *Lost in the Stars*, said that he and his collaborator, Maxwell Anderson, already had worked out the story line and that within a few days Anderson would start on the book.

Weill, who in Germany before World War II was one of Europe's eminent composers but got into Hitler's bad books through musical plays lampooning the fuehrer, said of the enterprise lying ahead:

"Both Maxwell and I are tremendously excited about the project. It will be Americana with the bark on. That raft upon which Huck floated down the Mississippi will of course be in evidence throughout the play and inevitably the river itself."

"Will you," we asked, "try for another 'Old Man River' number?"

The composer raised his hands with a frown. "That," he said emphatically, "is one of the things I shall carefully avoid. I haven't the slightest desire to compete against that particular song. But, of course, the soul of that great river and its bordering lands will be very much in the musical theme—as naturally, it will be in Maxwell Anderson's book."

In doing a work of this sort, does the composer set his music after reading the libretto, or does the music come first?

"I can see why you ask the question," he replied, "since in this country—not abroad—composers of musical comedies and ballads do the music first with the libertist [*sic*] following after. Personally, I write from Maxwell's script, taking usually a scene at a time; but occasionally two or three scenes. Of course, since the author and I have followed our custom of working out the story together, I know very well what lies ahead and so am in no danger of getting off the narrative motif."

Does he compose with a piano?

"I suppose," he said, "you have Wagner in mind—Wagner who had a desk above the piano keyboard and used the instrument [to make] notes on the desk. No, I use nothing but pencil and paper."

Lost in the Stars, his *Street Scene* score and a short opera, *Down in the Valley*, now much used in schools, come very close to opera. Will he proceed farther in this medium?

"I think not," he said. "The things I have done approximating opera are so close as to render anything further—short of a genuine opera—unnecessary. *Huckleberry Finn*, for instance, will be essentially a light musical comedy."
New York Times, 5 February 1950.

Weill (in New City) to William Henry, 28 January 1950: Thank you very much for your interesting letter of January 16. I agree with you that the performance of *Down in the Valley* by the Lemonade Opera was musically clearer and more interesting in the staging than the television performance of NBC. But you must not forget, after all, that television is a new medium and that the people who are working on it are still trying to find their way and are therefore far from any achievement. The time for rehearsals with cameras is very limited, and the sound men are still accustomed to the old radio rules to keep the orchestra down whenever there is any singing. Looking at it from this point of view, I thought that NBC made a very brave effort to show what opera on television could be, although I can certainly imagine a better performance of my work. I appreciate the progressive spirit behind this effort.

Weill (in New City) to W. Oberer of the Zurich Schauspielhaus, 15 February 1950: I was also greatly surprised to discover in the enclosed letter from Elisabeth Hauptmann to you that *Die Dreigroschenoper* is now handled by the Suhrkamp-Verlag—a fact which was completely unknown to me. As I have explained repeatedly both to you and to Dr. Hirschfeld, I have to insist on personal contracts and on my own terms for the use of the music of *Die Dreigroschenoper* as long as no contract, either with Brecht or with anybody else is in existence, and all my requests to send me such a contract remain unanswered. Therefore I cannot recognize any *Verteilungsschlüssel* [scheme for division of royalties]. Since I have no contract with Brecht, I am not interested in what his royalty is, and it is none of his business what my royalty is.

669. With his sheepdog Wooly, on the lawn at Brook House

670. One of the five numbers Weill drafted for *Huckleberry Finn*, "The Catfish Song."

671. Anderson's typescript of "This Time Next Year" and Weill's draft.

This Time Next Year

This time next year
Will tell a different story;
This time next year
Will shine with a trembling glory!
A stranger will look at me,
And I will look at him
While all the stars grow dim
This time next year!

This time next year
Some not too far-off night-time,
This time next year
The moon will bring the right time.
One certain one will turn
Searching for words to say
~~Who's loved me a year and a day~~ We've come to our magical day —
This time next year!

It's near,
It's almost here—
Maybe this ~~time~~ next year,
This time next year!

This time next year
Without a word of warning,
This time next year
He'll turn and he'll say, "Good ~~-morning!~~"
A stranger will pass this way
And his way will be mine,
And the spring-time will taste like wine,
This time next year!

This time next year
And that will be in May-time,
This time next year
At night-time or in day-time,
One certain one will turn,
Searching for words to say
~~Who's loved me a year and a day~~ We've come to our magical day —
This time next year!

It's near,
It's almost here,
Maybe this time next year,
This time next year!

672. Weill dies suddenly at Flower Hospital in New York City on 3 April 1950 after a slight period of improvement. His body lies in state at Brook House until he is buried two days later without religious rites at Mount Repose Cemetery in Haverstraw, in a plot high on a hill overlooking the Hudson River. The mourners include Lenya, Maurice Abravanel, Max and Mab Anderson, Marc Blitzstein, Marc Connelly, Charles MacArthur and Helen Hayes, Rouben Mamoulian, Erwin Piscator, Jo Révy, Elmer Rice, and Arthur Schwartz. Maxwell Anderson selects an excerpt from "Bird of Passage" from *Lost in the Stars* to be engraved on the tombstone, a song he and Weill once envisioned as part of a "service for those who die without faith, except in man."

From a typewritten transcription of Maxwell Anderson's handwritten diary, transcriber unknown.

Thursday, March 16
Mab and I went to Kurt's, where I read the new scene and new lyrics. Kurt in bed, but had done the "Catfish Song." I left Mab and Lenya at cards.

Friday, March 17
Kurt ill, very ill. Called Lenya, found that Kurt had a very bad night. Doctor came in the morning.
Lenya came in the afternoon. The doctor (Rumstein) had given Kurt an injection to make him sleep. Kurt had oppression round his heart. R. thinks it may be the first sign of coronary. Lenya in tears and we near them. He must rest two weeks.

Saturday, March 18
No work, Kurt ill. Stopped at Kurt's, not wanting to telephone, but Margaret said they weren't up yet. It developed later that Kurt had had a terrible night, coronary pain. Mab frantically trying to get a doctor for Kurt. Martha suggested Weishaar who came and seemed capable. Said it was coronary. Arranged for day and night nurse. Mab and I at Kurt's all afternoon. I saw him for a moment. He looked ghastly.
After dinner Mab, Hep, Bunny and I at Kurt's, sitting with Lenya. At 12 he slept and I came home with Hep. Mab and Bunny will stay with Lenya. The nurses have taken over.

Sunday, March 19
A terrible day. Kurt on the verge.
Went with Mab to Kurt's to confer with doctors. Rumstein, Weishaar and Schraf (?)
Decided to take him to NYC.
Got an ambulance. "Scully/Walton."
Flower Hospital. Kurt in an oxygen tent. Left him there, went to Rumpelmeyer's. Back to Flower. Found Kurt worn. In precarious condition. Mab and Lenya stayed at the hospital.

KURT WEILL
1900 —— 1950

TO TAKE HOLD OF A MOMENT
BY ERWIN PISCATOR

(A poem written on the day of the funeral of Kurt Weill, and given by the author to Lotte Lenya.)

Woeful the air around the house, heavy like an iron chain.
Not ever will his face shine from here again.
Emptiness lies scattered 'round the columns of the porch
where Kurt no longer stands.

Yesterday will merely be another tomorrow.

I look at things the same way as did he;
my sloping glance meets trees—his property.
A cloudy, lowly sky most anxiously is trying to prevent
the cobweb branches sensing the advent of lent.
April and Spring and stillness all are dead
The sky merely a cloth upon the coffin's lid instead.

At 2:30 they announced: it will be half an hour yet.
I saw the face—the coffin and the lid !
Merely half of such an hour yet!

It was, as if through *his* ears I listened to the brook,
the brook from which the house's name he took.
A house, in which not silence reigned,
but founts of wondrous melodies remained
with music as eternal law sustained.
But now the face is still—peacefully restricted in the coffin.
The flower still blooming in his hands
slipping away in yellow sands.—
As if he had lived fifty years, and every hour
had come to end, just to hold this flower—
At the beginning of night.

I groped with *his* hands o'er the grass.—
They did not look as small as they look now.
They now are folded.
Never had I seen these hands this way.
These hands which have held music.
Larger was the hand that now I saw—
almost like part of some place by the forest's cool
which he had shown me a few weeks ago and said:
"This year—we're going to build a swimming pool."

675. Theodor W. Adorno's influential obituary from the *Frankfurter Rundschau*, 15 April 1950, reinforced the "two-Weill" theory. (Excerpt)

KURT WEILL IS BURIED

Maxwell Anderson Speaks at Rites for Noted Composer

Special to THE NEW YORK TIMES.

NEW CITY, N. Y., April 5— Kurt Weill, composer, was buried this afternoon in Mount Repose Cemetery at near-by Haverstraw after a brief ceremony by his friends at his home here on South Mountain Road.

There was no religious service. Maxwell Anderson spoke. He is a next-door neighbor and had been a collaborator with Mr. Weill in several Broadway shows. Mr. Anderson told of Mr. Weill's career and their close association.

Leo Sohn, a brother-in-law, also spoke. Mr. Weill's parents and brother are in Palestine and Mrs. Sohn, the former Ruth Weill, was the only close relative here.

Among those at the burial were Mrs. Maxwell Anderson, Mr. and Mrs. Rouben Mamoulian, Mr. and Mrs. Max Dreyfus, Robert Sherwood, Mr. and Mrs. Elmer Rice, Mrs. Walter Huston, Mark Blitzstein, Charles MacArthur, Arthur Schwartz, Mr. and Mrs. Milton Caniff and Marc Connelly.

673. A report of Weill's funeral appeared in the 6 April 1950 issue of *The New York Times*.

674. Shortly after Weill dies, Lenya writes to his brother Nathan, a doctor living in Israel. Here are her notes derived from Nathan's reply about the cause of death.

> Nathan
>
> coronary trombosis
> Ecg showed extensive
> fresh ant. lateral wall
> infarctio. complications,
> paroxymal auricular
> tachycardia, azotemia,
> death caused by
> cerebral embolism

Kurt Weill — Musiker des epischen Theaters
Von Theodor W. Adorno

Samstag, 15. April 1950

Die Figur des Komponisten, der in Amerika starb, wird vom Begriff des Komponisten kaum recht getroffen. Seine Begabung wie seine Wirkung beruhte weit weniger auf der musikalischen Leistung als solcher, auf Gebilden, die nach Substanz und Faktur für sich selbst bestünden, als auf einem außerordentlichen und originalen Sinn für die Funktion von Musik auf dem Theater. Nicht, daß die seine „dramatisch" gewesen wäre, etwa wie die Verdis. Im Gegenteil: der unterbrechende Charakter seiner Nummern, die eher die Handlung stillstellen als weitertreiben; seine enge Verbindung mit der Idee des „epischen Theaters" fordert die überkommene Vorstellung des Dramatischen heraus. Aber gerade darin lag sein Eigenes. Er hat, wie kaum ein anderer, davon sich Rechenschaft gegeben, daß das Verhältnis von Musik und Szene als einer bloßen psychologischen Verdopplung fragwürdig geworden ist, und er blieb nicht bei der Einsicht stehen, sondern hat, bis zur Selbstpreisgabe, die Konsequenz daraus gezogen. Aus der Not begrenzter Gestaltungskraft hat er die Tugend der Unterordnung unter den Zweck—den artistischen und zu einigem Grade auch den politischen—gemacht. Den Gedanken an den Effekt suchte er zum Prinzip künstlerischer Arbeit selbst umzudenken. Er verkörperte mit Flair, Beweglichkeit und einem sehr spezifischen Ausdruckston einen neuen Typus: den des Musikregisseurs. […]

Er selber hat zunächst über den etwas engen, übrigens keineswegs amerikanischen Songstil hinausgewollt und an großen Opern sich versucht. Die prätentiösenste war die „Bürgschaft". Das Unzulängliche daran hat er wohl gesehen, auch dem Zwang und der Lockung des Exils nachzugeben, ohne sich volle Rechenschaft darüber abzulegen. Ihm verkehrte die geistesgegenwärtige Bereitschaft, Musik als Pointe dem Theater einzufügen, sich zum Konformismus, zur Fügsamkeit schlechthin. Vom Surrealisten blieb wenig übrig; er wurde, mit einer schüchtern verschlagenen Unschuld, die entwaffnete, zum Broadwaykomponisten, mit Cole Porter als Vorbild, und redete sich ein, die Konzessionen an den kommerziellen Betrieb seien keine, sondern lediglich ein Test des „Könners", der auch in standardisierten Grenzen alles vermöchte.

KURT WEILL DEAD; COMPOSER, WAS 50

Wrote Music for 'One Touch of Venus,' 'Lady in the Dark' and Other Broadway Hits

ALSO TURNED OUT OPERAS

'Der Protagonist' and 'Tsar Has Himself Photographed' His Best-Known Works

Kurt Weill, the composer, died at 7 o'clock last night in the Flower-Fifth Avenue Hospital, after an illness of two weeks. He was 50 years old.

Mr. Weill, whose melodies like "September Song" and "Speak Low" won the plaudits of Broadway, and whose more serious musical achievements were hailed in concert halls throughout the world, was exiled from his native Germany on stock Nazi charges of being a "Kultur Bolshevist."

The small composer with the enormous eyes was born in Dessau on March 2, 1900. Under the influence of his father, a cantor, he began to compose while still in primary school.

At the age of 18 he went to Berlin to study with Engelbert Humperdinck, the noted composer of *Hansel and Gretel*. From there he moved to Lüdenscheid in Westphalia, where he became conductor of the opera.

In the early Nineteen Twenties Mr. Weill returned to Berlin to join a group of young artists studying with the pianist and composer Ferruccio Busoni. He continued his studies until 1924, meanwhile composing his works of that period including symphonies and chamber music.

Ballet Started Him on Way

A Russian company that visited Berlin at the time commissioned Mr. Weill to do a children's ballet, and it was in the composition of this work that he adapted his style to the theater, the medium through which he was to attain eventual fame.

In 1926, collaborating with Georg Kaiser, he wrote the opera *Der Protagonist*, which was produced by the Dresden State Opera.

After composing two other operas, *Royal Palace*, with Ivan Goll, and *The Tsar Has Himself Photographed*, again with Herr Kaiser, Mr. Weill joined Bertolt Brecht in 1928 to compose *Die Dreigroschenoper* (*The Threepenny Opera*). It brought international acclaim to the team and ran for more than 2,000 performances in Germany.

With Herr Brecht he wrote several other operas, including *Mahogany* [sic], which also was well received. In 1932 he collaborated again with Herr Kaiser on *The Silver Lake*, which opened simultaneously in eleven German cities. A fantasy, which contained reflections on the fast-growing creed of Nazism and its Fuehrer, the production was followed with an official ban on Mr. Weill's works in Germany.

Mr. Weill and his wife left the Reich for Paris in 1933. There his work included a ballet for Tilly Losch, called *The Seven Deadly Sins*, and a musical play, with Jacques Deval, entitled *Marie Galante*.

Came to U. S. in 1935

From Paris the Weills went to London and in 1935 the composer was brought to America by Max Reinhardt to write the music for *The Eternal Road*. Other Broadway productions for which he was the composer included *Johnny Johnson*, *Knickerbocker Holiday*, *Lady in the Dark*, *One Touch of Venus*, *The Firebrand of Florence* (in which his wife appeared), *A Flag Is Born*, *Street Scene*, *Love Life* and *Lost in the Stars*. The last named opened at the Music Box Theatre on Oct. 30, 1949.

For *Knickerbocker Holiday* and *Lost in the Stars* Maxwell Anderson, who lived near Mr. Weill's home at New City, N. Y., wrote the lyrics. At the end of 1949 they began work on a musical play based on *Huckleberry Finn*. He had completed five songs for the production when he was stricken last month.

The drama critic of The New York Times said of Mr. Weill in 1941: "He is not a song writer but a composer of organic music that can bind the separate elements of a production and turn the underlying motive into song."

For the screen Mr. Weill wrote the music for such films as *You and Me* and *Were Do We Go From Here?* He also was the composer of the folk opera, *Down in the Valley*, with Arnold Sundgaard.

Mr. Weill became a United States citizen in 1943. He was an active member of the Playwrights' Company and the council of the Dramatists' Guild.

In 1928 [sic] Mr. Weill married Lotte Lenya Blamauer, who had been well known on the German operatic and concert stage as Lotte Lenya. She survives, as do his parents, Mr. and Mrs. Albert Weill, who live in Israel.

Music in Review
Kurt Weill
By VIRGIL THOMSON

Kurt Weill, who died last Monday at the age of fifty, was a composer who will be missed. Nothing he touched came out banal. Everything he wrote became in one way or another historic. He was probably the most original single workman in the whole musical theater, internationally considered, during the last quarter century.

His originality consisted in an ability to handle all the forms of the musical theater with freedom, to make them expressive, to build structures with them that serve a story and sustain a play. He was not a natural melodist like Richard Rodgers or George Gershwin, though he turned out some memorable tunes. Nor was he a master of thematic development, though he could hold a long scene together impeccably. He was an architect, a master of musico-dramatic design, whose structures, built for function and solidity, constitute a repertory of models that have not only served well their original purpose but also had wide influence on composers as examples of procedure.

His German Contribution

Weill came to the light musical theater, for which most of his American works were conceived, from a classical training (he was the pupil of Humperdinck and of Busoni) and long experience of the artistic, the experimental theater. His literary collaborators were consistently writers of distinction. Georg Kaiser, Ivan Goll, Bertolt Brecht, Arnold Sundgaard and Maxwell Anderson were among them. Brecht was the librettist of the epoch-making works of his German period—*Der Jasager*, *Die Dreigroschenoper*, and *The Rise and Fall of the City of Mahagonny*. Also of a ballet with words, composed in Paris, *The Seven Deadly Sins*, played in England as *Anna-Anna*.

These works have transformed the German opera. Their simplicity of style and flexibility of form have given, indeed, to present-day Germany its only progressive movement in music. Without them the work of Boris Blacher and Hans [sic] Orff would be inconceivable. Without their example also we would not have had the American Marc Blitzstein's powerful *The Cradle Will Rock* and *No for an Answer*. Whether Weill's American works will carry as far as his German ones I cannot say. They lack the mordant and touching humanity of Brecht's poetry. The also lack a certain acidity in the musical characterization that gave cutting edge to Weill's musical style when he worked in the German language.

His Value to America

Nevertheless, they are important to history. And his last musical play, *Lost in the Stars*, for all that it lacks the melodic appeal of *Mahagonny*, and even of *Lady in the Dark*, is a masterpiece of musical application of dramatic narrative; and its score, composed for twelve players, is Weill's finest work of orchestral craft. His so-called "folk opera," *Down in the Valley*, is not without strength either. Easy to perform and dramatically perfect, it speaks an American musical dialect that Americans can accept. Its artfulness is so concealed that the whole comes off as naturally as a song by Stephen Foster, though it lasts a good half hour.

Weill was the last of our local light theater men to orchestrate his own scores and the last to have full mastery of composition. He could make music move in and out of a play with no effect of shock. He could write a ballet, a song, a complex finale with equal ease. (A successful Broadway composer once asked me, "What is a finale?") These skills may turn up again in our light theater, but for the present they are gone. Or they may be replaced by the ability of Menotti, Blitzstein and other classically trained composers to hold public attention through constructed tragic music dramas. Just at present the American musical theater is rising in power. But its lighter wing has lost in Kurt Weill a workman who might have bridged for us the gap, as he did in Germany, between grand opera and the *singspiel*. The loss to music and to the theater is real. Both will go on, and so will Weill's influence. But his output of new models—and every new work was a new model, a new shape, a new solution of dramatic problems—will not continue. Music has lost a creative mind and a master's hand.

---

676. *The New York Times* published an obituary on 4 April 1950.

677. Composer Virgil Thomson's tribute to Weill appeared in the 9 April 1950 issue of the *New York Herald Tribune*.

THREE EULOGIES BY MAXWELL ANDERSON

At the funeral, 5 April 1950:

A bird of passage out of night
    Flies in at a lighted door,
Flies through and on in its darkened flight
    And then is seen no more.
This is the life of men on earth:
    Out of darkness we come at birth
Into a lamp-lit room and then
    Go forward into dark again.

I think we both believed that, yet Kurt was a happy man, happy in his work, happy in his life with Lenya, happy with his friends and in his hope for our democratic way of life in America. He left Germany forever behind him when Hitler came to power. He didn't even want to speak German. His dreams were in English. This was his country and he was happy in it. This was his countryside, right here, in Rockland County, and nobody was ever happier in this countryside.

He has left a great legacy in his music and in our memory of him.

Forgive me for speaking here. He'd rather just be buried quietly, and if he were alive he'd poke fun at me for saying these things. I'm afraid I say them for myself, not for him. My loss is very great, Lenya's loss is utter and terrifying, the world's loss is even greater, for he'll write no more music. But what he left must be saved, and we who are still here must save it for him. After a while, if we don't falter, the world's memory of him and his work will be like ours.

I say it again: He was a very great man—and as lovable as he was great, as lovable as his own music.

At the memorial concert, 10 July 1950:

This is a memorial concert, as you know, a memorial for a man who died on the third of April, this year. I find these words difficult to write, difficult to say. Kurt Weill was not only my friend and neighbor. We had worked so closely together, had exchanged ideas and criticism so constantly, that in losing him I am crippled and lost.

Something has gone out of this spring for me, and out of this year, that will not return. There is only one thought that comforts me at all—I have sometimes thought I would like to have known great men of genius whose work I especially admired. I would have liked to know John Keats or Franz Schubert, and many others. Well, for fifteen years I had a very great man for my neighbor and friend. How helpful and loving and keen he was as a person the world will never know. That goes when a man dies and cannot be recaptured. But how great Kurt Weill was as a composer of music the world will slowly discover—for he was a much greater musician than anyone now imagines. It takes decades and years and centuries to sift these things out, but it's done in time—and Kurt will emerge as one of the very few who wrote great music. I wish you could have known him—for his wit, his gentleness and the swift intuition that took him to the heart of any subject. That is no longer possible. But he left his music for us, and his music will keep his name and his spirit alive. It will not console us who have lost him—but it will live—long, long after we are forgotten, along with our grief.

In *Theatre Arts* magazine, December 1950, p. 58:

Working with Kurt Weill was one of the pleasantest experiences I have had in the theater, partly because he was a warm and amusing friend, partly because he was the only indisputable genius I have ever known. It's all very well to praise the gigantic musicals that overawe our public and the press agents, but the fact is that nobody before Kurt Weill brought great music to our theater, and it may be a long time before anybody does it again. We have had no other rounded and complete composer, able to help on the book and lyrics, consummate as arranger and orchestrator, bubbling with original and unhackneyed melodies. It's tragic that he's gone and will do no more toward the making of opera for Broadway, which was his dream. It's tragic too that there is nobody of his endowments to take his place. But what he had time to do has such stature, meaning and enchantment that he will be long remembered. I think he will be counted among the great composers.

678. 10,000 people attended a memorial concert at Lewisohn Stadium on 10 July 1950. Maurice Levine conducted highlights from *Lost in the Stars*, the complete *Down in the Valley*, and four of Weill's "popular classics" sung by Todd Duncan: "Green Up Time," "Here I'll Stay," "Speak Low," "September Song." Weill's German works were still largely unknown to American audiences. Olin Downes assessed Weill's American career in a *New York Times* article preceding the concert.

STADIUM PROGRAMS • SEASON OF 1950

THE PHILHARMONIC-SYMPHONY ORCHESTRA

Monday Evening, July 10, at 8:30

(In case of rain this program is postponed until the next clear night)

KURT WEILL MEMORIAL PROGRAM

MAURICE LEVINE, Conductor

TODD DUNCAN, Baritone

in excerpts from

"LOST IN THE STARS"

with

Virginia Paris   Herbert Coleman

Narrator: ALAN JAY LERNER

1. Hills of Ixopo .... Duncan and Chorus
2. Train to Johannesburg .... Chorus
3. Thousands of Miles .... Duncan

(Program continued on page 21)

Steinway is the official piano of the Stadium Concerts

Last minute news of Stadium programs is announced daily over WNYC at 5, 6, and 7 P. M.
WLIB at 7:00; WABF (FM) at 6:00 and 7:00; WQXR at 7:05

The Wednesday evening concerts will be broadcast over WNYC and WNYC-FM

Advance sale tickets may be purchased at the Box Office at Convent Avenue gate during intermission

(Program continued from pages 18 and 19)

4. Little Gray House .... Duncan and Chorus
5. Trouble Man .... Virginia Paris
6. Lost in the Stars .... Duncan and Chorus
7. Big Black Mole .... Herbert Coleman
8. Fear .... Chorus
9. Tixo .... Duncan
10. Stay Well .... Virginia Paris
11. Cry the Beloved Country .... Duncan and Chorus
12. Finale .... Duncan and Chorus

INTERMISSION

Spoken Tribute to Kurt Weill by MAXWELL ANDERSON

"DOWN IN THE VALLEY"

One-Act Folk Opera

Libretto by Arnold Sundgard

with

Elaine Malbin   Victor Clarke, Tenor   Norman Atkins, Baritone   Randolph Symonette, Baritone

Staged by: DINO JAMOPOULOS   Dances by: ANNA SOKOLOFF

POPULAR CLASSICS BY KURT WEILL

TODD DUNCAN

Virginia Paris

1. Green Up Time .... Chorus
    (from "Love Life" — Lyrics by Alan Jay Lerner)
2. Here I'll Stay .... Todd Duncan
    (from "Love Life" — Lyrics by Alan Jay Lerner)
3. Speak Low .... Duncan and Virginia Paris
    (from "One Touch of Venus" — Lyrics by Ogden Nash)
4. September Song .... Todd Duncan
    (from "Knickerbocker Holiday" — Lyrics by Maxwell Anderson)

Musical supervision by: MAURICE LEVINE

(Program continued on page 23)

MEMORIAL TO WEILL

Program Honoring a Man Who Aided U. S. Opera

By OLIN DOWNES

ONE of the most important programs of the present season of the Stadium Concerts is scheduled for to-morrow evening — the memorial program of works by the late Kurt Weill. This program, sadly enough, had been arranged by Weill himself before his death on the third of last April, and it embraces, so far as a single concert may, a number of his most significant achievements.

It is sheer necessity of practical program-making that there cannot be included in this concert passages from "Street Scene," the setting of Elmer Rice's drama, which Weill thought of as an opera of city life as contrasted with "Down in the Valley" as a kind of rustic pendant of American existence.

Rarely Equipped

He came to our popular musical theatre with the rarest sort of equipment. He was a brilliant master of composition and of every practical exigency of the theatre. He was probably the only composer for Broadway who knew how to orchestrate and who composed with an authority and dexterity entirely unmatched in this field. Weill had a strong, if not most distinguished, melodic gift. He was fascinated, as this writer well knows, by American popular song and folk song of all sorts, at the same time that he knew perfectly his Schoenberg and his Puccini. He has created sheer tunes which have become almost classics of their kind, and he has written for the stage with a technic and imagination and heart which make him one of the central figures in the development of an American form of opera.

679. Lenya preserved Weill's study after his death. On the desk is a freshly written, non-autograph score of "River Chanty." For the next thirty years she would work tirelessly to promote Weill's music in both Europe and America.

APPENDIX

The appendix contains English translations for most of the foreign-language documents reproduced as facsimiles as well as the original language for documents in the main text that have been translated into English. The following people contributed translations: Christopher Hailey, Stephen Hinton, Elmar Juchem, Stephen Kampmeier, Kim Kowalke, Dave Stein, and Lys Symonette.

CHAPTER 1

Emma Weill erinnert sich… (1955)
Es war der erste März u. es war der Freudentag „Purim" bei den Juden genannt, u. da es der Geburtstag meiner seligen Mutter war, bin ich jedes Jahr mit einem unserer Kinder nach Hause gefahren, obgleich es eine sehr weite Reise gewesen war. In diesem Jahr war der liebe Kurt an der Reihe, u. der war ein süßer Reisegenosse und voller Freude. Doch als es dann Abend wurde u. die Kinder der kleinen Stadt mit allerhand Masken und Allotria unsere Wohnung bestürmen, wie das so Sitte war, hat sich der l.[iebe] Kurt gefürchtet; er war 5 Jahre u. hatte furchtbare Angst bekommen u. hat geweint u.s.w. Als ich ihm das ernstlich verboten hatte u. böse war, stürzte meine Mutter auf mich zu, nahm mir den Kurt aus der Hand u. rief ganz laut: „Das Kind rührst Du mir nicht an, der ist etwas Besonderes."

Und in diesem Haus, das nebst der riesengroßen Synagoge ein Geschenk an die jüd. Gemeinde von der Baronin v. Cohn-Oppenheim in Dessau gewesen war, nebst einem großen Gebäude für alle Gesellschaften. Da konnte dann der l. Kurt seine fleißigen und glücklichen Jugendjahre verbringen, und die interessanten Menschen, die sich um unsere Familie sammelten, hatten auch sehr viel an Kurts Entwicklungen teilgenommen. Ich will noch eine Bemerkung einschalten, daß der Kurt ein *äußerst* gewissenhafter Schüler gewesen ist u. besonders die herrlichsten und interessantesten Aufsätze verfaßte. Und daß die 3 Jungens überhaupt in der Schule sehr beliebt waren u. nachdem wir einen Smoking besorgt hatten, regelmäßig abwechselnd die Schülerkonzerte dirigierten. . . . Die Schüler nannten ihn immer den *Musikerappel*.

Und nun schreibe ich von seinem ersten Klavierunterricht bei unserem l.[ieben] Vater, der aber bald durch eine junge Französin, die in Leipzig Musik studierte, unterbrochen wurde, bis er dann Bing als Lehrer bekam. . . . Wie glücklich der Junge war, als es uns dann möglich war, einen herrlichen Flügel zu kaufen."

Es war so weit, daß wir als Eltern uns entschließen mußten, ob Kurt Musik studieren soll. Unser l.[ieber] Vater wollte, daß er nebenbei noch Medizin studieren soll, der Sicherheit halber. Da kamen aber Nathan und Hanns u. haben gebettelt: „Vater, laß ihn doch Musik studieren, wir werden schon helfen. Der Nathan wird ein tüchtiger Arzt und ich, der Hanns, werde ein sehr tüchtiger Kaufmann und Commerzienrath, u. wir werden den Kurt schon durchbringen."

Dr. Willy Krüger erinnert sich… (1984)
Unsere Schule war die Herzogliche Friedrichs-Oberrealschule, in einem Gebäude mit dem Herzoglichen Friedrichs-Gymnasium untergebracht. Weill und ich waren Klassenkameraden von 1909 bis 1917. Kurt war ein sehr begabter Schüler. Allerdings nie ein Streber, er belegte viele Jahre den vierten bis sechsten Platz in der Klasse, das genügte ihm. Während wir nach dem Unterricht oft zum Sport gingen, Fußball oder Völkerball spielten, übte Kurt fast an jedem Nachmittag drei oder vier Stunden Klavier oder Orgel. Kurt galt alsbald in der Schule als Musikspezialist, und unser Musiklehrer, August Theile—der auch den Schulchor und das Schulorchester leitete—erkannte ebenfalls schon früh sein Talent. Ich erinnere mich an ein Schulkonzert 1916, bei dem der Schulchor auch einige von Kurt komponierte Kriegschöre sang. Sein Bruder Nathan dirigierte dabei den Chor.

In der zehnten Klasse mußten wir uns alle in einem sogenannten „Rede-Akt" üben, bei dem wir vor der Klasse dreißig Minuten lang über ein selbstgewähltes Thema frei zu sprechen hatten. Kurt entschied sich für den Komponisten Felix Mendelssohn-Bartholdy, worauf Theile ihm eine ganze Stunde einräumte und den Vortrag in der Aula vor allen Schülern der oberen Klassen arrangierte. Alle waren äußerst beeindruckt von Kurts Vortrag, und auch davon, wie er seine Ausführungen am Klavier durch Beispiele aus Mendelssohns Musik begleitete. Zu dieser Zeit, es muß wohl Ende 1916 gewesen sein, schickte Kurt auch seine ersten Kompositionen an einen Musikverlag in Leipzig. Der Verlag (ich erinnere mich nicht mehr, welcher es war) antwortete, die Musik sei sehr interessant, man meine aber in Anbetracht des jugendlichen Alters des Einsenders, es sei wohl angebracht, noch einige Jahre mit der Publikation zu warten.

Kurt war auch sehr belesen, er kannte die meisten Bücher in der Bibliothek seines Vaters. Unser Deutschlehrer, Dr. Preitz, war ein begeisterter Bibliophile. So beauftragten wir Kurt vor schwierigen Stunden, besonders wenn eine Arbeit anstand, den Lehrer doch zunächst abzulenken, was mehrfach gelang. Bei Stundenbeginn meldete sich Kurt und fragte Dr. Preitz nach dieser oder jener besonderen Klassiker-Ausgabe. Der Lehrer ließ sich nur zu gern auf solchen Spezialdisput ein und vergaß darüber manchmal, die anstehenden Hausaufgaben zu prüfen.

Einige Male lud Kurt uns auch in die Synagoge ein. Ich erinnere mich, ihm so manche Stunde beim Orgel-Üben zugehört zu haben. Einen besonders beeindruckenden Besuch bewahre ich im Gedächtnis. Dabei durften wir an einem jüdischen Fest teilnehmen, dem Laubhüttenfest. Wenn ich die Augen schließe, sehe ich heute noch ein Bild lebendig vor mir: Wie nämlich die ganz Familie Weill zusammen durch einen der großen Dessauer Parks spazierte: der Kantor (stets mit dem Hut auf dem Kopfe, auch im Hochsommer), voller Harmonie und Unbeschwertheit im angeregtesten Gespräch mit seiner Frau und den vier Kindern.

Dr. Werner Spielmeyer erinnert sich… (1984)
Ja, es stimmt, daß Weill Kriegschöre komponiert hat. Wie Ihnen bekannt ist, führte der Erste Weltkrieg zu einer großen nationalistischen Gefühlswelle in Deutschland. Als Jungen von vierzehn Jahren waren wir alle, auch Kurt, in unserer politischen Unerfahrenheit damals angesteckt vom „nationalen Geist", der in Deutschland umging, und wollten alles in unseren Kräften stehende tun, um auch „dabei" sein zu können. Der ganze Unterricht in der Schule richtete sich auf nationalistische Themen aus. Alles „typisch Deutsche" wurde in den Himmel gehoben: in Sprache, Literatur, Kunst, sogar in der Musik. So wurden wir darauf vorbereitet, den Dienst für Kaiser und Vaterland anzutreten.

Alle Jungs traten dem „Dessauer Feldkorps" bei, einer Organisation nach Art der Pfadfinder, natürlich in nationalem Geiste, wo wir unter Leitung des Lehrers Gerlach Kriegs-Geländespiele übten. Wie erhielten Uniformen, es gab verschiedene Ränge wie „Hilfskornett", „Feldwart" und „Kundschafter". Kurt war Kundschafter. Neben den Übungen, die zumeist am Wochenende stattfanden, veranstalteten wir auch manchmal öffentliche Abende, bei denen vorgetragen, rezitiert und gesungen wurde. Ich besitze noch den Programmzettel eines solchen Abends, vom Januar 1915 im Saal des Restaurants „Zentrale". Dabei trat Kurt als Klavierbegleiter auf. Als erste Nummer nach der Pause kam „Für uns". Das war wohl der erste öffentliche musikalische Auftritt von Kurt Weill überhaupt, damals war er noch keine fünfzehn Jahre alt.

1915/16 wurden die ersten Schüler zur Armee einberufen. Wenig später kamen dann auch die ersten Gefallenenmeldungen. Bei den Trauerfeiern in der Schule sprach zumeist Kurt als Vertreter der Schüler. Dabei fand er stets die passenden Worte.

Weill (in Dessau) an Nathan und Hanns Weill, 22. März 1917: Im ersten Teil der Woche hatte ich mit Proben, Stundengeben u.s.w. kolossal zu tun; dazu war immer schlechtes Wetter, sodaß die Laune gerade nicht sehr gut war. Dienstag war eine furchtbar lächerliche „Kriegsanleihenfeier" (Dr. Wichtig natürlich). Donnerstag um 19 Uhr bin ich dann mit Fr. Feuge nach Cöthen gefahren; Bing wollte durchaus mit, da ich ihm den „Liebestod" sehr schön vorgespielt hatte; er wollte sogar im Ernst abends zurücklaufen. In Cöthen habe ich bei Thormeyers wieder wunderbar gespeist. Grüne Erbsen mit Salzkartoffeln und 2 Spiegeleiern (in Butter) u. wunderbaren Schokoladenpudding. Nachmittags habe ich dann im Saal noch allein geübt, war dann im Café, bei Hofgaardens[?] und um 9 gings los. Das Konzert war gut besucht und ich wurde gleich bei meinem Auftreten (ich machte den Anfang) tüchtig beklatscht. Ich habe—ohne Selbstüberhebung—sehr gut gespielt, besonders meine auswendigen Sachen, den Liebestod u. die Jensen Liederbegleitungen, bei denen der Applaus eher mir als Fr. Feuge galt. Ich habe kolossalen Applaus gehabt, besonders beim *Tristan*. Nach dem „Grieg" wurde mir ein riesiges Blumenbukett überreicht, von Herrn Thormeyer; nett, was? Daraufhin musste ich dreimal herauskommen. Das Konzert hatte auch im übrigen grossen Beifall, am meisten natürlich Fr. Feuge, die so viel Blumen gekriegt hatte, wie sie kein Dessauer Blumengeschäft auftreiben kann. Wir waren dann noch in kleinem, gemütlichen Kreise beisammen. Thormeyers, Bankewitzens, Fr. Feuge u. ich; es gab Kaffee u. Kuchen und nachher wunderbaren Sekt; um 12h sind wir heim gegangen, wo es noch einmal Abendbrot gab; um 1/2 2 bin ich zu Bett gegangen, um 3/4 5 aufgestanden (die erste Nacht, in der ich keine Minute geschlafen habe!), um 3/4 6 ging mein Zug, da ich unmöglich schon wieder die Schule schwänzen konnte. Nun könnt Ihr Euch denken, daß ich heute todmüde bin. Auf die Kritik bin ich natürlich sehr gespannt. Sie kommt wieder in den *Staatsanzeiger.* Nebenbei habe ich 40,- M. gekriegt. Das Rittergut ist bald fertig.

Weill (in Dessau) an Hanns Weill, 30. März 1917: Hier in der Schule ist—ähnlich wie im Herbst 16 bei der Musterung der 98er—ziemliche Aufregung; denn gestern Abend stand die Ausmusterung der 99er in der Zeitung; es geht nächste Woche los, Ostern wird ausgesetzt, sodaß du, lieber Hans, Mittwoch den 11. IV. daran kommst. Du müßtest dich demnach dort erkundigen, ob es ratsam wäre, dich in Halberstadt oder hier mustern zu lassen, u. darüber deine Entschlüsse treffen. Doch darüber wird dir Vater noch schreiben. Jedenfalls hoffe ich, daß du dich durch nichts einschüchtern lassen wirst, und daß du deine bekannte große Klappe tüchtig gebrauchen wirst u. den Herrn Ärzten einen tüchtigen Bären aufbindest; du darfst nur auf keinen Fall Soldat werden! Verstanden?—Rührt Euch! — …

Ich habe eine sehr schöne vierstimmige Fuge geschrieben; Herrn Köhler war sie natürlich wieder zu modern, zu chromatisch, aber er konnte keinen Fehler entdecken u. gab zu, daß „viel musikalisches Zeug drin steckt." Ich hatte mir gerade bei der Arbeit vorgenommen, recht einfach zu schreiben; ich kriege es aber nicht fertig; ob das ein gutes Zeichen ist? Jetzt arbeite ich an vier größeren Fugen über „Danket dem Herrn, denn er ist freundlich, seine Güte währt ewiglich," außerdem will ich in den Ferien ein Kanon für 2 Frauenstimmen mit einfacher Klavierbegleitung schreiben, das ich Fr. Feuge versprochen habe; ich habe aber noch keinen geeigneten Text.

Weill (in Dessau) an Hanns Weill, 17. April 1917: Ich hatte auch Klavierstunde und zwar eine sehr interessante. Nach den Etüden (ich habe die erste von Moscheles angefangen), kamen wir auf das Orchester zu sprechen; ich soll nun ernstlich mit Partiturlesen beginnen; zu diesem Zwecke zeigte er mir Stellen aus der *Tristan*-Partitur; dabei verzögerten wir uns so, daß wir die Fortsetzung der Stunde auf Montag verschieben mussten. . . . *Hänsel u. Gretel* war einfach herrlich. Obwohl Humperdinck ganz nach Wagnerschem Vorbild arbeitet, sowohl in der Durcharbeitung der Themen als auch in der Instrumentation (er gehört ja, wie mir Bing erzählte, zu den begeistersten [sic] Anhängern und Mitarbeitern Bayreuths, ist Cosimas bester Freund und soll sogar das meiste an Siegfried Wagners Machwerken geschaffen haben), so geht er doch in der Wahl der Themen und im ganzen Aufbau neue, vorbildliche Bahnen. . . . Auf höchsten Wunsch seiner Hoheit mußte die Hexe als Fee erscheinen, damit die Kinder sich nicht fürchteten. Das wirkte furchtbar lächerlich, ebenso wie der Schluß, in den Humperdinck, um sich beim Herzog anzuschleißen, den Dessauer Marsch eingeflochten hat; das verdirbt den ganzen Effekt des herrlichen Schlußchores. . . .

Gestern nachmittag hatte ich nun wieder Stunde. Um Schlüssel lesen zu lernen, hat mir Bing vierstimmige Chöre von Bach mitgegeben, die in 4 verschiedenen Schlüsseln geschrieben sind, von denen ich nur den Baßschlüssel kenne. Ich muß in jeder Stunde einige vorspielen, „aber nur, wenn mein jüdisches Herz nicht beleidigt würde durch die kirchlichen Choräle." Dadurch komme ich nun sehr schön ins Partiturlesen hinein. . . .

Weill (in Dessau) an Hanns Weill, [20. April 1917]: Morgens bin ich immer bis 1/2 12 in der Schule—ich habe bis jetzt noch nicht gefehlt, da ich in Mathematik u. Physik tüchtig aufpassen muß—nachmittags arbeite ich privat u. abends bin ich meistens im Theater. Freitag abend war ein sehr schönes Konzert. Dem Bachkonzert war Mikorey natürlich wieder nicht gewachsen. Dagegen hat er die Romantische Symphonie v. Bruckner sehr schön herausgebracht. Ich habe durch Partiturlesen u. Durcharbeiten des Klavierauszuges, den mir Bing mitgegeben hat, das Werk ziemlich genau kennen gelernt als eine der schönsten Symphonien. . . .

Ich glaube, eine anständige *Tristan* Aufführung wird für mich immer ein Erlebnis sein. So viel steckt wohl in keiner Opernpartitur weiter; so kann man sich wohl in keine Musik weiter hineinversenken beim Anhören und Hineinknien beim Einstudieren und darstellen. Gestern abend war ich zur *Verlorenen Tochter* von Ludw. Fulda. Um Mutter einmal mit hineinzubringen, habe ich eine List gebraucht: Ich habe an der Theaterkasse einen Parkettsitz gekauft u. habe gesagt, Ruth hätte ihn in der Schule für 1 M. gekriegt. Ruth u. ich waren Stehplatz. Das Stück ist ein sehr nettes, ziemlich freies Lustspiel, bei dem wir viel lachten.

Weill (in Dessau) an Hanns Weill, 1. Mai 1917: Ich bin gespannt, ob er die Chordirigiererei lange aushalten wird, da es, wie er mir sagte, sehr anstrengend ist, in einer Schar von Leuten zu stehen u. die auf sich losbrüllen zu lassen; auch hat er noch niemals einen Chor dirigiert. Sonntag hat er mir die letzte Stunde vorläufig gegeben. Ich habe die 1. Webersonate aufgekriegt, schön aber schwer; ausserdem muss ich nach verschiedenen Büchern die

Holzbläser ganz genau studieren, Schlüssel lesen u. sehr fleissig Moscheles-Etüden arbeiten; habe also ganz schön zu tun. Das Kanon ist bald fertig; ich habe im Ausarbeiten desselben viel Vergnügen u. Freude gehabt, da die Begleitung zu meiner Überraschung ganz kontrapunktisch u. orchestral geworden ist. Ich glaube, ich komme dem Begriff des Orchesters allmählich immer näher.

Weill (in Dessau) an Hanns Weill, Mitte Mai 1917: Mäkke quängelt stundenlang an mir herum, ich soll meinen Vortrag halten; dabei habe ich ihn kaum angefangen. Daß ich über Mendelssohn-Bartholdy sprechen muß, weißt du wohl? Ich habe mir dazu ein sehr schönes Buch aus der Sammlung *Aus Natur und Geisteswelt*: „Die deutsche Blütezeit der musikalischen Romantik" v. Edgar Istel gekauft. Ich werde mich besonders über die Fragen Mendelssohn-Wagner u. Mendelssohn als Jude vorbereiten (er hat natürlich musikalisch so wenig jüdisches wie Mozart). . . .

Neben den üblichen, klaviertechnischen- u. Schlüsselleseübungen machen wir jetzt folgendes: Wir nehmen irgend eine Opernpartitur u. den Klavierauszug dazu; dann spielt zuerst Bing aus dem Auszug u. ich dirigiere aus der Partitur, nachher umgekehrt; so hat er mir jetzt für zu Haus die 1. Szene von Fidelio aufgegeben: 1). aus der Partitur zu spielen, 2). zu dirigieren und zwar ganz genau mit jedem Einsatz auf der Bühne u. im Orchester u. jeder Steigerung. Du kannst dir denken, was mir das für Spaß, aber auch für Mühe macht. . . .

Haben deine Friedenshoffnungen sich gebessert? Gestern haben wir ganz plötzlich 4 St. franz. Aufsatz geschrieben. La guerre sous-marine allemande. Große Scheiße!

Weill (in Dessau) an Hanns Weill, 16. Mai 1917: Montag halte ich meinen Vortrag, den ich dir dann schicken werde. Ich werde als Erläuterungen das Scherzo aus dem *Sommernachtstraum* und etwas aus einem Oratorium spielen. Außerdem muß ich zu Freitag eine geschichtliche Novelle von Gottfr. Keller lesen u. erzählen. Dann muß ich das Schülerorchester (?) u. den Männerchor reorganisieren. Das letztere wird mir vielleicht gelingen. Ich glaube, daß an einem Männerchor ziemliche Beteiligung sein wird. . . .

Bei Köhler habe ich ein kleines Streichquartett angefangen, natürlich noch ganz einfach.

Weill (in Dessau) an Hanns Weill, [16.] Juni 1917: Was sagst du zum *Palestrina*? Ich habe eine große, sehr interessante Rezension aus der Frankfurter Zeitung vom 15. u. 16. d.[es] M.[onats] gelesen, die sich Bing von Bömly geholt hat. Es scheint ja wirklich etwas ganz Gewaltiges zu sein, denk einmal 24 große Männergesangsrollen! Und vor allen Dingen scheint es auch wegweisend zu sein: Weg von der übermodernen Chromatik, zurück zum Wagner der *Meistersinger*! Allerdings bezeichnet es Paul Bekker als das letzte, höchst vergeistigte Werk der musikalischen Romantik, als den Abschluß einer großen Musikepoche. Ob das wohl stimmt? Jedenfalls ist es dem bescheidenen Pfitzner nun doch endlich gelungen, die ihm gebührende Achtung im deutschen Musikleben zu erringen, obwohl es über ein paar Aufführungen mit wenig allgemeinem Erfolg kaum hinauskommen wird.

Weill (in Dessau) an Hanns Weill, 26. Juni 1917: Die Gedichte v. Fr. Werfel (ist er Jude?) sind wirklich gut. Bing riet mir zwar von einer Komposition ab, ich will es aber doch versuchen; es würde vielleicht meine erste „philosophische Komposition" à la *Palestrina* werden.

Weill (in Dessau) an Hanns Weill, 20. August 1917: Ach, ich möchte jetzt so ein nettes kleines Zimmer haben, in Berlin, in Leipzig, in München, und ein Schrank voll Partituren u. Büchern u. Klavierauszügen u. Notenpapier u. arbeiten, daß die Schwarte knackt u. einmal ohne Hausvatersorgen, ohne Schulkram, ohne Einberufungssorgen hintereinander aufschreiben, was mir meinen Kopf manchmal fast bersten macht u. nur Musik hören u. nur Musik sein. Ja, ja, was man so alles will, u. Herr Hindenburg macht nicht mit. Aber du brauchst nicht denken, daß ich nun den Kopf immer so hängen lasse u. alles schwarz sehe. Nein, erstens glaube ich ja immer noch, daß der Krieg dieses Jahr noch aufhört, glaube ja immer noch, daß „Wenn die Not aufs Höchste steigt, Gott der Herr die Hand uns reicht."

Weill (in Dessau) an Hanns Weill, [Januar 1918]: Nun habe ich nur noch eine Angst: daß mir das Abitur bei meinen Konzerten dazwischenkommt. Ich gebe nämlich mit Fr. Feuge Abschiedskonzerte in Cöthen, wo ich auch Solo spiele (Türkischer Marsch, Raff u. Perpetuum mobile), u. wenn Mikorey nicht dazwischenpfuscht, hier, wo auch von 2 Damen das *Maikaterlied* gesungen werden soll. Ich muß allerdings mächtig hinterher sein beim letzteren u. muß das Kanon auch selbst einstudieren. Aber das macht ja mehr Spaß als Abitur. . . . Die Brahms Sonate macht schöne Fortschritte; den 1. schwersten Satz bewältige ich fast.

Weill (in Dessau) an Hanns Weill, [19. März 1918]: Endlich komme ich dazu, Dir einen genauen Bericht über meinen Berliner Aufenthalt zu geben. . . . Montag früh bin ich dann stundenlang herumgelaufen, um einen Platz zu *Salome* am Dienstag zu bekommen; es war aber nichts zu machen. Dienstag früh bin ich dann nochmal an die Kasse gegangen u. habe einen Sitzplatz 4. Rang 1. Reihe bekommen. Meine Freude kannst Du Dir denken. Es war denn auch der höchste Genuß, den ich bis jetzt überhaupt gehabt habe. *Salome* ist das genialste musikalische Werk, das Du Dir denken kannst. So gut wie garnicht leitmotivisch, sondern in echt Straußischer Art nur auf Klangwirkungen berechnet, die so meisterlich malen, daß mir auch nicht der zarteste Moment der Handlung entging, obwohl ich doch keine Ahnung davon hatte u. auch wenig Text zu verstehen war. So kommen Eindrücke zustande, die einen in einen förmlichen Rausch versetzen u. am Schluß konnte ich nichts tun, als „Strauß" zu rufen u. immer wieder „Strauß", bis er endlich kam u. mit ganz bescheidener Geste den Erfolg des Abends der Kemp zuschrieb, die auch wirklich eine Salome gab, wie sie unmöglich besser gegeben werden kann. Daß das Riesenorchester (20 I.Viol!) unter Strauß selbst wunderbar spielte, kannst Du Dir denken.

CHAPTER 2

Weill (in Berlin) an Hanns Weill, 2. Mai 1918: Ich sitze hier in dem schönen Lesezimmer der Hochschule, um Dir für Deine verschiedenen Nachrichten zu danken. . . . Ich habe mich nun schon soweit hier eingewöhnt, daß sich schon allmählich der jüdische Zug in mir, die Kritiksucht, zu regen beginnt. So fand ich heute nach der 2. Stunde, daß der Klavierunterricht bei dem alten Heymann ziemlich minderwertig ist; . . . Einige ganz nette Kommilitonen habe ich gefunden, die mir in manchem wie freie Improvisation, Kontrapunkt u.a. überlegen sind, in anderem wieder wie Klavierspiel, Partitur, Orgel, Dirigieren u. Theorie nicht an mich heranreichen. Sie kommen meistens von berühmten Lehrern wie Paul Ertl, Leop. Schmidt u.s.w.

Weill (in Berlin) an Hanns Weill, 9. Mai 1918: Ich habe nun schon zweimal beim alten Humperdinck Unterricht gehabt. Zum 1. Mal war ich in die Wohnung bestellt u. fuhr dann auch an einem strahlenden Maimorgen hinaus nach dem idyllischen Wannsee, wo H. eine herrliche Villa, in einem großen Park hat. Das Mädchen kannte schon meinen Namen u. führte mich durch die Diele, wo mir ein heller, eichener Flügel auffiel, ins Musikzimmer. Der Meister war noch sehr krank, war nur meinetwegen aufgestanden u. konnte kaum japsen; auf dem Flügel lag eine neue Opernpartitur von ihm im Manuskript. Er fragte mich nach diesem u. jenem, gab mir einige Aufgaben, dann konnte ich mich trollen. Gestern kam er dann in die Hochschule, gab mir neue Aufgaben u. sagte mir, ich solle ihn in der nächsten Stunde eine Skizze meines Streichquartetts zeigen; ich habe es gleich herausgekramt u. arbeite nun daran. . . . Obwohl die Herren Professoren ziemlich abfällig von ihm reden, bin ich ganz zufrieden mit der Sache u. hoffe, daß ich, wenn ich arbeite, bei ihm mindestens so viel lerne wie bei Herrn Prof. Koch, mit dessen Oper das Deutsche Opernhaus seine liebe Not hat. Und jedenfalls bedeutet es schon etwas, überhaupt bei Humperdinck gewesen zu sein.

Auf der Universität habe ich schon 2 herrliche Vorlesungen gehört. In Dessoirs „Philosophie der Kunst" ist für mich jedes Wort eine Offenbarung u. auch Cassirers Abhandlung über die Philosophie der Griechen folge ich mit viel Freude u. Interesse. Roethe (Literaturgeschichte von 1830 an) u. Reich (Antikes Drama) lesen noch nicht. Es ist doch eine schöne Sache, den vollständig eigenartigen Gedankengängen dieser erlauchten Geister folgen zu können. Da gehen einem ganz neue Gedankenwelten, neue Begriffe u. neue Anregungen auf. Und doch ist es mit dem Studentenleben eine komische Sache; die richtige Befriedigung kann man dabei wohl kaum finden, weil man niemals weiß, wofür man arbeitet u. weil man vor allen Dingen nicht regelmäßig genug arbeitet. G.s.D. ist das bei dem Musikstudium nicht in dem Maße der Fall, obwohl man auch hier fast ganz auf sich selbst angewiesen ist u. ich bis jetzt auch hierin noch nicht die richtige innere Befriedigung finde; das ist aber auch nach einem 14tägigen Studium kaum möglich.

Weill (in Berlin) an Hanns Weill, Anfang Juni 1918: Eine Freistunde in der Hochschule benutze ich dazu, deinen Brief zu beantworten, mit dem ich mich riesig freute. Wenn du nochmal meinen Titel „stud mus et phil" in den Dreck deiner Spötterei ziehst, kannst du dich auf eine Forderung gefasst machen, alter Kaufmannsstift du!—Von meinem „1. Auftreten in der Reichshauptstadt" darfst du dir keine übertriebenen Begriffe machen. Es ist ein Schülerkonzert von 14 Nummern mit 3 Begleitern, u. etwas außergewöhnliches ist es höchstens, weil es 1). das Abschlußkonzert des Sternschen Konservatoriums für dieses Semester ist, weil ich 2). der jüngste bin, u. weil es 3). das 1. Mal ist, daß einer, der nicht vom Sternschen ist u. dazu noch Hochschüler, dort begleitet. Daß 3 Begleiter hier sind ist für mich eine Ehrung; denn daran sehe ich, daß Rothmühl mich nicht in der Not nimmt, weil er mich unbedingt braucht, sondern weil ich etwas kann.– Ob das Streichquartett schon fertig ist, kann nur so ein unwissender Laie wie du fragen; ich bin froh, dass ich gestern Humperdinck die fertige Partitur des 1. Satzes zeigen konnte, nachdem ich die letzten Tage wie ein Blödsinniger geschuftet hatte. Es ist ein etwas getragener, aber sehr leidenschaftlicher Satz, mit folgenden Themen: 1). Hauptthema: [siehe Faksimile] Der 2. Satz, an dem ich jetzt arbeite, ist ein schneller Satz, den ich „Nachtstück" überschreiben will, pp, sehr schnell, mit viel Pizzikato u. chromatischer Umkleidung der Hauptmelodie u. folgende Themen: [siehe Faksimile] Als 3. Satz werde ich auf H.'s Rat ein langsames Intermezzo wählen u. zum Schluß das übliche Presto.

Weill (in Dessau) an Hanns Weill, 9. August 1918: So leicht ich in Berlin gearbeitet habe, so schwer geht es nun hier in dieser öden Umgebung. Da sieht man eben, wie sehr ich noch von der Anregung von seiten des Lehrers, der Mitschüler, der Oper u. Konzerte abhängig bin. Ob ich es wohl zu wahrer Kunst im Schaffen bringen kann, solange ich das nicht abstreife? Na, daß ich kein zweiter Schubert oder Beethoven werde, wissen wir ja u. die anderen haben, glaube ich, größtenteils auch an dieser „Krankheit" gelitten.

Weill (in Berlin) an Hanns Weill, 8. November 1918: Obwohl es kaum anzunehmen ist, daß dieser Brief in Deine Hände gelangt, will ich ihn doch nicht ungeschrieben lassen. Es ist ja nun glücklich durch die unglaubliche Einfalt der Melechs soweit gekommen, daß man heute jede Minute mit dem Ausbruch der Empörung hier rechnen muß. Ich weiß nicht, ob Ihr noch Zeitungen bekommt u. ob Du über alles informiert bist. Berlin ist nach außen hin vollständig abgeschlossen, u. da ich keine Nachricht von zu Haus habe, wollte ich Dich bitten, Sonntag nachmittag oder Montag früh einmal zu versuchen, mich anzuklingeln. Nach dem lauten Jubel über den bevorstehenden Abschluß des Waffenstillstandes ist noch am selben Abend die ungeheure Spannung u. Nervosität gefolgt, die, durch die Vorgänge in den norddeutschen Städten erregt u. durch die Vorsichtsmaßregeln der Polizei erhöht, nun von Minute zu Minute wächst, besonders nach dem Ultimatum an den Kaiser. Die Ordnung wurde bis jetzt so gewaltsam aufrecht erhalten, daß man fürchten muß, daß es, wenn es doch losgeht, eine der gewaltigsten Evolutionen [sic] der Geschichte werden wird. Aber die Hauptsache: Das Ende des Weltkrieges. . . . Die Suite macht langsame Fortschritte u. wird mehr als Studie denn als Opus geschaffen.

Weill (in Berlin) an Hanns Weill, 12. November 1918: Ich habe in den letzten Tagen Unbeschreibliches erlebt, unbeschreiblich besonders auch, weil es noch zu frisch ist. Die große Revolution am Sonnabend brach mit so elementarer Gewalt u. so fabelhafter Geschwindigkeit los, daß man es wohl draußen im Land garnicht begreifen kann. Ich war schon die ganze Nacht vorher unterwegs u. habe da schon gemerkt, wie glänzend alles vorbereitet war. Freilich waren da nur Vorsichtsmaßregeln gegen die Revolution zu sehen. Am Sonnabend war ich den ganzen Tag am Reichstag, habe die Überrumpelung der Kasernen, die Bildung der A.[rbeiter]- u. S.[oldaten]-Räte, die Umzüge, die Reden Liebknechts, Hoffmanns, Ledebours u. a.—u. schließlich abends das schwere Gefecht am Marstall erlebt. Auch bei der regelrechten Schlacht gestern am Reichstag war ich dabei. Die Offiziere verteidigen sich mit Hilfe unterirdischer Gänge mit solcher Tapferkeit, daß sie bis jetzt unbesiegt sind u. die Nacht wieder tüchtig schießen werden. Die Universität ist geschlossen u. ich würde mich gern dem A.- u. S.-Rat zur Verfügung stellen. Doch ist die Hochschule noch offen. Ich könnte Bände schreiben. Bin aber zu müde.

Weill (in Berlin) an Hanns Weill, 15. November 1918: Manchmal kann ich es garnicht glauben, daß nun die Waffen gänzlich ruhen, daß alles so anders gekommen ist, daß ich nun nicht mehr dieses dunkle Etwas der Einziehung in der Zukunft Schoß zu fürchten habe und—daß ich nicht mehr königlicher Generalmusikdirektor werden kann. Die Revolution ist nun auch hier in ruhige Bahnen gelenkt worden, u. einige hervorragende, vollständig vertrauenswürdige Männer haben die Zügel in die Hand genommen. Alles wäre gut, wenn man nicht eines fürchten müßte: Daß wir statt einer Diktatur der Aristokratie nun eine Diktatur des Proletariats kriegen können. Freilich ist das nur das Ziel der Spartakusgruppe; aber die bürgerlichen Parteien haben sich hier in Berlin so gänzlich ihres Einflusses berauben lassen, daß es nur schwer gut zu machen ist. Dringen diese nicht ganz energisch auf Einberufung der Nationalversammlung—die keineswegs zugunsten der Unabhängigen ausfallen wird—u. auf bürgerlicher Beteiligung an der Regierung, so haben wir russische Zustände zu erwarten u.—Progrome [sic], die, als wirksames Mittel, das Volk an sich heranziehen, durch Unabhängige u. Altdeutsche gemeinsam in Flugzetteln warm empfohlen werden. Daran ändert auch Herr Haase nichts trotz seiner beiden orthodoxen Söhne in Königsberg. Die Juden werden von jeder Partei, die bedrängt wird, als wirksames Ableitungsmittel benutzt werden. Dagegen können wir natürlich arbeiten, besonders indem wir bürgerlich oder höchstens mehrheitssozialistisch wählen. Eine Politik, wie sie die deutschen Staatsbürger jüd.[ischen] Gl.[aubens] treiben, die allem Geschehen unbeteiligt zuschauen wollen, ist unmöglich. Von zionistischen Kreisen ist hier übrigens eine jüdische Schutzwehr (geheim!) gegründet worden, die sich aus ehemaligen Soldaten rekrutiert. Der Mob wartet doch nur auf eine Parole zum Plündern u. Meutern u. richtet sich am liebsten gegen die Juden. Genug davon! . . .

An Konzerten habe ich ein Großes erlebt: Sauer. Er stellt alle Klaviervirtuosen, die ich bis jetzt gehört habe, in den Schatten, erinnert in allem kolossal an Liszt u. spielt ganz ideal. Morgen Harden, Montag *Missa solemnis* unter Ochs, Dienstag Hubermann-Strauß, Mittwoch das *Deutsche Requiem* v. Brahms im „Opernhaus Unter den Linden" unter Herrn Rüdel. Im Deutschen Theater sah ich den „Shylock" mit Wegener; als schauspielerische Leistung hervorragend, aber ungeheuer gehässig, absichtlich entstellt und unnatürlich. Die Aufführung an sich natürlich meisterhaft.

Weill (in Berlin) an Hanns Weill, 3. Dezember 1918: Humperdinck war einmal wieder vom 2. Satz der Suite ganz begeistert u. hat mich fest umarmt. . . . Ich bin nun auch noch in den Studentenrat der Hochschule gewählt. Habe nur angenommen, um gegen Risches zu kämpfen.

Weill (in Berlin) an Hanns Weill, 7. Dezember 1918: Überhaupt muß ich bemerken, daß sich gerade bei uns an der Hochschule ein ganz modern gerichteter Stamm entwickelt—seltsamerweise, denn die Lehrer sind es doch gewiß nicht; Humperdinck höchstens in Bezug auf kühne Rücksichtslosigkeit in der kontrapunktischen Stimmführung, Koch ist ein steifer Kontrapunktiker, als Komponist ein hypermoderner Viel-Lärm-um-Nichts-Schreiber u. Kahn ganz naiver Mendelssohnianer, dem ein übermäßiger Akkord wie eine Ohrfeige ist. Und da wächst ein—allerdings kleiner—Kreis von Schülern auf, unter denen man sich schämen muß, wenn man nicht den ganzen Richard Strauß u. Reger, aber auch Korngold, Debussy, Schreker, Bittner, Marx u.s.w. kennt. . . . Das regt natürlich an.

Weill (in Berlin) an Hanns Weill, 18. Februar 1919: Heute hörte ich, daß der Kandidaten für den Hochschuldirektorposten einer der modernsten aller Modernen sein soll: *Busoni*. Natürlich sträubt sich die altdeutsche, rückständige, idiotische Hammelherde von Hochschullehrern u. -Schülern mit Händen und Füßen. Aber gesund wäre dieser Mann für die alte Bude, obwohl ich nicht weiß, ob er der geeignete Kompositionslehrer ist. Auch halte ich es für ausgeschlossen, daß er ankommt. Sie sagen schon, er sei Jude, u. wenn das ein Student von Dir sagt, dann Gnade Dir Gott.

Weill (in Berlin) an Hanns Weill, 21. Februar 1919: Vorläufig neige ich noch zu einer fein gearbeiteten komischen Oper; doch scheine ich jetzt durch den Umgang mit meinem Mitschüler Kämpfer, mit dem ich nur modernste Musik (Schreker, Reger, Schönberg, u.s.w.) studiere, [scheine ich jetzt] wieder in modernes Fahrwasser zu kommen. Ich bin eben noch garnicht ausgeglichen in musikalischer Hinsicht. Entschieden bin ich in der Suite einen Schritt zurückgegangen. Das fiel mir erst so recht auf, als ich bei der ersten Probe meines Streichquartetts hörte, wie modern, wie Regersch das noch gearbeitet ist. Dieser Rückschritt ist nur dadurch zu erklären, daß ich mich noch etwas krampfhaft an die Form halte, die ich allerdings fast völlig beherrsche. Ich bin noch kein durchaus modern empfindender Mensch, wie es Mahler vorbildlich war, ich rieche noch nach Provinz, ich bin noch nicht mit den Kulturen der Gegenwart genug getränkt. Gerade darum plane ich jetzt nach der fertigen Konzeption der Suite (die übrigens eher eine Symphonie zu nennen ist) ein größeres modernes Orchesterwerk, bei dem ich mich an einen modernen literarischen Vorwurf halten will. Mein ursprünglicher Plan eines Vorspiels zu Grillparzers *Des Meeres u. der Liebe Wellen*, das sich recht modern gestalten ließe, ist mir noch immer recht teuer, würde allerdings das nicht treffen, was Kämpfer sich von mir wünscht: Modernstes Gestalten einer modernsten Dichtung, z. B. die *Weise von Liebe u. Tod* als bloße symphonische Dichtung mit dem hehren Vorbild des Straußschen *Don Juan*. . . . Mit meinem neuen Lehrer bin ich außerordentlich zufrieden. Da ich auch bei ihm einziger Kompositionsschüler bin, beschäftigt er sich eingehend (1 1/2 Std.) mit mir, ist ein durchaus moderner Musiker u. ich kann mir besonders was Orchesterklang, Instrumentationsfarben u.s.w. anbelangt (wovon ich bis jetzt so gut wie keine Ahnung hatte) bei ihm mehr positives Wissen anhäufen, als das bei Humperdinck je möglich gewesen wäre. . . . Das Streichquartett ist natürlich blödsinnig schwer, doch zeigen die Schüler viel Interesse. Heß' Urteil: „verteufelt modern, verteufelt schwer u. verteufelt schön!" Ich bin fast jeden Abend in Konzerten; im letzten Nikisch habe ich *Tod u. Verklärung* genau kennen u. ewig lieben gelernt.

Weill (in Berlin) an Hanns Weill, 27. März 1919: Natürlich geht die Konzeption der symphonischen Dichtung unter diesen Umständen auch nur langsam vorwärts. Ich will das Ganze in 3 Teilen gestalten, d.h. in einem Satz natürlich. Der 1. Teil schildert die düstre Stimmung des Ritters, die nur ab u. zu durch einen Lichtschein—den mutigen Tatendurst der Knaben—unterbrochen wird, der 2. Teil wird lyrischen Charakters sein u. die Liebesnacht schildern, dann im Übergang das jähe Erwachen des Schlosses, das Gerenne, der Brand u. im 3. Teil Schlacht u. Tod. Natürlich will ich nicht rein programmatisch vorgehen. Meine Musik soll zwar durch die verschiedenen Stimmungen der Dichtung angeregt werden, doch soll sie auch ohne jedes Programm verständlich sein. Das ganze ist eine schwere, aber lohnende Arbeit. Schade, daß ich so viel Anderes zu tun habe. Krasselt stellt an den werdenden Korrepetitor immer höhere Ansprüche. Mit dem, was Bing mich in Dessau lernen lassen wollte, will er mich jetzt schon ausrüsten. Jetzt verlangt er auch, daß ich klaviertechnisch wieder einen Schritt vorwärts komme, u. ich sehe selbst ein, daß ich den Sommer über tüchtig Klavier üben muß, um meine Technik wieder aufzuholen. Da ich fast jeden Abend besetzt bin, gehen die Tage herum, lange ehe mein Tagewerk vollbracht ist. Und wenn ich bedenke, daß voraussichtlich im Winter das Komponieren ganz aufhören muß. . .– Dienstag war großes Ereignis: *Elektra* unter Strauß mit der Gutheil-Schoder aus Wien. Es ist entschieden der Höhepunkt Straußschen Bühnenwerkes, kein Musikdrama, keine Musik mehr, sondern Musik—um nicht zu sagen Geräusch—nur noch als Mittel zum Zweck, als Erhöhung der dramatischen Wirkung, aber, von diesem Gesichtspunkt aufgefaßt—ganz genial u. meisterlich.

Weill (in Berlin) an Hanns Weill, 29. April 1919: Nun bin ich wieder mitten im Berliner Getriebe u. komme nicht zum Arbeiten, bis ich nicht mit der Wohnung im Reinen bin. Nach langem Suchen habe ich gestern eine alte Frau ausfindig gemacht, die, in Tante Evas Nähe, mir ein Zimmer für—sage u. schreibe—30 M geben will, allerdings ziemlich primitiv u. einfach u. in bedenklicher Nähe der Stadtbahn; doch daran gewöhnt man sich. Ein Klavier sollte 40 M kosten, bis ich vorhin durch Onkel Markus eins für 20 M angeboten bekam; morgen will ich es mir ansehen. Ich würde auf die Weise also billiger als jetzt wohnen.—Mit Krasselt sprach ich auch schon. Er hat auch gegen den Volontär nichts, wenn ich beschäftigt werde. Doch meint er, nachdem ich ihm zum 1. Mal mein Alter gesagt hatte, ich könnte auch noch einen Winter in Berlin bleiben; wir kriegen bestimmt ein Dirigiersemester u. ich könnte auch konzertieren. Wenn Bing nichts für mich findet, wäre das noch zu überlegen. Ich möchte natürlich, je eher, je lieber, losgehen.

Weill (in Berlin) an Hanns Weill, 9. Mai 1919: Die Stadtbahn höre ich, nach 2 fast schlaflosen Nächten, kaum noch u. hoffe bald soweit abgebrüht zu sein, um auch bei offenem Fenster schlafen zu können. Das Klavier ist sehr gut u. das Zimmer so abgelegen, daß ich ganz ungestört arbeiten kann. Allerdings werde ich viel zur Universität gehen. Ich höre: Cassirer, „Philosophie von der Renaissance bis Kant", Riehl, „Logik", Herrmann, „Geschichte des Theaters in Deutschland", Friedländer, „Das deutsche Lied", u. einige öffentliche Vorlesungen. Die philosophischen machen mir viel Freude. Und nun auch noch „Zarathustra"; das kann fein werden! Von Konzerten ist nichts zu berichten. Zu Weingartner traue ich mich nicht, da ich Angst habe, daß der tiefe Eindruck den Nikischs Beethoven-Interpretation auf mich gemacht hat, hier etwas verwischt wird. In hinreißender Aufführung sah ich die *Faschingsfee*; eine, auch musikalisch, recht bedeutende Operette vom „Czardasfürstin"-Fabrikanten. Ich glaube, daß dieser Mann nicht nur um Geld, sondern auch impulsiv, aus innerem Drang heraus schreibt; denn er bringt eine so schwungvolle—wenn auch abgenutzte—Musik, daß ich einen Zweifel bekam, ob ich das auch könnte. Es gehört doch mehr dazu, als einen annehmbaren Walzer zu schreiben.– Gestern abend hatte ich wieder einmal das höchste der Gefühle: *Figaro* unter Strauß. Ich erkannte das Werk, das ich genau studiert hatte, garnicht wieder; zum ersten Mal in meinem Leben begriff ich Mozart ganz u. was das heißt: Mozart. Das war eine große Freude, zu bemerken, daß ich nun auch dafür reif bin.

Weill (in Berlin) an Hanns Weill, 15. Mai 1919: Wegen Dessau brauchst Du keine Angst zu haben; ich schreibe den Mädels garnicht, sonst würde ich mich doch verplappern. Und verstehen tun sie uns doch nicht, dazu können sie viel zu wenig denken. Ich muß Dir allerdings sagen, daß mir für mein Teil diese Art Mädels—als Frau—lieber sind. In den anderen, mit denen ich mich mehr oder weniger geistreich unterhalten kann, sehe ich allenfalls einen Kameraden, einen Gesinnungsgenossen. Das aber, was ich von der Frau verlange, was jeder von uns, wir Künstler am meisten, vom Weibe brauchen, nicht nur in sinnlicher sondern auch in geistig-seelischer Beziehung, das wovon Goethes „Ewig-Weibliche" die schönste Potenzierung ist, das findet man bei den intelligenten Mädels so selten, das haben die Dessauer, die anderen in ausgiebigstem Maße für sich gepachtet. Und wo ist die, die das richtige Mittelmaß zwischen beiden bietet?

Weill (in Berlin) an Ruth Weill, [ca. 20 Juni] 1919: In meiner Nachbarschaft wohnen ein paar junge Mädchen, die jeden Abend—eben fangen sie wieder an—mehrstimmig allerlei Volkslieder singen. Ich habe solche frischen, unverdorbenen Mädchenstimmen gern. . . . Ist unter Deinen Mädchen nicht etwas heiratsfähiges für mich (Bedingungen: sehr hübsch, sehr dumm, unmusikalisch, 1 Million Mitgift)?

Weill (in Berlin) an Hanns Weill, 27. Juni 1919: Immer wieder wälze ich es mir durch den Kopf: Kannst Du hier bleiben? Und immer die Antwort: Nach Wien! Und dann jedesmal die Enttäuschung: Es ist ziemlich ein Ding der Unmöglichkeit für mich, diesen Plan jetzt zu verwirklichen. Denn die Teuerung in Wien u. die damit verbundene Hungersnot soll jeder Beschreibung spotten. Und ob das in 2 Monaten besser wird? Wenn ich eine Stelle hätte u. ein Jahr lang Vater nicht auf der Tasche liegen würde, könnte ich mich ohne weiteres auf nächsten Herbst vertrösten, zumal ich dann erst für die gewaltigen Eindrücke Wiens u. für einen Unterricht bei Schönberg ganz ausgereift wäre. . . . Dank der Vorsehung, daß ich nach Neuem suche u. das Neue verstehe. Strauß ist verblaßt. Denke Dir alles, was an Strauß unecht, trivial, übertüncht, gesucht ist, ersetzt durch höchste Modernität im Mahlerschen Sinne, durch tiefstes Herausschöpfen aus einer großen Persönlichkeit: dann hast du Arnold Schönberg, so wie ich ihn jetzt aus seinen *Gurre-Liedern* kennen lerne. . . . Wie es nun kommt, ist es mir recht, aber nach Wien muß ich—früher oder später.– Es ist etwas so Neues, was dieser Schönberg mir bringt, daß ich ganz sprachlos war.

An ersprießliches Arbeiten ist natürlich nicht zu denken. Nicht einmal ein kleines Lied formt sich; heute hatte ich eine sehr schöne Idee für den Anfang einer Cellosonate u. habe sie gleich notiert; jetzt hätte ich schon wieder Lust, es zu zerreißen. Ich war schon fast bei dem Entschluß angelangt, die Schreiberei aufzustecken, u. mich nur auf die Kapellmeisterei zu werfen. Wir Juden sind nun einmal nicht produktiv, u. wenn wir es sind, wirken wir zersetzend u. nicht aufbauend; zu wenn die Jugend in der Musik die Mahler-Schönberg-Richtung für aufbauend, für zukunftbringend erklärt (ich tue es ja auch!), so besteht sie eben aus Juden od. aus jüdelnden Christen. Niemals wird ein Jude ein Werk wie die Mondscheinsonate schreiben können. Und die Verfolgung dieses Gedankenganges windet einem die Feder aus der Hand. So weit will ich kommen—nur durch Schönberg könnte ich's—daß ich nur schreibe, wenn ich muß, wenn es mir ehrlich aus tiefstem Herzen kommt; sonst wird es Verstandesmusik, u. die hasse ich. Die *Weise* kommt mir von Herzen, in dieser Musik lebe ich; aber—auch das beschämend! Eine Dichtung brauche ich, um meine Phantasie in Schwung zu bringen; meine Phantasie ist kein Vogel, sondern ein Flugzeug. Ein kleiner Trost ist, daß die jungen Komponisten um mich auch nicht besser daran sind, oft noch schlechter, aber sie wollen nicht gleich so hoch hinaus wie ich, setzen ihre Ziele niedriger u. erreichen sie eher.

Weill (in Berlin) an Hanns Weill, 14. Juli 1919: Hatte ich Dir eigentlich geschrieben, daß ich von Schönberg aus Wien eine überaus nette Karte hatte, in der er mir in der vornehmsten Weise Entgegenkommen in jeder Hinsicht ankündigt. Die Karte ist so modern abgefaßt, daß wir hier, aber auch die Eltern, ganz begeistert davon sind.

Weill in Dessau an Hanns Weill, 5. September 1919: Ich bin Dir einen Bericht über die Ereignisse der letzten Tage schuldig. Gleich in der ersten Probe mit Elisabeth hatte ich gemerkt, daß meine übertriebensten Vorstellungen von ihren Leistungen berechtigt waren; sie hat eine ganz glänzende Stimme, versteht zu singen, ist musikalisch wie keine zweite u. legt in jedes Werk eine ganz eigene Note. Daß die Stimme in der Höhe noch nicht ganz ausgeglichen ist, merkt nur der Musiker u. ist in Anbetracht ihrer Jugend u. der Kürze ihres Studiums zu verstehen. Im Cöthener Konzert war sie natürlich sehr aufgeregt u. hat daher ein bischen gepatzt, ohne daß es jemand gemerkt hatte. Der Beifall war so stark, wie der bei den Cöthener Kuhbauern eben möglich ist; sie war natürlich ein wenig enttäuscht, da sie Beifallsstürme erwartet hatte, wie sie es aus Münchener Konzerten gewohnt war. Dafür haben wir gestern abend ein Konzert hingelegt, wie es Dessau selten gehört hatte. Das Programm, das ich Dir mit allen Kritiken einschicken werde, war äußerst wirkungsvoll zusammengestellt und umfaßte außer 3 Arien nur moderne Lieder, der Hoftheatersaal war bis zum Brechen überfüllt mit allerersten Publikum, besonders Adel, da der ganze Hof erschienen war. Das ganze atmete festliche Erwartung u. wirkte so auf uns, daß wir schöner musizierten als in der besten Probe. Besonders meine Lieder sang sie berückend schön, doch stießen sie durch ihre strenge Modernität auf blödes Mißverstehen bei der großen Menge. Wenn der Beifall auch für mich außerordentlich groß war, so hatte ich das wohl meiner Begleitung, die ich ganz vollendet ausführte, u. dem reichen Blumensegen zu verdanken, mit dem wir beide überschüttet wurden (zu Mutters größter u. meiner geringsten Freude). Elisabeth war dann beim Prinzen Aribert u. sie u. ich wurden für nächste Woche zur Erbprinzessin zum Musizieren eingeladen. In Dessau will das auch nach dem 9. Nov. 1918 etwas heißen! Da auch das ganze Theater im Konzert war, habe ich mich in meiner neuen Stellung glänzend eingeführt. Der erste Bariton ist schon gekommen u. hat mich gebeten, gegen gute Barzahlung jeden Tag eine Stunde mit ihm zu korrepetieren. An Neid fehlt es natürlich auch nicht.

Figure 46. E.H. "Kunst und Wissenschaft: Elisabeth Feuge—Arien und Liederabend." ***Anhalter Anzeiger*, 5 September 1919.** "Art and Sciences: An Evening of Arias and Lieder by Elisabeth Feuge" . . . Whether the young artist sang Meyerbeer, Rossini or Thomas, whether in her richly selected program she advocated Liszt, Wolf, Reger, Pfitzner or Herrmann, everywhere she met with astonishing security the style of these masters and created with astonishing insight and vividness many a fine showpiece. Surely, Miss Feuge will additionally profit from her mother's schooling in order to join other masters of singing and interpretative arts and mature into an artistic world of her own. Miss Feuge was accompanied at the grand piano by Mr. Kurt Weill, technically excellent in every regard and musically poetic, was a collaborator who, in every way, stood on the same high level. Also, of great interest were this young and promising musician's two song compositions, which—especially the first one—were composed in an expressionistic manner and proved to be of a strong, totally individualistic talent. Finally, it should be mentioned that the concert hall was filled to the last seat, and the two artists were practically overwhelmed with applause.

Weill (in Dessau) an Hanns Weill, 19. Dezember 1919: Die *Weise* ist bis auf die dynamischen Zeichen fertig. Bing, dem ich die Partitur zeigte, war sehr begeistert davon, hält das Werk für aufführungsreich u. will bei Nikisch u. Strauß vermitteln. Ich glaube nicht recht daran. Der Stellennachweis der Bühnengenossenschaft, an den ich mich wegen einer Stelle wandte, hat mir schon einen sehr günstigen Vertrag für sofort als 2. Kapellmeister in Lüdenscheid in Westf.[alen] gesandt. Ich habe gleich unterschrieben u. warte nun auf die Gegenzeichnung der Direktion. Meine Tage in Dessau sind also wahrscheinlich gezählt.

Weill (in Lüdenscheid) an Ruth Weill, 28. Januar 1920: Ich habe vorläufig die Absicht, falls mir das Theaterleben einmal wieder ein wenig Zeit und Muße zu eigenem Schaffen läßt, den Einakter von Erich Hardt, dessen Vertonung ich begonnen habe, zu vollenden. Ich würde in diesem Werke nur eines geben u. nur eines geben wollen: Schönheit. . . . Wenn ich nun mit einem Dichter zusammen ein Kunstwerk schaffen würde, so schwebten mir auch dafür ganz neue Ideen vor. . . . Was das Wort nicht zu sagen vermag—u. das wird viel sein—wird die Musik, die Pantomime, der Tanz (in modernem Sinn), die Farbe, das Licht sagen müssen, am meisten die Musik, denn sie kann am besten ungesagtes aussprechen. Das wäre vielleicht ein Lebenswerk u. ich würde nicht viele finden, die mich verstehen würden. . . . Vorläufig ist ja an eine kompositorische Tätigkeit garnicht zu denken. Es kann mir kein Mensch nachfühlen, wie ich darunter leide. Hoffentlich kann ich es mir zum Sommer besser einrichten. . . . Ich werde die nächsten Tage wieder angestrengt zu tun haben. Drei neue schwere Sachen, von denen mir eine viel Freude macht, da es die erste Oper ist, die ich dirigiere, u. dazu noch eine der schwersten, *Die schöne Galathea*. Natürlich muß ich es wieder mit einer Probe machen; das kostet wieder Nerven. Ich habe neulich einen sehr anregenden Abend bei Bekannten aus Benneckenstein in Gelsenkirchen verlebt, habe einen kolossal begabten jungen Komponisten kennen gelernt u. mit beiden bei wundervollem Rotwein bis 1/2 drei debattiert u. musiziert. Das war einmal eine angenehme Abwechslung.

Weill (in Lüdenscheid) an Engelbert Humperdinck, 16. März 1920: Sie werden sich wundern, so lange nichts von mir gehört zu haben, aber mein neues Betätigungsfeld bringt soviel Arbeit mit sich, daß ich erst heute in einer späten Nachtstunde dazu komme, Ihnen recht herzlich für Ihre lieben Zeilen zu danken. Ich bin in der kurzen Zeit, die ich hier bin, ein gewaltiges Stück in meiner Entwicklung zum Kapellmeister vorwärts gekommen. Was ich erreichen will, ist das: So über der Sache zu stehen, daß ich in jeder Dirigentenstelle noch Zeit genug finde, um mich mit eigenen Arbeiten zu befassen. Dazu gehört ja vor allen Dingen Routine, u. die kann ich mir hier in hohem Maße aneignen. Ich muß alles selbst einstudieren u. habe fast jeden Abend zu dirigieren. Außer der gesamten klassischen und modernen Operette habe ich auch schon einige Opern herausgebracht (*Freischütz, Waffenschmied*), das hat besonders viel Freude, aber auch genug Arbeit gemacht. Diese Woche habe ich *Zigeunerbaron*, dann wahrscheinlich *Martha.* Man bestätigt mir von allen Seiten, daß die musikalischen Leistungen des Theaters seit meinem Hiersein einen entschiedenen Aufschwung genommen haben.

Die Akademie schreibt den 2. Preis der Michael Beer'schen Stiftung aus (ein Werk für großes Orchester u. ein Kammermusikwerk). Bedingung ist das vollendete 22. Lebensjahr, ich bin erst 20 Jahre alt. Wäre wohl trotzdem—durch Ihre Fürsprache—eine Beteiligung von mir möglich? Meine symphonische Dichtung liegt sein einigen Wochen bei Prof. Nikisch. Könnten sie nicht ein gutes Wort für mich einlegen? Eine Aufführung dieses Werkes würde mich zum glücklichsten Menschen machen. . . .

Ich habe für den Sommer ein gutes Angebot als 1. Kapellmeister am Kurtheater Norderney. Was ich im Winter mache, weiß ich noch nicht. Ich hoffe im Mai einige Tage in Berlin zu sein u. dann auch bei Ihnen vorzusprechen.

Weill (in Lüdenscheid) an Hanns Weill, 1. April 1920: Ich habe Ostern folgende Aufgaben: Sonntag nachmittag *Fledermaus*, abends *Cavalleria*, Montag nachmittag *Zigeunerbaron*, abends *O schöne Zeit, o selige Zeit* (Uraufführung). Du kannst Dir denken, was ich diese Woche für Arbeit habe. Schon allein die große *Cavalleria*-Partitur auf mein minimales Orchester zu reduzieren u. es mit diesem einstudieren, dann der kleine Chor, die schwierigen Bühnenverhältnisse usw. Ich bin auch ziemlich am Ende meiner Kräfte. Nach Ostern tue ich nichts mehr. Heute abend habe ich Hauptprobe *Cavalleria;* vorher hatte ich nur 2 Proben mit dem halben Orchester. Das kann heiter werden. Aber Spaß macht es, sich in diese leidenschaftliche Musik hineinzuknien. Allerdings sind die Schwierigkeiten mit dem Orchester unglaublich.

Weill (in Berlin) an Albert Weill, 29. November 1920: Ausserdem hätte Busoni schon Bie geantwortet, daß ich ihn besuchen soll. Ihr glaubt nicht, wie schwer es ist, an Busoni heranzukommen, der Portier ist angewiesen, jeden fortzuschicken. Trotzdem habe ich einen überaus interessanten Nachmittag bei Busoni verbracht, er spricht kolossal anregend, verlangt auch im Umgang völlige Freiheit u. Offenheit mit einer solchen Konsequenz, daß es für unsereinen schwer ist, mit ihm umzugehen. Etwas Positives erreicht habe ich noch nicht. Er ist erstaunt über meine Jugend, hat meine Kompositionen dabehalten, will sich aber nicht entscheiden, da sich so viele Kapazitäten gemeldet haben, daß für so junge Burschen wie ich kaum noch ein Platz übrigbleibt.

Weill (in Berlin) an Ferruccio Busoni, 20. Januar 1921: Sehr verehrter, lieber Meister, erlauben Sie mir, meinem Herzen auf diesem Wege Luft zu machen u. Ihnen nochmals für Ihre überaus freundliche Hilfsbereitschaft zu danken. Ich konnte Ihnen heut nachmittag meinen Dank nur so flüchtig hinstammeln in meiner Überraschung darüber, daß ein Mensch sich meiner so tatkräftig annehmen konnte, dazu noch der Mensch, den ich von allen am glühendsten verehre. Ich war Ihnen schon vor dem heutigen Tage so dankbar für jedes Wort aus Ihrem Munde, für den freundschaftlichen Verkehr, dessen Sie mich würdigten, für die ungeahnten Ausblicke, die Ihre Musik mir eröffnete, daß ich nun kaum weiß, wie ich diese ganze Dankesschuld abtragen soll. So werden Sie es verstehen, wenn ich mit meinem heutigen Dank eine Bitte verbinde: Lassen Sie mich Ihnen weiter helfen, soweit Sie mich brauchen u. ich es vermag, lassen Sie es als selbstverständlich gelten, daß ich mit allem, was ich habe, Ihrem Werk u. Ihrem Leben zur Verfügung stehe. Ich wäre sehr glücklich, immer gelten zu dürfen als Ihr aufrichtig ergebener „famulus" Kurt Weill

Weill (in Berlin) an Hanns Weill, 12. April 1921: Tausend Dank für die Übersendung des Geldgeschenkes, es kam gerade in dem Augenblick, als ich mir was pumpen wollte. Ich bin nun also wohlbestallter Chordirigent an der Synagoge Münchenerstr., bekomme 400 M, habe aber vorläufig nur für einen Monat angenommen. Ich muß den Chor erst gründen u. bis Peßach einstudieren, was mit viel Aufregungen verbunden ist, besonders wegen der kurzen Zeit. . . . Die einzige Abwechslung bieten die Besuche bei Busoni, der heute nach Italien fährt (auf kurze Zeit).

Ferruccio Busoni (in Berlin) an Raffaello Busoni, 15. Juli 1921: Ich erlebe den Unterschied mit meinen Schülern, mit denen ich in diesem Jahr den Unterricht begonnen habe. Es sind bis jetzt ihrer vier: ein eigensinniger Russe, der stets Recht behält und wenig zustande bringt; ein etwas parfümierter Kroate, der in Agram schon Professor ist; einen ganz feinen kleinen Juden (der sicherlich weiterkommen wird und schon ein bischen Factotum im Hause ist); u. endlich ein kleiner, runder, wie aufgeblasenes Gummi aussehender Jüngling, mit zwei enormen Linsen auf der Nase, der ohnezweifel begabt ist. Die beiden letzteren sind erfreulich. Aber *wo* den Unterricht beginnen? Das ist in diesem Moment recht schwierig. Sie können viel, und wiederum nicht Das Einfachste, sind kompliziert u. doch nicht reich an Formen, und sie nehmen für sich das heutige allgemeine Recht der Jugend in Anspruch, jede schiefe Linie als Individualität und Freiheit zu verkünden. Wo beginnen? Das kann nur allmählig, mit Geduld geschehen, daß man sie zur Einsicht bringt. Würde ich sie „gleich vor den Kopf schlagen", so machte ich mich in ihren Augen lächerlich, ohne sie zu überzeugen. Bin ich nicht einer der „Führer der Moderne"? Erfüllen sie nicht—so fühlen sie—meine kühnsten Träume?—O, der Misverständnisse!

Weill (in Berlin) an Ferruccio Busoni, 13. Februar 1922: Der verhängnisvolle Eisenbahnstreik ist schuld daran, dass ich erst heute in den Besitz ihres Briefes gelangte. Ich bin aber sehr glücklich, dass Sie an mich gedacht haben u. danke Ihnen aufrichtig. Das *Athenaeum* habe ich in Ihrer Wohnung vorgefunden u. habe den Aufsatz des Mr. Dent mit grossem Interesse gelesen. Es ist tatsächlich erstaunlich, welches Verständnis der Mann Ihrem hiesigen Wirkungskreise u. der Art Ihres Einflusses entgegenbringt. Wie er die Atmosphäre Ihres Hauses schildert, wie er von der günstigen Einwirkung des Romanentums auf deutsche Kunst spricht, wie er von dem warmen Verhältnis zwischen Ihnen u. uns erzählt, das alles sind Sätze, die unsere eigenen Gedanken u. Empfindungen während des letzten Halbjahres ansprechen. Freilich ging Ihr Einfluss noch viel tiefer als bis zu jenen kompositorischen Angelegenheiten: bei mir selbst gipfelt er in der Erkenntnis, dass wir erst—durch alle Kompliziertheit hindurch—unser Menschentum auf die einfachste u. knappste Formel bringen müssen, ehe wir ein wahres Kunstwerk schaffen können.—

Von hier gibt es nicht viel zu berichten. Der Streik—in seinen Auswirkungen wohl der schlimmste, den Berlin erlebt hat—hatte doch das Gute, dass er den Amerikanismus, von dem Berlin seit einigen Jahren erfasst ist, wenigstens für eine Woche lahmgelegt hat. Einige Bilder blieben haften: Ein Herr im Pelz u. Zylinder als Wasserträger am Kurfürstendamm, eine Dame, die nachts Begleitung durch den stockfinsteren Tiergarten sucht u. schliesslich die Charlottenburger Chaussee, dem Roten Meer gleichend, durch das die Israeliten trockenen Fusses gen Westen ziehen. . . .

Ich selbst habe mich wieder viel mit Mozart beschäftigt, u. was ich oben über das innere Gleichgewicht meinte, bezieht sich auf ihn u. alle, die seinen Spuren folgen. Unter den letzteren habe ich Bizet genauer studiert; seine *L'arlésienne*-Suite hat mich in helles Entzücken versetzt durch die Wärme des Ausdrucks u. die Meisterschaft, mit der sie gemacht ist. Mit grosser Freude u. viel Drang arbeite ich an einer Passacaglia für Orchester, die, wie ich hoffe, bis zu Ihrer Rückkehr fertig sein wird.

Weill (in Berlin) an Ruth Weill, September/Oktober 1922: Die Pantomime beginnt nun nach den Freuden der Komposition in das sorgenreiche u. aufregende Stadium der Proben zu treten, u. ich fürchte, ich werde in den nächsten Wochen mehr Ärger damit haben, als die ganze Sache wert ist. Aber auch das soll Schule sein. Außerdem die anderen Aufführungsmöglichkeiten; die hängen wieder alle an einem Faden u. es heißt nun bloß mit der größtmöglichen Ruhe abwarten, bis der Faden gerissen ist. Am sichersten erscheint noch eine Aufführung in Dessau, wo Bing nun so gut wie sicher 1. Kapellmeister zu werden scheint. Er hat mir einen sehr lieben u. freundschaftlichen Brief geschrieben.– Menschlich erlebe ich sehr viel; wenig, sehr wenig Schönes, aber manche sehr dramatische Szenen. Und ich sehe, daß kein Dichter je etwas erfunden hat, was nicht jeder auch erleben kann. Das schlimmste ist, daß ich jeden u. jeden Tag diese langweiligen Stunden geben muß. Natürlich ist es mit der Arbeit bei all dem schlecht bestellt, zumal ich mit der Partitur der Pantomime noch reichlich 3–4 Wochen zu tun habe.

Figure 61. R.S. "Aus den Konzertsälen." ***Berliner Börsen-Courier*, 15 December 1922.** "From the Concert Halls." In the Academy of Voice, the state-sponsored students of Professor Dr. Ferruccio Busoni's master class—now one knows what the fuss is all about—came on stage one by one to conduct the Philharmonic Orchestra and present their creations to the audience. How well these young people have it nowadays! One lives decidedly openhanded after the war. One finds ideal uses for scraps of paper, and the Master no longer hovers over his entrusted ones in fretting nervousness. Amazing, how these young folks deftly utilize this formal-technical apparatus. No more idiocy. In the arts as well as everywhere else. Let's advance the age of foolishness for fifteen years! As can be seen in the student biographies on the last page of the program, Walther Geiser and Robert Blum have only been with Busoni since 1922, but already their snappy tone and witty episodes are already inextricably related to him. Wherever Geiser tries to furrow deeper it falls by the wayside and is without conviction. In the *Intermezzo* Blum develops a tranquil plane, which even if somewhat empty, it still is noticeably there. No exaggerations occur, and technically the composition has turned out well. Another case is Kurt Weill—by the way, the only German among all those students who are here on the State's expense. He is the metaphysician, self-willed, and writes rather abstract music. He could gain significance once he acquires an additionally sensuous form; otherwise he could easily dry up into a bare stump. Luc Balmer is the most perfect representative of a "master student." His symphonic settings contain theme, counter-theme, recitative, reprise, finale. How wonderful I feel! Splendid know-how, solid workmanship, but also more architectural in concept as well as partially in the language of the Brahmsian style moves him to the center of this circle of pupils. He also is more versed in conducting than the aforementioned, all of whom provided their little pieces with some unintentional comedy. The outsider, the "enfant terrible" is Vladimir Vogel. His is the last word of this "symphonic happening," yet cleverly remains in the background and leaves the clarification of "course of events" to Dr. H. Unger. With loving and most intensive knowledge Unger dove into the difficult score and by way of a truly excellent performance as conductor he gave a taste of what a conductor should be all about. There is only one way for the conductor to "illuminate a work": a "stringer," however, leafs through the score as if from afar, because he feels secure in any saddle. Vogel gave into new-Russian excesses, instrumentally with Stravinsky, melodically flirting with Scriabin, thereby proving that this is permitted by Busoni as well. His was the most self-assured composition of the evening, which is meant as a compliment. This piece does not need to be in a pupil's concert. The gray heads were horrified, but the youth was enthusiastic and stamped their feet in approval. An orchestrally brilliant performance, but internally whimsical, because the piece still lacks a compelling strength of expression. Altogether an impressive evening, one which some thirty or fifty years ago would have been considered a fairy tale of the future. In the end there were calls for the Meister, but he remained invisible, like Wotan for his scion Siegmund.

Weill (in Leipzig) an Ferruccio Busoni, 31. März 1923: Sie werden schon erfahren haben, dass mein Divertimento (in der Fassung zu 5 Sätzen) am 10. Juni in der Singakademie unter Ungers Leitung aufgeführt wird. Die Änderung des Streichquartetts nimmt mich augenblicklich sehr in Anspruch. Ich hörte aber aus Donaueschingen, dass die Programme schon so gut wie fertig seien u. dass grösste Eile geboten sei, u. entschloss mich daher, das Quartett vorläufig in der ersten Fassung abzuschicken.

Weill [in Frankfurt] an Ferruccio Busoni, 21. Juni 1923: Dann gab es noch ein Experiment, das aufhorchen liess: Stravinskis *L'histoire du soldat*. Das ist eine Art „Volksstück mit Gesang u. Tanz", ein Mitteding zwischen Pantomime, Melodram u. Posse; die Musik ist, soweit das diese Art zulässt, meisterlich gestaltet, u. auch das Suchen nach dem Geschmack der Strasse ist erträglich, weil es sich dem Stoff einfügt. Mein Quartett höre ich heute zum ersten Mal, weil die Hindemith-Leute sehr überlastet sind. Merkwürdigerweise scheint der letzte Satz—für mich ebenso wie für Sie der reifste—bei den 4 Herren den geringsten Anklang zu finden. Ich fürchte, dass Hindemith schon etwas zu tief in das Land des Foxtrotts hineingetanzt ist.

Ferruccio Busoni (in Berlin) an Emil Hertzka, Universal Edition, Juli 1923: Ich habe meinem Schüler Kurt Weill einen Brief gegeben, der an Sie adressiert ist und den sie in Kürze erhalten werden. Er betrifft Weills Streichquartett, ein Werk hervorragender Qualität mit Kraft und Erfindungsgeist. Ich kenne kaum ein anderes Stück eines heute 23jährigen, das so attraktiv und lohnend ist.—Es ist durch und durch „modern", ohne jedes unangenehme Merkmal. Ich habe in dem Brief nachdrücklich unterstrichen, daß Sie dieses Talent unverzüglich ergreifen sollten. Außerdem (und deshalb ist es so wichtig) ist Weill ein Mann, der nachdenkt und belesen ist, ein Mann des aufrechtesten Charakters.

Weill (in Berlin) an Ferruccio Busoni, Oktober 1923[?]: Es gibt nur eine Entschuldigung für mein langes Schweigen: das ist der Wunsch, Sie vor Lamentationen zu bewahren. Es sah hier fast so aus, als ob keine Hoffnung mehr sei; der Übergang von der Million zur Milliarde war so gewaltsam, dass er selbst Leute, denen Gelddinge gleichgültig sind, fassungslos machte. Jetzt hat man sich auch daran gewöhnt u. greift nach neuen Strohhalmen. Vom Ausland wird sich alles noch schlimmer ansehen, als es ist. Schliesslich kann dieses Land kaum verloren sein, wenn es die jüngsten Krisen überstanden hat; u. die Geduld dieser Bevölkerung ist bewunderungswürdig.

Berlin hat sich—soweit man das von hier aus beurteilen kann—seit Ihrer Abreise kaum verändert. Die Konzertsaison hat mit demselben Wagemut wie immer begonnen. Bruno Walter, der seine Entwicklung zum amerikanischen Heldentenor jetzt zu vollenden scheint, dirigiert Mozart überpräzise, maniriert u. zuckersüss. Ich kann diesen Typus „mauschelnder" Dirigenten nicht leiden, deren Geist nichts zu tun hat, als sich einen Spiegel zu schaffen, in dem sie ihre eigene schöne Rückenlinie bewundern. Ich bin manchmal versucht, zu bezweifeln, dass Mahler von diesem Fehler ganz frei war; oder darf man aus den Kompositionen keinen Rückschluss auf den Interpreten wagen?– Schnabel scheint mir gegen früher—in seinem Spiel!—männlicher, bestimmter geworden zu sein, es gelingt ihm alles, wie er es beabsichtigt, aber die Mängel liegen in der Absicht selbst, u. die ist Sache der Grundeinstellung, des Temperaments. Claudio Arrau müht sich redlich, in Ihrem Geist zu spielen; das gelingt ihm weniger in Ihrer *Carmen-*, als in Liszts *Don Juan*-Fantasie.

Ja, und der neue Generalissimus der Oper! Von der ausgezeichneten *Fidelio*-Aufführung erzählte ich Ihnen. *Aida* hat mir weniger gefallen, denn Verdi verträgt nicht dieses Stilisieren, dieses Hineinknien in jede Phrase, u. wenn einer ein deutscher Kapellmeister ist, so kann er auch durch die willkürlichsten Temposchwankungen kein italienisches Theaterblut vortäuschen. Und doch ist Kleiber ein famoser Musiker u. auch der richtige Mann am Ort, weil er von unten auf das Repertoire erneuert. Vorläufig lässt er sämtliche Bayreuther Viertel-, Halb-, Dreiviertel- u. Ganzgötter der Reihe nach aufmarschieren.

Ein Blick auf das Publikum der Konzertsäle genügt, um zu erkennen, dass dieses Berlin die Musik nicht aufgeben wird. Freilich sitzen in den Philharmonischen Konzerten noch die Scharen, die bei Mozart „niedlich", bei Beethoven heroisch u. bei Bach streng auszusehen versuchen; das linke Bein klopft die Viertel dazu u. die rechte Hand klimpert die Achtel. Aber allen Gesichtern gemeinsam ist ein rührender Ausdruck von Glückseligkeit, dass sie bei allem Geschehen noch in einem erleuchteten Konzertsaal sitzen u. Musik hören dürfen. Dadurch wird das Urteil des Laien naiver, aufrichtiger u. wertvoller für den Künstler. Und an den Kassen hört man Fantasiepreise für Billets. (Bis zu einer Milliarde am Montag abend).

Von mir gibt es wenig neues zu berichten. Den Kampf um ein Zimmer gebe ich jetzt auf u. bleibe vorläufig hier in der Wohnung meiner Freunde. An Arbeiten war kaum zu denken, obwohl ich in guter Verfassung dazu wäre. Aber gelesen habe ich manches: viel Mozart-Quartette, unter denen ich dem in C dur aus dem Jahre 1785 die Palme reiche; Sie erinnern sich an die Adagio-Einleitung mit dem berühmten Querstand am Anfang—einer der ergriffensten u. dabei kühnsten Sätze, die ich kenne. Dann viel Berlioz-

Partituren; das ist mir nun aufgegangen, dass es einen Instrumentations-Stil nicht gibt, sondern nur eine bestimmte Art, für Orchester zu komponieren, so wie der Maler bei einer Radierung anders zeichnet, als bei einer Bleistiftskizze.

Figure 64. "Friedrich-Theater: Letztes Abonnements-Konzert." *Volksblatt für Anhalt*, 15 June 1923. "Friedrich-Theater: Last Subscription Concert." A world premiere at the beginning of the evening: the orchestral suite from the children's pantomime "Magic Night," opus 9. A work by the Busoni student Kurt Weill, whose two songs Feuge sang here some years ago, and which were written by the glow of his study-lamp. It is an ardent endeavor that succeeds in presenting a lively sample of his musical knowledge, but nothing more. The work gives proof of a lot of knowledge, has little strength, extraordinary awareness of mixing orchestral sounds, but no complexity of organization. It doesn't provide a hint of the music of the future; the score provides a slight breeze of the rarefied air from the laboratory. (A talented famulus as compared to Busoni's *Faust* music.) Consequently, a mere byproduct, but not an end product, yet with father and son Bing's support, certainly worthwhile. (Krenek is even performed nowadays, isn't he?) It would be desirable if this over-zealous young man from Dessau could come forward with a more self assured "I must" instead of the his beaming, "I can." The audience remained cool to the four movements of this premiere and tried to make sense of the pantomime. This youthful music was not able to electrify. But one hopes to hear more of Weill's music in the future, and often.

Ferruccio Busoni (in Paris) an Philipp Jarnach, 7. Oktober 1923: Ein Frauentanz von Weill ist mir unbekannt. Die Produktivität dieses Jungen ist überraschend, bei seiner spröden Ader u. der umständlichen Arbeit. Die „Einfälle" sind—wie sie sagen—häufig, aber versteckt u. angedeutet, so daß nur „Unsereiner" sie entdeckt u. bewundert. Er—Weill—scheint sich nicht bewußt zu sein, wenn er an der rechten Stelle ist; sondern schreitet über sie hinweg, wie über Sand u. Gestein, wozwischen hübsche u. eigenartige Blüthen sprießen, die e nicht zertritt aber auch nicht pflückt, bei denen er nicht verweilt. Sein Reichtum ist groß, seine Wahl vorläufig unaktiv. Man beneidet, man möchte helfen.—Aber er kommt von selbst auf das Richtige!—Die ewige Frage: ist er noch im Werden, oder schon bei seinem Höhepunkt?

Weill (in Berlin) an Emil Hertzka, 16. Februar 1924: In Ihrem Schreiben vom vergangenen Herbst kündigten Sie mir an, dass Sie die Absicht haben, Anfang 1924 „mein gesamtes Schaffen in Ihre Kataloge aufzunehmen." Ich halte es darum für eine angenehme Pflicht, Sie heute, wo ich kurz vor dem Abschluss von Verträgen mit einem deutschen u. einem ausländischen Verlag stehe, nochmals um endgültigen Bescheid zu bitten. Da ich jetzt einige grosse Erfolge gehabt habe, brauchen Sie nicht mehr einen ganz Unbekannten aus der Versenkung zu holen. Ein hiesiger grosser Bühnenverlag hat soeben zwei Stücke von mir erworben: die Kinderpantomime *Zaubernacht*, die im Herbst in New York aufgeführt wird (im hiesigen Theater am Kurfürstendamm 1923 uraufgeführt), sowie ein abendfüllendes Bühnenwerk, an dem ich augenblicklich arbeite, u. zu dem mir *Georg Kaiser* den Text schreibt. Mein Streichquartett op. 8 wird jetzt vom Roth-Quartett öfter gespielt werden; für dieses Stück macht mir soeben ein bekannter ausländischer Verlag ein Angebot, aber falls Sie sich dafür interessieren, wäre es mir sehr lieb, bald Ihre Vorschläge zu hören. Op. 9 ist *Quodlibet*; eine Unterhaltungsmusik (4 Stücke für kleines Orchester nach der oben genannten Kinderpantomime); es hatte grossen Erfolg in Dessau, ist gefällig, leicht spielbar u. nicht prätentiös (auch darüber stehen gute Kritiken zu Ihrer Verfügung). Der *Frauentanz* op. 10 (7 Lieder für Sopran, Bratsche, Flöte, Klarinette, Horn, Fagott) wurde durch die I.N.M.G. mit Frau Pisling u. Stiedry aufgeführt; es wird Sie besonders interessieren, dass *Ferruccio Busoni* eines dieser Lieder für Gesang u. Klavier bearbeitet hat u. voraussichtlich die übrigen ebenso behandeln wird. Op. 11 ist ein a-capella-Chorwerk mit lateinischem Text (5. Kapitel der Klagelieder Jeremiae), 4-stimmig mit Kinderchor. Es soll, wie ich höre, auf dem diesjährigen Tonkünstlerfest des A.D.M.V. uraufgeführt werden. Meine nächsten Pläne sind: ein Violinkonzert (bereits angefangen), ein neues Streichquartett u. eine neue (komische) Oper.

Weill (in Davos) an Ferruccio Busoni, 25. Februar 1924: Es ist hier oben eigentlich das erste Mal, dass mir das Nichtstun zum Genuss wird; es gibt so viel Überraschendes, wenn man von einem Tag auf den anderen Berlin mit einem Hochgebirgsort vertauscht, dass kaum ein anderer Gedanke in einem aufkommt, als der des Staunens. Wir wohnen hier ganz idyllisch an einem Bergabhang 100 m über dem Ort Davos; auf der einen Seite sehen wir in einen steil ansteigenden Wald, in dem die Sonne auf dem bläulich schimmernden Schnee die lieblichsten Farbenspiele treibt; u. nach Süden zieht eine lange Bergkette, deren Kuppel sich schneidend scharf gegen den Himmel abhebt, u. dieser Himmel ist von einer Bläue, die ich nie gesehen habe, u. die mir erste Vorahnung des Südens zu sein scheint. Schon in Helgoland empfand ich freudig eine Art Erdverbundenheit, weil die Geschehnisse des Tages abhängig gemacht werden vom Wetter, von Naturvorgängen; das ergibt jene Gleichmässigkeit des Tagesverlaufs, die doch nie in Eintönigkeit ausartet. Morgens bin ich in den Bergen, der Schnee liegt zwei Meter hoch u. man geht ohne Überkleider in strahlender Sonne. Mittags liegt man dann auf der offenen Terrasse nach Süden, die Sonne ist so heiss, dass man sich vor ihr schützen muss, u. dabei kommt zum ersten Mal der Wunsch auf, der sich wohl auf dieser Reise öfter wiederholen wird: wenn Sie doch hier wären! Man ist immer in „gehobener" Stimmung, wenn einen diese glühende Wintersonne erreicht, wenn man diese reine, dünne Luft atmet, u. wenn man tief unten die Wolken liegen sieht, die das flache Land verdüstern.—

Sie werden lachen, wenn Sie hören, dass ich Sport treibe; aber es ist ein schönes Gefühl, auf einem kleinen Schlitten eine eisglatte Bahn von 4 km herunterzusausen u. durch einen leisen Druck des Körpers eine Kurve zu nehmen. Und da ich es ohne Ehrgeiz tue, ist es auch ungefährlich. . . . Von Hertzka hatte ich ein erfreuliches Telegramm: „Habe für Übernahme Ihrer Werke lebhaftes Interesse, erbitte Vorschläge betreffs Bedingungen." Trotzdem ich in Verlegersachen sehr skeptisch bin, will ich doch über Wien zurückfahren u. versuchen, mit Hertzka mündlich einig zu werden.

Wenn ich an Berlin denke u. das, was hinter mir liegt, so bin ich fast ausschliesslich bei Ihnen u. bedauere lebhaft, noch von keiner Seite Nachricht über Ihr Befinden zu haben. Ich hoffe u. wünsche so sehr, dass die entschiedene Besserung, die wir vor meiner Abreise beobachten konnten, angehalten hat, u. dass Sie bald imstande sind, den Süden aufzusuchen u. dort alles zu finden, was Sie noch immer schwer vermissen.

Weill (in Bologna) an Ferruccio Busoni, 6. März 1924: Schon seit einigen Tagen bin ich in diesem Land, aber das, was ich mir unter Italien vorgestellt hatte, habe ich erst heute u. hier gefunden. . . . Ich habe den kürzeren u. schöneren Weg über die Bernina genommen. Es ist überwältigend, wenn man von einer Höhe von 2400 m. unten grüne Täler liegen sieht u. sich dann in kreisendem Abstieg einem blauen italienischen See nähert. In Poschiavo schien eine warme Sonne u. in Tirano erlebte ich schon eine regelrechte italienische Strassenszene mit Zigeunern, Rauferei, u. so schönen Tenorstimmen, dass ich mit Wehmut an die Berliner Staatsoper dachte. Für den Comer See ist die Jahreszeit noch zu früh u. das vielgerühmte Bellaggio verfehlte ein wenig die versprochene Wirkung. Auch Mailand enttäuschte mich ein wenig. Für solche Schönheiten wie der Dom u. das erzbischöfliche Palais ist die Stadt ein bischen zu durchschnittlich. Aber die Scala! Was für ein herrliches Theater! Welch restlose Erfüllung des Begriffs „Theater"! Wie festlich das Bild des weiten, breiten Parterres u. der 5 Reihen von Logen! Und was für eine Aufführung!

Von allem szenischen, das ich gesehen habe, kommt das dem Mahlerschen Ideal des „konzessionslosen" am nächsten. Man gab *Louise* von Charpentier. Toscanini dirigierte, u. das allein war ein Ereignis, um das sich diese ganze Reise lohnt. Ich wusste nicht, dass man mit solcher Freiheit, mit solchen willkürlichen rubati „auf" einem Orchester spielen kann. Es wurde famos gesungen, der Chor war verblüffend in der musikalischen u. darstellerischen Gestaltung seiner Aufgabe. Ich weiss nicht, ob das Stück durch die Aufführung so gewonnen hat,– ich fand es stellenweise (wie am Anfang des 4. Aktes) schön. Sie können sich denken, mit welchem Schwung die grosse Ausstattungsszene des 3. Aktes herausgebracht wurde. An diesen Abend werde ich lange denken. . . . Und nun sitze ich in einem Café, die Kapelle spielt *Traviata* u. alles singt mit, man wird froh u. leicht u. wünscht nichts sehnlicher, als dass Sie bald gesund genug sind, um hier zu sein.

Weill (in Florenz) an Ruth Weill, 8. März 1924: Die Reise nach Florenz war amüsant. Man bekommt für 6 Lire eine Düte mit Cervelatwurst, ein Stück kalten Kalbsbraten, eine Gurke, Apfelsinen u.—eine Korbflasche Chianti. Nun sitzt der ganze Zug u. frisst und säuft. Dann kommt eine Familie, die hat ein ganzes Huhn mit, das unter allgemeiner Beteiligung verzehrt wird. Und alle singen u. schwatzen u. schreien—ein glückliches Volk! Wenn es nicht so glücklich wäre u. so vollkommen verwachsen mit dem Begriff Schönheit, so könnte es nicht eine Stadt wie Florenz geschaffen haben. Man spürt in dieser Stadt, wie die Väter ihre Söhne gelehrt haben, welche Steine gut genug für den Dom sind, man spürt, wie dieses Volk sich ganz bewusst diese Ewigkeitswerte geschaffen hat u. wie jeder, der begabt war, sich freiwillig in den Dienst dieser Sache stellte. Und jede Generation setzt da ein, wo die vorige geendet hat, sie bring ihre Individualität zum Ausdruck, aber sie vergisst nicht den Zusammenhang mit dem Gewesenen. . . . Ich erlebe so stark hier u. falle so von einem Wonneschauer in den andern, dass ich nachts nicht schlafen kann, u. mich oft zusammen nehmen muss, um nicht wie ein Kind zu weinen. Alles lebt: die Kirchen sind bevölkert von knieenden Menschen, Pfaffen sind wie Sand am Meer, das Volk lacht u. trinkt Chianti u. neapolitanische Sänger schlagen jeden Kollegen von der Berliner Oper aus dem Feld—für 2 Soldi! Gestern abend war ich trunken von aller Schönheit u. betrunken vom Wein.

Figure 75. Contract between Kurt Weill and Universal Edition, 22 April 1924.

1. I hereby cede to you—as far as all of my compositions inclusive of the music-dramatic works I will produce within the next 8 years are concerned—the priority claim in such a way that—on basis of royalties paid to me—you will own the exclusive and sole copyright, which include especially the publishing-distribution-performance and translation rights as well as the rights for mechanical instruments or similar appliances, all of which you are entitled to acquire by simple declaration of acceptance.

2. The Gold mark price set at coming out of publication is to be the basis of the royalty calculation. The royalty is to be 12% of the retail price for the first three, 15% for the next five years.

3. The accounting and payment of the royalty takes place in such a way that after the printing the royalty for half of the edition will be paid to me in advance every time. After the edition has been sold payment for the rest of the edition follows at the same time with the advance for half of the next edition. No royalties are to be paid for free copies of each work which are used as complimentary copies, or as copies given to authors, critics, artists, etc. You have the right to deduct 10% of each first edition but at least 50 copies of the copies to be printed not being subject to royalties. Should special circumstances require that free copies exceed the figures agreed to, it will be announced separately and taken into consideration at the next accounting.

4. The edition royalty is not meant for theaters, chorus and orchestral works and its components incl. piano vocal scores with text and libretti. Of these works the royalty will be paid per sold copy, or materials through half-yearly payments.

5. At the signing of the contract I will receive an advance for the edition royalty of the first 5 works in the amount of 300 Gold Marks.

6. For your theater activities you will receive from all German performances in Germany and German-Austria for resulting stage performance-income 20%, from foreign stage-performance-income 30%, which you are entitled to deduct for yourself. In case the work has been done with a collaborator, I have to pay the same with the stage performance and publishing income coming to me, and I have the obligation to inform my collaborator of my agreements with you and I will tie a condition to my collaborative work that the collaborator is agreeable with the conditions of this contract.

7. I am obligated to submit to you all of my compositions completed during the duration of this contract after they are finished (with stage works in book and full score) and it is your choice to accept the works concerned within the time space of 4 weeks after submission according to above mentioned conditions. In case the declaration of acceptance on your part does not occur within 4 weeks, your priority claim is invalid and I have the unlimited right to dispose of the works in question.

By acceptance of a work you at the same time accept an obligation to publish the composition in question within the time of one year. Should publication not have taken place within this year, the copyright of same, if I so desire, returns to me again.

8. Income from performances in concerts will be distributed in such countries, in which there exist institutions for the controlling of concert performances, by the author's societies entitled to this on the basis of statute.

9. For the purpose of advertising and popularization I permit you to publish single compositions or fragments from a work in newspapers, magazines, collections, anthologies, without making any claim on royalties or other indemnities.

10. If I should act in any way against the obligation I have accepted you are within your right, without detriment to your additional incumbent rights, to stop the accounting of the royalties granted to me in this agreement.

Weill (in Rom) an Ferruccio Busoni, 15. März 1924: Diese Tage in Rom gehören zu den schönsten meines Lebens. Ich erlebe den vielgerühmten römischen Frühling u. ich kann nicht aufhören, den Anblick dieser wahrhaft göttlichen Stadt, wie sie da weiss u. glitzernd in der Sonne liegt, in mich einzuschlürfen. Dieses Bild vom Pincio aus über die Stadt hinweg nach den grünen Höhen, dieses Bild des marmornen Gemäuers u. schwarzer Zypressen, das die Hintergründe von Raffaels Madonnenbildern darstellen,—es ist zu einem Teil meines Fühlens geworden, u. ich werde immer Sehnsucht danach haben.

Und ich erlebe die Kunstschätze des Vatikans. Drei Stellen besuche ich täglich: die Sixtinische Kapelle, Raffaels Stanzen u. seine Ausschmückung der Villa Farnesina, u. immer von neuem liege ich auf den Knien vor dieser Vollendung. Ich bin zu voll von allem, um Worte dafür zu finden, aber ich weiss wohl, dass es eine Erklärung für diese ergreifende Wirkung gibt, dass diese Leute unendlich viel konnten u. dass ihr Gefühl von jener Lauterkeit war, die allein dazu berechtigt, göttliche Dinge menschlich zu gestalten. Die Beziehungen zur Musik Bachs u. Mozarts sind mannigfaltig, sie gehen bis in die formalen u.—melodiösen Einzelheiten; aber wem sind die Zusammenhänge so vertraut wie Ihnen? . . . Heut ist ein warmer Frühlingstag, ich war in den Grotten bei den Wasserfällen, die das schönste Scenarium für den *Freischütz* bilden; u. nun liege ich auf einem Ölberg am Abhang des Sabinergebirges, eine Schafherde weidet neben mir u. der Hirt singt mit seiner Phyllis neapolitanische Lieder. Ich spüre eine nie gekannte Leichtigkeit, eine Fülle, einen Überfluss—u. ich singe mit: [see facsimile]. Das ist schöner als die Musik, die ich gestern in einem Konzert der „Corporazione delle nuove musiche" (nicht „Internationale") gehört habe. Es war der 2. Abend von fünf, deren Programme ausschliesslich französische u. italienische Musik enthalten (bezeichnend dafür, was man sich hier unter „neuer Musik" vorstellt). Das beste war noch ein Quartett von Milhaud u. kleine Witze von Poulenc. Stravinskis Suite für Klavier, Violine u. Klarinette klingt scheusslich. Das erfreulichste an dem Konzert (das Casella leitete) war, dass ich dort Edward Dent traf u. sprach. Er bestätigte mir, was Jarnach in einer Karte andeutete: dass mein *Frauentanz* für Salzburg angenommen ist. Das freut mich ungemein, zumal ich nie gewagt hatte, es zu erhoffen.

Figure 76. Kurt Weill. [Richard Strauss.] *Musikblätter des Anbruch* 6, no. 5 (May 1924): 207. What Richard Strauss means to me: Crossing the threshold from the 19th to the 20th century, looking back to the past while holding promise for the future. He marks the end of an era whose means were not always the choicest, and whose inevitable destination was Naturalism. And he marks the beginning of a new one, because in his hands all "portraits" become transformed into pure, unencumbered music-making. He creates a form that makes us forget the non-musicality of the intended tone-painting. He creates a harmonic language that avails itself of dissonances as an expressive means; his voice-leading results in the expanded concept of tonality that helped pave the way for the complete abandonment of tonal harmony. He creates an orchestra that casts all ideas, even uninspired ones, in the most flattering light, possessing a certain lightness and ease, even though it is incapable of renouncing completely the viscosity of Wagnerian scores.

Weill (in Berlin) an die Familie, 29. Mai 1924: Ich war von meiner Arbeit sehr in Anspruch genommen u. die Verpflichtungen nach aussen hin steigern sich auch. Vom Violinkonzert sind 2 Sätze fertig, aber jetzt stockt es seit 3 Tagen, sodass mein Plan, das ganze Stück bis zu meinem Besuch bei Euch zu vollenden, nicht durchzuführen sein wird. Aber schön wird es! Kaiser liefert noch immer nicht den Schluss des Buches. Aber ich mache mir nichts draus, weil ich unendlich viel Pläne habe. Erdmann, bisher einer meiner Feinde, scheint sich plötzlich bekehrt zu haben, denn er bestellte ein grosses Klavierwerk bei mir. Im *Anbruch* (Mai-Heft) sind in sehr ehrenvoller Umgebung meine Sätze über Richard Strauss erschienen. In Salzburg wird Lotte Leonard, die bedeutendste deutsche Konzertsängerin, den *Frauentanz* singen. Ich war noch einmal in Dresden u. diesmal den ganzen Tag mit Busch zusammen—eine in jeder Beziehung wertvolle Bekanntschaft. In meiner Entwicklung hängt jetzt sehr viel, vielleicht alles von mir selbst ab: ich muss in den nächsten Jahren enorm arbeiten, um den etwas günstigen Anlauf, den ich jetzt nehme, auszunützen. Pekuniär habe ich kaum noch Befürchtungen, nicht nur findet sich jetzt für mich öfter Gelegenheit, etwas zu verdienen, sondern allmählich werden sich auch laufende Einkünfte einstellen.

Weill (in Berlin) an die Universal Edition, 3. Juni 1924: Zusammen mit dem *Frauentanz* sende ich Ihnen die beiden anderen Kompositionen: das I. Streichquartett, das zum ständigen Repertoire des Roth-Quartetts gehört u. von diesem auch im Ausland gespielt wird—u. das Orchesterstück: *Quodlibet*, eine Unterhaltungsmusik, für das verschiedene Aufführungen in Deutschland (u.a. Dresden u. Bochum) sowie in New York in Aussicht stehen. Es ist nämlich aus der Musik meiner Kinderpantomime *Zaubernacht* zusammengestellt, die—wie ich eben von dem Unternehmer u. Autor des Buches, Herrn Dr. Wladimir Boritsch, erfahre—mit ziemlicher Gewissheit in New York durch Fokin herauskommen soll. Sowie ich über diese Aufführung Definitives erfahre, will ich eine neue Partitur des Werkes für Mozartsche Besetzung herstellen (die Partitur der hiesigen Aufführung hatte nur 9 Instrumente). Haben Sie an der Übernahme des Stückes schon jetzt Interesse u. würden Sie an dem Zustandekommen der New Yorker Aufführung mitarbeiten? Das gesamte Material ausser Partitur ist schon in Amerika. . . .

Noch eins: ich arbeite an einem *Konzert für Violine u. Blasorchester*, mit dem ich in 2–3 Wochen fertig zu sein hoffe. Das Stück ist angeregt durch den—bisher noch nie ausgeführten—Gedanken, die konzertante einzelne Violine einmal einem Bläserchor gegenüberzustellen. Nun kommt mir eben das Preisausschreiben von Schott in die Hände, das ganz ähnliche Ziele anstrebt. Es wäre mir daher lieb, wenn Sie schon jetzt, vielleicht im *Anbruch* unter der Rubrik „Manuskript", auf dieses Werk hinweisen würden.

Weill (in Berlin) an Leo und Ruth (Weill) Sohn, Juni? 1924: Ihr dürft über mein Schweigen nicht bös sein; Busoni ist todkrank u. wir wissen alle nicht, wo uns der Kopf steht. Selbst zu leiden wäre nicht so schlimm, als einen solchen Menschen so entsetzlich leiden zu sehen. Wenn ich nicht bei ihm bin, muss ich mich in die Arbeit stürzen, um den Anblick etwas zu vergessen. Vorige Woche war ich—leider bei Regenwetter—in Grünheide bei Kaisers, die mir liebe Freunde geworden sind u. vielleicht die einzigen sein werden, die mir einen Teil von dem ersetzen können, was ich an Busoni verliere. Ich habe ein neues grosses Stück vollendet, ein Violinkonzert. Nun wird es endlich wieder an die Kaisersche *Pantomime* gehen. Ich habe die Absicht, im August nach Salzburg zu gehen, falls ich das Geld zusammenkriege.

Figure 84. Adolf Weissmann. "Das zweite internationale Kammermusikfest in Salzburg." *Die Musik* 17, no. 1 (October 1924): 52. Starting here a connection spans itself to Kurt Weill, the Busoni student, whose *Frauentanz*, a song cycle on medieval texts dressed in a peculiar instrumental wrapping, was even more impressive than at its first performance in Berlin thanks to a stylish adaptation into contemporary language. For Lotte Leonard uplifted these seven songs by the beauty of her voice and her intelligent interpretation inasmuch as Jarnach's baton knew how to blend the players of mixed ability into unity.

Weill (in Berlin) an die Universal Edition, 10. Oktober 1924: Anbei sende ich Ihnen den druckreifen Klavierauszug vom *Frauentanz* u. hoffe, dass Sie ihn gleich der Stecherei übergeben können. Halten Sie die Anmerkung betr. Busoni auf dem Titelblatt für angebracht? Oder erscheint Ihnen folgende Fassung besser: „Die Klavierbearbeitung von Nr. 3 ist die letzte musikalische Arbeit von Ferruccio Busoni"?

Der *Frauentanz* wird, wie Sie vielleicht schon wissen, im Dezember durch Walter Straram in Paris aufgeführt. Straram will auch das Violinkonzert in Paris herausbringen, sobald ich über das Material verfügen kann, wenn möglich schon im Januar. Ausserdem spielt das Roth-Quartett in Paris mein I. Streichquartett.

Wegen der Uraufführung des Violinkonzerts schweben hier noch Verhandlungen. Sollten sie sich zerschlagen, so schicke ich Ihnen gleich Partitur u. Klavierauszug.

Vom *Stundenbuch* habe ich noch keinen Klavierauszug.

Hätten Sie (ev. in Wien) die Möglichkeit, mein a capella-Chorwerk *Recordare* (4-stimmig mit Kinderchor) zur Aufführung zu bringen. Es enthält einige Schwierigkeiten, die aber kein Hindernis bieten, wenn ein tüchtiger Chormeister sich der Mühe des Einstudierens unterziehen würde.

Schliesslich wäre ich Ihnen dankbar, wenn Sie sich wegen der Übernahme von *Quodlibet* bald entscheiden würden, da ich soeben von anderer Seite eine Anfrage speziell nach Orchesterwerken erhalte. Sie forderten s. Z. dringend die Partitur ein u. sprachen von einer Wiener Aufführung. Furtwängler hat mir eine Aufführung des Stückes im Gewandhaus nach seiner Amerikareise in Aussicht gestellt. Auch sonst hätte ich für dieses Werk verschiedene Möglichkeiten, wenn es publiziert wäre. Bitte teilen Sie mir Ihre diesbezüglichen Absichten mit.

Weill (in Berlin) an Lotte Lenya, 15. oder 22. Dezember 1924: Die Erinnerung an Deinen heutigen Ausbruch ist nicht schmerzlich. Du warst sehr schön—u. hattest Recht. Die Schuld war auf meiner Seite. Meine Einstellung war immer noch falsch. Aber jetzt—endlich, endlich—habe ich begriffen, wo Du mich haben willst. Und jetzt weiß ich auch, daß das garnicht so schwer ist. Eine Umstellung, nicht mal eine Abschwächung meiner Gefühle—das ist alles. Wie glühend ich Dich liebe—heut mehr als je—das ist meine ganz private Angelegenheit. Die Äusserung dieser Empfindung muß unabsichtlich sein u. nur für Dich spürbar—so wie Deine Liebe, die mir sogar aus dem heutigen Zornesausbruch entgegensprang. Denn in allem hattest Du recht, nur darin nicht, daß Du mich nie „gern" hattest; Du hast mir zu oft das Gegenteil bewiesen (u. geschrieben: daß Du gegen mich härter bist, als gegen andere, das macht mich froh, denn das ist oft der stärkste Beweis Deiner Zuneigung). Nur eines sollst Du mir noch glauben: diese kleinen Auseinandersetzungen sind nicht das Ende, sie sind die unbedeutenden Reibereien des Anfangs, die einzig durch meine Unerfahrenheit verschuldet sind. Das ist jetzt vorbei. Heute erst schenke ich Dir: mich; Du darfst dieses Geschenk ruhig annehmen, es wird Dir nur gutes bringen. Laß mich Dein „Lustknabe" sein, das ist mehr als ein Freund—u. weniger als ein Gatte. Ich bin für Dich auf der Welt—das ist zu selbstverständlich, als daß es Dich zu irgend etwas verpflichten könnte. Du wirst es jetzt spüren. Gib mir nur ein kleines Zeichen, daß Du das Geschenk annimmst. Bitte.

Weill (in Berlin) an die Universal Edition, 28. Dezember 1924: Unterdessen hat sich eine neue unangenehme Situation ergeben. Meine 6 Orchesterlieder *Stundenbuch* sind als einziges neues Werk von der deutschen Sektion der Intern. Ges. f. neue Musik für das Prager Musikfest vorgeschlagen; die Partitur ist in Winterthur, wo vom 27. d. M. ab die Jury tagt.

Dasselbe Stück soll aber am 22. Januar durch Unger in der Philharmonie (Gesellschaft der Musikfreunde) uraufgeführt werden. Wenn also die Partitur rechtzeitig zurückkommt, muss ich sofort die Stimmen herausschreiben lassen. Ich wäre Ihnen sehr dankbar, wenn Sie die Kosten der Material-Anfertigung übernehmen würden. Für mich ist es kaum erschwinglich u. Sie werden doch voraussichtlich das Werk nach der Uraufführung übernehmen. Bitte teilen Sie mir *umgehend* Ihre Meinung darüber mit. Ich habe Herrn Dr. Wellesz dringend um sofortige Rücksendung der Partitur gebeten. Hoffentlich klappt es.

Weill (in Berlin) an Emma Weill, 31. Dezember 1924: Da Du heute abend allein bist, sollst Du Dich morgen früh wenigstens über diesen Brief freuen. Tröste Dich, ich werde am Silvester auch daheim bleiben; ich habe nachmittags Proben (wie jetzt bis zum 22. I. jeden Tag!) u. werde es nicht mehr schaffen, nach Grünheide zu fahren. Und wo anders will ich nicht sein. Ich hasse es, im Rausch einer bezechten Nacht in einen neuen Lebensabschnitt hinüberzutaumeln, u. ziehe vor, in solchen Stunden zu Hause zu sitzen u. nachzudenken. Du schreibst da eine halb spaßige, halb bissige Bemerkung über Chanucka, die Anlaß zu einigen wichtigen Erklärungen gibt. Religion ist in jedem Fall eine Frage der Überzeugung. Drei Wege führen zu ihr: der erste beruht auf Erziehung u. Gewohnheit; Ihr habt eine gute Pflicht erfüllt, uns diesen Weg zu zeigen, aber wir denken zu viel u. unserer junger, zersetzender Geist kann es nicht fassen, dass wir auf Grund eines reinen Kinderglaubens Handlungen vollbringen sollen, die uns außerhalb der Gewohnheit stellen. Heute, nachdem ich auch den zweiten Weg hinter mir habe, fühle ich mich diesem ersten viel näher. Der zweite nämlich ist die Gesellschaft. Es erleichtert die Ausübung religiöser Dinge, wenn man sie als Glied einer Gemeinschaft erfüllt. Ich habe den Anschluß an diese Gemeinschaft gesucht, ich glaubte in dieser Gesellschaftsschicht eine Freundschaft gefunden zu haben, aber sie scheiterte gerade an dieser Gesellschaft, u. es blieb eine so gründliche tiefe Verachtung gegen diese jüdischen Kreise übrig, dass ein Umgang mit ihnen unmöglich ist. Und die anderen Juden (Assimilanten u. Zionisten) sind sowieso unmöglich. Bleibt also nur der dritte Weg: aus seiner eigenen menschlichen Entwicklung heraus ganz allmählich zu seinem Kinderglauben zurückzufinden. Das dauert lang u. führt über viele Umwege—aber es ist das Ziel jeder grossen Entwicklung—denn die grosse Wahrheit muss etwas ganz einfaches sein.

Und Freundschaft suche ich nur noch unter meinesgleichen, nachdem ich sie in Busoni so schnell gefunden u. schnell verloren habe. Kaisers versuchen die Lücke in meinem Leben auszufüllen u. schon dieser rührende Versuch lässt mich sie lieben.

Was ich geschenkt gekriegt habe: eine wunderschöne Tischdecke, 6 bastseidene Taschentücher, 6 Hutschenreuth Teetassen, Bücher u. Cigaretten u. von Lello u. Hide einen grossen Korb mit Obst, Tabak, Eingemachtes, Chianti, Schnaps, Süßigkeiten u.s.w.

CHAPTER 3

Figure 92. Kurt Weill. "Möglichkeiten absoluter Radiokunst." *Der deutsche Rundfunk* 3, no. 26 (29 June 1925): 1625-28. "Possibilities of Absolute Radio Art." A few weeks ago a collective of young Berlin artists, the November Group, stepped forward with a series of experiments that had been initiated and prepared at different places some time ago, but which reached their first and definitive result only here. The absolute film as it has progressed so far was presented in one of UFA's big theaters to an illustrious audience consisting of scientists, scholars, artists, and critics. This event again provides an occasion to take up the comparison between the movies and radio, which is all too often abused, in order to think it through thoroughly. If considered merely as entertainment institutions, the possibility of a comparison between these two gigantic technical achievements is obvious. Both are supplied by sources outside their own field: movies rely on theater and vaudeville, radio on music and spoken word. Viewed from an economic perspective, the two represent a new form of old popular entertainment, a new kind of diverting journalism. Both, however, do possess value of their own, unique to them, and which can grow into a new form of art by gradual development. New art can come into being only if new technique has become a matter of course. That is: new art is already bringing along the new technical innovations it requires as finished achievements. The cyclorama existed when the naturalistic stage needed it. Clarinets were invented when a new orchestral era began with Mozart. Technical devices await their use in the world of art, which must not itself be dependent on the former. The best example is quarter-tone music: today, in its early stages, it is regarded as a mere technique; it can only become an art form when several generations have dealt with it, when quarter-tone sonorities have become familiar to the general public.

The early stages of the movies consisted of groping toward new possibilities. It started with sensationalism. The first Sherlock Holmes movies from America as well as sentimental love stories coming out of Paris depended on basic instincts. Next came borrowing from literature: screen adaptations of plays and novels of all kinds, of all languages. Nature had to serve as the set. Countries were combed for new and sensational scenery. The quandaries of life, science, and politics were brought in. Finally one began to recognize the unique ways, the special opportunities of these movies in two areas: for the time being it was a continuation and perfection of the naturalism of the stage; literature passed on the exact representation of life to the movies, which possessed every possible technical device, the harsh realism of the big historical movies perhaps comprising the genre's final climax. After a while, however, the movies' other goal became the representation of the fantastic, the mysterious, and the transcendental, made possible only by tricks in the studio. *Dr. Caligari*, *Sumurun*, the dream sequence in Chaplin's *The Kid* are the finest results along that line. However, it always had to be pleasantly entertaining or at least didactic. The inspired combination of both directions in the American grotesque-movies [*Groteskfilm*] showed the dawning of a concept of a true film-art of its own, which possesses special means of expression, tempo, and dynamics. Various Parisian painters (e. g. Léger) designed movies that depicted the crazy jumble of thoughts and notions in the brain of a modern urban human being, while renouncing any kind of plot, theme, or interior connections. Here (and similar to Chaplin's touching comic elements) things can border on the tragic, if in the midst of crowded boulevards, in the midst of speeding trains a straw hat appears over and over again. Taking a look at the Germans—Ruttmann, Eggeling, etc.—the endeavors toward a film-art of its own lead to complete abstraction. A geometric "theme" is exposed and subsequently reworked into all different shapes according to purely musical laws. The diversified line-up of purely optical design-forces, the flowing into one another in a contrapuntal manner—of lines and circles, which are joined at the climax by the most expressive component, color—all of this is apt to evoke the outward impression of a musical piece, but it only offers the outline, the contour of the music. It can communicate an expression very well; but what is meant to be expressed is missing: the spiritual essence, the inner chant. This lack of essence turns the absolute film into commercial art [*Kunstgewerbe*]. But even as such it is entitled to a place of its own.

It is not difficult to predict that the development of radio will follow very similar patterns, except that the dependence on other branches of art will be much stronger, because up to this point radio as means of entertainment is an institution which only serves the propagation of musical and literary masterworks. As an educational institution it significantly helps millions of listeners eager to learn. Its artistic significance, however, lies above all in the quantitative rather than in the qualitative. Already a great deal has been accomplished by the possibility of carrying art to the masses, of allowing existing art to having an impact on the widest level, of broadcasting to the man on the street as well as the member of the propertied class not only the greatest creations of music and theater, but also their master performers. Even nature is being acoustically represented: the London station transmits the singing of nightingales and the breaking of waves on England's coast. Just as with the development of film, this will lead to a clear separation between radio and other art institutions, the latter still perceiving the former as competition for the time being. The arts will dispose some of their elements, whose transmission will be left to the microphone alone. Naturally these will be phenomena that are especially supported by radio transmission or only now are made possible by it. It is likely at this point that mainly those works are going to be considered, which require the invisibility of the whole apparatus, which perhaps make it necessary that the activity of the eye is completely shut off. In the sphere of the radio play people are already dealing with this issue. There is already talk of an audio play completely separate from the traditional theater, which will be developed into a new art genre according to its own set of rules and according to the aims of the studio facilities. Also, within the music world, radio will occupy its own special niche—probably through the gradual disappearance of stardom, by emphasis on intimate, private cultivation of music. In addition, however, there will be a process of perfection for radio technology, less with respect to the receiver but with respect to the studio. The goal would be too low if it were considered only to be the best possible transmission of music or readings. The movies brought along several innovations: the continuous change of scenery, the simultaneity of two events, the tempo of real life and the faster-than-life tempo of slapstick, the marionette-like truthfulness [*Wahrhaftigkeit*] of the animation film, and the possibility to follow a line from its genesis until its transition to different forms—all of which (transferred to acoustic conditions) has to be accomplished by the microphone. Just as the film has enriched optical means of expression, the broadcasting telephony has to enlarge the acoustic ones in ways yet to be discovered. The "acoustic slow-motion" has to be invented—and many other things. And all of this could lead up to an absolute radio art. The absolute movie faces the difficulty that our visual senses are tied too closely to the transmission of concepts based on nature and life in order to be perceived as a purely "melodic" art. The visual arts' expressionism, too, having aimed at similar goals, eventually failed because the spectators, and quite frequently even the artists themselves, have taken these abstract realms as a symbol of some kind of event. This danger is ruled out as far as music and the art of words [*Wortkunst*] are concerned. The dilettante view that one has to "think of something" while listening to a musical piece, that the enjoyment of music is linked to some sort of dramatic or idyllic notion, is proven false in practice time and again. The unspoiled audience, free of prejudices, will perceive music always as music per se, the enchanting merging of melodies and harmonies, which is illuminated by the creator's internal experiences as the nocturnal woods are lit up by the clear silvery moon. Now we can imagine very well that the sounds and rhythms of music will be joined by new sonorities, sonorities from different spheres: calls from human and animal voices, voices of nature, rushing of winds, waters, trees and then a host of new, unheard sounds, which the microphone could create artificially if sound waves were being raised or lowered, arranged in layers or merged, faded out or born anew. To emphasize the most important point once again: such an opus is not supposed to represent an atmospheric picture, no symphony of nature striving for the most realistic usage of all existing means, but it should be an absolute, spiritual work of art floating above the earth, with no other goal than the goal of every true art: to provide beauty, to turn mankind good with beauty, and making it indifferent toward the trivia of life.

Whether all this will remain utopian depends upon the progress of technology. Considering today's state of broadcasting telephony such an enterprise is hardly imaginable—but, on the other hand, in 1910 the absolute film would have been technically inadequate if not impossible. The whole broadcasting movement is not yet strong enough to approach the realization of its ultimate plans—a fact that should not keep us from considering all kinds of possibilities. To take up an earlier point, a first step will be turning the radio into a part of every-day life for the masses, a matter of course for the public instinct [*Volksempfinden*]. Something of substance can only be erected on the basis of an established concept, within a very familiar and well-liked situation. Considering only the sound, we can imagine such a work of art already today. We can even imagine that a certain sensation will be expressed, which may be more superficial than the content of a musical composition, but which can nevertheless spring from a deeper experience of the soul. Only the tension, the feeling of being filled up, and the form of such an artistic undertaking is beyond our grasp. Music, of all the arts, has been the only one so far that has been tied to the course of time. A painting and a sculpture are subject only to spatial considerations, they exist in form of a single copy only, and their impact is a continuous one. The impression of a poem is ubiquitous due to its readability and the abstractness of its thoughts. Only music unfolds its impact over time, but it possesses the most beautiful of all artistic means: the melody is the spirit, the pulsating life of music, and only by the melodies' ambiguity the form of a composition is created. But how can a melody happen within the frame of an absolute acoustical art [*Hörkunst*] that is not music? Which sounds and noises could replace melody in a near-perfect manner so that a period of time can be filled with the most intense experience? It is at this point that our imagination fails; here the creative force of a personality will set in, which will raise all previous attempts from the morass of the experiment to the purified sphere of art.

Weill (in Berlin) an Albert und Emma Weill, 15. Juli 1925: Die Rundfunkleute sprechen immer deutlicher davon, dass sie mich als musikalischen Redakteur fest anstellen wollen. Das hat für sie den Vorteil, dass sie mir nicht jede Zeile extra bezahlen müssen, u. für mich, dass ich ein ganz anständiges Fixum beziehe. Andrerseits bin ich natürlich dann noch mehr gebunden, muss oft auf die Redaktion u.s.w. Aber die Vormittage bleiben mir ja für meine Arbeiten—das ist die Hauptsache. Und über kurz oder lang müssen ja doch einmal stärkere Gelder aus den Kompositionen fliessen (Ich sehe Mutters Gesicht beim Lesen dieses Satzes). Die Pariser Aufführung hat mir sehr genützt.

Weill (in Berlin) an die Universal Edition, 18. August 1925: In der *Revue musicale* finde ich eine Besprechung des Violinkonzertes von Prunière. Ich sende Ihnen (übersetzt) die wichtigsten Sätze daraus: „Der erst 25jährige K. W. ist einer der begabtesten Musiker der jungen deutschen Schule ... er ist im Besitz eines Handwerks von ganz aussergewöhnlicher Sicherheit. Man muss den polyphonen Sinn des Autors anerkennen sowie die bemerkenswerte Geschicklichkeit, die Orchesterklänge abzuwägen u. auszugleichen. In seiner Art ist K. W.'s Konzert ein vollkommen gelungenes Werk."

Soeben vollendete ich ein neues Stück: *Der Neue Orpheus*, Concertino für Sopran, Geige u. Orchester (Text von Iwan Goll).

Weill (in Berlin) an die Universal Edition, 22. August 1925: Wichtige Neuigkeiten! Busch hatte mich für gestern telefonisch nach Dresden gebeten. Er hat die Absicht, so schnell wie möglich (wahrscheinlich am 8. Oktober!!) den *Protagonist* herauszubringen. Taucher, der beste Tenor für die Titelrolle, von dessen Entscheidung die Annahme abhing, hat im Prinzip bereits zugesagt. Dienstag zeigt ihm Busch den Klavierauszug; dann fällt die letzte Entscheidung. Aber Taucher fährt schon Ende Oktober nach Amerika, dann müsste ich mit der Uraufführung bis Mai warten. So aber wäre es (auch für Berlin) das erste Ereignis des Winters. Dass die Aufführung unter der Eile leiden wird, ist nicht zu befürchten, da ja Busch selbst dirigiert.

Weill (in Berlin) an die Universal Edition, 28. August 1925: Besten Dank für Ihre Nachricht. Ich bin sehr froh, dass es mir nun doch gelungen ist, die überraschende Annahme in Dresden zustande zu bringen. Generalm.[usikdirektor] Busch sagte mir, dass der Klavierauszug in Dresden autographiert u. von Ihnen übernommen wird. Ich bitte Sie nun gleich zu veranlassen, dass die Widmung

„Für Lenja"

auf dem Titelblatt angebracht wird (Sie steht nicht auf dem Manuskript, aber ich lege Wert darauf, dass sie eingefügt wird!). Den Titel habe ich geändert, das Werk heisst jetzt: „Kulissen", ein Akt Oper von Georg Kaiser, Musik von K.W.—Wegen weiterer Annahmen verhandle ich mit Szenkar u. Schulz-Dornburg. Besonders günstig steht es auch mit Coburg, wo mein Freund Albert Bing Opernleiter geworden ist (der mir begeistert über meine Oper geschrieben hat.)

In wenigen Wochen werde ich das fertige Textbuch zu einem neuen (abendfüllenden) Bühnenwerk, einer Art Operette, bekommen, das ich im Laufe des Winters komponieren will. . . . In Anbetracht der günstigen Lösung der Opernfrage werden Sie es nicht für unbescheiden halten, wenn ich noch einmal die pekuniäre Frage anschneide. Der Herbst lässt sich für mich sehr böse an. Ich habe keine Schüler, u. irgend eine andere Beschäftigung würde mich daran hindern, das neue Bühnenwerk zu schreiben. Nun hat mir Herr Direktor Hertzka fest u. mehrfach zugesagt, dass im Fall einer Annahme in Dresden einer Erhöhung u. Verlängerung meiner Rate nichts mehr im Wege steht, darum kann ich Sie jetzt ruhigen Gewissens ersuchen, die monatliche Summe (möglichst sofort) auf 200.- M. festzusetzen.

Weill (in Berlin) an Albert und Emma Weill, 17. September 1925: Sonntag bekomme ich den Besuch meines Dresdner Regisseurs Gielen zum Zweck einer gründlichen Vorbesprechung. Bisher habe ich weder die Dekorationsentwürfe noch eine Probe gesehen, u. Ihr könnt Euch denken, wie ich gespannt bin. Aber Ihr wisst, wie zermürbend schon die Probe eines Orchesterwerks für den Komponisten ist. Wie soll das erst bei einem Bühnenwerk sein. Da hilft nur eine tüchtige Portion Frechheit u. Wurschtigkeit– u. beides hab ich mir ja im Laufe der Zeit zugelegt. Mein Streichquartett pilgert in diesen Tagen durch 9 Städte Spaniens. Ein komisches Gefühl. Aber mein bestes Stück ist fertig geworden: *Der neue Orpheus*, Kantate für Sopran, Soloviolin u. Orchester. Lotte Leonard wird es singen.

Weill (in Berlin) an die Universal Edition, 26. September 1925: Gestern war ich nochmals in Dresden u. bin endgültig zur Einsicht gelangt, dass es für mich doch von grossem Vorteil ist, die Premiere des *Protagonist* zu verschieben. Das Werk war schon mehr als 3/4 einstudiert, u. man hätte den Termin vom 8. Oktober mit Leichtigkeit einhalten können, wenn nicht Taucher plötzlich in der Nervosität vor seiner Amerikareise den Kopf verloren hätte. Dazu kommt, dass Taucher, der tatsächlich der idealste Vertreter dieser Partie ist u. auf den ich nur sehr ungern verzichten würde, schon am 12. 11. nach Amerika abreist, dass die Oper also 2, höchstens 3 mal gegeben worden wäre. Das wäre natürlich sehr nachteilig für den Erfolg. Taucher selbst, Busch u. der Regisseur Gielen sind fest überzeugt, dass mit Taucher in der Titelrolle der *Protagonist* ein Sensationserfolg werden kann. Man versichert mir immer wieder, wieviel Freude man an dem Werk hat u. wie ungern man es aufschiebt. Taucher hat fest versprochen, am *1. März* mit der fertig studierten Rolle aus Amerika zurückzukommen, am 20. März soll dann die Premiere sein, worauf das Stück den ganzen April auf dem Spielplan bleibt u. vor allem als einziges Werk eines jungen Komponisten innerhalb der grossen Opernfestspiele herauskommen soll, die die Dresdener Staatsoper für Mai plant. Schliesslich vertraue ich Ihnen an, dass ich innerhalb kürzester Zeit ein neues Libretto (halb Oper, halb Ballett) bekommen werde, das ich bis Anfang 1926 zu vollenden u. noch für den gleichen Abend in Dresden anzubringen hoffe.

Weill (in Berlin) an die Universal Edition, 15. Oktober 1925: Es ist mir völlig unbegreiflich, warum Sie mit dem Erscheinen meiner Werke so zögern. Nachdem Frenkel schon vor mehreren Tagen einen Bürstenabzug des Klavierauszuges vom Violinkonzert bekommen hat, warte ich noch immer vergeblich auf die Korrekturabzüge. Auf diese Weise wird es dann natürlich unmöglich sein, das Violinkonzert zu dem Dessauer Termin, den Sie seit Monaten kennen, herauszubringen. Der Schaden liegt auf Ihrer Seite, da ich in Dessau sehr bekannt bin u. Sie wahrscheinlich eine beträchtliche Anzahl von Exemplaren abgesetzt hätten. Auch das *Quodlibet*, das seit einem Jahr bei Ihnen ruht u. das ich schon vor Monaten Korrektur gelesen habe, erscheint zu spät, um noch eine Aufführung durchzusetzen. Ich hoffe, dass es mit dem *Neuen Orpheus* nicht ebenso geht. Es liegt mir unendlich viel daran, dieses Stück so bald als möglich herauszubringen. Ich habe bei Furtwängler, Klemperer und Scherchen Chancen, die ich aber nur ausnützen kann, wenn ich mit grösster Beschleunigung Partitur u. Klavierauszug bekomme. . . .

Heute kann ich Ihnen mitteilen, dass ich an einer neuen Oper arbeite, einem ballettartigen Einakter *Royal Palace*, Text von Iwan Goll (ein herrliches Libretto). Ausserdem habe ich ein Ballett *Maschinen* von Terpis begonnen, das hier an der Staatsoper herauskommt. Auch von Georg Kaiser bekomme ich ein neues Libretto, u. schliesslich arbeitet ein hiesiger junger Literat nach meinen Angaben an einem abendfüllenden Operntext. Da ich eine günstige Zeit zum Arbeiten habe, hoffe ich viel von diesen Plänen in diesem Winter zu schaffen.

Weill (in Berlin) an Emma und Albert Weill, [Ende Oktober 1925]: Ich wünschte manchmal, ich könnte mehr, als ich es tue, Euer Leben mitleben. Aber ich mache jetzt die Jahre durch, wo der Künstler ständig auf dem Pulverfass ist, wo unverbrauchte Energien sich explosiv entladen müssen, wo eine gesteigerte Überempfindsamkeit einen ständigen Zustand der Spannung, der Erregung erzeugt. Nur so könnt Ihr manches begreifen, was Euch an mir vielleicht unverständlich erscheint. Jetzt hat es mich wieder gepackt. Ich bin eingegraben in diese neue Oper, ich gehe nur zur Erledigung der wichtigsten äusseren Dinge aus dem Hause. Ich muss einen Ausdruck meistern, der mir noch neu ist. Und ich stelle zu meiner Freude fest—was ich schon bei dem *Neuen Orpheus* entdeckt hatte—dass ich allmählich zu „mir" vordringe, dass meine Musik viel sicherer, viel freier, lockerer u.—einfacher wird. Das hängt auch damit zusammen, dass ich äusserlich unabhängiger, sicherer, heiterer u. weniger verkrampft geworden bin. Daran hat natürlich das Zusammenleben mit Lenja wieder starken Anteil. Das hat mir sehr geholfen. Es ist ja die einzige Art, wie ich einen Menschen neben mir dulden kann: ein Nebeneinander zweier verschiedener künstlerischer Interessen, ohne innere Bindung, jeder auf seinem Weg durch den anderen gefördert. Wie lange das geht? Ich hoffe: recht lang.

Weill (in Dessau) an Lotte Lenya, [28. Oktober 1925]: Hoesslin ist tatsächlich sehr untüchtig. Er kann weder dirigieren noch probieren—das ist bös. Die Leute lachen, spielen dauernd falsch (was er nicht einmal merkt), u. von Disziplin ist keine Spur. . . . Von mir ist es eine Dummheit, den Dessauern, die von allen die Dümmsten u. Spießigsten sind, dieses etwas rauhe, begrifflose, ganz dissonante Stück vorzusetzen. Es wird auf einmütige Ablehnung stossen. Man muss schon mit allem guten Willen eine Portion Schönberg verdaut haben, ehe man diese Musik begreifen kann.

Weill (in Berlin) an die Universal Edition, 30. Oktober 1925: Gestern war ich zur deutschen Uraufführung des Violinkonzertes in Dessau. Es war keine ideale Aufführung, aber Frenkel hat famos gespielt. Der Erfolg war stark für ein so reaktionäres Publikum, das die vorausgegangene Tanzsuite von Bartok völlig ablehnte. Zu schade, dass der Klavierauszug nicht fertig geworden ist!

Weill (in Berlin) an Emma und Albert Weill, 7. November 1925: Dieses gottverdammte Drecknest Dessau hat einen so düsteren Eindruck auf mich hinterlassen, dass ich tagelang unbrauchbar war. Ich habe noch nie eine so hochmütig ablehnende Atmosphäre erlebt wie bei diesem Gesindel. Da sie die Tanzsuite von Bartok, eines der wertvollsten u. leichtverständlichsten Werke unserer Zeit, das in 60 Städten Beifallsstürme erzeugt hat, mit völligem Schweigen aufgenommen haben, konnte ich für mein Konzert keinen Erfolg erwarten. Dazu kommt die unglückliche Konstellation. Hoesslin ist sehr unbeliebt. Und das mit Recht. Einen solchen Grad von Untüchtigkeit habe ich nicht für möglich gehalten. Die Aufführung war bös—bis auf den Geiger, der ausgezeichnet war. Die Kritiken sind vollkommen negativ, u. solange Herr v. Hoesslin dort ist, sieht mich Dessau nicht wieder.

Weill (in Berlin) an Emma und Albert Weill, 14. Dezember 1925: Ich habe jetzt eine böse Woche. In der Redaktion müssen wir hintereinander 3 Hefte fertig machen, da muss ich jeden Tag in die Stadt. Aber ich fühle mich sehr wohl, besonders wenn ich hinter meinem Schreibtisch sitze. Vorige Woche sollte ich an einem musikalischen Tee bei Stresemann teilnehmen; als das Sekretariat bei mir anrief, sagte ich, sie sollen sich an Jarnach wenden, das sei der einzige Komponist, der einen Frack hat. Dafür war ich gestern auf einem Ball beim Redaktion des *Börsencourier* u. heute bin ich mit Kaiser zur Première von *Wozzeck* von Alban Berg, einer ganz modernen Oper. In der öffentlichen Generalprobe war schon Skandal. In 3 Monaten bin ich auch so weit.

Weill (in Berlin) an Albert Weill, 1. Januar 1926: Ich glaube nicht, dass Ihr Euch eine Vorstellung machen könnt, was es heisst, in 2 1/2 Monaten eine Oper von fast einer Stunde Dauer fertigzustellen. Wenn ich nicht diese himmlisch ruhige Wohnung hätte u. mir nicht allen Verkehr vom Halse geschafft hätte, wäre das ja nicht möglich gewesen. Ich verspreche mir von der neuen Oper ziemlich viel u. glaube, dass sie einen bedeutsamen Schritt in meiner Entwicklung darstellt. Weihnachten war ich einen Tag bei Kaiser in Grünheide, musste aber am anderen Abend schon wieder in der Redaktion sein. Kaisers sind sehr freundschaftlich, mit Georg hatte ich eine lange, sehr aufrichtige Unterredung.

Figure 99. Kurt Weill. "Bekenntnis zur Oper." ***Blätter der Staatsoper Dresden*, Spielzeit 1925-26, no. 13 (April 1926): 97–99.** "Commitment to Opera." We cannot approach opera from the snobbish position of disinterested abstention. We cannot write operas while bemoaning at the same time the shortcomings of the genre. We cannot see opera as the fulfillment of a purely superficial responsibility while expending our true ideas in other forms. We must hold the conviction that our formal ideal can be realized within the parameters of the stage, that a theatrical work is capable of conveying the essential elements of our music. We must make a jubilant commitment to opera.

The awareness that nothing more could be added to, or coaxed from, the genre of music-drama made us fanatics of absolute music. We wanted to assert our own century against the preceding one, which we charged with a literary bent, with having caused a materialization of art. Music, as an end in itself, was to become again the sole purpose of our creative work. The study of Bach and pre-classical composers and the cultivation of chamber music led to an intensification of our musical experience. Even so, we could still not bring ourselves to neglect the operatic stage altogether. Some were attracted by the possibility of a wider impact, others by the difference from their own sensibilities. People wrote ballets—that is to say, they enhanced the effect of concert music by adding a visual dimension. But the dance was also structured according to musical laws, and the pacing of the stage was absent. And many thought that by despising this theatrical pacing they were offering proof of their exclusive musicianship.

Central to all this is the realization that we cannot approach the creation of a work for the stage by changing our musical thinking; we must make music in opera with the same abandon and imagination as in chamber music. It is not a matter, however, of transferring the elements of absolute music to opera; that would lead to cantatas, to oratorios. On the contrary: the dramatic impetus demanded by opera can be an essential component of all musical creation. Mozart taught me this. Whether composing an opera, a symphony, or a string quartet, he stays the same. He always exhibits the pacing of the stage, which is why he can remain an absolute musician, even when he has the infernal din come crashing over *Don Giovanni*. If our music possesses typically operatic elements—strict accentuation, concise dynamics, eloquently moving melodic lines—opera can once again become the most precious vessel for capturing our inner song.

It was only when I sensed that my music contains the tension of scenic events that I turned to the stage. I wrote the pantomime *Zaubernacht* for a Russian troupe at the Theater am Kurfürstendamm. The intense concentration of Russian theater taught me two things: that the stage has its own musical form whose laws derive organically from the unfolding of the action, and that something significant can be said on stage only with the simplest, most modest means. A nine-piece orchestra, a female singer, two female dancers and a group of children—such were the forces of this danced dream. I was thrilled when Georg Kaiser offered to write me the scenario for a full-length ballet. We set about working together. In ten weeks almost three-quarters of the piece was written. The score of the prelude and the first two acts was complete. Then came a block. We had grown out of the subject matter, the muteness of the characters bothered us, we had to burst the chains of the pantomime: it had to become opera. Georg Kaiser reverted to an earlier piece which he had at one point conceived in his mind in terms of opera, the one-act play *Der Protagonist*. Here we had what we were looking for: an unforced, unintended dovetailing of opera and pantomime. The melodramatic acting of the protagonist could only be conveyed by an operatic character; the high points of the action could only be expressed by music: the dialogue between brother and sister, the clandestinely hasty love scene, the transition to dance and the sudden shift from comedy into tragedy. The two pantomimes afforded an opportunity for lyrical expansion. In order to lend the proceedings a musical framework I gave the eight musicians something akin to the role of the chorus in Greek tragedy: they are supposed to open the drama, passively accompany it until they themselves intervene and, at the end, create the impression that we are guests of the Duke and have witnessed the exceptional performance of the protagonist.

Weill (in Berlin) an Emma und Albert Weill, 1. April 1926: Was sagt Ihr zu der fabelhaften Presse. Die Kritik von Bie, die ich eben schickte, ist nach seiner eigenen Aussage das beste, was er bisher über Oper geschrieben hat. Fabelhaft sind auch *Dresdener Neueste Nachrichten* von heute (Dienstag). Es ist doch recht aufregend, über Nacht eine Weltberühmtheit zu werden. Auch die paar schlechten Kritiken kommen mir sehr gelegen, weil bei einer einstimmig günstigen Presse die Ansprüche an mich ins Masslose steigen würden.

Weill (in Berlin) an Emma und Albert Weill, 8. April 1926: Seid nicht böse über mein Schweigen. Wir sind vorigen Sonnabend zu Kaisers hinausgefahren. Es war ganz herrlich draussen, wir haben schon stundenlang gesegelt, jeden Nachmittag gab es eine grosse Radtour, abends wundervollen Bordeaux. Kaiser hat eine sehr gute Zeit, u. wir arbeiten schon am Entwurf zu einem neuen Opernstoff. Ich bin gestern hereingekommen. Lenja bleibt noch bis Anfang nächster Woche, da sie sehr erholungsbedürftig ist.

Täglich kommen noch Kritiken aus Provinzblättern. *Frankfurter Zeitung*, die ja besonders wichtig ist, war ausgezeichnet, ebenso Breslau, Mannheim, Wien u.s.w. Ich habe bis jetzt schon mehr als 20 restlos anerkennende Kritiken, darunter ungefähr 10 in sensationeller Aufmachung. Es war eben tatsächlich „der" grosse Opernerfolg der Saison. Über die Auswirkung weiss ich noch nichts. . . . Bei mir war davon nicht so viel zu merken, weil mein Bekanntenkreis sich ja meistens aus „Kollegen" zusammensetzt, deren Begeisterung sich begreiflicherweise nicht so laut äussert. Jetzt wird mit allen erdenklichen Mitteln gegen eine hiesige Annahme intrigiert, u. da mich mein Erfolg noch mehr isoliert hat, wird die Berliner Aufführung kaum zustande kommen.

Figure 104. Oskar Bie. "*Der Protagonist*: Dresdner Opernhaus." *Berliner Börsen-Courier*, 29 March 1926. During the days of old England this lead actor and director of a strolling troupe would not have been such an estimable human being without his urge to maintain his love of truth against the deceptions of the actor's mask, notwithstanding his passionate love for his own profession. His sister becomes a mirror of truth for him. With just one glance into her eyes, he is able to rid himself of the stage's demons. She has never deceived him. But just this once she has remained silent about her own affair of the heart. She staggers into love. During a rehearsal of the Pantomime, she staggers into his work. The discovery of her secret disturbs the actor to such a degree that he actually stabs her to death in the frenzy of playing his role. The profession takes a life, and life destroys the profession.

Georg Kaiser first brought out this double play of stage and real life as a freestanding one-act play, then, with only minor changes, turned it into an opera libretto. Stressing a double meaning, he concerns himself with a performance before a Duke, which at first is rehearsed as a buffo-esque pantomime, and then, on new orders from the duke, as a tragic pantomime. Tragic stage action spills over into real life. He imagines two orchestras—one for the happenings on stage and one for the play itself—allowing everything to be reduced to two opposing sides: playfulness and seriousness, comedy and tragedy, theater and real life. One could call it a crossing of Schnitzler motifs with those of *Ariadne* and *Pagliacci*, if only the symbolism of ideas weren't so typically Kaiser's: the ingenious worsening of the matter, the affected curling of language. It is not so much that the text is perceived and expressed musically, but rather that its fate rests on the sort of music that genius can hear and shape for itself.

Kurt Weill, a pupil of Busoni, whose previous works have drawn instant attention to his outstanding talent, is capable of finding such music. He seeks it at the play's beginning but sways uncertainly; then he finds it, grabs hold of it, intensifies it and deepens it to such an extent that at the dreadful catastrophe, in which the characters on stage seem to resemble something like dancing ideas, the music overarches them completely.

Weill employs his instrumental resources very originally and very effectively: there are two orchestras, the one below [in the pit] representing "real life", with strings, oboes, bass clarinet, horns, trombones, percussion—the other above, on stage, an octet made up of two flutes, two clarinets, two trumpets, two bassoons. But this is no longer the traditional division between orchestral and stage-music. It now has two souls. After an announcement, the stage musicians (in costume) descend to a podium in the orchestra pit, participating in the general symphony, since the stage at first is real life. For the performance itself they climb up and accompany the first, merry, pantomime without the lower orchestra. For the second, tragic, pantomime, they play with the orchestra in the pit. Real life reenters. Since only one of them is victorious, they grow silent only to re-appear at the end of the piece to announce real life with mockingly solemn fanfares from the stage. Up to now, there has never been an opera, where a multitude of orchestras has been so spiritually, so symbolically conceived. It is not a question of orchestral versus chamber music; there are elements of expression from diverse worlds, whose conflicts are the essence of this piece. It is also a drama of the orchestra.

Weill, who does not think in naturalistic but in stylized terms, treats the human voice as a vocal instrument, not in a declamatory or instrumental way, but rather as a voice per se. Therefore, he favors a new melody over respect for words. This is an important step toward a modern way of singing, toward the future of opera. In crucial cases words are dropped altogether, as in interjections of solemn, tragic, or mocking sentiments, which indulge themselves in melodies and lyric intensification and express themselves only in coloraturas. Or as in this new coloratura, which takes words—secrets, lies, love—these insinuatingly playful words onto singing lips, letting them melt into the absolute musical language of the duet like spring snow on the warm ground. How often have I recommended this kind of perspective for opera. Now I am experiencing it.

Weill's musical style is somewhere between Busoni's psychological intellectualism and the finely etched wind-graphics of Stravinsky. Yet he is totally his own person, independent, not relying on anyone. He loves the sound of the brass, which everywhere today reacts against the string sound of romanticism. Every romanticism, every ecstasy is passé, landscapes and soulful shadows laid out over them, but the expression of emotion is somehow bound up in music, which forms its great and powerful nuances and its silent depths from its own nature. It is this class of antiromantic music, basically absolute despite all characteristical types, responsible only to itself, which settles softly over the world nowadays. Its language is of the latest modern freedom, without grimace or malice. In the course of the piece it steadily matures.

The architecture is grandiose. The first breakthrough ensues with the actor's foreboding of his approaching insanity. A tremendous intensification, upon which the great *sordinato* of the sister's love scene has been built. A duet which dissolves into pure music. The stupid, haughty chords of the majordomo, who orders the buffo pantomime. The dance-like transition. The exquisite parodic octet of the upper wind-group as an illustration of the buffo-esque. The droll vocalization of the pantomime players, the vocal quartet accompanying the brass chords. The first outpouring of the sisterly confession. The tragic pantomime, dark colors, a gradually emerging continuo of timpani played with wooden mallets, elementally increasing in sound, B and C sharp, the giant strokes of tragedy, shrieks of dissonant instruments breaking out, pure D-major of the upper trumpets as judges, remaining G-minor of the lower trombones as a lingering sound.

Once again one went to Dresden, the suburb of modern opera, although its feats can be challenged only by the unique *Wozzeck*, the flower of its genre. The achievement is astonishing. Busch conducts the divided and all-embracing score as if had never rehearsed anything else. Josef Gielen creates a very effective staging, the main room of an inn with scaffolds before which Mahnke hangs the exquisitely made balcony backdrops, at first colourful and happy, then, reversed, black and gloomy. The two couples' acting styles of the cheerful and the tragic pantomimes are clearly and sharply distinguished. Curt Taucher is simply magnificent as a wildly moved, adventurously imaginative, truly tragicomic hero of a refreshing strength and vividness in voice, profile, movement, sentiment. The sister is sung by Stünzner with great love for the new style, supported by a practiced technique. Schöpflin is the realistically portrayed innkeeper. Everything has been well and smoothly coached, and no inhibitions toward an unfamiliar task seem to have hampered or confused anyone.

Was it a purely mental enjoyment? Was it an intellectual discovery of new operatic worlds? Perhaps it was a bit of that, but only in the consciousness of a critic, who holds the threads of the development of this insurmountable genre in his hands and examines them. For the non-philosophical theatergoer it was immediate effect, a stage adventure in a new form, the fact of a musical talent, which looks into the future not only on the basis of knowledge, but will conquer on its own ability, nourished by the compelling power of invention and imagination. This is the student's step beyond the master Busoni.

Figure 105. Schwesternbund der Leipzig-Loge, XXXIII Nr.496 U.O.B.B. Dear Mrs. Weill, dear Sister! The *Schwesternbund* most heartily wishes to congratulate you, as the mother, and your dear family, for the extraordinary success of your son Kurt on the occasion of the world premiere of his first opera! With sisterly greeting! Fanny Rosenthal, President; Lily Joske, Recording Secretary.

Figure 106. "Pressestimmen zum *Protagonist*." "Press Clippings about *Der Protagonist*."

Dresdner Neueste Nachrichten. Without further ado: this "act opera" renews one's faith in the future of musical theater. A way has been found—by brazenly turning away from the playground of romantic sentimentality, briefly to blunder through the anarchic neighborhood of Schönberg, suddenly with enlightened explanations the spirited guide Busoni showed his searching pupil a path leading to unchartered territory. The stranger remains as yet somewhat astonished and confused, but the road—if followed leads to great heights. . . .

The dramatic impulse was unmistakable; the musician has been seduced by the contrary nature of the two pantomimes. And he succeeded indeed to intensify the poetic idea through the means of music. He even succeeded where least expected: in the great disputes between the Protagonist and his sister, that problematic, philosophical dialogue, which contains the entire philosophy of the play. He succeeded, because his music remains absolutely with sensuality, because it does not try to expound, but it is loaded with the same dramatic tension as the play.

Weill succeeds in characterizing the change of mood through use of purely musical means, exploiting them with a true sense of theater. He splits up his orchestra and through this division emphasizes the poetic idea of the libretto, an excellent inspiration, which up to that point contained only theoretical and no actual dramatic power. These strolling players now perform the music in the style of a puppet play traversing pantomime, which is effective because of its grotesque comedy. The actor's fantasy is within himself, turned away from life, intensified by a sense of happiness over his own delusions. Into the great madness of this improvised comedy of jealousy a quartet enters, in which the four voices of the performers sing only vowels, in its bluntness belonging to the best of the score. The protagonist's world of madness now gains its strongest intensity. But there is a sudden turn of events. Comedy turns to Tragedy. The imaginary Duke, a sort of Jourdain (*Ariadne*), a higher, invisible force, demands a serious play. Life intervenes, the larger orchestra in the pit gets involved. Reality and madness are mixed. The mood is one of unsettling power. During charged moments it's as if the tragic Muse herself bursts forth. The scene becomes transparent. The music says what the play alone could not. The resounding D-major fanfares by the fantastic 8 musicians gruesomely announce the catastrophe of madness. The curtain over the play on the stage have fallen; the play has become reality. There no longer is a difference between real and enacted madness.

Weill's pronounced talent for the stage proves itself also through the way he treats the figure of the ducal *Hausmeister*. At first he appears as a garrulous, sycophant to his easy-go-lucky master, he sings silly coloraturas and pleases himself with senseless tirades. The second time he appears—and this is entirely Weill's own idea—he is a somber messenger who evokes a tragic fate. This is no empty symbolism, this is gripping demonic nature made effective through theatrical means. The protagonist's jubilant intoxication of happiness, abruptly turns into ghastly desperation. The dramatic concept of music and thereby play fuse into one cohesive union.

Weill (in Berlin) an die Universal Edition, 29. April 1926: Eben schreibt mir ein bekannter deutscher Generalmusikdirektor: „Wann beginnt eigentlich die U.E. mit der sonst üblichen Propaganda? Die Stille kommt mir etwas merkwürdig vor." Es ist also glücklich so weit, dass aussenstehenden Musikern Ihr Schweigen bez. des *Protagonisten* auffällt. Ich gestehe Ihnen, dass ich darüber aufs tiefste verstimmt bin. Die Intendanten sagen sich natürlich: wenn sich der Verleger so ausschweigt, kann es mit dem Erfolg nicht so weit her sein. Wenn der Prospekt noch nicht fertig ist, hätten Sie wenigstens eine Mitteilung herausgeben müssen. Der Erfolg des *Protagonist* stand in nichts hinter dem des *Wozzeck* zurück, die Presse ist genau so sensationell, u. überall, wo von moderner Oper gesprochen wird, werden beide Werke nebeneinander genannt. Jeder, der dabei war, kann Ihnen bestätigen, dass noch keine Erstlingsoper eines 25jährigen einen solchen Erfolg gehabt hat. Durch Ihr Verhalten sieht es nun so aus, als sei es der übliche Achtungserfolg gewesen. Sie setzen sogar Ihre Taktik fort, mir die weiteren Annahmen zu überlassen. Wenn Ihnen an einer Annahme der hiesigen Staatsoper liegt, so muss ich Sie dringend ersuchen, die Sache sofort u. energisch in die Hand zu nehmen. Solange ich persönlich verhandle, bemühen sich einige mir wenig wohlgesinnte Leute, die Verhandlungen zum Stillstand zu bringen—was ihnen jetzt vollkommen gelungen ist, da ich weder von Kleiber noch Hörth etwas höre.

Weill (in Berlin) an Emma und Albert Weill, 27. Mai 1926: Im übrigen werde ich immer mehr zum Einsiedler, u. wenn ich Lenja nicht hätte, die meinem Lebensgefühl immer neue Frische zuströmen lässt, wäre ich wohl schon der vollendete Hypochonder. So kann ich mir es leisten, den äusseren Abstand von den Menschen im gleichen Maasse [sic] wachsen zu lassen, wie ich mich innerlich von ihnen entferne. Und aus dem Hochmut gegen die anderen erwächst die Demut vor sich selbst (die man auch Frömmigkeit nennen kann).

Weill (in Berlin) an Maurice Abravanel, 9. Juni 1926: Ich habe in den 10 Wochen seit der *Protagonist*-Premiere wie im Fieber gearbeitet u. war für meine Umgebung überhaupt nicht vorhanden. Vielleicht nimmt es einen Teil meiner Schuld Ihnen gegenüber, wenn ich Ihnen sage, dass ich in dieser Zeit den ganzen 1. Akt meiner neuen (3.) Oper (1 Stunde Musik!) komponiert habe. . . . Kleiber hat meinen 2. Einakter *Royal Palace* zur Uraufführung erworben. Das Stück soll Anfang Februar unter Kleiber u. Hörth mit Dekorationen von Chagall herauskommen. . . .

Die Arbeit am neuen Werk, der Musiquette *Na und?*, beschäftigt mich stärker als alles vorher. Es ist auffallend, wie meine dramatische Begabung selbst bei einem ganz leichten, graziösen Stoff die Theaterwirksamkeit durchsetzt.

Weill (in Alassio) an Emma und Albert Weill, [nach dem 26. Juni 1926]: Endlich nach 2tägigem Aufenthalt am Meer habe ich mich von den Züricher Strapazen soweit erholt, dass ich Geduld habe, Euch ausführlicher zu berichten. Diese Musikfesttage waren doch furchtbar anstrengend. Man stellt sich die Berühmtheit viel leichter vor, als sie ist. Abgesehen von den aufreibenden Proben, den persönlichen Verpflichtungen, den fast 100 Menschen, die mich „ausführlich" sprechen wollten, gab es täglich feierliche Empfänge, mittags, abends u. nachts, u. a. ein märchenhaftes Gartenfest auf dem Schloss der reichsten Seidenhändler sowie ein Déjeuner mit 25 Gängen, von Frau MacCormick im vornehmsten Hotel veranstaltet. . . . Wir sind dann über Mailand u. Genua hierher gekommen. Es ist unsagbar schön. Ein tiefblauer Himmel, die tropische Vegetation, Palmen, Kakteen, Feigen, das salzige Meer u. die heisse Sonne—da vergisst man alles andere.

Weill (in Berlin) an Lotte Lenya, [Juli 1926?]: Jetzt vor einer Woche saßen wir in Verona auf der Piazza Signori u. fingen allmählich an zu merken, wie schön es da war. Jetzt, wenn ich daran zurückdenke, habe ich doch gehörig Sehnsucht nach Dir—also weg mit den Erinnerungen, übermorgen sehe ich Dich ja. Das war schon früher so: wenn ich mich nach Dir sehne, so denke ich am meisten an den Klang Deiner Stimme, den ich wie eine Naturkraft, wie ein Element liebe. In diesem Klang bist Du (für mich) ganz enthalten, alles andere ist nur ein Teil von Dir, u. wenn ich mich in Deine Stimme einhülle, bist Du ganz bei mir. Ich kenne jede Nuance, jede Schwingung Deiner Stimme, u. höre genau, was Du sagen würdest, wenn Du jetzt neben mir wärest—u. wie Du es sagen würdest. Und plötzlich ist mir dieser Klang wieder ganz fremd u. neu und dann ist es höchste Seligkeit, zu wissen, wieviel streichelndes Liebkosen diese Stimme für mich hat—das ist dann wie in den ersten Wochen, als ich schon den Gedanken an Dich für Vermessenheit hielt. Das ist aber das Schöne: daß ich heute wie in der ersten Stunde eine Ehrfurcht vor Dir empfinde, die es mir fast unbegreiflich erscheinen lässt, daß Du zu mir gekommen bist, und daß es so schön geworden ist. Und jetzt, wo es wieder wie am ersten Tag ist, bin ich auch nicht mehr traurig darüber, daß da irgendwo Deine Stimme klingt—u. ich sie nicht höre.

. . . Dienstag bei Frau von Nostitz war es ulkig. 2 Etagen am Lützowplatz, mit schloßartiger Einrichtung und sehr schönen echten Sachen, dazu Diener u. alles was dazugehört. Darin eine schöngeistige Dame mittleren Alters, literarisch orientiert, im Vorstand des Penclubs, Gattin eines Diplomaten, bekannt mit sämtlichen internationalen Größen von Literatur und Politik. Nur die jungen Musikgrößen haben ihr noch gefehlt—also muß ich ran. Gäste außer Arrau und mir: der frühere (kaiserliche) Intendant von Wiesbaden, 2 junge Schriftsteller (ein hysterischer jüdischer und ein monoklig arischer) sowie die letzte Liszt-Schülerin, die in fantastisch vorsintflutlicher Weise Klavier spielte. Später sprach man über den „Durchbruch bei Goethe", die Temperatur Stravinskis, u. die geheimnisvolle Macht des Katholizismus. Ich spielte den gewandten Unterhalter, indem ich weder meine Limonade umwarf, noch mit der Zigarette etwas verbrannte, dafür aber alle halbe Stunde eine treffende Bemerkung von mir gab. Worauf die Gnädige der Hoffnung Ausdruck verlieh, mich im Herbst wieder bei sich zu sehen. Meine Verbeugung war korrekt. Der Diener bekam eine Mark. Im angeregten Gespräch über den auch mir so gänzlich unerwarteten Ausgang des letzten Tennistourniers betraten wir die Straße. Du siehst—ich bin gänzlich mondän geworden. . . . Jeder Notenkopf im *Protagonist* ein B-u-s-s-i für Dich!!

Weill (in Berlin) an Emma und Albert Weill, 22. Juli 1926: Meine 4 wöchige Abwesenheit hat mein Freund Jarnach benutzt, um einen Sturm von Intrigen gegen mich zu entfesseln. Da man mir künstlerisch nicht beikommen kann, stellt man mich jetzt als einen charakterlosen Schieber hin, u. beeinflusst alle maßgebenden Kreise in diesem Sinne. Jeden Tag höre ich eine neue Klatscherei gegen mich, u. alle laufen sie bei dem Einen zusammen. Etwas dagegen zu tun, wäre sinnlos. Man muss sie ausklaffen lassen.

Weill (in Berlin) an Peter Bing, 3. September 1926: An meiner Bühnenmusik zu Grabbes *Herzog Theodor von Gothland* hättest Du Deine Freude gehabt. Ich habe selten so farbig, dramatisch u. einfallsreich geschrieben u. vor allem klingt jetzt alles, wie ich es mir vorstelle. Besonders gelungen sind ein kleiner türkischer Marsch, ein Lied mit Harfe u. Saxophon, ein schwungvolles Schlachtlied, Kriegsmusik, Choreffekte u. ein grosser Trauermarsch. Die Aufführung war musikalisch sehr gut, aber die Regie versagte gänzlich u. das Ganze hatte keinen starken Nachhall—ausser meinen 1000.- M. Sonst wenig Neues. Jarnach schweigt nach der Aussprache, die mir in allen Punkten recht gab. Hertzka kommt in diesen Tagen. Er trieft vor Liebenswürdigkeit. Wie steht es mit Papas Konzert. Uraufführung *Orpheus* kann er haben. Grüss ihn!

Weill (in Berlin) an die Universal Edition, 25. November 1926: Ich danke Ihnen sehr für die Übersendung des Libretto-Entwurfs von Hans Kafka, mit dem ich mich eingehend befasst habe. Die Idee des Stückes ist ganz ausgezeichnet, u. wenn sie mir auch vorläufig eher für ein Schauspiel als für eine Oper zu passen scheint, so bin ich doch überzeugt, dass in gemeinsamer Arbeit hier ein sehr schönes Textbuch zustande kommen könnte, u. ich hoffe, dass sich in nächster Zeit einmal Gelegenheit für mich bieten wird, mit dem Autor persönlich die Möglichkeit einer solchen Zusammenarbeit zu besprechen. Nun habe ich allerdings die feste Absicht, nach *Na Und?* zunächst einmal meine Opernproduktion für einige Zeit zu unterbrechen, u. die Auswirkungen meiner bisherigen Bühnenwerke nicht immer durch die Ankündigung einer neuen Oper zu stören. (So konnte ich jetzt in Dresden anlässlich der *Cardillac*-Premiere beobachten, dass augenblicklich schon beinahe mehr Interesse für *Na Und?* als für *Royal Palace* herrscht.) Falls Sie daher für Kafkas Libretto Interessenten haben, die sofort an die Ausarbeitung herangehen würden, so würde ich selbstverständlich im Interesse des Autors verzichten. In jedem Fall danke ich Ihnen für Ihre Anregung.

Als Erklärung meines gestrigen Telegramms teile ich Ihnen mit, dass Stanislawski von dem Inhalt des *Protagonisten*, den ihm der Übersetzer (mit einer kleinen Änderung nach der revolutionären Seite hin) mitgeteilt hat, ausserordentlich begeistert ist. Er will so schnell wie möglich die Musik kommen lassen, u. es ist möglich, dass er das Werk noch in diesem Winter herausbringt. . . . Die Bearbeitung, die er vorhat, ist sehr geschickt; sie würde allerdings breiter angelegt sein u. daher einige musikalische Erweiterungen verlangen; doch würde sich diese Arbeit im Fall einer Annahme wohl lohnen, da Stanislawski das Werk serienweise spielen würde.

Figure 115. Karl Holl. "Kurt Weill: *Royal Palace*: Uraufführung in der Berliner Staatsoper." *Frankfurter Zeitung*, 4 March 1927. After Krenek's *Johnny*: one step closer towards "Opera of Today." An experiment in theatrical production of contemporary topics, on the border between straight play, pantomime, and opera, incorporating film. Krenek, who wrote his own librettos, who was able to write his own librettos, received better counsel than Weill, who collaborated with Ivan Goll. Krenek, well versed in stagecraft, even where he wants to be lofty, writes solid, good all-around theater for music. Goll, the lyrical surrealist, almost disrupts the playful themes with a world of total sentiment and *revue* with music. But on its own, this music, the opera's greatest asset thanks to its sensitivity to its own time, stands in long passages in inner opposition to the soft scenery.

Royal Palace? . . . A hotel, near one of Upper Italy's lakes. This name is merely a cue for the action, and that's the end of it. A play about the misunderstood modern woman. Honk-honk—and she makes her entrance on the terrace with her three gentlemen. The Husband, who "holds" her and promises to remain true 'til bankruptcy doth do them part, who promises her the lake, an airplane, and indeed, the entire continent. Her "yesterday's lover," who "needs" her, offers her pearls and "The Heaven of our Nights." "Tomorrow's lover" first lays flowers, then the vast realm of fantasy at her feet. Attention! Film! Dance! Pantomime! The Magic of Behind-The Stage-Atmosphere! Despite of all of this, love's labor lost. Because Dejanira, Janirade, Rajedina, Nirajade are tired: tired of the sun, of champagne and tears. Disgusted with the ubiquitous male ego, unrecognized and impure she gives herself back to Nature; at night, she strides towards the foaming lake. The husband cries in front of the curtain: Help! Someone has drowned!

Upon closer scrutiny, the problem is more of yesterday than of today; it is late romanticism in contemporary make-up. Novelty, in its dramaturgical packaging (with cars, airplanes, film, revolving stage, panorama etc.) appears slapped-on. And the whole thing—viewed in the twilight of grotesque and sentimentality—grows into a matter for aesthetes. Nobody who actually lives in the present and is able to look beneath this era's skin would likely to be mourning for Dejanira. Except perhaps for the composer, who entered the scene early with his young works, and like this opus 17, are evidence of great technical talent and solid ability. If by the virtue of its libretto *Royal Palace* is more lyrical than *Protagonist*, with which Weill made his successful operatic debut last winter, one still experiences an unusual inner tension in his new score, which accommodates the scene's dramatic moods and its intentions. Most striking is the tonal mastery of the dance-like time element [*Zeitgestus*], with all of its rhythmical and colorful peculiarities ("Ballet of the Waiters and the Bellhops," "Pantomime of Nights"). Also effective is the "horizon of sound" this Busoni student has created to animate the proceedings in "Voices from the Water" (Soli and Female Chorus). Add to that, the piano solo as a realistic soundtrack for film. And above all: the code of spiritual static and sensuous economy worthy of better theatrical material. One found the composer's preferences well looked after in his cantata *Der neue Orpheus*, text by Goll as well, moving and essentially related to the ideas of *Royal Palace*, which preceded the opera as a quasi-overture. Orpheus: today's artist; rides the express from Athens to Berlin; meets Eurydike at the *Schlesischer Bahnhof*; unable to draw her away from Orcus; stranded in daily life; shoots himself in the heart in the waiting room. A variety number elevated to intellectuality. For a melodramatically capable soprano, solo violin and an unusually diaphanous orchestra. Delia Reinhardt—actually much too straight-forward for this role, had to make the best of it in front of the footlights of the Staatsoper.

The performance tried to atone for the opera's shortcomings. Kleiber modeled the sound with every stratagem, finesse of ear and with a great effort. Hörth played a superb game with arms and legs, levers and wheels, clouds and water, film reels, large and small skylights. Aravantinos starred as designer, Terpis as choreographer assisted in a not thoroughly convincing manner. In the principal roles: Reinhardt, Schützendorf, Kern and Jöken. Thus, from the outset, success had been assured. In order to complete the evening—and possibly also as a precaution—the problematic Weill was accompanied by the unproblematic de Falla: *Maestro Pedro's Puppet Play*, which last summer delighted the guests of the Zurich Music Festival in its original form as a puppet play. Transplanting this high romantic form of culture onto the opera stage was not to the best idea. Yet Kleiber and Hörth did everything to make it tasteful to Berlin audiences with the help of Henke, Scheidl and Genia Guszalewicz and an ensemble of children as real life dolls.

Weill (in Berlin) an die Universal Edition, 4. April 1927: Es ist der erste Versuch, in einer Oper das Wesen unserer Zeit von innen her zu beleuchten, nicht von den selbstverständlichen äusseren Requisiten. Das Thema dieser Oper: Das Aneinandervorbeireden und -Handeln der heutigen Menschen. . . . Es ist der Typ einer heiteren Oper, wie er seit dem *Rosenkavalier* nicht weitergeführt wurde, und wie ihn die Theater suchen,—nicht grotesk oder parodistisch, sondern heiter und musikantisch. Die musikalische Form: Siebzehn abgeschlossene Nummern, dazwischen Rezitative oder gesprochene Dialoge mit Klavier oder kammermusikalischen Besetzungen.

Weill (in Berlin) an die Universal Edition, 2. Mai 1927: In Eile die Mitteilung, dass ich meine Absichten bez. Baden-Baden geändert habe. Ich habe plötzlich einen sehr schönen Einfall gehabt, an dessen Ausführung ich jetzt arbeite. Titel: *Mahagonny*, ein Song-Spiel nach Texten von Brecht. Ich denke, das kleine Stück bis Mitte Mai zu vollenden. Kann ich es Ihnen dann zur Herstellung des Materials u. Klavierauszugs schicken? Sie werden übrigens auch ausserhalb Baden-Badens Verwendung dafür haben.

Weill (in Berlin) an die Universal Edition, [26. Mai 1927]: Heute ging der Rest der *Mahagonny*-Partitur an Sie ab. Eben bekomme ich Ihren Brief vom 23. ds. u. sende Ihnen sofort ein Exemplar der *Hauspostille*, um dessen *Rücksendung* ich bitte. Diese Texte sind aber *nur* zur Orientierung für den Kopisten bestimmt. Der genaue Gesamttext mit Zwischentiteln, Finale u. Szenerieangaben geht Ihnen in den allernächsten Tagen zu zur Verwendung für das Textbuch. Vielleicht könnten Sie das kleine Textbuch besonders reizvoll ausstatten, wenn Sie die 5 Bühnenbilder, die der bekannte Theatermaler Caspar Neher für Baden-Baden machen wird, als Buchillustrationen beigeben würden.

Weill (in Berlin) an Lotte Lenya, [3.? Juni 1927]: Endlich habe ich Zeit, Dir ausführlich zu schreiben. In Essen war das nämlich ganz unmöglich. Das wirst Du einsehen, wenn ich Dir jetzt der Reihe nach erzähle. Der Flug war herrlich. Das Sicherheitsgefühl ist geradezu erstaunlich u. man ist viel weniger nervös als in der Eisenbahn. Der schönste Moment ist der, wenn das Flugzeug sich ganz langsam in die Luft hebt. Montag Nachmittag hatten wir dann eine Vorbesprechung [mit den Essener Behörden] u. abends gingen wir quer durch die Werke, wobei einige überwältigende akustische Eindrücke mir plötzlich eine ganz neue Klangvorstellung für das Stück gaben. Dienstag sind wir 10 Stunden mit dem Auto durchs ganze Ruhrgebiet gefahren, bis zum Rhein. Koch kennt die Gegend sehr genau u. konnte uns alles erläutern. Als wir aus dem giftigen Qualm des Ruhrtales an den klaren hellen Rhein kamen, dachten wir schon: bloss nicht mehr zurück in die Giftgase! u. weiter: wie schön wäre es, die bunte Lebendigkeit dieses Stromes zu gestalten anstelle der düstergrauen Fabriken da hinten. Aber als wir dann am anderen Mittag aus dem Bergwerk wieder ans Tageslicht kamen; da war es klar: das furchtbare Grauen da unten, die masslose Ungerechtigkeit, dass Menschen 700 Meter unter der Erde in völliger Finsternis, in einer dicken schweligen Luft eine unerträglich schwere Arbeit verrichten, nur damit Krupp zu ihren 200 Millionen jährlich noch 5 hinzuverdienen—das muss gesagt werden, u. zwar so, dass es keiner mehr vergisst. (Aber es muss überraschend kommen, sonst stopfen sie uns den Mund!). Wir waren 4 Stunden im Bergwerk, 6-700 Meter tief, 2 Stunden gelaufen, dann auf allen Vieren durch 2 Schollen geklettert, dann auf Leitern 150 Meter nach unten—schliesslich pechschwarz in die Badewanne. Heute tun mir noch alle Glieder weh. Donnerstag haben wir noch einen Flug übers Ruhrgebiet gemacht, dann waren wir stundenlang in den Stahlwerken bei Krupp, das war ungemein erfrischend u. beruhigend nach dem schrecklichen Eindruck. Dazwischen waren wir im Rathaus, in Bochum u. Duisburg, in Museen u. Archiven. Wir haben einen sehr günstigen Vertrag aufgesetzt, hoffentlich kommt er zustande. Wir bekommen 5-7000.- M (Jeder) Honorar, das Stück gehört aber uns. Der Titel soll wahrscheinlich sein: „REP" (Ruhrepos), Essen Dokumentarium. Spesen haben sie so anständig bezahlt, dass ich noch 30.- M übrig habe.

Weill (in Berlin) an die Universal Edition, 6. Juni 1927: Es handelt sich nun darum, ob Sie nur die Texte der 5 Songs aus der *Hauspostille* oder (was natürlich besser wäre) den vollständigen Text mit Szenarium, Zwischentexten u. Finale drucken wollen. Im letzten Falle müssten Sie sich zunächst mit Bert Brecht (Berlin W. Spichernstr. 16) in Verbindung setzen. Ich würde es für am besten halten, wenn Sie den vollständigen *Mahagonny*-Text mit den Bildern Nehers als *besonderes* kleines Heft herausbringen würden, da das Stück als Einlage in Revuen u.s.w. sehr gute Auswertungsmöglichkeiten hat. Bitte senden Sie mir sofort nach Fertigstellung einen Klavierauszug, den ich zur Einstudierung der „Bessie" hier brauche.

Weill (in Berlin) an die Universal Edition, 22. Juni 1927: Soeben schreibt mir Iwan Goll aus Paris, dass er mit Diaghilew über *Royal Palace* u. *Orpheus* ausführlich gesprochen u. ihm beide Klavierauszüge übergeben hat. Die Sache steht günstig, u. Goll schlägt vor, mit Ihnen zusammen eine Art von „Generaloffensive" auf Diaghilew zu unternehmen. Ich bitte Sie nun sehr, Diaghilew sofort u. mit grösstem Nachdruck zu schreiben (jetzige Adresse: S. de Diaghilew, Director of Russian Ballets, Princess Theatre, London). *Royal Palace* ist ohne Änderung als Ballett darzustellen, denn so war es ja immer gedacht.

Weill (in Berlin) an die Universal Edition, 4. August 1927: Der sensationelle Erfolg von *Mahagonny* in Baden-Baden hat sich unterdessen in einer Fülle glänzender Kritiken ausgewirkt, die ich Ihnen in den nächsten Tagen zugehen lasse, da Sie ja (wie besprochen) das Stück in grossem Stile propagieren wollen. Klavierauszug u. Partitur haben Sie wohl aus B.-B. zurückerhalten. Den „Alabama Song", den Sie für Gesang, Klavier u. Geige herausbringen wollen, lassen Sie vielleicht von Ihrem Spezialisten für diese Schlager-Ausgaben bearbeiten u. schicken es mir zur Durchsicht. Bei den Ausgaben für Salonorchester könnte man sehr stark das Original benutzen.

Weill (in Prerow, Ostsee) an die Universal Edition, 16. August 1927: Schon vor mehreren Tagen hatte man mit mir über eine Aufführung von *Mahagonny* im Rahmen einer grossen Ausstattungsrevue verhandelt. Ich hatte mich damals hinhaltend geäussert, zumal die Sache nicht unmittelbar akut war.

Gestern nun bekam ich ein ähnliches Angebot, nur mit bedeutend günstigeren Begleiterscheinungen. Es handelt sich ebenfalls um eine Revue, aber ernsthaften künstlerischen Charakters, mit hervorragenden Mitarbeitern u. glänzenden Möglichkeiten (ein bekanntes Berliner Theater, berühmter Regisseur u.s.w., *Serienaufführung*, keine einseitige Festlegung wie bei Piscator!). Ich würde in einer solchen Aufführung die einzige Möglichkeit sehen, den Baden-Badener Erfolg äusserst wirkungsvoll auszunützen, ohne der Wirkung einer späteren grossen *Mahagonny*-Oper(ette) Abbruch zu tun. Im Gegenteil bin ich überzeugt, dass eine solche Eingliederung des Baden-Badener Stückes in eine grosse Publikumsrevue die Oper glänzend vorbereiten würde. (Ausserdem ergibt sich folgende Möglichkeit: die gleiche Theaterdirektion würde die grosse *Mahagonny*-Oper, nachdem wir sie an einer Provinzoper zur Uraufführung gebracht haben, für eine Berliner Serienaufführung annehmen). Die Ausnutzungsmöglichkeiten des Notenverkaufs (Alabama-Song!!) bei einer solchen Revueaufführung sind ja für Sie klar ersichtlich.

Figure 129. Eberhard Preussner. "Deutsche Kammermusik 1927." *Die Musik* 19, no. 12 (September 1927): 887-88. The *enfant terrible* of the music festival was without question the *Songspiel Mahagonny*, with which Bert Brecht and Kurt Weill vividly made their presence known. As always for forward-looking children of the Muse, hidden behind widespread disbelief and disapproval of the grief-stricken in-group, alias audience, was unbridled astonishment at the baldness of such frank expression. Bert Brecht, contemporary poet, singer of ballads, songs and dramas, which already are partly musical, has taken these "Mahagonny-Songs" from his volume of poems: *Die Hauspostille.* Musicians must be especially fascinated and inspired by Brecht. He is a folk singer in the Age of Skyscrapers, who has the bad luck not to have a receptive nation or public behind him. Otherwise, quite a few of his ballads, certainly the "Legend of the Dead Soldier," would have long since become the general property of the people. While we assiduously search for new and old folk songs, here we have songs from our times.

That a composer would find his way to Brecht's text was predictable. Kurt Weill, contemporary musician, creator of theatrically effective operas, ready to seize a poet's world of ideas, is the lucky one. He expresses Brecht inventions in sound with great aptitude; in this case, however, the real creativity rests with the poet and not with the musician. In Hindemith's sketch one could still perceive the contour of a plot—which degenerated into absurdity when it reversed itself — but there is no such dramatic development whatsoever in the *Mahagonny* Songs. A pure *play* of songs to German and American lyrics rules here. Because there is nothing in this world to hold onto, Brecht creates an ideal State of Mahagonny with the figures of the Men of Mahagonny, which—beyond all Good and Evil—sing as the mood of the moment strikes them. And what a mood they are in! When God himself appears in the midst of their whisky, the men of Mahagonny are going on strike:

You can't pull us by the hair to get us to go to Hell,
Because we have always been in Hell.

In Mahagonny there is no whitewash or sentimentality. The singers climb into the boxing ring, the world of ropes conquers the opera stage; in front of a motion picture screen they sing of horseflesh and women's flesh, of whisky and of the poker table.

The following sample proves how music-driven these lyrics are:

Shine on, you beautiful green Moon of Mahagonny!

And that the American hit has entered the scene, without losing any of its punch, can be seen in "Benares Song": [lyrics not reproduced]

It is possible that in all of this, the operatic stage may already have been abandoned while cabaret is making its happy entrance; yet there still appears to be a new and serious movement in all of this. It seems to me that up until now no one has succeeded in putting so many songs together, approximating the form of a cantata on stage, with such a lively, intense, almost dramatic effect. From a purely musical point of view, one has to admire the way Weill has perfectly absorbed what we understand to be contemporary music especially in rhythmic, but also in melodic ways, which he now lets roll by in one great succession of images. But at the same time it must be recognized that the singer as solo virtuoso has been dethroned, the music-making is now done by a fully engaged ensemble of two female and four male voices instead, where each voice nonetheless is offered great autonomy. A new form of theatrical presentation is evident. And even if a lot is sacrificed for the spirit of the times, these sacrifices have not been made in vain. The Baden-Baden catcalls, meant for the men of *Mahagonny*, were apparently enjoyed by them; because they always have been in hell.

Universal Edition (in Wien) an Weill, 23. August 1927: Wir haben den „Blues" aus *Mahagonny* für die Einzelausgabe von einem unserer Arrangeure durchsehen und in eine, für diese „populäre" Ausgabe geeignetere Form, bringen lassen. Wir senden Ihnen gleichzeitig das Manuskript dieser Ausgabe ein, mit der Bitte, es durchzusehen und uns Ihre Meinung hierüber mitzuteilen. Wir selbst sind der Ansicht, dass der 1. Teil (bis zum Refrain) noch erleichtert und vereinfacht werden müsste, vor allem in der linken Hand, da die Sekunde auf das 1. und 3. Viertel überall sehr schlecht klingt. Wir würden vorschlagen, dass man beim 1. und 3. Viertel aller dieser Takte auf die zu scharfen Dissonanzen verzichtet und eventuell nur den ersten Ton als Oktave spielen lässt. Der groteske Ton dieses Teiles kommt wohl durch die dann noch verbleibende Harmonie genügend zum Ausdruck und das Ganze wird auf dem Klavier viel besser klingen.

Weill (in Berlin) an Lotte Lenya, [25. August 1927]: Übrigens brauchst du mich nicht allzusehr zu bedauern. Ich fühle mich nach den paar Tagen Grünheide jetzt sehr frisch u. sehe auch nicht mehr ganz so schlecht aus. Ich glaube eher, daß ich nicht lang brauche, um mich ganz zu erholen. Es scheint festzustehen, daß Mami u. Anselm mitkommen. Mami ist ein sehr lieber Kerl u. ich bin schon darum gern bei ihr, weil sie dich so gern hat. Die Kinder sind jetzt in einer günstigen Zeit, nett, gescheit u. anständig. Anselm ist schlank u. sieht reizend aus. Gestern war ich abends bei Wurms, um *Mahagonny* vorzuspielen. Salter u. Papi waren da. Alle waren einfach erschlagen. Ich mußte dreimal spielen. Sie wollen jetzt die Sache mit Haller mit Hochdruck betreiben u. Salter will versuchen, den „Alabama-Song" für Amerika von der U.E. freizukriegen, weil er sich drüben ein tolles Geschäft verspricht. . . . Du, es gibt einen himmlischen amerikanischen Film *Rivalen* (ich war mit Mami da) beglückend in der pazifistischen Haltung u. in der künstlerischen Durchführung.

Figure 134. "Kurt Weill, Bert Brecht: *Mahagonny.*" *Pult und Taktstock*, September–October 1927.

B.Z. Am Mittag (A. Weissmann). With devilish skill and downright tragic impertinence, Kurt Weill has created music which is steeped in the spirit of nonsense. . . . This Kurt Weill is able to do what others simply cannot.

Berliner Börsencourier (H. Strobel). The sensation of this evening of operas was *Mahagonny.* It starts out like a revue. Its music blends Jazz, cabaret-chansons and lyrical elements in a most original manner. Gilded everyday music. Little by little social and political inclinations force themselves into that which begins as pure musical whimsy. Plot elements develop. Closely related is the imperceptible growth of the music from dancelike to dramatic. The last song, a rebellion against traditional world order in revue-like packaging, stretches into a precipitous dramatic curve. In intensity of expression, this exceeds the *Protagonist.* This is electrifying. It tells again of Weill's eminent talent for the theater, his ability of dramatic concentration . . . received with demonstrative applause.

Vossische Zeitung (Max Marschalk) . . . one cannot escape the stimulating effect; one is on tenterhooks and doesn't quite know why; and doesn't know what for. . . . The music is lively, glowing all over; the strongest music Weill has written up to now. A *Songspiel*: how strange, a "song play," a dream play. . . . The Alban Berg Suite and *Mahagonny* by Kurt Weill were the jackpots to be won at this festival.

Neue Leipziger Zeitung (A.Baresel). Weill's was the most elemental success. Up to now, Weill has made the strongest, most uninhibited use of jazz, extricated it from dance, tracked down the sentimentalities of Negro music. . . . For indulgent theater audiences and music lovers hungering for novelty the piece was a smash hit.

Hamburger 8 Uhr Abendblatt. Weill wrote music from an inner necessity, always heartfelt, always original. . . . For the first time, here resounds Jazz, raised to "permanent art form." . . . that such a work exists, that it has been allowed to resound, this fact as well as the influence it is bound to have on whatever comes after, can no longer be ignored by future developments in the arts.

Weill (in Berlin) an die Universal Edition, 25. August 1927: Was mich zu Brecht hinzieht, ist zunächst das starke Ineinandergehen meiner Musik mit seiner Dichtung, das in B.-B. alle massgebenden Beurteiler überrascht hat. Dann aber glaube ich bestimmt, dass aus der intensiven Zusammenarbeit zweier gleichermassen produktiven Leute etwas grundlegend Neues entstehen kann. Es steht doch ausser Zweifel, dass gegenwärtig eine völlig neue Art von Bühnenkunstwerk entsteht, das sich an ein anderes u. ungleich größeres Publikum wendet, u. dessen Wirkung in ganz ungewohnter Weise in die Breite gehen wird. Diese Bewegung, deren stärkster Faktor auf dem Gebiete des Schauspiels Brecht ist, hat bisher nirgends (ausser in *Mahagonny*) auf die Oper übergegriffen, obwohl die Musik eines ihrer wesentlichsten Elemente ist. In langen Unterredungen mit Brecht habe ich die Überzeugung gewonnen, dass seine Ansichten von einem Operntext mit den meinen weitgehend übereinstimmen. Das Stück, das wir schaffen werden, wird nicht Aktualitäten ausnützen, die nach einem Jahr veraltet sind, sondern es will unsere Zeit in einer endgültigen Form gestalten. Daher wird seine Auswirkung sich weit über seine Entstehungszeit hinaus erstrecken. Es gilt eben das neue Genre zu schaffen, das die völlig veränderten Lebensäusserungen unserer Zeit in einer entsprechenden Form behandelt.

Weill (in Berlin) an die Universal Edition, 10. November 1927: Soeben aus Leipzig zurückgekehrt, möchte ich Ihnen gleich berichten. Ich habe mit Brecher lange gearbeitet. Er ist ungeheuer pedantisch u. auf eine ganz bestimmte Theorie der Deklamation festgelegt, die er ausnahmslos bei allen Opern anwendet. Bei mir trifft er da auf besondere Schwierigkeiten, weil ich von jedem Deklamationsstil weit entfernt bin. Mit einiger Hartnäckigkeit habe ich erreicht, dass er sich in den meisten Fällen mit geringfügigen Verschiebungen in den Gesangsstimmen, oft sogar mit blossen Textänderungen begnügte, die an der Struktur des Werkes nicht das geringste ändern. In ganz wenig Fällen (4 oder 5) werden Taktwiederholungen nötig sein. All diese Änderungen, die ich durchaus verantworten kann (ohne sie von meinem künstlerischen Standpunkt unbedingt nötig zu finden), haben doch den einen praktischen Vorteil: dass sie die Einstudierung des Werkes wesentlich vereinfachen u. erleichtern. Daher wäre ich doch dafür, sie, soweit möglich, in den Klavierauszug aufzunehmen.

Universal Edition (in Wien) an Weill, 24. November 1927: Wir möchten nun noch eine andere wichtige Frage mit Ihnen besprechen. Wir müssen den Bühnen ausser dem üblichen Notenmaterial beim *Zaren* ja auch die Grammophonplatten des Tango mitliefern. Wir möchten Sie nun bitten, nachdem ja in Berlin die besten Aufnahmemöglichkeiten bestehen, sich wenn möglich gleich mit einer der grossen Grammophonfirmen in Verbindung zu setzen und bezüglich der Aufnahme des Tango Verhandlungen zu führen.

Weill (in Berlin) an die Universal Edition, [1. Dezember 1927]: Mit Bezug auf meine Unterredung mit Herrn Dir. Hertzka sprach ich heute nochmals mit Georg Kaiser wegen des Titels „Der Zar lässt sich...." Auch er ist unterdessen von verschiedenen Seiten darauf aufmerksam gemacht worden, dass der Titel etwas anstössig sei, u. er schlägt vor, es doch bei *Der Zar lässt sich photographieren* zu belassen. Ich weiss nicht, ob diese Änderung im Klavierauszug noch durchzuführen ist.

Emil Hertzka, Universal Edition (in Wien) an Weill, 16. Dezember 1927: Im Besitze Ihres Schreibens vom 8. d.M. und der Inhaltsangabe von *Mahagonny* gestehe ich Ihnen offen, dass ich von diesem Exposé ein bisschen enttäuscht war. Ich hatte doch geglaubt, dass es Ihnen und Herrn Brecht gelungen sein wird, dem *Mahagonny*-Stoff eine symbolhafte fassbare Opernhandlung zugrundezulegen. Das, was aber aus dem Exposé hervorgeht, ist ja zwar ein neuer Opernstil, der aber doch immerhin nur aneinandergereihte, allerdings manchmal sehr spannende und originelle Szenen bedeutet und gewissermaßen einen neuen Typ „Opern-Revue" bilden kann. Es ist ja kein Zweifel, dass eine gute und interessante Opern-Revue noch immer unendlich viel wertvoller sein kann, als eine schlechte Oper; ich glaube aber, dass man den *Mahagonny*-Stoff und die Idee, die wir ja wiederholt besprochen haben—ohne dass das Lebendige, Ihnen so reizvoll Erscheinende hätte wegbleiben müssen, doch auch noch in eine Handlung, die dem Werke sicherlich die Wege ebnen würde, hätte formen können. In dieser Handlung hätte unbedingt als Gegengewicht zu der allzu stark betonten Wildwest-Realistik eine Dosis positiver menschlicher Eigenschaften, ob nun Freundschaft, Liebe, Treue mit derartigen Dingen zusammenhängende lyrische Auswirkung gehört. Wenn Sie auch von einem *Mahagonny*-Idyll schreiben und ja vielleicht ein derartiges Bild auch vorgesehen haben, so überwiegt doch Boxkampf, Mord, Totschlag, Trunkenheit und dergl. und das könnte wohl für einen ganzen Abend schwer erträglich werden. Ich war vor wenigen Tagen in Wiesbaden bei der Aufführung von *Romeo und Julia auf dem Dorfe* (nach einer Novelle von Keller). Da gab es zweieinhalb Stunden beinahe nur Lyrik ohne nennenswerte dramatische Explosionen und nur von einem Faden von Handlung zusammengehalten. Trotz der wunderschönen Musik von Delius ist das Werk als Oper unmöglich. Ein Gegenbeispiel zu dieser blassen, farb- und harmlosen Szenenfolge scheint mir *Mahagonny* zu sein mit seiner immer blutroten und blutrünstigen, leider ebenfalls nur an einem Faden hängenden Handlung.

Weill (in Berlin) an die Universal Edition, 27. Dezember 1927: Ich hatte nicht erwartet, dass Ihnen *Mahagonny* auch in dieser Form noch zu „handlungsarm" erscheinen würde. Wenn Sie bedenken, dass es mir in Baden-Baden gelungen ist, den Hörer *ohne eine Spur von Handlung* 25 Minuten lang in erregtester Spannung zu erhalten, so müsste Ihnen für die Oper eine derart logische und geradlinig durchgeführte Handlung u. eine solche Fülle spannender Einzelvorgänge doch als ausreichend erscheinen. Wenn ich 3 Monate lang Tag für Tag mit Brecht zusammen an der Gestaltung dieses Librettos gearbeitet habe, so bestand mein eigener, diesmal sehr starker

Anteil an dieser Arbeit fast ausschliesslich darin, eine möglichst konsequente, geradlinige u. leicht verständliche Handlung zu erreichen. Der Vergleich mit Delius' *Romeo u. Julia* hat mich ein bischen erschreckt; denn der grosse Nachteil dieser Oper besteht ja darin, dass sie—entschuldigen Sie das harte Wort—langweilig ist. Und so viel kann ich Ihnen schon jetzt versichern, dass in *Mahagonny* auch nicht einen Moment lang Langeweile auftreten wird. Allerdings hat in dem Opernstil, den ich hier begründe, die Musik eine weit wesentlichere Rolle als in der reinen Handlungsoper, da ich an die Stelle der früheren Bravourarie eine neue Art von Schlager setze. Infolgedessen kann ich Sie auch vollständig beruhigen, wenn Sie befürchten, dass das Stück irgendwie von der Sprechbühne herkomme. Ich habe mit vieler Mühe Brecht so weit gebracht, dass es ihn gerade reizte, einen Text rein für die Bedürfnisse der Musik zu schreiben, u. jedes Wort darin ist von mir auf die Erfordernisse der Opernbühne hin geprüft worden. Es ist seit langen Jahren zum erstenmal ein Libretto, das vollkommen auf die Musik, ja sogar auf meine Musik angewiesen ist.– Sehr interessant war für mich, dass Sie ein Überwiegen der rohen, grausamen Elemente gegenüber einfachen menschlichen Regungen feststellen. Das hat mich sehr zum Nachdenken angeregt, u. ich beschäftige mich bereits mit einer Änderung, durch die die Liebeshandlung Jimmy-Jenny stärker in den Vordergrund rückt.

Weill (in Berlin) an Erwin Stein, Universal Edition, 5. Januar 1928: Im Besitz des Klavierauszugs meiner *Zaren*-Oper möchte ich nicht versäumen, Ihnen für Ihre Arbeit herzlich zu danken u. Ihnen zu sagen, dass ich über die ausgezeichnete Durchführung des Auszugs, besonders über die Durchsichtigkeit u. leichte Spielbarkeit des Klaviersatzes sehr erfreut bin. Ich hoffe, es wird möglich sein, dass Sie auch bei *Mahagonny* den Klavierauszug machen.

Weill (in Berlin) an die Universal Edition, 23. Februar 1928: Beachtenswert erscheint mir der Plan, den *Zaren* in einer Bearbeitung für Kammerorchester in Amerika anzubringen. Das wäre sicher auch dadurch erleichtert, dass Kaiser in Amerika sehr beliebt ist, und dass man Stoffe dieser Art drüben sehr gern hat. Vielleicht könnten Sie diesen Plan schon sehr bald in Angriff nehmen, damit ich bei einem eventuellen Abschluss die Instrumentation für kleines Orchester beginnen kann. Ein derartiger Abschluss würde sich ja auch hier kolossal auswirken. Übrigens glaube ich auch, dass der *Zar* in Russland anzubringen ist, wo man sich ja schon lange für den *Protagonist* interessiert. In der russischen Bearbeitung und auch in einem eventuellen Exposé für die russischen Bühnen müsste die Figur des Zaren noch mehr ins lächerliche gezogen werden, als wir es uns hier erlauben konnten.

Figure 144. Alfred Baresel. "Neue Requisiten der Opernbühne." *Neue Leipziger Zeitung*, 17 February 1928. "New Props for the Operatic Stage: Concerning Leipzig's World Premiere of Kurt Weill's New Opera." Successful opera of the last few years quite obviously is searching for an expansion of its scenic domain of action. Many such sought-after stage props relied on the topicality of the times: Johnny's automobile cannot be more surprising than the Walküre's horse was at its time. Moreover, the operatic stage's searching for new ways will have to keep up with the kind of attraction cinema and revues hold. It will have keep up with the kind of scenic effects which now are overpowering the world of entertainment, unless it wants to lose the greater part of its reconstructed public. Now, the average operagoer poses one principal demand: *never be boring!* They now call for conciseness of expression, for the barest formulation of text as well as of music: the days of the *da capo* aria, the philosophical monologues, and the importunate relation of music to the concreteness of drama now is passé. The present demands are for colorful substitutes, for the scenic diversity that film and revue are able to provide.

Therefore the medium of film itself had been harnessed into the frame of operatic action—most remarkably in *Royal Palace*, where it advanced the action partly through "movie music." In fact, totally non-musical props are meant to heighten the appeal of the scenic. Musically buzzing toboggans and a prowling boxer have already appeared in Strauss (*Intermezzo* and *Josephslegende*). But a sports platform, which has no immediate connection to music, turns into an opera podium in Weill's *Mahagonny*. In the abovementioned opera Weill also includes an airplane as an extramusical prop, after Krenek's *Schnellzugslokomotive* (a different concept than Honegger's *Pacific*) had already appeared earlier than this performance. The pursuit of this kind of development has already been reported on these pages. For some time now, we have been moving away from the illustrative musico-dramatic, and ever since Busoni strove once more toward absolute operatic music, one is able to bring "unmusical" subject matter to the operatic stage once more as well.

This is where logically Kurt Weill's new opera *Der Zar lässt sich photographieren* fits in. A *dangerously loaded camera* dominates the stage. The librettist of this buffo-opera, Georg Kaiser, uses it in an ingenious way as a prop for an assassination. The Tsar who whiles away the time in a Paris-of-Foxtrot-Rhythms, is supposed to be assassinated. The assassin's gun is hidden in a camera in the studio of the notoriously beautiful photographer Angèle. "Smile, please!" The place close to the heart .... please a little bit more toward the left!.... Now, just hold still ..... there is no need to preserve this film to make copies later! -A devilish idea indeed, worthy of being put to music by the Mahagonny-Weill!

One can characterize this Weill—who at one time was conducting male choruses in a suburb of Leipzig—as a master of the comic in musical situations. Also this time he has placed a male chorus in Leipzig's orchestra pit, which "elucidates the action" in the manner of a Greek tragedy, always at the wrong moment when the suspense of the assassination-gun as well as that of the audience has reached a peak. Whereas he let his Songspiel *Mahagonny*, about which we reported from Baden-Baden, be broadcast live, there now are further concessions to mechanical sound transmissions, and the telephone and gramophone scenes offer an opportunity for intensification of the text's humor.

Not entirely new, but at the present scale still utterly astounding is the sung telephone conversation. To be more precise: one naturally hears only the singing and the answering voice on the receiving end, at different times replaced by new monitoring devices because of the monstrousness of the message; until finally the photographer herself gains the necessary aplomb to publicize this telephone conversation: the Tsar himself condescends to be photographed in the flesh by the court photographer *in spe*....

And thus, this happy play is full of non-committal irony and anonymous parody in both text and music. A climax is reached, when the really "false" Angèle, that conspirator who has carried on with the Tsar an exciting battle between love and deadly photography, puts on the "*Tango Angèle*", which signifies the *gramophone as substitute orchestra.*

Angèle takes advantage of the tango to escape over the roofs from the approaching police force. Kurt Weill uses it to let his multifariously pulsating jazz rhythms lead into a pure and chaste hit song. And the Lindström Company makes use of it in order to produce an ingenuous "Odeon" recording, which in this most tricky moment of the operatic happenings replaces an orchestra by sending its bewitching airs out into the audience—and which in any case will have to be preserved for repeat orders.

This recording is in no way a substitute for musical illustration as in, let's say, Respighi's tone poem "I pini di Roma" (being played at the Gewandhaus), which is a live recording of a real nightingale's singing. In this new opera, it serves as a means to heighten the comic situation. Weill illustrates this with a completely original musically witty brainstorm, which is based on the preceding happenings.

Finally, it has to be emphasized once more, that all of these new devices are not attractions in an external sense, they rather are the new props for the operatic stage. Weill and his librettist have used them as a means to express their artistic ideas, with the desire to create contemporary *opera buffa*. This splendidly accomodates the present demand for lively musical theater without ideological background. At the very end, the piece triumphs over highly political apprehensions when a defiant Tsar finally assumes a merry photographic pose in front of the unloaded camera, while his officers salute him to the accompaniment of a military march.

Weill (in Berlin) an die Universal Edition, 8. März 1928: So viel ich weiss, hat Sie die Piscator-Bühne telegraphisch um die Option für den *Zaren* gebeten. Piscator will das Stück als Serienaufführung im Lessingtheater herausbringen. Ich bin begierig zu erfahren, was Sie zu diesem Plan sagen. Piscator fährt zur Aufführung am 14. nach Leipzig und will sich dann sofort entscheiden. Ich verkenne nicht die Schwierigkeiten dieses Projekts (Orchester, Sänger usw.), sehe aber auf der anderen Seite sehr starke geschäftliche Möglichkeiten und eine erfreuliche Durchbrechung des alten Opernbetriebes.

Weill (in Berlin) an die Universal Edition, 15. März 1928: Bei Piscator scheint man noch ziemlich unentschlossen zu sein. Man hätte aus Spielplangründen den *Zaren* schon Mitte April herausbringen müssen, und das erscheint mir doch so gut wie unmöglich. Ich habe in den nächsten Tagen mit Piscator eine eingehende Besprechung, über deren Ergebnis ich Ihnen berichten werde. Bei Klemperer sieht die Sache günstiger aus, und ich hoffe dort Ende der Woche eine Entscheidung zu erzielen. Man beabsichtigt dort im Mai, den *Zaren* zusammen mit Ravels *L'heure espagnol* herauszubringen—übrigens eine ausgezeichnete Zusammenstellung. Allerdings ist es keineswegs sicher, ob dieser Plan zur Ausführung kommt, und ich möchte Ihnen doch vorschlagen, von sich aus an Hoerth zu schreiben, auf die Verhandlungen mit Klemperer und Piscator anzuspielen und ihm die gemeinsame Aufführung von *Protagonist* und *Zar* zu empfehlen. Nach der ganzen Situation würde ich eine Berliner Aufführung des *Zaren* in dieser Saison für sehr günstig halten, aber wenn Hoerth den *Protagonist* dazu nimmt, könnten wir bis Anfang nächster Saison warten.

Figure 146. "Erstaufführung im Großen Haus: *Oedipus Rex* und *Der Zar lässt sich photographieren.*" Stravinsky's *Oedipus Rex*, a serious matter, quite unseriously introduced by a Speaker, "relevant" music of "irrelevant" qualities. At the occasion of an intense performance, the audience remained cool.

Weill: The Tsar has himself—after many instants before a camera with a nihilist's gun built-in—finally *really* photographed. An amusing "Krimi." One says: a hopeful opera buffa. There was no lack of voltage. There were many curtain calls at the end. Rightfully so, for all that hard work.

Weill (in Berlin) an die Universal Edition, 20. März 1928: In der Angelegenheit der Berliner *Zaren*-Aufführung hat sich durch meine heutige Unterredung mit Dr. Curjel die Lage wieder verschoben. Er glaubt nicht, dass Klemperer sich das Stück entgehen lassen wird, und will lieber in Abwesenheit Klemperers durch telefonische Verständigung mit ihm eine Entscheidung herbeiführen, bevor er das Werk Walter überlässt. Da Klemperer den *Cardillac* macht, ist es möglich, dass er den *Zaren* Zemlinsky übergibt, und für diesen Fall wäre es garnicht ausgeschlossen, dass man den *Protagonist* hinzugibt, der Zemlinsky ganz besonders gut liegt. Das wäre natürlich eine glänzende Lösung, und ich möchte Sie sehr bitten, in diesem Sinne Ihren ganzen Einfluss bei Klemperer und auch bei Zemlinsky geltend zu machen. Die Leute hier haben den grossen Premierenerfolg des *Protagonisten* scheinbar ganz vergessen und können sich die starke Publikumswirkung des Werkes nicht vorstellen. Sie waren ganz überrascht, als ich von den 46 Vorhängen der Dresdener Uraufführung erzählte.

Universal Edition (in Wien) an Weill, 20. März 1928: Die „Electrola", Berlin, telegraphiert uns, wie folgt: „Sollte Tango Angèle aus Weill *Zar* für Jazz oder Salonorchester erschienen sein, sendet postwendend per Flugpost an Electrola."

Wir haben den Herren geschrieben, dass wir Material des *Tango Angèle* noch nicht besitzen und dass sie sich diesbezüglich an Sie wenden sollen, nachdem die Stimmen der ursprünglichen Aufnahme bei Ihnen vorhanden sind. Wir bitten Sie, sich freundlichst umgehend mit der „Electrola" in Verbindung zu setzen. Wir haben ja keinerlei ausschliessliche Abmachung mit der „Lindström" getroffen, sodass wohl kein Grund besteht, der „Electrola" eine neue Aufnahme zu verweigern. Im übrigen haben Sie ja seinerzeit die Unterhandlungen mit Lindström selbst geführt, sodass Sie ja wohl selbst am besten wissen, ob eine neuerliche Aufnahme durch die „Electrola" stattfinden kann. Wir bitten Sie, uns von dem Resultat Ihrer Besprechungen mit der „Electrola" orientieren zu wollen.

Universal Edition (in Wien) an Weill, 29. März 1928: Es wird Sie interessieren, welchen Bescheid wir von einem unserer russischen Vertrauensleute erhalten haben. Der Betreffende, Konsulent der Moskauer Staatsoper, schreibt uns: „Kurt Weills Oper ist ein hervorragendes Werk. Ich möchte auch seine anderen Werke kennenlernen. Sie ist natürlich sehr amüsant, aber die Ideologie dieser Oper macht eine Aufführung in Sowjetrussland ausgeschlossen. Der Komponist ist nur satirisch. Er stellt sich auf keine Seite. Er betrachtet den Zaren ebenso satirisch, wie die Revolutionäre, ja diese spielen sogar den komischen Teil in der Oper und wir lieben es absolut nicht, komische Revolutionäre auf der Bühne zu sehen. Ich will immerhin über die Oper in unseren Blättern berichten und will darüber nachdenken, wie man den Inhalt für unsere Verhältnisse verändern könnte."

Figure 154. Weill (in Berlin) to Alfred Einstein, 26 July 1928: Enclosed I send you the requested information for the *Lexikon*: Kurt Weill (with two l's!), of Badenish descent, born on 2 March 1900 in Dessau. First instruction by Dessau's kapellmeister Albert Bing. 1918 Hochschule für Musik in Berlin, for only one semester, studies with Humperdinck and Krasselt. Conductor in Dessau and at Civic Theater in Lüdenscheid (Westphalia). 1921 return to Berlin, studies with Busoni and close friendship with him until his death. Now living in Berlin.

Published works: (all with Universal Edition, Wien): Op.8: String Quartet; Opus 9: *Quodlibet* for orchestra; Opus 10: *Frauentanz*, 7 songs to medieval poems for soprano, viola, flute, clarinet, horn, bassoon. Opus 12: Concerto for violin and wind orchestra (Paris 1925); Opus 15: *Der neue Orpheus*, cantata for soprano and orchestra.

Stage works: *Der Protagonist*, opera in one act, libretto by Georg Kaiser (Dresdner Staatsoper, 1926); *Royal Palace*, opera in one act, libretto by Iwan Goll (Staatsoper Berlin, 1927); *Der Zar lässt sich photographieren*, opera buffa in one act, libretto by Georg Kaiser (Leipzig 1928); *Mahagonny* Songspiel, libretto by Bertolt Brecht (Baden-Baden, 1927). The latter is a study for the forthcoming three-act opera *Mahagonny*, libretto by Bertolt Brecht.

After that there will be a completely new score for the *Beggar's Opera*, a German version of the old English ballad opera (adapted by Bert Brecht).

Unpublished: Aside from a number of early works (among them a symphony, an orchestral work *Fantasia, Passacaglia and Hymnus*; also chamber music and songs, an a capella choral work *Recordare*, (Opus 11), Orchestra Songs to a text by Rilke, (Opus 14 and 15), a Ballad *Vom Tod im Wald* for bass and 10 brass instruments (Opus 23).

In addition: Various incidental music to legitimate plays, among them Strindberg's *Gustav III*, Bronnen's *Katalaunische Schlacht*, Brecht's *Leben Eduards II*.

One unpublished two-act opera, completely finished, *Na und?* (written in 1926).

Weill (in Berlin) an die Universal Edition, 21. August 1928: Ich bin sehr erfreut, dass das Material der *Beggars Opera* hier hergestellt wird, da es sonst sehr knapp geworden wäre. Die Orchesterproben beginnen am 26. ds., die Premiere ist am 31.—Ich möchte Sie heute um einen Gefallen bitten. Ich glaube nach Abschluss der Arbeit an der *Bettleroper*, dass mir hier ein gutes Stück gelungen ist, und dass einige Stücke daraus jedenfalls musikalisch die grössten Aussichten haben, in kürzester Zeit populär zu werden. Dazu ist aber unbedingt nötig, dass in der ganzen äusseren Aufmachung der Premiere der Musik der ihr gebührende Platz eingeräumt wird. Man scheint im Theater (wie immer bei der Literatur) ein bischen Angst vor der Durchschlagskraft der Musik zu haben, und ich befürchte, dass man die Musik in Ankündigungen, Pressenotizen usw. mehr als Bühnenmusik ausgeben wird, obwohl sie mit ihren 20 Nummern weit über den Rahmen einer Schauspielmusik hinausgeht. Ich möchte Sie nun bitten, vom Theater am Schiffbauerdamm (NW 6 Schiffbauerdamm 4a) kategorisch zu verlangen, dass in allen Veröffentlichungen, Notizen, Plakaten, Inseraten usw. mein Name als Mitautor genannt werden muss, dass mein Bild in das Programmheft kommt usw., da Sie sonst rein aus geschäftlichen Gründen die Musik nicht zur Aufführung hergeben können. Sie wissen, dass ich persönlich auf diese Dinge keinen grossen Wert lege, aber wir müssen ernstlich befürchten, dass uns alle Auswertungsmöglichkeiten dieser Musik verloren gehen, wenn sie jetzt bei der Uraufführung nicht genügend propagiert wird.

Figure 168. Walter Steinthal. *"Die Dreigroschenoper:* Uraufführung im Theater am Schiffbauerdamm." *12-Uhr Blatt.* No two ways about it—this was a great victory.

It seems that the poet Bertolt Brecht—for many years probing, struggling against constraints from the outside and erroneous paths within himself, is about to find his very own formula. Together with the composer Kurt Weill, he has created a dramatic Something, a mixture of drama, parody, conscious *Kitsch* and lofty values, the unusual character of which brought about an almost sensational public success. These two authors approach theater with a new (pre)supposition. Their dramaturgy resolutely rejects a one-track grouping of humor versus seriousness, or of tragedy versus comedy. They offer a new cross-section for the theater. The ridiculousness of the tragic, the unimportance of any single existence, the tight closeness of contrasting sentimental values in life: all of this lets them discover a new form of art. They cut the Gordian knot, in which all the problems of our theater have found themselves entangled, by totally dissolving a troubled species which has gotten stuck in its own tracks.

There is no way of denying that at first, a foreign tone emerges. But it is a very fertile element, this lyricism of soberness, this overwhelming in-your-face formulation of life's problems, this immoral heresy of expression. It is Brecht's style that he says everything that convention of the last one hundred years has not permitted to be said on any stage, and shows everything that shouldn't be shown. Together with his musico-dramatic buddy he goes back to the roots of the sentimentally dramatic theater, back to opera, and on from there to horror-tale-ballads, and from there on to a liberating, courageous grip to unadulterated Kitsch. Both authors' distancing themselves from this Kitsch is artificial; in reality they revel in it to their heart's content. They accomplish this effect because they create on the basis of their ideology, because they call things by their names, because they don't try to embellish or conceal their intent for the sake of exterior effects. *Dreigroschenoper*—that's Theater of the Sentiment for the simple person, for the illiterate, for the poor. The subject matter has been taken in all honesty from *that* world from which romanticism and sentimentality flow the richest. The play takes place in London's [under]world of beggars and crooks. A melodramatic story of Macheath, King of Burglars, a charming crook by the grace of God, who has the breaking of doors and of women's hearts on his conscience, who enjoys a correct, yet comfortably fraternizing relationship with the Chief of Police, whom whores betray to the Instruments of Justice, and who—because of the poet's personal chivalry—is spared the gallows in the finale of the last act. Around him, an army of a variety of differently profiled crooks, to each one's right and left a gangster's moll—and within that radius, extras make up the lot of London's beggars, tightly organized by the crafty and worldly-wise beggar king Peachum. All of this has been developed tightly and with increasing intensity: the story of an English *Schinderhannes* [a famous German robber] in wonderfully woven fantastic episodes. But this is not the important thing; rather the principal matter is that strangely honest, seemingly unconcerned, presupposing manner of the poetic substance. This substance is aggressively ready to burst, while at the same time it is being covered with a breath of true poetry. Its language is full of social and moral irony, but all the more fascinating is the tenderness, with which the creator Brecht touches his creatures. Still, there is plenty of swearing, cursing and talking dirty. It is difficult to describe the unusual, amazing, breathtaking tone which swings through all of this, one can only say that it is of greatest effect, it is the pouring out of a demonic gaiety as well as of the release of forces of the deepest seriousness, with which this form of a horror-tale-ballad touches the lowlands of boorishness with the left, while with the right it gropes for glowing stars, through which the driving forces of backstairs are seen honestly, yet through a filter of an enormously tender poetic psyche being let loose on us, and which prove to be of unusual artistic strength. Almost all of the scenes climax into a linguistically conditioned final point, an in-between-thing ballad and *chanson*, sometimes according to foreign models, but always ravishing, always with a shattering spiritual sharpness. In such matters, the best spirit of Nestroy and Karl Kraus hovers over the poet Brecht. The most enjoyable about all of this is demonstrated by the broad effect it all had on the audience. Since for some time now, a younger generation had merely been slashing theatrical forms, one now can sense here a new element for rebuilding, a seed of a new kind of drama.

It is almost scary the way poet and composer complement each other. Kurt Weill is just as inartistic as Brecht, he goes after effects wherever they are to be found, he will not be scared by either the pathetic nor by the sentimental. He purifies the various ingredients of *Kitsch* and uses each single one in full conscience and with magnificent impudence. His musical invention, his orchestrations, his ability to change his expression between the outermost poles of musical formation—all of this shows once again his enormous talents. Perhaps Weill has the stuff to become the most popular composer of his time—popular not because of the aptitude of a popular songwriter, but because of the depth of a truly new feeling for a novel kind of popular music. He has a downright exciting way to make illustrations, but he also has an entirely rough-and-ready heaviness and depth, and he has the astonishingly unorthodox courage to use these gifts of his. Those operatic sketches he has scattered here, have a positively significant poignancy, even when he makes fun of them. Perhaps the team Brecht-Weill might someday create a authoritative *Revue* for us—both their talents point in this direction—not only because it would be timely, but because it would put them in total command of a bridge between laughing and crying; because such a tune—letting a tinge of parody resonate without hiding behind the pretense of parody—that would be the tune for our time. Life at best is never a happy affair. Strange, that the theater has drawn the consequences of this old wisdom only at such a late date. Otherwise today's drama could not have ended up in the present cul-de-sac. Perhaps this type of Revue (of course not the glitzy kind) could be a way out, because the dense next-to-each-other-mood characterizes its very nature. In that case, Brecht and Weill are born pioneers.

Especially when there is a congenial stage director like Erich Engel at their side. One rarely has seen a performance of such equally high standards, of such precision of character, of such an enlivening of each single point of acting. Engel knows exactly the crucial elements of this piece, those which turn the victory of creative thinking into the success of the evening. With him Harald Paulsen, charming as well as ice-cold, at the same time a tenorish gentleman-crook. The discipline with which he, but also Roma Bahn, Rosa Valetti and Kate Kühl throw themselves into the spiritual explosion of the Brecht-Weill *chansons* is admirable. For the first time, Kurt Gerron is not merely a cabaret performer, but transported onto the stage as a very impressive actor. He should remain in Erich Engel's school. And lastly Erich Ponto, so far Germany's strongest actor not from Berlin, has finally arrived here. He plays the Beggar King. The subjectiveness of his face, his human truthfulness and the concentration of his acting are gifts, for one who has met him somewhere outside of Berlin, to be admired for a long time. Nobody should get the idea of ever letting him leave again!

In the course of a season, only a few evenings like this take place in Berlin. On the outside, a success of totally unexpected impact. The audience—first resisting, then from scene to scene drawn more and more into the spell of these novel thoughts of expression—reserved at first, eventually no longer resisting—and in the end jubilant. One would wish that this play could run for 500 performances, because sensational successes in such a straight forward manner and on such a significant level cannot be realized often.

Universal Edition (in Wien) an Weill, 8. September 1928: Nun zu der Frage der Salonorchester-Ausgaben. Diese aparten Stücke müssen auch apart arrangiert werden und unter den hiesigen Fachleuten ist leider niemand, der hierzu genug Fantasie und Originalität besitzt. Dagegen sind in Berlin mehrere ausgezeichnete moderne Arrangeure und wir würden Ihnen daher vorschlagen, dass Sie sich freundlichst selbst mit einem der in Betracht kommenden Herren in Verbindung setzen und das Arrangement der wichtigsten Songs in Auftrag geben. Sie haben ja noch Material als Unterlage dort und könnten die Technik gleich selbst mit dem Arrangeur besprechen. Die uns eingesandten Teile der Partitur haben wir bereits zur Lichtpause gegeben, sodass Sie diese ebenfalls in einigen Tagen, falls Sie sie benötigen werden, zurückerhalten können. Wir bitten Sie, uns in dieser wichtigen Frage zu unterstützen, damit alles geschieht, um Klavierauszug, Textbuch, Einzelausgaben für Klavier, Solo-Orchesterausgaben, gedruckte Orchesterpartitur für die Bühne möglichst rasch herauszubringen. In Berlin kommen folgende Arrangeure in Betracht:

Jerzy *Fitelberg*, Berlin-Halensee, Westfälische Strasse 58.
Nico *Dostal*, Berlin W.30, Hohenstaufenstr. 33.
Hermann *Krome*, Berlin S.W.48, Verl. Hedemannstr. 5/III.
Hartwig v. *Platen*, Berlin-Wilmersdorf, Prinz Regentenstr. 65

Weill (in Berlin) an die Universal Edition, [Eingangsstempel: 24. September 1928]: Herr Karl Koch, einer unserer besten Filmproduzenten, hat grosse Teile der *Dreigroschenoper* während der Aufführung filmisch aufgenommen. Aus diesem Material könnte man etwa 50 hervorragend gelungene Fotografien, in denen dann sämtliche für eine Aufführung wichtigen Stellungen und Stellungswechsel zu sehen wären, auswählen, vergrössern und auf vier Seiten dem Klavierauszug beifügen. Dies wäre eine ganz moderne, bisher einzigartige Neueinführung, die den Wert des Klavierauszugs für die Bühnen, aber auch für das kaufende Publikum ausserordentlich steigern würde, zumal diese Berliner Aufführung der *Dreigroschenoper* schon einen grossen Ruf geniesst. Das nötige Material könnte ich Ihnen sofort beschaffen. Die Kosten dieser Bilderseiten würden nach vorläufiger Schätzung des Herrn Koch sich auf etwa M. 250.- betragen. Bitte, telegrafieren Sie mir sofort darüber.

Weill (in Berlin) an die Universal Edition, 2. Oktober 1928: Zunächst zur Frage des Aufsatzes: ich war sehr erfreut, dass Sie, lieber Herr Dr. Heinsheimer, im neuesten Heft des *Anbruch* so energisch in einer Richtung vorgestossen haben, die ich, wie Sie wissen, für absolut wegweisend halte. Auch dass Sie in dieser Linie weiter vorgehen wollen, ist äusserst begrüssenswert. Ich weiss nur nicht, ob es taktisch richtig ist, wenn ich selbst jetzt diesen Weg, der doch vorläufig von mir allein beschritten wird, theoretisch zu begründen versuche. Ich müsste doch in einem solchen Aufsatz fast ausschließlich von dem sprechen, was ich in der *Dreigroschenoper* gemacht habe, denn in *Mahagonny* werde ich wieder ein ganzes Stück weiter sein. Ich habe, wie Sie ja auch wissen, immer eine leise Scheu, mich über das, was ich tue, schriftlich zu äussern, weil mir diese Äusserungen bisher stets falsch ausgelegt worden sind. Glauben Sie nicht, dass ein anderer das, was unbedingt gesagt werden muss, leichter und präziser sagen kann als gerade ich selbst? Denn ein anderer könnte ja auch das feststellen, was eigentlich einer der wesentlichsten Punkte ist, nämlich dass meine Musik in der *Dreigroschenoper* (und damit eben die ganze Richtung dieses Werkes) einen Publikumserfolg von breitesten Ausmaassen hat. Vielleicht ist es möglich, eine Form zu finden, in der ich das alles sagen kann, etwa so, dass Sie darüber schreiben: „Aus einem Brief Weills an den Verlag", und dass das ganze tatsächlich wie aus einem Brief herausgenommen wirkt.

Weill (in Berlin) an die Universal Edition, 11. Oktober 1928: Übrigens höre ich aus Frankfurt, dass man dort schon anfangen will, allerhand Reduzierungen im Orchester bei der *Dreigroschenoper* vorzunehmen. Ich halte das für sehr gefährlich und bitte Sie, Herrn Direktor Hellmer streng zu verbieten, irgendwelche Änderungen in der Musik oder in der Instrumentation vorzunehmen, ohne meine Zustimmung einzuholen.

Weill (in Berlin) an die Universal Edition, 17. Oktober 1928: Über den günstigen Ausgang der Charlottenburger Aufführung habe ich Ihnen telegrafisch berichtet. Der Erfolg war nach dem *Zaren* ausserordentlich stark und wurde durch Pfeifer auf 20 Vorhänge hinaufgetrieben. Glänzende Kritiken von Kastner, Schrenk (besonders gut!), Pringsheim, Bie u. a. haben Sie wohl gelesen (falls nicht, kann ich sie schicken). Besonders erfreulich ist der gänzliche Umschwung Weissmanns. Ich glaube jedenfalls, dass das Ergebnis dieser Aufführung so günstig ist, wie es unter den gegebenen Umständen kaum zu erwarten war.

Anbei schicke ich Ihnen den Aufsatz in Form einer Antwort auf Ihren Brief. Ich hoffe, dass er noch rechtzeitig kommt. Ich würde Sie nur bitten, in Ihrem Brief, den Sie mit abdrucken werden, den Satz „Weill als Humperdinck" fortzulassen, da ich eine ganz persönliche Antipathie gegen diesen Komponisten habe. Vielleicht können Sie statt dessen irgend etwas in dieser Art: „Von Offenbach zu Weill" oder dergl. sagen.

Figure 185:"Korrespondenz über *Dreigroschenoper.*" *Anbruch* 11, no. 1 (January 1929) 24-25. "Correspondence Concerning *Threepenny Opera.* Dear Mr. Weill, the sensational success of the *Threepenny Opera*, whereby a work with a thoroughly new, forward-looking style has suddenly been turned into a box-office hit, gratifyingly confirms the prophecies repeatedly made in this journal. The new, popular opera-operetta, drawing as it does the right conclusion from the artistic and social premises of the present, has succeeded in splendid and exemplary fashion.

Your practical achievement and proven success gives you an evident advantage over our sociological and aesthetic ratiocinations. May we now ask you to give our journal your theoretical opinions about the path you have chosen?

Dear Anbruch, I thank you for your letter and am pleased to let you have a few words about the path that Brecht and I have chosen to take with this work and which we intend to pursue.

You refer in your letter to the *Threepenny Opera*'s sociological significance. The success of our piece does indeed prove that the creation and realization of this new genre not only came at the right moment for the situation of art but that the audience seemed actually to be waiting for the renewal of a favorite type of theater. I'm not so sure that our type of theater will replace operetta. With Goethe having reappeared on earth through the medium of an operetta tenor, why shouldn't another series of historical or at least aristocratic personalities utter their tragic outcry at the end of the second act? That will take care of itself, so I don't believe any niche worth occupying is opening up here. More important for all of us is the fact that for the first time a breakthrough has been achieved in a consumer industry previously reserved for a completely different kind of musician and writer. With *The Threepenny Opera* we are reaching an audience which either did not know us at all or, at any rate, never considered us capable of interesting a circle of listeners much wider than the average concert- and opera-going public.

Seen in this way, *The Threepenny Opera* aligns itself with a movement that involves nearly all of today's young musicians. The abandonment of the *l'art pour l'art* standpoint, the turning away from an individualistic principle of art, the ideas on film music, the contact with the youth music movement, the simplification of the musical means of expression connected with all these things—these are all steps along the same path.

Only opera still persists in its "splendid isolation". The opera-going public still represents a closed group seemingly removed from the large theater-going public. "Opera" and "theater" are still treated as two completely separate concepts. In recent operas the dramaturgical style employed, the language spoken, and the subjects treated would all be quite unthinkable in contemporary theater. And one still hears: "That might work in the theater, but not in opera!" Opera was established as an artistic genre of the aristocracy, and everything one calls "operatic tradition" only underlines the class basis of this genre. Today, however, there is no other artistic form in the entire world whose bearing is so unabashedly engendered by established society [*gesellschaftlich*]. The theater in particular has moved quite decisively in a direction that can rather be described as socially regenerative [*gesellschaftsbildend*]. If the bounds of opera cannot accommodate such a rapprochement with the theater of the times [*Zeittheater*], then its bounds must be broken.

Only in this way can one understand the fact that nearly all worthwhile operatic experiments in recent years have been basically destructive in character. With *The Threepenny Opera* reconstruction became possible, since it allowed us to start again from scratch. What we were aiming to create was the prototype of opera [*Urform der Oper*]. With every musical work for the stage the question arises: how is music, particularly song, at all possible in the theater? Here the question was resolved in the most primitive way possible. I had a realistic plot, so I had to set the music against it, since I do not consider music capable of realistic effects. Hence the action was either interrupted, in order to introduce music, or it was deliberately driven to a point where there was no alternative but to sing. The piece, furthermore, presented us with the opportunity to make "opera" the subject matter for an evening in the theater. At the very beginning of the piece the audience is told: "Tonight you are going to see an opera for beggars. Since this opera was intended to be as splendid as only beggars can imagine, and yet cheap enough for beggars to be able to watch, it is called "The Threepenny Opera." Thus the last "Dreigroschenfinale" is in no way a parody. Rather, the idea of opera was directly exploited as a means of resolving a conflict and thus shaping the action. Consequently it had to be presented in its purest, most pristine form.

This return to a primitive form of opera entailed a far-reaching simplification of musical language. The task was to write music that could be sung by actors, that is, by musical amateurs. At first this appeared to be a limitation. As work progressed, however, it proved to be an enormous enrichment. Only the realization of a coherent, identifiable melodic line made possible *The Threepenny Opera*'s real achievement: the creation of a new type of musical theater. Yours truly, Kurt Weill

Weill (in Berlin) an die Universal Edition, 25. Oktober 1928: Ich hätte gern noch einmal mit Ihnen ausführlich über die Auswirkungsmöglichkeiten meiner schlagerartigen Kompositionen gesprochen. Ich bin über die bisherigen Erfolge dieser Stücke und über die Aussichten, die sie augenblicklich haben, tief beunruhigt. Ich höre täglich von allen Seiten, aus allen Kreisen des Publikums, dass von diesen Stücken eine populäre Wirkung ausgeht wie seit Jahren von keiner Musik. Jeder Mensch bestätigt mir, dass an den etwa fünf Stücken dieser Gattung, die ich jetzt geschrieben habe, mit Leichtigkeit ein kleines Vermögen zu verdienen wäre. Ich sehe aber augenblicklich überhaupt keine Möglichkeit, irgendwelche nennenswerte[n] Beträge mit diesen Stücken zu verdienen. Ich bitte Sie dringend, das nicht etwa als einen Vorwurf gegen Sie aufzufassen. Ich weiss genau und bin fest überzeugt davon, dass Sie mit grösster Energie und mit allen Ihnen zu Gebote stehenden Mitteln sich für mich einsetzen. Wenn ich überhaupt dieses Thema anschneide, so ist es nur, weil ich ernstlich befürchten muss, dass ich mir durch eine zu geringe Ausnützung dieser Schlager die günstigste Gelegenheit entgehen lasse, mich auf Jahre hinaus finanziell sicherzustellen. Ich bin überzeugt, dass meine Begabung, eine völlig neue Art volkstümlicher Melodien zu schreiben, heute vollkommen konkurrenzlos ist. Wenn diese Sache in einer ganz grosszügigen, neuartigen Weise aufgezogen wird, so besteht kein Zweifel darüber, dass meine Schlagerkompositionen an die Stelle der jetzt gerade etwas abgelebten amerikanischen Jazzkompositionen treten können. Das ist auch die einstimmige Meinung aller ausländischen Hörer der *Dreigroschenoper*. Ich möchte daher vorschlagen, dass wir so bald wie möglich einmal, am besten wohl beim nächsten Berliner Besuch von Direktor Hertzka, ganz ausführlich die Möglichkeiten durchsprechen, die sich hier ergeben. Besonders möchte ich Ihnen den dringenden Vorschlag machen, die besten Nummern aus der *Dreigroschenoper* für Amerika einem der dortigen Schlagerverleger zu übergeben, da ich sonst keine Möglichkeit einer Ausnützung der ungeheuren Chancen meiner Musik in Amerika sehe. Der Notenverkauf hier in Berlin funktioniert überhaupt nicht. Von Herrn Huebner habe ich seit Wochen nichts gehört. Kein einziges Notengeschäft hat die beiden Nummern ausgestellt. In Zeitungen kommen Anfragen aus dem Publikum, warum es keine Noten und Grammophonplatten von der *Dreigroschenoper* gibt. Es ist so schade, wenn Ihre so energische und rasche Herstellungsarbeit an diesen Stücken auf diese Weise wirkungslos bleiben soll. Und ich weiss nicht, wieviel Stücke von der Durchschlagskraft des Alabamasongs, des Kanonensongs, des Tangos, des angenehmen Lebens und der Moritat mir noch gelingen werden.

Weill (in Berlin) an Maurice Abravanel, [Ende 1928]: Sei nicht weiter böse über unser langes Schweigen. Du gehörst ja Gott sei Dank nicht zu denen, die einem so etwas übel nehmen. Ich kann dir nur sagen, dass mich meine eigene Berühmtheit allmählich schon ankotzt. Die Ausmaasse des *Dreigroschenoper*-Erfolgs brauche ich dir wohl nicht zu schildern. Ich habe mit einemmal Dinge erreicht, die ich frühestens in 10 Jahren erwartet hatte. Das hat natürlich grosse Vorteile, und zwar nicht nur materieller Art, sondern ich kann mir in den nächsten Jahren auf Grund meines Namens (der eben jetzt Geld wert ist!) allerhand leisten. Du kannst versichert sein, dass ich von diesen Möglichkeiten reichlich Gebrauch machen werde.

Hast du denn eigentlich die *Dreigroschenoper* schon gesehen? Du müsstest sie dir möglichst in Berlin ansehen. Es ist wirklich ein schönes Stück und sicher das beste was mir bisher gelungen ist. Und die Berliner Aufführung ist musikalisch unbedingt hörenswert. Augenblicklich ist das Stück ja ein Riesenerfolg in Leipzig und vielen anderen Städten.

Du kannst dir denken, was für eine endlose Kette von Erledigungen aller Art meine plötzliche Weltberühmtheit nach sich zieht. Ich kann mich wirklich manchmal überhaupt nicht mehr retten. Dabei habe ich allerhand neues gemacht, u.a. eine kleine Kantate *Das Berliner Requiem*, die Anfang Februar im Frankfurter Sender herauskommen soll. An *Mahagonny* arbeite ich noch weiter und bringe es erst Anfang nächster Saison heraus. . . .

Lenja ist eine berühmte Schauspielerin geworden und spielt augenblicklich am Staatstheater eine grosse Rolle nach der anderen. Wir haben jetzt eine sehr hübsche eigene Wohnung und einen kleinen Fiat-Wagen.

Weill (in Berlin) an die Universal Edition, 29. Dezember 1928: Ich war unterdessen zur Premiere der *Dreigroschenoper* in Leipzig, wo das Stück einen ganz grossen Erfolg von Berliner Ausmaassen hatte. Es ist vorläufig auf 14 Tage jeden Abend angesetzt und die ersten Aufführungen sind längst ausverkauft. Anbei 2 Kritiken, die für mich ganz besonders günstig sind.

Ich habe jetzt die für den Frankfurter Sender bestimmte Kantate vollendet und glaube, dass es eines meiner besten und neuartigsten Stücke geworden ist. Es heisst *Das Berliner Requiem* und bildet eine Folge von 7 Stücken teils feierlich tragischen, teils ironischen Charakters. Aufführungsdauer 20-25 Minuten. Besetzung: 3 Männerstimmen und 15 Instrumente (Bläser, Banjo, Schlagzeug und Orgel). Ich glaube sicher, dass dieses Werk durch die leichte Aufführbarkeit und durch die Annäherung an meinen gegenwärtigen Bühnenstil seinen Weg durch die Konzertsäle machen wird, und es wäre daher zu überlegen, ob Sie das Stück nicht baldmöglichst herausbringen sollten, da ja zahlreiche Dirigenten und Konzertinstitute gerade jetzt auf ein Konzertstück von mir warten. . . .

Ich veranlasse jetzt die Rundfunksender, soweit ich Beziehungen habe, die Songs der *Dreigroschenoper* für sich aufzuführen, da das natürlich für die Verbreitung der Stücke viel beitragen würde. . . . Die Schallplatte der Deutschen Grammophon A.G. ist erschienen. Sie ist sehr wirkungsvoll, obwohl sie aufnahmetechnisch nicht ganz auf der Höhe ist. Leider konnte ich noch nicht durchsetzen, dass richtige Gesangsaufnahmen der Songs gemacht werden.

Indem ich Ihre Neujahrswünsche aufs herzlichste erwidere, wünsche ich der ganzen U.E. ein schönes und „fruchtbares" 1929!

CHAPTER 4

Weill (in Berlin) an die Universal Edition, 5. Februar 1929: Die *Kleine Dreigroschenmusik* (ich habe absichtlich das Wort Suite vermieden) habe ich gestern auf der Probe gehört und bin sehr zufrieden damit. Es sind 8 Nummern in ganz neuer, konzertanter Fassung, teilweise mit neuen Zwischenstrophen und durchweg neu instrumentiert für 2 Fl., 2 Kl., 2 Sax., 2 Fagotte, 2 Tr., 1 Pos., 1 Tuba, Banjo, Schlagzeug, Klavier. Ich glaube, dass das Stück enorm viel gespielt werden kann, da es genau das ist, was alle Dirigenten suchen: ein schmissiges Schluss-Stück.

Figure 193. Kurt Weill. "Über den gestischen Charakter der Musik." ***Die Musik*** **21, no. 6 (March 1929): 419-23.** "Concerning the Gestic Character of Music." *In this essay composer Kurt Weill, who has created typical* Gebrauchsmusic *for our time, discusses the constructive principles of his operatic works. [The Editor.]*

In my attempts to arrive at a prototype for works of musical theater, I have made a few observations which at first seemed to me to be completely new perceptions, but which with closer consideration can be classified as being well within the historical continuum. While working on my own compositions, I continually forced myself to consider the question: "What are the occasions for music on the stage?" In retrospective consideration of my own or others' operatic works another question emerged: "How is music for the theater constructed, and are there definite characteristics that identify it as theatrical music?" It has been confirmed often that a number of significant composers either have not been involved with the theater at all or have attempted in vain to conquer the stage. Therefore, there must be specific features that permit music to seem appropriate for the theater, and I believe that these qualitites can be summarized under the concept that I am inclined to call the gestic character of music.

In so doing I take as a given that form of theater which seems to me to offer the only possible basis for opera in our time. The theater of the preceding era was written for its sensual palatability [*Geneissende*]. It sought to titillate, excite, stimulate, and upset the spectator. It pushed the material aspects into the foreground, and for the presentation of the material it enlisted every theatrical device from authentic grass to conveyor belts. And what it offered to its spectators could not be denied to its creator: when he wrote his work, he was an epicurean [*Geniessender*] too; he experienced the "intoxication of the creative moment," the "ecstasy of the creative impulse of the artist," and other pleasurable emotions. The other form of theater, which is beginning to be successful today, counts on a spectator who follows the proceedings with the quiet composure of a thinking man and who, since he really wants to think, perceives any demand on his pleasure centers [*Genussnerven*] as an annoyance. This theater seeks to show what man does. It is interested in material aspects only up to the point where they provide the framework or pretext for human relations. Therefore, this theater puts greater value on actors than on stage apparatus, and it denies its creator the epicurean posture that its audience renounces. To the highest degree, this theater is unromantic; for "romanticism" in art precludes thinking, it involves narcotic properties, it shows mankind in an exceptional state, and in its golden age (Wagner) it generally relinquished any representation of mankind.

If both forms of theater are employed in opera, it becomes evident that today's composer may no longer approach his text with the attitude of the epicurean. In the opera of the nineteenth and early twentieth century the task of music consisted of manufacturing atmosphere, supplying the background for situations, and emphasizing the dramatic accents. Even that form of musical theater which only utilized the text as an occasion for free, uninhibited music-making is ultimately only a final consequence of the romantic ideal of opera, since here music participated in development of the dramatic idea even less than in music drama.

The form of opera is an absurdity if it does not succeed in granting music a predominant position in its overall structure and in execution of even the most particular details. The music of an opera cannot abandon the whole task of the drama and its idea to the text and the stage setting; it must take an active role in the presentation of the proceedings.

And since the primary goal of today's theater is the representation of human beings, the music must also be related solely to mankind. Now, as is well-known, music lacks all capacity for psychological or characterizing effect. Instead, music possesses one capability which is of decisive significance for the representation of man in the theater: it can reproduce the *gestus*, which elucidates the events on stage. It can even create a type of fundamental *gestus* which prescribes a definite attitude for the actor and eliminates any doubt or misunderstanding about the respective incident. In the ideal case, it can fix this *gestus* so powerfully that a false representation of the relevant action is no longer possible. Every observant theater-goer knows how often the simplest and most natural human occurrences are presented on stage by counterfeit sounds and untruthful movements. Music has the potential to define the basic tone and fundamental *gestus* of an event to the extent that at least an incorrect interpretation will be avoided, while it still allows the actor abundant opportunity for deployment of his own individuality of style. *Naturally, gestic music is in no way bound to a text*, and if, in general, we perceive Mozart's music, even the non-operatic compositions, as "dramatic," we do so because it never abandons its gestic character.

Generally we find gestic music wherever an incident relating men to one another is presented musically in a naïve manner. The most striking examples are in the recitatives of Bach's Passions, in Mozart's operas, in *Fidelio* ("Nur hurtig fort, nur frisch gegraben"), and in the compositions of Offenbach and Bizet. In "Dies' Bildnis ist bezaubernd schön" the attitude of a man who is gazing upon a picture is fixed by the music alone. He can hold the picture in either his right or left hand; he can raise or lower it; he can be illuminated by a spotlight or he can stand in the dark—his basic *gestus* is correct because it is correctly dictated by the music.

What are the gestic means of music? First of all, the gestus is expressed in a rhythmic fixing of the text. Music has the capacity to notate the accents of language, the distribution of short and long syllables, and above all, pauses. Thereby, the sources of the most serious errors in the treatment of the text are eliminated from the stage. Furthermore, one can interpret rhythmically one phrase in the most diverse ways, and the same gestus may be expressed in various rhythms; the critical factor is only whether the proper gestus is found. This rhythmic fixing which is obtained from the text in this way forms only the basis for gestic music. The specific creative work of the composer occurs when he utilizes the remaining means of musical expression to establish contact between the text and what it is trying to express. Even the melody is stamped by the gestus of the action that is to be represented, but, since the stage action is already absorbed rhythmically, much wider latitude exists for the essential means of musical expression—the formal, melodic and harmonic construction—than in purely descriptive music or in music which parallels the action under constant danger of being concealed. Thus, the rhythmic restriction imposed by the text is no more severe a fetter for the operatic composer than, for example, the formal schemes of the fugue, sonata, or rondo were for the classic master. Within the framework of such rhythmically predetermined music, all methods of melodic elaboration and of harmonic and rhythmic differentiation are possible, if only the musical spans of accent conform to the gestic proceeding. Thus, a coloratura-type dwelling on a single syllable may be completely suitable if it is based on a gestic lingering at the same spot.

I will give an example from my own practice. Brecht, out of the necessity of making the *gestus* clear, had earlier sketched tunes for a few of his poems. Here a basic *gestus* has been defined rhythmically in the most primitive form, while the melody adheres to the totally personal and inimitable manner of singing with which Brecht performed his songs. In this version, the "Alabama-Song" appears as follows:

[music example]

One sees that this is nothing more than an inventory of the speech-rhythm and cannot be used as music at all. In my composition of this text the same basic gestus has been established, only here it has actually been "composed" for the first time with the much freer means of the musician. In my case the song has a much broader basis, extends much farther afield melodically, and even has a totally different rhythmic foundation as a result of the pattern of the accompaniment—but the gestic character has been preserved, although it occurs in a completely different outward form:

[music example]

It is still necessary to say that by no means can all texts be set in a gestic manner. The new (or renewed) form of theater which I take as a basis for my exposition concerns only a very few poets nowadays, and only this form permits and makes feasible a gestic language. Therefore, the problem raised here is to an equal extent a problem of modern drama. But for the theatrical form that aims at saying something about mankind, music is indispensable because of its capacity for fixing the gestus and elucidating the action. *And only a form of drama for which music is indispensable can adapt itself fully to the needs of that purely musical work of art that we call opera.*

Weill (in St. Cyr) an die Universal Edition, 25. Mai 1929: Ich bin nach einer herrlichen Autofahrt von 6 Tagen am Donnerstag hier eingetroffen. Brecht, der in seinem Wagen mitfuhr, ist in der Nähe von Fulda, wo wir zum Essen verabredet waren, mit seinem Wagen verunglückt, und ich musste ihn mit einem Kniescheibenbruch nach Berlin zurückschaffen lassen. Dadurch haben sich leider meine ganzen Pläne verschoben, da wir ja zusammen hierher gehen wollten, um zu arbeiten. Wir wollten die Songtexte für *Happy End* machen und uns mit neuen Plänen beschäftigen. Vor allem aber wollte ich mit Brecht eine Änderung für *Mahagonny*, die mir in den letzten Tagen eingefallen war, besprechen und ausarbeiten. Die einzige Stelle, die nämlich einer Verbreitung des Werkes unter Umständen Schwierigkeiten bereiten könnte und die z. B. auch Klemperer für gefährlich hält, ist die Darstellung der Liebe im 2. Akt, die Szene mit der langen Reihe von Männern vor dem Bordell. Ich habe nun die Idee, die Szene in eine Art von „Statistik des

Liebeslebens in Mahagonny" umzuwandeln, die teilweise gesungen, teilweise mit Lichtbildern oder Trickfilm dargestellt werden müsste, wobei der „Song von Mandelay", der jetzt an dieser Stelle steht, in irgend einer Form eingearbeitet werden müsste. Falls Brecht mit dieser Änderung einverstanden ist, werde ich versuchen, so schnell wie möglich die nötigen textlichen Unterlagen von ihm zu bekommen. . . . Schwieriger ist es schon mit meiner Absicht, die fertigen Teile des Klavierauszugs jeweils mit Brecht noch einmal einer gründlichen Revision der Texte und Regieanweisungen zu unterziehen. Da ja die Drucklegung des Klavierauszuges nicht verzögert werden darf, gibt es keine andere Möglichkeit, als diese textlichen Ausfeilungen im Juli, wenn ich mit Brecht zusammen bin, an Hand der Korrektur-Abzüge vorzunehmen.

Weill (in St. Cyr) an die Universal Edition, 4. Juni 1929: Das *Berliner Requiem* scheint in Frankfurt einen sehr guten Erfolg gehabt zu haben. Ich bitte Sie aber, das Stück erst nach der Uraufführung von *Mahagonny* für weitere Aufführungen frei zu geben, da ja der Song „Können einem toten Mann nicht helfen" in *Mahagonny* eine wichtige Rolle spielt. Ich würde Ihnen dann folgendes vorschlagen: ich schreibe für Baden-Baden mit Hindemith zusammen den *Lindberghflug*. Die Teile, die ich gemacht habe (mehr als die Hälfte des ganzen), sind so gut gelungen, dass ich das ganze Stück durchkomponieren werde, also auch die Teile, die Hindemith jetzt macht. Wir könnten dann einen sehr schönen Band herausbringen: 3 Songspiele von Weill und Brecht. 1). *Mahagonny Gesänge* (d. i. die Baden-Badener *Mahagonny*-Fassung), 2). *Das Berliner Requiem*, 3). *Der Lindberghflug*. Ich habe auch die Absicht, diese drei Stücke zusammen aufzuführen, in einer neuen Form zwischen Konzert und Theater, mit Bildern usw., und zwar will ich dafür in Berlin eine Truppe zusammenstellen, die ich dann auf Reisen schicken will, nicht für die Theater, sondern für die Konzertinstitute oder Cabarets.

Weill (in St. Cyr) an Hans Curjel, 13. Juni 1929: Unterdessen habe ich die ganze Berliner Presse der Hindemith-Oper bekommen. Dass eine so dumme Sache in Berlin kein Erfolg sein kann, war mir immer klar. Dass es aber eine Pleite von solchen Ausmaassen werden könnte, hatte ich nicht erwartet. Ich hatte geglaubt, man würde doch noch einmal auf diesen Pseudo-Humor hereinfallen. . . . Für *Mahagonny* habe ich eins gelernt: es war ein richtiger Instinkt, *Mahagonny* nicht als „lustige Oper" anzulegen, und wir müssen die ganze Aufführung darauf anlegen, dass sich alles mit einem tödlichen Ernst abspielt. Der sogenannte Buffocharakter kotzt mich nämlich gewaltig an. Die Spielfreudigkeit hat nun wohl endgültig ausgespielt.

Weill (in St. Cyr) an die Universal Edition, 25. Juni 1929: Bei den Zusammenstellungen des Baden-Badener Programms haben sich (in meiner Abwesenheit) Dinge ereignet, die meine früheren unangenehmen Eindrücke dieser ganzen Veranstaltung nur bestätigen. Ich werde Ihnen die näheren Einzelheiten mündlich schildern, möchte Sie heute nur bitten, eine Notiz folgenden Inhalts an die Presse zu geben: „Die neuste Komposition Kurt Weills ist eine Kantate *Lindberghflug* zu einem Text von Bert Brecht. Das Werk wird im Herbst zur Uraufführung gelangen. Einige Sätze aus dieser Komposition werden auf dem diesjährigen Baden-Badener Musikfest aufgeführt." Es ist aus taktischen Gründen sehr wichtig, dass diese Notiz bald erscheint.

Weill (in Berlin) an Hans Curjel, 2. August 1929: In Baden-Baden war es sehr beschissen. Hindemiths Arbeit am *Lindberghflug* und am *Lehrstück* war von einer kaum zu überbietenden Oberflächlichkeit. Es hat sich klar erwiesen, dass seine Musik für Brechtsche Texte zu harmlos ist. Erstaunlich ist, dass auch die Presse das gemerkt hat und mich als leuchtendes Beispiel hinstellt, wie man Brecht komponieren müsse.

***Figure* 208. Alfred Kerr. "*Happy End?* : Schiffbauerdamm." *Berliner Tageblatt*, 3 September 1929.**

I. A master player like Erich Engel, who is capable of many shades, can do a lot for an author—but there is one thing he cannot do: write for him. There's the rub.

If a play can neither come to life nor die, and never seems to come to an end until 11:30 . . . that's like someone on a bicycle who, after having been helped onto it, only knows how to pedal and can't dismount, and keeps pedaling and pedaling much to the viewer's overall ennui: one thing is for sure: no angel [*Engel*] can save him.

II. The resulting impression, a little before midnight on the telephone: "In this play, run by Brecht and a probably non-existent business partner, Brecht has plagiarized himself. A few nice flashes of wit. Flattering music. But at times, the height of stupidity. Applause from a chosen part of the audience. ("chosen" is not meant as a participle.) In the end: a theatrical scandal.

III. Why did they whistle right in the middle of it? Because someone masked as "Time-Dramaticus" had previously only referred to the death—Marlowe (three hundred and fifty years), John Gay, (two hundred years), Rimbaud (seventy years), Büchner (one hundred years), Villon (five hundred years), the anniversary of the Tauchnitz Publishing House; yet this time he referred to someone called "Miss Helyett" (approximately 50 years of age).

IV. A Helyett of the Salvation Army to the right; a plucky criminal; once again Mackie Messer "business is business" to the left, in the end . . . a couple.

Many would have predicted this, either in today's revolutionary poetry, or operetta reform.

What was not foreseen is that these criminals became soldiers of the Salvation Army. Under Brecht's slogan: "Happily borrowed" [*happy entlehnt*].

V. Madame Weigel, articulating brilliantly, spoke—no: read a bit of social criticism at the close of this stalled evening, from a scrap of paper. Tacked on, so to speak. Whereby the ignominious Helyett business had to throw in something communistic, in order to hastily stuff the mouths of our times with garbage. That was the worst of it.

Spoken words—hardly grown on Brecht's own farmland. (Had they been wittier, they could have been Tucholsky's.)

VI. Let's pause for a panoramic view. To pass off these Anglo-Saxon trifles, which smell of decay, as present-day dramatics—that's the last straw!

The excuse, that such worn-out stuff is "parody" goes, of course, into the files. But careful here. Parody of whom?

Contemporary drama means: Cadging [i.e. from other writers] with vocal inserts.

VII. One vocal insert uses the word sh-t as refrain. Several times. Again and again. I am hardly squeamish; but the fascinating-darling, magically-sweet, folksy-simple human flower named Neher-Carola, perhaps a future [Käthe] Dorsch, seemed to be embarrassed by such insipid garbage.

Another phrase recurs: "in the kisser." Endlessly: "in the kisser." A third one: "you can kiss my . . ." Repeatedly, repeatedly. If only something were meant by it . . . after all, one is open to reason.

The struggle against smut and trash is exposed and brought in question, so exposed and brought in question as the criticism of wretched social conditions; exposing everything left in the shadows. It's an absolute low point for this commercial venture.

Let's take a moment for reflection: enough!

(I fudged the actual time elapsed).

VIII. Homolka's effect is a precious one, one of dilapidated force, juicy and forceful right next to that heavenly Klabund-wife.

The musician Weill . . . it's like this: Brecht has turned away from newer theater (which, as he claims, he has never been active in) and gone back to Brecht. For which Weill composed melodies, which had already existed for an even longer period of time.

Having been rewarded four hundred times by Weill in the *Threepenny Opera*, the audience welcomed these fond memories. Which, in a humorous way, went to the head of the deceased John Gay, while Brecht turned in his grave.

IX. That's how with older, existing, reliable melodies, that's how Weill clad in a facade of jazz lured the audience away from new music. But Weill . . . Flatterer! At least he charmingly sets to music what people will sing after they have paid for their tickets. He is quite exquisite among the non-exquisites. A thief of hearts! with a program. Should one first make sure that he won't bewitch us?

X. Caspar Neher's half-curtain. Inscriptions. Laboriously distanced through film. (Of course, a parody.) Lorre, Günther, Hoerrmann, Radecki, Carell, Schöller, Lingen, Oswald. From time to time it pleases me to see the old Gerron [play on a quotation from *Faust*].

XI. Acting masterful throughout (as far as it can be in this many-authored play), in cutting, in fine shades of expression, in variety. Just not in poetry.

When, Mr. Engel, are you going to write the next drama yourself?

Weill (in Berlin) an die Universal Edition, 1. Oktober 1929: Mit gleicher Post schicke ich Ihnen die Neufassung der 14. Szene (Liebesszene) druckfertig für Textbuch und Klavierauszug. Es ist ein vollkommenes neues und, wie ich glaube, sehr gelungenes Stück geworden. Wir haben es mit Absicht im Gegensatz zu der bisherigen Fassung gestaltet und geben in der neuen Fassung ein grosses Gespräch zweier Liebenden in einem strengen Stil. Ich glaube, dass die Szene in dieser Form eine wichtige Stellung innerhalb des ganzen Werkes einnehmen wird. . . . Ausserdem vollende ich den *Lindberghflug*, der Ihnen ungefähr in 2 Wochen in Partitur zugeht. Es liegt mir sehr viel daran, dass der *Lindberghflug* im Laufe des Winters möglichst viel und möglichst an auffallender Stelle aufgeführt wird, da ich vor *Mahagonny* unbedingt meinen *Song*-Arbeiten ein derartiges ernstes Werk gegenüberstellen muss.

Figure 211. Rudolf Arnheim. "Krankenkost." *Weltbühne* 30, no. 37 (10 September 1929): 406-407. "Food for the Sick." Brecht and Weill - the first names are casually suppressed (soon the program will probably list him as Brecht,: also known as *Shiffbowerdammbert*)—Brecht and Weill characterize their new work *Happy End* as a magazine story by Dorothy Lane. Be that as it may concerning the source, the choice is typical: one helps himself to a literary genre which clearly is not literature, one adds a woman author to give the enterprise a dubious tinge, and as background, America, where people measure works of art with a stopwatch and think of Sophocles as some European contemporary of indistinguishable nationality. It is the dear and already no longer original belief in the inane and ordinary, the flirting with bankruptcy, the desertion by the artists who under the battle cry, "Who would want to know all this!" surrender to the enemy camp, where straddlers punch each other in the nose, where one puts a dime in the juke box when there is need for an artistic experience, where one eats and discusses with the knife, and where any cracker-barrel philosophy is at home, that we know from Brecht's songs; that there is nothing doing any more with the dear Lord, that everything happens as it should, and that today's world is a sad one.

The stage director Erich Engel has developed astonishing virtues of a housewife in order to make our stay in Bill Brecht's Ballhaus comfortable. He carves his figures sharply, making them impish, but still giving them a shot of reality, thus preventing them from turning into marionettes. Only the intellectually hardened Helene Weigel is made of granite, through which every stage director tries to bite in vain. This energetic lady loves to storm across the stage with hunched shoulders, her lower jaw like a battering ram wherever Theater is to be had. She should at long last let go of this silly dilettantism; acting is a not a private affair. Oskar Homolka, in contrast, is without inhibitions or critical reserve in his role, and dissolves in his part like a cube of sugar in water. Blissful dreams swim before his naked eyes, his lips rise thirstily, and on those lips appear head and body, determination and reason seem to hang helplessly, to be dragged ahead to a goal that the drunk eyes can't see, an unsurpassed impersonation of an animalistic, sensual being. And from Carola Neher, Erich Engel, a tender-fingered gynecologist, delivers the child hidden in her, the precipitous, obstinate, yet dreaming, lovely, child.

Lots of good meat on a non-existent skeleton. The play is conceived as a parody of detective stories, although it's been done in too slipshod a manner to dare to come out as a serious thriller. Edgar Wallace, with his cigarette holder raised, would immediately fire the guilty Pseudo-Poet on the spot if his literary department presented him with a draft in which a lady causes death by asking for a match, or needs a complicated loudspeaker to ask for something she could ask for in person. In the last act the conspirators, suddenly cut off from the power of religion, land on the Salvation Army's bench, and now water needs to run through the arena, drowning the criminals and their helpers, and the whole thing could be a pantomime with decor by Paula Busch.

From whence such a play, and where will it lead? The blame certainly lies with that widely held snobbism which considers intellect as having no brain; but stupidities don't fall from heaven. It's all due to man's fatigue. Just as in the evening a lot of doctors, lawyers, and scientists need to see "The Bloody Triangle" or "The Three Loves of Mabel Savage" in order to relax, people on both sides of the footlights are tired, our theaters often try to entertain with inferior, often craftily served-up acrobatics, since war and inflation have ruined their nerves, and they can't raise their spirits or their enthusiasm to either enjoy or create anything meaningful. We are all stuck in this crisis, but a lot depends on how one generally manages the consequences; whether one rolls up ones sleeves and noisily goes along, or whether one quietly and sadly steps aside.

Hans Heinsheimer, Universal Edition (in Wien) an Weill, 10. Oktober 1929: Wir haben uns ja in Baden-Baden über prinzipielles und taktisches so ausführlich unterhalten, dass ich daran anknüpfend folgendes sagen möchte: Die Situation, in der Sie augenblicklich sich befinden, ist nicht einfach. Der Stil, der in der *Dreigroschenoper* und in *Happy End* festgelegt war und der auch in *Mahagonny* . . . beibehalten bleibt, dieser Stil ist, darüber sind wir uns ja alle einig, nicht auf die Dauer kopierbar. Er ist, wenn ich ihn in der Entwicklung Ihrer Person richtig beurteile, gleichsam der Durchbruch zu einem populären einfachen Musikstil, der Sie aus dem Bezirk jenes Darstellungsstiles, der etwa in *Frauentanz* aufscheint, radikal gelöst hat. Auf die Dauer gesehen wird aber dieser Songstil nur die Plattform bilden, auf der Sie nun doch wieder zu tieferen und wesentlicheren musikalischen Schöpfungen zurückfinden und ich habe, das will ich bei dieser Gelegenheit sagen, mit geradezu freudigem Schreck die neue Szene aus *Mahagonny* durchgespielt. Hier, lieber Freund Weill, trifft das ein, was ich immer in der letzten Zeit erwartet und ausgesprochen habe, nämlich die Synthese zwischen dem durch die Songtechnik gelockerten und dem Verständnis der Allgemeinheit erschlossenen melodischen und rhythmischen Gut Ihrer Phantasie und zwischen der Gestaltung und Formung, die das Kennzeichnen wirklicher auf hoher Warte stehender künstlerischer Verantwortung trägt. Aus diesem Grunde halte ich diese Szene in *Mahagonny* für so besonders wesentlich. Hier machen Sie mit dem Stil von 1928 Schluss, hier wird der neue Klang der nächsten Jahre hörbar, jener Klang, den ich mir gebildet denke aus einer neuen Romantik, einer neuen Sehnsucht, einem neuen Suchen nach dem „Unerreichbaren", kurz einer Gefühlswelt, welche die neue Sachlichkeit ganz begreifen musste, um sie nun aber zu überwinden. . . .

Der starke Widerstand, der jetzt überall in Deutschland gegen die Berliner Vorherrschaft sich zeigt, ist für mich nicht im entferntesten überraschend. Er liegt vielmehr ganz genau im Rahmen einer Entwicklung, die zwangsläufig ist. Die deutsche Provinz führt ihr eigenes, starkes und bewundernswertes geistiges Leben. Die lebendigen Kräfte, die in ganz Deutschland wirken, sie bestimmen, davon bin ich absolut überzeugt, das geistige und das künstlerische Gesicht der nächsten Jahre. . . . Wenn ich also meine Ansicht zum Schluss ganz klar formulieren soll, so ist es die: Sie sollen und müssen endlich aus der industriellen Kunstbetätigung, die in Berlin geübt wird, wieder loskommen.

Weill (in Berlin) an Hans Heinsheimer, Universal Edition, 14. Oktober 1929: Ich danke Ihnen herzlich für Ihr ausführliches Schreiben. Ich habe mich ausserordentlich gefreut, dass Sie mir mit soviel Verständnis, mit soviel Intensität und wirklich freundschaftlicher Gesinnung über meine gegenwärtige Situation schreiben, und das was Sie sagen ist so richtig und entspricht so sehr meinen eigenen Anschauungen. . . . Da Ihr Brief so grundsätzlich gehalten ist, und da mir Ihre Stellungnahme so sehr zusagt, erlauben Sie mir wohl auch, zu diesen prinzipiellen Äusserungen einiges hinzuzufügen. Ich habe mich vor allem gefreut, dass Sie das Wesen der Stilwandlung, in der ich mich befinde, so richtig erkannt haben. (Es gibt nämlich nicht viel Leute, die das merken). Nur ist der Zeitpunkt dieser Stilwandlung viel früher anzusetzen, als Sie es tun. Schon der weitaus überwiegende Teil von *Mahagonny* ist doch bereits von dem Songstill völlig losgelöst und zeigt schon diesen neuen Stil, der an Ernst, an „Grösse" und an Ausdruckskraft alles übertrifft, was ich bisher gemacht habe. Fast alles, was zu der Baden-

Badener Fassung neu hinzugekommen ist, ist in einem vollkommen reinen, durchaus verantwortungsbewussten Stil geschrieben, von dem ich fest annehme, dass er länger bestehen wird, als das meiste was heute produziert wird. Auch *Happy End* ist in dieser Beziehung völlig verkannt worden. Stücke wie der grosse „Heilsarmeemarsch" und das „Matrosenlied" gehen über den Songcharakter weit hinaus, und die ganze Musik stellt formal, instrumental und melodisch eine so deutliche Weiterführung über die *Dreigroschenoper* hinaus dar, dass nur so hilflose Ignoranten wie die deutschen Kritiker es übersehen konnte[n]. Es handelt sich hier um eine grosse Entwicklung, die bisher *keinen Moment lang* stehen geblieben ist, und die, wie Sie richtig erkennen, jetzt in der neuen *Mahagonny*-Szene und im *Lindberghflug* wieder einen neuen Vorstoss gemacht hat. Wir dürfen uns auch nicht dazu verleiten lassen, das, was durch die *Dreigroschenoper* nicht nur für meine, sondern für die allgemeine musikalische Situation erreicht worden ist, jetzt zu bagatellisieren, weil meine neuen Arbeiten zufällig einmal in einem schlechten Stück schlecht eingebaut waren. Dass meine Musik zur *Dreigroschenoper* industrialisiert worden ist, spricht ja nach unserem Standpunkt nicht gegen sondern für sie, und wir würden in unsere alten Fehler zurückfallen, wenn wir einer Musik ihren künstlerischen Wert und ihre Bedeutung absprechen würden, nur weil sie den Weg zur Menge gefunden hat. Sie haben recht: für *mich* ist dieser Songstil auf die Dauer nicht kopierbar, und ich habe durch meine Arbeiten seit *Mahagonny* bewiesen, dass ich nicht die Absicht habe, ihn zu kopieren. Aber wir können nicht verkennen, dass dieser Stil Schule gemacht hat, und dass heute mehr als die Hälfte der jungen Komponisten der verschiedensten Richtungen davon leben. Daher übersieht die Allgemeinheit sehr leicht, dass ich selbst, der erst vor einem Jahr diesen Stil geprägt hat, unterdessen in aller Ruhe meinen Weg weitergegangen bin. Sie sehen also, dass Ihre Ausführungen sich im Endziel vollkommen mit meinen eigenen Anschauungen decken.

In einem Punkt allerdings kann ich mich Ihrer Meinung nicht anschliessen: das ist das, was Sie über Berlin und die deutsche Provinz sagen. Ich kenne die deutsche Provinz. Ich bin dort aufgewachsen, ich komme jetzt oft in die Provinzstädte und ich lese Zeitungen. Der Geist der deutschen Provinz, so wie ihn die Presse darstellt, ist tief reaktionär, und es ist völlig undenkbar, dass aus einer dieser Städte eine neue, zukunftweisende künstlerische Bewegung hervorgehen kann. Und der Widerstand gegen Berlin kann jedenfalls im Theaterleben nicht so gross sein, da die *Dreigroschenoper*, das kühnste und revolutionärste Produkt dieses vielgeschmähten Berliner Geistes, überall volle Häuser macht. Nein, lieber Freund Heinsheimer, der Kampf, der in ganz bestimmten Kreisen der Provinz-Bevölkerung gegen Berlin geführt wird, ist ein Teil jener grossen Offensive, die die Reaktion in den letzten Jahren eröffnet hat, und die durch dieses Mittel auch auf das Kunstgebiet hinübergetragen werden soll. Die geistigen Kräfte der Provinz, von denen Sie sprechen, haben keinen sehnlicheren Wunsch, als nach Berlin zu kommen. Die Entwicklung des deutschen Theaters in den letzten Jahrzehnten ist einzig und allein von Berlin ausgegangen, von Brahm, von Reinhardt, von Jessner und Piscator und zuletzt vom Theater am Schiffbauerdamm. Glauben Sie wirklich, dass man diese Leistungen, die Berlin heute zur unumstritten ersten Theaterstadt Europas gemacht haben, mit dem Ausdruck „industrielle Kunstbestätigung" abtun kann? Und glauben Sie wirklich, dass man diesen Ausdruck auf das anwenden kann, was ich mache? Ich arbeite seit Jahren als einziger schaffender Musiker konsequent und konzessionslos gegen den Widerstand der Snobs und der Ästheten, an der Schaffung von Urformen eines neuen, einfachen, volkstümlichen musikalischen Theaters. Auch die geringfügigste Theaterarbeit, die ich in dieser Zeit gemacht habe, ist unter dem Gefühl dieser Verantwortung entstanden, unter ständigem Bemühen, eine Entwicklung, die mir die einzig mögliche erscheint, weiterzutreiben. Ist das industrielle Kunstbestätigung? Und wäre es nicht viel leichter (und industriell viel einträglicher), wenn ich ebenfalls wie die meisten den überkommenen Opernstil ein wenig weiterführen und variieren und mich von vornherein auf den Geschmack und auf die Geistigkeit eines provinziellen Opernbesuchers einstellen würde? Niemand kennt so gut wie ich die Gefahren des Berliner Literatentums. Aber ich habe ja bewiesen, dass gerade aus dieser Atmosphäre, wenn man ihren Gefahren nicht erliegt, die wesentlichsten und reinsten künstlerischen Leistungen hervorgehen können.

Weill (in Berlin) an die Universal Edition, 19. November 1929: Ich muss Ihnen noch einige Worte in der Angelegenheit meiner *Gema*-Einschätzung schreiben. Ich bin diesmal mit 125 Punkten eingeschätzt worden und glaube zunächst, mich damit abfinden zu müssen. Jetzt erfuhr ich zu meinem Erstaunen, dass andere Kollegen, die mir offensichtlich weder an Bekanntheit des Namens noch an effektiver Aufführungsziffer überlegen sind, bedeutend günstiger eingeschätzt wurden. So erhalten, um nur einige Beispiele zu nennen, d'Albert und Hindemith genau die doppelte (!) Punktzahl der meinigen. Man hat offenbar bei meiner Einschätzung übersehen, dass ich sowohl für ernste Musik als auch für Unterhaltungsmusik eingeschätzt werden muss. Ich werde natürlich in Konzerten weniger gespielt als etwa Hindemith, dafür sind doch aber „Kanonensong," „Tangoballade" und *Dreigroschenoper*-Potpourris in zahllosen Programmen von Gaststätten, Kinos, Rundfunksendern usw. zu finden. Jedenfalls ist es ungerecht, mich um die Hälfte geringer einzuschätzen als etwa gleichgestellte Kollegen.

Weill (in Berlin) an die Universal Edition, 16. Dezember 1929: Sie werden durch Herrn Loewy die Kritiken des *Lindberghflugs* erhalten haben und vieles darin gefunden haben, was für eine Propagierung dieses Werkes sehr gut zu verwenden ist. Die Aufführung hat hier grosses Aufsehen gemacht und wird wegen der Neuartigkeit dieses Versuches noch jetzt überall diskutiert. Ich freue mich jedenfalls, dass meine (und Ihre) Absicht, mit einem ausgesprochenen Konzertwerk herauszukommen, so erfolgreich durchgeführt werden konnte, und ich bin überzeugt, dass eine grosse Anzahl von Konzertinstituten des In- und Auslandes das Werk aufführen werden. Unabhängig davon werde ich versuchen, allmählich zu einer Aufführung in Schulen vorzudringen. Das ist eine Lieblingsidee von mir, und ich bin mir bewusst, dass ihre Verwirklichung vorläufig noch grossen Schwierigkeiten begegnet.

Figure 220. Karl Westermeyer. "Musikleben—Berlin: Konzert." *Die Musik* (January 1930): 229. The execution of this fine concert is due for the most part to the efforts of the talented conductor Karl Rankl. Be that as it may, a few remarks on the topic of "Worker's Music" come to the fore, because the musical perceptiveness of the real worker does not suffice at all for the high strung cultural experiments of their intellectual spokesmen. Because of his economic dependency, the worker is always ripe for class-struggle and class-hatred, open and receptive only when enjoying something that has more than pure entertainment value and only when his economic situation can be improved, thereby moving him toward the bourgeois level.

In contrast, the attraction for every worker of tendentious art was evident during a evening concert of Berlin's "Schubert Chorus." New choruses by Kurt Weill and Hanns Eisler had their world premieres: very critical of our time, aggressive in content, blatantly revolutionary choruses. This same Chorus performed with great effect Eisler's new choruses last year (*Bauernrevolution* [Revolution of the Peasants], for example). This time, the most pleasing ones were *Auf den Strassen zu singen* [To Be Sung In The Streets], followed by *Streikbrecher* [Strike Breaker] and *An Stelle einer Grabrede* [In Place of a Eulogy]. Eisler's choral tone is balladlike and with realistic expressiveness, with thoroughly idiosyncratic voices and complex sentences, proof of personal inspiration. Kurt Weill who set some very highly peppered poems by Bert Brecht to music, *Legende vom toten Soldaten* [Legend of the Dead Soldier] and the satire *Zu Potsdam unter den Eichen* [To Potsdam, under the Oak trees] was perhaps not as original as Eisler, but the heightened satirizing effect was therefore all the more striking. This concert too took place under the breathtaking conductor Karl Rankl, who, by the way, is the chorus director of the Staatsoper on the Platz der Republik as well.

Weill (in Berlin) an die Universal Edition, 31. Dezember 1929: Übrigens hat sich aus meinen neuerlichen Besprechungen mit Brecher noch etwas sehr wichtiges ergeben. Schon nach *Happy End* machten mich meine Freunde darauf aufmerksam, dass die Verwendung amerikanischer Namen für *Mahagonny* eine Gefahr bedeutet, da unterdessen die Jimmys, Jackys, Bills usw. schon in vielen Stücken vorkamen und die Gefahr einer Festlegung auf völlig falsche Begriffe von Amerikanismus, Wildwest oder dergl. in sich schliessen. Schon seit Wochen haben mich diese abgenützten und missverständlichen Namen mit schwerer Sorge erfüllt, und ich bin sehr froh, dass ich jetzt mit Brecht eine sehr günstige Lösung gefunden habe, und zwar zur gleichen Zeit, als auch Brecher mich auf die gleiche Gefahr aufmerksam machte. Wie werden also bereits in Leipzig und in den anderen Städten *Mahagonny* mit grösstenteils deutschen Namen geben, und ich bitte Sie, in die Klavierauszüge (etwa dort wo die Orchesterbesetzung steht) sowie in die Textbücher einen Zettel folgenden Wortlauts einzukleben:

Da die menschlichen Vergnügungen, die für Geld zu haben sind, einander immer und überall aufs Haar gleichen, da die Vergnügungsstadt Mahagonny also in weitestem Sinne international ist, können die Namen der Helden in jeweils landesübliche umgeändert werden. Es empfiehlt sich daher, etwa für deutsche Aufführungen folgende Namen zu wählen:

Statt Fatty	Willy
„ Jim Mahoney	Johann Ackermann (auch Hans)
„ Jack O'Brien	Jakob Grün
„ Bill	Sparbüchsenheinrich (auch Heinz)
„ Joe	Josef Lettner, genannt Alaskawolfjo.

Ich bitte Sie sehr, diese kleine Änderung noch durchzuführen, da ich überzeugt bin, dass wir dadurch, besonders bei der Presse, einen schweren Angriffspunkt beseitigen.

Figure 221. Kurt Weill. "Vorwort zum Regiebuch der *Oper Aufstieg und Fall der Stadt Mahagonny*." Musikblätter des *Anbruch* 12, no. 1 (January 1930): 5-7. "Foreword to the Production Book for the opera *Aufstieg und Fall der Stadt Mahagonny*." In *Die Dreigroschenoper* an attempt was made to renew the prototypical form of musical theater. The music no longer advances the plot. Rather, wherever the music occurs it interrupts the plot. The epic form of theater is a cumulative juxtaposition of situations. For this reason, it is the ideal form of musical theater: only situations can be set to music in a closed form, and a juxtaposition of situations according to musical principles produces the heightened form of musical theater called opera.

In *Die Dreigroschenoper* the plot had to be unfolded between the musical numbers; the result was a form of "dialogue opera," a mixed genre combining play and opera.

The subject-matter of the opera *Aufstieg und Fall der Stadt Mahagonny* made possible a construction according to purely musical laws. The form of a chronicle that we chose is nothing less than a "juxtaposition of situations." Each new situation in the history of the city of Mahagonny is introduced by a caption which creates a narrative transition to the new scene.

Two men and a woman, fleeing from the police, get stuck in a desolate area. They decide to found a city in which men coming from the Gold Coast will have their needs satisfied. In the "paradise city" that emerges people lead a tranquil, idyllic life. In the long run, however, such a life cannot satisfy the men from the Gold Coast. Dissatisfaction prevails. Prices go down. In the night of the typhoon that approaches the city Jim Mahoney invents the new law of the city. The law is: "You may do everything." The typhoon changes course. People continue to live according to the new laws. The city flourishes. Needs increase—and with them, prices. You may do everything—provided you can pay for it. Jim Mahoney himself is condemned to death when he runs out of money. His execution gives rise to a huge demonstration against the inflation that heralds the city's demise.

That is the story of the city of Mahagonny. It is represented in a loose juxtaposition of "images of twentieth-century customs." It is a parable of contemporary life. The main character of the piece is the city, which emerges from people's needs. It is people's needs that bring about the city's rise and fall. We merely show the individual phases in the city's history and how they affect people. Just as people's needs influence the city's development, so in turn the city's development changes people's attitudes. All the opera's songs are an expression of the masses, even where they are performed by the individual as spokesman of the masses. The group of founders at the beginning confronts the group of new arrivals. At the end of the first act the supporters of the new law struggle against its opponents. The fate of the individual is portrayed only where it exemplifies the fate of the city.

Looking for psychological or contemporary relevance beyond this basic idea would be wrong.

The name "Mahagonny" connotes merely the name of a city. It was chosen for timbral (phonetic) reasons. The city's geographical location is immaterial.

Presenting the work with either an ironic or a grotesque slant is to be discouraged. Since the action is not symbolic but typical, the greatest economy is recommended in the use of scenery and theatrical expression. The directing of the singers, the movement of the choir, the whole style of presentation of this opera—all are determined by the style of the music. At no point is this music illustrative. It attempts to reproduce people's attitudes in the various situations brought about by the rise and fall of Mahagonny. That attitude is already captured in the music in such a way that a natural interpretation of the music itself indicates the style of presentation. Those on stage can restrict themselves to the simplest and most natural gestures.

Any staging of the opera must take into account the fact that the musical forms are self-contained. An essential task is to ensure purely musical continuity, and to block the players on stage in such a way that an almost concert-like form of music-making is possible. The style of the work is neither naturalistic nor symbolic. Rather, it could be described as "real," since it depicts life as presented in the sphere of art. Any exaggeration in terms of pathos or balletic stylization is to be avoided.

Caspar Neher's projection screens comprise part of the performance materials (and are to be shipped to theaters along with the music). These screens independently illustrate the scenic events, with the means available to the artist. They supply a visual aid to the city's history, which is projected sequentially onto a screen, either during or between the individual scenes. The performers perform their scenes in front of this screen, and it is sufficient here to set up the most indispensable props for the performers to elucidate their parts. It is unnecessary in this opera to employ any complicated stage apparatus. More important are a few good projectors and a skillful arrangement of projection screens that make it possible to see clearly from any seat in the house the pictures and, above all, the explanatory inscriptions. The scenery should be simple enough to be readily transplantable from the theater to any kind of platform. The scenes for soloists should be played as close as possible to the audience. For this reason, it is advisable to put the orchestra not in a pit but level with the front house seats, and to extend the stage across the pit so that some scenes can be played in the middle of the orchestra.

Weill (in Berlin) an Lotte Lenya, 27. Januar 1930: Gestern war ich den ganzen Tag unterwegs: mittags bei Hans zum Essen, dann im Theater, wo ich Strawinsky gesprochen habe, dann mit Aufricht im Café, und abends in einem Rundfunkkonzert, das Strawinsky dirigiert hat. Er war richtig begeistert über die *Dreigroschenoper*, sagte, es sei im Ausland das bekannteste und meistbesprochene deutsche Kunstwerk der Gegenwart. Es sei ein Stück, wie es nur auf deutschem Boden entstehen könne, aber trotzdem eine ganz neuartige Mischung aus Shakespeare und Dickens. Die Musik sei „hundertprozentig". Ich soll ihm sofort alle Grammophonplatten und Noten schicken, weil er es immer bei sich haben will.

Weill (in Berlin) an Lotte Lenya, 31. Januar 1930: In Leipzig habe ich unausgesetzt zu tun gehabt, sodass ich nur eine knappe Stunde bei meinen Eltern war. Wir haben ausschliesslich mit Brügmann gearbeitet. Er hat sich zuerst entsetzlich doof angestellt sodass wir am ersten Abend ganz verzweifelt waren. Dann hat er plötzlich Feuer gefangen, als das Wort „Masken" fiel. Da ging ihm (soweit das bei einem solchen Esel überhaupt möglich ist) plötzlich der Knopf aus. Das Ergebnis: wir spielen das ganze Stück in Masken, die genau nach der Gesichtsform der einzelnen Darsteller hergestellt werden, sodass sie keine andere Aufgabe erfüllen, als die, das Gesicht der Darsteller vollkommen unbeweglich zu machen. Das ist natürlich ein Riesengewinn. Da wir es ganz konsequent durchführen wollen, kann es tatsächlich die modernste Theateraufführung werden, denn alle Leute reden seit Jahren von Masken, und niemand hat es gemacht. Und den Spilastikern sind auf die Weise noch mehr die Hände gebunden. Ich habe gleich einen herrliche Einfall gehabt: am Schluss muss der „Gott in Mahagonny" den Männern die Masken vom Gesicht nehmen. Daraufhin bricht der Aufstand aus. (Ist das nicht schön?).

Alfred Polgar, "Krach in Leipzig," *Das Tagebuch*, 22 March 1930. Hier, dort, oben, unten im elektrisch geladenen Raum zuckten Widersprüche auf, riefen Widersprüche gegen die Widersprüche wach, die ihrerseits Widersprüche zur dritten Potenz weckten. Und bald griff die epische Theaterform von der Bühne auf das Parkett über, wo sich das etablierte, was das Programmbuch als das Wesen der „idealen Form des musikalischen Theaters" erkennt, nämlich: eine Aneinanderreihung von Zuständen. Zustände von Zuständen! In nächster Umgebung meines Platzes geschah allein schon folgendes: Die Nachbarin links wurde von Herzkrämpfen befallen und wollte hinaus; nur der Hinweis auf das Geschichtliche des Augenblicks hielt sie zurück. Der greise Sachse rechts umklammerte das Knie der eigenen Gattin und war erregt! Ein Mann hinten redete zu sich selbst: „Ich warte nur, bis der Brecht kommt!" und leckte sich—in Bereitschaft sein ist alles—die Lippen feucht. Kriegerische Rufe, an manchen Stellen etwas Nahkampf, Zischen, Händeklatschen, das grimmig klang wie symbolische Maulschellen für die Zischer, begeisterte Erbitterung, erbitterte Begeisterung im Durcheinander. Zum Schluß: levée en masse der Unzufriedenen, und deren Niederschmetterung durch den Hagel des Applauses. . . .

Weill (in Berlin) an Maurice Abravanel, 2. Februar 1930: Unter uns gesagt: ich habe Angst, dass Geis die Aufführung stark nach der literarischen Seite abbiegen will. Hoffentlich kommt ihr nicht in den Fehler, den du der Leipziger Aufführung des *Zaren* zum Vorwurf machst! *Mahagonny* ist eine Oper, eine Gesangsoper. Eine Besetzung mit Schauspielern ist so gut wie unmöglich. Es darf nur das gesprochen werden, was ich als gesprochen notiert habe, und irgendwelche Änderungen sind nur mit meinem Einverständnis möglich.

H.H. Stuckenschmidt "Mahagonny", *Die Scene* (1930).
Seit langer Zeit ist kein dramatisches Kunstwerk leidenschaftlicherem Widerstand ausgesetzt gewesen als Brecht-Weills *Mahagonny*, seit langer Zeit wohl auch keine Uraufführung mit größerer Spannung erwartet worden. Wenn überhaupt schon jetzt eine Lösung der musikdramatischen Produktionskrise erhofft werden konnte, so mußte sie aus jener Ecke kommen, wo Brecht und Weill ihre ideologische Erneuerung überlieferter Mittel ausüben. Über Mangel an Begabung kann weder in der Literatur noch in der Musik ernstlich geklagt werden. Die Entwicklung der modernen Oper leidet geradezu unter einem Übermaß an großen Talenten. Aber all diese Werke haben uns kaum weitergebracht. Auf Entscheidung kam es an; Entscheidung für eine neue Form der Oper, für eine radikal andere Art Theater zu spielen. Dieser neuen Form strebt der nun dreißigjährige Kurt Weill seit seinen musikdramatischen Anfängen zu. In der Dreigroschenoper wurde sie erstmalig erreicht. Ihre wesentlichsten Merkmale sind: totale und unverbrämte Erneuerung der ideellen Struktur; Verzicht auf Pomp und falschen Heroismus, rücksichtslose Abschaffung der narkotischen Elemente; ausgiebige Verwendung von Kunstmitteln des Films und des Kabaretts. Dazu kommt eine ausgesprochen soziale Note, die beileibe nicht als Lokalkolorit gedacht ist (wie etwa die Armeleutedichtung um die Jahrhundertwende), sondern ihre kulturelle Funktion haben will. Und hier kann die Musik Hebel ansetzen; hier beginnen die Möglichkeiten breitester Wirkung. Hier darf mit dem Prinzip des Gassenhauers gearbeitet werden, und die Erinnerung an längst Bekanntes tritt als künstlerisches Reizmoment in Kraft. Nicht die Originalität der Mittel ist da entscheidend, sondern ihre Suggestion. . . .

Die primitive und rohe Großartigkeit dieser durch moritatenhafte Zwischentitel verbundenen Vorgänge verlangte nach einer durchaus elementaren Musik. Weill hält an dem Prinzip fest, das den Erfolg der Dreigroschenoper gemacht hat. Er löst die Handlung in songhafte Episoden auf und schafft so Opernnummern von großer melodischer Eindringlichkeit. Nicht nur die bestechendsten Einfälle wie der Alabama-Song, die Moritat „Wie man sich bettet, so liegt man" oder das herrliche Liebesduett von den Kranichen, auch die vermittelnden Strecken sind äußerst genau und oft mit unmittelbarem Anschluß an vorklassische Beispiele (Händel) gearbeitet. Das neunte Bild mit den Klaviervariationen über das Gebet einer Jungfrau ist ein Kabinettstück modernen Opernstils, in Farbe und Kraft durchaus der Schenke in Bergs *Wozzeck* zu vergleichen.

Das Werk steht entwicklungsgeschichtlich an der Spitze der musikdramatischen Produktionen der Gegenwart. Es trägt, all seinen Bierulk, all seine gymnasiastische Romantik zugegeben, aufs wirksamste zur Legitimierung des neuen Theaters bei und ist schon aus diesem Grunde leidenschaftlich zu bejahen. Es macht die Möglichkeiten der Oper für Gegenwart und Zukunft wieder plausibel und sprengt gleichzeitig ihre Grenzen.

An diesem Werk mußte jede liberale Kritik Schiffbruch leiden. Es gab hier nicht mehr die Ausflucht des „Einerseits-Andrerseits" und die geschmeidigsten Federn sahen sich zum Bekenntnis gezwungen. Und auch das ist von unschätzbarer Wichtigkeit. Denn so wurde dieses Werk (wobei seine spezifische Qualität ganz gleichgültig ist) zum Orientierungspunkt für die moderne Oper und darüber hinaus für das künftige Theater und die neue Musik.

Weill (in Berlin) an die Universal Edition, 18. März 1930: Hier in Berlin ist unterdessen ein anderes grosses Projekt aufgetaucht, von dem allerdings noch niemand etwas wissen darf. Charell interessiert sich brennend für *Mahagonny* und würde es schon im Mai im Grossen Schauspielhaus (3500 Plätze!) herauszubringen versuchen, ev. als Einladung an die Leipziger Oper. . . . Aufricht weiss noch nichts von diesem Plan.

Weill (in Berlin) an die Universal Edition, 20. März 1930: Ich bin sehr erfreut, dass Sie die Propaganda für *Mahagonny* jetzt gleich in Angriff genommen haben. Was würden Sie davon halten, im Prospekt einen Anhang zu machen, der den Leipziger Skandal behandelt, und zwar ebenfalls als Aneinanderreihung von Zeitungsnachrichten. Man könnte dadurch eine völlige Isolierung der *Leipziger Neuesten Nachrichten* und der paar nationalistischen Blätter, die ebenfalls für die Zensurierung eintraten, erreichen und könnte, was sehr wichtig wäre, die Theaterleiter darüber aufklären, dass es sich lediglich um verabredete Machenschaften rechtsradikaler Elemente handelte (wie ja Braunschweig deutlich zeigte).

Unterdessen höre ich auf Umwegen, dass man in Essen und Dortmund mit dem Gedanken umgeht, *Mahagonny* „auf unbestimmte Zeit" zu verschieben. Gegen diese Absicht müssen wir uns mit allen zu Gebote stehenden Mitteln wehren. Es handelt sich offenbar um Treibereien aus Zentrumskreisen, die sich auf die Dauer zu einer schweren Schädigung für jede moderne Unternehmung auf dem Theater auswachsen würden, wenn man sie durchgehen liesse. Ich bitte Sie daher, alle rechtlichen Mittel, die Ihnen zur Verfügung stehen (Konventionalstrafe, Schadenersatz), anzuwenden, um durchzusetzen, dass die Aufführungen auf jeden Fall zustandekommen. Das Werk liegt heute in einer Fassung vor, die auch vor einem katholischen Publikum gespielt werden kann, und es ist blinde Voreingenommenheit, wenn man jetzt schon, bevor man diese Fassung gesehen hat, gegen die Aufführung hetzt.

Figure 235. *"Aufstieg und Fall der Stadt Mahagonny*: Uraufführung in Leipzig." *Zeitschrift für Musik* 97, no. 4 (April 1930): 292. Hello, fine gentlemen Brecht and Weill, your days must be as numbered as they are for your scum city *Mahagonny*! Did the happenings on the occasion of the premiere of this unfathomably evil, low-down, above all artistically impotent piece not produce such an honest, splendid theatrical scandal with a clear separation between decent, and let's say, oppositionally oriented audience members; a scandal, at least at this point in time, and in Leipzig, which could not have been more unequivocally hoped for. Such energized whistling, fueled by an inner need, topped by cat calls like: "Shame!" "Cut it out!" has certainly never happened before in the *Neues Theater*, and so there developed afterwards a most amusing battle between those who applauded and those who whistled, which—and there can't be any doubt—will bring about a decisive turnabout in the attitude toward the dirty poetry of Mr. Brecht, as well as to the like-minded machine-jazz-music of Mr. Weill. The evening was nothing but a "People's Court," going much further than the usual theater scandal even if the fashionable riffraff of the arts—whom we congratulate most heartily—on the surface still appear to be stronger, and succeeded in as far as calling the authors before the curtain is concerned. But what lies behind all of these theatrical battles? The minority (for now) of the audience had to reach out for self-help; it had to, out of respect for the arts and their own dignity—first to protect themselves from an unscrupulous big city press which insists on praising everything modern and trendy to the skies, and second betrayed and trampled into the dust by civic and state-art authorities. Self-help for the better part of the audience and complete failure of the press and administrative bodies, that's what is behind this battle of the theater. And if by now the partly homogenous press, which had surrounded not only a *Johnny*, but also a *Threepenny Opera* with a halo, immediately turns around and boxes itself on the ears, as an immediate consequence of the People's Court. In the last hour before copy deadline we ascertain that *Mahagonny* is essentially less common than the *Threepenny Opera*, of which it is to some extent a continuation. There it is: "First feed your self, then comes morality," the motto here is: "Don't forget, that first comes the eating, second there is love (by which Mr. Brecht means only the bordello), third don't forget boxing, fourth drink as much as you can, and above all don't forget that everything is permissible." What was permissible after 1928, one can no longer do in 1930! That's the solution of the puzzle! We must wait for the consequences the theater battle has in store, especially for Leipzig. But this aside: March 9th for Leipzig certainly signifies a day for urgent self-contemplation; the golden days for the poets of pimpdom are over!

Weill (in Berlin) an die Universal Edition, 25. März 1930: Sie werden sehen, dass durch unsere Änderungen (die jetzt endgültig sind) klar und eindeutig zu erkennen ist, dass *Mahagonny* nichts anderes ist als Sodom und Gomorrha. Wir zeigen deutlich, dass Anarchie zum Verbrechen führt und Verbrechen zum Untergang. Noch moralischer geht es nicht. Dramaturgisch hat das Ganze jetzt noch sehr gewonnen. Besonders der Schluss des zweiten Aktes ist viel wirkungsvoller geworden, weil die Arie des Jim an den Anfang des 3. Aktes und statt dessen das wirkungsvolle Chorstück „Lasst euch nicht verführen" an den Schluss des 2. Aktes gestellt worden ist. „Gott in Mahagonny" wirkt jetzt in keiner Weise mehr aufreizend, da es nicht ins Publikum gespielt wird sondern dem Verurteilten vorgespielt wird. Ich finde übrigens, dass wir am Tag nach der Premiere bei den von Herrn Brecher und Herrn Dr. Heinsheimer gewünschten Änderungen, die Sie unterdessen auch den anderen Bühnen mitgeteilt haben, etwas zu weit gegangen sind. Der Satz mit der Wäsche (S. 62) hat in Kassel keinerlei Anstoss erregt, ebenso ist auch der erste Teil von Jims Lied „Wenn es etwas gibt" S. 139 vollkommen ruhig aufgenommen worden. Ich habe daher nur die Änderungen ausgeführt, die mir nach ruhiger Überlegung und nach den Kasseler Erfahrungen als notwendig erschienen.

Weill (in Berlin) an die Universal Edition, 5. April 1930: Ich erhielt soeben Ihr Schreiben betr. *Seemannslos*. Ich bin zunächst aufs äusserste erstaunt über Ihre merkwürdige Stellungnahme in dieser Angelegenheit. Ihre Behauptung, dass Sie „keine Ahnung von dieser Angelegenheit" hatten, ist absolut unrichtig. Das Textbuch der *Mahagonny*-Oper ist Ihnen seit einem Jahr, die Partitur seit 2 Jahren bekannt, und ich bin erstaunt, dass Sie zugeben wollen, eine Oper, deren Textbuch, Partitur, Klavierauszug und Orchestermaterial Sie gedruckt haben, so wenig zu kennen. . . . Übrigens war es auch ein Ergebnis unserer Besprechungen über diesen Punkt, dass ich beim *Gebet einer Jungfrau* die Fußnote „unter Benutzung des Gebet einer Jungfrau" beigefügt habe. Bei dem *Seemannslos* schien uns das unnötig, da es ja im gesprochenen Text ausdrücklich heisst:

„Am besten ist, wir singen: „Stürmisch die Nacht, um den Mut nicht zu verlieren."

„Stürmisch die Nacht ist vorzüglich, wenn man den Mut verliert.

„Wir wollen für alle Fälle gleich einmal singen."

Dadurch ist unzweideutig ersichtlich, dass es sich um ein reines Zitat und zwar in deutlich karikierender, parodistischer Absicht handelt. Das geht auch aus der musikalischen Verarbeitung hervor: ich habe (S. 234) die Vorstrophe und den Refrain des Liedes zusammen kontrapunktiert und dazu noch in den Rhythmus eingebaut, der der ganzen Szene zugrundeliegt. Musikalische Zitate dieser Art gibt es doch sehr häufig. Wenn ich überall, wo meine *Dreigroschenoper*-Songs parodistisch zitiert werden, Ersatzansprüche anmelden könnte, so wäre ich bald ein reicher Mann.

Figure 241. Kurt Weill. "Über meine Schuloper *Der Jasager*." "About My Didactic Opera *Der Jasager*." The intention to write a didactic opera [*Schuloper*] occurred to me about a year ago. From the beginning the word "Schuloper" encompassed for me several possibilities of combining the concept of "training" ["*Schulung*"] with the concept of "opera." First of all, an opera can be training for composers or for a generation of composers. At precisely this time, when it is a matter of positing new foundations for the genre of "opera" and of redefining the boundaries of this genre, an important task is to create prototypes of this genre, in which the formal and thematic problems of a primarily musical form of theater are examined afresh on the basis of new hypotheses. In this sense, one could also label Busoni's *Arlecchino*, Hindemith's *Hin und zurück*, Milhaud's *Le pauvre matelot* and *Die Dreigroschenoper* as didactic operas, for each of these works seeks to establish a prototype of opera.

An opera can also be training for operatic production. When we succeed in fashioning the entire musical design of a stage work so simply and naturally that we can designate children as the ideal interpreters of these works, then such a work would also be suitable to force opera singers (or those who wish to become opera singers) to achieve that simplicity and naturalness in singing and in presentation that we still so often miss in opera houses. In this sense, the didactic opera can serve somewhat like an "etude" for operatic training and undertakings (to be performed once daily before the start of rehearsal).

The third interpretation of the word "Schuloper" is one that contains the first two: opera that is intended for use in schools. It is to be classified among the attempts to create a musical production in which music is not an end in itself, but serves those institutions that need music and for which a new musical production represents something of value. Now principally two new market outlets have emerged next to the old (concert, theater, radio): the workers' choral movement and the schools. Therein, a rewarding task exists for us: to create for these new areas works of greater scope, which are nonetheless restricted in the external means to such a degree that the possibility of performance in the intended places is not hindered. Therefore, I have arranged *Der Jasager* in such a way that it can be performed by students in all parts (chorus, orchestra, and soloists), and I can even envision students designing the scenery and costumes for this play. The score has been arranged appropriately for the instrumental possibilities of a student orchestra: a basic orchestra of strings (without violas) and two pianos, with three woodwinds (flute, clarinet, saxophone), percussion, and plucked instruments added *ad libitum*. But I do not believe that one should reduce the level of difficulty of the music for a didactic opera too far or that one should write particularly "child-like," easily singable [*nachsingbare*] music for this purpose.[1]

The music of a didactic opera must absolutely be calculated for careful, even lengthy study. For *the practical value of didactic opera consists precisely in the study*, and as far as the performers are concerned, the performance of such a work is far less important than the training that is linked to it. At first this training is purely musical, but it should be at least as much intellectual. For the pedagogical effect of the music can arise in the course of intensive musical study because the student in the process of study occupies himself with a specific idea, which presents itself to him more flexibly through the music and which establishes itself in him more strongly than if he had to learn it from a book. It is absolutely worth every effort, therefore, to see that a didactic piece offers the students the opportunity of learning something in addition to the joy of making music.

While the old Japanese play that we (Brecht and I) selected as the textual basis for the first didactic opera seemed to us suitable in its basic character for immediate use in schools, the events still lacked that foundation which allows a pedagogical utilization to appear justified. Therefore, we added the concept of "acquiescence" [*Einverständnis*] and changed the play accordingly: now the boy is no longer (as in the old play) involuntarily thrown into the valley. Rather, he is questioned beforehand and proves through the declaration of his "acquiescence" that he has learned to take upon himself all the consequences for the sake of a community or for an idea to which he had attached himself.

Hans Heinsheimer, Universal Edition (in Wien) an Weill und Brecht, 1. Juli 1930: Wir möchten Ihnen kurz über das Resultat der Berliner *Jasager*-Aufführung und über die weitere Propagandaarbeit, die wir planen, Mitteilung machen. Das Kritikenergebnis ist ganz ausserordentlich günstig. Als besonders interessant ist wohl hervorzuheben, dass die Presse aller Parteirichtungen das Werk einmütig anerkennt. Besonders gute Kritiken sind erschienen im *Vorwärts, Deutsche Tageszeitung, Tempo, Deutsche Allgemeine Zeitung, Berliner Tageblatt, Berliner Börsencourier, B.Z. am Mittag, 8 Uhr Abendblatt, Frankfurter Zeitung,* etc. Wichtig ist auch, dass ein gewisser Dr. Arno Huth, der in cca. 30 Provinzzeitungen schreibt, eine geradezu enthusiastische Kritik verfasst hat, die für die Provinzauswirkung besonders bedeutsam sein kann. Wir sind nun bereits dabei, einen, wie wir hoffen besonders wirkungsvollen Prospekt, der besonders für die Schulen gedacht ist, zusammenzustellen. In diesem Prospekt werden auch die im Programmheft erschienenen Aufsätze enthalten sein.

Weill (in Berlin) an die Universal Edition, 6. August 1930: Wir haben jetzt endlich mit Hilfe eines Rechtsanwalts durchgedrückt, dass die uns vertraglich zugesicherte entscheidende Mitarbeit an dem Tonfilm 3-Gr.-O. in befriedigender Weise fixiert worden ist. Die Nero, rein industriell eingestellt und dabei von einer seltenen Organisations-Unfähigkeit, wollte ganz offensichtlich aus der 3 Gr.-O. einen harmlosen Operettenfilm machen. Dagegen mussten und müssen wir uns mit allen Mitteln wehren. Die Arbeit am Drehbuch ist jetzt im Gange. Ich beschäftige mich unterdessen hier damit, die technischen und akustischen Voraussetzungen genau zu studieren und danach die Instrumentation zu ändern. . . . Was meine neuen Pläne betrifft, so beschäftige ich mich augenblicklich viel mit Jack London, dessen Werke mir allerhand neue Ideen bringen. Ferner verdichtet sich der Plan einer Oper nach Franz Kafka (dieses alles natürlich vertraulich). Ich hoffe bestimmt, dass sich einer von allen diesen Plänen im Laufe der kommenden Wochen so verdichten wird, dass ich im Herbst mit einer grossen neuen Arbeit beginnen kann.

Weill (in Berlin) an die Universal Edition, 24. August 1930: In der Angelegenheit Scheer hat uns die gesamte Presse in rührender Weise in Schutz genommen und von rechts bis links ist ein förmlicher Sturm der Entrüstung losgegangen. Trotzdem können die Neroleute nicht einsehen, dass sie besser täten, uns in Ruhe und ohne ständiges Drängeln arbeiten zu lassen, als sich in ständige Kampfstellung gegen uns zu begeben. Eine grauenvolle Industrie!

Weill (in Berlin) an die Universal Edition, 27. August 1930: Ich arbeite seit etwa 2 Wochen mit Caspar Neher an einem Operntext. Das bisherige Ergebnis dieser Arbeit ist überraschend gut. Wir haben eine sehr starke und einfache Handlung konstruiert und haben jetzt das Vorspiel niedergeschrieben. Ich halte für sehr möglich, dass in dieser Zusammenarbeit ein Libretto entstehen kann, wie ich es jetzt brauche. Der Titel der (abendfüllenden) Oper wird vielleicht sein: *Die Bürgschaft.*

Weill (in Berlin) an die Universal Edition, 28. September 1930: Über die Frankfurter *Mahagonny*-Angelegenheit bin ich ein bischen beunruhigt. Ich bekam vor einigen Tagen von Dr. Graf den beiliegenden Brief, der ja, offen gesagt, nicht sehr vertrauenerweckend klingt, und ich fürchte, die Herren befolgen bei mir die gleiche Taktik wie bei Schönberg, den man bekanntlich zu Proben nicht zugezogen hat und den man aus der Generalprobe hinauskomplimentierte, als er seine Ansicht äussern wollte. In der Frage „Gott in Mahagonny" habe ich geantwortet, die vorgeschlagene Änderung mit dem „Glück" (ich hoffe, Herr Dr. Graf hat nicht das ganze Stück so missverstanden wie diese Szene) käme nicht in Frage, ich sei aber einverstanden, wenn die Szene überhaupt gestrichen wird, und auch Brecht hat sich damit einverstanden erklärt. Das sei allerdings sehr schwer, da damit die ganze musikalische Steigerung zum Schluss hin fortfiele. Man solle mir also mitteilen, wie man diese Schwierigkeit lösen wolle. . . . Die grösste Gefahr liegt meiner Ansicht nach darin, dass man aus lauter Angst das Stück jetzt so verwässern und verdünnen wird, dass von der aufreizenden oder erschütternden Wirkung, die ja in Leipzig unbedingt vorhanden war, nichts mehr übrigbleibt.

Weill (in Berlin) an die Universal Edition, 6. Oktober 1930: Sie werden erfahren haben, dass es wegen des Tonfilms *Dreigroschenoper* zum Prozess kommt. Die Leute haben sich unglaublich benommen, und es ist nach den letzten Vorgängen nicht mehr daran zu zweifeln, dass man vorsätzlich jeden Versuch von unserer Seite, gegen den Kitsch, der dort fabriziert wird, Einspruch zu erheben, mit Gewalt und mit Mitteln, wie man sie nur aus Wildwestromanen kennt, unterdrücken wollte. Als ich zum ersten Mal von meinem vertraglichen Mitbestimmungsrecht Gebrauch machen wollte und gegen eine Szene, die mir besonders schädlich schien, Einspruch erhob, wurde mir ohne jeden Grund mein Arbeitsvertrag gekündigt. Darauf hat mein Anwalt Otto Joseph sofort die Klage eingereicht. Termin (mit Brechts Prozess zusammen) findet am 17. Okt. statt.

Weill (in Berlin) an die Universal Edition, 21. Oktober 1930: Durch den Prozess war ich bis heute verhindert, Ihnen zu schreiben. Die Frankfurter Premiere war, wie Sie ja aus den Zeitungen entnehmen konnten, ein einmütiger grosser Erfolg. Prof. Turnau, die städt. Dezernenten und alle Beteiligten waren sich darüber einig, dass es eine Serie wie bei *Land des Lächelns* geben würde. Die Premiere war vollständig ausverkauft, ein Parkett von Fräcken und Smokings, man spürte, wie schon nach einer Viertelstunde der Widerstand, der künstlich geschürt worden war, völlig verschwand, dann gab es mehrfach Applaus bei offener Szene, nach dem 1. Akt 12 und am Schluss 23 Vorhänge (5–6 Vorhänge hält man in der Frankfurter Oper schon für einen Erfolg!). Es ist also eindeutig erwiesen (nämlich an dem stumpfesten und altmodischsten Publikum Deutschlands), dass *Mahagonny* in der vorliegenden Fassung ganz ausserordentliche Erfolgsmöglichkeiten hat und vor jedem Publikum bestehen kann (s. *Frankfurter Zeitung*). Diese Fassung hat übrigens dramaturgisch gegenüber der früheren Fassung grosse Vorteile, das Ganze wirkt klarer und geschlossener. Ich möchte allerdings keinen Zweifel darüber lassen, dass die etwas gemilderte Wirkung keineswegs durch unsere Bearbeitung (die ja in Wirklichkeit gar keine ist) entstanden ist, sondern durch die etwas ängstliche, unentschiedene und (unter uns gesagt) nicht gerade überwältigende Aufführung in Frankfurt. . . . Es ist natürlich ein ausgemachtes Pech, dass die 2. Aufführung in Frankfurt von Nazis gestört wurde. Dieser Skandal richtete sich natürlich in keiner Weise gegen das Werk.

Figure 249. "Nationalsozialistische Theaterskandale." *Vossische Zeitung.* 20 October 1930. "National Socialist Theater Scandal." Severe riots erupted during the second performance of the opera *Mahagonny,* which was given during the 50th anniversary of the Frankfurt Opera. During the first intermission, approximately 150 National Socialists stormed through the lobby, where they made a deafening noise. Their whistling, screaming, and growling rumbled through the entire house, and on the square in front of the opera house their allies trumpeted their battle cry: "Germany, awake!" Only after the police had, with difficulty, established some order could the second act begin. But it wasn't long before a veritable hailstorm of stink bombs poured over people sitting in the orchestra seats. Several rocket-type fireworks exploded, and the performance was interrupted again. The Japanese Prince Takamatsu and his wife were in attendance but left in indignation. After the performance, the National Socialists continued their passion for disturbance by demonstrating throughout Frankfurt's streets, but the police were soon able to disperse them. Several arrests were made.

Weill (in Berlin) an die Universal Edition, 25. Oktober 1930: Es zeigt sich hier, welche Leute (Schlächter und Eisenbahndiebe) von jetzt an in Deutschland über das Schicksal von Kunstwerken entscheiden sollen. Die demokratische Presse sieht seelenruhig diesem Treiben zu. Sie bringt den Skandal als Sensationsnachricht, aber sie nimmt nicht Stellung dazu. Jeder weiss, dass diese Zustände unerträglich sind, aber keiner traut es sich zu sagen oder gar zu schreiben.

Weill (in Berlin) an die Universal Edition, 5. März 1931: Sie werden sicher auch die ganzen Zeitungsschmierereien um die Beendigung meines Prozesses herum verfolgt haben. Ganz plötzlich wollte man mir nicht erlauben, diesen Prozess zu beenden, der tatsächlich anfing, mir schwer auf die Nerven zu gehen und mich von meiner wichtigeren Arbeit abzuhalten, und den ich bis zu Ende mit einer Courage und mit einer Konsequenz geführt habe, wie sie bei den Herren von der Zeitung kaum zu finden sein dürfte. Man hat dann versucht, das ausserordentliche Ergebnis dieses Prozesses: dass ein Musiker die Möglichkeit einer unabhängigen und unbeeinflussbaren Filmarbeit erhält, einfach zu verschweigen oder zu verfälschen. Tatsächlich ist ein Vertrag geschlossen worden, nach dem mir die Tobis für meine künftige Filmarbeit weitestgehende künstlerische Zugeständnisse macht, wie sie noch niemals ein Autor erreicht hat.

Weill (in Berlin) an Erwin Stein, Universal Edition, 7. August 1931: Ich freue mich sehr, dass Sie, wie mir die "U-E" mitteilt, den Klavierauszug zur *Bürgschaft* machen. . . . Was den Klavierauszug betrifft, so möchte ich vorschlagen, ihn dies Mal nicht, wie bei *Mahagonny,* lediglich auf Spielbarkeit für das grosse Publikum zu bearbeiten, sondern einen Auszug herzustellen, der genau die Struktur der Musik, mit allen wichtigen Nebenstimmen, rhythmischen, harmonischen und stimmführungsmässigen Varianten wiedergibt, der dabei aber doch die Durchsichtigkeit der Partitur, die für mich ja das Wesentlichste ist, auf den Klaviersatz überträgt.

Weill (in Berlin) an die Universal Edition, 19. November 1931: Wir müssen also alles daran setzen, um die *Mahagonny*-Aufführung gegenüber der *Bürgschaft* nicht zu wichtig erscheinen zu lassen. Es müsste an verschiedenen Stellen mit aller Deutlichkeit gesagt werden, dass *Mahagonny* der Schlusspunkt einer von mir bereits überholten Schaffensperiode ist, die mit dem Baden- Badener *Mahagonny* ihren Anfang nahm, dass dagegen die *Bürgschaft* das erste grössere Ergebnis einer neuen Ausdrucksform ist, die vom *Lindberghflug* und vor allem vom *Jasager* ihren Ausgang nimmt. Ich würde es sehr begrüssen, wenn Sie in irgend einer Form diesen Gedankengang jetzt in den Wochen bis zur *Mahagonny*-Premiere publizistisch ausführen lassen würden.

Weill (in Berlin) an die Universal Edition, 1. Dezember 1931: Die Proben zu *Mahagonny* sind im vollen Gange. . . . Ich mache eine ganze Reihe von Änderungen und komponiere auch einige Stücke neu.

Existieren eigentlich von *Mahagonny* schon Schlagerausgaben? Im Falle eines grossen Erfolges müsste man doch sehr rasch Material für Café- und Tanzkapellen haben. Ich würde es in diesem Falle am besten finden, wenn man alles auf *eine* Nummer konzentrieren und die gross aufziehen würde. Dazu eignet sich am besten (textlich und musikalisch) „Wie man sich bettet", das von einem erstklassigen Bearbeiter (der lediglich die Vorstrophe etwas vereinfachen müsste) zu einer interessanten und leicht spielbaren Nummer gemacht werden kann.

Hans Heinsheimer, Universal Edition (in Wien) an Weill, 7. Dezember 1931: Ich möchte Ihnen heute nur mitteilen, dass die gestrige Wiener Erstaufführung des *Jasager* in einer ganz hervorragenden, vor allem orchestral und chorisch glänzend studierten Aufführung durch den Arbeiterchor „Stahlklang" einen sehr grossen Erfolg hatte und eine ganz tiefe, erschütternde Wirkung auf das Publikum hatte. Ich selbst habe das Werk ja nun zum ersten Male in der Aufführung kennengelernt und ich möchte Ihnen auch noch sagen, wie ausserordentlich stark mein persönlicher Eindruck gewesen ist. Die Wirkung auf das Publikum war viel stärker, als man es überhaupt annehmen konnte, insbesondere die Abschiedsszene („Seit dem Tage, da uns der Vater verliess") hatte eine unerhört erschütternde Wirkung, so dass man vor lauter Schluchzen kaum mehr die Musik hörte.

Weill (in Berlin) an die Universal Edition, 9. Dezember 1931: Neher hatte unmöglich Zeit, mir etwas für Ihr Titelbild zu geben. Ich habe daher mein schönes *Begbick*-Bild von Neher aus dem Rahmen genommen und Ihnen gestern (leider etwas verspätet) geschickt. Das ist ein sehr schönes Titelbild für ein *Mahagonny*-Album.

Figure 272. "Heute hat Geburtstag: Kurt Weill." [March 1932]. He must be somewhere around thirty, somewhere around that age when youth is unrecoverable. He looks like some devilishly clever university candidate behind those large flashing Greek eyeglasses. It is he who represents the state of twentieth century theater music. He has liberated modern music from the iron bars of the guildhall. Creative at the highest level, he is popular as well. This symbiosis alone happens only once every 300 years. His development starts where most radical events come to an end— yet the audiences are with him just the same. *The Threepenny Opera* was what its name said, the very best; yet for the masses. In the period when he worked happily with Brecht, the principle of the very best for the masses became a kind of philosophy of art. Weill's music: breathless and with deep rhythmically, aggressive yet truly melodic, cold-blooded yet full of great theatrical strength, restrained yet passionate, this music was able to raise the level of even Brecht's lesser works. But that period lies behind him. The apportioning of their effect of two temporarily homogeneous authors, has passed. Weill can now serve only himself; he stands in the middle of the reshaping of German opera.

Weill (in Berlin) an die Universal Edition, 2. Februar 1932: Wir stecken seit einer Woche unaufhörlich zusammen: Ebert, Stiedry, Neher und ich. Das ist ein sehr angenehmes und intensives Arbeiten. Dazu kommt noch, dass ich Anfang März in mein neues Häuschen in Zehlendorf übersiedle.

Weill (in Berlin) an die Universal Edition, 2. März 1932: Vielen Dank für Ihre verschiedenen Nachrichten betr. *Mahagonny,* die mich natürlich lebhaft interessieren. Allerdings möchte ich mit Ihnen, lieber Dr. Heinsheimer, zunächst noch einmal ganz ausführlich über diesen Plan sprechen, denn es scheint doch, dass Sie das Werk sehr weitgehend verändern wollen. Die von Herrn Simon angedeuteten Instrumental-Änderungen stellen natürlich eine vollständige Verschiebung des für mich typischen Klangbildes dar, und gerade die *Mahagonny* Partitur ist in ihrem völlig eigenen Klangbild so sorgfältig gearbeitet, dass eine einfache Einbeziehung von fehlenden Instrumenten in andere Gruppen garnicht möglich ist. Über all das müssen wir also noch ausführlich sprechen.

Figure 275. "Parabel von Herder." ["Der afrikanische Rechtsspruch" by Johann Gottfried von Herder] Alexander of Macedon once arrived in a remote and wealthy African province. The inhabitants brought him bowls of perfect golden fruit. "Eat this fruit at home," said Alexander; "I have not come to see your riches, but to learn of your customs." Then they led him to the marketplace, where their king was sitting in judgment. At that moment a citizen stepped forward and spoke: "O King, I have bought from this man a sack of grain and have found in it an unexpected treasure. The grain is mine but not the gold; and this man will not take it back. Speak to him, O King, for it is his." And his opponent, who was also a citizen of that place, answered: "You are afraid of keeping something not your own: should I not be afraid to accept such a thing from you? I sold you the sack, including everything that was in it. Take what is yours. Speak to him, O King!"

The King asked the first man if he had a son. "Yes," he answered. The King then asked the other if he had a daughter, and again the answer was yes. "Good," said the King, "you are both righteous people; join your children in marriage, and give them the treasure as dowry—that is my decision."

Alexander was astonished at this verdict. "Are you astonished because I have pronounced unjustly?" asked the King. "By no means," answered Alexander, "but in our country the verdict would be different." "In what way?" asked the African King. "Both parties would lose their heads," Alexander replied, "and the gold would go to the King."

The King clasped his hands, and said: "Does the sun shine in your land too, and does the rain still fall from the heavens?" "Yes," replied Alexander. "Then," said the King, "that must be because of the innocent animals who live in your land; for on such a people no sun can shine and no rain can fall."

Figure 278. [Annotations from *Die Bürgschaft* program.] Boredom is the death of the didactic play.—Herder's parable has 20 lines; Weill, who admittedly mixes into his work many other elements, almost four hours, the musical substance not being diversified and multifarious enough to hold one's interest over such a long period of time. It's a shame, because the work represents a splendid try, and I am sure that with reasonable cuts in the 2nd and 3rd act the opera would be a lot more effective. The first act can stay as it is, by far the most beautiful both in story and music. Especially the three crooks with their cabaret songs—pieces that recall *Threepenny Opera* and *Mahagonny* the most, are very funny, with characteristic musical coloring. Orth's aria is also beautiful, and—one of the best scenes—the duet of the two leading characters on their boats. The chorus, which takes on a prominent position in this work, represents a gain, but also a danger. The inclination toward effects of antique drama results in a certain numbness, which in the last two acts has a paralyzing effect. Here, several of the plots run parallel and independently (among them a quite unnecessary subplot involving the daughter); furthermore, the work is driven off the operatic path towards oratorio; the work pontificates (chorus!). The thesis about mankind's unchangeability (to me, the opposite seems to be proven by the piece itself) is dragged in again and again, and the music is not strong enough to give these acts fresh momentum. And so one grows wearier and wearier, and the fine beginning is soon forgotten. However, this seems to me to be only a fault of the technique and not the opera itself. It is rich enough in isolated moments of beauty. Together with *Macbeth* this performance belongs to the best this poor season has given us, both works with Ebert as stage director and Stiedry as conductor.—As a stage director, Ebert especially has something his colleagues from the opera (Hörth!) are lacking: ideas and a sure taste.—Except for two, the singers are irrelevant: but Reinmar and, even more, the returned Rode (Vienna can no longer pay him!) sang magnificently.

Weill (in Berlin) an die Universal Edition, 30. März 1932: Sie können den Bühnen, mit denen Sie in Verhandlungen stehen, schon jetzt mitteilen, dass die *Bürgschaft* bereits jetzt in stark gekürzter Form aufgeführt wird. Die gestrige Berliner Aufführung, in der wir die ganze Beamtenszene Nr. 14 gestrichen haben, hat alles in allem 3 Stunden 20 Minuten gedauert, und in Düsseldorf hoffe ich durch weitere Striche auf 3 Stunden (incl. Pausen) zu kommen. Darüber hinaus aber arbeite ich mit Neher an einer vollkommenen Neufassung des 2. Aktes, den wir zu einem kurzen dramatischen Akt machen wollen (von höchstens 20 Minuten Dauer), sodass dann die Oper bei einer Pause von 20 Minuten kaum mehr als 2 Stunden 50 Min. dauern würde.

Weill (in Berlin) an Maurice Abravanel, 3. Mai 1932: Ich bin erst gestern von einem 14tägigen Aufenthalt in Wien zurückgekommen, wo *Mahagonny*, von einer Truppe ganz junger Leute sehr gut aufgeführt, ein grosser Erfolg war. Ich war inzwischen keineswegs untätig in deiner Angelegenheit, aber ich muss dir offen sagen, dass alle meine Bemühungen ganz erfolglos waren. Iltz, der die Stelle von Martin neu besetzt, sagte mir sofort: „Ich weiss, Sie werden mir Abravanel empfehlen, und ich weiss niemand, den ich lieber engagieren würde. Aber ich habe solche Schwierigkeiten, Horenstein zu halten, dass ich mir nicht noch einen Juden mit französischem Namen aufhalsen kann." So und ähnlich antwortet man mir überall: bei Ebert, bei Brecher. Es ist zum Verzweifeln.

Weill (in Berlin) an die Universal Edition, 4. Mai 1932: Nach Berlin zurückgekehrt, möchte ich Ihnen zunächst noch einmal sagen, dass dieser Wiener Aufenthalt für mich besonders interessant war. Ich glaube, dass Wien augenblicklich für neue musikalische Bestrebungen ein günstigerer Boden ist als die meisten deutschen Städte. Ich bin darum sehr froh darüber, dass die saubere, lebendige, von wirklich jugendlichem Geist erfüllte *Mahagonny*-Aufführung diesem Werk in Wien einen Erfolg gesichert hat, wie es ihn bisher eigentlich noch nirgends gehabt hat. Darüber hinaus möchte ich noch einmal zum Ausdruck bringen, dass mir der Weg, den die „Wiener Opernproduktion" beschritten hat, sehr beachtenswert erscheint, und dass ich es sehr begrüssenswert fände, wenn es möglich wäre, gerade jetzt bei der fortschreitenden Verkalkung der grossen staatlichen Opernbetriebe ganz von unten her eine neue, junge Opernkultur aufzubauen.

Hans Heinsheimer, Universal Edition (in Wien) an Weill, 14. Mai 1932: Endlich kam aus Coburg, wo ich auch mit dem Intendanten in besonders enger Verbindung stehe, folgende Nachricht:

„Zur *Bürgschaft* werde ich mich infolge der besonderen Konstellation Coburgs kaum entschliessen können. Wie Sie wissen, hat die gesamte rechtsstehende Presse gegen das Werk ausserordentlich scharf Front gemacht und es wäre sinnlos, gerade der Stadt Coburg das Werk aufzwingen zu wollen."

Dann kam ein Brief aus Hamburg, wo ich neuerlich energisch wegen der *Bürgschaft* vorstellig geworden war. Dr. Böhm schreibt folgendes:

„*Bürgschaft* kann ich leider vorerst nicht machen. Es ist mir dies direkt nicht erlaubt worden. Da wir, wie Sie wissen, jetzt mit gewissen Strömungen zu rechnen haben, muss man sich einfach fügen."

Weill (in Berlin) an Walter Bruno Iltz, Intendant der Oper in Düsseldorf, 16. Mai 1932: Ich möchte heute noch einmal auf unsere Gespräche in Düsseldorf und hier in Berlin zurückkommen. Ihre Stellungnahme gegenüber der Theaterpolitik der Rechtskreise erscheint mir über den Rahmen Ihrer dortigen Tätigkeit hinaus so wichtig und von so grundlegender Bedeutung, dass ich es für unbedingt nötig halte, Ihr Vorgehen weiteren Kreisen bekannt zu machen. Wie Sie wissen, unterwerfen sich die meisten deutschen Theaterintendanten bereits seit Jahren einer Zensur, die es überhaupt nicht gibt. Die überwiegende Mehrzahl der Theaterleiter hat sich schon seit Jahren, also zu einer Zeit, wo sie nicht die geringste Veranlassung dazu hatten, bei jeder Entscheidung feige zurückgezogen. Damit haben sie den Zustand heraufbeschworen, in dem wir uns jetzt befinden. Dagegen zeigt Ihr Fall, dass das alles garnicht nötig gewesen wäre und auch heute nicht nötig ist. Sie haben immer genug persönliche Überzeugung und persönliche Courage gehabt, um das, was Sie als künstlerisch richtig und notwendig erkannt haben, auch durchzusetzen. Die Bedeutung Ihres jetzigen Vorgehens besteht darin, dass Sie bei jedem Verlangen der Rechtskreise, das Ihnen unbillig erscheint, den Versuch unternehmen, diese Kreise aufzuklären, ihnen klarzumachen, dass sie ihre Schlagworte falsch anwenden und dass die Durchführung ihrer Forderungen schwer blamabel wäre für die, die die Forderungen aufstellen, und für die, die sie durchführen.

Es ist geradezu haarsträubend, was ich auf diesem Gebiete jetzt wieder mit der *Bürgschaft* erlebe. Die leitenden Männer fast aller führenden deutschen Bühnen stehen mehr als positiv zu dem Stück und sind von der künstlerischen Bedeutung des Werkes überzeugt, die meisten sind auch entschlossen, es aufzuführen. Aber sie trauen sich nicht. Niemand verbietet es ihnen. Aber Andeutungen genügen, um ihre Entschlüsse umzuwerfen. Es wäre nun von grösster Bedeutung, diesen Leuten einmal zu zeigen, dass es auch anders geht. Ich bitte Sie darum sehr herzlich, mir doch einmal die Vorgänge vor der Premiere der *Bürgschaft* (den Protest des rechtsgerichteten Kulturbundes, Ihre aufklärende Antwort und die loyale Aufnahme dieser Antwort bei dem Kulturbund) in wenigen Sätzen darzustellen und mir die Erlaubnis zu geben, diesen Bericht durch die Universal-Edition an andere Bühnenleiter weiterzugeben, als Ermutigung oder als Beschämung.

Ich würde ausserdem einen der maßgebenden Berliner Journalisten (etwa Kerr, Stefan Grossmann oder Manfred Georg) ersuchen, Ihren Bericht zum Ausgangspunkt einer Betrachtung über das gleiche Thema, das ich in diesem Brief angeschnitten habe, zu machen. Ich bin überzeugt, dass es sich jetzt in diesen Monaten entscheidet, ob wir überhaupt in den nächsten Jahren in Deutschland noch so etwas ähnliches wie eine Theaterkultur haben werden. Darum ist gerade jetzt eine erhöhte Aktivität nötig.

Weill (in Berlin) an die Universal Edition, 17. Mai 1932: Dass in Coburg, der Nazi-Burg, die *Bürgschaft* kommen kann, habe ich nie ernsthaft angenommen. . . . Sicher ist, dass man jetzt sehr aktiv werden muss. Ich werde jetzt den Versuch unternehmen, eine Reihe von Leuten zusammenzubringen mit dem Entschluss, sich zur Wehr zu setzen.

Weill (in Berlin) an die Universal Edition, 3. Juni 1932: Ich habe immerhin schon erreicht, dass man überall die Notwendigkeit einer entscheidenden Opposition einzusehen beginnt. Ich habe heute eine Unterredung mit Preussner, nächste Woche mit Kestenberg. Ich möchte zunächst erreichen, dass eine Gruppe fortschrittlicher Künstler Material über die fortschreitende Barbarisierung der deutschen Provinztheater zusammenstellt und der ihr nahestehenden Presse übergibt, u. zwar mit voller Namensnennung aller Beteiligten. Ein neues Beispiel: in Dresden hat Herr Reucker inhibiert, dass Lopatnikoff dem ihm befreundeten Busch seine Danton-Oper *vorspielt*! Ich werde Sie zu gegebener Zeit bitten, mir Ihr ganzes Material zu dieser Sache aus den letzten Jahren (*Wozzeck, Totenhaus, Hahnrei, Mahagonny, Bürgschaft* usw.) zusammenzustellen. . . .

Es tauchen in Umrissen allerhand Projekte auf, die, wenn sie sich verwirklichen würden, auch für Sie von grösstem Interesse sein könnten. In jedem Fall scheint die Entwicklung dahin zu gehen, dass die grossen öffentlichen Kunstinstitute kaum noch in Frage kommen. Es gibt aber ausserhalb dieser Institutionen noch genug Möglichkeiten. Ich denke dabei nicht nur an die Organisationen, für die ich den Typus „Laienoper" machen will, sondern auch an alle Privattheater-Unternehmungen, für die ich einen Typus von Oper machen will, der mit sehr kleinem Apparat, ohne Chor sehr leicht aufführbar sein soll, sodass ein solches Stück überall unabhängig von den öffentlichen Institutionen gespielt werden könnte. Ich beschäftige mich jetzt damit, die Grenzen zwischen dieser Gattung und der Gattung „Laienoper" abzustecken und die Möglichkeit zu untersuchen, beides zu vereinen.

Weill (in Berlin) an die Universal Edition, 29. Juni 1932: Charell hat vor einigen Tagen den entscheidenden Einfall gehabt für das, was er als nächste Theaterproduktion machen wird, und zwar ist dieser Einfall ausschliesslich von dem Gedanken an die Zusammenarbeit mit mir ausgegangen. Es soll ein zu 90% musikalisches Stück *Das Cabinett des Dr. Caligari* sein. . . . Es ist geplant (dies alles unter dem Siegel strengster Verschwiegenheit!), das Stück in Wien zu starten, dann nach Paris und London und zuletzt erst nach Berlin zu bringen.

Das klingt alles sehr schön. Nun kommen aber die Schwierigkeiten, die allerdings auf rein künstlerischem Gebiete liegen. Ich habe mir gestern mit Charell und Neher den Film vorführen lassen. Für mich bietet dieser Film ausser dem Titel nichts, was man in ein Theaterstück übernehmen kann. Charell sieht es rein vom Atmosphärischen her. Er sieht Rummelplatz, Hypnose, Somnabulismus, Mystik—alles private, abnorme, bürgerliche Erscheinungen, die ich doch nun nicht plötzlich zum Inhalt eines Stückes machen kann, nachdem ich seit Jahren mit grösster Hartnäckigkeit den Standpunkt vertreten habe, das Theater müsse sich den grossen tragenden Ideen der Zeit widmen. Eine anschliessende 6stündige Debatte ergab auf beiden Seiten das Gefühl, dass zwischen seiner und meiner Einstellung zum Theater ein weiter Abstand besteht, und dass es nicht ganz leicht sein wird, diesen Abstand zu überbrücken.

Weill (in Berlin) an die Universal Edition, 29. Juli 1932: Unterdessen hat sich aus den Gesprächen, die ich anlässlich des Charell-Planes mit Georg Kaiser hatte, ein sehr schöner neuer Plan entwickelt. Kaiser will mit mir ein musikalisches Volksstück schreiben. Er hat dafür eine sehr schöne, echt Kaiserische Idee, an der wir jetzt seit einigen Tagen arbeiten. Ich denke, dass bis Anfang nächster Woche bereits ein Entwurf dieses Stückes vorliegen kann. Es soll keinesfalls eine Oper werden, sondern ein Zwischengattungs-Stück. Es bleibt mir vorbehalten, ob ich daraus ein „Stück mit Musik", also mit ganz einfachen Liedern mache, die von reinen Schauspielern gesungen werden können, oder ob ich doch mit etwas grösseren musikalischen Ansprüchen herangehe und eine Musik im Umfang und im Schwierigkeitsgrad etwa einer Offenbach-Musiquette schreibe. Das letztere würde mich mehr reizen, weil ich hier über den in der *Dreigroschenoper* geschaffenen Typus hinausgehen könnte.

Weill (in Berlin) an Hans Heinsheimer, Universal Edition, 20. September 1932: Die politische Lage hat sich in den letzten Wochen entscheidend verändert. Alle jene Stellen, die in ehrerbietiger Erwartung des dritten Reiches bereits offen Nazi-Politik betrieben haben, sind jetzt ganz offen und eindeutig von Hitler abgerückt. Die ganze sogenannte „Generalanzeiger"-Presse in der Provinz tritt jetzt mit der gleichen Schärfe gegen Hitler auf, mit der sie vor einigen Wochen alle Hitler-Feinde verdammt hat. Die antisemitische Frage spielt überhaupt keine Rolle, da ja jetzt ausschliesslich Gewittergojim gegeneinander kämpfen. Selbst an den Theatern muss es sich bereits herumgesprochen haben, dass Hitler ausgespielt hat, und es wird für die Herren Theaterdirektoren höchste Zeit, ihre Mauselöcher zu verlassen, weil sie sonst garnicht merken, dass sich einiges verändert hat.

Weill (in Berlin) an die Universal Edition, 14. November 1932: Die Pariser Sache steht günstig. Noailles hat uns noch einen anständigen Mehrbetrag bewilligt, damit wir die Berliner *Jasager* Aufführung von Martens nach Berlin bringen können (vorausgesetzt, dass wir den Schulurlaub bewilligt kriegen). Wir wollen es vorläufig nicht publik werden lassen, damit uns das Kultusministerium nicht dazwischen funkt.

Weill (in Berlin) an die Universal Edition, 24. November 1932: Es ist natürlich *ganz unmöglich*, dass bei diesem Werk der Klavierauszug als Partitur verwendet werden kann. Es handelt sich ja nicht um eine Operette, bei der es auf die Instrumentierung nicht ankommt, sondern um eine ganz ausgewachsene, sehr sorgfältig gearbeitete Partitur. Das Werk ist an allen Theatern für die ersten Kapellmeister bestimmt, die es sicher und mit vollem Recht ablehnen werden, eine so umfangreiche und verantwortungsvoll gearbeitete Musik aus dem Klavierauszug zu dirigieren. Ich erinnere Sie, lieber Dr. Heinsheimer, daran, dass ich es hier in Berlin, als Sie mich danach fragten, *ausdrücklich* abgelehnt habe, dass von diesem Werk ein sogenannter Dirigentenauszug gemacht wird. Schon bei der *Dreigroschenoper* (wo es sich nur um 7 Instrumente handelte) hat sich der Dirigierauszug nicht bewährt, weil kein Mensch sich von dem Klangbild, das bei mir ja immer besonders wichtig ist, eine Vorstellung machen konnte.

Weill (in Berlin) an die Universal Edition, 26. Dezember 1932: Die *Sérénade* wird natürlich, nachdem sie von der Presse dazu aufgefordert worden ist, alles daransetzen, um in der Frühjahrsaison *Mahagonny* in der kleinen Fassung noch einmal zu machen. Daran ist besonders die Leiterin und Begründerin der *Sérénade*, die Marquise de Casa Fuerte, stärkstens interessiert, und auch Curjel arbeitet mit Hochdruck an diesem Plan. Dabei ist nur die grosse Schwierigkeit: was gibt man zu diesem *Mahagonny* dazu (die gleiche Frage hat auch Aufricht an mich gerichtet, der ja mit Ihnen über eine Tournee gesprochen hat; übrigens dazu: grösste Vorsicht! Aufricht taucht überall auf, wo ein Geschäft zu wittern ist, er hat jetzt die Methoden gelernt, und man muss mit allem, besonders mit Tantiemen, sehr aufpassen). Es wäre natürlich sehr wünschenswert, wenn man für diese Tournee auch ein Stück von mir zu *Mahagonny* dazu geben würde, und für Paris wäre das geradezu unerlässlich. Ich wäre auch bereit, für diesen Zweck noch etwas zu schreiben oder einzurichten. Das Naheliegendste wäre natürlich (ein alter Plan von mir), die Songs aus *Happy End* ebenfalls zu einer Art von Songspiel mit kleinen gesprochenen Spielszenen usw. einzurichten, etwa in der Art: Szenen aus dem Leben eines Heilsarmeemädchens. Das könnte natürlich Brecht machen, aber es ist ein schrecklicher Gedanke, wegen einer so kleinen und leichten Sache alle Schwierigkeiten einer Arbeit mit Brecht wieder auf sich zu nehmen. . . . Jedenfalls werde ich diesen Plan weiterverfolgen, da man auf diese Weise vielleicht einen sehr schönen Theaterabend für 6 Darsteller und 11 Mann Orchester bekommen könnte.

Weill (in Berlin) an Lotte Lenya, 7.? Januar 1933: Ich versuche mir dieses Leben so erträglich wie möglich zu machen. Das ist sehr sehr schwer, wenn man so ganz anderes gewöhnt war. Ich bin froh, daß ich dich gesprochen habe—u. doch nicht froh. Ich hoffe nur, Du glaubst mir, was ich dir gesagt habe.

Weill (in Berlin) an Lotte Lenya, 9. Januar 1933: Bidi hat Aufricht tagelang gequält, mich mit ihm zusammenzubringen. Ich habe schließlich vorgeschlagen, Aufricht soll uns zusammen einladen. Das hat Freitag stattgefunden, ist aber ziemlich ergebnislos verlaufen. Ich war ganz kühl u. zurückhaltend, er ganz beflissen, devot, anscheißerisch. Er will ein kürzeres Stück, als Ergänzung zu *Mahagonny* schreiben, mit einer schönen Rolle für Dich. Er behauptete, dafür gute Stoffe zu haben. Als ich dann zu Haus war, rief er um 2 Uhr nachts an, um mir einen Vorschlag zu machen. Na was meinst Du? Du rätst es nicht: den *Lindberghflug* will er für diesen Zweck „dramatisieren". Ist das nicht idiotisch? Jetzt ruft er dauernd an, ich soll mich mit ihm treffen, aber ich mag noch nicht. Diesmal bekommt er von mir Dinge zu hören, die ihm noch keiner gesagt hat. . . . Ich habe einen großen Filmantrag. Gab Frank ist jetzt tatsächlich eine ganz große Kanone im Film. Er hat in einem halben Jahr den „Europa-Verleih" aufgebaut, der jetzt bereits die einzige

Konkurrenz der UFA ist. Er hat mir vorgeschlagen, im Laufe der nächsten 2-3 Jahre vier Filme bei ihm zu machen. Ich habe sehr weitgehende Mitbestimmungsrechte, besonders was die Wahl des Regisseurs, den Stoff, den Drehbuchmann usw. betrifft. Der erste Film soll sofort gemacht werden, u. zwar hat er einen Stoff, den ich ohne weiteres akzeptieren kann: *Kleiner Mann—was nun?* von Fallada. . . .

Es sind auch persönliche Gründe, warum ich den Film annehmen möchte. Ich habe in den letzen Wochen wieder gemerkt, daß ich ganz zusammenklappe, wenn ich nicht arbeite. Dieser Film, der schon Anfang März ins Atelier soll, zusammen mit der *Silbersee*-Premiere, würde mich in einen solchen Arbeitswirbel hineinreißen, daß ich keine Zeit für Depressions-Zustände mehr habe.

Wie geht es Dir, Tuetilein? Ich dachte, Du würdest mir nach dem Telefongespräch mal schreiben. Aber Du darfst wahrscheinlich nicht. Ich habe in der letzten Zeit sehr viel an Dich gedacht u. mir so sehr gewünscht, daß es einmal wieder so wird wie früher.

Weill (in Berlin) an Lotte Lenya, 28. Januar 1933: Das Leben ist eine komische Einrichtung: heute vor 7 Jahren um diese Zeit trafen wir uns vor dem Rathaus Charlottenburg mit der Gratenau, der Lind u. Caten Zeit sehr viel an Dich gedacht u. mir so sehr gewünscht, daß es einmal wieder so wird wie früher.

Das Leben ist eine komische Einrichtung: heute vor 7 Jahren um diese Zeit trafen wir uns vor dem Rathaus Charlottenburg mit der Gratenau,Wie geht es Dir, Linnerl? Bist Du gesund u. froh? Wenn ich so lange Zeit nichts von Dir höre, dann kann ich mir garnicht vorstellen, dass Du überhaupt noch manchmal an mich oder gar: an uns denkst. Wann wirst Du nun kommen? Ich freue mich schon mächtig, besonders dass Du mit mir nach Leipzig kommst.

Weill (in Berlin) an Erika Neher, 29. Januar 1933: Ich glaube übrigens, dass das die einzige Möglichkeit für die innere Weiterbildung eines Menschen in dieser Zeit ist—u. vielleicht immer war: mit einem grossen Gefühl im Herzen ein Stoiker zu werden. Darum bin ich auch immer mit einem solchen Gefühl von Dankbarkeit für dich erfüllt, mein liebstes süssestes zartestes, reichstes Engelein du, weil ich ohne dich nie dahin gekommen wäre u. (davon bin ich überzeugt) zu Grunde gegangen wäre.

Weill (in Berlin) an Hans Heinsheimer, Universal Edition, 6. Februar 1933: Ich arbeite unausgesetzt daran, eine Basis zu schaffen, auf der trotz aller Schwierigkeiten meine Mitarbeit an dem Film möglich ist, und es sieht jetzt eigentlich wieder so aus, als ob die Sache doch zustandekäme. Ich weiss nicht, ob Sie sich eine Vorstellung machen können, welches Maass von Geduld, von Vorsicht, von Ausdauer dazu gehört, auch nur die Grundlagen herzustellen, auf denen diese Leute einen in Ruhe arbeiten lassen. Sie haben eine ständige Angst vor nichts anderem als vor meiner festen Absicht, einen künstlerisch wertvollen Film [herzustellen]. Das genügt schon. Aber ich sitze sehr fest bei den eigentlichen Geldgebern und hoffe daher, doch durchzukommen. Ich habe jetzt fertiggebracht, dass Viertel mitarbeitet. Das ist eine sehr günstige Kombination. Aber vorläufig hat er ebenso wenig wie ich einen Vertrag. Trotzdem arbeiten wir jetzt regelrecht 8–10 Stunden pro Tag an dem Manuskript.

Hans Heinsheimer, Universal Edition (in Wien) an Weill, 8. Februar 1933: Ihre Meinung, der neue Kurs in Deutschland könnte nur ein Alptraum von einigen Monaten sein, vermag ich nicht zu teilen. Ich bin von tiefstem Pessimismus erfüllt weil ich glaube, dass die Unterschätzung des Gegners sich nun erst rächen, dass es sich nun zeigen wird, dass jene alles besser, sicherer und rücksichtsloser halten werden, als es sich die Republikaner durch 15 Jahre getraut haben. Wie wird sich diese Lage nun im konkreten Fall *Silbersee* auswirken? Ich meine, dass ein Ausweichen jetzt, etwa eine Verschiebung der Premieren bis nach den Wahlen, nutzlos ist. Der Gedanke wäre aber immerhin zu diskutieren. Wir müssen es wohl ruhig darauf ankommen lassen und einmal sehen, was die neuen Regierungsblätter und Stellen nun zu Weill in einer derartigen unagressiven Umgebung sagen. Es wird jedenfalls eine sehr wichtige und aufschlussreiche Kontrolle Ihres augenblicklichen Rufes in diesen Kreisen sein. So glaube ich, dass wir dem Schicksal, auf alles gefasst, seinen Lauf lassen sollen.

Hans Heinsheimer, Universal Edition (in Wien) an Weill, 24. Februar 1933: Wir brauchen uns ja nichts vorzumachen: so schön der Leipziger Erfolg war, die Situation ist genau so ernst, wie wir es die ganze Zeit empfunden und gefühlt haben. Dass man gegen dieses harmlose Stück in Magdeburg so erfolgreich losgeht: es handelt sich eben nicht um die Sache, sondern um Ihre Person. Haben Sie die Kritik der *Leipziger Tageszeitung* (Nazi) gelesen? Nochmals, lieber Freund, bitte, las Sie herzlich, unser Gespräch zu überlegen, die Fragen, wie Film, Übersiedlung nach Paris, Amerikareise, die Einrichtung einfach auf ein Vakuum bei den deutschen Bühnen, Schulen, Radios auf längere Zeit, zu prüfen und in einer neuen unerbittlichen Situation Entscheidungen zu treffen.

Weill (in Berlin) an die Universal Edition, 26. Februar 1933: Die Filmsache stand natürlich nach dem Erfolg des *Silbersee* sehr günstig. Der Vertrag wurde fertig gemacht, die Punkte, die ich mit Ihnen besprochen hatte, wurden in Ihrem Sinne abgeändert, der Vertrag war fix und fertig zur Unterschrift, plötzlich stockt wieder alles, unter irgend einer Ausrede wird mir der Vertrag wieder nicht zugestellt und gestern wird mir auf einmal mitgeteilt: auf Grund der Magdeburger Vorgänge, die hier in der *Nachtausgabe* furchtbar aufgebauscht wurden, müsse man befürchten, dass auch bei einem Film mit Musik von mir Störungen eintreten können, durch die etwa 300.000 Mark, die in den Film investiert werden, gefährdet werden würden. Man sei zwar noch nicht ganz entschlossen, aber wahrscheinlich müsse man mich in den nächsten Tagen bitten, von der Mitarbeit zurückzutreten. Ich habe sofort erklärt, dass ich das nicht machen werde und dass ich gezwungen bin, mich auf den Vertragsstandpunkt zu stellen, da ja meine Verträge bis zur Unterschrift fix und fertig sind. Wahrscheinlich wird man mir als Ausgleich anbieten, den nächsten René-Clair-Film zu machen. Das wäre allerdings eine Lösung, die ich sehr begrüssen würde.

Rolf Nürnberg. "Großer Kaiser-Weill-Erfolg." ***Leipziger Feuilleton,*** **30 February 1933.**
. . . Zumal Kurt Weill eine Musik beigesteuert hat, die Georg Kaisers Werk bindet und vorwärts treibt, die von einer großartigen Geschlossenheit und Eindringlichkeit ist, die nicht einige Musiknummern bietet, sondern ein virtuos durchgeführtes einheitliches Handlungsgemälde, von einer erregenden, bezwingenden Schärfe. Weills Musik kommt Kaisers Diktion entgegen, sie hält sie aufrecht, sie führt sie durch. Eine glanzvolle Partitur zu einem schönen Libretto. Der Klang dieser klaren, sinnvollen, beschwingten Töne fundiert und verstärkt den Erfolg des Abends. Weills Musik wurde durch das Leipziger Symphonie-Orchester, das Gustav Brecher mit bewundernswerter Disziplin und Verve dirigierte, zu fulminanter Wirkung gebracht.

F. A. Hauptmann. "Uraufführung in Leipzig." ***Völkischer Beobachter,*** **Berlin section, 24 February 1933.** . . . Einem solchen Komponisten muß man mit Mißtrauen begegnen, noch dazu, wenn er sich als Jude erlaubte, für seine unvölkischen Zwecke sich einer deutschen Opernbühne zu bedienen! . . . Das Beschämendste an dieser Angelegenheit ist, daß sich der Generalmusikdirektor der Stadt Leipzig, Gustav Brecher, zu derartigen musikalischen Belanglosigkeiten hergab! Ein Mann mit einigem Feingefühl hätte an diesem verantwortungsvollen Posten—ausgerechnet fünf Tage nach dem 50. Todestage Richard Wagners, mitten in den Gedenkfeiern in der ihm leider noch immer anvertrauten Oper!—auf solche Darbietungen verzichtet! . . . Herr Brecher hat sich neulich im Gewandhaus zur Gedächtnisfeier . . . unseren Führer, den Führer des deutschen Volkes, recht genau betrachtet. Ich hatte Gelegenheit, das zu beobachten. Nun, er wird ihn und die von ihm ausgehende, alles Ungesunde und Schädliche hinwegfegende Kraft noch genauer kennenlernen!

Figure 303. Funk-Stunde Berlin. "Keine Jazzmusik mehr im Programm der Berliner Funk-Stunde." 8 March 1933. "No More Jazz Aired by the Berlin Radio." During the first few years after the war, Germany became acquainted with "Jazz-Music", a kind of dance music dominated by unrestrained, sharply over-accentuated rhythms, characterized by the garish tone colors of groups of brass instruments and a multifaceted complex of percussion and other noise-making instruments.

This musical degeneration was first introduced by America, where the folk music of the North American Negroes had given the stimulus to the creation of jazz. As it has developed over the last few years, most of the ugly, grotesque and provocative effects have been removed. The jarring sound colors have softened, the rhythmical undercoating is more discrete, random improvisations have been tuned out and a melodic line has developed. In three-quarter time dances, and in the tango, the violin has regained its rights, and once more a melodic line can swing in serenity.

Berlin Radio [Funk-Stunde] has banned all questionable "Negro Music," so called by a healthy public, where provocative rhythms dominate and the melody might be defiled. The Funk-Stunde will keep on cultivating modern dance music, as long as its musical elements are not inartistic and won't hurt German sensibilities. The mere use of instruments favored by jazz, like for example the saxophone or banjo, does not necessarily characterize music as jazz music.

Weill (in Berlin) an Hans Heinsheimer, Universal Edition, 1. März 1933: Ich habe nun, um möglichst rasch disponieren zu können, auf sofortige Entscheidung gedrängt, und ich werde heute einen Vertrag unterschreiben, wonach ich zwar aus der Arbeit an dem Film *Kleiner Mann, was nun?* ausscheide, wonach aber der Europa-Verleih zusammen mit der deutschen, französischen und englischen Tobis im Laufe eines Jahres einen anderen Film mit mir machen will.

Weill (in Berlin) an Hans Heinsheimer, Universal Edition, 14. März 1933: Ich habe ein bischen den Eindruck, dass Sie jetzt vollkommen die Flinte ins Korn werfen, und, wohl auch unter dem Einfluss der zahlreichen Berliner Miesmacher, die Sie jetzt dort treffen, in eine Lethargie verfallen, die gerade im jetzigen Moment ganz unangebracht ist. Ich finde es einfach ganz falsch und unhaltbar, dass Sie alle jetzt in Wien sitzen und Trübsal blasen, anstatt das zu machen, was in Ihrer und unser aller Lage heute das einzig mögliche ist: ins Ausland zu gehen und dort alle Möglichkeiten zu untersuchen, um für Ihre Verlagswerke neue Absatzmärkte zu finden, neue Beziehungen anzuknüpfen, neue Aufführungsmöglichkeiten aufzuspüren oder zu schaffen. Warum sind Sie, lieber Dr. Heinsheimer, jetzt nicht in Paris? Sie haben gesehen, der Riesenerfolg, den ich dort hatte, ist überhaupt nicht auszunützen ist, wenn niemand an Ort und Stelle ist, der wirklich daran arbeitet. . . . Es ist einfach ein Jammer, dass die ungewöhnlichen Möglichkeiten, die Paris jetzt für mich bietet (und sicher auch für Krenek und Alban Berg), vollkommen ungenützt bleiben sollen. Ich selbst tue, was in meiner Macht steht. Seit Monaten führe ich Verhandlungen, anstatt meine Nerven für meine Arbeit aufzusparen.

Hans Heinsheimer, Universal Edition (in Wien) an Weill, 15. März 1933: Von Wreede kommt heute die Nachricht, dass er mit Ihnen vereinbart hat, dass Sie vorläufig nicht nach Amerika reisen. Ich wäre Ihnen sehr für eine Nachricht dankbar, wie nun Ihre Dispositionen für die nächste Zeit sind. Ich hatte Sie eigentlich längst hier erwartet, auch Herr Renoir hatte geglaubt, Sie würden schon zu ihm kommen. Ich bin äusserst erstaunt, dass Sie Ihre Absichten geändert haben und kann mir das gar nicht erklären. Geben Sie uns doch bitte recht bald Nachricht.

Figure 306. Alfred Kalmus. [Changes to Weill's contract with Universal Edition], 30 March 1933. Financially, the contract of 15 April 1929 will be altered for the time of May/1/1933 until November/1,1933 as follows:

a) In case Mr.Weill does not receive any commissions during this time, his monthly rate of 750 Marks for this period shall be reduced to 500 as an advance, and 250 Marks as actual remuneration.

b) In case Mr. Weill receives a commission of at least 25,000 francs (about which he is to inform U.E. immediately) the monthly subsidy will be reduced to 500 M., 350 as advance and 150 as remuneration. Should Mr. Weill receive such a commission by the end of July, the payment will be reduced to 500 M. for at least 4 months after such a commission has been obtained.

Weill (in Paris) an Hans Heinsheimer, Universal Edition, 3. April 1933: Ich danke Ihnen mit aller Herzlichkeit für Ihren Brief. Sie können sich vielleicht nicht vorstellen, welche Freude und Beruhigung für mich in meiner jetzigen Situation ein solcher Freundesgruss bedeutet. Es ist ja jetzt ein Zeitpunkt, wo sich wirkliche Freundschaft und wirkliches Zusammengehörigkeitsgefühl erweisen muss. Wir müssen uns genau merken, wer jetzt zu uns hält. Es kommt auch wieder einmal anders rum.

Natürlich wäre es wunderschön gewesen, wenn wir uns jetzt einmal hätten aussprechen können. Sie wissen, welches Vertrauen ich zu Ihnen habe und wie gern ich Ihren Ratschlägen Folge leiste. Aber meine Anwesenheit hier war dringend notwendig, und Sie sehen aus den neuesten Ereignissen, wie richtig mein Instinkt war, hierherzugehen.

Ich habe in den 10 Tagen, die ich jetzt hier bin, schon allerhand erreicht. Überall zeigt sich, was für ein Glück es war, dass ich im Dezember diesen *Mahagonny*-Abend hier hatte. Die Verhandlungen wegen des Films mit Renoir stehen günstig. Es gibt für die Finanzierung dieses Films 3 Möglichkeiten: eine mit Pathé-Natan, der grössten französischen Film-Firma, and 2 andere mit kleineren Firmen, von denen besonders die eine (Braunberger) äusserst günstig wäre, weil sie die grösste künstlerische Freiheit gewährleistet. Ich hoffe zuversichtlich, dass eine dieser 3 Kombinationen gelingen wird. Wir hoffen, im Laufe dieser Woche so weit zu kommen, dass wir von einer dieser drei Stellen eine bindende Zusage haben, damit wir mit der Manuskript-Arbeit beginnen können. Ich wollte zu diesem Zweck gegen den 10. April mit Renoir nach dem Süden gehen. Das scheint sich aber nun durch eine andere Sache wieder zu ändern:

die besten und jüngsten Tänzer jenes russischen Balletts, das aus den Resten und Schülern Diaghilews zusammengestellt wurde, haben sich unter künstlerischer Leitung von Balanchine und geschäftlicher Leitung von Boris Kochno zu einer ganz ausgezeichneten Ballettgruppe zusammengeschlossen, die am 27. Mai hier eine Saison starten wird und anschliessend zu einer grossen Saison nach London gehen wird. Kochno quält mich seit ich hier bin, ich soll ihm etwas schreiben. Er hat bereits Originalballette von Milhaud und Sauguet zur Uraufführung. Ich war sehr zurückhaltend, da ich zu der ganzen Sache kein rechtes Zutrauen hatte. Nun ist gestern ein englischer Finanzmann, Mister James, Gatte von Tilly Losch, aufgetaucht, der die ganze Sache finanzieren will, unter der Voraussetzung, dass ich etwas schreibe. Ich habe gestern mit ihm verhandelt. Er scheint meine finanziellen Forderungen (30.000 francs) bewilligen zu wollen. Künstlerisch habe ich die Zusammenarbeit mit einem gleichwertigen Dichter verlangt. Denn ich habe einen Plan, für den ich gute Texte haben muss, da ich auf keinen Fall ein Ballett schreiben will, wie alle anderen es tun. Ich habe Cocteau vorgeschlagen. Ich gehe jetzt zu der entscheidenden Verhandlung in dieser Angelegenheit und schreibe Ihnen dann weiter, wenn ich zurückkomme.

Also: ich habe mit Mr. James allein gesprochen. Die Sache hängt nur noch davon ab, ob er in London ein geeignetes Theater findet, da das Alhambra-Theater, das ihm angeboten ist, zu gross ist. Er will mir nicht mehr als 25.000 francs zahlen. Ich habe ihm gesagt, ich könnte es nur dann zu diesem Preis machen, wenn er wirklich (was seit langem seine Absicht ist) in London in Verbindung mit der gleichen Season *Mahagonny* (in der Pariser Form) und *Jasager* geben würde. Auf dieser Basis scheint nun tatsächlich eine Einigung zustandezukommen. Er spricht heute mit Cocteau und morgen mittag soll die Sache perfekt werden.

Hans Heinsheimer, Universal Edition (in Wien) an Weill, 3. April 1933: Wir erhielten Ihr Telegramm und haben Ihnen gleichzeitig 500.- Mark überwiesen. Was die weiteren Beträge anlangt, so müssen wir Sie bitten sich zu gedulden. Die letzten 8 Tage haben eine so katastrophale Zuspitzung gebracht, dass wir augenblicklich über die Weiterführung des deutschen Geschäftes noch völlig um Unklaren sind. Herr Direktor Winter ist nach Berlin abgereist, um an Ort und Stelle Informationen einzuholen und festzustellen, welche Arbeitsmöglichkeiten überhaupt noch vorliegen. Unter diesen Umständen müssen wir Sie bitten zunächst für April mit 500.- Mark sich einverstanden zu erklären. Wir werden sofort nach Rückkehr von Herrn Direktor Winter und nachdem wir die Situation etwas besser überblicken können, Ihnen weitere Nachricht geben.

Weill (in Paris) an Direktor Hugo Winter, Universal Edition, 9. Mai 1933: Ich danke Ihnen herzlich für Ihre Nachrichten und für Ihre Bemühungen in der Angelegenheit der Überweisung meines Privatgeldes. Ich hoffe, dass der von Ihnen eingeschlagene Weg der richtige ist, und dass mir durch diese Überweisung keine Unannehmlichkeiten entstehen. Ich hatte, offen gesagt, nicht damit gerechnet, dass in dieser Angelegenheit mein Name überhaupt genannt werden muss. Aber hoffen wir, dass alles glatt geht.

Weill (in Paris) an Erika Neher, Mai 1933: Die furchtbarste Tatsache für mich ist die, dass ihr (es ist schrecklich, dass ich „ihr" schreiben muss) zu mir überhaupt kein Vertrauen habt. Jeder der mich ein bischen kennt, weiss, dass für mich ein Text lediglich ein Anlass ist, dass jeder Text, den ich komponiert habe, völlig verändert aussieht, wenn er durch meine Musik hindurchgegangen ist. . . . Nein, Liebling, seien wir ehrlich: die Gründe liegen anderswo. Seit Wochen hält mich C. durch seine Unentschlossenheit hin. Du selbst hast mir am Telefon bestätigt (u. auch er schriftlich), was ich längst vermutet hatte: dass er aus durchaus begreiflichen Gründen Hemmungen hat, eine Arbeit mit B. und mir zu machen. [. . . Das ist] derselbe Cas, der es *niemals* gewagt hat, über B. etwas zu sagen, der geschwiegen hat, wenn einer geschimpft hat, der mich bei *Mahagonny* in Berlin vollkommen im Stich gelassen hat in meinem Kampf gegen B., der noch immer mit ihm zusammengekommen ist, als ich verfeindet war. . . . Engelein, liebstes, geliebtestes, süssestes Engelein, sei nicht bös, dass ich das alles schreibe. Ich muss doch alles mit mir allein ausmachen. Seit 6 Uhr gestern nachmittag laufe ich hier im Zimmer herum u. denke über diese Sache nach, nun ist noch Dein Brief gekommen. . . . Ich bin in einer verdammten Situation. Ich muss einen anderen Maler suchen, dies in einem Moment, wo ich Tag u. Nacht an der Partitur sitze, Schwierigkeiten mit den Scheidungsanwälten, Schwierigkeiten mit der Dresdner Bank, Schwierigkeiten mit den Ballettproben u. in den Gliedern die Nachwirkungen eines schweren Schwindelanfalls, den ich Sonntag mittag hatte. Aber dieser Brief soll nicht schliessen, ohne Dir zu sagen, dass mich trotz allem der Gedanke an Dich ruhig u. froh macht u. dass ich traurig, aber sehr schön an Dich denke.

Figure 317. Weill (in Paris) to Bertolt Brecht, [May 1933]: Dear Brecht, [Edward] James is finally back and I asked him immediately to send you the money. He promised to do it right away. Tilly is here as well. I have not seen her yet, but Abravanel says she seems to be talented. By the way, James is terribly impressed by the poetry and everything will be done the way we want it.

I am working like a dog, but I'm enjoying it a lot. Five numbers are finished. I think it will be very beautiful. Otherwise, there's nothing new, except that you will be getting the snapshot on the motorbike very soon.

Figure 318. Weill (in Paris) to Bertolt Brecht, 1 June 1933: It is the usual chaos [*The Seven Deadly Sins*]. Of course, a small clique has developed among the devotees of the old Russian ballet, for whom our ballet isn't "ballet" enough, not enough "pure choreography." Because of that there were tremendous fights during the last few days and I succeeded in getting one man 'put on ice.' Though Balanchine is teetering between two factions, he has done a marvelous job, and he has found a performance style which is very 'balletic' but still sufficiently realistic. Lenja and the family will be very good, as well as the sets by Cas [Neher] and the music, of course. The rest depends on whether Balanchine will overcome his innate laziness—which the other faction actually stirs up—and whether he will work meticulously on the dances or not. On that point we can neither help nor influence him.

Of course, all of us would be delighted if you could come. James, with whom I have discussed this, said the same thing (he is already thinking about other things and is entirely uninterested in Tilly at this point). He has already half promised me to pay for your trip in case you come, and I believe I can squeeze out 1,000 francs, if you want to do that.

The *Hauptprobe* [the rehearsal before final dress] is on Monday, the dress rehearsal on Tuesday (exact time not known yet), opening night on Wednesday, and the second performance is on Saturday. You can arrange this anyway you like, since you probably want to combine it with your move to Denmark.

I have had not further news about the *Dreigroschenoper* matter. However, I'm thinking about the idea of the *Spitzköpfe und Rundköpfe* [Roundheads and the Pointed Heads], which I had proposed to you—I mean in association with Steinthal, who might want to work with me in the theater here. First, though, the following points would have to be clarified: you know that for quite some time now I've been thinking about a sort of "operetta" based on this play, and that this idea is exclusively mine. Now, Aufricht seems to have mentioned to Steinthal that you want Eisler to write the music for this piece. Since I don't want to touch your plans with Eisler in any case, and because I want to work only under very specific and unambiguous conditions, I would like to ask you to clear up this question before I consider it further.

By the way, right now I am planning two months of real vacation, which I need urgently. I have a very kind invitation to go to Italy and I guess I'll be leaving around 12 June.

Universal Edition (in Wien) an Weill, 7. Juni 1933: Sie Sache steht nun so, dass durch den gänzlichen Ausfall des Deutschlandgeschäftes bei Ihren Werken die Einnahmen aus Ihren Kompositionen auf ein nicht nennenswertes Minimum zurückgehen müssen, zumal wir auch im Auslande mit der grossen Anzahl Ihrer Werke so gut wie keinen Absatz erzielen können, da für Bühnenaufführungen keine Abschlüsse zu erzielen sind, die materiell in Betracht kommen. Auf diese Weise wird Ihr Saldo von über Mk.15.000.- sich in diesem Jahre kaum durch Einnahmen verringern und von diesem Standpunkt aus ist es in materieller Beziehung eine schwere Belastung, den Saldo durch weitere Monatszahlungen zu erhöhen. Wir hätten es daher sehr begrüsst, wenn Sie trotz Ihrer jetzigen Situation, die sich hoffentlich immer mehr bessern wird, dem Verlag, der die ganze Zeit sich mit seiner vollen Kraft für Sie eingesetzt hat, mit Rücksicht auf die gegenwärtige Lage in Deutschland entgegenkommen und für die nächsten Monate den Vertrag auch ohne monatliche Zahlungen aufrecht erhalten wollten. Wenn Sie sich zu dieser Lösung jedoch nicht bereit finden, so machen wir Ihnen einen Vorschlag, der sicher Ihren Interessen entspricht, und zwar, dass wir Ihr gesamtes Schaffen auf ein Jahr freigeben. Sie sind dann in der Lage, über Ihre nächsten Kompositionen zu verfügen und daraus auch verlagsmässig separate Eingänge für sich zu erzielen. Drei Monate vor Ablauf dieses Jahres wäre dann ein neuerliches Abkommen über die Fortführung unseres Vertrages zu treffen.

Yvon Novy. "Lorsque Tilly Losch, Balanchine et Kurt Weill parlent des Ballets 1933 entre un cocktail et d'exquises tartes aux fraises." *Comoedia*, 22 May 1933. Accoté au chambranle d'une porte un petit homme, le regard ironique derrière les lunettes, le visage intelligent et narquois, répond avec une imprécision aimable aux questions qui s'abattent sur lui, dru comme grêle. C'est Kurt Weill, l'auteur aujourd'hui fameux de l'«Opéra de quat'-sous» et qui a écrit la partition des "Sept péchés capitaux," une oeuvre qui sera créée aux Ballets 1933.

Est-il depuis longtemps en France? . . . Trois mois. S'il a des projets? . . . Parbleu . . . Lesquels? . . . Eh bien! d'aller dans le Midi, par exemple! . . . Mais le cinéma? . . . Ah, le cinéma. . .Ici, une précision.

—Je suis en pourparlers avec plusieurs maisons françaises de cinéma. Peut-être en sortira-t-il quelque chose. Je voudrais réaliser des films musicaux, mais. . .

Geste éloquent.

Jean Cocteau (à Paris) à Weill, [8] juin 1933: Vous avez dû sentir combien je souffrais hier soir de la frivolité tragique de cette salle. Mais vous l'avez "eue"—vous lui avez imposé votre ombre. C'était superbe, en quelque sorte, la lutte entre ce confort—cet égoïsme et le malaise et l'altruisme de votre oeuvre.

Les deux dames était étonnantes, remuaient autour d'elles un air surhumain. Tendre et cruel, voilà [?] le tempo de votre oeuvre où j'habite depuis 2 jours. Je vous embrasse.

Pierre-Octave Ferroud. "Le premier spectacle des "Ballets 1933." *Paris-Soir*, 12 June 1933. *Les sept péchés capitaux*, pour ce qui est d'eux, nous font reprendre contact par la tangente avec cette sorte d'esthétique du désespoir, ou tout au moins la déception, qui a fleuri, si l'on ose dire, depuis la guerre en Allemagne, et contre laquelle semblent s'insurger actuellement les forces vives de cette nation: romantisme, exotisme, «expressionisme». Nous enregistrons tout cela comme autant de phénomènes instructifs, certes, mais qui sont aujourd'hui révolus pour tout le monde, et auxquels Paris, s'il faut parler franc, n'a pas de raison spéciale de donner asile. Nous aussi, nous avons les yeux tendus vers l'avenir, et refusons donc de prendre à notre compte certaines erreurs qui n'ont même pas eu l'excuse d'être générales. A cet égard, nous ajouterons que la partition de M. Kurt Weill, cantate plus que ballet, ne nous révèle rien que nous ne connaissions déjà. Elle sonne remarquablement, mais ses sonorités nous sont familières.

Weill (in Positano) an Lotte Lenya, 16. Juli 1933: Schamlos u. gemein sind die Berichte aus Deutschland über die *7 Todsünden*. Sie lügen einfach einen Mißerfolg zusammen u. behaupten, auch Paris wolle von meinen Machwerken nichts mehr wissen, die das „neue Deutschland" längst abgestoßen habe. Von Paris selbst habe ich rückblickend den Eindruck, daß es dort auch schon eine recht rührige Anti-Weill-Clique gibt u. daß in wütender Weise dort gegen mich gehetzt wird. Ich denke mir manchmal, ob ich es wirklich nötig habe, mich dort in einen neuen Hexenkessel zu setzen u. meine Nerven im Kampf gegen dieses Intriganten-Geschmeiß verbrauchen soll. Bestimmt würde ich, wenn ich nach Paris ziehe, weit draußen wohnen u. nur arbeiten. Oder wäre es vielleicht besser, sich irgendwo im Tessin, Garda-See oder dergl. ganz billig einzurichten u. nur nach Paris zu fahren, wenn es nötig ist.

Weill (in Positano) an Emma und Albert Weill, 23. Juli 1933: Vielen Dank für deinen Brief, lieber Hans. Ich freue mich, dass du dich erholt hast und dass es euch so gut geht. Mir geht es auch gut. Der Ausschlag ist jetzt ganz weg u. die Psoriasis kann auch als fast geheilt bezeichnet werden. Ich habe allerdings 4 Wochen in einer glühenden Sonne gebraten. Jetzt wird es aber so heiss, dass es kaum noch erträglich ist. Wir fahren Dienstag hier ab, bleiben ein bischen in Rom u. Florenz u. wollen dann noch 2 Wochen in die Dolomiten. Ueber den weiteren Verlauf meines Lebens bin ich mir noch nicht klar, mache mir aber keine Gedanken—ein Zeichen, dass ich erholt bin. Allerhand Arbeitspläne stellen sich allmählich ein—auch ein gutes Zeichen. In London waren die *7 Todsünden* der grosse Erfolg der Saison u. besonders Lenja hat ganz gross eingeschlagen. Könntest ihr mir wohl nach Trento (Italien) poste restante folgende Bücher besorgen:

1). Die Reclam-Ausgabe von *1001 Nacht*.
2). Alle Calderon-Bände bei Reclam (ausser *Richter von Zalamea*).
3). Die deutsch erschienenen Werke von Schalom Asch.
4). Eine deutsche Ausgabe der Talmud-Erzählungen.

Lotte Lenya (in Berlin) an Weill, September 1933: Die Scheidungssache ist in Ordnung. Man braucht (glaube ich) nichts mehr beschleunigen. Das genügt so jetzt. Ich hoffe nur, daß Du bald was findest, damit Du Ruhe hast und aus den Hotelzimmern herauskommst. . . . Das Haus einem Vermittler zu übergeben halte ich auch für das richtigste. . . . Ich tue, was sich machen läßt um es möglichst rasch los zu werden.

Figure 333. Weill (in Paris) to Engelhardt, 5 October 1933: I still have a credit with the Dresdner Bank, Trust Funds, Berlin-Charlottenburg, Berlinerstrasse 58, which amounts to approximately 1750.00 marks and which has been frozen as a foreign account. Since my divorced wife, Mrs. Karoline Weill, nee Blamauer, still has rights to alimony from me, I hereby order the transfer of the above credit to her as part payment of her claims, with the request that you kindly so inform her.

Figure 335. Weill (in Paris) to Jean Cocteau, 18 November 1933: I have finished composing your poem "Es regnet" [It's raining]. I think you will like it a lot. I am not satisfied yet with the other one, "Der Lügner" [The liar]. It's quite difficult to find a form of expression both excited and calm.
I'm still in Louveciennes, and I'm really happy to have my own four walls all to myself. I will call you at the beginning of next week and will come see you very soon.

Weill (in Paris) an Lotte Lenya, 29.? November 1933: Ich bin froh, dass ich Nachricht von dir habe. Ich kann mir denken, dass es dich wurmt, dass in dem schönen Haus nun bald diese Spiesser wohnen. Mir geht es ebenso, aber dann sage ich mir wieder, dass es doch für dich kaum möglich gewesen wäre, in dieser Umgebung zu existieren, u. dass schliesslich alles was man dort aufgegeben hat, nicht unersetzlich ist. Du siehst ja, wie sie es mit unsereinem machen: die Gema setzt mich ohne jeden Grund von 125 Punkten auf—5 Punkte herunter, d. h. von 4000.- Mark auf 150.- Das ist praktisch nichts anderes als Enteignung, man kann es auch Diebstahl nennen. . . . Ich habe grossen Ärger gehabt: in dem Konzert waren die 3 Lieder ein grosser Erfolg. *Caesar* wurde da capo verlangt, da stand ein französischer Komponist, Florent Schmitt (ungefähr so begabt wie Butting) auf u. schrie: Heil Hitler! Genug mit der Musik von deutschen Emigranten usw. Das Publikum benahm sich sehr anständig u. brachte ihn zur Ruhe, das Lied wurde noch einmal gesungen u. war dann wieder ein Erfolg. Aber fast die ganze Presse stellt sich auf die Seite des „französischen Meisters", gegen mich, dieselben Leute, die vor einem Jahr bei *Mahagonny* Luftsprünge vor Begeisterung machten, sind jetzt kühl und zurückhaltend. Merkwürdig anständig benimmt sich Milhaud. Die Sache scheint ihm doch etwas zu weit zu gehen. Ich habe mich ein paar Tage sehr geärgert, trotzdem es mir eigentlich wurscht sein kann, da der Verleger mir gesagt hat: dieser Schmitt ist ein Irrer, u. vollkommen unzurechnungsfähig.

Figure 336. Paul Achard. "On a crié "Vive Hitler!" á la Salle Pleyel." *Comoedia*, 27 November 1933. "Someone shouted "Heil Hitler" in the Salle Pleyel in order to protest a few "chansons" by Kurt Weill." During a concert given yesterday afternoon at the Salle Pleyel, which our correspondent Paul Le Flem will review elsewhere, Mme. Madeleine Grey gave the first performance of three songs by Kurt Weill, the composer of *Threepenny Opera*, who had to leave Germany some months ago because of the anti-Semitic movement there. The first chanson, "The Salesgirl" was successful and so was the second one, "The Poor Relation". But the third one, pretentiously called "Ballad of Caesar" was not to the taste of two spectators; when she had finished, they shouted in a loud voice: "Vive Hitler!"

This came as a surprise, and it was answered by applause. But the protesters were stubborn; they repeated, "Vive Hitler! Vive Hitler!" One of them added: "We have enough lousy musicians in France without having them send us all the Jews in Germany."

Madame Grey took the hall's applause as encouragement, and, amused by the incident, she encored the "Ballad of Caesar."

Once more the protesters made themselves heard with their cry: "Vive Hitler!" By this time the other spectators, somewhat taken aback, understood their intention. The interpreter's merits were rewarded by applause. Policemen appeared. There was some bustle at the back of the hall; the protesters left, and the discussion continued inside the hall and out on the sidewalks of the Faubourg Saint-Honoré.

This incident might appear trivial. But it is significant; it is the first time that a Frenchman has cried, "Vive Hitler!" in a public place. And this Frenchman, if I may be permitted to name him, is Mr. Florent Schmitt, an important French composer, accompanied by one of his friends, who assisted him in the protest.

Make no mistake: this is the first drop of water before the storm comes. If only Mr. Kurt Weill had really brought us anything good! Judge for yourself : here's the "corpus delicti":

[French translation of the lyrics to Caesar's Ballad]

As a very intelligent man said, "It's music that isn't worth the effort." And the same goes for the words.

Figure 339. Weill (in Paris) to Marlene Dietrich, 17 December 1933: Dear Marlene Dietrich, as a little New Year's greeting, I'm sending you the manuscript of the song I wrote for you last fall. When you have a pianist play through it for you, please tell him to look it over beforehand. I don't know whether the key is right; in any case, you would have to sing it an octave lower than written.

I am sitting in my little house thirty kilometers from Paris, working a lot. I am preparing something for the theater which Reinhardt is going to do this fall.

How are you? How is Katharina? Would you be inclined to do a "musical film" at some point? A while ago, someone came to me with an idea for a story which would have a marvelous role for you—something new. With best wishes for 1934 and very best regards, your Kurt Weill

CHAPTER 5

Weill (in Paris) an Lotte Lenya, 11. Januar 1934: Bei den Eltern war es sehr nett. Sie haben sich riesig gefreut, dass ich gekommen bin. Wenn sie so von der übrigen Familie weg sind, sind sie ja wirklich sehr nett. Sie jammern übrigens garnicht sondern sind ganz fidel. Ich habe mir für nicht ganz 100.- Mark einen sehr schönen Winteranzug machen lassen. Außerdem hat mir ein Karlsbader Arzt gegen den Ausschlag einen—Aderlass gemacht. Es ist jetzt am Kopf ganz und an den Händen fast ganz weg, nur am Körper noch ein bischen. Ich weiß nur nicht, was nun geholfen hat: die Diät, der Tee, die Spritzen, die Höhensonne, die Salbe oder der Aderlaß. Wahrscheinlich nichts von all dem. Immerhin werde ich weiter Diät leben, weil ich gemerkt habe, daß mir das besser tut.

In Wien war ich nur 1 1/2 Tage. Wenn man dort die Emigranten sitzen sieht, dann kann man wirklich froh sein, daß man da nicht dabei ist. Ich finde es ist dort viel schlimmer, weil das übelste Literaturpack beisammen sitzt, u. weil es dort ganz unproduktiv ist. Mit Martin hatte ich mich verabredet in der Imperialbar, da hockten sie alle beisammen: Pallenberg (der widerlichste von allen), Polgars, Martins, Bois u. die übrigen Versteller. Sie schimpfen u. jammern, aber es geht ihnen immer noch viel zu gut. Auf Paris haben sie alle eine Wut, weil man da für sie keine Verwendung hat. Wenn ich dagegen daran denke, wie nett u. lustig wir alle jetzt wieder in Rom beisammen waren, dann sehe ich, daß wir es doch richtig gemacht haben. Dich soll ich natürlich von allen grüßen. Am nettesten war Stiedry, der gerade aus Russland zurückkommt. Er hat in Berlin Kaiser gesehen, das scheint furchtbar zu sein. Er ist vollkommen am Ende, spricht nur von Selbstmord u. Stiedry hat ernstlich Angst, dass es eine Katastrophe gibt, wenn man ihn nicht herausholt.

Weill (in Louveciennes) an Lotte Lenya, 25. Januar 1934: Ich war die ganze vorige Woche hier draußen u. habe sehr schön gearbeitet. Die Partitur ist zu zwei Drittel fertig. Diese Woche hatte ich sehr wichtige Verhandlungen, die (unberufen) fast perfekt sind. Es handelt sich um folgendes: Jacques Deval, der meistgespielte u. begehrteste französische Theaterdichter der Saison, dessen Stück *Tovarich* der größte internationale Theatererfolg des Jahres ist, will sein neues Stück mit mir machen. Wir wollen seinen erfolgreichsten Roman *Marie Galante* dramatisieren. Ein ausgezeichneter, *ernster* Stoff: ein französisches Bauernmädchen wird, weil sie mit einem Mann mitgeht, nach Panama verschlagen; sie hat keinen anderen Wunsch, als wieder nach Haus zu kommen, sie verdient sich in Bordellen das Geld u. als sie es beisammen hat u. schon die Schiffskarte für die Rückfahrt gekauft hat, stirbt sie. Das Stück soll, wenn irgend möglich, schon im Mai in dem schönsten Pariser Theater (Marigny) herauskommen, im Herbst in London u. New York. Es sieht so aus, als ob das die große internationale Chance ist, auf die ich gewartet habe.

Weill (in Louveciennes) an Lotte Lenya, 20. Februar 1934: Die Vorgänge in Österreich sind wirklich schwer deprimierend für jeden Menschen, der noch einen Rest von Gerechtigkeitsgefühl hat. Die Tiere sind barmherziger als diese Menschen. Politisch sind wir an einer ganz gefährlichen Ecke. Wir waren noch nie so nahe am Krieg seit 1914 wie jetzt. Ich persönlich glaube nicht, dass es dazu kommt, aber die Kriegsstimmung macht immer weitere Fortschritte und diese Vandalen werden keine Ruhe geben, bis sie es so weit haben.

Weill (in Louveciennes) an Lotte Lenya, 3.–6. März 1934: Das war ein aufregender Tag. Gestern abend wurde ich angerufen, ich solle sofort Marlene meine Adresse telegrafieren, was ich gleich tat, u. heute morgen war schon folgendes Telegramm da: „Würde es Sie interessieren, herzukommen u. mit Sternberg u. mir an einem musikalischen Film zu arbeiten. Dauer ungefähr 6 Monate. Drahten Sie an mich, ob Sie wollen u. können. Alles weitere erledigt Paramount. Herzliche Grüsse. Marlene." Da machst du Augen, was? Ich rufe dich morgen früh an, um mit dir darüber zu sprechen. Ich glaube, da kann man nur Ja sagen, was? Sternberg u. Marlene u. 6 Monate Arbeit—das bietet sich nicht so oft.

Weill (in Louveciennes) an Hans Curjel, 19. April 1934: Bei mir haben sich jetzt deutlich 3 Pläne herauskristallisiert, die sich mit der für diese Zeit bezeichnenden Langsamkeit aber doch ganz sicher weiterentwickeln: die *Marie Galante* mit Deval kommt nun endgültig hier im Oktober heraus, ich werde sie aber erst im Sommer schreiben können, da Deval in Hollywood ist (es ist nicht ganz ausgeschlossen, dass ich auch im Sommer hinübergehe). Der grosse Plan eines szenischen Oratoriums nach Worten des alten Testaments, mit dem sich Reinhardt in Verbindung mit mir seit langem beschäftigt, macht gute Fortschritte, wird aber kaum vor Ende der nächsten Saison spruchreif werden. Es soll in London in grossem Stile herauskommen. Der dritte Plan, der mir am meisten Spass macht und auch am weitesten fortgeschritten ist, ist die Operette, die ich mit Vambery schreibe. . . . Es ist ein ausgezeichnetes Buch, an die beste Tradition der Operette anknüpfend, aber weit weg von dem Operetten-Schund. Es ist im Bau vollkommen fertig, 12 Musiknummern, die ich komponiert habe und die glänzend gelungen sind, sind schon textiert, das Buch wird im Mai ganz fertig. Ich bin schon mit einem grossen hiesigen Theater sowie mit Cochran in London in Unterhandlung. Wir würden aber sehr gern vor der französischen und englischen eine deutsche Aufführung haben.

Weill (in Louveciennes) an Hans Curjel, 23. April 1934: Anbei schicke ich Ihnen das Exposé der Operette. Der Titel kann natürlich nicht so bleiben. Ich bitte Sie, dieses Exposé lediglich als das zu lesen, was es sein will: Unterlage für meine Musik. Was ich bisher komponiert habe, erregt überall Aufsehen, wo ich es zeige, besonders ein sehr populäres Marschlied des Generals, eine Barcarole, ein ausgesprochener Schlager: *Auf Wiedersehn* (English Waltz), das Lied vom grossen Pharaoh und das Lied von der Kuh mit dem sehr schönen Text:

Ich habe eine Kuh gehabt
Ich hab die Kuh nicht mehr.
Ich hab dafür
Gott helfe mir
Jetzt ein Maschinengewehr.

Die Hauptrollen sind: der General (glänzende Komikerrolle), Juanita (gut singende Schauspielerin oder gut spielende Sängerin), Juan (lyrischer Tenor), der Präsident (guter Schauspieler). Wenn Sie den General starmäßig besetzen, so käme dafür sehr gut Wallburg in Frage, aber es könnte, von einer ganz anderen Seite her, auch Pallenberg machen, für den es mal etwas ganz anderes wäre, als was er bisher gemacht hat. In diesem Fall könnte man Juanita in unserem Sinne besetzen, d.h. wohl am besten mit Lenja, die aus der *Ballade vom Räuber Esteban* eine ganz grosse Nummer machen würde. Oder aber man besetzt Juanita starmäßig, dann käme entweder eine begabte Operettensängerin in Frage, am besten die Nowotna oder Lizzie Waldmüller, oder aber ein Filmstar, etwa Renate Müller oder Magda Schneider. In diesem Fall würde ich den General in unserem Sinne besetzen, und zwar mit Gretler. Für Juan müsste man einen jungen, gut aussehenden, spielbegabten Tenor finden. Alles übrige ist leicht zu besetzen. Mit einem Orchester von 17 Mann würde ich, glaube ich, auskommen, wenn ich mir die Besetzung des Orchesters ein bischen nach meiner Art zusammenstellen kann. Die Chöre schreibe ich denkbar leicht, man würde aber doch, wie übrigens in jeder halbwegs anständigen Operettenaufführung, etwa 15–20 Personen brauchen. . . . Die grossen Vorteile des Stückes liegen darin, dass es an die beste Tradition der Operette, die seit Jahrzehnten verschüttet war, endlich wieder anknüpft, eine sehr geschickte Dosierung von ernst und heiter, von lyrisch und dramatisch darstellt und die aktuellsten Dinge (Dinge, die viel aktueller sind als das dritte Reich) in liebenswürdiger, komischer Weise zeigt.

Figure 348. Bruno Walter (in Salzburg) to Weill, 23 August 1934: My interest in your work is steadily growing, and I'm seriously considering a performance of it in New York as well as in Amsterdam, but, if at all possible, not as a "symphony." Certainly, the form is symphonic. But the treatment of the orchestra certainly is not, e.g.: clarinet solo with the ensuing trumpet melody, bolero-rhythms in the strings, finally also the "accompaniment" of the trombone solo in the 2nd movement and similar things. After all, the work's special appeal is created by the strange, ironic, tragic, popular tone, which you so coyly try to avoid when you use the word "Symphony."

I don't want to suggest any titles to you. Instead, I'm asking you to please mention a possible title to me which might suggest a concise reflection of your feelings and your state of mind when this work was conceived. A revision of the bowings for the strings and more detailed nuances in the dynamics would be most important for the performance; also, I think it would be desirable if you could look over the entire work and consider the necessity of adding percussion.

I hear that you would like to have your full score back. Would it be time enough, if you have it by the end of September or could you leave it with me altogether?

Weill (in Louveciennes) an Lotte Lenya, 16. September 1934: Die Bibelsache wird musikalisch sehr schön u. sehr reich. Daran merke ich erst, wie ich seit der *Bürgschaft* weitergekommen bin. Es ist ebenso ernst, aber im Ausdruck viel stärker, reicher, bunter—mozartischer.

Weill (in Louveciennes) an Lotte Lenya, 23. September 1934: Die *Marie galante* spielt Florelle. Das ist für hier glänzend, da sie sehr zieht und die Chansons anständig bringen wird (für hiesige Verhältnisse). Den Japaner spielt Inkischinow (aus *Sturm über Asien*) und für die 3. Hauptrolle wollen wir Harry Baur haben. Das wäre dann eine tolle Besetzung.

Weill (in Louveciennes) an Max Reinhardt, 6. Oktober 1934: Seit ich aus Salzburg zurück bin, arbeite ich buchstäblich Tag und Nacht an unserer Sache, mit einer Begeisterung, wie ich sie seit langem nicht verspürt habe. Ich glaube (und jeder, dem ich etwas davon zeige, bestätigt es mir), daß es die schönste Musik wird, die ich bisher geschrieben habe. Vor allem glaube ich, daß es mir gelungen ist, die formale Frage zu lösen, indem ich, ohne am Text das geringste zu ändern, doch große musikalische Formen schaffe, die von gesprochenen Szenen unterbrochen werden. Dadurch bekommt das Ganze ein festes Gerüst, und die Gefahr, daß es zerfließen könnte, (die bei der Lektüre des Buches oft auftaucht), ist dadurch beseitigt. Es ist eine Musik, die, gegenüber den anderen Elementen der Musik, hauptsächlich die Melodie in den Vordergrund rückt, wobei ich von originalen jüdischen Motiven nur sehr sparsam, d.h. nur dort, wo eine Beziehung zur Liturgie besteht, Gebrauch mache. Die jüdische Liturgie ist ja sehr arm an wirklichen „Melodien", sie besteht hauptsächlich in melodischen Wendungen und kurzen Motiven, die ich besonders den Lesungen des Rabbi manchmal zu Grunde legen konnte. . . . Werfel hat mir jetzt alle 4 Teile des Werkes geschickt. Ich finde großartig, was er gemacht hat. . . . Besonders freudig überrascht bin ich von dem letzten Schluss des Werkes. Diese Messias-Vision ist in ihrer echten Naivität und Einfachheit von einer wirklichen Größe, und alle Fragen der „Tendenz" des Stückes sind damit gelöst, da der Sinn des ganzen Werkes damit vollkommen aufgehellt ist. . . . Tatsächlich bin ich jetzt mehr als eh überzeugt, daß es nötig sein wird, einen Teil der Rollen mit Sängern, allerdings Sänger jenes großen Formats, das Ihnen vorschwebte, zu besetzen. Sie werden wohl kaum Schauspieler finden, die ihren Naturalismus vergessen und wirklich einen „gehobenen Stil" spielen können. Dagegen sind Sänger gewohnt, gehobenen Stil zu spielen, und es wird leichter sein, ihnen das falsche Pathos abzugewöhnen als den Schauspielern den Naturalismus und die unechten Töne. . . . Eine andere Frage, die mir große Sorge macht und die ich gern baldigst gelöst wissen würde, ist die Dirigentenfrage, da ja von dieser Entscheidung für mich so viel abhängt. Bei der Kürze der Zeit und der Neuartigkeit der Aufgabe halte ich es für unerlässlich, daß wir einen Dirigenten mitbringen, der diese Art von musikalischem Theater, das wir anstreben, sofort und ohne lange Diskussionen versteht und zu realisieren vermag, der mit Begeisterung und Aufopferung an dem Aufbau dieser Sache mitarbeitet. Ich halte für den idealen Mann den jungen Jascha Horenstein, der ja der begabteste und fanatischste unter den jungen deutschen Dirigenten ist und auch in Amerika bekannt ist.

Weill (in Louveciennes) an Maurice Abravanel, 21. Januar 1935: Inzwischen spielte sich die ganze Passion um *Marie galante* ab. Deval hat sich als das übelste Schwein entpuppt, das mir in meinem Leben begegnet ist. Er hat hintereinander alle die mit dieser Sache zu tun hatten, betrogen, belogen, begaunert, dazu noch, ohne selbst etwas davon zu haben. Da ihn der Verleger auf Grund des Vertrages gezwungen hat, das Stück zu schreiben und die Aufführung des Théatre de Paris durchzusetzen, hat er dann die Aufführung selbst systematisch sabotiert, mit Mitteln, von deren Existenz ich bis dahin nichts wusste. Auf diese Weise ist eine schaurige Aufführung zustandegekommen, aber die Musik hatte einen Bombenerfolg, eindeutig glänzende Presse, im Gegensatz zum Stück, das schwer verrissen wurde. Der Erfolg der Musik hätte immerhin die Sache in Schwung bringen können, aber Deval hat hinter meinem Rücken mit allen Finessen daran gearbeitet, es zu Fall zu bringen, und schliesslich wurde es nach 3 Wochen wieder abgesetzt. Ein schmählicher Durchfall.

Die Symphonie hat Walter glänzend gemacht. Er war ehrlich begeistert, hat es auswendig dirigiert und fabelhaft probiert. Das Orchester hat mit einer Hingebung gespielt, wie ich es bei einem neuen Stück noch nie gesehen habe. Grosser Publikumserfolg—katastrophale Presse („banal", „abgebraucht", „leer", „Beethoven im Biergarten" usw.) Trotzdem hat Walter es noch in Rotterdam und Haag gemacht, dann am 13. Dez. in New York. Er hat mir telegrafiert: „Grosser Erfolg. Gratuliere." Darauf kam die Presse an: katastrophal, kein einziges auch nur freundliches Wort. Offenbar hat dieses Stück den Widerstand der Fachleute gegen mich, der latent immer vorhanden war, in der wildesten Weise entfesselt. Die haben es bisher geschluckt, dass einer für das Theater eine Musik schreibt, die direkt, ohne Vermittlung der Fachleute, ans Publikum herangeht. Dass das nun auch im Konzert einreissen soll, dass auch hier eine unmittelbare Wirkung auf den Hörer erreicht werden soll, das geht ihnen über die Hutschnur.

Ihr seht, es ist nicht gerade erfreulich oder ermutigend, was sich bei mir in der Zwischenzeit zugetragen hat, und es gehört schon eine gehörige Portion Selbstvertrauen und Widerstandskraft dazu, diesen ganzen Dreck noch länger mitzumachen. Gottseidank macht mir die Arbeit reines ungestörtes Vergnügen, und ich bin überzeugt, dass ich auf einem guten Weg bin. Die Symphonie klingt hervorragend, Walter war ganz ausser sich über meine Fähigkeit, nur das notwendigste zu instrumentieren und doch einen vollen, schönen Klang zu erreichen. Er ist übrigens ein wirklich feiner Kerl, wir haben uns sehr gut verstanden.

Die Operette ist jetzt fertig. Ich schreibe augenblicklich den Klavierauszug der Bibel und der Operette gleichzeitig, nachher die beiden Partituren. Morgen fahre ich nach London um eine Generaloffensive für die Aufführung der Operette zu unternehmen. Es wird nicht leicht sein, einen Abschluss zustande zu bringen, denn die Sache ist doch auf einem sehr hohen Niveau, es ist eine regelrechte komische Oper, mit zwei grossen, bunten, gut gebauten Finales. Wenn es mir gelänge, dieses Stück, das ich für meine wichtigste Arbeit halte, so herauszubringen, wie ich möchte, dann bin ich über den Berg. Aber wird man mir das erlauben? Halte mir jedenfalls, wenn Du Generalmusikdirektor von Melbourne bist, ein Pöstchen als Orchesterdiener frei.

Weill (in Louveciennes) an Lotte Lenya, 10.–11. Juli 1935: An London mag ich nur denken, soweit es dich betrifft. Alles andere muß ich erst vergessen. Aber du hast mir diesmal wieder ganz besonders gut gefallen, ich finde, daß du eine großartige Pison bist und daß dein menschliches Format sich immer parallel mit meinem entwickelt und daß du mir (nach 10 Jahren!) immer noch Dinge gibst, die niemand sonst mir geben kann und die entscheidend sind. Ich habe mir auf der Rückfahrt gedacht, daß wir eigentlich die Frage des Zusammenlebens, die doch für uns besonders schwer ist, auf eine sehr schöne und richtige Art gelöst haben. Findest du nicht? Ich habe für dich und deine Arbeit ein sehr gutes Gefühl für England und Amerika. Wir werden es schon schaffen, nicht?

Weill (in Novi, Jugoslawien) an Lotte Lenya, 26. Juli 1935: Ich bin noch immer nicht über diesen Londoner Durchfall hinweg und liege nachts stundenlang wach und grüble darüber nach. Der einzige Trost sind die Verdi Briefe, die ich wieder lese. Diese Ähnlichkeit ist verblüffend.

Weill (in Salzburg) an Lotte Lenya, 26. August 1935: Wir sind mitten in den Verhandlungen mit Weisgal. . . . Die Entscheidung fällt heute nachmittag. Wenn sie so ausfällt, wie ich es hoffe, soll ich schon mit Weisgal am 4. Sept. auf der *Majestic* fahren. . . . Wir können nun überlegen, wie wir es mit deiner Reise machen. Es wäre natürlich fein, wenn wir zusammen fahren könnten und ich habe auf jeden Fall mal eine Doppelkabine reservieren lassen. . . . Lebe, Kleene. Ich freu mich auf dich. Aber du wirst ja so frech geworden sein!

Weill (in New York) an Max Reinhardt, 27. November 1935: Nachdem Sie gestern eine Streichung nicht nur der ganzen Salomon und Tempelszene sondern auch des grossen Abschiedsgesangs von Moses für möglich erklärt haben, möchte ich Ihnen noch einmal meinen Standpunkt in dieser Frage präzisieren.

Wie Sie wissen, habe ich vom ersten Tag unserer Zusammenarbeit an immer den Standpunkt vertreten, daß ich keine Bühnenmusik zu schreiben habe, sondern eine Musik, in der der Gesang, d.h. eine neue, aufgelockerte Art von Gesang eine hervorragende Rolle spielen soll. Auf dieser Grundeinstellung ist nicht nur meine Musik sondern auch Werfels Dichtung aufgebaut, deren Steigerungen ja immer in Musik hineinführen, sodaß eine Streichung der musikalischen Höhepunkte absolut gleichbedeutend wäre mit einer Streichung der Höhepunkte des Stückes.

Diese musikalischen Höhepunkte sind jetzt, nach Berücksichtigung Ihrer und Werfels Wünsche und nach langer Arbeit, vollkommen durchgeformte musikalische Gebilde, an denen man nicht herumstückeln kann, ohne sie ganz zu zerstören. Ich halte die Form nicht nur für den wesentlichsten Bestandteil künstlerischer Arbeit sondern auch für den wichtigsten Erfolgsfaktor, und ich habe in meiner eigenen Entwicklung gesehen, daß ich immer durchgefallen bin, wenn ich mir meine Form habe zerstören lassen. Die Opferung und Befreiung Isaaks, der Abschiedsgesang und Tod Moses', das Buch Ruth, der Tempelbau mit Salomos Tempelweihe und den Jubelchören, all das sind künstlerische Gebilde, die nach musikalischen und theatralischen Gesetzen geformt sind und denen man einfach ihre Wirkung nehmen würde, wenn man anfangen würde, sie zu sezieren.

Kurt Weill (à New York) à Heugel, le 31 janvier 1936: Les répétitions sont presque finies et la pièce pourrait être prête pour la première représentation dans deux semaines. Mais il paraît que la direction du théâtre est en certaines difficultés financielles [*sic*] qu'il faut surmonter avant de finir le spectacle. La reconstruction du théâtre a coûté beaucoup plus cher que l'on avait pensé. On a déjà dépensé plus que 250.000 dollars et les financiers du spectacle ont refusé de donner plus d'argent avant qu'on fait un budget définitif. Alors on a fait ce budget et on a trouvé qu'il faut encore 200.000 dollars pour finir. La somme de 450.000 dollars est tout à fait normale pour un grand spectacle ici surtout au cas d'une reconstruction entière du théâtre. Mais il n'est pas facile de trouver cet argent. . . . On a interrompu tous les travails pour 10 jours pour ne pas faire des dépenses inutiles et pour donner à M. Weisgal l'occasion de fixer [*sic*] la situation financielle. . . . Moi j'ai un peu de temps maintenant de faire nouveaux projets de théâtre ici et d'en à mes amis américains. Il y a beaucoup de chances d'avoir un autre spectacle ici au début de la saison prochaine. Je suis en pourparlers avec Ben Hecht et Charles MacArthur. Ce sont les auteurs célèbres du spectacle *Jumbo* qui est le plus grand succès de théâtre à New York. Ils ont l'intention de faire une pièce musicale avec moi et nous sommes en train de chercher un sujet. De même j'ai des conversations très intéressantes avec les membres du Group Theatre, le théâtre le plus moderne et le plus jeune de New York. Là aussi il y a un intérêt énorme pour moi. Enfin je suis en pourparlers avec deux maisons de cinéma à Hollywood (Metro-Goldwyn-Mayer et Paramount). Je leur ai proposé de faire un contrat pour trois films avec moi.

Il serait merveilleux si Yvonne Printemps jouerait *Marie galante*. Je suis sûr qui ce serait un très grand succès et je viendrai sûrement à Paris si ça se réaliserait.

Weill (in Chapel Hill, North Carolina) an Lotte Lenya, [3. Mai 1936]: Es ist herrlich hier. Ich bin ein vollkommen anderer Mensch, wenn ich aus der Stadt weg bin. Ich habe im Zug ganz gut geschlafen; als ich am Morgen aus dem Fenster sah, war ich in einer richtigen grünen Sommerlandschaft u. es roch wie in Südfrankreich, heiss und nach Blumen. . . . Dies ist die älteste Universität Amerikas, der ganze Ort wirkt sehr englisch, aus jedem Fenster schaut man auf grüne Blumen u. Wiesen. Ich habe ein reizendes Zimmer mit Dusche und mache richtiges Feinlebe. Diese Ruhe ist einfach himmlisch. Man sieht nur junge Leute hier u. lernt eigentlich erst, was Amerika ist u. wie unwichtig New York ist für das Land. Paul Green macht einen sehr guten Eindruck, frisch, jung, lustig, fast wie Zuckmayer. Ich glaube, er ist ein guter Mann für mich. Wir haben schon den ganzen Nachmittag u. Abend sehr schön gearbeitet.

Weill (à New York) à Heugel, le 4 juin 1936: C'est avec le plus grand regret que je regarde notre collaboration comme interrompue pour le moment. Cette collaboration était toujours une joie profonde pour moi parce que je sentais tout le temps que vous avez confiance en moi et en mon travail. C'est pourquoi il n'y a pas de doute pour moi que nous trouverons un jour, et j'espère bientôt, l'occasion de continuer nos relations vraiment amicales. Pour le moment je veux tâcher de créer pour moi une position dans la vie théâtrale de l'Amérique. Ce sera très difficile et j'aurai besoin de toute ma patience et de toute mon énergie. Si j'aurai fondé cette position ici, je peux revenir aux travaux qui correspondent à mon talent et à mon ambition, et ce sera le moment de vous offrir des oeuvres d'opéra d'une valeur internationale qui, j'en suis sûr, seront intéressantes pour vous.

Je vais faire tous les efforts de faire représenter ici les oeuvres que j'ai écrit pour vous. Les chances pour *Eternal Road* ne sont pas mauvaises. Un excellent directeur de théâtre du Broadway, M. Crosby Gaige, a pris dans ses mains toute l'affaire, Il a beaucoup d'optimisme de trouver l'argent pour une représentation en automne et il croit qu'il sera un très grand succès.

Weill (in Nichols, Connecticut) an Erika Neher, 28. Juli 1936: Ich trage seit Tagen diese beiden furchtbaren Briefe mit mir herum. Ich wusste vom ersten Moment, was ich Dir darauf antworten muss, aber ich habe Angst davor, weil es doch ein tiefer Einschnitt in mein Leben ist. . . . Aber was konnte ich Dir bieten, was Dich halten konnte? Ein Vagabund, von Pech verfolgt, in einem ewigen Kampf gegen die Ungerechtigkeit, ohne Heimat u. ohne Recht. . . . Du hast vergessen, wie ich Dir tausendmal gesagt u. geschrieben habe, dass Du für mich der einzige Mensch bist, der imstande ist, mich froh u. zufrieden zu machen, dass es für mich kein anderes Glück gibt u. nie geben wird, als das ich bei Dir gefunden habe. . . . Was mir bleibt, ist nur diese ganze Seite, die Liebe, Gefühl, Zärtlichkeit, Glück heisst, aus meinem Leben zu streichen, u. versuchen, ohne all das weiterzuleben. Das ist anderen vorher passiert u. sie haben es überstanden. . . . Bitte, mein Liebstes, tu jetzt alles was nötig ist, damit Du glücklich u. ruhig bist, denn nur dann kann ich ruhig u. glücklich sein, u. dann wird es ja auch zwischen uns wieder schön werden—wenn auch ganz anders.

Figure 379. Kurt Weill. "[Handwritten annotations to] What is Musical Theater?"

musik. Theater kann realistischer sein als poet. Drama [musical theater can be more realistic than poetic/verse drama]

Keine Psychologie [no psychology]

Form of musical play, whole play written in a style that music fits in

Dialektische Kraft der Musik [dialectic power of music]

Gestischer Charakter der Musik [gestic character of music]

Letztes Kapitel: Oper muss Isolierung verlassen. Stravinsky "L'histoire", Strauss "Bourgeois (?)", Gershwin "Porgy", meine eigene 3 Gr. O., Mahagonny, Silbersee, Eternal Road ?

[last chapter: opera must leave its isolation. . . . my own *Dreigroschenoper* . . .]

Weill (in Nichols, Connecticut) an Franz Werfel, 3. August 1936: Je länger ich hier bin und je mehr ich das Land kennen lerne, desto besser gefällt es mir—und es gibt ja im Moment nicht viel, was einen nach Europa zurückzieht.

Ich habe Reinhardt auf der Durchfahrt nach Europa in New York gesehen. Von der *Eternal Road* hatte ich seit einigen Monaten nicht gehört, außer daß Weisgal seine Bemühungen, die Sache zu retten, nicht aufgegeben hat (was wohl jeder andere an seiner Stelle getan hätte). Weisgal gab nun Reinhardt und mir einen Bericht über das, was er erreicht hatte, und zwar in Gegenwart eines sehr bekannten und geschätzten Anwalts (Louis Niger), der auf Reinhardt und mich einen denkbar günstigen Eindruck machte. Weisgal hat wirklich das unmögliche zustandegebracht und die Sache auf einer neuen Basis vollkommen neu organisiert, die Mißstände der alten Gesellschaft beseitigt und eine neue Gesellschaft, mit neuem Geld und neuem Finanzierungsplan auf die Beine gebracht. . . .

Es sind drei Dinge, die meiner Ansicht nach geregelt werden müssen: 1. die Terminfrage, die ausschließlich von Reinhardt abhängt. . . . 2. müßte Reinhardt bei Geddes darauf bestehen, daß er die für den Erfolg des Stückes unerläßlichen Änderungen macht, eine permanente Synagoge schafft, leichtere Verwandlungsmöglichkeiten und besondere Kostüme. . . . 3. glaube ich, daß wir an dem Stück selbst noch einige Arbeit leisten müssen. Ich bin jetzt fast ein Jahr hier und habe das amerikanische Theater und Publikum sorgfältig studiert, und nach allem was ich gesehen und gelernt habe, glaube ich, wir sollten alles tun, um die Synagogenhandlung zu einer einheitlichen, spannenden Handlung aus[zu]bauen, die in der ersten Szene beginnt und sich durch das ganze Stück zieht und die Bibelszenen stärker zusammenhält, als es jetzt der Fall ist.

Alma Maria Werfel (in Wien) an Weill, 20. August 1936: Einen herzlichen Dank Werfels für Deinen Brief. Es ist zu schade, dass Ihr nicht nach Europa gekommen seid, wenngleich *ich auch* lieber dort, als hier leben möchte! Werfel ist nicht dafür, die Synagoge umzubauen—es könnte da leicht ein Reisser mit musikalischen Bibeleinlagen daraus werden. Wenn schon die Veranstalter keine Vornehmheit besitzen, so muß doch die *künstlerische* Vornehmheit gewahrt bleiben. Wenn wahrscheinlich auch das gewöhnliche jüdische Publikum von N.Y. auf eine reisserische Handlung positif reagieren würde, so würde diese Handlung unbedingt den Zweck und Kern das Ganzen, die Bibel—erdrücken.

Bisher hatte *ich* immer das Gefühl, dass zu viel galizisch jüdisches Element vorhanden war. Diese Synagogenhandlung muss zurücktreten, damit die wirkliche Dichtung und Musik so rein wirkt *wie* sie concipiert ist.

Weill (in New York) an Hanns und Rita Weill, 15. Januar 1937: Tausend Dank für euer Telegramm, das mich riesig gefreut hat. Der Erfolg des Stückes ist wirklich ausserordentlich, nur die Kasseneinnahmen sind vorläufig nicht so wie wir es erwarteten nach der Presse, und das Stück ist ja so furchtbar teuer in den wöchentlichen Ausgaben. Aber wir hoffen, es wird sich auch finanziell durchsetzen.

Für mich ist es jedenfalls wunderbar, da ich jetzt hier einen fantastischen Namen habe und endlich auch anfangen kann, meine arg zerrütteten Finanzen wieder ein bischen aufzubessern. Ich habe darum ein Angebot für einen Film angenommen und gehe Ende nächster Woche auf 8–10 Wochen nach Hollywood. Lenja bleibt vorläufig, so lange sie spielt, hier. Ich freue mich natürlich sehr auf die Reise und die neue Umgebung, trotzdem ich mir in meinem augenblicklichen Zustand nicht recht vorstellen kann, wie ich eine neue Arbeit anfangen soll. Aber ich hoffe mich in dem schönen Klima dort ein bischen zu erholen, bevor die richtige Arbeit anfängt.

Weill (in Hollywood) an Lotte Lenya, 28. Januar 1937: Ich bin also gestern, am 27. (!) Januar, hier eingetrudelt. Es war niemand an der Bahn außer einem Angestellten der Agentur, der mich gleich ins Walter Wanger Office gebracht hat, wo Milly und Cliff auf mich warteten. Ich habe sofort angefangen, am Manuskript zu arbeiten und nach einer Stunde hatte ich schon durchgesetzt, daß ich einen Song schreiben kann, der glänzend in die Handlung eingearbeitet wird. Es wird eine Art revolutionärer Song sein, der aber gleichzeitig als *love song* fungiert. . . .

Der erste Eindruck hier ist ziemlich verheerend. Es ist ein furchtbares Dorf, man kann keine fünf Schritte gehen, ohne Bekannte zu treffen. Die Landschaft ist herrlich, mit Bergen im Hintergrund wie Salzburg. Aber was sie da hineingebaut haben! Es sieht genau aus wie Bridgeport—nur daß New York 3000 Meilen entfernt ist. Das Klima bekommt mir vorläufig noch nicht gut. Es ist nicht warm und nicht kalt, und ich habe dauernd Kopfschmerzen. Aber das ist wohl nur die ersten Tage. . . . Ich glaube, ich habe hier sehr große Chancen und ich halte es glatt für möglich, daß ich einen sehr großen Vertrag hier bekomme, weil jeder sagt, es gibt überhaupt keine Konkurrenz für mich hier und man braucht dringend Leute wie mich. . . . Heute ist es 11 Jahre, daß wir zum ersten Mal geheiratet haben, und jetzt bist du schon zum zweiten Mal ein Weillchen, du mußt eben alles doppelt haben, du Ameisenblume.

Weill (in Hollywood) an Lotte Lenya, 1. Februar 1937: Die Arbeit an dem Film geht langsam vorwärts, aber es ist ganz interessant, die Technik eines Filmmanuskripts zu lernen. Einfallen tut mir vorläufig noch nicht viel, es ist doch ein ganz neues Medium u. ich fühle mich noch recht unsicher.

Weill (in Hollywood) an Lotte Lenya, 4. Februar 1937: Ich habe einen Max gekauft, einen primi. Nachdem ich schon fast entschlossen war, einen neuen Ford auf Abzahlung zu nehmen, bin ich plötzlich auf die Idee gekommen, mir einmal gebrauchte Wagen in der Klasse unseres Buick anzusehen, die hier viel billiger sind, und tatsächlich einen 1934er Oldsmobile gefunden, in glänzendem äußeren und maschinellem Zustand, ein grünes Zweisitzercoupé, sehr eligant und mit einer fabelhaften Maschine. Er fährt sich genau wie der Buick und es sieht natürlich für hier viel besser aus, mit einem schönen Wagen herumzufahren—und er ist 350 Dollar billiger als der Ford. Ich zahle nur 200 Dollar an und zahle dann monatlich 30 Dollar, alle Versicherungen, Steuern usw. einbegriffen.

Weill (in Hollywood) an Lotte Lenya, [25. Februar 1937]: Montag war ich den ganzen Tag und die Nacht bis 4 Uhr morgens im Studio und habe zugeschaut, wie der musical director (der sehr tüchtig ist) Musik für einen neuen Wanger Film (*History is made at night*, Charles Boyer and Jean Arthur, reizend) recorded hat. Ich habe viel gelernt. Der Ton in diesem Studio ist wunderbar, lustig, sachlich, ohne Krăche, aber mit viel Whisky.

Weill (in Hollywood) an Lotte Lenya, [3. März 1937]: Heute hat Wanger beschlossen, den Film vorläufig nicht zu produzieren, sondern zu warten, bis er eine richtige Starbesetzung dafür findet. Die ganze Produktion ist abgeblasen. Du kannst dir denken, was das für eine Aufregung war—allerdings nicht für das Klugi. Ich bekomme das ganze Geld, sobald ich die Musik abliefere. Ich fange also morgen an, die Musik auszuarbeiten, Szene für Szene. Ich hoffe bis 1. April alles fertig zu haben. Dadurch wird es natürlich ein sehr gutes Geschäft für mich, da ja nun die Bezahlung der Länge der Arbeit entspricht. Der Agent versucht jetzt für 1. April einen anderen Job für mich zu finden. Wenn er bis zu dem Tag, wo ich meine Musik abliefere, nichts gefunden hat, reise ich sofort ab.

Weill (in Hollywood) an Lotte Lenya, 10. März 1937: Antheil habe ich neulich gesehen. Er hat einen Höllenrespekt vor mir und hat offenbar (was alle Leute bestätigen) hier grosse Reklame für mich gemacht (wahrscheinlich um sich als Weill-Kenner aufzuspielen). Seine Frau, die übrigens schwanger ist, hat hier eine moderne Bildgalerie eröffnet, die hier ganz gross in Mode ist, da ja Snobbismus [sic] hier eine grosse Rolle spielt (sie bereitet eine grosse Max Ernst-Ausstellung vor und verspricht sich einen grossen Erfolg davon). Sie wollen als erstes gesellschaftliches Ereignis in ihrer Galerie einen Empfang für mich machen und dabei den *Jasager* und den *Dreigroschenoper*- Film aufführen. Ich glaube, das wäre sehr gut für mich, weil die Leute hier zu wenig von mir wissen, und da würden sie alle hinkommen. Wenn du hier wärest, könntest du Songs singen, aber es wird in jedem Fall leicht sein, hier für dich einen Songabend zu arrangieren.

Weill (in Hollywood) an Lotte Lenya, [13. März 1937]: Nachmittags war ich bei Wanger, habe ihm einige Platten vorgespielt und fing gerade an, einiges von der Musik für Cliff's Film zu spielen (die ja Wanger gehört), als die Tür aufging und—Charlie Chaplin hereinkam. Das ist nun wirklich der bezauberndste Mensch, den ich ja gesehen habe, man riecht auf 10 Meilen Entfernung das Genie. Ich hatte sofort Kontakt mit ihm. Sowas von Begeisterung über die Musik kannst du dir nicht vorstellen, er sprang dauernd auf, sagte: Ach spielen Sie das noch mal, und alles was er sagte, zeigte ein ausserordentliches Verständnis. Er war ganz außer sich über den Anfang des Films, wo ich mit einer wilden spanischen Musik anfange, mit vielen Kastagnetten, die dann plötzlich in Maschinengewehr-Geknatter übergehen, während die wilde Musik weitergeht. „That's one of the greatest ideas I ever heard," sagte er. Wir waren 1 1/2 Stunden zusammen, haben farbige tests für den neuen Wanger Film (Vogues of 1938) gesehen, und er hat sich nur mit mir unterhalten. Du kannst dir denken, was das auf Wanger für einen Eindruck machte. Bevor Chaplin kam, sagte Wanger, er wüsse nicht, ob ich amerikanisch genug bin für den Film 52nd Street, aber dann als ich wegging, sagte er: Let's get together on 52nd Street, und gestern hat er schon Allenberg angerufen und gesagt, ich solle mit dem Mann zusammenkommen, der das Manuskript schreibt. Das alles will natürlich noch nicht heissen, dass ich den Film kriege. Ich würde ihn schrecklich gern machen, weil es ein wirklich musikalischer Film ist, mit einer glänzenden Idee und grossen Möglichkeiten. Also drücke den Daumen.

Weill (in Hollywood) an Lotte Lenya, [15. März 1937]: Aber es scheint, dass Wanger zweifelt, ob ich „amerikanisch" genug für diesen Film bin. Ich habe ihm geantwortet der „amerikanischste" Komponist, Irving Berlin, ist ein russischer Jude—und ich bin ein deutscher Jude, das ist der ganze Unterschied.

Weill (in Hollywood) an Lotte Lenya, [28. März 1937]: Dann war ich den ganzen Nachmittag und Abend bei den Spevacks. Das sind reizende Leute, sie werden Dir ungeheuer gefallen. Die Frau hat ein bischen was von Madeleine Milhaud. Wir haben einen wundervollen Stoff ausgearbeitet und sind alle drei sehr begeistert: ein Stück über die refugees. Es beginnt im Mannheimer Opernhaus auf einer Opernprobe, die plötzlich durch einen Nazi unterbrochen wird, der sie alle entlässt, weil sie Nichtarier sind. Sie gehen alle nach New York und wir zeigen nun ihre Erlebnisse, natürlich mit viel Humor, aber auch z. B. eine Szene, wo ein Brief aus Mannheim kommt von einem ihrer Freunde, der nicht mehr lebt, wenn der Brief ankommt. Am Schluss kommt einer ihrer Freunde aus Deutschland an und sagt, er habe alles arrangiert, sie können zurückkommen, aber dann sagen sie, sie wollen nicht zurück, und der Schluss ist, dass sie in einem Kino in einem kleinen Nest in Amerika die Oper aufführen, die sie im ersten Akt probiert haben. Ist das nicht ein wundervoller Stoff?

Weill (in Hollywood) an Lotte Lenya, [8. Mai 1937]: Es sieht sehr so aus, daß der Fritz Lang Film bei Paramount zustandekommt. Sie sind einverstanden, 10.000 für den ganzen Job zu zahlen. Ich würde jetzt ungefähr 4 Wochen an dem Film arbeiten und versuchen, in dieser Zeit so viel wie möglich zu schaffen. Gleichzeitig müßte ich hier die wichtigsten Nummern für die show schreiben. Dann würde ich ungefähr am 10. Juni in New York sein und könnte ungefähr 3 Monate an der show arbeiten. In dieser Zeit bereitet Lang den Film vor und fängt an zu drehen, und ich komme erst hierher zurück, wenn er mich braucht. . . . Sie haben Sylvia Sydney und George Raft für die Hauptrollen, und ich glaube, es kann ein sehr interessanter Film werden. Es ist bestimmt keine leichte Nuß mit Lang, der natürlich ein ekelhafter Kerl ist (obwohl er zu mir vorläufig rührend ist), und es wird die tollsten Kämpfe geben. . . .

Wir wollen mit dem Geld sehr vorsichtig sein, Blumi, weil doch schließlich das alles, was ich jetzt mache, nur eine Berechtigung hat, wenn ich genug damit ersparen kann, um dann endlich mal wieder etwas ganz großes, auf meinem früheren Niveau zu machen. Ich möchte nicht in den Fehler verfallen, den hier alle machen (Cliff und alle anderen), daß man das Geld, das man verdient, ausgibt und dann wieder einen neuen Job annehmen muß und allmählich ein vollkommener Sklave von Hollywood wird. Ich weiß ja, daß das auch deine Ansicht ist. Wenn wir aufpassen, könnten wir im Herbst, wenn dieser Film fertig ist, ungefähr 16.000 Dollar in der Bank haben und könnten uns in der Nähe von New York ein kleines Haus mieten, ein Mädchen, ein Auto, und dieses Zigeunerleben aufgeben, das einen ja garnicht zur Besinnung kommen lässt. . . . Geld kann nur dazu dienen, sich unabhängig zu machen.

In der vorigen *Sunday Times* war ein Bericht aus Wien, daß Walter meine Symphonie aufgeführt hat. Es war zum ersten Mal, dass Toscanini zu einem Konzert eines anderen Dirigenten gegangen ist. Der Bericht sagt, daß das Publikum auf das Werk positiver reagiert hat, als auf irgendein anderes modernes Werk. Das freut einen, besonders wenn man hier in Hollywood sitzt und sich mit Boris Morros herumstreiten muss.

Ich war einen Abend mit Stokowski, der sehr nett zu mir war.

Weill (in Santa Monica) an Lotte Lenya, [29. Mai 1937]: Donnerstag haben wir in der Antheil Galerie den *Lindberghflug* aufgeführt, nur mit ein paar Sängern und zwei Klavieren. Es ist erstaunlich was für eine gute Musik das ist und wie frisch es noch wirkt, nach fast 10 Jahren. Ausserdem haben wir den *Dreigroschenoperfilm* aufgeführt, aber wir haben nur die französische Version bekommen, die recht schlecht ist, und bei dem Film konnte man, im Gegensatz zum *Lindberghflug*, leider schon sehen, dass er etwas veraltet ist und dass er nie gut war. Es war alles da, was in Hollywood an neuen Sachen interessiert ist: Gershwins, Mirjam Hopkins, Litwak, Milestones, Lang, Luise und Cliff und viele andere. . . . Gestern war in Los Angeles Premiere von *Johnny Johnson*. Ich bin zu ein paar Proben gegangen und habe ihnen ein bischen geholfen. Es war die grösste WPA Aufführung, die sie bisher gemacht haben, viel frischer und unbekümmerter als die New Yorker Aufführung, natürlich schlechtere Schauspieler, aber ein reizender ganz junger *Johnny* (das Stück wirkt ganz anders mit einem jungen *Johnny*), mit grossem (schlechtem) Orchester, Chören und sehr interessanten *sets*. Dass die Aufführung anders war als New York, kannst du daran sehen, dass der zweite Akt weitaus am stärksten wirkte. Sie haben den *french wounded* Chor gemacht und den ganzen Tanz der Generäle, der ausserordentlich wirkte. Es war gestern abend, bei der Premiere, noch sehr roh und unfertig, besonders musikalisch, aber es war ein ausgesprochener grosser Erfolg, die Leute haben glänzend reagiert, viel gelacht, Totenstille bei dem *gun song* (der grossen Applaus hatte wie überhaupt alle *songs*), Riesenapplaus am Schluss. Auch die Presse scheint gut zu sein. Sie werden es 6–8 Wochen spielen.

Madeleine Grey (à Paris) à Weill, le 29 theater 1937: J'espère que vous vous souviendrez encore de mon nom; car moi je vous suis fidèle—mieux encore j'ai avec vos mélodies mes plus grands succès.

Si je vous disais qu'avec l'air de la "pauvre parente" de *Silbersee*, je fais le bonheur du public italien et suisse—quant au "Roi d'Aquitaine" de *Marie galante*, il est devenu, à Naples, depuis trois ans que je leur chante, presque aussi populaire que "Sole mio."

Je crois que maintenant je rend ces choses là parfaitement bien et que je suis d'essence votre interprète—c'est pourquoi, je vous en prie, de faire pour moi une suite de chansons de caractère pour que je puisse les créer dans mon récital de la rentrée.

Je viens d'en donner un ce 11 theater, où vous étiez aussi avec le plus grand succès—je crois que Madeleine Milhaud vous a envoyé mon programme.

Faites vite, Kurt Weill, j'ai très besoin de choses nouvelles écrites pour moi. Je vous rappelle que je suis mezzo.

Weill (in New York) an Alfred Kalmus, Universal Edition, 28. Juli 1937: Wenn ich Ihnen heute, nach langer Zeit, einmal wieder schreibe, so ist es zunächst, um Sie zu bitten, mir doch sobald als möglich mehrere Exemplare aller meiner bei der Universal-Edition erschienenen Werke zukommen zu lassen. Meine Situation hier in Amerika ist jetzt, was die Anerkennung meines Könnens anbetrifft, eine so gute, dass ich daran denken kann, meine früheren Werke hier mehr als bisher bekannt zu machen, und ich bekomme auch von den verschiedensten Seiten Anfragen nach meinen früheren Konzert- und Theaterwerken. Ich möchte besonders die verschiedenen hier entstehenden Operngesellschaften für die *Bürgschaft* und auch für die anderen Opern interessieren, aber ich habe leider keinerlei Material hier, das ich den in Betracht kommenden Leuten zeigen könnte.

Weill (in New York) an Ernst Aufricht, 18. August 1937: Anbei sende ich Ihnen die beiden Chansons für Yvette Guilbert. Beide Texte sind ausgezeichnet, und ich glaube, es sind zwei sehr gute *Dreigroschenoper*-Chansons geworden. Das erste Chanson („Ahh Polly, Polly, tu me démolis") muss ziemlich rasch genommen werden, der Rhythmus hat eine leicht spanische Färbung; der dritte Vers (wo sie schon schwer betrunken ist) ist wie eine Art Trauermarsch komponiert, geht dann aber im Refrain plötzlich wieder in das lustige Tempo über. Das zweite Chanson habe ich als ein Menuett komponiert. Es ist sehr im Stile der *Dreigroschenoper*, diesen etwas obszönen Text zu einer sehr graziösen und anmutigen Musik zu singen. Ich habe das Chanson auf die Frage „Qui?" aufgebaut und lasse an bestimmten Stellen im Chanson dieses „Qui?" dazwischensprechen, was natürlich jedesmal mit wechselndem Ausdruck gemacht werden müsste. Die Antwort „C'est moi…" ist dann jedesmal ein Ausbruch von Verzweiflung und Kummer.—Falls die Chansons zu hoch sind, können sie leicht um ein paar Töne transponiert werden. . . .

Ich habe mich sehr über Ihren Bericht gefreut. Ich bin natürlich sehr begeistert, dass die Guilbert die Madame Peachum spielt, und ich bin überzeugt, wenn der Rest der Aufführung so gut wird, wie sie sicher sein wird, so kann es ein grosser Erfolg werden. Bitte imitieren Sie nicht die Berliner Aufführung sondern versuchen sie es so weit wie möglich zu französisieren. Und vergessen Sie nicht, dass unsere Berliner Aufführung jetzt fast 10 Jahre alt ist, und manches heute schon etwas veraltet wirken muss.

Weill (in New York) an Hans Nathan, 30. Mai 1938: Sofort nach meiner Rückkehr von Hollywood habe ich die Bearbeitung der beiden Volkslieder in Angriff genommen, habe sie soeben beendet und an "Masada" abgeschickt.

Ich glaube, daß mir beide Bearbeitungen gut gelungen sind. „Havu l'venim" habe ich mit einer kurzen Einleitung versehen und das Ganze sehr auf einen gehaltenen Marschrhythmus gestellt, der, glaube ich, recht wirkungsvoll ist. Das ganze Lied kann wiederholt werden, die „prima volta" führt direkt in das Vorspiel.

Für „Ba'a M'nucha" habe ich eine Art von durchkomponierter Form gewählt, ohne aber das Schema der Strophenform zu zerstören. Die ersten 12 Takte sind in den drei Strophen verschieden behandelt, entsprechend dem verschiedenen Charakter der Texte. Der Refrain ist in den drei Strophen gleich, nur in der letzten Strophe sind die letzten Takte zugunsten der „Nachtstimmung" frei behandelt. I hope you like it."

Weill (in Hollywood) an Lotte Lenya, 19. April 1938: Heute morgen um 1/2 9 hat mir Fritz ungefähr 2/3 des Films vorgeführt. Es ist ein sehr schöner, teilweise aufregend schöner Film, aber zu lang, (d.h. zu lang und zu Lang), oft sehr schleppend und sehr deutsch, aber im Niveau unvergleichlich besser als alles was sie hier machen. Die Songs sind absolut die Höhepunkte und man könnte weinen (oder lachen), wenn man bedenkt wie alle meine Ideen in diesem Film sich wieder als richtig und neu und aufregend erweisen—und daß nie jemand wissen wird, daß es meine Ideen sind. Der „Right Guy" wirkt großartig, der „Song of the Lie" kommt viel besser durch als ich dachte. Am schönsten ist der „Cashregistersong" im Anfang, aber den verstehen sie natürlich alle nicht (außer Lang) und ich bin sicher, daß sie ihn streichen werden. Na ja, ich habe mir vorgenommen, mich nicht aufzuregen, und ich bin mehr als je überzeugt, dass es nicht wert ist, sich aufzuregen, weil man es ja nur mit dem Ausschuß der Menschheit zu tun hat. Den Boris habe ich ins Gesicht gefragt, was bei Wanger passiert ist, und aus seinem Gestotter war deutlich zu erkennen, daß er auch seine Dreckfinger drin hatte. Da sind sie alle beisammen, wenn es eine Schweinerei zu machen gibt.

Weill (in Hollywood) an Lotte Lenya, 5. Mai 1938: Die erste freie Minute benutze ich, um dir ein paar Zeilen zu schreiben. Ich habe seit mehr als einer Woche keine Nacht mehr als 4 Stunden geschlafen, immer bis 3 gearbeitet und dann um 7 wieder raus. Die Arbeit wäre ja nicht schlimm, weil mir das ja immer Spaß macht, aber diese Ärgereien, Stänkereien und diese entsetzliche Dummheit und Ungebildetheit, gegen die man zu kämpfen hat, dazu die heimlichen Schweinereien von Borris [sic] und natürlich auch von dem geliebten Fritz [Lang], der bei jeder passenden Gelegenheit gegen mich Stellung nimmt, und der derartig unmusikalisch ist, daß man sich die Haare ausraufen könnte. Ich habe herausgefunden, daß hier nur eins hilft: furchtbar frech zu sein und allen ins Gesicht hinein zu sagen, was man denkt. Seit ich diese Technik angefangen habe, ging es plötzlich viel besser, die haben Respekt vor mir, mehr als vor irgend jemand mit dem sie bisher gearbeitet haben, und ich habe allerhand durchdrücken können, so wie ich es wollte.

CHAPTER 6

Figure 487. "Kurt Weill" in *Lexikon der Juden in der Musik*.

Weill, Kurt (Curt) Julian, b. Dessau 3 March 1900, composer, conductor—formerly of Berlin. The name of this composer is inseperably connected to the worst corruption of our art. His stage works show baldly and unscrupulously the Jewish-anarchistic tendency. Having completed various works in the realm of chamber, chorus and entertainment music, the Lied, cantata and opera, together with Bert Brecht (text) he achieved a sensational success with *Dreigroschenoper* (1928) (over 200 performances in one Berlin season). Created as an adaptation of, and partly remodeled with obvious plagiarisms from the old *Beggar's Opera* created by Gay and Pepusch, this work with its undisguised pimps' and criminals' morality, its song-style and its shrewdly-primitive mixture of chorale, foxtrot and negroid jazz was touted by Jews and and their panders as a revolutionary upheaval of all musico-dramatic art. For instance, Hans Mersmann, pioneer of musical decadence and editor of the journal *Melos*, still in 1934 wrote in his *History of German Music*: "This is in every way an entirely new form of theater—neither cheap entertainment nor ethical morality, rather a reflected consequence (as the two authors formulate it in some other places) of the existing social stratum's unstoppable decay. Therein lies the meaning of the text, which instead of a hero puts on stage the human being who fights for his bare life, thus trying to grab the listener by reminding him of the instinctive basic forces of his own existence. Therein also lies the power of the music, which seems to consist of nothing but interludes, loosely connected to the action, which are hammering the text's maxims into the listeners with the power of a pop song."

Within this same direction also lies *The Rise and Fall of the City of Mahagonny* (1929). There, one finds amongst other things the verse:

"If you're short of cash
For a thing you want to buy
Then go get the cash.
Just head for the street and find a rich man
Hit him on the head and take all his cash:
Just do it!"

In another place the chorus sings:

"First, don't forget the joys of eating
Second comes the sexual act.
Third, go and watch the boxers fighting.
Fourth comes drinking as per pact.
But mainly get it through your head
That nothing is prohibited!"

At this point, when Weill's musical emptiness showed all too clearly, and the storm of protests formed by all sane people reacting against this scorn for the most fundamental concepts of decency on the stage grew stronger and stronger, Weill turned away from the glorification of class warfare and subhuman creatures toward school opera, didactic play and radio cantata: *Lindbergh-Flug, Der Jasager* (1930), which in spite of all its basic Jewish-Marxist attitude was officially sanctioned and propagated: The chorus of the Hochschule of the Institute for Church Music even traveled to Paris with *Der Jasager*.

Weill (in New City) an Bertolt Brecht, 9. März 1942: Vielen Dank für Ihren Brief, den ich zusammen mit einem Telegramm von Marton hier vorfand, als ich von einer Reise nach Washington und Detroit zurückkam. . . .

Ich hoffe, daß Sie noch nicht zu tief in diese Angelegenheit verwickelt sind, da ich sie, nicht nur von meinem, sondern besonders von Ihrem Standpunkt aus gesehen, für nicht günstig halte. Es ist schade, daß Sie mir nicht die Möglichkeit gegeben haben, Sie in einem früheren Stadium der Verhandlungen zu beraten. Ich glaube, ich hätte Sie besser beraten können als die meisten Leute in Hollywood, und besonders in der Angelegenheit einer amerikanischen Wiederaufführung der *Dreigroschenoper* bin ich ja eine Art „expert", da [ich] mich seit 7 Jahren immer wieder mit diesem Problem beschäftigt habe. Nach der ganzen Struktur des amerikanischen Theaters ist es sehr schwierig, ein Stück, das einmal durchgefallen ist, wieder herauszubringen, selbst wenn es so eine gute Reputation hat wie die *Dreigroschenoper.* Aber es ist ausser Zweifel, daß wir eines Tages eine erstklassige „revival" der *Dreigroschenoper* haben werden, wenn wir auf die beste Kombination von Übersetzer (für das Stück und, was besonders schwierig ist, für die Gesangstexte), Regisseur, Producer und Schauspieler warten. Ich habe in den letzten Monaten mehrere Verhandlungen mit Charles MacArthur, einem der besten jüngeren Dramatiker in Amerika, langjährigem Mitarbeiter von Ben Hecht, gehabt. Er war sehr interessiert, und mein Plan war, entweder von ihm allein oder zusammen mit Ben Hecht, mit dem ich sehr befreundet bin, eine wirklich erstklassige amerikanische Adaption zu bekommen. (Was wir brauchen, ist nicht eine Übersetzung, sondern eine Adaption für das amerikanische Theater, denn einer der Hauptgründe für den Durchfall in 1933 war, daß sie eine wörtliche Übersetzung gemacht haben). Wenn ich eine solche gute Adaption hätte, wäre es nicht schwer für mich, einen erstklassigen Producer und eine hervorragende Besetzung zu finden. Eine solche Aufführung der *Dreigroschenoper*, wie ich sie beabsichtige, würde für Sie nicht nur wirkliche finanzielle Vorteile bringen, sondern würde Sie als Theaterautor in Amerika etablieren.

Dieser Plan würde wahrscheinlich für immer, mindestens aber für die nächsten 10 Jahre undurchführbar werden, wenn wir die *Dreigroschenoper* von einer Negertruppe in Californien aufführen ließen. Ich habe, wie ich Ihnen früher schrieb, schon vor Jahren mit einem amerikanischen Autor an einer Negerfassung der *Dreigroschenoper* gearbeitet. Wir hatten zunächst versucht, wie Ihre Leute es scheinbar tun, die *Dreigroschenoper*, wie sie ist, von Negern spielen zu lassen. Aber es stellte sich heraus, daß die Idee, eine deutsche Bearbeitung einer englischen *ballad opera* des 17. Jahrhunderts von amerikanischen Negern darstellen zu lassen, so „sophisticated" war, daß es das Publikum vollständig verwirrt hätte. Wir versuchten dann, das Stück so zu bearbeiten, daß die Probleme wirklich Negerprobleme bekamen—aber das hätte bedeutet, daß ein vollkommen neues Stück geschrieben werden müsste.—Ich kenne Clarence Muse nicht und weiß nicht, ob er einen besseren job machen kann als die Leute, mit denen ich es versucht hatte. Ich weiß aber, daß in den sieben Jahren, seit ich in Amerika bin, immer wieder der Versuch gemacht wurde, Stücke in Californien zu starten und dann nach New York zu bringen (das ja, leider, immer noch das einzige Theaterzentrum in Amerika ist)—und daß es nie gelungen ist, und zwar aus dem einfachen Grunde, weil die Dinge, die sie in Californien gemacht haben, nicht gut genug waren. Das bedeutet, daß eine solche Aufführung für Sie vom finanziellen und vom künstlerischen Standpunkt aus fast bedeutungslos wäre. Selbstverständlich kann ich sehr wohl verstehen, daß Sie ungeduldig werden, etwas hier in Gang zu bringen und das wahrscheinlich auch Ihre finanzielle Situation einen baldigen Theatererfolg wünschenswert erscheinen lässt. Aber ich hatte gehofft, daß Sie durch Freunde in Hollywood einen Start im Film finden würden, sodaß wir mit der *Dreigroschenoper* warten können, bis wir die großen Chancen, die diese „property" für uns enthält, wirklich ausnützen können. Aber Sie werden wahrscheinlich sagen, das ist ein typisch kapitalistischer Standpunkt.

Was mich persönlich anbetrifft, so müsste ich natürlich zunächst die Übersetzung des Stückes und der Gesangstexte sehen, bevor ich irgendetwas entscheiden kann. Die songs der *Dreigroschenoper* sind hier in Kennerkreisen ausserordentlich bekannt und beliebt. Ich habe immer und immer wieder versucht, Übersetzungen der Gesangstexte machen zu lassen, die dem Stil der Musik entsprechen und die Schönheiten Ihrer Originalverse auch nur annähernd wiedergeben. Bisher ist mir das nicht gelungen, und ich möchte die Musik nicht freigeben, bevor die Frage der Übersetzung nicht einwandfrei gelöst ist. Also senden Sie mir bitte zunächst das Buch ein. Was den Wunsch des Theaters anbetrifft, meine Musik selbst zu instrumentieren, so kann ich mir recht gut vorstellen, wie meine Musik aussehen würde, wenn ich das zulassen würde. Ich habe, besonders hier in Amerika, immer streng darauf gehalten, daß meine Musik im Theater nur in meiner eigenen Orchestration gespielt wird, und ich müsste an diesem Prinzip auch in diesem Fall festhalten.

Weill (in New City) an Bertolt Brecht, 13. März 1942: Soeben erhielt ich Ihren zweiten Brief. Zunächst vielen Dank für den wunderschönen Song. Ich werde ihn komponieren, und wenn Sie wollen, werde ich ihn den Leuten anbieten, die die short-wave Sendungen nach Deutschland machen. (Es ist übrigens möglich, daß ich in einiger Zeit ein eigenes Programm dieser Art machen werde, für Radio nach Deutschland, und dann würde ich mehr Material von Ihnen brauchen).

Was die *Dreigroschenoper* anbetrifft, so haben Sie ja inzwischen meinen ausführlichen Brief bekommen, der Ihnen meinen Standpunkt klargemacht hat. Ich verstehe natürlich vollkommen, wieviel Ihnen an dieser Aufführung liegt, und Sie können überzeugt sein, dass ich Sie in der Angelegenheit vollkommen unterstützen werde, sobald ich festgestellt habe, ob wir wirklich eine Chance haben mit dieser Aufführung. Schauen Sie, Brecht, ich habe in den sieben Jahren hier in Amerika immer wieder gesehen, daß Leute von drüben sich Hals über Kopf in irgendein Projekt gestürzt haben, das ihnen dann mehr geschadet als genützt hat, und es ist mindestens ebenso in Ihrem wie in meinem eigenen Interesse, wenn ich versuche, auf Grund meiner Erfahrungen im amerikanischen Theater uns vor ähnlichen Irrtümern zu bewahren. Wir wollen doch beide nicht, daß das noch einmal geschieht, was 1933 hier in New York und später wieder in Paris mit der *Dreigroschenoper* geschehen ist. Wir können es verhindern, wenn wir ein bischen vorsichtig sind. Wenn die Leute es ernsthaft meinen mit ihren Plänen für die *Dreigroschenoper*, so werden sie gewiss nichts dagegen einzuwenden [haben], dass ich das Buch sehen möchte und mich über die Details der Aufführung informieren möchte.

Figure 510. Theodor Adorno (Los Angeles) to Weill, 31 March 1942: It must be a surprise after such a long time and a failed rendezvous in New York to suddenly hear from me again. However, independent of the wish to keep alive a relationship which has meant a lot to me and perhaps something to you too, I am writing to you on for a particular reason. It is the topic of an American performance of the *Threepenny Opera.*

As you know, Brecht lives here and we are together a lot. He told me that there is an opportunity to organize a performance of *Threepenny Opera* by a Negro ensemble, and he also mentioned your own reluctance to endorse this project. Please do not consider it presumptuous of me if I express my unsolicited opinion concerning this matter, a matter which, as nobody knows better than you, is most dear to me and whose possibilities in America, musical and sociological I feel qualified to evaluate.

The Broadway premiere ten years ago apparently was what Karl Kraus called a *verbroigten Leubusch.* My strong feeling is that in an intellectual environment where artistic productions are judged in terms of tests, contests or, at best raffles, a repeat of the experiment on Broadway would not be guaranteed success, unless the *Threepenny Opera* was established earlier in some other venue, so as to conquer New York by storm from the outside. Furthermore, the ideological situation in America cannot be compared to the German one of 1929; it is in no way a "critical situation" and therefore as yet not ready to accept the authentic *Threepenny Opera*, which is so inseparably tied to a climate of crisis.

On the other hand, there is Brecht's situation, which, as far as I can judge, is so precarious that he can hardly afford to wait indefinitely for a *Threepenny Opera* revival. Of course, a personal point of view cannot and should not be the decisive factor in a question of artistic responsibility; however, it is this same artistic responsibility which gives impetus to try anything to allow the creative powers of Brecht to reproduce themselves in a dignified way so that he is relieved of the most trivial daily worries.

Now as far as the performance itself is concerned: we are talking here about the founding of a Negro theater of national import, backed by Paul Robeson and the so-called Negro Lodges, therefore considerable moral backing, with financial consequences, if successful, which offer you and Brecht good prospects. The *Threepenny Opera* should be the first work to be showcased on this stage by this group. However, the thought which actually motivated me to intervene, is the following: From the very beginning the performance style of the *Threepenny Opera* has been based on the jazz arrangement. In my opinion, there exist only two possibilities for a worthwhile performance, namely the strict, tone for tone rendition of the original full score—a process which your own intention, and your and Brecht's vision of montage, rejected. Or one has to present the work in an actual jazz adaptation. This, however, can only be successful over here, if the principle of jazz variation would be applied in a far more radical way than would have been necessary in Europe. You surely will agree with me that the method of someone like Mackeben would not be successful here, because it lags way behind the American rhythmic style. If one handed over the jazz adaptation to one of the commonly employed white jazz arrangers, even the very best, there would be the danger that something tame and bland would be made out of *Threepenny Opera*, that it would lose its bite and its special peculiarity. I cannot counter Brecht in his assertion that the only chance—a paradox—to achieve success and at the same time retain its defiant categorization, at least for the moment, lies on a really far-reaching "re-structuring" using a Negro ensemble working on both text and music. One should strive for a somewhat economically self sufficient performance, one in which the Negroes, whose reactions never could completely understood by us anyway, would largely be left to themselves and who would improvise the work in their own way. I would go so far as to say that *Threepenny Opera* depends either on the utmost faithfulness and literality, or on the crassest and most infringing improvisational liberties, and the work itself is laid out from the beginning for the latter, such that it would find solace in it, until such a day when it can celebrate its negative-theological resurrection once more, like on the first day of creation in the Theater am Schiffbauerdamm.

To show you that I have not become music-sociologically half-witted in my period of silence, I am sending you under separate cover my last two publications in that field.

Weill (in Los Angeles) an Emma und Albert Weill, 5. November 1943: Endlich finde ich ein bischen Zeit, um euch wieder mal zu schreiben. Ich habe ein paar sehr schwere und aufregende Monate hinter mir, aber, wie ihr schon gehört habt, hat sich all die Arbeit auch diesmal wieder gelohnt und das neue Stück ist ein grosser Erfolg geworden. Es war eine besonders schwierige Aufgabe, weil ich diesmal keinen Moss Hart oder Ira Gershwin dabei hatte und ganz auf mein eigenes Urteil angewiesen war, alle Entscheidungen allein, und oft sogar gegen den Willen meiner Mitarbeiter treffen musste und ausser der Musik auch am Libretto, an der Besetzung, den Bühnenbildern und der ganzen Organisation einer grossen Broadwayshow arbeiten musste. Während 7 Wochen, bevor die show eröffnete, habe ich keine Nacht mehr als 2–3 Stunden geschlafen, da ich tags auf der Probe war und nachts orchestrieren musste. Aber das merkt man ja garnicht, wenn man so „im Schwung" ist und Lenya hat dafür gesorgt, dass ich regelmässig gegessen habe. Am schlimmsten war es während der drei Wochen in Boston, wo es zuerst so aussah, als ob das Stück ein gewaltiger Durchfall werden würde und ich musste in kurzer Zeit die ganze Sache zusammenreissen. Aber das ist nun alles vergessen—Gottseidank! . . .

Ein anderes grosses und freudiges Ereignis: ich bin vor einigen Wochen amerikanischer Bürger geworden! Das habe ich seit Jahren angestrebt und ich bin sehr glücklich darüber.

Wir sind vor einigen Tagen hier in Hollywood angekommen, wo ich für einige Monate an einem Film arbeiten und mich gleichzeitig ein bischen erholen werde. Wir haben ein reizendes kleines Haus gemietet, mit einem schönen Garten, in dem wir unsere eigenen Zitronen vom Baum pflücken, und einem „swimming pool". Wir haben unser Mädchen mitgebracht, damit wir nicht in Restaurants essen müssen, da wir das in den letzten Monaten dauernd machen mussten. Das Klima ist wunderbar hier in dieser Jahreszeit: kühl während der Nacht und angenehm warm unter Tag. Ich denke, dass wir bis Anfang Februar hier bleiben werden.

Ernst Aufricht (in New York) an Weill, 24. Dezember 1943: Ein mir bekannter Berliner Bühnenmaler Leo Kerz hat Brecht das Angebot gemacht, sein Stück „Das gute Mädchen von Sezuan" jetzt am Broadway aufzuführen. Brecht bat mich, den Mann und seine Möglichkeiten zu untersuchen. Ich habe Folgendes festgestellt: Der Mann hat 50 000 Dollars zur Verfügung. Er hat die alte Fassung und die neue gelesen; er will die alte spielen, die neue gefällt ihm nicht. Er ist bereit sofort eine Drei Monats Option zu kaufen, um in dieser Zeit die Möglichkeiten für Besetzung, Theater usw. festzustellen. Brecht will unter keinen Umständen etwas abschließen, bevor er weiß, ob Sie auf sein Stück noch reflektieren. Bitte telegrafieren Sie Brecht oder mir. Brecht will den Mann gern fallen lassen, wenn Sie mit ihm zu einem Abschluss kommen.

Weill (in Los Angeles) an Albert und Emma Weill, 30. April 1945: Endlich finde ich ein wenig Zeit euch zu schreiben. Die letzten Monate waren, wie immer wenn ich ein Stück herausbringe, voll von Aufregungen und so vollkommen konzentriert auf meine Arbeit, dass ich zu nichts anderem Zeit hatte. Es war diesmal besonders schwer, weil der Dramatiker, der das Buch geschrieben hat, ein vollkommener Versager war, und ich hatte ein besonderes Gefühl von Verantwortung, weil es eine sehr teure und grosse show war, und natürlich auch weil Lenya darin gespielt hat. Musikalisch war es das beste was ich in Jahren geschrieben habe, eine richtige Oper mit grossen Chören und Ensemble-Nummern, voll von melodischer Erfindung, unter Ausnützung des ganzen handwerklichen Könnens, das ich durch die Jahre mir angeeignet habe. Auch Ira Gershwin, der die Gesangstexte geschrieben hat, hat sich selbst übertroffen. Aber das Libretto war sehr schwach, und die Aufführung liess viel zu wünschen übrig. Abgesehen von Lenya (die eine grossartige Darstellung der Herzogin von Florenz gab) war die Besetzung nicht sehr gut und wir hatten diesmal keinen grossen Star-Namen. Kurz und gut—diesmal war es kein so grosser Erfolg wie die letzten Stücke. Persönlich hatte ich einen grossen Erfolg mit meiner Musik, aber im übrigen waren die Kritiken sehr schlecht. Dazu kommt, dass wir gerade in einer Zeit eröffneten, wo die Spannung über die Ereignisse in Europa so gross ist, dass die Leute keine grosse Lust haben ins Theater zu gehen.– Abgesehen von der momentanen Aufregung und dem Ärger, der immer mit diesen Dingen verbunden ist, hat mich der geringe Erfolg des *Firebrand of Florence* nicht sehr berührt, und auch ihr braucht euch darüber absolut keine Kopfschmerzen zu machen. Ich habe mich längst an diese Auf-und-Ab-Kurve des Erfolgs gewöhnt, und ich war mir seit langem bewusst, dass nach diesen beiden Riesenerfolgen, die ich in den letzten Jahren gehabt habe, einmal wieder ein Rückschlag fällig war. Irgendwie bin ich sogar zufrieden, dass ich nicht in die Routine einer gleichmässigen Erfolgskarriere verfalle. Solange ich mit jedem neuen Stück etwas neues versuche, das in vielen Fällen meiner Zeit voraus ist, muss ich solche möglichen Rückschläge in Kauf nehmen—was natürlich umso leichter ist, als ich es finanziell gut aushalten kann. Also Schwamm darüber—und auf zu neuen Taten! . . .

Alles was man persönlich erlebt ist ja jetzt weit überschattet durch die gewaltigen Ereignisse, die sich auf dem Welttheater abspielen. Es erfüllt einen mit Hoffnung und Zuversicht, wenn man den Sieg der Gerechtigkeit miterleben darf, wenn man sieht, wie nach kurzer Zeit das Böse bestraft wird und das Gute siegt. Ich glaube nicht, dass jemals in der Geschichte der Menschheit eine Nation eine so furchtbare Niederlage erlitten hat wie Deutschland—und dass niemals vorher ein Volk eine Demütigung so verdient hat wie diese Barbaren, die sich angemasst haben, alles Gute und Anständige zerstören zu dürfen, was der Mensch durch Jahrtausende aufgebaut hat. Wenn man daran denkt, mit welchem Mut und Stolz die Engländer, die Holländer, die Franzosen, die Russen, die Jugoslaven [sic] und, vor allem, die Juden ihre Niederlage ertragen haben, dann erfüllt es einen mit tiefem Abscheu, wenn man die Feigheit, die Erniedrigung, die krankhafte Selbstzerstörungswut, die die sogenannte Herrenrasse in der Zeit ihrer Niederlage zeigt. Was die alliierten Armeen in vier kurzen Jahren vollbracht haben, grenzt an das Wunderbare und war nur möglich, weil es so offensichtlich ein Krieg des Guten gegen das Böse war. Nun erwarten wir jeden Tag die Nachricht von dem „unconditional surrender"—und es ist sicher, dass, wenn ihr diesen Brief erhaltet, der Krieg in Europa vorbei sein wird. Lenya und ich beginnen schon davon zu sprechen, dass wir, sobald private Reisen erlaubt sein werden, euch besuchen kommen wollen—und wenn alles gut geht, mag das schon nächsten Winter sein, oder nächstes Frühjahr.

CHAPTER 7

Weill (in New City) an Caspar Neher, 2. April 1946: Mir ist es gut gegangen. Ich habe eine wirkliche Heimat hier gefunden, einen interessanten Wirkungskreis, Freunde und im ganzem eine viel gesundere Atmosphäre als irgendwo in Europa. Es ist ein wundervolles Land, dieses Amerika, und ich kann mir nicht vorstellen, dass ich irgendwo anders leben könnte. Ich habe unausgesetzt gearbeitet und meine Arbeit hat viel Anerkennung gefunden, besonders die beiden großen Theatererfolge *Lady in the Dark* (1941) und *One Touch of Venus* (1943). Leider gibt es in diesem grossen Lande nur eine Theater-Institution: „Broadway", d.h. das kommerzielle Theater in New York, und das ist ein sehr enges Feld und ein sehr harter Kampf—aber das Publikum ist grossartig—naiv, wissensbedürftig—und sehr aufnahmefähig.

Weill (in New City) an Caspar Neher, 2. Juli 1946: Gestern abend, als ich aus der Stadt nach Haus kam, fand ich deinen und Erika's Brief vom 27. Mai vor. Welche Freude, nach all den Jahren endlich wieder von euch zu hören, zu wissen, dass ihr diese Katastrophenjahre überlebt habt und in Sicherheit seid, dass du wieder arbeiten kannst und beginnst Pläne für die Zukunft zu machen. Es ist merkwürdig: als ich eure Briefe sah, war es plötzlich, als ob diese 11 Jahre seit 1935 zusammenschrumpften und es schien wie gestern, seit ich zum letzten Mal von euch Abschied nahm, und all die wilden, hässlichen, unsagbar grausamen Dinge, die sich in diesen Jahren abgespielt haben, schienen plötzlich ausgewischt, und unsere alte, gute Freundschaft knüpfte ruhig wieder an, wo sie unterbrochen worden war. Du kannst dir vorstellen, welchen Abscheu ich empfinden musste gegen die Dinge, die sich in Deutschland abspielten in diesen Jahren, und gegen die Menschen, die nicht nur ihr eigenes Volk sondern die ganze Welt ins Verderben zu stürzen drohten. Dieses Gefühl, zusammen mit einem grossen Gefühl von Dankbarkeit und Anhänglichkeit für die neue Heimat, die ich hier gefunden habe, entwickelten in mir eine Art Gleichgültigkeit und Interesselosigkeit für das Schicksal der Leute, die ich früher in Deutschland gekannt hatte. Du und Erika waren die einzigen Ausnahmen, und es verging kaum ein Tag, wo ich nicht in irgendeinem Zusammenhang an euch dachte—beruflich natürlich, wenn ich Schwierigkeiten mit meinen Librettisten hatte und an unsere Zusammenarbeit dachte oder wenn ich wieder und wieder eine Bühnenausstattung hier mit deinem Werk vergleichen musste, nur um immer wieder festzustellen, dass niemand hier dir auch nur das Wasser reichen kann. . . . Die ersten Jahre hier waren natürlich sehr schwer. Das biblische Bühnenwerk mit Reinhardt war ein Misserfolg, aber meine Musik wurde sehr gelobt und ich entdeckte, dass für meine spezielle Begabung als Theater-Komponist hier ein fruchtbarer Boden war. Da es ja hier keine subventionierten Theater gibt und (abgesehen von der altmodischen, unzugänglichen „Metropolitain" [sic]) keinerlei Operntheater existieren, beschloss ich die Form des musikalischen Stückes mehr und mehr nach der Seite der Oper auszubauen und so allmählich den Boden für eine Art amerikanischer Oper vorzubereiten. Damit war ich sehr erfolgreich, und in den 11 Jahren meines Hierseins hat sich das musikalische Theater am Broadway ausserordentlich entwickelt.

Weill (in New City) an Emma und Albert Weill, 9. September 1946: Ich arbeite unaufhörlich an *Street Scene*. Es ist das grösste und gewagteste Projekt, das ich bisher hier unternommen habe, da ich diesmal eine wirkliche Oper für das Broadway Theater schreibe. Wenn es gelingt, wird es ein neues, grosses Feld für mich eröffnen, da ich auf diesem Gebiete der populären Oper heute fast ohne Konkurrenz bin. Ich verwende daher mein ganzes Talent und Können und Energie für dieses Werk, um es so gut wie möglich zu machen. Die Komposition ist ungefähr 80% beendet und seit 4 Wochen bin ich nun an der Orchestration und sitze an meinem Schreibtisch von 8 Uhr morgens bis spät in die Nacht und schreibe ungefähr 15 Seiten jeden Tag. Aber Lenya passt auf, dass ich mich nicht überarbeite, und dass ich zwischendurch etwas für meine Gesundheit tue, Radfahren, Gartenarbeit usw. . . .

Wir sind natürlich fortgesetzt besorgt und aufgeregt über die Vorgänge bei euch, die ja nur ein Teil der ganzen sehr beunruhigenden Weltlage darstellen. Es scheint ja mehr und mehr, dass wir in einer Periode leben, die wahrscheinlich unter dem Titel „Der hundertjährige Krieg" in die Geschichte eingehen wird. Die ideologische Spaltung in der Welt führt mehr und mehr zu einem Aufeinanderprallen der wirklichen grossen Mächte, das bisher vermieden werden konnte, weil sekundäre Mächte wie Deutschland und Japan sich in den Vordergrund zu schieben versuchten. Jetzt scheinen wir uns dem wirklichen, fundamentalen Konflikt zu nähern, und nur die weiseste, genialste Staatsmannschaft könnte uns vor neuen Katastrophen bewahren. Gottseidank ist im Moment niemand in der Welt für einen neuen Krieg geneigt oder interessiert, und der alte Selbsterhaltungstrieb der Menschheit wird wohl wieder wie so oft einen Ausweg finden aus dem allgemeinen „Shlamassel".

Ich glaube, ich habe euch schon in meinem letzten Brief geschrieben, dass ich nun zu einem Mitglied der „Playwrights Producing Company" ernannt worden bin. Das ist eine grosse Auszeichnung, da diese Company die feinste Gruppe schaffender Künstler fürs Theater umfasst (es sind, ausser mir, nur noch 3 Mitglieder: Maxwell Anderson, Elmer Rice und Robert E. Sherwood—alle 3 erstklassige und anerkannte Dramatiker).

Alfred Schlee (in Wien) an Weill, 26. September 1946: Ich weiss nicht, ob Sie sich meiner erinnern. In der letzten Zeit Ihres Berliner Aufenthaltes war ich einige Male als Vertreter der Universal-Edition bei Ihnen und hinterliess Ihnen einen denkbar schlechten Eindruck.

Inzwischen habe ich nach der Befreiung Wiens die Leitung der Universal-Edition übernommen, wie Sie wahrscheinlich von Heinsheimer schon gehört haben. Wir haben sofort die *Dreigroschenoper* neu gedruckt, eine geplante Aufführung jedoch nicht forciert, da die derzeit vorhandenen Regisseure uns fragwürdig erschienen.

Während der Nazizeit waren mit mir noch einige Beamte in der Universal-Edition (insbesondere Frl. Rothe und Herr Decsey), die sich alle Mühe gegeben haben, wenigstens den Bestand zu retten. Leider konnten wir nicht verhindern, dass einiges doch von der Gestapo beschlagnahmt und weggeführt wurde. Dazu gehört zu meinem grossen Bedauern *Mahagonny*. Da für dieses Werk, insbesondere in der ersten Fassung, jetzt wieder Aufführungsmöglichkeiten bestünden, bitte ich Sie um eine Nachricht, ob Sie irgendwelches Material davon besitzen. Wenn ja, senden Sie es bitte so bald wie möglich.

Gibt es irgendwelche neue Orchester- oder Kammermusik, die wir hier spielen könnten? Ich höre, dass Sie sehr erfolgreich am Broadway arbeiten. Vielleicht haben Sie aber trotzdem einmal etwas geschrieben, das nach Europa passt.

Weill (in New City) an Caspar Neher, 16. Februar 1947: Ich war nach der Premiere von *Street Scene* so erschöpft, dass ich mich für Wochen nicht einmal zu einem Brief aufraffen konnte. Das war eine harte Nuss zu knacken diesmal. Ich hatte mir in den Kopf gesetzt, diesmal wirklich eine Oper für Broadway zu schreiben, was ich ja seit Jahren geplant und vorbereitet hatte. Wenn du „Broadway" ein bischen besser kennen würdest, könntest du dir vorstellen, was für ein gewagtes Unternehmen das war. . . . Der grosse Reiz für mich bestand darin, eine Form zu finden, die den Realismus der Handlung in Musik setzt. Das Resultat ist etwas ganz neues und, wahrscheinlich, die „modernste" Form von musikalischem Theater, da es die Technik der Oper verwendet, ohne jemals in die Unnatürlichkeit der Oper zu verfallen. Es ist eine Art Nummernoper, aber der gesprochene Dialog zwischen den Musiknummern ist „durchkomponiert" wie Rezitativ, sodass der Dialog vollkommen mit dem Gesang verschmelzt und eine Einheit von Drama und Musik entsteht, wie ich sie nie vorher erreicht hatte (der erste Akt *Bürgschaft*, unter allen meinen früheren Werken, hatte dieselbe Einheit von Drama und Musik).—Wir hatten eine grossartige Besetzung, wundervolle Stimmen mit grosser schauspielerischer Begabung, und während der Proben hatten wir alle das Gefühl, dass wir auf der Spur von etwas neuem waren. Es ist Sitte hier, ein Stück für einige Wochen ausserhalb New Yorks zu spielen, bevor man es nach Broadway bringt. Wir eröffneten am 16. Dezember in Philadelphia—ein vollkommener Misserfolg. Wir hatten nicht erwartet, dass diese Provinzstädte noch immer so weit zurück sind—die Kritiken verständnislos und feindselig, leere Theater jeden Abend für 3 Wochen, allgemein Mutlosigkeit und Zweifel. Aber du kennst mich ja in solchen Situation[en]. Ich arbeite ruhig weiter, machte Striche und Änderungen. In New York hatte sich das Gerücht verbreitet, dass wir ein Misserfolg waren und man bereitete eine erstklassige Beerdigung vor. Aber sobald die Musik begann in der Premiere (9. Januar), hatte sich das Ganze Bild verändert und nach 10 Minuten wusste ich, dass ich dieses Publikum vollkommen in meiner Hand hatte. Der Erfolg an diesem Abend und am nächsten Morgen in den Zeitungen übertraf alle meine Erwartungen. Die Presse begrüsste es als die erste amerikanische Oper und nennt mich den grössten Theaterkomponisten in Amerika (was kein so grosses Kompliment ist, wenn ich mir die Konkurrenz anschau). Das wichtige ist, dass seit 6 Wochen in einem Broadway Theater ohne Subsidierung eine Oper läuft. Der Klavierauszug wird in einigen Monaten gedruckt sein und ich werde ihn dir schicken.

Weill (in New City) an Caspar Neher, 25. März 1947: Vielen Dank für deinen Brief und deine Geburtstagswünsche, die mich sehr gefreut haben. Ich habe sehr schwere Wochen hinter mir. Ich hatte gerade begonnen mich eine bischen von den Anstrengungen dieses Winters zu erholen, als mich ein schwerer Schicksalsschlag ereilte: mein Bruder Hans starb am Tag vor meinem Geburtstag. Er war vor ungefähr 2 Jahren an hohem Blutdruck (infolge von Nierenschwund) erkrankt. Seine Ärzte hatten mich heimlich gewarnt, dass er nicht lange leben wird, aber ich versuchte mit allen Mitteln, diese Krankheit zu bekämpfen und es schien erfolgreich, zuerst eine strenge Diät, dann eine schwere Operation, die er glücklich überstand, sodass alle ihn gerettet glaubten—und plötzlich bekam er einen Herzschlag. Er ist unerbittlich, der grosse Unbekannte, er nimmt sein Opfer und wir müssen stillhalten und die Zähne zusammenbeissen. Es ist ein schwerer Schlag, da mein Bruder mir sehr nahe war, besonders in den Jahren hier in Amerika. Es ist furchtbar für meine Eltern (die es noch nicht wissen) und ich habe nun beschlossen, nach Palestina [sic] zu gehen, sobald ich Visa und Schiffskarten bekomme. . . .

Was du von der *Bürgschaft* sagst, interessiert mich sehr, da ich vielfach daran gedacht habe, es zu bearbeiten. Ich glaube, es ist, neben *Dreigroschenoper* und *Jasager*, das wichtigste und lebensfähigste Werk, das ich in Deutschland geschrieben habe. Der zweite Akt müsste ganz umgeschrieben werden, da er sehr verwirrt, und musikalisch schwächer als der erste und dritte Akt ist. Aber wir müssen erst das ganze Thema wieder untersuchen und eventuell eine neue Konstruktion machen. Es wäre schön, wenn mir das, und vieles andere, im Frühjahr besprechen könnten. Ich besitze nur einen Klavierauszug. Mit Klemperer müssen wir vorsichtig sein, da ich nicht sicher bin, ob er ganz geheilt ist. Aber das wären spätere Fragen, auch die Frage, ob die *Bürgschaft* noch der Universal Edition gehört oder nicht.

Weill (in New City) an Margarethe Kaiser, 1. Mai 1947: Ich freue mich sehr, dass Martin den *Silbersee* am Hebbel Theater aufführen will, und ich habe auch an sich gegen die Aufführung des *Protagonist* und *Der Zar lässt sich photografieren* an deutschen Opernbühnen nichts einzuwenden. Leider ist es aber sehr schwer für mich, von hier aus etwas Klarheit in die ganze Verlags-Situation zu bringen. Ich hatte einen Brief von der Universal-Edition mit der lakonischen Mitteilung, dass alle meine Partituren seinerzeit von der Gestapo geholt und weggenommen wurden. Das ist natürlich eine unglaubliche Vernachlässigung der Verpflichtungen eines Verlegers gegenüber seinen Autoren. Ich besitze keinerlei Partituren meiner europäischen Werke, und ich kann daher im Moment nicht sagen, wie man sie beschaffen kann.

Weill (in New City) an Emma und Albert Weill, [November/Dezember 1947]: Das grosse Ereignis der letzten Wochen war natürlich die Partition, und ich kann mir denken, welch freudige Erregung ihr alle gespürt haben müsst in diesen Wochen. Im Moment sind natürlich die Folgeerscheinungen noch etwas unklar und es wird einige Zeit brauchen, bis sich die Dinge in ein ruhiges Fahrwasser begeben. Aber die Tatsache, dass die grossen Völker sich zusammentun konnten und einer machtlosen Minorität zum Recht verhelfen konnten, ist das erste Zeichen, dass wir besseren Zeiten entgegengehen. Für Palestina [sic], den Zionismus und die Jewish Agency ist es ein grosser Sieg, besonders für Weizmann und Shertok. Am 25. November fand ein grosses Galadiner (250.- dollar pro Person) für Weizmann statt, bei welchem das Boston Symphonie Orchester (das beste Orchester in der Welt) unter Serge Koussevitzky zu Ehren Weizmann's ein Konzert gab. Weizmann rief mich an und bat mich für diese Gelegenheit die Hatikvah zu orchestrieren, was ich natürlich tat.

Traute von Witt, Universal Edition (in Wien), an Weill, 5. Juli 1948: Die Songs der *Dreigroschenoper* waren in der Nazizeit in gewissen Privatkreisen eine Art Hymne und diente zur seelischen Auffrischung mancher bedrückter Gemüter!! Sie ahnen nicht, wie geliebt und geehrt Sie waren.

Weill (in New City) an Alfred Schlee, Universal Edition, 11. Dezember 1948: Die Situation mit der *Dreigroschenoper* scheint ziemlich verworren zu sein. Vor einigen Wochen habe ich einen Bericht aus München erhalten, dass in der dortigen Neuaufführung des Werkes die Musik beträchtlich geändert war, und dass sogar neue Musik hinzugefügt war. Ich wäre Ihnen sehr dankbar, wenn Sie herausfinden könnten, ob das wahr ist, da ich natürlich jede, auch die kleinste Änderung, in dieser Partitur strengstens verbieten und im Falle der Wiederholung gerichtlich verfolgen würde.

Weill (in New City) an Bertolt Brecht, 17. Januar 1949: Ich habe heute endlich die Änderungen in der *Dreigroschenoper* erhalten und beeile mich, Ihnen zu antworten.

Ich muß Ihnen ehrlich gestehen, daß ich nicht verstehe, was Sie mit diesen Änderungen beabsichtigen. Es mag sein, daß ich von hier aus die Situation in Deutschland nicht genügend beurteilen kann, aber es scheint mir sicher zu sein, daß von Ihrem Standpunkt, als Dichter der *Dreigroschenoper*, diese neuen Texte eine Abschwächung der Originaltexte darstellen, da diese mehr kabarettartige Anspielung auf „aktuelle" Ereignisse einfach nicht auf dem Niveau der *Dreigroschenoper* ist (abgesehen davon, daß doch Göring, Schacht und Keitel schon heute kaum mehr aktuell sind).

Sie werden vielleicht sagen, daß mich das eigentlich einen Dreck angeht, da die Änderungen ja der Musik folgen. Aber da diese Musik zu Ihren Originaltexten geschrieben war, und das Ineinanderschmelzen von Wort und Musik einer der Haupteigenschaften der *Dreigroschenoper* war, so befürchte ich, daß diese drastischen Änderungen (z. B. im „Kanonensong") von einem Publikum, das diese Lieder seit 20 Jahren gesungen hat, als störende Eingriffe empfunden werden müssen.

Bertolt Brecht (in Berlin) an Weill, 28. Januar 1949: Vielen Dank für Ihre schnelle Antwort. Die Szenenänderungen habe ich gemacht aus sehr einfachen Gründen: Die Krüppelkopien des Herrn Peachum sind im Augenblick in Deutschland nicht attraktiv, da im Zuschauerraum selbst zu viele echte (Kriegs-) Krüppel oder Anverwandte von Krüppeln sitzen. Es musste da einfach ein Ersatz gefunden werden. Glücklicherweise konnten die Änderungen so klein sein, daß sie den Charakter des Stückes nicht verändern. Hier wie in den Zusatzstrophen der Songs handelt es sich tatsächlich *nur* um eine zeitweilige Änderung, die nur für diese Zeit gelten (und auch nicht gedruckt werden) soll.

Ihren Einwendungen gegen die Monotonie evtl. zweier weiterer Strophen in der „Ballade vom angenehmen Leben" finde ich ganz richtig und auch den Schluß der letzten Ballade werde ich so revidieren, daß er zum Charakter der Musik passt. Von einem Verbot der *Dreigroschenoper* in München weiß ich nichts. Es handelt sich wohl nur um Quertreiberei.

Mit Bloch Erben, glaube ich, komme ich zu einer gütlichen Einigung. Diese Firma wird auf den weiteren Vertrieb verzichten, und bevor ich diese Regelung fix mache, geht Ihnen natürlich der Wortlaut zu, so daß Sie Vorschläge dazu machen können. Interimistisch wollte ich für das Albers-Gastspiel den Vertrieb und die Überwachung Jacob Geis überlassen, der dann Ihre Tantiemen an die Universal-Edition (falls Sie dies wünschen) übergeben wird. Er ist absolut zuverlässig. Natürlich sind das alles ganz zeitweilige Maßnahmen, und zu endgültigen Regelungen müssen wir uns einfach persönlich treffen. Sie können mir glauben, daß ich gegen Ihre Interessen nichts, aber auch gar nichts, unternehmen und Ihre Meinung jeweils einholen werde, schon da ich ja immer noch sehr auf weitere

Zusammenarbeit hoffe. Ich wäre sehr froh, wenn Sie Ihre Zustimmung zu dem Albers-Gastspiel bald erteilen könnten, damit Albers losgehen kann.

Weill (in New York) an Karlheinz Gutheim, 31. Januar 1949: Ich bin Ihnen sehr dankbar für den eingehenden Bericht über die Dreigroschenoper-Angelegenheit. Um kein Missverständnis aufkommen zu lassen, habe ich Ihnen sofort nach Erhalt Ihres Briefes ein Kabel geschickt, in dem ich jede Änderung der Musik und der Instrumentation strikt untersagt habe.

Falls die Direktion der Kammerspiele von Ihnen die Gründe für meine ablehnende Haltung wissen will, werde ich Ihnen eine kurze Erklärung geben, obwohl ich sicher bin, dass Ihnen, als Musiker, meine Stellungnahme durchaus verständlich sein wird. Die Dreigroschenoper ist in den 20 Jahren ihrer Existenz ein klassisches Werk geworden und hat immer wieder, in tausenden von Aufführungen, ihre künstlerische Stärke und ihre Schlagkraft auf das Publikum erwiesen. Die Partitur wird in Musikschulen als ein Beispiel für gutklingende Instrumentation mit geringen Mitteln gelehrt, und niemand ist bisher auf die Idee gekommen, dass diese Partitur verbessert werden müsste. Wenn die Aufführungen in deutschen Theatern in letzter Zeit nicht erfolgreich waren, so kann ich mir das nur erklären, weil entweder die Musik schlecht gespielt (und wahrscheinlich gesungen) wurde, oder dass das deutsche Publikum unter den gegenwärtigen Zuständen für ein Werk wie die Dreigroschenoper nicht empfänglich ist (was ich mir durchaus vorstellen kann). Für mich kann das nur bedeuten, dass man eben dieses Stück momentan in Deutschland nicht aufführen kann. Keinesfalls kann ich mich aber dazu einverstanden erklären, dass man meine Musik willkürlich verändert, um sie dem gegenwärtigen Niveau in Deutschland anzupassen. Ich habe übrigens dieselbe Stellung zu den Textänderungen eingenommen, die mir Brecht geschickt hat, und deren „Aktualisierung" ich in keiner Weise billige.

Weill (in New City) an Emma und Albert Weill, 11. Juli 1949: In der Zwischenzeit habe ich eine grosse freudige Überraschung gehabt, von der ich euch erzählen will. Meine Volksoper *Down in the Valley*, die ihr ja am Radio gehört habt, und die nun schon in 100 amerikanischen Städten aufgeführt worden ist, ist nun in New York herausgekommen, in einem kleinen Theater, wo eine Gruppe von jungen Sängern seit einigen Jahren mit grossem Erfolg Opern aufführen. Sie nennen sich „Lemonaden-Oper", weil sie in der Pause Lemonade [sic] verkaufen, und um den Gegensatz zur pomphaften grossen Oper zu betonen (wie wir es seinerzeit mit der *Dreigroschenoper* taten). Es war eine glänzende Aufführung und ein enormer Erfolg aber ich hatte nicht erwartet, was am nächsten Morgen geschah: die Zeitungen begrüssten meine Oper als das grosse Ereignis im amerikanischen Musikleben. Der Kritiker der *Times* vergleicht es mit der originalen *Beggar's Opera*, die der Ursprung der englischen Oper wurde, und sagt, *Down in the Valley* wird in die Geschichte eingehen als der Ursprung („Fountain head") der amerikanischen Oper. Ein anderer Kritiker beginnt seinen Aufsatz: „Kurt Weill, der in Dessau in Deutschland geboren wurde und in unser Land kam, um hier zu leben, wird in späteren Geschlechtern der Begründer der amerikanischen Oper genannt werden". Ihr könnt euch denken, was das für mich bedeutet, da diese Anerkennung meiner Bestrebungen mir nun erlaubt, wieder auf dem Gebiete der Oper zu arbeiten, das ja immer mein eigentliches Betätigungsfeld war. Mein nächstes Werk nach dem Stück, an dem ich jetzt arbeite, wird eine Oper sein, für die Maxwell Anderson den Text schreiben wird, und in der der berühmte amerikanische Bariton Lawrence Tibbett die Hauptrolle singen wird.

Weill (in New City) an Emma und Albert Weill, 6. September 1949: Gestern habe ich die Komposition der Musik beendet und jetzt arbeite ich mit Hochdruck, um so viel Orchestrierung wie möglich zu vollenden, bevor die Proben beginnen, am 19. September. Der neue Titel für das Stück ist *Lost in the Stars*, das heisst auf deutsch „In den Sternen verloren" und ist auch der Titel der wichtigsten Gesangsnummer. Wir haben den ganzen Sommer an der Besetzung dieses Stückes gearbeitet. Es war ausserordentlich schwierig, und manchmal dachten wir, dass wir das ganze Projekt aufgeben müssten, weil wir nicht die Darsteller finden konnten. Aber nun, nach all diesen Bemühungen, haben wir eine ausgezeichnete Besetzung, mit dem berühmten Neger-Bariton Todd Duncan in der Hauptrolle und dem berühmten englischen Schauspieler Leslie Banks in einer wichtigen weissen Rolle, dazu eine Reihe sehr guter Neger-Sänger und -Sängerinnen. Wir eröffnen diesmal direkt in New York, am 30. Oktober. Es ist eine sehr schwierige Arbeit, aber, gerade deswegen, sehr interessant.

In der Zwischenzeit hat sich ja allerhand mit meinen früheren Werken ereignet, und es sieht fast so aus, als ob ich nun eine Art Erntezeit, nach 25 Jahren schwerer, unermüdlicher Arbeit, haben würde, nicht im materiellen Sinne sondern rein idealistisch. Nach dem Erfolg von *Down in the Valley* und der *Street Scene*- Konzertaufführung, die auch in Hollywood ein grosser Erfolg war, bin ich nun plötzlich zu einer Art Klassiker befördert worden, und man beginnt allgemein von der „historischen Bedeutung" meiner Werke zu sprechen. Jetzt will man in Los Angeles mein erstes amerikanisches Stück *Johnny Johnson* wieder aufführen, und soeben erfahre ich, dass das Opernstudio der Metropolitain [sic] Opera am 27. Januar (3 Tage vor meiner Premiere) meine alte Oper *Der Zar lässt sich photographieren* mit jungen Opernstars der Metropolitain zur Aufführung bringt.

Weill (in New City) an Bertolt Brecht, 7. Januar 1950: Ich habe seit sehr langer Zeit nicht von Ihnen gehört. Das letzte Mal, dass Sie mir schrieben, war, als Sie mir mitteilten, dass der Vertrag mit Felix Bloch Erben gelöst war, und dass Sie beabsichtigten, den Bühnenvertrag der *Dreigroschenoper* dem Suhrkamp-Verlag zu übergeben. Ich hatte Ihnen damals geantwortet, dass ich mit einer solchen Lösung einverstanden wäre, vorausgesetzt dass ich mit dem Suhrkampverlag eine Einigung über die Vertragsbedingungen erziele. Ich hatte Sie gebeten, den Suhrkampverlag zu veranlassen, mir einen Vertragsentwurf zuzuschicken. Leider habe ich seither weder von Ihnen noch von dem Suhrkampverlag etwas gehört. Ich glaube nun nicht, dass wir diese Sache länger anstehen lassen können. Da ich die Universal-Edition angewiesen habe, keine musikalischen Aufführungsrechte zu erteilen, bis die Frage des Bühnenvertriebes vertraglich erledigt ist, so ist die gesamte Rechtslage der *Dreigroschenoper* im Moment ungeklärt und jede Aufführung des Werkes wäre illegal. Dr. Kurt Hirschfeld, der im Herbst hier war, hat mich um die Rechte für Zürich gebeten, und ich sagte ihm, dass das Züricher Schauspielhaus mit mir einen persönlichen Vertrag machen müsse. Das ist aber nur möglich, solange es sich um Aufführungen ausserhalb Deutschlands handelt, während Aufführungen in Deutschland vollkommen brachgelegt sind, bis wir uns vertraglich auf einen Bühnenvertrieb geeinigt haben.

Ich hatte Sie seinerzeit auch gebeten, mir mitzuteilen, was mit meinen Tantiemen von München geschehen ist, und, falls es dort noch gespielt wird, wohin diese Tantiemen für mich ausgezahlt werden. Auch darauf habe ich nie eine Antwort bekommen.

Erwin Piscator: „Um einen Moment zu fassen"
(Ein Gedicht verfaßt am Tag der Beerdigung von Kurt Weill)

Die Luft ist weh um das Haus,
Drinnen das Gesicht schaut nicht mehr heraus.
Um die Säulen der Veranda ist Leere verstreut
Kurt steht nicht mehr davor. Gestern und heut'
Sind beide gleich.

Mit seinen Augen gehe ich herum;
Mein Blick trifft schräg die Bäume, sein Eigentum,
Die ein wolkiger niedriger Himmel verängstigt begrenzt,
Die spinnweben Zweige schon zärtlich belenzt.
April und Frühling und die Stille ist tot
Und der Himmel ein Deckel zum Sarg—seufze nicht Gott.

2.30 sie sagten: eine halbe Stunde noch
Und sah auf das Gesicht—den Sarg und den Deckel!—
Eine halbe Stunde doch!

Auch den Bach hörte ich mit seinem Ohr,
Merkmal des Platzes, des Hauses, der Veranda davor.
Es war keine Stille und sie war auch nicht tot.
Melodien kamen von dort, Musik ein Gebot,
Des ewigen Klingens, das rinnt an und fort—
Aber still ist das Gesicht—friedlich begrenzt im Sarge dort.
Noch blüht die Blume in seiner Hand,
Ein rinnendes Gelb im Stundensand—
Als ob er fünfzig Jahre gelebt hätte und geschafft,
Um am Ende diese Blume zu halten—zum Anfang der Nacht.

Mit *seinen* Händen tastete ich über das Gras—
Nicht schmal, wie jetzt, gefaltet waren sie,
Ich hatte diese Hände nie so gesehen.
Die Hände die Musik gehalten hatten——
Groß war die Hand jetzt, die ich sah
Beinah wie ein Teil des Platzes am Wald,
Den er mir zeigte, ein paar Wochen zurück, sagend:
Noch in diesem Jahr—— werden wir einen Swimming-pool bauen.

Figure 675. Theodor W. Adorno. "Kurt Weill: Musiker des epischen Theaters." *Frankfurter Rundschau*, 15 April 1950. [Excerpt:] The image of this composer, who died in America, hardly fits our notion of composers. His gift, like his influence, rests far less on his musical achievement as such (on creations whose substance and structure would stand on their own) than on an extraordinary and original sense of the function of music in theater. Not that his music would have been considered "dramatic," like, say, that of Verdi. Just the opposite: The discontinuous nature of his numbers brings the action to a standstill rather than driving it forward; his close relation to the idea of "epic theater" challenges the inherited perception of the dramatic. But therein lies his very own idea. He had, like hardly anyone else, embraced the insight that the relationship of music and scene as a mere psychological redoubling had become questionable, and he did not rest with that, but drew consequences to the point of self-indulgence. Working with limited powers of organization, he made a virtue of necessity subordinating his purpose, the artistic and to some degree even the political. He sought to take the very thought of the effect and develop it into a principle of the artistic effort. With flair, mobility and a very specific expressive tone, he defined a new role: that of musical stage director. . . .

He himself wanted for the moment to rise above the somewhat cramped, in other respects not at all American manner of songwriting to try his hand at grand opera. The most pretentious attempt was *Die Bürgschaft.* He recognized the inadequacies of it, giving in to the constraints and enticements of exile, without demanding an account of it from himself.

For him, the contemporary willingness to add music to the theater's conformism stood as case in point, to docility pure and simple. Not much remained of the surrealist; with a disarmingly coy, crafty innocence, he developed into a Broadway composer, with Cole Porter as his model, and talked himself into believing that concessions to commercial enterprise were in fact nothing but a test of his ability, of one who was capable of everything, even within standardized limits.

Plate 2. Georg Kaiser. "Die erste Pantomime." *Der Protagonist.* Universal Edition Nr. 8388, 1925. "The First Pantomime." (It is to be presented in dance-like, unrealistic fashion with exaggerated gestures, in total contrast to the later second pantomime, which should be played dramatically, with lively expression and passionate movements.)

(The Woman [second actor] turns towards the back, and with languishing gestures lures her Husband [the Protagonist] to come toward her. The Husband finally comes and grudgingly endures her caresses. He gives her to understand that he must leave the house. The Woman is desperate, but eventually calms down. The Husband disappears, comes out of the door downstairs and locks it. The Woman leans out of the window, begging him to stay home. The Husband points to the street through which he will have to go. The Woman sends kisses after him. The Husband leaves. Overwhelmed by grief, the Woman puts her head on the window sill. After a while the Husband returns, sneaks under the window at the right and begins a serenade. The Young Lady [third actor] becomes attentive and shyly looks down. The Woman at the left listens — looks up, sees the Husband and begins to rage. Stiffly, the Young Lady sits down. The Husband runs under the window at the left and wants to calm down the Woman. The Woman makes terrible threatening gestures toward the window below. The Husband sadly sits down next to the door, listens, and jumps into the street from where he pulls close a Monk [1st Actor]. He gesticulates vigorously, pointing toward his Wife and giving him the key to the door, always dancing back and forth in excitement. Finally, the Monk enters the house with an amused smile. The Woman looks behind her, changes her attitude and waits in humility. The Monk appears next to her and after some pious skirmishing he becomes importunate. The Woman still resists. Meanwhile the Husband shows up again under the Young Lady's window and throws his mandolin up to her. The Young Lady ties the key to her door on a ribbon and lets it down. The Husband unlocks the door, enters and becomes visible near the Young Lady. From here on progressive amorous play on both sides (Quartett). The mutual love pressure comes to a climax, the Monk lying over the Woman, who hangs out of the window and therefore can see her Husband in similar position with the Young Lady.

WOMAN:"Traitor!"
THE OTHERS:"Psst!"
Renewed urgency by Monk and Young Lady, reversed positions: Woman over Monk, Young Lady over Husband, who discovers his
WIFE: "Faithless one!"
THE OTHERS: "Psst!"

The Woman pushes the Monk back and threatens the Husband. The Husband responds, pointing to the Monk. The Monk disappears— the Woman after him. The Monk comes out the door—the Woman still after him. The Monk escapes into the street. The Woman knocks at the door on the right. The Husband and the Young Lady in an embrace lean out and scoff at the Woman. The Woman becomes tame and begs her Husband to come on down. The Husband points to the Young Lady whom he wishes to bring along. The Woman consents. Husband and Young Lady away from window, coming out of the door. The Husband kisses both. The Monk re-enters from the street in order to exercise his rights on the Woman. He is chased away by both Husband and Woman, gets caught, beaten up and scared away. The Husband sends both Woman and Lady back to their separate windows, then runs from one house to another and finds endearments for both of them.

MUSIC COPYRIGHTS AND ILLUSTRATION CREDITS

A NOTE ON EDITORIAL PROCEDURES, ARCHIVAL REPOSITORIES, AND LACUNAE

Music Copyrights

All music by Kurt Weill reproduced in this book is protected by copyright and has been used with permission of the publisher. For further information about specific compositions, consult *Kurt Weill: A Guide to His Works* (compiled and edited by Mario R. Mercado, 2d edition, 1994) or contact either the Kurt Weill Foundation for Music (7 East 20th Street, New York, NY 10003; telephone: 212-505-5240; e-mail: kwfinfo@kwf.org) or European-American Music Corporation (P.O. Box 4340, Miami, FL 33014; telephone 305-521-1604; e-mail: eamdc@warnerchappell.com).

Illustration Credits

The following persons and institutions provided photographic reproductions for this book or own an original document reproduced herein. Any illustrations not listed below originated from the Weill-Lenya Research Center, Kurt Weill Foundation for Music, New York. The numbers refer to the figure numbers that are printed in bold at the beginning of each caption.

Academy of Motion Picture Arts and Sciences: 409, 425, 429 (top), 564
Akademie der Künste, Berlin: 190
Bertolt-Brecht-Archiv, Akademie der Künste: 142, 167 (all), 317–18
Bildarchiv Preußischer Kulturbesitz: 125
Alfred Einstein Papers, Music Library, University of California, Berkeley: 154
Ernst Toch Papers, Music Library Special Collections, University of California, Los Angeles: 120
Jean Cocteau Foundation: 335
Leah Salisbury Papers, Rare Book and Manuscript Library, Columbia University: 572, 667
Commanday, Irma: 672
Corbis-Bettmann: 447
Culver Pictures: 309, 385, 418, 443, 481, 493, 539, 540–41, 543, 611, 637, 660
Dessau Stadtarchiv: 1, 6, 7 (both), 16 (top), 17, 20–21, 25, 43 (both), 46, 48, 64 (both)
Deutsche Stiftung Kinemathek: 339 (top), 355
Margo Feiden Galleries: 639, 662
Fuld, James: 286 (top)
Olin Downes Papers, University of Georgia: 665
Frederick R. Koch Collection, The Harvard Theatre Collection, The Houghton Library: 330
Hochschule für Musik, Berlin: 33, 36, 44, 47
Huynh, Pascal: 68, 303
School of Music, Indiana University: 630–32
Jewish National and University Library: 422
Levy Sheet Music Collection, Johns Hopkins University: 237

Institut für Theater- Film- und Fernsehwissenschaft, Universität zu Köln: 103, 146, 188 (right), 206, 209–10, 214, 230, 267–69, 277, 279, 280–85, **plate 3 (top left, bottom right), plate 4 (all), plate 8 (both)**
Klemperer, Lotte: 173
Leipzig Stadtgeschichtliches Museum: 224, 227 (no. 4, 12, 14, 19), 299
Levitz, Tamara: 36
Music Division, Library of Congress: 18
Lüdenscheid Stadtarchiv: 52 (all)
Raymond Mander & Joe Mitchenson Theatre Collection: 362, 365
Mannheim Stadtarchiv: 93
Museum of the City of New York: 438, 442, 444, 457, 479–80, 482, 584
Lotte Jacobi Archives, University of New Hampshire: 294
New York Public Library for the Performing Arts: 439 (top left), 530, 628 , **plate 9 (bottom), plate 21 (bottom right), plate 24 (bottom)**
Paul Green Papers, Southern Literature Collection, University of North Carolina: 377
O'Connor, Patrick: 357
Bildarchiv und Porträtsammlung der Österreichischen Nationalbibliothek: 286 (bottom)
Photofest: 610
Polignac Estate: 340
Universal Edition–Kurt Weill Archives, Sibley Music Library Eastman School of Music, University of Rochester: 62, 63 (both), 67, 82 (both), 83, 95 (both), 136, 157 (left two), 159, 161 (all), 188 (bottom), 192 (left), 204 (left), 219, 238–39, 276, 287, **plate 1 (both), plate 2 (left), plate 6 (top right), plate 7 (both)**
Rodgers and Hammerstein Organization, 556
Roger-Viollet, Paris: 288, 328, 337, 354
Schebera, Jürgen: 5, 8, 16 (bottom), 34, 80 (both), 166, 192 (right)
Staatsbibliothek Preußischer Kulturbesitz: 74
Galston-Busoni Archive, University of Tennessee: 81
Maxwell Anderson Papers, Harry Ransom Humanities Research Center, University of Texas: 647
Ullstein Bilderdienst: 116, 149 (bottom), 263, 291
Universal Edition: 73, 91, 117, 134
Maurice Abravanel Papers, University of Utah Libraries: 107, 449
Wiesloch Standesamt: 3 (right)
Beinecke Library, Yale University, Beinecke Library: **plate 9 (top right)**
Papers of Kurt Weill and Lotte Lenya (MSS 30),Yale University Music Library, 14, 57–59, 78, 121 (both), 135 (both), 152 (left), 183, 248, 271, 305 (both), 307, 311, 319, 323, 325, 329, 331, 339 (bottom), 348, 356, 368, 371, 378, 379 (both), 381, 403, 406 (left), 413, 415–17, 420 (right), 429 (left), 439 (bottom

left), 451–52, 456, 458–59, 461–62, 469, 471, 476–78, 488, 498 (both), 507 (top), 509, 510 (both), 511–14, 517–19, 527, 536, 547, 550, 552, 556, 563, 571, 573–74, 576, 579 (left), 589, 591–92, 598–99, 601–602, 604–605, 608, 613, 621, 622 (top), 628, 633, 634, 643 (both), 651–53, 661, 666, 668, 670–71, 674, **plate 12, plate 14 (right), plate 15 (left), plate 17 (bottom left)**

Editorial Procedures

The compilers followed a number of editorial procedures to impose a level of consistency on the text. Obvious errors of spelling and grammar were corrected, and the use of italics and quotation marks for titles of musical works was regularized. For the most part, the peculiarities of Weill's written English grammar and syntax were maintained. The translations from German to English attempt to capture an idiomatic tone. The translations in the appendix tend to be more literal. The translations of the letters between Weill and Lenya and of Weill's writings conform to previously published versions. Most of the letters and reviews are excerpts. Salutations and closings of letters are not included. American spellings are used for geographic names. "Holograph," the formal term to indicate a signed document in the author's hand, is avoided in preference to the more general term, "autograph." To determine the original language of a text, consult the appendix, where the original versions of most documents not in English are reproduced.

Over half of the photographs were reproduced from digital images, many of which were minimally edited to adjust contrast or brightness, or to remove annotations or distracting imperfections caused by dust or scratches. All of the black and white photographs are printed in duotone. The main text is set in Janson type; display, captions, and subheadings are set in the Futura family.

Archival repositories

Most of the documents reprinted in this book come from one of three major Weill-related collections. In 1980, acting on the advice of Kim Kowalke and with the encouragement of librarian Harold Samuel, Lotte Lenya placed on deposit at the Yale University Music Library all of Weill's musical scores that were in her possession (mostly for the American musicals) and a large collection of photographs, programs, correspondence, and documents. In 1983, the Board of Trustees of the Kurt Weill Foundation established the Weill-Lenya Research Center,

which has developed into a central repository for research materials related to both Kurt Weill and Lotte Lenya. The Research Center has worked to acquire copies of materials located in other institutions and has acquired a substantial collection of new material through gifts and purchase. Finally, in 1998, Universal Edition placed on deposit at the Sibley Music Library, Eastman School of Music/University of Rochester its collection of Weill's holograph scores. At the same time it donated a collection of archival material related to the production of original scores and parts to the Weill-Lenya Research Center. Universal Edition also provided the Kurt Weill Foundation with color photocopies and microfilm copies of the collection on deposit at Eastman.

Lacunae

The compilers attempted to bring together photos and documents accessible in libraries and archives in the U.S. and Europe according to predetermined selection criteria. However, much of the material required to construct a complete picture of Weill's life and works remains lost, primarily due to Nazi persecution, the war, and Weill's two emigrations. For instance, the autograph score of every major, unpublished work Weill composed in Germany is partially or completely missing. Also missing from his years in Germany are diaries, address books, notebooks, and business correspondence (except for a large collection of roughly 1,500 letters preserved by Universal Edition). Especially regrettable is the loss of his Berlin library, which would have revealed much about his compositions and unrealized projects. Programs and posters of Weill's German stage works remain very difficult to find. Most of his business correspondence from the French years remains missing, except for letters retained by Heugel and a few with the collaborators on *Der Weg der Verheißung* (which Weill probably brought with him to America). The American years fare slightly better. Lenya preserved a moderate collection of business correspondence (including carbon copies of Weill's responses), which is now at the Yale University Music Library. The Weill-Lenya Research Center has assembled a representative selection of his correspondence with collaborators from diverse sources over the years, but virtually all of his correspondence with Chappell is missing. Weill seldom kept copies of letters sent to him, and he never kept copies of his personal letters to others.

SELECTED BIBLIOGRPAHY

Writings by Weill

Weill, Kurt. *Ausgewählte Schriften*. Edited by David Drew. Frankfurt am Main: Suhrkamp, 1975.

_____. *Kurt Weill de Berlin à Broadway*. Edited and translated by Pascal Huynh. Paris: Éditions Plume, 1993.

_____. *Kurt Weill: Musik und musikalisches Theater: Gesammelte Schriften mit einer Auswahl von Gesprächen und Interviews*. Edited by Stephen Hinton, Jürgen Schebera, and Elmar Juchem. Mainz: Schott International, 2000.

Weill, Kurt and Lotte Lenya. *Speak Low (When You Speak Love): The Letters of Kurt Weill and Lotte Lenya*. Trans. and ed. by Lys Symonette and Kim H. Kowalke. Berkeley: University of California; London: Hamish Hamilton, 1996.

_____. *Sprich leise (wenn du Liebe sagst): Der Briefwechsel Kurt Weill, Lotte Lenya*. Trans. and ed. by Lys Symonette and Kim H. Kowalke. Cologne: Kiepenheuer & Witsch, 1998.

Weill, Kurt and Universal Edition. *Kurt Weill und die Universal Edition: Ein kommentierter Briefwechsel*. Ed. by Nils Grosch. Freiburg: Rombach, 2000.

Reference Books

Drew, David. *Kurt Weill: A Handbook*. London: Faber; Berkeley: University of California, 1987.

A Guide to the Weill-Lenya Research Center. Compiled and edited by David Farneth, John Andrus, and Dave Stein. New York: Kurt Weill Foundation for Music, 1995.

Mercado, Mario R., compiler. Kurt Weill: *A Guide to his Works*. 2d ed. New York: Kurt Weill Foundation for Music, Inc.; Valley Forge: European American Music Corp., 1995.

Nesnow, Adrienne, comp. MSS 30: *The Papers of Kurt Weill and Lotte Lenya*. New Haven: [Yale University Music Library], 1984.

Biographies

Bélicha, Roland. *Kurt Weill et la France*. Villejuif: Editions du Reveil des Combattants, 1996.

Farneth, David, ed. *Lenya the Legend: A Pictorial Autobiography*. New York: Overlook Press; London: Thames and Hudson, 1998.

(German edition: Cologne, Könemann, 1999)

Hirsch, Foster. *How Can You Tell an American?: Kurt Weill on Stage from Berlin to Broadway*. New York: Knopf, 2000.

Sanders, Ronald. *The Days Grow Short: The Life and Music of Kurt Weill*. New York: Holt, Rinehart and Winston, 1980.

Schebera, Jürgen. *Kurt Weill: Eine Biographie in Texten, Bildern, und Dokumenten*. Leipzig and Mainz: VEB Deutscher Verlag and B. Schott, 1990.

_____. *Kurt Weill: An Illustrated Life*. Translated by Caroline Murphy. New Haven: Yale University, 1995.

_____. *Kurt Weill*. Reinbek: Rowohlt, 2000.

Spoto, Donald. *Lenya: A Life*. Boston: Little, Brown, 1989.

Taylor, Ronald. *Kurt Weill: Composer in a Divided World*. Boston: Northeastern University, 1991.

Essays and Other Books

Block, Geoffrey. *Enchanted Evenings: The Broadway Musical from* Show Boat *to* Sondheim. New York: Oxford University, 1997.

Busoni, Ferruccio. *Selected Letters*. Trans. and ed. by Antony Beaumont. New York: Columbia University, 1987.

Brinkmann, Reinhold and Christoph Wolff, eds. *Driven into Paradise: The Musical Migration from Nazi Germany to the United States*. Berkeley: University of California, 1999.

Cook, Susan, C. *Opera for a New Republic: The Zeitoper of Krenek, Weill, and Hindemith*. Ann Arbor: UMI, 1988.

Csámpai, Attila and Dietmar Holland, eds. *Bertolt Brecht/Kurt Weill, Die Dreigroschenoper; Igor Strawinsky, The Rake's Progress: Texte, Materialen, Kommentare*. Reinbek bei Hamburg: Rowohlt Taschenbuch, 1987.

Diehl, Gunther. *Der junge Kurt Weill und seine Oper "Der Protagonist."* Kassel: Bärenreiter, 1994.

Drew, David, ed. *Über Kurt Weill*. Frankfurt am Main: Suhrkamp, 1975.

Engelhardt, Jürgen. *Gestus und Verfremdung: Studien zum Musiktheater bei Strawinsky und Brecht/Weill*. Berliner musikwissenschaftliche Arbeiten, Band 24. München: Katzbichler, 1984.

Geuen, Heinz. *Von der Zeitoper zur Broadway Opera: Kurt Weill und die Idee des musikalischen Theaters*. Sonus: Schriften zur Musik, Band 1. Schliengen: Argus, 1997.

Giles, Steve. *Bertolt Brecht and Critical Theory: Marxism, Modernity and the Threepenny Lawsuit*. Berne: Peter Lang, 1997.

Gilliam, Bryan, ed. *Music and Performance During the Weimar Republic*. Cambridge; New York: Cambridge University, 1994.

Grismer, Kay L. *Cheryl Crawford Presents: A History of Her Broadway Musical Productions, 1936-1949*. Ann Arbor: UMI, 1993.

Grosch, Nils. *Die Musik der Neuen Sachlichkeit*. Stuttgart: Metzler, 1999.

Grosch, Nils, Joachim Lucchesi, and Jürgen Schebera, eds. *Kurt Weill-Studien*. Stuttgart: M & P Verlag, 1996.

CONTENTS: "'Junge Klassizität' zwischen Fortschritt und Reaktion: Ferruccio Busoni, Philipp Jarnach und die deutsche Weill-Rezeption" by Tamara Levitz; "Zum Verhältnis von dramaturgischer Konzeption und kompositorischer Gestaltung in Kurt Weills früher Oper *Der Protagonist*" by Gunther Diehl; "'Notiz' zum *Berliner Requiem*: Aspekte seiner Entstehung und Aufführung" by Nils Grosch; "'Du kannst in jeder Sache einen Haken finden': Überlegungen zu Kurt Weills *Bürgschaft* anhand der Entstehungs- und Aufführungsgeschichte" by Andreas Hauff; "Amsterdam, 11. Oktober 1934: Einiges zur Uraufführung von Weills Sinfonie Nr. 2" by Jürgen Schebera; "*Der Weg der Verheißung*: Die Genese als via dolorosa" by Guy Stern; "Kurt Weills Aneignung des amerikanischen Theaterliedes: Zur Entstehungsgeschichte von 'Johnny's song'" by J. Bradford Robinson; "Kein Geld für 'Gold!': Finanzierung einer Broadway-Produktion am Beispiel von *Lost in the Stars*" by Elmar Juchem; "Weill hasn't changed, I have': Zur Ästhetik des Komponisten Marc Blitzstein" by Elisabeth Schwind; "Klare Kompetenzen" by Kurt Weill; "Zu meiner Kantate *Das Berliner Requiem*" by Kurt Weill; "Notiz zum *Lindberghflug*" by Kurt Weill; "Mit geistigen Mitteln ist nichts zu machen!" by Kurt Weill; "Über die Sinfonie Nr. 2" by Kurt Weill.

_____. *Emigrierte Komponisten in der Medienlandschaft des Exils 1933-1945*. Stuttgart: M & P Verlag, 1998.

INCLUDES: "'Der Zerfall der alten Formen durch neue musikalische Produktionsmittel': Eisler, Weill und das Komponieren für die technischen Massenmedien im Exil" by Nils Grosch; "Kurt Weills Schaffen in der französischen Medienlandschaft 1933-1935" by Pascal

Huynh; "Kurt Weill und die Radiokunst in den USA" by Elmar Juchem; "Klaus Pringsheims Jasager-Projekt in Tokyo 1932 und weitere japanische Weill-Erstaufführungen der dreißiger Jahre" by Erina Hayasaki; "Kurt Weill, moderne und populäre Kultur: Öffentlichkeit als Stil" by Kim H. Kowalke.

Hinton, Stephen, ed. *Kurt Weill: The Threepenny Opera*. Cambridge Opera Handbooks. Cambridge: Cambridge University, 1990.

CONTENTS: "Brecht's Narration for a Concert Version of *Die Dreigroschenoper*"; "'Matters of Intellectual Property': The Sources and Genesis of *Die Dreigroschenoper*" by Stephen Hinton; "The Première and After" by Stephen Hinton; "*The Threepenny Opera* in America" by Kim H. Kowalke; "The Threepenny Opera" by Bertolt Brecht; Correspondence Concerning *The Threepenny Opera* between Hans Heinsheimer and Kurt Weill; "*The Threepenny opera*: A Berlin Burlesque" by the Berlin Correspondent of *The Times*; "*The Threepenny opera*" by Theodor Wiesengrund-Adorno; "*The Threepenny opera*" by Ernst Bloch; "Three-groats Opera" by Eric Blom; "*L'opéra de quat'sous*" by Walter Benjamin; "*The Threepenny Opera*" by Hans Keller; "Motifs, Tags, and Related Matters" by David Drew; "The Dreigroschen Sound" by Geoffrey Abbott; "Misunderstanding *The Threepenny opera*" by Stephen Hinton.

Huynh, Pascal. *La musique sous la République de Weimar*. Fayard, 1998.

John, Eckhard. *Musikbolschewismus: Die Politisierung der Musik in Deutschland 1918-1938*. Stuttgart: Metzler, 1994.

Kater, Michael H. *The Twisted Muse: Musicians and Their Music in the Third Reich*. New York: Oxford University, 1997.

Kortländer, Bernd, Winrich Meiszies, and David Farneth, eds. *Vom Kurfürstendamm zum Broadway: Kurt Weill (1900-1950)*. Düsseldorf: Droste Verlag, 1990.

CONTENTS: "*Der Weg der Verheißung* — *The Eternal Road*" by Bernd Kortländer; "Grußwort" by Lys Symonette; "Hin und zurück: Kurt Weill heute" by Kim H. Kowalke; "Das ist 'ne ziemliche Stadt': Kurt Weill in der Kunst- und Geisteslandschaft von Berlin 1918-1933" by Jürgen Schebera; "Zur Urform der Oper" by Stephen Hinton; "Kurt Weill-Musiktheater: Theaterarbeit in Deutschland, Frankreich und Großbritannien 1919-

1935" by Winrich Meiszies; "Das amerikanische Musical in den dreißiger und vierziger Jahren und die Rolle Kurt Weills" by Henry Marx; "Weills Kontakte zur amerikanischen Literaturszene" by Michael Nott; "Erfolg in einem neuem Land: Weills amerikanische Bühnenwerke" by Mario R. Mercado.

Kowalke, Kim H. *Kurt Weill in Europe.* Studies in Musicology, no. 14. Ann Arbor: UMI Research Press, 1979.

_____, ed. *A New Orpheus: Essays on Kurt Weill.* New Haven: Yale University, 1986.

CONTENTS: "Looking Back: Toward a New Orpheus" by Kim H. Kowalke; "Creating a Public, Addressing a Market: Kurt Weill and Universal Edition" by Christopher Hailey; "Kleinkunst and Küchenlied in the Socio-Musical World of Kurt Weill" by Alexander L. Ringer; "Kurt Weill's Operatic Reform and its Context" by John Rockwell; "Weill: Neue Sachlichkeit, Surrealism, and Gebrauchsmusik" by Stephen Hinton; "*Der Zar lässt sich photographieren*: Weill and Comic Opera" by Susan C. Cook; "Crossing the Cusp: The Schoenberg Connection" by Alan Chapman; "Music as Metaphor: Aspects of *Der Silbersee*" by Ian Kemp; "Weill and Berg: *Lulu* as Epic Opera" by Douglas Jarman; "Most Unpleasant Things with *The Threepenny Opera*: Weill, Brecht, and Money" by John Fuegi; "'Suiting the Action to the Word': Some Observations on Gestus and Gestische Musik" by Michael Morley; "The Genesis of *Die sieben Todsünden*" by Ronald K. Shull; "Reflections on the Last Years: *Der Kuhhandel* as a Key Work" by David Drew; "The Road to *The Eternal Road*" by Guy Stern; "Weill in America: The Problem of Revival" by Matthew Scott; "Musical Dialects in *Down in the Valley*" by John Graziano; "*Street Scene* and the Enigma of Broadway Opera" by Larry Stempel; "Chronology of Weill's Life and Works" by David Farneth.

Kowalke, Kim H. and Horst Edler, eds. *A Stranger Here Myself: Kurt Weill-Studien.* Haskala wissenschaftliche Abhandlungen, Band 8. Hildesheim: Olms Verlag, 1993.

CONTENTS: "Fragwürdiges in der deutschen Weill-Rezeption" by Stephen Hinton; "Formerly German: Kurt Weill in America" by Kim Kowalke; "'Fremd bin ich

eingezogen': Anmerkungen zu einer geteilten Biographie" by Joachim Lucchesi; "Der literarisch-kulturelle Horizont des jungen Weill: Eine Analyse seiner ungedruckten frühen Briefe" by Guy Stern; "Von der Provinz in die Stadt: Die frühe musikalische Ausbildung Kurt Weills" by Tamara Levitz; "*Der Jasager*: Weill's Composition Lesson" by Ian Kemp; "The *Bürgschaft* Debate and the Timeliness of the Untimely" by David Drew; "Elemente romantischer Tradition im Musiktheater Kurt Weills—Überlegungen zur Nebelszene der *Bürgschaft*" by Andreas Hauff; "'I Cannot/Will Not Sing the Old Songs': Some Observations on Weill's Adaptations of Popular Song Forms" by Michael Morley; "Psicosi per musica: Re-examining *Lady in the Dark*" by bruce mcclung; "Der 'alien American' Kurt Weill und seine Aktivitäten für den War Effort der USA 1940-1945" by Jürgen Schebera; "The Enigma of Kurt Weill's Whitman Songs" by Jürgen Thym; "Propaganda der Trauer: Kurt Weills Whitman Songs" by Werner Grünzweig.

Levi, Erik. *Music in the Third Reich.* New York: St. Martin's, 1994.

Levitz, Tamara. *Teaching New Classicality: Ferruccio Busoni's Master Class in Composition.* European University Studies, Series 36 [Musicology], vol. 152. Frankfurt: Peter Lang, 1996.

Lindenberger, Herbert. *Opera in History: From Monteverdi to Cage.* Stanford: Stanford University, 1998.

Metzger, Heinz-Klaus and Rainer Riehn, eds. *Kurt Weill: Die frühen Werke 1916-1928.* Musik-Konzepte 101/102. Munich: edition text + kritik, 1998.

CONTENTS: "Zwischen Synagoge und Herzoglichem Hoftheater: Kurt Weill: Kindheit und Jugendjahre in Dessau" by Jürgen Schebera; " '. . . wenn Sie doch auch hier wären!': Briefe von Kurt Weill an Ferruccio Busoni" by Jutta Theurich; "'. . . mich so zu geben, wie ich bin, und nichts gewollt modernes zu suchen': Konturen zu einer Schaffensästethetik und ihre kompositorische Vermittlung im frühen Œuvre Kurt Weills" by Gunther Diehl; "Kurt Weill, die 'Novembergruppe' und die Probleme einer musikalischen Avantgarde

in der Weimarer Republik" by Nils Grosch; "Der Rundfunk, die Öffentlichkeit und das Theater: Kurt Weill, der Komponist als Kritiker, der Kritiker als Komponist" by Andreas Hauff; "Eurydike folgt nicht mehr, oder Auf der Suche nach dem neuen Orpheus: Skizze der musikalisch-dichterischen Zusammenarbeit zwischen Kurt Weill und Yvan Goll anhand der Kantate *Der neue Orpheus*" by Ricarda Wackers; "*Die Dreigroschenoper*: ein Mißverständnis" by Stephen Hinton.

Meyer-Rähnitz, Bernd. *Kurt-Weill-Discographie: Die Grammophon-Schallplatten 1928-1961.* Dresden: Bibliophilen Verlag, Albis International, 1998.

Potter, Pamela M. *Most German of the Arts: Musicology and Society from the Weimar Republic to the End of Hitler's Reich.* New Haven: Yale University, 1998.

Smith, Wendy. *Real Life Drama: The Group Theatre and America, 1931-1940.* New York: Knopf, 1990.

Sullivan, Jack. *New World Symphonies.* New Haven: Yale University, 1999.

Wharton, John F. *Life Among the Playwrights.* New York: Quadrangle, 1974.

Weber, Horst, ed. *Musik in der Emigration, 1933-1945: Verfolgung, Vertreibung, Rückwirkung: Symposium Essen, 10. bis 13. Juli 1992.* Stuttgart: Metzler, 1994.

Willett, John. *Art and Politics in the Weimar Period: The New Sobriety 1917-1933.* London: Thames and Hudson; New York: Pantheon, 1978.

_____. *The Theatre of the Weimar Republic.* New York: Holmes & Meier, 1988.

Dissertations

Published dissertations are listed under Essays and Other Books.

Citron, Atay. "Pageantry and Theatre in the Service of Jewish Nationalism in the United States: 1933-1947." Ph.D. dissertation, New York University, 1989.

Harden, Susan Clydette. "The Music for the Stage Collaborations of Weill and Brecht." Ph.D. dissertation, University of North Carolina, Chapel Hill, 1972.

Hennenberg, Fritz. "Neue Funktionsweisen der Musik und des Musiktheaters in den

zwanziger Jahren: Studien über die Zusammenarbeit Bertolt Brechts mit Franz S. Bruinier und Kurt Weill." Ph.D. dissertation, Martin-Luther-Universität Halle, 1987.

Humphreys, Paul W. "Expressions of Einverständnis: Musical Structure and Affective Content in Kurt Weill's Score for *Der Jasager*." Ph.D. dissertation, University of California, Los Angeles, 1988.

Huynh, Pascal. "Kurt Weill et la République de Weimar: une vision de l'avant-garde dans la presse (1923-33)." Ph.D. dissertation, Conservatoire National Supérieur de Musique de Paris/Université de Tours, 1990.

Juchem, Elmar. "Die Entwicklung eines amerikanischen Musiktheaters in der Zusammenarbeit von Kurt Weill und Maxwell Anderson." Ph.D. dissertation, Georg-August-Universität Göttingen, 1999.

Kilroy, David Michael. "Kurt Weill on Broadway: The Postwar Years (1945-1950)." Ph.D. dissertation, Harvard University, 1992.

mcclung, bruce d. "American Dreams: Analyzing Moss Hart, Ira Gershwin, and Kurt Weill's *Lady in the Dark*." Ph.D. dissertation, Eastman School of Music, University of Rochester, 1994.

Robinson, J. Bradford. "Der Jazz in der Oper: Beiträge zum musikalischen Zeittheater der zwanziger Jahre." Technische Universität Berlin, 1996.

Sheppard, William Anthony. "Modernist Music Theater: Exotic Influences and Ritualized Performance." Ph.D. dissertation, Princeton University, 1996.

Spindler, Howard Robert. "Music in the Lehrstücke of Bertolt Brecht." Ph.D. dissertation, University of Rochester, 1980.

Strangis, Francis Anthony. "Kurt Weill and Opera for the People in Germany and America." University of Western Ontario, 1987.

Thornhill, William. "Kurt Weill's *Street Scene*." Ph.D. dissertation, University of North Carolina, Chapel Hill, 1990.

Von der Linn, Michael. "Degeneration, Neoclassicism, and the Weimar-era Music of Hindemith, Krenek, and Weill." Ph.D. dissertation, Columbia University, 1998.

INDEX OF NAMES

INDEX OF WORKS BY WEILL